LEADING EDGE
MARKETING RESEARCH

LEADING EDGE
MARKETING RESEARCH
21st-Century Tools and Practices

EDITORS

Robert J. Kaden
The Kaden Company

Gerald Linda
Gerald Linda & Associates

Melvin Prince
Southern Connecticut State University

Los Angeles | London | New Delhi
Singapore | Washington DC

Los Angeles | London | New Delhi
Singapore | Washington DC

FOR INFORMATION:

SAGE Publications, Inc.

2455 Teller Road

Thousand Oaks, California 91320

E-mail: order@sagepub.com

SAGE Publications Ltd.

1 Oliver's Yard

55 City Road

London EC1Y 1SP

United Kingdom

SAGE Publications India Pvt. Ltd.

B 1/I 1 Mohan Cooperative Industrial Area

Mathura Road, New Delhi 110 044

India

SAGE Publications Asia-Pacific Pte. Ltd.

33 Pekin Street #02-01

Far East Square

Singapore 048763

Acquisitions Editor: Patricia Quinlin

Editorial Assistant: Katie Guarino

Production Editor: Brittany Bauhaus

Copy Editor: Codi Bowman

Typesetter: C&M Digitals (P) Ltd.

Proofreader: Jennifer Gritt

Indexer: Jeanne Busemeyer

Cover Designer: Gail Buschman

Marketing Manager: Helen Salmon

Permissions Editor: Adele Hutchinson

Copyright © 2012 by SAGE Publications, Inc.

Printed in the United States of America

Library of Congress Cataloging-in-Publication Data

Leading edge marketing research: 21st-century tools and practices / editors, Robert Kaden, Gerald Linda, Melvin Prince.

p. cm.
Includes bibliographical references and index.

ISBN 978-1-4129-9131-5 (pbk. : alk. paper)

1. Marketing research. I. Kaden, Robert J. II. Linda, Gerald. III. Prince, Melvin.

HF5415.2.L383 2012
658.8′3—dc23   2011030238

This book is printed on acid-free paper.

11 12 13 14 15 10 9 8 7 6 5 4 3 2 1

Brief Contents

Detailed Contents

3 Combining Data Mines and Attitude Research   50

Paul Gurwitz, PhD, Managing Director, Renaissance Research & Consulting, Inc.

4 The 21st Century Development of Products: Where Customer Guidance Is Taking Us   71

*Howard R. Moskowitz, PhD, Bert Krieger, and Linda Ettinger Lieberman,
all of Moskowitz Jacobs, Inc.*

5 Behavioral Economics: A Blueprint for New Aha Moments   89

Crawford Hollingworth, Founder, The Behavioral Architects

6 State-of-the-Science Market Segmentation: Making Results Actionable for Marketers 119

Kevin Clancy, PhD, Chairman, Copernicus, Inc. and Ami Bowen,
Vice President, Director, Corporate Communications, Copernicus, Inc.

7 Marketing Accountability: Understanding Performance and Drivers of Brand Success 139

William Pink, PhD, Partner, Client Solutions, Millward Brown; Phillip Herr,
Senior Vice President, Millward Brown; and Dorothy Fitch, Global Analyst, Millward Brown

PART III. QUALITATIVE MARKETING RESEARCH

8 Taking Qualitative Research to the Next Level 156

Judy Langer, President of Langer Qualitative and Sharon Dimoldenberg,
Divisional Director, GfK NOP

9 Consumer Anthropology as a Framework for the Use of Ethnography in Market Research   178

*Jamie Gordon, Vice President of Consumer Anthropology,
Northstar Research Partners and Larry Irons, PhD, Principal,
Customer Clues, LLC*

10 Diving Deep: Using ZMET to Unearth Insights About Unconscious Consumer Thinking   195

*Joseph Plummer, PhD, Columbia University and Senior Adviser, Olson Zaltman Associates;
James Forr, Director, Olson Zaltman Associates; and Katja Bressette, Director,
Olson Zaltman Associates*

11 Crowdsourcing and Consumer Insights   211

Robin Pentecost, PhD, Lecturer, Griffith University and Mark T. Spence, PhD, Associate Professor of Marketing at Bond University

PART IV. CUSTOMER MOTIVATION

12 Understanding Consumer Emotions: How Market Research Helps Marketers Engage With Consumers   230

Alastair Gordon, Managing Partner at Gordon & McCallum Consultants

13 Neuroimaging and Marketing Research: Hook Up, Love Affair, or Happy Marriage?   252

Sean Green, PhD, University at Buffalo, The State University of New York, SIM UB Program and Neil Holbert, PhD, University at Buffalo, The State University of New York, SIM UB Program

14 Using Empathy and Narrative to Ignite Research   273

Neil Gains, PhD, Founder of Tapestry Works

15 Standing Waves: Stasis, Contagion, and Consumer Trends   287

J. Walker Smith, PhD, Global Executive Chairman, The Futures Company

PART V. MARKETING RESEARCH INDUSTRY TRENDS

16 Mixed Methods in Marketing Research   300

Melvin Prince, PhD, Professor of Marketing at Southern Connecticut State University;
Mark A. Davies, PhD, Senior Lecturer of Marketing, Heriot-Watt University;
Chris Manolis, PhD, Professor of Marketing, Xavier University; and
Susan Tratner, PhD, Associate Professor, Empire State College, SUNY

17 Improving a Firm's Financial Performance Using Advanced Analytical Insights   319

Marco Vriens, PhD, Senior Vice President for The Modellers LLC and David Rogers,
Principal, ConvertClick LLC

18 Panel Online Survey and Research Quality   337

Raymond C. Pettit, EdD, Vice President of Market Research, PRN Corporation

19 RFID in Research: 19 Things You Can Do With RFID That You Couldn't Do Before   365

Mickey Brazeal, Associate Professor of Marketing at Roosevelt University

20 Is the Future in Their Hands? Mobile-Based Research Options and Best Practices   379

Darren Mark Noyce, MMRS, MCIMA, Founder and
Managing Director at SKOPOS Market Insight

Epilogue: The Futures of Marketing Research   414

Robert Moran, President U.S. Region, StrategyOne

Preface

When we began thinking about this book, we knew we had a good idea because there was a great deal of buzz about the need for the industry to change. For example, there was an explosion in potential new research tools because of the Internet and mobile telephony. And at the same time, there were concerns about data quality. Also, interesting technological developments in brain science had broad implications for assessing marketing stimuli. Also, the practically brand-new use of radio frequency identification (RFID) technology was allowing researchers to accomplish things never before possible. And much work in cultural anthropology and behavioral economics was starting to creep into mainstream research thinking.

Then, too, serious thinkers were starting to codify much of what had been happening in product development research, in segmentation, in advanced analytics, and in qualitative research.

Indeed, the very philosophical underpinnings of the discipline were shifting. There were new ideas about how research information should be shared, about roles that researchers must play in the future, about how to justify expenditures in research, and even an entire new sense of what might be expected from research.

So this is what *Leading Edge Marketing Research: 21st Century Tools and Practices* is about.

To bring the book to fruition, we found contributing authors, who are well-known, thought-provoking marketing research experts. As important as theories are, we were not looking for concepts that hadn't been fully field-tested; we specifically sought *actual practices* that represented guideposts for the future development of the industry. As we searched, it turned out we had a tapped into a *global* phenomenon—something that we had not anticipated. We found serious thinkers around the world, who were interested and interesting. So these authors, engaged in a common cause, come from the United States, England, Singapore, New Zealand, Australia, and Scotland.

All are experienced marketing researchers from leading client-side companies, veteran consumer insights managers, executives from blue-chip research and consulting companies, and thought-leading marketing and marketing research academicians. Many have a foot in both the domain of academe and the world of practitioners; and many have previously written or edited noteworthy books on their own.

They have joined us by writing chapters in *Leading Edge Marketing Research: 21st Century Tools and Practices,* and if you like this book and think it makes a contribution, all praise goes to these 38 men and women, who are practicing on the emerging landscape of the research profession and have been willing to openly share and explain in detail what they are doing.

Each chapter in this book presents a rich, innovative discussion of an emerging area of marketing research. The articles are broad enough to fully cover the topic and the methods employed and contain case histories, such that a sophisticated reader should be able to fully understand the underlying theory and research process and even replicate it, should they be willing to make the effort.

Each chapter contains the following elements:

- Where applicable, a brief historical review of traditional approaches that have led the research community to the need/opportunity for a new approach, which will be described in the rest of the chapter
- A comprehensive review of a single topic reflecting the newest work in the field and, where applicable, how it may be combined productively with earlier approaches
- A detailed enough explanation of methodologies so that a sophisticated reader could actually try to use the new approach described
- Real-world examples of how the approach is being used, how it works, or how it offers something no other tool does or how it provides something quicker, more accurately, or in a less expensive manner
- Ethical issues, if any, associated with the use of these latest methodologies
- Illustrations to enhance the exposition, such as pictures, diagrams, graphs, tables, and so on
- Footnotes, as well as recommendations for further reading

Five key sections and an epilogue structure *Leading Edge Marketing Research: 21st Century Tools and Practices*. The sections include new developments in the following:

- Quantitative marketing research
- Qualitative marketing research
- Customer motivation research
- Marketing research industry trends
- Epilogue: The Future of Marketing Research

Leading Edge Marketing Research: 21st Century Tools and Practices broadly covers the latest practices of marketing research. As such, it will appeal to those with specialized interests in the field as well as those who are seeking a panoramic view of the field in its entirety. It will also appeal to nonresearch executives—those who faced with profit and loss responsibilities and who are looking to bring fresh insights to the marketing issues facing them by using leading-edge research approaches and, in doing so, to maximize the value of their research investments.

Certainly, *Leading Edge Marketing Research: 21st Century Tools and Practices* is a touch-stone for today's research professionals. They will find it a valuable and up-to-date reference; one that provides tools and techniques to better understand and predict consumer behavior. In doing so, we hope that today's marketing researchers will achieve greater distinction for their contribution to managerial decision making and add a renewed vitality to an industry clearly in need of transformation.

Important as well, *Leading Edge Marketing Research: 21st Century Tools and Practices* is ideally suited for teachers and students of either undergraduate or graduate courses in marketing or marketing research. Whether used as a primary or supplemental text, *Leading Edge Marketing Research: 21st Century Tools and Practices* will enrich the curriculum, help develop assignments or initiate projects, be a source of topics and methods, and fully enlighten students about the future of marketing research and how leading-edge research methods will bridge the chasm between academic and practical skills.

We hope that you find *Leading Edge Marketing Research: 21st Century Tools and Practices* useful, challenging, and a strong motivation for raising the marketing research bar to heretofore unimagined heights. When you finish, we know you'll be excited and hardly able to wait until you can try some of these new techniques.

We understand; we feel the same way, too.

—Bob Kaden
—Gerald Linda
—Melvin Prince

Acknowledgments

If having a research career that spans 40 years provides anything, it is perspective. And so today, at this very moment, more than ever before, the time for a paradigm shift in the way marketing research is practiced is at hand. For students and research practitioners to learn from and embrace even some of the leading-edge approaches they will find here, and as a result bring a new vibrancy to my lifelong profession, would be acknowledgment enough for me.

So I will simply applaud the courage of the many visionaries and who contributed to *Leading Edge Marketing Research,* and who continue to toil day in and day out to open minds to the many ways we can be a more important force to those we serve

So, too, I thank my coeditors for their patience and perseverance in working with me and, thus, allowing me to put an exclamation point on what has turned out to be a pretty decent career.

—Bob Kaden, Lincolnwood, IL

The origin for *Leading Edge Marketing Research: 21st Century Tools and Practices* stems from what at first seemed like casual "attaboy" congratulations from Mel Prince to Bob Kaden and me for a coauthored prior publication. In addition, he said something like, "You know, your last chapter on the future of marketing research could be the basis for an entire book itself." Bob and I thought, "Now isn't that nice."

This was in early 2010. Little did we understand what lay ahead because once Mel gets an idea, he is relentless in pursuing it to completion. He cajoled, he argued, he pushed, and he ignited our interest. About two and a half months later, we had a contract with Sage, and we have been running hard ever since.

So thanks Mel, for being the first to realize that there was a need for this book. And thanks, too, for being an indefatigable partner and coeditor in bringing this project to completion.

I also wish to thank longtime friend and coeditor Bob Kaden, for being a true partner. This is the second book we have worked on together, and I couldn't find a better peer, a sharper research mind, or a better writing collaborator.

Of course, I want to praise the 38 authors of the 20 chapters and epilogue in this book. As the chapters started to come in, we three coeditors became more and more excited at their quality, lucidity, and meaningfulness. These contributors, from around the world, truly made our dream for a pragmatic book about work actually being done on the leading edge of the research industry into a reality.

Finally, I want to thank my wife Claudia, source of all good things in my life, who occasionally questioned whether working on this book was the best use of my time, instead of say, billing more hours or pursuing new clients.

May she be proved wrong!

—Gerald Linda, Glenview, IL

In principle, this innovative and intriguing book will transport marketing practice and marketing education into the 21st century, much as the editors envisioned. By strategic diffusion of the latest research techniques and practices, the book will be instrumental in enhancing the quality of marketing practice. In addition, it will increase the value and relevance of marketing education.

I congratulate the distinguished contributors to *Leading Edge Marketing Research* for their generosity and courage in openly sharing with our readers previously unavailable trade technologies. Your superb efforts in writing and rewriting while immersed in your professional pursuits are sincerely appreciated.

My coeditors, Bob Kaden and Gerry Linda, enabled this project to get off the ground. We worked very closely and intensively to develop a clear vision of where *Leading Edge Marketing Research* was positioned. They did yeoman's service in recruiting talented contributors, and brought the work to a high professional level. A project of this magnitude demanded a mix and match of editors, with our diverse backgrounds and perspectives. As editors, we represent a fortuitous assortment of industry and academic perspectives, methodological expertise, writing styles, and substantive research knowledge.

Heartfelt thanks are also due to our associates at Sage publishing. Their experience, patience, understanding, and helpful suggestions made our lives ever so much easier and pleasant. We will most certainly remain friends.

Finally, I must convey my personal gratitude to Sheila for her constant inspiration, help, and guidance over the course of this challenging and productive book project.

—Melvin Prince, Darien, CT

Challenges to Marketing Research

New Roles for Marketing Researchers

IAN LEWIS

SIMON CHADWICK

Cambiar LLC

INTRODUCTION

The marketing research profession will experience major changes in the years ahead, with new roles and opportunities emerging for marketing researchers. Importantly, though, we begin with a historical perspective, and then look at how marketing will change in the next 5 to 10 years. With this as a base, we discuss the future expectations for marketing research from the perspective of senior management.

We also highlight emergent information sources and marketing research methodologies. Then, we examine how marketing research departments will need to operate and what this means for the roles of marketing researchers—those in client marketing research departments and those working for marketing research companies.

We delve deeply into the evolving roles and responsibilities, identifying needs, opportunities, and career path implications, and then we look into how the taxonomy of marketing research companies will evolve and what that implies for the changing role of the researcher.

Our chapter concludes with a reprise of the new roles, the drivers, and the keys to success.

A PERPLEXING HISTORY

On November 14, 1938, the newly minted director of customer research staff at General Motors, Henry "Buck" Weaver, was featured on the cover of *Time* magazine. He was the first—and, perhaps, the last—market researcher to be so honored. Such was the status of research at the time. It only went downhill from there. As marketing research became more and more the norm in corporate America, as methodologies became more and more standardized, and as an entire profession progressed from "cottage" to "industry," its orbit perplexingly gravitated further and further away from the C-suite and from strongly influencing corporate and marketing strategies.

In 1991, this green British market researcher (Simon Chadwick) arrived in the United States to take the helm of a respected market research company. What he found stunned him. His clients rarely saw, let alone conversed, with their CEOs; his survey results were invariably packaged in thick, boring reports that nobody read; his brilliant researchers were never allowed to make recommendations; and the first conference he attended—the Research Industry Leaders Forum—was dominated by research directors from Fortune 500 companies bemoaning their "lack of a seat at the table."

Marketing research had declined from the strategic top floor to the basement of tactics and hygiene. Luckily, this was to be its nadir, and over the last 20 years, research has regained much of its strategic luster. That it has done so is due in large part to a generation of research directors and vice presidents who realized that only they could make research more relevant and have more of an impact. To do that, they had to overhaul the product and the entire way in which they and their staff interacted with senior management. It was going to be a long journey.

In 2003, Roper Consulting (a division of the research firm NOP World), under the leadership of veteran Boston Consulting Group (BCG) consultant Richard Hermon-Taylor, set out to track that journey. Through an exhaustive study of the research departments of 30 major corporations, Roper constructed a taxonomy of research and the way it impacted the organization in the value added. Figure 1.1 highlights his thinking.

The taxonomy posits five levels of the research process. The first two—primary data collection and project management—define research at its tactical basics and are primarily about its *inputs*. Beyond that, we start to think about its *outputs*. At Level 3, there are two possible outputs:

1. Studies that yield insights from that study alone (we call this Level 3a)

2. Insights that are derived from multiple studies from a particular source (for example, a single research provider—Level 3b)

It is beyond Level 3 that the research function starts to become more strategically critical for an organization. At Level 4, the function derives insights from the integration of information generated across multiple sources—that is, it has become a source of holistically generated insights that have strategic value to the organization. Level 5 is the Holy Grail of

Figure 1.1   Taxonomy of Research Process

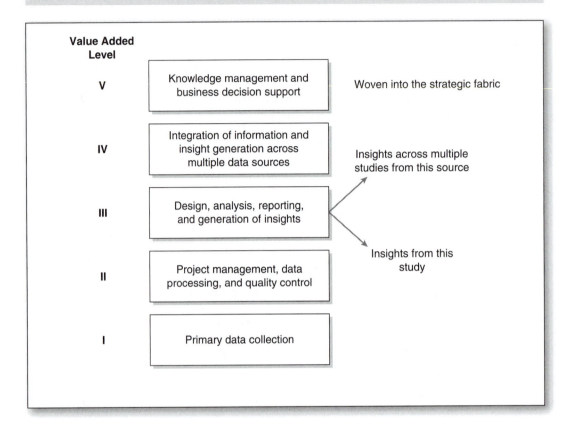

research departments and CMOs; it integrates all sources of information and insight into a cohesive knowledge management and business decision support system.

When we started our analysis of this taxonomy in 2003, about one third of companies in our study were at Level 3b or above. That is to say, 70% of companies were treating research as a tactical, hygienic necessity. Seven years later, we would estimate that more than half the companies in our database view their research functions more strategically, and they are driving for (level) five. Certainly, the Advertising Research Foundation's (ARF) initiative in pushing for research transformation would suggest that this drive has assumed strategic importance in many key Fortune 100 companies.

However, we are not there yet.

TAKING STOCK OF TODAY'S SITUATION

Numerous sources paint a picture that is troubling for how marketing research is performing while the need for consumer insight to inform business decisions grows. Dissatisfaction in the performance of marketing research is voiced by clients and marketing researchers.

Company and marketing executives want to see greater business impact from marketing research while researchers want to be in the role of the "most sought after" for advice and counsel. Market Research Executive Board (MREB) reports that 61% of senior executives/business partners want research to be a strategic partner, but only 29% currently view the research function as such. Furthermore, business partners who view research as a strategic partner are much more likely to have changed decisions based on research than those who view research as an analytic resource (54% versus 34%).

In 2009, the BCG conducted a study of 40 global, consumer-facing companies, among researchers and business partners. They found that "Nearly 90% of blue-chip companies aren't fully leveraging their market research functions. Less than 45% believe that their marketing research/consumer insight function provides a competitive advantage or high ROI" (Egan, Manfred, Bascle, Huet, & Marcil, 2009).

Dissatisfaction with the status quo is voiced by marketing researchers and their clients. An ARF survey conducted in 2008 reported, "85% of research leaders are neutral or dissatisfied with the impact of marketing research in their company" (Rubinson, 2010, slide 6).

Some industry leaders have been highly vocal about how marketing research needs to respond. Stan Sthanunathan, vice president of marketing strategy and insights, Coca Cola, is a frequent speaker at industry events and espouses, "We need to go from insight providers to creative problem solvers, storytellers, disruptive thinkers and visionaries, acting to shape change and light the way" (personal communication).

HOW MARKETING WILL CHANGE IN THE COMING YEARS

A working committee of the ARF Research Transformation Super-Council (RTSC) looked ahead to 2020 and highlighted nine overarching trends that will impact marketing (ARF RTSC General Council meeting, August 3 2010). They are listed here:

1. *Changing economic power balance, driven by the ascent of China.* By 2020, it is forecast that China will overtake the United States and equal the European Union (EU) in gross domestic product (GDP; Avruch, 2010).

2. *Technology/digitalization.* In 2000, we didn't have Facebook, which in July 2010 had 500 million users (Zuckerberg, 2010). There were no Blackberries, iPhones or iPads. We can count on several major tech innovations in the next decade; we just don't know what they will be! We do know that the march toward digitalization of everything will continue.

3. *Privacy.* Increasing digitalization will have the effect of increasing privacy concerns.

4. *More connected, more empowered consumers.*

5. *Media makeover.* Media brands will increasingly become multimedia brands, the need for 360 media planning and measurement will escalate, and geosynchronous targeting will be ascendant.

6. *Globalization.* Companies will increasingly need to operate globally yet act locally. Brand Z/Interbrand reported that 6 of the 10 fastest growing global brands are from outside the United States.

7. *The challenges for developed markets.* Developed markets such as the United States, Japan, and major European nations have aging populations, and face challenges with the escalating cost of healthcare and pension costs.

8. *The multicultural world.* In the United States, the aggregate U.S. minority population is expected to become the majority in 2042.

9. *Sustainability.*

THE FUTURE OF MARKETING RESEARCH DEPARTMENTS

What will the marketing and C-suite expectations be for research?

A recent IBM study polled more than 1,500 corporate heads and public sector leaders across 60 nations and 33 industries. Eighty-eight percent of all CEOs and 95% of standout leaders believe getting closer to the customer is the top business strategy over the next five years. This spells opportunity for marketing researchers (Carr, 2010)!

On an analyst call in 2009, P&G CEO Bob McDonald said, "Consumer research has an integral part to play in achieving these [growth] goals" (McDonald quoted in Tarran, 2009, para. 3).

Looking ahead, Monika Wingate of the UW-Madison School of Business noted, "There is an increasing expectation on the part of management for researchers to uncover breakthrough insights" (Wingate quoted in Shepard, 2006, para. 7).

THE EVOLVING ROLE OF MARKETING RESEARCHERS

While there were only *data* sources in the 1990s, there are now broader and richer *information* feeds, with video, pictures, emotions, eye movement, facial tracking, body and brain responses, and more. Today, we have mountains of information, and research has a huge need to synthesize the information, tell the story, and take a stand to create business impact.

In 2010, the ARF Research Transformation Super-Council defined the new mission for marketing research as "Inspiring better business futures by listening, learning, and translating humans and markets to bring them to life, in order to anticipate and give knowledge to the enterprise" (personal communication).

Researchers must spend their time productively, addressing the key strategic needs of client corporations rather than the myriad tactical issues. To achieve this, researchers must make the journey to become consultants. The journey requires a shift in how researchers define their purpose, in what they provide their clients, in how they define value, in how they work, and in their ability to influence others. We organize this transformation into four pillars: (1) mindset, (2) principles, (3) tools, and (4) practices.

A consulting mindset is focused on making change happen, going beyond information to provide solutions and provoke action. It measures value creation by the impact on client actions. It's not about lengthy PowerPoints—it's about figuring out the important few things that the company needs to act on and being the catalyst for action. At the ARF Industry Leaders Forum October 28, 2010, Margaret Coughlin, CMO of Digital Globe, said, "The presentation should last 10 minutes; the discussion should continue for hours" (personal communication).

Consulting principles include understanding the different levels of client value, stakeholder alignment, empathy, collaboration, individual and organizational value creation, and more. Unfortunately, these principles aren't taught to researchers progressing through the ranks—researchers are trained to operate independently, with a focus on technical mastery.

Consulting tools include problem/opportunity definition, determination of important deliverables, and solution development. Learning these tools can ensure that research is better focused, with clearer expectations and with higher-level actionable findings.

Consulting practices include being a first mover, synthesizing knowledge and collaborating to leverage expertise, creating intellectual property, communicating for impact, and more. These practices are far from commonplace among researchers today, but are well known to management consultants, and are essential for the new value creation model.

Marketing researchers who step up to the plate and embrace the consulting pillars can make a huge impact in their companies.

As we look ahead, some of the trends are readily apparent. The volume of available information will continue to grow rapidly, driving the need for synthesis; processing power will continue to increase, and advanced analytics will flourish. The need for closeness to the customer and the increasing challenge to differentiate products and services will drive innovation, especially in *unprompted* consumer feedback (i.e., other than answers to questions).

Leading corporations will ultimately develop fluid, searchable knowledge collection capabilities—an "insights on demand" capability that won't require stopping to initiate individual studies to answer business questions—although this is still in the distance and will develop much more quickly in some industries (such as consumer packaged goods [CPG]) than in others.

To address these many challenges, the future role of marketing researchers can be boiled down to four headlines: (1) consult, (2) synthesize, (3) tell a story, (4) take a stand.

EMERGENT INFORMATION SOURCES AND RESEARCH METHODOLOGIES

Back in the 1990s, the structure of data sources for marketing research was straightforward. There were just two buckets. One bucket was for company data, retailer data, syndicated marketing and sales data, and syndicated media data. Then there was a second bucket for survey research, which came in a few flavors and sizes—custom survey research, which was conducted mostly by phone or in malls; traditional qualitative research, including primarily focus groups and individual depth interviews (IDIs); and syndicated survey research studies.

In the years following Internet adoption, and especially with the growth of broadband, things changed rapidly. Change accelerated in marketing, in media, in technology, in consumer empowerment and communications, and in marketing research.

Figure 1.2   Left and Right Brain

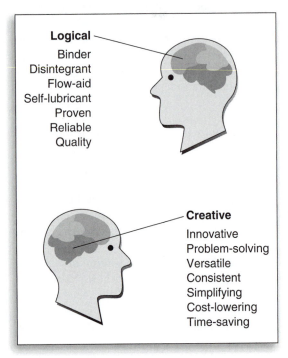

Logical
Binder
Disintegrant
Flow-aid
Self-lubricant
Proven
Reliable
Quality

Creative
Innovative
Problem-solving
Versatile
Consistent
Simplifying
Cost-lowering
Time-saving

The decade starting in 2000 saw the ascent of Google and social media taking off, dramatic Internet advertising growth, and a host of new measurement systems. The rise of mobile communication and smart phones fueled new modes of communication. These changing events have prompted marketing research to expand from two buckets to four buckets.

One new bucket formed containing mountains of company and syndicated digital data from websites and mobile and social media, that primarily feeds the left side of the brain, or the logical side of the mind, and is illustrated in Figure 1.2. Another new bucket developed from unprompted consumer feedback—from listening, search analysis, ethnographies, virtual shopping, neuroscience, biometrics, eye tracking, metaphor elicitation, emotion mining, behavioral economics, and more—that primarily feeds the right side of the brain, or the creative side of the mind.

As the ARF noted, a major paradigm shift is under way: "Research used to be discrete events, now there's a continuous flow of insights that we can tap into" (Rubinson, 2009). And the survey research bucket didn't stay still as online surveys replaced much of what was done by phone or in malls. Additionally, online access panels, custom online panels and hosted online communities flourished; do it yourself (DIY) surveys sprang up and new online capabilities emerged.

The rapidly expanded toolkit for researchers has major implications for research talent, which we will explore later in this chapter.

HOW WILL MARKETING RESEARCH DEPARTMENTS NEED TO OPERATE AND ENGAGE TO CREATE BUSINESS IMPACT?

In November 2009, Mediapost reported, "According to BCG, low ROI on consumer insight in part results from many companies continuing to run the function in an outmoded fashion: they ask marketing researchers to take orders rather than to act as strategic partners generating breakthrough insights." Findings were based on a BCG survey of 800 executives (half consumer insight, half line management) at 40 global consumer-facing companies with $1.5 billion or more sales (Lukavitz, 2009).

Marketing research departments need to develop formal agreements with their management about how to engage and operate with the business, something that we've termed The Management Contract.

Figure 1.3   The Management Contract

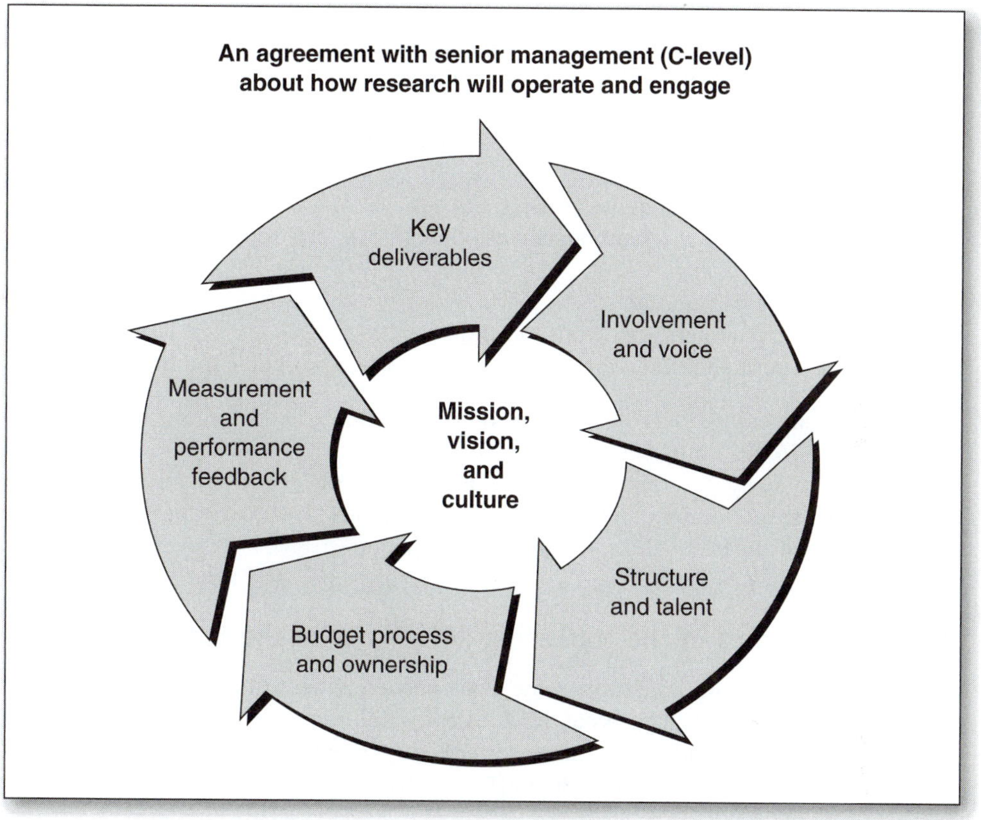

**An agreement with senior management (C-level)
about how research will operate and engage**

Key
deliverables

Involvement
and voice

Mission,
vision,
and
culture

Measurement
and
performance
feedback

Structure
and talent

Budget process
and ownership

WHAT DOES THIS IMPLY FOR NEW ROLES FOR RESEARCHERS?

It will be helpful to look at this from a number of vantage points, as defined by the part of the marketing research business one works in or desires to work in. Two broad categories are as follows:

1. *Client marketing research departments.* This is where the purchasing of research services happens. Industries range from consumer packaged goods to financial services to media to healthcare, and so on. And the size of the client research department ranges from one to perhaps 1,300 at Procter & Gamble.

A 2009 BCG study found that the most successful market research departments have impact across multiple functions in the organization, well beyond marketing. These departments are likely to be responsible for competitive intelligence, new product forecasting, and/or measuring return on investment (ROI) for marketing investment, broadening the range of career possibilities for marketing researchers.

2. *Marketing research providers, often called "suppliers" in the United States.* This is largely where the research is conducted and sold. There is a wide range of providers, the most prominent being for the following:

- Custom quantitative survey research
- Syndicated marketing and sales information
- Syndicated media information
- Syndicated web/mobile and search data and analytics
- Copy testing
- Traditional qualitative research
- Observational research (such as ethnography, anthropology, or virtual shopping)
- Online panels
- Online communities
- Consumer listening (from social media, blogs, etc.)
- Neuroscience, biometrics, eye tracking, and other body and brain information

The larger providers often offer multiple services, and the largest company has approximately 25,000 employees.

Additionally, the rapid and continuing expansion of the range of services since the 1990s has led to many more types of research roles, with correspondingly varied educational and experiential background requirements.

Defining the Roles of the Marketing Researcher in the Future

In this section, we'll look at the skills needed, where the opportunities are, what this implies for career paths, what this means for different constituencies, and what it means for someone considering a career in marketing research.

A European Society for Marketing Research (ESOMAR) sponsored debate in London held in April 2010 noted,

> There was general agreement, from the floor, the chair and the speakers, about the need for the next generation of market researchers to be better than their predecessors in being their clients' 'wide angle lens'. That is having the ability to: handle formal survey data; glean insights from the 'social media', tease out clues from the web and then explain what it all means in simple stories. Indeed Bill Blyth (TNS Director of Global Research) "highlighted the importance of researchers having the skills needed to 'triangulate' different sources of data." (Smith, D. V. L., 2010, p. 4)

What are the mindset, skills, and background needs?

Historically, the majority of researchers have been left-brain oriented, having a heavily quantitative orientation. However, the best researchers have been able to integrate both left- and right-brain approaches. Some have even referred to the need for a "bionic marketing researcher" to fulfill all of the needs. This is illustrated in Figure 1.4.

Figure 1.4   Mindset, Skill Set, and Expertise Needs

Mindset

- Change agent
- Bold, provocative
- Curious
- Open-minded
- Collaborative
- Integrative
- Future-focused

Skill Set

- Conceptual
- Visionary
- Creative
- Analytical
- Problem solver
- Storyteller
- Relationship builder
- Empathetic
- Persuasive

Expertise

- Knowledge of the business, brands, and company capabilities
- Marketing research knowledge
- Advanced statistics and modeling
- Synthesis
- Media and consumer technology understanding
- Consumer understanding
- Insight identification

The list is somewhat daunting, and few (if any) people will be masters of the entire list. As such, there will be an increasing segmentation of roles. Generalists who are grounded in research and are strong conceptual thinkers, strategic, future-focused change agents will be in demand. Yet, there will be a growing need for those with specialized skills and who have mastered the intricacies of specific research methodologies, such as modeling data mining or accessing social networks to improve insights into consumer behavior.

Looking ahead, what are the opportunities?

Opportunities for **specialized capabilities** will increase for both left- and right-brain application areas.

The rapidly growing mountains of digital data will fuel growth of applications that feed the left-brain; the ability to work with mega-databases and to apply advanced analytics will clearly grow for the foreseeable future. The growing need for marketing accountability will also fuel growth in analytics.

An Inside Research survey reported in the June 2010 (volume 21 number 7) issue noted, "More than half of IR's buyer Roundtable respondents embraced 'listening' to social media as wave of future, and additional third called it potentially goldmine of useful information," even though many struggle applying it today. It's a good bet that right-brain oriented approaches, such as consumer listening, online communities, and observational research will be growth areas for several years. The same trend is likely for what we call "body and brain" measurement, which includes neuroscience, biometrics, eye tracking, emotion mining, and more.

Other growth areas are not strongly left- or right-brain leaning, such as information synthesis, shopper insights, global expertise, or multicultural expertise.

Figure 1.5 summarizes the major growth drivers that will lead to new marketing research opportunities.

Figure 1.5 Growth Drivers for Market Research Opportunities

Left-Brain Oriented	Right-Brain Oriented	Dual
Mega databases Advanced analytics Marketing accountability	Consumer listening Online communities Body and brain measurement	Synthesis of information Shopper insights Global Multicultural

The source of talent for these growth areas will come from a wider range of sources than has been the case historically. The marketing research industry will need many more people with specialized expertise in the following areas:

- *Management of extremely large data sets.* Google processes about 24 petabytes of data per day. AT&T has about 19 petabytes of data transferred through their networks each day (Petabyte, n.d.). [A petabyte is 10^{15} bytes of information.] Marketers will increasingly seek to search the rivers of information that are available in real time.
- *Advanced statistics and analytics.* The enormous data sets open new avenues for advanced analysis—to connect the dots and mine multiple information sources, to understand behavior, to segment and target more granularly (with mobile facilitating geo-targeting), and for predictive modeling.
- *Web analytics.* Search and web behavior can be mined for search engine marketing (SEM), language optimization, content development, ROI, and more.
- *Modeling.* Models are built to understand and guide, to explain variation, or for prediction (e.g., direct marketers use models for prediction without focusing on the underlying causation). A return on marketing model is used to measure and explain variation and to guide future marketing investments. Cross-platform (TV, Internet, print, social media, etc.) media models will measure the impact of individual platforms and the synergies between platforms. Once again, the surge in data availability opens new modeling applications.

The industry will also recruit more of the following:

- *Neuroscientists and biometricians.* Success stories have been cited at conferences by Hyundai, The Weather Channel, Frito Lay, Yahoo, and Microsoft. Millward Brown added a Neuroscience practice in March 2010, and expanded it across four continents in July.

- *Ethnographers and anthropologists*. Marketers and marketing researchers need to understand how to connect at an emotional level with their customers and prospects to differentiate their brands. Ethnography is not new, but has experienced resurgence with the increased need for emotional connection. Ethnographers and anthropologists can get to a deeper level than with the traditional focus group approach, and we expect the growth to continue.

- *Trade insights experts*. CPG companies now have a growing business to business (B2B) marketing function that is focused on the trade customer. The balance of power has been shifting from the manufacturer to the trade. Trade insights functions at clients are typically self-contained units either within the marketing research function or reporting to sales/customer marketing. Major research companies have substantial trade insight divisions

- *Global and international experts*. With the ascendancy of China and the other Brazil/Russia/India/China (BRIC) countries, and with the opportunity presented for growth in other developing markets, there will be an increase in demand for marketing researchers who are knowledgeable about marketing research capabilities for international markets. This includes an understanding of language, cultures, values, habits and practices in any number of worldwide geographies.

- *Multicultural experts*. In the United States, the aggregate minority population is expected to be the majority in 2042 (U.S. Census Bureau, 2008). Other countries are also experiencing increased multicultural populations pointing to the need for multicultural minority experts.

- *Behavioral economists*. Daniel Ariely's (2008) best-selling book *Predictably Irrational* is an excellent primer on the insights that are possible using behavioral economics to understand how shoppers make decisions.

- *Futurists*. Marketing research needs to be more future focused, and this will lead to more attention on processes and expertise.

Opportunities for **generalists** will require talent that has more consultancy-based skills—people who are strong conceptual thinkers, strategic, and who are always looking to go beyond the "what," or findings, to the "so what," or implications, to the "now what," or outcome from their work.

Masters of business administration (MBAs) are likely to remain one of the preferred educational qualifications for entry-level generalists in market research departments, along with psychology and social science graduates. At the most-senior management levels, we believe that marketing research positions will be filled more frequently than today from backgrounds that include the following:

- *Management consultants whose orientations are to be change agents and who understand the big picture and understand the business*. Starbucks and Novartis hired heads of strategy and research from BCG and McKinsey in 2010.

- Strategic planners, who have a big picture orientation and understand key business needs and drivers.
- Agency planners who use personal experience to be strong conceptual thinkers with a holistic understanding of consumers, are facile at integrating information from multiple sources, and open to new approaches and thinking.

CAREER PATH IMPLICATIONS

It's pretty clear that few, if any, people could be experts across all the growing range of marketing research approaches. As we've pointed out, this will lead to increasing specialization and to an increase in dual career paths—one being a specialty career path, the other being a generalist career path. For instance, a research company may develop a neuroscience unit with opportunities for neuroscientist staff to progress within that unit, or a web analytics unit staffed with modelers, or a qualitative research unit staffed with moderators, ethnographers, and anthropologists. Likewise, a manufacturer might have a group dedicated to advanced analytics or the return on marketing investment (ROMI) measurement.

The adoption of dual career paths is dependent on the size of the research company and the nature of their business or the size of the client research department. Obviously, larger organizations will have the greatest opportunity to implement dual career paths.

The message here is that there will be increasing opportunity for specialists in the growth areas to advance.

WHAT DOES THIS MEAN FOR DIFFERENCE CONSTITUENCIES AND LEVELS?

Client Marketing Research Departments

Size of department and the combination of willingness and ability to change will drive how client marketing research departments evolve and the corresponding job opportunities. This is illustrated in Figure 1.6.

Research Companies

The changes that we have outlined are already making themselves felt on the supply side of the industry. So much so that industry associations such as ESOMAR and the UK's Market Research Society have embarked on a major project to redefine the marketing research industry. But more of this later.

In full-service research companies, as we define them today, the changes that we are seeing regarding how accounts are serviced are already making themselves felt.

Where the project was once king, now the relationship dominates. That relationship is anchored in not only understanding the client's real business needs but also bringing a

Figure 1.6   Change Orientation and Size: Impact on Staffing

	Change Averse Environment or Department	Environment and Department Embraces Change
Large Department (*N* = 50+)	Staffed with project focused traditional researchers and syndicated analysts Late adopters for testing emergent approaches, reacting to management requests	Have senior-level generalists with strong conceptual and consultative skills Have specialist functions for emergent approaches Outsource low value-add work
Small Department (*N* < 30)	Staffed with project focused traditional researchers and syndicated analysts. The latest adopters for testing emergent approaches.	Staffed with generalists with strong conceptual and consultative skills. Outsource low value-add work, and to leverage emergent specialties, and onboard this when scale sufficient.

holistic array of information and insights from a variety of sources to bear on the client's problem. More to the point, the research company needs to identify itself with those problems and needs and become an advocate within the client company for their resolution.

In short, the supply-side researcher will become more of a consultant, which clearly has major implications for the types of people who research companies will need to hire. At the forefront will be the rapidly changing role of the account manager.

Evolution of Account Manager and Research Manager Positions

Whether account manager at a supplier or research manager at a company, a number of changes are emerging. To illustrate these changes, we're deliberately examining researchers with at least five years of experience and looking out five years. Figure 1.7 shows the increase in what will be demanded of these evolving positions.

Emerging Research Manager or Account Manager Role

Even in looking out five years or more for the generalist position, there will remain plenty of jobs with the "was" profile for years to come. For client organizations with small research departments, staff will continue to be generalists. For larger client organizations, there will be an increasing need for specialists—in shopper insights, consumer listening, ethnography/anthropology, global knowledge, multicultural, data mining, advanced analytics, behavioral economics, and the others we have mentioned. Some clients will even hire journalists to help improve storytelling capabilities.

At very senior levels, the need to consult, synthesize, tell a story, and take a stand will be paramount. Research department leaders will need to be effective operating with the

Figure 1.7 Emerging Research Manager or Account Manager Role

Was	Emerging Role
Research or account manager position exists to design, execute, identify insights, and report on projects for client/marketing.	**Research or account impact manager** position exists to leverage a wide range of information sources to drive business impact.
Key Responsibilities	**Key Responsibilities**
• Design studies requested by client/marketing and develop questionnaires • Manage supplier implementation of study—field, tabulation, costs, and timing • Write reports, identify insights, and present to client/marketing	• Understand specific business needs of client/marketing and other business functions • Mine information sources • Supplement information sources with research studies, if needed, managing implementation • Synthesize information, identify insights, and recommend actions • Communicate and follow-up to create business impact
Success Factors	**Success Factors**
• Ability to manage all aspects of project independently • Efficient processing • Responsiveness • Identify insights • Storytelling	• Business knowledge • Consulting skills • Understanding of wide range of information sources • Ability to synthesize from a wide range of information sources • Storytelling

C-suite. We expect clients to hire from management consultants, strategic planners, and agency planners.

In August 2009, Inside Research (Volume 20 Number 8) asked vice presidents and directors at marketing research buyers and suppliers to, "Imagine what you'd tell a son or daughter or another bright young person who had decided to become a marketing/advertising/public opinion research practitioner and asked your counsel on career preparation." Their advice was to get a social science degree, then an advanced degree (either an MBA or a masters in marketing research). Some quotes are provided next.

"I think a strong undergraduate program is very valuable. While I chose the social sciences as number one, I think a broad exposure to literature, arts, science is very important. I think the number one factor in choosing MR as a career is if you truly enjoy this kind of work—analytical, psychological—aimed at solving business problems."

"As our industry has become more 'specialized,' I think a career path in MR today is highly dependent on one's area of interest. If mathematically oriented, a supplier focus may be most relevant. If communications, an advertising agency, or if understanding consumer motivations and behavior, a manufacturer."

"I'm toward the end of my career. . . . I would urge a young person to get both global research experience and digital research experience. Technology is changing the field quickly. Some of the best opportunities will be for young people who pioneer in using new ways to gather useful information from cyber space."

HOW WILL THIS EVOLVE BY INDUSTRY? WHAT ROLE DOES CORPORATE CULTURE PLAY?

The nature of the business and the culture of the client organization will impact rate of adoption of these changes. Consumer packaged goods (CPG or FMCG in Europe) and consumer technology will be among the first to embrace the emerging roles, and this process has already begun. For these companies, and especially for those with brands that need ongoing product and communications innovation, it is already happening.

Technology companies, for example, have been early adopters of consumer listening; Dell and Kodak now have chief listening officers (Slutsky, 2010). However, the adoption process will be slower in B2B industries and where the corporate culture is more resistant to change.

The importance of corporate culture was perhaps best stated by Jane Altobelli, EVP, Chief People Officer, Human Resources for SymphonyIRI, at a recent ARF Industry Leaders Forum, "Culture eats strategy for lunch!"

The model in Figure 1.8 illustrates how corporate culture and the culture of the research function impact the adoption process. The top right of the quadrant promotes rapid adoption.

HOW WILL THE TAXONOMY OF RESEARCH COMPANIES EVOLVE?

The rate at which client marketing research evolves will determine the pace of change for research companies. First of all, what exactly is a research company? Is it a company that specializes in primary research, based on quantitative or qualitative interviews with consumers and customers? Or is it a company that integrates information from a variety of sources, primary and secondary, passive and active? Or is it perhaps a new breed of company—for example, a company that specializes in web or marketing analytics?

One way to assess where the winds of change are blowing is to follow the money. Where is venture capital going? Prior to the Great Recession, the answer was technology-oriented research companies. Today, overwhelmingly, the answer is companies specializing in marketing and web analytics. This has not gone unnoticed by the major research companies, who are forming and/or acquiring analytics capabilities.

Figure 1.8 Impact of Culture on the Adoption Process

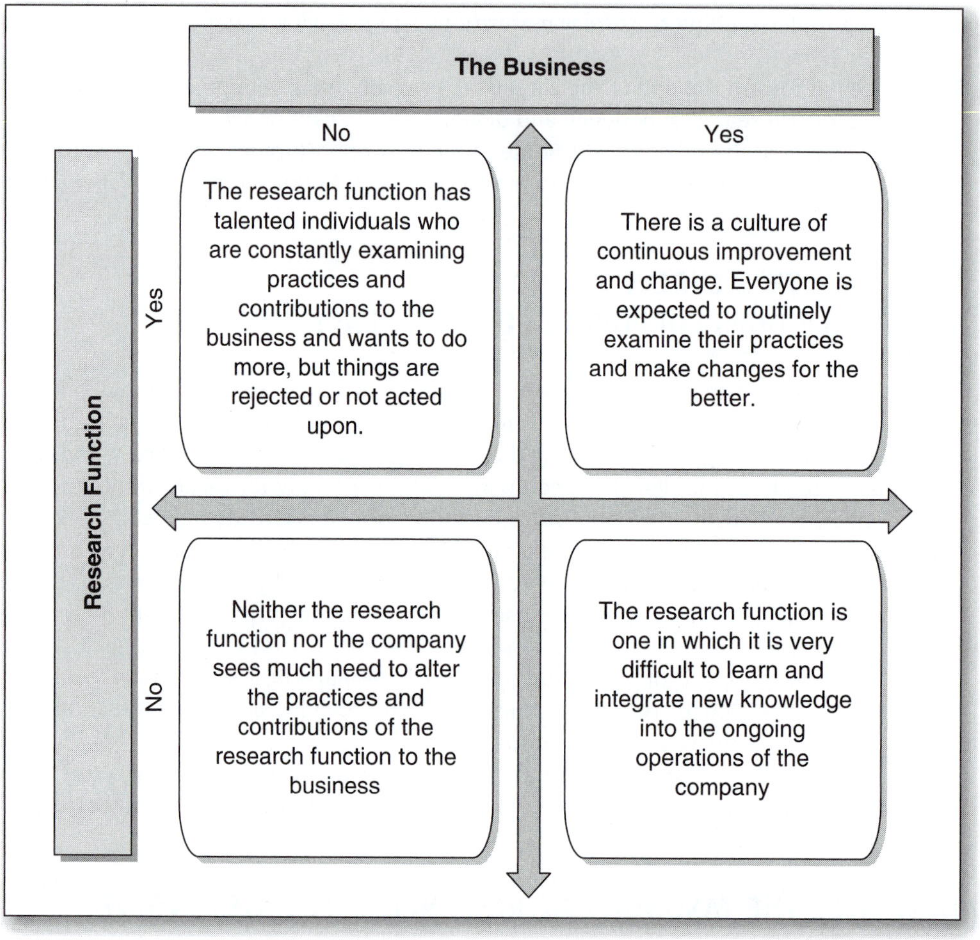

The Business

	No	Yes
Yes	The research function has talented individuals who are constantly examining practices and contributions to the business and wants to do more, but things are rejected or not acted upon.	There is a culture of continuous improvement and change. Everyone is expected to routinely examine their practices and make changes for the better.
No	Neither the research function nor the company sees much need to alter the practices and contributions of the research function to the business	The research function is one in which it is very difficult to learn and integrate new knowledge into the ongoing operations of the company

Research Function

Source: Wayne R. McCullough, PhD, Institute for Social Research, University of Michigan.

Increasing demand for integrated, left- and right-brain solutions has meant that there is much more appetite on the part of clients to experiment. As technology opens new vistas for listening and for conducting research and ethnographic studies, solutions are beginning to emerge for clients to widen the scope of insights generation.

As a result, we are now seeing entire new segments of the research industry begin to emerge and grow with many breakthrough innovations coming from new entrants and start-ups. These vary considerably in nature, but all share the same common theme: using new people who can harness new technology to enable and produce insights that were previously unattainable. Interestingly, they fit into the taxonomy at all levels.

Level 1: Data Collection. With the advent of social media as a primary form of communication, entertainment and connectedness, the traditional (online) mode of interacting with people for the purpose of collecting information has started to break down, especially in the younger demographics. This has led to the emergence of the *social media data collection* company. Pioneered by firms such as Peanut Labs, itself an offshoot of a social network, the art and science of deriving samples and collecting data from social media users—including game sites—has now become part and parcel of the online data-collection toolkit. If you want to reach young males, for example, you have to look to social media.

Level 2: Project Management. Just as online data collection revolutionized the way in which we sample people for research purposes, the social media genre is beginning to change the way in which we manage projects. Indeed, it is changing the way in which we *define* projects. The online qualitative and ethnographic platform offered by Revelation, for example, promises to "unleash the power of qualitative research."

By using a social media interface, firms such as these are able to engage consumers in a much deeper and broader way over a longer period of time—where once a focus group perhaps elicited 12 minutes of contribution from a participant, now that same participant can contribute two to three hours of time and thought using a variety of qualitative and ethnographic exercises. They can participate in bulletin boards, do specific exercises, upload photos and video, annotate and tag what they upload with their thoughts and feelings and so on. For the qualitative researcher, this means not only a faster, easier, and cheaper approach to projects but a much richer set of derived insights and a bigger information set.

This redefinition of what a project is—and what it can generate in terms of insights—stretches across the spectrum of what we currently consider to be research and beyond.

Online communities, such as those offered by Communispace and Passenger, allow multiple interactions between clients, researchers, and participants and can be used for multiple purposes within a relatively short time. The online virtual environments created by Decision Insights and others allows testing of hundreds of variations of packaging, promotions, and in-store display situations where before a shelf test would have allowed only a handful. New product development projects by companies, such as InsightsNow! artfully combine online and off-line, quantitative and qualitative, questioning and observation to leverage the time and contribution of each respondent to a level undreamed of only five years ago.

Indeed, today a project may not even involve respondents as such. Web analytics companies, such as Conversion, instead carefully set up multiple listening posts on the web, sampling sites by their known demographic makeup, and glean insights both qualitative and quantitative in nature.

Or take the example of "Digividuals," a new service offered by the British research company BrainJuicer. These are research robots (or "bots") profiled to look like a target audience that are let loose to garner web talk on sites such as Twitter and that then re-Tweet to the same audience to stimulate reaction to certain concepts or themes of interest to the researchers. Such Digividuals have been known to garner reaction from as many as 100,000 individuals on the web.

Levels 3 and 4: Insight generation. In these examples, we have seen how new platforms have engendered entirely new ways of collecting information and have come to redefine what data collection and, indeed, a project actually are.

These new entrants are not just about new ways of collecting data. In virtually every case, they are about generating insights that would not otherwise have been available. Additionally, the insights that they generate are rarely singular or point in time. These companies are accumulating insight norms and databanks against which to measure and assess the quality of the insight being generated, and they are formulating hypotheses of human behavior against an ever-richer context of background information. As such, their input becomes more valuable over time.

One might say that such accumulation of knowledge and wisdom was perfectly possible under the old paradigm of surveys and focus groups. However, the ugly truth is that few companies would progress beyond our Level 3a—that is, they would look for insights from the project itself but rarely compare these to an extensive library of similar projects in the past.

True, some companies, such as BASES and Millward Brown, built norm-based systems designed to enable decision hurdles, but all too often, neither the research company nor the client would take the time or trouble to mine the information that they already had in their possession. Very simply, such an undertaking would have been too costly in time and money, and there was always the next project that needed to be dealt with.

Today, another type of new entrant is resolving those issues of cost and time: the off-shore extension team. These are teams of highly qualified people in countries, such as India, that are assembled to provide an extension to the client's research or consumer insights function. Costing perhaps less than half what it would take to staff an equivalent function in the United States or Europe, these teams are there not only to deal with peak loads of demand but also to provide data mining services for existing data to generate new insights, high-end analytical services, and listening services, such as blog mining, that can be integrated with more traditional survey research.

Level 5: Business decision support (or research impact). Truth be told, very few of the new entrants cited previously will rise to Level 5 in their impact on the organization. However, it is possible that certain business intelligence platforms could do so through various kinds of decision support systems that integrate knowledge gleaned not only from research but from a myriad of other sources (competitive intelligence, CRM, business analytics, secondary data, financial data, and so on).

There are those who believe that such platforms could subsume the role of consumer insights in impacting strategic decision making. We are not so sure, as we believe that the impact of right-brain information is equally as powerful as that of left-brain—and machines are often lacking (at present at least) in of deriving insights from the right brain. We shall see.

The 1990s and 2000s saw a period of unprecedented consolidation in the research industry, as major research companies not only expanded their geographic reach but also filled in various niches in their portfolios that could lead them to the nirvana of one-stop shopping. The great thing about this is that it led to a period of refragmentation, as the principals of the acquired companies recycled themselves and became serial entrepreneurs.

Today, those entrepreneurs have been joined by many others who understand the role of technology in redefining research, and are not afraid to bring new solutions to the market. The list of the types of companies that they have brought to the scene—types that were not there 5 or 10 years ago—is a long one:

1. Social media data collection companies
2. Providers of online communities
3. Builders of proprietary online panels
4. Virtual environment specialists
5. Web analytics firms
6. Advertising analytics providers
7. Crowdsourcing and predictive markets specialists
8. Qualitative and ethnographic platforms
9. Offshore extension teams
10. Neuroscience specialists
11. Biometric firms
12. Business intelligence platforms

The boundaries are blurring as to what constitutes a real research firm. And to compound the situation, research suppliers are determined to blow up the old model of market research, an objective publicly espoused by BrainJuicer, for example. Whether they succeed in this objective, the landscape for the supply-side researcher is changing forever, as Figure 1.9 demonstrates.

The Changing Role of the Researcher

The researcher of the future will have more advanced skills than today's equivalent. While the basic mindset and background relevant to survey and qualitative research will still have relevance, tomorrow's researcher will need not only to have a much broader set of skills and interests but also have the ability to understand when and how to search for and bring in skills not possessed. They will need to understand how to manage, integrate, and analyze data from a multiplicity of sources, both right-brained and left-brained.

And then, they will have to be an excellent communicator and storyteller.

While all of this might seem daunting, in actuality, it is not all that different from the profiles of researchers that European suppliers of research searched for 30 years ago. Some of the most brilliant minds in European research—John Samuels, Kit Molloy, Julian Bond, Sven Arn, and Cecilia Gobbi are all good examples—came from backgrounds similar to the above and possessed skills and mindsets that were near identical to those we say are critical to the future success of the profession. And today, many of the most successful young European research companies carry on that tradition—Nunwood, FreshMinds, Incite Consulting, HTP, and BrainJuicer are just a few that are blazing trails of which their forefathers would approve. Perhaps the American research industry could do worse than look across the ocean for inspiration.

Figure 1.9   The Changing Role of the Researcher

Was	Will be
Roles and Responsibilities • Study design • Questionnaire design • Sample design • Analysis plan • Analysis • Reporting and presentation	**Roles and Responsibilities** • Definition of insight needs • Choice of instruments for inclusion in integrated design • Sourcing of expertise • Integration of insights from sources and from historical data • Analysis • Building and telling the story
Mindset and Skills • Quantitative or qualitative training and capabilities • Statistical training • Analytical frameworks • Writing skills	**Mindset and Skills** • Broad appreciation and understanding of a variety of tools and approaches • Statistical and qualitative analytical skills • Ability to detect patterns in a variety of data forms • Curiosity about new forms of insight generation • Story telling
Background Needs • Economics • Statistics • Psychology	**Background Needs** • Behavioral economics • Statistics • Psychology • Geography • Political science • Social media • Communications • Business

For that to happen, however, and for the younger generation to view marketing research as exciting and sexy (which it undoubtedly *should* be), our educational system will need to catch up to modern reality; our associations will need to adjust their training priorities, and our practitioners—both on the client side and on the supplier side—will need to reassume their role as professors for the modern generation.

Education surrounding marketing research today, whether as an undergraduate or graduate course, tends to focus too much on the basics. Curricula stress research as we knew it—probability theory, sampling, questionnaire design, how to analyze tables, and rudimentary qualitative approaches. There needs to be awakening in universities as to the changing nature not only of research itself but of what it is designed to achieve.

Similarly, our associations are stuck in the same universe and need to broaden their educational and certification horizons to a new world. Certification, in particular, causes considerable concern, as there is a danger that it will preserve in aspic our old precepts of what research is and cause us to miss the opportunities that the new research affords us.

Some research companies and end users are beginning to awaken to the new reality and adjusting their training programs accordingly. GfK is an excellent example of this, having designed its graduate training program around the power of social media.

SymphonyIRI Group is a major syndicated research company and is at the forefront of transforming the role of its market research function—and their story is worth telling.

Besides recruiting a new profile for the client account teams, SymphonyIRI is also implementing a comprehensive business insights training program. Their program is a five-stage client engagement continuum starting from Stage 1 "vendor" to Stage 5 "trusted business adviser." Skills, competencies, and client outcomes are mapped to each stage. Most critical is the creation of an insights competence group differentiated from a services competence group.

Starting early in 2010, they rolled the training out to the client insights teams on their top strategic accounts. Their strategic clients expect insights that are actionable, compelling, with clear recommendations, and a point of view that ultimately advances their business outcomes.

The insights training program has led to specific actions being implemented by clients who attribute many positives to the new skill sets being provided to SymphonyIRI client insight team members. Because of the training, client insights teams are being asked to meet with more senior people at the client organization—both within and outside of market research. Several clients are clearly showing interest in being part of this new business partnership and cite the clear benefit that their account teams are providing to the business. They range from recommendations on brand building to market mix to price and promotion to shopper-centric strategies.

Jane Altobelli, EVP & chief people officer at SymphonyIRI Group, stated,

> In order to deliver these insights, we needed to recruit a new professional with consultative experience and skill set. In parallel, we needed to train our existing teams on how to better create and communicate insights and to reach the right individual at our clients. . . . A consulting framework and methodology must be the centerpiece of insight creation and delivery with the researcher having skills to identify, build, communicate and deliver the insight. (personal communication)

The importance of consulting or consultative skills is underlined by the fact that CEO John Freeland came to the firm in 2007, after a 25-year successful career at Accenture.

Whether others will follow is a matter of speculation, but one can only hope that they will and, in doing so, attract the best and brightest of the upcoming generation. We certainly know that the right training can and does affect the impact of research, both in end-user organizations and in research suppliers.

Another example is that of a major telecom company, where an entire insights and intelligence function was retrained in what constitutes insight and how to communicate it. Here, the emphasis was on the fact that insight requires a complete change in body, mind, and soul. *Body* refers to the structure and processes that needs to be present in an organization for insight to take place. *Mind* references not only the data and analysis that are necessary for insight to emerge but also the behaviors of the people mining data and doing that analysis.

And, most important, *soul* encompasses the attitudes of those charged with producing insight—are they empathetic with both the business and the consumer? Do they have intuition and imagination? And, most important of all, do they have the storytelling capabilities to communicate the insight effectively? After all, an insight is not an insight unless it is effectively communicated and results in actions and behaviors that are different from what would have taken place had the insight not emerged.

In the instance of the telecom company, body-mind-soul insight training resulted in a complete transformation of the research function, from reactive order taker to proactive and strategically vital decision maker, and all within nine months.

Training does work, as long as the will to transform is there. Transformation works, as long as the training is there.

In today's world, training and education play a crucial role in achieving research impact. To ensure that we have impact, we need to train in both the science of deriving insight and in the art of communicating the impact that it can have. Nothing less will work.

KEYS TO A SUCCESSFUL MARKETING RESEARCH CAREER

We have discussed the history of the role of marketing researchers, looked at the trends that will impact marketing, discussed what marketing and the C-suite will demand from marketing researchers and how researchers must respond, and explored the emergent marketing research capabilities. With this as background, we then discussed the implications for new roles for marketing researchers working for client (buyer) research departments and for those working for marketing research suppliers.

The future offers great opportunities for marketing researchers that align themselves with the trends. The opportunities can be summarized in two areas:

1. Generalists who are strong conceptual thinkers, strategic, future focused, and change agents who understand the intricacies of businesses they serve. They need to become great consultants who seek alignment on key management needs, synthesize information from multiple sources, build strong relationships, tell compelling stories, and persuade management to take action.

2. Specialists who align themselves with one or more of the numerous growth areas. Growth areas include consumer listening, advanced analytics (e.g., statistics, modeling, data mining, web analytics, media measurement, and analytics), online

communities, co-creation capabilities, business intelligence platforms, shopper insights, neuroscience/biometrics, behavioral economics, global and multicultural experts, ethnography, and anthropology.

The key drivers behind these opportunities are threefold:

1. Technological innovation and digitization
2. The need for researchers and marketers to get closer to customers and prospects to create competitive advantages
3. The changing global economic landscape

Keys to Success

If you are starting out or in the early years of your career, we suggest that you explore how your skills, mindset, interests, and sources of satisfaction fit in with the growth opportunity areas that we've discussed.
Seek to

- review the generalist and specialist growth areas, and ask yourself where your passion lies. Your passion will fuel your curiosity and engagement, which will enhance your success;
- learn as much as you can about the area(s) that attract you and then reassess critically. Are you still passionate about it? Is it a good fit with what you're good at?
- seek ways to get started on your chosen direction. This may involve further education, an appropriate entry-level position, an opportunity to change responsibilities where you are working, or a complete job change; and
- if you are thinking of a generalist path, be honest with yourself about your ability and aptitude to be a change agent, conceptual thinker, synthesizer, and storyteller. These capabilities will be increasingly necessary as your level of responsibility increases.

For those who have already been in the profession for several years, critically evaluate yourself and seek to determine

- if you want to follow a specialty growth path and how your particular skills mesh with the many specialties that are emerging and
- if you have the strong leadership abilities necessary for becoming a generalist and can master the four skills necessary for this career path: the ability to (1) consult, (2) synthesize, (3) tell a story, and (4) take a stand.

We believe that marketing research and the role of marketing researchers will change more rapidly in the next 5 to 10 years than at any time in the past, and that this will open enormous, wide-ranging opportunities.

There are many paths to success, and we hope we've touched on one that speaks directly to you. Best of luck.

FURTHER READING

Burby, J., & Atchison, S. (2007). *Actionable web analytics.* Indianapolis, Indiana. Sybex.

Chadwick, S. (2006, May). Client driven change: The impact of changes in client needs on the research industry. *International Journal of Market Research, 48*(4).

Garcia, G. (2004). The new mainstream. New York, NY: HarperCollins.

Hill, D. (2003). *Body of truth. Leveraging what consumers can't or won't say.* Hoboken, NJ. John Wiley & Sons.

Johansen, B. (2007). *Get there early.* San Francisco, CA. Berrett-Koehler.

Kaushik, A. (2007). *Web analytics.* Indianapolis, Indiana. Sybex.

Lewis, I. (2010, March). High impact research. *Research World, 18.*

Micu, A., Dedeker, K., Lewis, I., Moran, R., Netzer, O., Plummer, J., & Rubinson, J. (2011, March). The shape of marketing research in 2021. *Journal of Advertising Research, 51*(1).

PART II

Quantitative Marketing Research

Research ROI Analysis

A Powerful Tool for Marketers

DIANE SCHMALENSEE

Schmalensee Partners

A. DAWN LESH

A. Dawn Lesh International

INTRODUCTION

Return on investment (ROI) analysis can be a powerful tool for marketing researchers in two basic kinds of situations. First, it can be used as a decision tool to help researchers and their clients make the most of their research spending. ROI analysis can help determine appropriate research budgets for projects, prioritize research spending across various projects, and focus clients on their role in getting the most value out of the research investment. Second, ROI analysis can also be used as a marketing tool to enhance relationships with clients and secure needed resources in the future. When marketing researchers discuss financial returns on research with their clients and prepare reports that demonstrate what they have helped their organizations earn or save, they show that they understand their clients' goals and can be valued partners in their clients' success. While it is helpful to point out the theoretical distinctions between these two applications of ROI analysis, in practice the distinction between the two uses is not always clear-cut. In fact, researchers often find that by using ROI analysis to prioritize research spending (and perhaps even eliminate less valuable projects), they are actually enhancing their relationships with their clients.

This chapter discusses how ROI analysis can be valuable as a decision tool and then as a marketing and relationship tool for marketing researchers whether located in a business line or in a centralized marketing research function. Formulas for measuring ROI (as well as some alternative methods of assessing value) are presented, and then a number of examples that illustrate the various situations in which ROI analysis can be used are discussed. The chapter concludes with a description of how some marketing research groups have incorporated their ROI analysis into annual reports and budget requests.

ROI Analysis as a Decision Tool

Most marketing research departments have limited budgets and resources and need to find ways to reconcile the potential value of projects with the amount of monies and people available. ROI analysis computes financial measures of the payoff of marketing research projects, so it is a valuable decision tool that that is understood by CFOs, CEOs, and other top executives. ROI analysis can be used as a decision tool to help create an appropriate budget for a research project, prioritize or rationalize spending on research projects, make the research design more actionable, and focus clients on their role in getting the most out of the research investment.

To illustrate just one of these decision situations, consider the case of the head of a corporate marketing research department. He was asked by a marketing executive to initiate a customer satisfaction measurement and tracking project that would identify ways to build repeat sales and recommendations from current customers to grow revenues. At the same time, a different marketing executive asked the marketing research head to conduct a massive customer segmentation project to identify the most valuable customer segments and to develop new products/services and marketing/sales approaches that would increase sales to those customer segments. The marketing research head knew that he had a limited research budget (including limited staff) and that conducting both of these projects on a grand scale would mean that he would have to secure additional funding or drop other marketing research projects that had already been approved.

Both projects might be very important strategically to his firm. Both had high-level executive sponsors or champions within his firm. Both might have strong impact on the revenues and competitive success of his firm. And both might be very expensive to conduct the research and staff time.

How did the marketing research head handle this situation? He analyzed the investment needed for each of these research projects and compared that to the anticipated payoffs or financial returns of the projects. This use of ROI analysis as a decision tool provided him with a rational, objective, and defensible way of making budgeting decisions by prioritizing projects and spending. After using ROI analysis, the marketing research head recommended accepting both the customer satisfaction and segmentation projects because they each had substantial returns even though the budgets were large. At the same time, he recommended eliminating a previously approved project with low returns to help pay for the satisfaction and segmentation projects. In this marketing research head's case, ROI analysis provided a methodology for responding to research requests in a way that the executives could understand. It avoided the appearance of favoritism or off-the-cuff decision making when determining how to spend or how to allocate the marketing research department's limited time and money. And it allowed him to decrease part of his budget and workload to add the new satisfaction and segmentation projects.

ROI Analysis as a Marketing Tool to Build Relationships and Secure Resources

Marketing researchers can use ROI analysis as a marketing tool to demonstrate their value to their organizations and clients and to make the case for budget and resource requests. Although most marketing research departments are perceived as adding value, those that aren't are the ones most likely to be asked to justify their budgets with an ROI analysis. As one researcher put it, "I developed my ROI measures as a defensive tactic. The marketing research function was under attack in my firm and I needed something concrete to convince our clients (and ourselves) that we were worth all and more of what we were spending on marketing research." An internal client provided a parallel point of view. "If I'm happy with my research group, I don't need to have them take their time and budget to measure ROI or prove to me how valuable they are. However, if I'm unhappy with them and don't think I'm getting good value for my money and time, then you bet I want to have some objective way of evaluating whether I'm getting value for what I'm paying for."

A woman who was in charge of the marketing research function in her firm knew that the economy and slowing demand for her firm's products meant that she might face a decline in her budget and staff. The end of the fiscal year was approaching, and she needed to put together her annual budget plan for the coming year. She knew that her marketing research group was highly regarded by senior management, that the number of research projects had been increasing from year to year, and that her group consistently received many compliments from the business managers. However, staff size had not grown, and people were working so flat-out that they had no time for training or ongoing skill development. They were routinely working overtime to deliver projects, and were in danger of burning out. In fact, several team members had said they would have to reduce their overtime or look for other jobs with better work/life balance. She was squeezed from both sides, with staff pushing for more resources and corporate looking for ways to cut back.

She was competing with other groups within the organization that were certain to provide evidence of their need for more resources, so she needed to provide an objective argument that allowed top management to assess the value of marketing research compared to the value provided by the other groups within the firm.

How did she handle this challenge? She created an annual report that had several sections. First, she determined the value that the marketing research group had produced in the past year for the organization and used this as a benchmark to estimate the future value that marketing research could produce in the coming year with proper funding. Second, she estimated the potential value of the research she hoped to conduct in the coming year. This was based on a series of conversations she held with top clients about their research needs and how research could help them accomplish their goals for the coming year. And finally, she listed what monies and staff she needed to implement the marketing research plan for the next year based on demand by business managers. This marketing research annual report clearly demonstrated to top executives that they either needed to cut back on marketing research that had been so valuable in the past or expand marketing research financial and staffing. She won some, although not all, of what she requested. However, if she could not demonstrate the value provided by marketing research, she probably would have had her budget and staff reduced.

ROI analysis was a powerful marketing tool in this case, just as it is a powerful decision tool for weighing research projects and spending. When using ROI analysis as a marketing tool, the researcher typically looks backward at what the ROI marketing research has provided in the past year for the organization as well as forward to the expected returns on the research that is being proposed for the coming year. The last section of this chapter describes in detail how to calculate anticipated ROI for future projects as well as how to estimate the actual ROI on projects already completed.

ASSESSING THE VALUE OF INVESTMENT IN RESEARCH

There are three methods for assessing the value of investment in marketing research. The simplest is called **negotiated value**. As its name implies, the marketing researcher and client negotiate the value they attribute to the research. The second method is **traditional ROI**, which uses a standard formula for computing returns as a percentage of investments. The third and most sophisticated method is **research ROI**. This adds the concepts of confidence and likelihood of acting to the traditional ROI measure, which makes it especially appropriate for use by researchers.

Negotiated Value Method

The negotiated value method is the easiest tool for evaluating the financial impact of marketing research projects. It begins with a negotiation conversation with the client that focuses on the potential value of decisions to be guided by the research. The conversations go beyond project objectives because the researcher and client agree on a monetary value of the research. There is no fixed way to estimate the value, which makes it less onerous than the usual ROI discussions, but negotiated value is also less standardized and more difficult to use for comparison purposes than ROI analysis. The researcher and the client know that the value estimate is just that: an estimate. However, the discussion helps them determine how much to spend on the research and may also help guide the research objectives and design. The following are just some examples of how negotiated value analysis might be used.

- For research on new products or new markets, the negotiated value estimate might focus on the expected value of each promising new idea identified and developed.
- For product, line extension, or enhancement research, the estimate might be based on the incremental revenue expected from improving the products or services.
- For advertising research, the estimate might be based on the advertising budget at risk.

One researcher explained her use of negotiated value this way. "I meet with my clients before the research projects begin and ask how they will use the research and what value they hope to gain by conducting the research. Sometimes they will say that it will help them spend their marketing budget more wisely, so we estimate the value as a portion of their marketing budget. Other times they may say that they hope to better understand the needs of a promising new market segment and that, if successful, this could have huge payoff for the entire firm. In that case, we might decide to attach a higher dollar value to the research."

In addition, some researchers "bank" the negotiated values of the projects they conduct in a year and then add that value together to estimate the overall annual value provided by the marketing research group. "Suppose I've conducted 20 major research projects this year for which my clients and I have estimated the negotiated value. Then, I prepare an annual report for the top executives summarizing the total value. It's a great way to demonstrate in financial terms what the firm has gained from its investment in the marketing research group and in our projects."

Traditional ROI

Historically, traditional ROI was used primarily as a way to assess the expected payoff of potential major investments, such as investments in new factories. Its formula reflects the importance of both the expected money to be gained and the money to be invested. Traditional ROI is defined as the ratio of money gained or lost on an investment relative to the amount of money invested.

$$Traditional\ ROI = \frac{\$Return\left[Final\ \$Value\ minus\ Initial\ \$Value\right]}{\$Investment\left[Initial\ \$Value\right]}$$

The final value term is the amount the organization expects to (or actually does) earn from the investment. The initial value term is the investment itself. And the numerator or the $ return is the difference between what is finally earned and what is initially invested.

Some marketing researchers have used traditional ROI as a tool to determine how much to spend on research projects. As one researcher put it, "Marketing was under pressure to estimate its ROI, so I decided to use the same tool when a marketing client asked me to conduct research on a potential new product. We talked about what the final value of the new project might be—that is, what we could hope for in sales from the new product if it were successful. Of course, we agreed that it was simply a guesstimate, but we came up with a total of $1 million over a five-year period. This helped us decide that we should invest a substantial sum in conducting the research because the potential payoff was so big. We spent $100,000 on the research, so our estimated [traditional] ROI was

$$Gross\ ROI = \frac{\$1,000,000 - \$100,000}{\$100,000} = \frac{\$900,000}{\$100,000} = 900\%$$

(There are many articles and books on how to compute traditional ROI. See the Further Reading section at the end of this chapter.)

The advantage of using traditional ROI over using negotiated value is that traditional ROI is more familiar and in much broader use among executives. This permits executives to compare the ROI estimates of marketing research with the ROI of other investments (such as investments in new IT systems or HR training). Using traditional ROI analysis also demonstrates that marketing researchers speak the same language and share financial goals with the clients, especially those at the top of the organization.

The main disadvantage of using traditional ROI is that it does not account for the unique but limited contributions of marketing research and may overstate the value of the research, which can cause executives to reject researchers' calculations. This has led some marketing researchers to use the research ROI method.

Research ROI

Research ROI adds the concepts of confidence and actionability to the traditional ROI because these are important benefits of conducting marketing research. The more that marketing research can increase the decision maker's confidence in making the correct decision, the greater the value of the research. Similarly, the more the marketing research increases the likelihood that executives will take action, the greater its value. Thus, some marketing researchers use the research ROI formula next because it includes an assumption about increased confidence (or reduced risk) and increased likelihood of taking action when research is conducted. The research ROI formula is as follows.

$$\frac{\$Return\left[Final\ \$Value - Initial\ \$Value\right] \times Increased\ Confidence \times Increased\ Likelihood\ of\ Acting}{\$Investment\left[Initial\ \$Value\right]}$$

Adding the Concept of Confidence

Marketing researchers know that many executives are willing to make decisions (even large and risky decisions) without the benefit of any marketing research, if the executives believe they already know the correct decision to make. Many researchers have been asked at the last minute to conduct marketing research that would merely bless a decision that an executive has already decided to make. If a firm regularly makes decisions without research, then research may not be able to increase the confidence in a decision, and the firm should not spend much money conducting marketing research. However, if the firm cannot imagine making decisions without research, then the marketing research has considerable value because it increases the confidence of making the best decision.

Adding the Concept of Actionability

Some research does not result in any action: Some decision makers choose, for reasons of their own, to take no action even when the research gives clear direction. Sometimes firms conduct research to increase their knowledge or as an input to developing a strategy without necessarily leading to action (as is often the case with exploratory research).

When the research does not lead to action, many people believe this means that the research is less valuable than research that does leads to action.

Adding estimates of confidence and actionability to the ROI calculation is not easy. As one marketing research director said, "I'm not sure if it's a good idea or not to try to measure return on research. Such as estimating the return on IT investments, there are so many assumptions necessary that you can never be sure your estimate will be close. For some kinds of exploratory research, like researching new products or markets, you don't know until you're done whether or not it will produce anything of financial value, and you certainly can't predict whether the executives will take action or not." Because these discussions are difficult, some marketing research groups prefer to avoid the research ROI method. And those who do use it admit that they compute research ROI only for larger projects.

In one case, the head of marketing research—a woman with many years of experience at the firm—was asked to research a new product concept and determine the product features and target market segments that would yield the greatest profits. This was a very important project for the firm, whose strategy called for having a steady flow of successful new products. So the researcher talked with executives in marketing, manufacturing, finance, and sales to estimate the most likely sales volume over the first five years of the product's life. Using a 10% cost of capital at the advice of the CFO (because that was the rate used for other investments), she determined the net present value of five years of revenues from the new product was $6.5 million. She then talked to the marketing and senior managers to determine how confident they were that they could make the right choice of product features and target markets without research. The clients said they were only 30% confident without research but would be at least 70% confident after the research was completed—an increase of 40%. Finally, she asked them how likely they were to introduce a new product—that is to take action—with and without the research. They determined that their likelihood of action would increase from 25% without research to 75% with research, for an increase in actionability of 50%. Then, estimating that the new product marketing research would cost $500,000, she calculated the research ROI of the project, as shown next, and determined that the research would be worthwhile for her firm.

$$\frac{(\$6,500,000 - \$500,000) \times 40\% \times 50\%}{\$500,000} = \frac{\$6,000,000 \times .2}{\$500,000} = \frac{\$1,200,000}{\$500,000} = 240\%$$

Which Measure of Value Is Best for You?

When calculating traditional or research ROI with their many assumptions and measures, it is important to be very clear with clients about the assumptions being made. For example, when marketing researchers talk to clients about their estimated likelihood of taking action with and without the research, it can start a valuable dialogue that emphasizes the importance of the client in the research process. On the other hand, it may annoy some clients.

Many researchers talk about how difficult it is to get estimates from their clients of the potential revenue and cost implications of the marketing research. One marketing researcher said, "What do I know? What do my clients know about manufacturing costs or the cost of capital to use in net present value? I don't know what financial or ROI hurdles the firm has set or what other opportunities they face. My clients and I are, for the most part, too junior to enter the circles where these conversations take place." Other researchers talk about how many assumptions go into the estimates. "We could make estimates, but it feels like pulling rabbits out of a hat. We could be right or wrong, and we wouldn't know the difference." Still others tell us that their clients lack the patience to sit down with them and make the estimates. "To a lot of these clients, I'm just an order-taker. They tell me what research they want, and they don't want a lot of guff from me about whether they will use the research and how certain they are about the results. I try to talk to them like a partner, but not all clients want that."

These are all valid comments; and therefore, most marketing researchers use the research ROI tool only for major projects. The choice of using negotiated value, traditional ROI or research ROI depends on the firm, the situation, and the client. The Table 2.1 compares some of the pros and cons of each measure as an analysis tool.

Since the research ROI is the most complete and challenging measure, the rest of this chapter focuses on research ROI implementation with examples of its many uses. Anyone who knows how to compute and use the research ROI analysis should be able to scale back to the traditional ROI or negotiated value analyses.

HOW TO USE RESEARCH ROI AS A DECISION TOOL

There are many ways to use research ROI as a decision tool. This section presents four common ways.

1. Create an appropriate budget for a research project.
2. Make the research design more actionable.
3. Compare alternative research options and prioritize them.
4. Focus clients on their role in getting the most value out of the research investment.

1. Create an Appropriate Budget for a Research Project

An ROI discussion can help the researcher and the client agree on how much to invest in a new piece of research. For example, if the dollar value of a decision is small and/or the expected decrease in uncertainty is low, then it may not be worthwhile to spend very much money conducting marketing research to guide that decision. However, a decision with large financial or strategic implications for the client or where there exists a great deal of uncertainty about the best course of action may make a substantial investment in marketing research cost effective.

For example, a marketing manager wanted to conduct research among potential customers to determine which of four promotional offers would be most effective. All the offers

Table 2.1 Pros and Cons of Methods for Assessing the Value of Investment in Marketing Research

Negotiated Value Method

Measures Used	Pros	Cons
Negotiated estimates of expected revenues or value of issues to be researched	• Easiest method • Is a way of assigning monetary value to marketing research • Can tie research budget to expected value it provides • Dialogue shows marketing researchers care about clients' values and needs	• Lack of consistent measures or methods of determining value means it can't be used to compare the value of projects to each other

Traditional ROI Method

Measures Used	Pros	Cons
• Estimates of return (final monetary value minus initial investment) • A ratio of return as a % of investment	• Same as negotiated value • ROI can be compared among research projects and between research and other spending • Formula and concept familiar to many executives	• Not easy to estimate expected returns with certainty, especially for inexperienced clients or researchers • Assumes all returns are attributable to MR, which they are not

Research ROI Method

Measures Used	Pros	Cons
Same as traditional ROI plus • Increase in confidence • Increase in actionability	• Same as traditional ROI • Provides a better estimate of the value of MR, which is not the sole cause of revenues but does increase confidence and actionability • Becomes easier with repeated usage	• Requires the most assumptions and discussion • Discussions about client likelihood of action and confidence in decisions can be uncomfortable for clients and MR

cost about the same amount to implement, so the challenge was to see which one was most preferred by customers with the highest reported purchase intent to increase revenues the most. In previous years, similar promotions had resulted in revenue increases of about $2 million. Given that there were four choices, the researcher and the client agreed that the odds of randomly picking the best one were 25%, which would increase to 100% once the research was complete (an increase in confidence of 75%). And the marketer agreed that he was certain to take action once the best promotion was determined. So the researcher and marketer computed how much to spend using the research ROI calculation. Note that they assumed that the research ROI had to be at least 100% or breakeven.

$$Research\ ROI = \frac{(\$2,000,000 - Cost\ of\ research) \times 75\% \times 100\%}{Cost\ of\ research} =$$

$$\frac{\$1,500,000 - .75 \times Cost\ of\ research}{Cost\ of\ research}$$

Research ROI x *Cost of research* = $1,500,000 - 0.75 x *Cost of research*
If *Research ROI* = 1.00: 1.75 x *Cost of research* = $150,000
Implies: *Cost of research* = $857,143 at break-even ROI of 100%

They concluded that a breakeven budget (where the research ROI was exactly 100%) was about $860,000. As long as they spent less than that and the costs of implementing the results were not a factor, the research would pay for itself at that level. Since even a first-rate project, with a large national sample of customers was priced at only $100,000, they agreed that this budget was very worthwhile.

2. Make the Research Design More Actionable by Comparing Options

Anil Menin and James Wilcox (1994) in their article, "USER: A Scale to Measure Use of Marketing Research" found that there are many reasons why marketing research is conducted. These include positive reasons (to guide decisions, to increase knowledge, or to build awareness of the reasons why decisions must be made) but also some cynical reasons (to play internal politics, to delay or confuse decisions, or to bless decisions that have already been made).

A major challenge for all researchers is to make their research actionable, which means to design the research so that it gives such clear guidance on the best course of action that the client will find it almost impossible not to take action. However, when research is done for cynical reasons (for example, when the client has already determined what action he or she wants to take and is using the research to bless a desired action or prevent an undesired action), then it is easy to determine that the projected research ROI is zero. Why?

If the action being researched is desired and the client is already certain it is correct, then the increase in confidence is zero, which means the ROI is zero. Similarly, if the action being researched is so unpopular with the client that she or he has already determined not to implement it no matter what the research may show, then the chances of acting on the research are zero, which means the ROI is zero. Thus, no monies or effort should be spent on conducting research.

Suppose that you are facing this situation, what can you do? One approach is to ask the client to let you design the research to test additional alternative action options. One researcher faced a situation where her CEO wanted to implement a new $10 million advertising campaign that was designed by his spouse and children. The CEO asked the researcher to conduct research on this campaign design but clearly was doing this only to confirm the decision he wanted to make. However, the researcher's gut reaction and the reaction of several other colleagues was that this campaign would actually damage rather than help the firm. They could also see that testing just this one option would have a research ROI of zero. No matter what was spent on the research or what it said, the increase in certainty and actionability would be zero. The researcher saw that she could either decide to spend almost nothing on the research because she assumed the research would not be acted on even if its conclusion recommended against the already made decision. Or she could offer to study other creative options as well as the wife's creative campaign since she wanted to see the $10 million advertising budget put to the best use. After some diplomatic pleading, she got the CEO to agree to let her add four creative options that appealed to the CEO's wife and children. Then she showed him the research ROI based on the following assumptions.

- The five creative approaches would cost the same amount, so the $10 million campaign cost was the final value estimate.
- Although the CEO was certain his campaign was the best of the five, no one knew for sure, so the confidence of randomly picking the best one was only 20%.
- After the research was complete, if the research showed another campaign was best, the CEO would be only 25% confident that the research was correct, so the increase in confidence would actually be only 5%.
- The researcher believed that the odds of the CEO actually implementing one of the other campaigns (if it proved to be best) were 50% because he had to advertise in some way.
- And she assumed that she could conduct the copy testing for $125,000.

Then the research ROI =

$$\frac{(\$10,000,000 - \$125,000) \times 5\% \times 50\%}{\$125,000} = \frac{\$9,875,000 \times .025}{\$125,000} = 198\%$$

Thus, there was substantial estimated return to conducting research that compared the CEO's wife's campaign with others, even if he was far from certain to implement another campaign. If the CEO's favorite campaign won, at least others in the firm would be convinced, and the CEO would be grateful to the researcher. If another option proved to be superior and the research convinced the CEO to use that option, then the researcher would have helped the firm avoid wasting the whole $10 million.

As this example shows, the research ROI is always enhanced by testing more than one option—whether it is new products, new advertising, new promotions, or new pricing schemes.

3. Compare and Prioritize Research Projects

Research ROI analysis can be used to compare and prioritize proposed new research projects. It is also a good way to assess the ROI of ongoing research projects on a periodic basis. Many ongoing projects (such as the purchase of syndicated research, ongoing satisfaction research, and tracking studies of all types) deserve an ROI analysis now and then. This allows marketing researchers to prioritize and potentially eliminate less valuable projects to make room for new projects that should have greater value to the organization. An ideal time to do this is when the research group is asked to do more than it can afford, when staff members are feeling overwhelmed by the volume of work, or during the annual budget process.

4. Focus Clients on Their Role in Making Research Valuable

The clients play a key role in determining the research ROI because they are the ones who have to take action based on the research. No matter how well designed the research, if the clients are unlikely to act, then they are better off not conducting that marketing research. The start of a marketing research project, when the clients are enthusiastic about the need for the research, is the ideal time for the researcher to focus the clients on their role in making research valuable and taking action.

The following is an example of focusing clients on getting the most out of the marketing research. A marketing research CMO asked for research to determine whether to enter a new market with a new marketing approach. If the decision were yes, the CMO estimated it would take $20 million in production and marketing costs to produce a new revenue stream of $50 million in the first year. The CMO suggested using only the first year's net income of $30 million ($50 minus $20) as the expected net value for the research ROI calculation because of the uncertainty of how quickly another competitor might jump into the market. (Note that sophisticated clients might use net present value of revenue streams even after competitive reaction to estimate research ROI, but using a one-year time horizon is always the most conservative approach to estimating research ROI.)

Although the CMO was very excited by this possible new market and hoped it would be the key to the firm's future growth, he knew that this was a risky undertaking. The CMO estimated he was only 10% confident that he would make the right decision without research. With the research (which he assumed would be good), he estimated he would be 90% confident, which is an increase of 80%. A very new group of C-suite executives (including the CMO) who had worked together for only a short time and had no clear sense of teamwork yet led this firm. Some of them were very risk averse and were not eager to enter a new market until they had more experience. In the process of discussing the research proposal with the C-suite executives, the marketing research director brought up the issue of the executives' role in taking action based on the research results. The marketing research director offered some hypothetical scenarios to them and asked them how they would respond.

- Who would take the lead on taking action?
- How would they make decisions and choices of the correct action as a team?
- How would they decide what financial and human resources to use and how much to spend?
- Who would be accountable for the results after action was taken?

They agreed that they would work together as a team to decide which actions to take because of the marketing research. However, they estimated that, even if the research gave clear direction, they might be unable or unwilling to act. So they agreed that the estimated likelihood of acting on the research was 30%.

The cost of the research was expected to be $1 million. So the marketing research director and CMO calculated the research ROI to decide whether the research was still worthwhile given the low likelihood of acting on the research. As the calculation shows, the research ROI was estimated to be 696% by the end of the first year, and they believed that the return would increase in future years.

$$Research\,ROI = \frac{(\$30,000,000 - \$1,000,000) \times 80\% \times 30\%}{\$1,000,000} = \frac{\$6,960,000}{\$1,000,000} = 696\%$$

While the C-suite executives did not commit to action, they realized that any inaction would be because of their indecision and not to a deficiency in the research. And after the research was completed, the marketing research director had the opportunity to meet with the executives to discuss why an actual decision was or was not made. This was an excellent way for the marketing research director to stay involved with his clients and in understanding the clients' changing needs and decision processes.

In this case, the marketing research director used the research ROI analysis as a decision tool before the research. Then, by checking back with the CMO and C-suite executives afterward to see what actions were or were not taken as a result, he also used the ROI analysis as a marketing and relationship tool.

A Word of Warning

There are going to be times when marketing researchers will be wise to provide the clients with what the clients want even if the expected research ROI is poor or even negative.

- If the CEO asks for a piece of research because her or his boss (perhaps the board) demands it, all the marketing researcher can do is try to design the research to maximize the ROI while still meeting the CEO's needs.
- Research that links directly to company strategy or business goals might be given a higher value than research that has only indirect links. The purpose of the ROI discussion is not just to make the best possible research spending and design decisions.
- If the clients resist participating in the ROI discussion, researchers probably will have to accept the situation and hope for a future opportunity for discussion. Although some clients prefer researchers to be order takers, most researchers' primary goal is always to show clients that they want to be and are partners in their clients' success.

HOW TO USE ROI ANALYSIS AS A MARKETING TOOL

The annual marketing research budget process is an ideal time for marketing researchers to meet with internal clients to ask for their feedback on the performance of the marketing research group in the past year, to understand the clients' business challenges and needs for the coming year, and to plan the appropriate research to support their expected business decisions and challenges. This interactive process can be enhanced with research ROI calculations for the planned research, which will result in priorities for the resources available for research and will also enhance the relationship process between the marketing researcher and the client.

Some of the ways to use research ROI analysis for marketing and relationship-building purposes are the following:

1. A year-end review of the value (financial and other) provided by the marketing research group

2. An annual listing of the highest priority research needs and their estimated ROIs

3. Support for the marketing research group's resource requests

In all three of these uses, the discussions with the client executives and the research ROI analyses act as both decision tools and marketing tools.

1. A Year-End Review of the Value Provided by the Marketing Research Group

Increasingly, marketing research groups are preparing annual reports for top executives and clients in their firms that demonstrate the value they have provided in the past year. The annual report not only demonstrates the actual financial returns from the past year's investment in marketing research, it also is a powerful marketing and relationship-building tool to show senior leaders and clients how effective the marketing research group has been and can be as a partner in their success.

These annual reports usually take several approaches to measuring the value provided by the marketing research group, and each of these approaches can be key sections in the annual report. Note that these are often similar to the balanced scorecard elements developed by Kaplan and Norton (1996) and marketing researchers working on their annual reports are strongly encouraged to read their publications. Typical sections in the annual report might include the following:

- The financial value or research ROI of marketing research during the last year
- Knowledge management or the contributions of research to the wisdom of the organization during the last year
- Client satisfaction or the effectiveness of the marketing research group during the last year
- Process or operating measures of the efficiency and magnitude of the research

Financial Value or Research ROI of Marketing Research

Research ROI analysis can be a powerful tool for demonstrating the value provided by the marketing research function in the past, just as it is for weighing alternative research projects. In the case of the annual report or balanced scorecard measure, only marketing researchers typically look backward at the ROI to show top decision makers what marketing research has actually contributed financially.

Estimating the annual research ROI of the marketing research investment begins by cataloging the research projects undertaken in the past year and estimating the actual research ROI that each project or activity produced. If the research ROI of a project was estimated before the project began, then the marketing researcher can go back to the decision maker or client after the research is completed and when enough time has passed for actions based on the research to have been taken. Then, by asking the client what actions were actually taken and how confident the clients felt in their actions, the researcher can recompute the research ROI.

To illustrate, let's return to the example of the new C-suite executive management team that had research conducted to assess the value of a new product in a new market. The estimated first year's net income from the new product was $30 million, the estimated increase in confidence was 80%, the estimated likelihood of taking action was 30%, and the cost of the research was $1 million. The marketing research director went back to the C-suite management team six months after the research was completed to assess the actual research ROI. The CMO told the marketing research director that the executives had committed to the new product and would be implementing it soon, although the research showed that the financial value would only be $15 million for the remainder of this year. The CMO said that he believed that the research had increased the executives' confidence that they were making the right decision by 80%—as they had estimated before the project was started. The CMO also said that the executives gave the marketing research director full credit for helping them commit to action by bringing up the actionability question in advance. So the marketing research director recomputed the actual research ROI as

$$\frac{(\$15,000,000 - \$1,000,000) \times 80\% \times 100\%}{\$1,000,000} = \frac{\$14,000,000 \times 80\%}{\$1,000,000} = 1,120\%$$

This was a very high research ROI, much higher than most projects' ROI. Research projects can also take a loss or have no credited value. For instance, if a business took action based on research that resulted in a loss, then the marketing research group would share in this loss and an amount for the loss would be deducted from the total sum that marketing research contributed over a year.

Finally, the annual report combines the actual research ROI of all the projects the marketing research group has completed in the year for which an ROI was calculated and computes an overall average research ROI for the year. In practice, most small-value projects will not have research ROI calculations because it is not worth the effort to the client or marketing research. And even some major projects may lack a research ROI calculation because the clients are not very interested in spending the time to estimate the necessary figures. For the projects that have been completed without measuring research ROI (or even traditional ROI or negotiated value with clients), the marketing research group's annual report can demonstrate value presented in the other sections of the report.

It is useful for the marketing research group and its senior clients to set an annual research ROI or financial goal for the marketing research group at the beginning of each year. This permits the marketing research group head and the senior executives of the organization to evaluate marketing research success, and bonuses for the marketing research group can be determined if actual research ROI meets or exceeds goal expectations. These research ROI goals can be set separately for each client, the business line or for the organization as a whole.

Knowledge Management

In this section of the marketing research group's annual report, the new insights or knowledge that have been provided by this year's research, are listed. This is primarily descriptive information about what has been learned and how it has been communicated. Many large marketing research groups put some of this information on the intranet so that qualified clients can see the topics that have been researched, and can request a conversation or data about what was learned that could apply in their business. The knowledge management section of the report can include surprising things that were learned from the research, how the research budget was aligned with the overall organization's strategic goals, and other factors that show how marketing research has contributed to the successful management of the organization.

Client Satisfaction or the Usefulness of the Marketing Research Group

This section of the annual report focuses on client perceptions of the value of the marketing research group. This could include measures of the usefulness of the research as rated by clients, client satisfaction with the way the research was conducted, and client ratings of the relationship they have with the marketing research group. These measures are perceptual rather than financial, but for many projects where no research ROI analyses are possible, they are often the most important available measures for the annual report.

Anil Menin and James Wilcox (1994) suggest the following measures of research usefulness, which some marketing research groups use to assess the usefulness of their research work:

- Degree to which results of the study were influential in the final decision
- Degree to which something new was learned from results or from doing the research
- Degree to which the research increased knowledge or led to action instead of being a show
- Comparative number of people using the research—the more who find it useful, the better
- Percentage of study that need not have been done or was beside the point

When measuring client satisfaction with the marketing research group, the model proposed by Rust, Zeithaml, and Lemon (2000) as shown in Figure 2.1 could be a useful tool.

Figure 2.1   Department Satisfaction Model

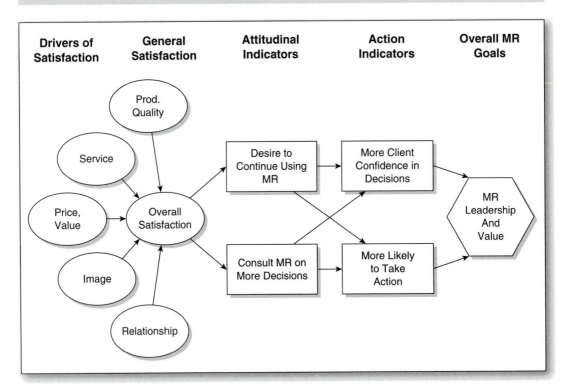

Operations or Process

The operating or process measures of the marketing research group are often fairly simple measures of the research work completed and the efficiency of the work. For instance, typical measures include the number and types of research projects or analyses, the cost of the projects, the ability of the group to complete projects on time and within budget, comparisons or benchmarks with other comparable marketing research groups, the costs of work done in house versus by suppliers, and so on.

Not every marketing research group has the resources or ability to prepare an effective annual report. However, when a high-quality annual report is shared in person with top management or key clients as part of an annual review, it becomes a powerful tool for building strong relationships and demonstrating the marketing research group is a committed business partner with the same professionalism as they would expect from themselves.

2. An Annual Listing of the Highest Priority Research Needs and Their Research ROIs

A best practice used by some leading marketing research heads is to have annual review discussions with their top clients. This ideally happens before the annual budgeting and strategic planning cycle begins so that the marketing research group's plans can be aligned with the needs of its clients. In these discussions, the marketing researchers typically ask the business executives about their marketing challenges, their strategic goals, and the risks they face in the coming year. Most researchers and clients report that the clients are more likely to clearly articulate their tactical issues (such as the need for a new campaign or the need to get a new product in the pipeline into widespread distribution) than their more unpredictable competitive or strategic challenges.

To help their clients think about the unpredictable but potentially very important challenges, some marketing researchers talk to their clients about **risk analysis**. This tool involves looking for the hidden, unanticipated risks that can threaten the survival of an organization. In marketing, these risks might be the failure to spot new technologies or competitive risks that could remake a market. As long as there are no new competitors or technologies, the failure to regularly conduct competitive and new product research may not be a problem. But if a new competitor or technology does appear, the failure to conduct this research can threaten revenue and even a firm's survival in some cases. In cases like this, the research ROI might be very low if no competitive threats are found, but it might be very high if the threats materialize. In this case, some wise marketing researchers compute two versions of the research ROI: one if the research does not turn up a threat (and does not lead to action) and one if the research does turn up a threat in time for the client to act to take action to address the threat.

How might this be done? One firm thought that a possible threat might come from a small competitor whose product had low market share at the moment but might steal sales in the future from the firm's main product, which produced $5 million in sales each year. If the marketing research group conducted research (costing $100,000) among their customer base on the appeal of the competitor's product and found that it was not a threat after all, then the firm estimated it might gain a great deal of confidence in deciding to take no action. So although they estimated their confidence would increase by 80% the likelihood of action would be zero and the research ROI would be zero as shown next. In essence, the marketing research group would have spent $100,000 with no monetary reward.

$$Research\ ROI = \frac{(\$5,000,000 - \$100,000) \times 80\% \times 0\%}{\$100,000} = \frac{\$0}{\$100,000} = 0\%$$

However, the executives also calculated that if the research revealed that the competitor posed a serious threat but that the firm could easily overcome that threat through a product modification (which the firm would certainly do), then the research ROI would be high.

$$Research\ ROI = \frac{(\$5,000,000 - \$100,000) \times 80\% \times 100\%}{\$100,000} = \frac{\$4,900,000 \times 80\%}{100,000} = 3,920\%$$

So the marketing researcher showed both calculations to the firm's executives and explained that the research could result in a zero research ROI or in a substantial research ROI, depending on what the research revealed. This helped the firm's executives understand that there was a risk in *not* conducting this research and that they should fund that research even if the threat did not materialize. This demonstrates that annual dialogues with executive clients (about their ongoing marketing research needs for the coming year, their strategic goals and the biggest threats they face that keep them up at night) are a good way to ensure that no important research needs are overlooked. And by adding the concept of risk analysis to the research ROI calculation, it is possible to get clients to see the value of some research projects that they might overlook otherwise.

The next step is for the marketing research group head to prepare a list of the major proposed projects for the coming year along with the budget requests and research ROI (if it can be calculated) for each one. In practice, no one list all projects. Most people list the most important projects that they envision for the coming year and try to create an estimate of the value for each of these important projects. Ideally, the research ROI will be calculated, but if this is not possible because of lack of information, then perhaps, a negotiated value assessment can be provided.

This listing of projects and their expected value might include the following groupings.

Proposed Research for Coming Year

1. Ongoing research (satisfaction and market tracking, for instance)
2. New tactical research (new media evaluation, pricing, etc.)
3. Strategic research (to allow the clients to support the firm's strategic goals, such as entering new markets, etc.)
4. Risk reduction research (to prepare the client to address competitive threats)
5. Budget request for emerging issues not known now

Another way of grouping projects could be according to the organizational structure of the company such as by business lines or client segments. The grouping that makes most sense to executives and the way the company thinks is the best grouping choice.

Under each grouping or heading, many specific projects could be listed, each with its own budget request and, where possible, research ROI analysis. Since some projects will have higher research ROIs than others, this permits the top managers in the firm to determine which projects to prioritize and how much to spend on them. Note that, by adding the final heading for "emerging issues," the marketing research group permits itself the time and resources to address the unexpected research requests that always arise each year.

3. Support for the Marketing Research Group's Resource Requests

The annual report combined with the listing of highest priority marketing research projects, when communicated properly, can help marketing researchers retain and grow the budget and other resources they need to continue to serve their clients effectively. Marketing researchers compete with other groups within the organization for resources, so it is important for marketing research to provide objective and persuasive evidence of their value compared to the value provided by the other groups.

CONCLUSION

ROI analysis is an important tool for marketing researchers that can be used in two ways that appeal to top executives. ROI analysis can be used as a decision tool with financial measures that are understood and meaningful to CFOs, CEOs, and other business executives within the firm. ROI analysis can also be a marketing or relationship-building tool because the process of agreeing on which research ROI assumptions and measures to use requires important conversations with clients that can demonstrate the value of the marketing research projects and group. These discussions demonstrate the marketing researcher's knowledge of the business, show that the marketing researcher is a team player with goals that are aligned with the client's, and increase the likelihood the client will accept and value the research. When marketing researchers hold postproject conversations with the clients to determine the actual research ROI of the research, the clients can see that the researchers are serious about providing value, and this makes clients willing to share more of their time and insights with the marketing research group in an effort to continue growing the relationship.

There is overlap between using research ROI as a decision tool and as a marketing tool because both uses of research ROI analysis require a deep discussion and interaction with the clients. In a typical, non-ROI-focused discussion between client and researcher at the start of a research project, the emphasis is on the research objectives and what issues to study. As long as the researcher understands the objectives or purpose of the research and designs the research to accomplish that objective, then the client and researcher both are usually satisfied with the research design. However, adding the discussion about the research ROI analysis requires interaction before, during, and after the research that strengthens the relationship between the marketing research group and its clients, allows them to prioritize research projects, and helps win client support for future projects and annual budget requests. And when this research ROI information is aggregated into a measurement system with a consistent methodology for calculating and reporting the predicted and actual value of research work, the stature of the marketing research group as a valued and important partner to its clients and the firm increases substantially. In fact, the consistent and proper use of research ROI analysis may be one of the most powerful tools the marketing research group can use to enhance its standing within the organization.

APPENDIX 2.1

DEFINING AND COMPUTING TRADITIONAL ROI

Defining Terms

The definitions of the value of the return and investment can vary according to different situations. In James Lenskold's book *Marketing ROI* (2003), there is a discussion of how to estimate the incremental **revenue** aspect of value. There is a range of choices available that include gross margins, total net profits adjusted for net present value, or net customer lifetime value. It is also possible to simply estimate the incremental **cost** aspect of value.

For example, a decision that involves using an entirely new marketing approach for a new market segment will probably have more money at risk than a decision about a minor change in packaging

The following are examples of calculating ROI with the gross measure approach and the net measure approach.

Gross value example. Assume that a business manager wants to know whether a new product will generate more new revenue than the existing product. If the marketing researcher used a gross value of revenue, the calculation would look only at the anticipated future gross revenue from the new product compared to that of the existing product. Let's assume that the new product is expected to provide $1 million more in revenue than the current product. Then, the ROI calculation would be based on this $1 million in gross revenue increase, minus the cost of the research (say $100,000), for an ROI of 900%. The calculation would be as follows:

$$Gross\ ROI = \frac{\$1,000,000 - \$100,000}{\$100,000} = \frac{\$900,000}{\$100,000} = 900\%$$

Net value example. Now we will calculate a net income ROI with the same scenario. In this example, all the additional incremental costs associated with the new product are considered. This could include the costs of new materials, new manufacturing capabilities, new marketing or advertising campaigns, and so on compared to the cost of materials, manufacturing, and marketing for the existing product. Suppose that the additional or incremental costs are $800,000, which means that the net income would be only $200,000 ($1,000,000 minus $800,000), and the ROI of the $100,000 research would be only 100%.

$$Net\ ROI = \frac{\$200,000 - \$100,000}{\$100,000} = \frac{\$100,000}{\$100,000} = 100\%$$

The gross income method of calculating ROI is easier than the net income method because it requires fewer estimates. Using the gross income method avoids the need to estimate the many variables on the cost side (such as cost of materials, labor costs, marketing and advertising costs, distribution costs, etc.) with which the researcher and client may have limited or no familiarity. For researchers and their clients who are just starting to use ROI, the gross income method could feel like all they could handle. Some researchers say that it's difficult enough to estimate revenues or sales and that they have no reliable way of estimating the manufacturing or other costs. However, other researchers have pointed out as mention by Brett Hagins (2010), it is best to make the ROI calculation as conservative as possible to maximize the credibility of the estimate. Failure to be conservative may diminish the client's willingness to accept the researcher's ROI estimate.

Regardless of the measure of value that is used, it is important for the marketing researcher and the client to agree on the most appropriate measure to use given the decisions to be made. It is also important to be consistent in the measures used in calculating ROI: Select and use either gross or net gain/loss, but do not switch back and forth between gross and net measures.

This is important so that comparisons can be made between different marketing research projects. One way to determine which method to use is ask the CFO or business managers for advice on which measure is more commonly accepted in the organization. The finance people in the firm can also be of assistance in calculating the ROI for the first few times.

Selecting Time Horizons and Net Present Value

ROI calculations also require decisions about what time horizons to use: Is it sufficient to project final value for just a single year, or will the value of the research investment endure over multiple periods, perhaps for many years? If it is appropriate to estimate ROI over more than one year, then the ROI analysis needs to calculate the net present value (NPV) of the final value in today's dollars (where future dollars are worth less than today's dollars based on the estimated cost of cash). For example, assume that a research project will result in a new product that will produce revenues for five years beginning the year after the research is conducted. If we use the gross revenues that we expect to flow from the new product as our measure of final value, then the NPV of the final value might be estimated as presented next, where the NPV is only $6.5 million instead of $7.5 million.

Year	$ Gross Revenues in 000's (does not include cost of production)	NPV of $ Gross Revenues (using a 10% cost of capital for illustration)
1 (year research is conducted)	0	0
2	500	455
3	2,000	1,653
4	2,500	1,878
5	2,000	1,366
6	500	310
Total Final Value	7,500	5,662

FURTHER READING

Ambler, T. (2003). *Marketing and the bottom line* (2nd ed.). London, UK: Pearson Education Limited.

Lesh, A. D., & Schmalensee, D. (2004). Measuring returns on research. *Marketing Research*, 22–27.

Likierman, A. (2009). The five traps of performance measurement. *Harvard Business Review*, 96–101.

Schmalensee, D., & Lesh, A. D. (1998). How to make research more actionable. *Marketing Research*, 23–36.

Schmalensee, D., & Lesh, A. D. (2007). Creating win-win relationships. *Marketing Research,* 16–21.

Schmalensee, D., & Lesh, A. D. (2010). How to transform marketing research from vulnerable to valuable. *Quirk's Marketing Research Review,* 36.

Wyner, G. A. (2006). Beyond ROI. *Marketing Management*, 8–9.

CHAPTER 3

Combining Data Mines and Attitude Research

PAUL GURWITZ

Renaissance Research & Consulting, Inc.

INTRODUCTION

Historically, market researchers have had access to data from two principal sources:

- *Data from surveys of representative samples of the market for a given product or service.* Typically, these data included respondent background variables, attitudes toward specific products or brands, and self-description statements (psychographics), as well as self-reports of consumption behavior such as usage, frequency, and volume.
- *Data from databases.* These are either internal databases (customers, subscribers, members, etc.) containing identifying information and specific transactional data or publicly available databases on a subset of the general population that include consumers' financial status, background data, media and purchasing behavior.

Note that each data source has its own advantages and disadvantages. Attitudinal data are only available from respondent-level surveys; however, behavioral data from such surveys are necessarily self-reported and, therefore, subject to bias. Conversely, behavioral data from databases are hard data, given that they are abstracted from a consumer's actual behavior, rather than his or her report of it; on the other hand, database data, being *only* behavioral, can lack richness, as they deal with the "what," rather than the "why" of marketing decisions.

For this reason, analysis of data from only one of these sources will *not* allow the research to answer certain questions that cross domains, such as, "What attitudes predict true purchase behavior?" That is why, over the last 30 years or so, marketing researchers have been interested in merging the two domains: pairing attitudinal data from consumer surveys with behavioral data from available databases. This article will review these efforts, discussing the following issues:

- Why combine data sources—what types of marketing questions can be answered uniquely by merging attitudinal and behavioral data?
- Data gathering considerations—what are the different strategies for combining data from different sources and levels of analysis, and what are the advantages and disadvantages of each?
- Analyzing multidomain data—what are the specific analytic challenges presented by multidomain data, and what types of analysis can best take advantage of the richness of such datasets?
- The future of multidomain data—what are likely to be the opportunities and challenges for combining and using attitudinal surveys and behavioral databases?

WHY COMBINING ATTITUDES WITH EXISTING DATA MINES IS IMPORTANT

The short answer is that, together, they potentially tell you more than either of them separately would.

Demographic and behavioral data can be used to identify the prime prospects for a product or service, where they are located, and what media can be used to reach him or her; product usage data can also be used to infer his or her product needs. However, neither can get at the attitudes that may underlie, and possibly influence, product choices—knowledge that can be crucial for understanding the purchase decision process, thereby, improving one's prediction of it.

Data from an attitude survey, on the other hand, can get at the consumer's self-image, product attitudes, and needs that are not directly expressed by actual behavior. Different consumers can make the same product choice for different reasons; therefore, they might be the object of very different marketing and advertising treatments, even though their behavior alone can't tell them apart.

Only direct questioning of a sample of consumers can elicit the "why" behind a purchase decision than can inform both marketing decisions and the content of the messages used to advertise them. However, while it's true that one may ask behavioral questions, for instance about product usage, in a survey, the answers to those questions are still not a record of true behavior because they are self-reported. Usage data from a survey are subject to many biases, including imperfect recall, under- or overestimation of volume, and in certain sensitive categories, social desirability effects that drive respondents to purposely over- or underreport (or frankly mislead about) a behavior. For this reason, the record of actual behavior is always preferable to self-report data.

Thus, each domain provides unique information that can be crucial for marketing decision making. Given that, it follows that the most reliable way of investigating the relationship between background, attitudes, and behavior would be to *combine* the two domains. Such a procedure would be necessary to answer a range of different marketing questions:

- *How accurate are consumer self-reports of purchase behavior?* Many marketing researchers use self-reported purchase and usage data from surveys as a surrogate for records of actual purchases, usually because of lack of access to the latter. Underlying this is the assumption that respondents can report past purchases and/ or usage in an accurate and unbiased way. But how true is that assumption? Under what circumstances, for what product categories, for what types of measures can we be more or less certain of respondents' accurate recall of their behavior? This could be tested by matching the product purchase records of a sample of customers to their answers to a product purchase and usage battery. The data from the two domains could then be cross-tabulated or correlated to determine the actual level of accuracy and bias of the sample's recall.

  For instance, a bank wants to know how accurate their customers can be about their relationships with the institution: what products they own, how much they have invested, and so on. They sample their customer database and survey the sample. Among the questions, respondents are asked what bank products they hold. These data are then cross-tabulated against the data in actual customer files.

  In this case, it turned out that there was only a 40% correspondence between what customers *thought* they owned and what they actually did: respondents reported owning products not on the bank's records, and failed to report those that are. The bank used this information to improve their customer information and communication systems—and to rely less on customer self-report when it came to measuring the size of their relationships.

- *How do consumer attitudes toward a product actually affect their purchasing behavior?* It is a commonplace in marketing that attitudes lead behavior—that a positive attitude toward a product is a necessary condition for its purchase, even if not necessarily a sufficient one. However, it is easy to imagine cases in which neither assumption might be true:
  - Consumers might have a high level of satisfaction with a brand, but buy another because of external influences such as availability or a price promotion.
  - Conversely, there can be instances in which consumers buy a particular brand even though their satisfaction with it is low, for instance, a product like a bank checking account where the start-up cost and inconvenience of switching banks may deter customers from moving their account from a bank that they are nonetheless dissatisfied with, or a cell-phone contract with large monetary penalties for early termination.

  Even the causal order between the two may sometimes be reversed, with behavior leading attitudes. The theory of cognitive dissonance, developed in the 1950s, maintains that people will change their attitudes toward an action that they were induced or compelled to perform for some external reason (Festinger, 1957). So consumers might actually increase their level of satisfaction about a product they bought because it was the only one available to justify the purchase to themselves.

In other words, the relationship between attitudes and behavior in brand purchase is a hypothesis; it can be tested by matching the brand attitudes and satisfaction of a sample of customers to their actual purchase behavior. Such a dataset can then be used to test the extent of the link between attitude and behavior in the specific instance and, more generally, to develop hypotheses about when that link holds and when it doesn't.

For instance, a packaged-goods marketer believed that color and brand name were the biggest drivers of customer satisfaction. However, when he attached the respondents' purchase records from a publicly available consumer panel, he found that they were not the biggest drivers of *purchase*—low price was.

- *How well does the behavior of different market segments follow their attitudes?* Attitudinal segmentation has been a mainstay of marketing research for decades. For example, to develop customized marketing and communications strategies for various targets, a market might be divided into attitudinal segments to ascertain different needs, varying self-images, and attitudes toward brands.

  However, since they were developed based on attitudinal measures alone, such segments may be distinct attitudinally, but not necessarily distinct in either background or behavior.

  o A given attitudinal segment may be spread across demographic groups (age, gender, location, etc.), making it hard to identify and locate to deliver segmented communication.
  o A particular attitudinal profile does not necessarily imply a unique pattern of purchase behavior. On the one hand, different patterns of attitudes can still result in the same purchase pattern; on the other hand, varying purchase behaviors can be the result of the same set of attitudes.

  Matching data from a segmentation study to its respondents' background and purchase behavior provides a way of testing the fit between the attitudinal segments and their demographic characteristics and their behavioral outcomes.

  Note that this kind of testing is not restricted to those who have access to internal databases of customer behavior. Thanks to publicly available proprietary databases maintained by companies, such as Axciom, Experian, InfoUSA, and FICO, those with access only to attitudinal survey data (for instance, CPG manufacturers), can often find demographic and behavioral data on their survey respondents that will allow them to establish a link between their attitudinal segment and behavioral information that can be used to target various populations for varying marketing communication. We will discuss the means, and the issues, around establishing that link next.

APPROACHES FOR COMBINING EXISTING DATA MINES WITH SURVEY DATA

Given the necessity (or at least the desirability) of being able to analyze attitudinal and behavioral indicators together, the question becomes how that is managed. Such an effort has to satisfy many criteria for data quality:

- *Validity*. The data should be as accurate as possible an indicator of the phenomena being measured. For example, actual purchase records are more valid an indicator of purchase behavior than self-reported purchase.
- *Completeness*. As many data points as possible should be available for every respondent that is sampled. In particular, there should be no systematic missing data (i.e., variables that are entirely missing for any given subset of respondents), which would tend to bias the analysis if they were used in it.
- *Representativeness*. The sample should be projectable to a larger population or market. This is particularly a question when data from multiple sources are merged because the effective sampling frame for the merged dataset is the smallest of the various sources.

    For instance, a marketer has access to the data from a previously conducted attitudinal survey of a random national sample of consumers. Merging his customer database with respondent attitude survey will produce a file of customers with both attitudinal and behavioral information in it. However, the merged dataset will be a projectable sample of customers only to the extent that those customers are representative of all the customers on the marketer's database.

- *Granularity*. The data should refer to the smallest unit of analysis possible. Individual-level data are preferable to data aggregated up to the state, regional, or national level because individual respondent variance is lost in the aggregation process.

As we will see, the various methods of combining attitudinal and behavioral information in the same dataset are all compromises, as all sacrifice some of the requisites of good data in favor of others.

Individual-Level Matching of Survey and Database Data

One method for combining attitudinal and behavioral indicators is to merge attitudinal survey data with database records at the individual level. This is most often done when the study is of a defined population (e.g., a company's customers, subscribers to a periodical, employees, or website visitors) where an individually identified behavioral database exists. Alternatively, there exist proprietary databases, maintained by companies such as Axciom, Experian, InfoUSA, and FICO, that contain behavioral data points on some portion of the general population that are gleaned from publicly available sources at an individual level. This source is especially useful for marketers without an internal customer behavior database, such as consumer goods manufacturers.

For a defined population such as a customer list, the behavioral database becomes the sampling frame. A random sample of data records is drawn (of a size that will allow sufficient statistical power, taking likely response rate into account), and the contact information on the database appropriate to the survey methodology (i.e., addresses, phone numbers, e-mail addresses) is collected. Respondents are then contacted and asked to participate in a survey, in which they are asked attitudinal and other questions not present on their database record. The chosen items in the respondent's database record are then appended to the survey record, producing a combined database for analysis.

For a general population survey, on the other hand, a random sample is first drawn from the intended frame (e.g., U.S. households, adults, licensed drivers, etc.). An attitude survey is administered to this sample. At the same time, an attempt is made to match the survey respondents to records in one or more proprietary demographic or behavioral databases; if a match is found, the selected demographic or behavioral data points are appended to the respondent's survey data record for analysis.

For either a defined or a general population, this approach has many advantages but also several problems. On the one hand, data matching potentially passes the test of validity in that it allows the combination of attitudinal data be merged with actual rather than self-reported behavioral indicators. (I use "potentially" here because validity depends in part on data quality.) It also yields data at the individual level, which is more useful for analysis than aggregate data.

On the other hand, data quality and representativeness can be major issues in respondent data matching. Although we can reasonably assume that internal databases such as customer, member, or subscriber files have a complete list of *individuals,* we often can't make the same assumption for the *variables*.

Because such files are gathered for other than research purposes, without systematic cleaning or updating procedures, inconsistent or missing data can be a frequent problem. Incompleteness in data limits their usefulness for analysis and systematic missing data (that is, data that is missing for an entire category of cases) can introduce bias. At the very least, use of internal databases usually implies a fairly onerous cleaning and coding job to make the data sufficiently consistent for research purposes.

When accessing proprietary national databases, there can be no assumption that all of the survey respondents are even in the database. The match rate of the database to the survey sample determines not only the usefulness of the behavioral data points but also the representativeness of the resulting dataset. No matter how carefully a survey sample has been designed, the actual representativeness of the matched dataset can be no better than that of the database being used.

Beyond considerations of the validity and representativeness of the data collected, matching of survey data to outside individual-level databases also involve ethical concerns, including respondent confidentiality, privacy, and informed consent.

Concern over confidentiality is especially acute in the case of matching survey data to client databases that may focus on customers, members, or employees. Since by definition, the identity of the respondents is at least potentially known to the client. The Code of

Standards and Ethics for Survey Research of the Council of American Survey Research Organizations (CASRO; 2011) says,

> It is essential that Survey Research Organizations be responsible for protecting from disclosure to third parties—including Clients and members of the Public–the identity of individual Respondents as well as Respondent-identifiable information, unless the Respondent expressly requests or permits such disclosure. (para. 1)

The CASRO (2011) code does make an explicit exception for data matching, but conditionally:

> Where Respondent-identifiable data is disclosed to clients so that the Survey Research Organization may analyze survey data in combination with other respondent-level data such as internal customer data . . . it is understood that the information will be used for model building, internal (Survey Research Organization) analysis, or the like and not for individual marketing efforts and that *no action can be taken toward an individual respondent* simply because of his or her participation in the survey. (para. 2)

In this case, it is the responsibility of the survey researcher to obtain an agreement to these terms from the client.

Another ethical issue surrounding individual data matching is that of respondent privacy. This is especially true when survey research data are merged with proprietary national databases. Informed consent to divulge personal information is an ethical requirement of survey researchers. CASRO (2011) again states,

> "Respondents should be:
> a. willing participants in survey research
> b. appropriately informed about the survey's intentions and how their personal information and survey responses will be used and protected" (Preamble)

However, national databases collect individual-level information without a person's informed consent, at least to the extent that they weren't informed that the information might be used for a particular research study. Therefore, appending database information on a respondent to the survey data record is potentially an ethical lapse, unless the researcher explains the intended augment, including a description of the variables and how they are to be used, to the potential respondent at the point the respondent is being asked to take the survey, which, to the author's knowledge, is *not* common practice despite the implications of the codes' ethical restrictions.

Matching Survey Data to Aggregate Databases

Another method for merging survey data with external information is to link individual survey responses with aggregate database information. An example of this is census information, which is made available on an aggregated basis to many geographic divisions, with the smallest available information of certain data being at the block level (U.S. Census Bureau, 2011). Another example of such databases are geodemographic segmentation schemes such as VALS or PRIZM, which classify the various neighborhoods (blocks) in the United States into lifestyle segments, using block-level census data.

To put all the data in an analysis in a consistent level of aggregation, one of two strategies is used:

- *Aggregation* (upward). Individual respondent data are pooled by summation, averaging or percentaging to the level of aggregation of the database. For instance, variables on all respondents in a given block are averaged, and the analysis is conducted at the block level.

  In this process, the choice of statistic (mean, count, top-box percentage) must be chosen with care. And the choice of aggregating statistic may well influence the results, and therefore, must be appropriate both to the variable and to the objective of the analysis.

- *Ascription* (downward). Database data from a given unit of analysis (e.g., ZIP code) are appended to every respondent belonging to that unit, which is how geodemographic segmentations are used. The segmentation code for a given census block is appended to the record of every respondent who lives in that block. Another example is appending aggregate data for a county to each respondent who lives in that county.

Aggregate matching tends to satisfy the requirements of validity, completeness, and representativeness. Nevertheless, aggregation tends to produce data at a low level of granularity because the behavioral variables are not measured at an individual level. In essence, the effective level of detail of a merged dataset is that of the *least* granular variables. Special analytical techniques are often needed to take into account the reduced variance introduced by aggregate variables ascribed to individuals.

Newer Data Matching Strategies

In addition, newer strategies for merging survey and database information have been developed over the last few years, which use statistical techniques to move away from one-to-one matching of data records without resorting to aggregation and its accompanying loss of granularity. Since these techniques are not yet as commonly used as the ones described previously, they will be discussed further later, regarding the future of database merging.

ANALYZING DATA FROM MULTIPLE DOMAINS

In many ways, analyzing a dataset that combines attitudinal survey and behavioral database data follow the same rules, and uses the same techniques as does analyzing either type of data alone. However, there are certain challenges posed specifically by mixed-domain data, and certain types of analysis are especially suited to it.

We will discuss both next, using as examples two types of analysis that are especially appropriate to such datasets:

- Using attitudes to predict behavior
- Segmenting a sample across both attitudes and behavior

Using Attitudes to Predict Behavior

One of the central reasons for combining attitudinal and behavioral data is to use the former to predict the latter (and, as a corollary, using the latter to validate the former). For this purpose, one of the most important tools in the analyst's arsenal is **multiple regression**. Regression predicts the value of an outcome variable (in this case, a behavior) as a function of a number of predictor variables (here, the attitudes) by assuming that the relationship between the two can be described as some variant of a straight line, whose equation is the following:

$$Y = A + \sum b_i x_i, \text{ where}$$

Y = The value of the behavioral variable
x_i = The value of the attitudinal variable i
b_i = The predictive weight assigned to attitudinal variable i
A = A constant

The task of the analysis is to assign weights to each attitude such that when the weighted attitude scores are summed, the result will be as close as possible to the value of the behavior. The b weights also, when standardized (and are known as *beta weights*), represent the importance of their corresponding predictors on a scale from zero to one.

Even though it is the most common predictive tool, multiple regressions have certain characteristics that complicate its use for predicting behavior. The first is the issue of variable scales. Linear regression is ideally suited to variables measured on an interval scale, preferably with no endpoints. A physical characteristic, such as temperature, comes closest; a multipoint attitude scale, while not infinite, is often well behaved enough to use in a regression.

On the other hand, while most attitudinal variables are relatively regression-friendly, not all behavioral variables are. In particular, linear regression can produce misleading or even nonsensical results when used to predict dichotomous (yes/no) variables such as actual product purchase.

The reason is that when one uses regression to predict product purchase, the result is always an estimate of purchase *likelihood*—the *probability* that the product is purchased, given the set of attitude scores. The problem is that purchase likelihood, like any probability, has a restricted range (from 0% to 100%), while linear regression (which always describes a straight line) is subject to no such constraint. As a result, as Figure 3.1 shows, it is possible for linear regression to produce nonsensical predictions (purchase likelihoods less than 0% or more than 100%), particularly if the predictor variables are not well distributed.

Accordingly, it is important when using behavioral variables as predictive outcomes to pay close attention to their form and to use the appropriate analytic techniques. For instance, when estimating the likelihood of a positive purchase decision, it is a much better idea to use **logistic regression**, otherwise known as logit analysis, which assumes the relationship being measured is a cumulative probability curve whose limits are 0 to 100%, rather than a straight line (see Figure 3.1).

Figure 3.1   Linear Versus Logit Prediction of Purchase

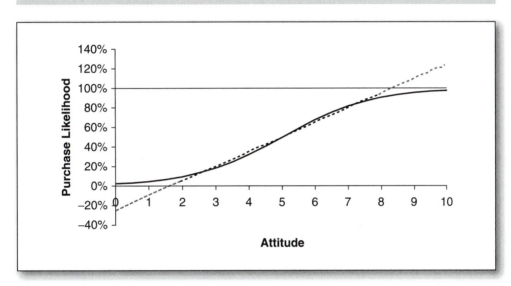

The linear prediction is represented by the dotted line and the logit prediction by the curve.

An even larger issue with using simple regression with multidomain data is the influence of **collinearity**. The predictors of a given behavior can also predict each other, as shown by high intercorrelations among them; these correlations can distort, or at least misrepresent, the effects of predictor variables on an outcome. These distortions can be of two types:

• The inclusion of a variable in a regression equation can severely reduce the apparent effect of another variable with which it is highly correlated, even though the other variable has almost as much effect on the outcome as the first one. This is because each regression equation calculates the effect of each variable on the outcome *over and above* that of all other variables in the equation; therefore, if two variables explain the same variation in the outcome, they will not both be given credit for it, even though both variables have an impact.

• The effect of a variable that influences an outcome in complex ways can be washed out in a simple regression model. For instance, if a background variable has a strong positive effect on one attitude and a strong negative impact on another, its effects can cancel one another out, suggesting (falsely) that the variable has no effect on either.

The reason for both of these problems lies in the fact that one is using a simple model (simple linear regression) to describe what can be a causally complex process. Often, the internal correlations among predictor variables represent a multilevel causal structure in the process being described, for instance see the following:

Respondent Characteristics ⇒ *Attitudes* ⇒ *Behavioral Outcome*

The inclusion of data from different domains in the same regression equation can increase the likelihood that there is such a complex structure in the data. This structure cannot be adequately described by a single regression equation, which makes the implicit assumption that the only relevant relationship in the data are between all the predictor variables, on the one hand, and the outcome, on the other. What is needed to describe the relationships properly is an analytic technique that explicitly includes *multiple* causal processes in the same system and evaluates them simultaneously.

These techniques have many different names, along with variations in their estimation algorithms: structural equation modeling, simultaneous equation modeling, or path modeling. What they all have in common is that they explicitly specify a complex causal structure among the variables, made of two or more interlocking regression equations in which the outcome of one equation is a predictor in another, eventually predicting the outcome variable. Such a model is often represented visually by a schematic, known as a *path diagram* (see Figure 3.2).

Figure 3.2   Hypothetical Path Model: Purchase Likelihood Predicted by Attitudes and Demographics

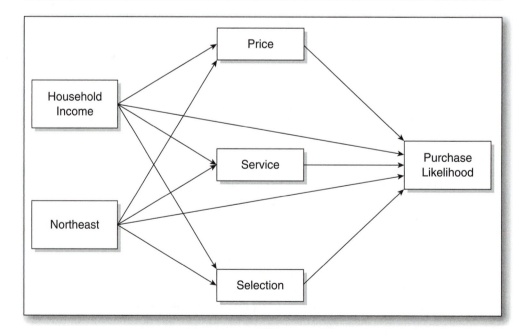

The several equations in the model are then evaluated, so a weight is calculated for each individual predictor-outcome relationship. These weights are then used to label the relationships (known as "paths") on the path diagram. By themselves, they represent the *direct effect* of one predictor on its proximate outcome in the model; more complex *indirect effects* of one variable on another through a third can be calculated by multiplying the weights of all the paths connecting the original predictor with its outcome. Such a model can faithfully describe more complex causal processes than can a single regression equation.

For example, a national retailer conducts a customer satisfaction survey among a sample of her current and lapsed customers. Among other questions, customers are asked to rate the store on its price/value, selection, and service. By matching the customer list to a commercial database, the retailer has detailed demographic background information on her customers, including where they live and their household income. She also knows which of them made a purchase in the past six months.

At first, the marketer attempts to predict whether the customer is a recent purchaser by creating a simple regression model. Table 3.1 shows the results of that analysis:

- Of the three store attributes, price is by far the most important, followed by selection; by contrast, service has virtually no impact on purchase.
- Customers who live in the Northeast are more likely to be recent purchasers than those who live elsewhere.
- By contrast, household income has virtually no impact on recent purchase.
- The model explains 42% of the variance in recent purchase (R^2, or coefficient of determination), which while highly significant still leaves a great deal of variance unaccounted for.

Table 3.1 Results of Single Predictive Regression

Variables	Regression Weights
Store Attributes	
Price	0.50
Service	−0.05
Selection	0.20
Customer Characteristics	
HH Income	0.00
Northeast	0.35
Variance Explained	42%

In an attempt to get a better handle on the antecedents of purchase behavior, the marketer specifies a path model of the relationships (recall Figure 3.2). The model can be viewed as a series of interlocking hypotheses:

1. Recent purchase is a function of both store attributes and customer background.
2. Store attribute ratings, in turn, differ based on the customer's background characteristics.

All of the hypotheses represented in the path model are tested by separate regressions: The destination of each arrow is regressed on all of the variables pointing to it. The regressions produce weights corresponding to each path in the model; paths associated with statistically insignificant weights are dropped from the diagram while the significant weights are used to label the corresponding paths. The result can be seen in Figure 3.3, and they tell a different story from that told by the simple regression equation.

- All three store characteristics have substantial effects on purchase. Price remains the most important. However, both service and selection also matter.
- Living in the Northeast does predict recent purchase, in two ways:
  - Customers in the Northeast are more likely to rate the store highly on selection.
  - They are also more likely to have purchased recently, even holding their rating of the store's selection constant.
- Household income has a significant effect on both price and service ratings, but in *opposite directions*: More upscale customers tend to rate the store higher on price/value but *lower* on service.

Figure 3.3   Path Model: Purchase Likelihood Predicted by Attitudes and Demographics

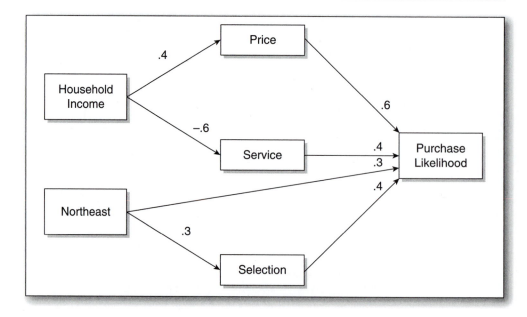

In addition, by multiplying and summing the relevant path weights, one can estimate the *total effect* of each variable, wherever it is in the model, on recent purchase. Table 3.2 shows the total effects thus calculated, which differ in important ways from the results of the simple regression equation.

- The effects of both living in the Northeast and of selection rating appear larger in the path model results than in a simple regression, in which they were confounded.
- The simple regression equation also underestimated the impact of both price and service ratings because they were confounded with household income. Once the effect of the latter was correctly specified in the path model, the effects of the two attribute ratings increased.
  - Note that the overall effect of household income on purchase likelihood remains nil in the path model. This is because its countervailing effects on price and service ratings cancel each other out. However, the path model, by specifying the *process* by which household income operates, still allows a marketer to take specific action with respect to given market segments.
- The total coefficient of determination (TCD) of the entire system of equations on purchase likelihood is 85%, suggesting that the model explains most of the variance in recent purchase.

Thus, when marrying marketing data from different sources, it is important to bear in mind the causal structure of the different data domains, and analyze it accordingly because misspecification of that causal structure can lead to erroneous conclusions.

Table 3.2 Path Model Example: Total Effects of Variables on Purchase Likelihood

Variables		Regression Weights	Regression Weights
Store Attributes			
	Price	0.50	0.60
	Service	−0.05	−0.40
	Selection	0.20	0.30
Customer Characteristics			
	HH Income	0.00	0.00
	Northeast	0.35	0.49
Variance Explained		42%	85%

SEGMENTING SAMPLES USING ATTITUDES AND BEHAVIOR

Another area for which multiple data domains present particular benefits and challenges is segmentation. Traditionally, consumers can be segmented either by background and behavior or by attitudes. Each type of segmentation provides a different look at how consumers are divided—one based on their observable characteristics: the other based on the attitudes and psychographics. Certainly, combining the two approaches would add a new dimension to a consumer segmentation model, or at least, by underlining the relationship between the two domains, would allow it to be seen in a new perspective.

Methodologically, however, segmenting on combined data domains is not simple, for two reasons. The first has to do with the different characteristics of behavioral and attitudinal data, which tend to call for different types of segmentation methodologies:

- Attitudinal variables are usually measured on an ordinal scale that is uniform across the whole attitude battery. Such data are the most amenable to cluster analytic techniques such as k-means, which searches for group commonalities and differences across a whole battery.
- Background and behavioral variables, such as marital status or purchase likelihood, are usually discrete and categorical, and they often have different, even incomparable, scales across the variable list. Because of the scale differences, cluster analytic techniques often stumble on this kind of data. A hierarchical splitting algorithm such as Chi-Square Automatic Interaction Detector (CHAID), which is more robust to scale differences, is more appropriate in this domain.

Second, segmenting on background, behavioral, and attitudinal data simultaneously can be problematic because of the overlap between the domains. To the extent that there is high correlation between background and behavior, on the one hand, and attitudes, on the other, the more strongly segmenting domain can take over the segmentation, so the other appears to have little or no effect on the segmentation at all. The scale issues discussed previously can magnify this problem: Given the sensitivity of segmentation techniques to the scales of the variables, the domain that dominates the segmentation is most likely going to be the one whose data best fits the technique being used.

There are two possible ways around this dilemma. The first might be called "metasegmentation": one segments the sample *twice*, once on background and behavior, once on attitudes, using a methodology appropriate for each type of data. Then, the two resulting segmentations are cross-tabulated to gain additional insights from examining their interrelationships:

- Does a particular behavioral segment tend to cluster within one or more of the attitudinal segments? This suggests that the segment is being defined by both behavior and attitudes, which are most likely correlated themselves.
- Conversely, is a given behavioral segment distributed across two or more attitudinal segments? In this case, the attitudinal data provide added information, distinguishing two subsegments with identical behavioral characteristics, which can be treated as separate segments for marketing purposes.

- Alternatively, is a given attitudinal segment distributed across different behavioral segments? This may suggest that more attention be paid the behavioral segmentation because the same cluster of attitudes may be leading to different behaviors.
- Is each segmentation distributed more or less randomly across the other? This is an indication that the two data domains profile essentially independent segments of the population. In that case, they are two alternative views of how consumers are divided; therefore, one would choose the most useful alternative for marketing purposes, or (if sample sizes permit) use the subsegments (attitude within behavior or vice versa) as the basis for marketing and communications decisions.

For example, a membership organization wants to segment its members. It has extensive background data on them from their original application forms and an extensive transactional record of the organization's services they used. The organization then administers an attitudinal battery of data to a random sample of the membership. Based on these data, it conducts two segmentations:

- A behavioral segmentation using CHAID. This divided the sample into four segments, defined by their background, that were differentiated in the volume of services they used.
- A *k*-means cluster analysis of the sample's attitudes, yielding three distinct attitudinal segments.

The distribution of the attitudinal segments was then cross-tabulated by that of the behavioral segments; Table 3.3 shows the relationship between the two.

Table 3.3 Relationship of Behavioral to Attitudinal Segmentation

	Behavioral			
Attitudinal	Segment 1	Segment 2	Segment 3	Segment 4
Segment 1	10%	45%	33%	35%
Segment 2	80%	45%	33%	30%
Segment 3	10%	10%	35%	35%

- The majority of respondents in Behavioral Segment 1 were also in Attitudinal Segment 2; this suggested that there was no need to subdivide this behavioral segment attitudinally.
- Behavioral Segment 2, on the other hand, was almost equally split between Attitudinal Segments 1 and 2. In this case, the same behavioral segment could be usefully split into two separate attitudinal subgroups, each of which *look* alike but *think* differently.

- Attitudinal Segment 3 is primarily found in *either* Behavioral Segments 3 or 4. Here, the decision was made to keep the two cells separate so that the segments could be identified more easily for marketing purposes, even though similar messages would be addressed to them.
- The remaining attitudinal/behavioral subsegments were treated as distinct entities for marketing communications purposes.

A more elegant way of dealing with multiple types of data in the same segmentation is **hybrid segmentation**. This method, which includes elements of both CHAID-like sequential splitting algorithms and battery-oriented segmentation schemes like *k*-means clustering, segments a population using *both* background and behavioral data simultaneously, while treating each type of data in a way that is statistically optimal.

Hybrid segmentation, like CHAID, clusters by optimization: It repeatedly splits a sample in two based on that demographic or behavioral variable that creates the *greatest difference* between the resulting subgroups in an outcome criterion. Unlike CHAID, however, that outcome is not the value of a single variable, but rather a measure of the clusteredness of the sample across *all* the attitudes in a battery, which is the criterion used in a *k*-means clustering routine. Thus, at each step, a hybrid clustering routine creates a new cluster that is defined by some combination of behavioral variables, and has as distinct an attitudinal profile as possible; in this way, it creates a cluster solution that is simultaneously behavioral and attitudinal.

We can best illustrate how hybrid segmentation works using the following example. An attitude and usage study was conducted among a series of consumers who were in the market for an automobile in the next 12 months. Among other measures, the study asked the importance (on a five-point scale) of a series of automobile attributes:

Cargo Room

Comfort

Fuel economy

Legroom

Luxury

Power

Price

Reliability

Safety

Sportiness

The study also collected a full battery of standard demographics on each respondent. Both the importance and demographic batteries were input into the segmentation algorithm (as separate domains).

The hybrid segmentation process is illustrated by the tree diagram in Table 3.4. It proceeds in a series of steps.

- The first split is made on gender. Breaking the sample by gender splits off a segment primarily concerned with safety (women), while the male cluster's motivations are still heterogeneous.
- In the next step, the best split divides the males on income: those with a household income of $75,000 or greater form a segment, for whom *luxury and comfort* are paramount.
- This time, men with incomes less than $75K are split by age, forming two segments:
  - Younger (less than 35), relatively less affluent men, whose primary needs are *sporty and cheap*
  - Older, less affluent men, whose primary needs are *economical and reliable*
- The scan is repeated once more, splitting women based on whether they had children younger than age 6. This created two final clusters:
  - Children younger than 6: safety, legroom, and cargo space
  - No children younger than 6: safety and power

At the end, the analysis has divided the sample into six segments, each with a unique demographic definition and a distinctive profile of needs. The automobile marketer can easily find each segment in the marketplace and knows what products and promises to offer them.

Whatever segmentation methodology is used should be chosen with the goal of preserving the richness of both data domains. Given that the purpose of using multidomain data in segmentation is to use multiple perspectives on the population, one should take care that they are not obscured by the analytic technique chosen

Table 3.4   Hybrid Segmentation of Automobile Needs

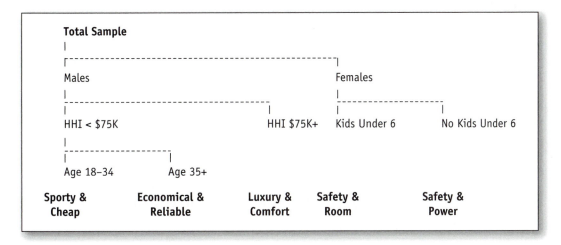

THE FUTURE FOR COMBINING
EXISTING DATA FROM DATA MINES WITH SURVEY DATA

As we have seen, the combination of attitudinal data and behavioral databases can greatly expand the marketer's research horizon, both in the questions asked and the validity of those answers.

But where will this technique go in the future? What might constitute new opportunities for matching behavioral and survey data, and what obstacles could conceivably stand in the way? From the perspective of today, two areas seem most likely to develop: the availability of new types of data and advances in methods of data collection and merging.

In new behavioral data *sources*, it seems that the most fruitful area in the immediate future will be online, especially in two areas: transactional data and social networks.

The growing importance of online shopping makes Internet transactions a potential treasure trove for marketers. Being able to capture data on both shopping and purchase, often in real time, can afford an online marketer an accurate and abundant source of behavioral data on the customers and prospects; marrying those data with appropriate attitudinal questions can provide insight into their motivations inexpensively and efficiently.

Such a marriage can be performed either in real time—for instance, by directing every *n*th customer of a website to a brief survey tapping her needs and wants for the product she has just bought or at a remove, as when a random sample of customers is contacted by e-mail and asked to take an online attitudinal survey. In both cases, the result is a database combining both attitudinal and behavioral data that can, by providing insight into *why* customers bought what they did, inform product, sales, and advertising decision making.

Even more interesting possibilities are afforded by the Web 2.0 user-centered messaging and networking applications that facilitate user-initiated content, including social networking sites such as Facebook and LinkedIn, blogs, and short-messaging systems such as Twitter. Sites such as these hold out the intriguing prospect of collecting data on respondents' social choices—for instance, the density and type of one's social network, which would allow sampling and segmenting people based on the characteristics of their friendship group; or a person's position in the social network, which could be used to identify and target opinion leaders, for example.

Messaging sites, such as Twitter, could potentially be used to identify social networks to use as sampling frames, by tracing webs of followers of users who tweet in specific content areas.

In addition, many of the Web 2.0 sites already incorporate survey applications, potentially allowing a marketer to deliver an attitudinal survey to a precisely targeted sample of social network participants.

Advances in *methods of combining data sources* will consist of dealing more effectively and with the problem discussed earlier: how to match attitudinal response data with behavioral databases in ways that preserve the validity, completeness, representativeness, and granularity of the data. In this area, two possible approaches to this problem can be envisaged.

One is the growth of and increasing reliance on single-source data, particularly from panels, which track both sides of the equation: attitudes and behavior. Certainly, the panel approach, because it is often cost-effective and makes respondent cooperation a given, is increasingly attractive. In addition, such a method provides data that are complete and as granular as one could wish. On the other hand, its validity and representativeness depend on the degree to which the panel was recruited randomly (or at least properly weighted to its population), as well as to the continuing level of its cooperation with often numerous survey interventions (which themselves bring up the question at what point do the panel members become professional respondents whose responses no longer necessarily reflect the views of those they are supposed to represent).

The other possible avenue is the development of new techniques that go beyond one-to-one matching of respondent data across databases. One such set of techniques is known collectively as "data fusion." They work by statistically matching an individual in one database with one or more individuals in a second database, based on their correspondence on one or more key variables (usually demographic). This can be done either by finding the one closest match in the second database for each case in the first or by creating new variables for individuals in the first database, based on a similarity-weighted average of individuals in the second.

Data fusion, thus, is theoretically an answer to the problem of correspondence of different databases at an individual level, without the loss of granularity inherent in aggregation. On the other hand, the validity of such databases can be questioned because some of a given respondent's data are borrowed from entirely different individuals. Some might even argue that such techniques might not be applicable to attitudinal data, which usually have a relatively low correlation with respondent background.

The marriage of attitudinal and behavioral data are also likely to face two apparently contradictory *challenges* in the future. One may come from the constantly increasing availability of behavioral data, particularly online. This embarrassment of riches could itself prove to be a problem for marketing researchers, as the sheer volume of data outstrips current methodologies for collecting it; storing it; and, above all, analyzing it. The issue of scalability for marketing research techniques will likely require the development of new data collection and analytic technologies to keep pace with the growth in data volume.

However, while technological improvements might potentially multiply the amount of behavioral data to which researchers have access, it is likely that respondent concerns about privacy will also grow, along with their concomitant effects on respondent cooperation. The continuing downward trend in survey cooperation (Brennan, Benson, & Kearns, 2005; Council for Marketing and Opinion Research [CMOR], 2003) is likely to extend to online behavioral measurement as pressure grows for the institution of a do-not-track facility, along the lines of the do-not-call list for telephone solicitation (Angwin & Valention-Devries, 2010). Thus, researchers may face the paradox of having to deal with a spiraling amount of behavioral information on a smaller and smaller, and possibly less representative, segment of their market.

The challenge of responding to consumers' growing demands for privacy will require increasing efforts to actively procure their cooperation, as well as greater attention to the representativeness of research databases and the further development of techniques to come to grips with the sampling issues raised by respondent noncooperation.

FURTHER READING

Aaker, D., Kumar, V., & Day, G. (2001). *Marketing research*. Chicago, IL: American Marketing Association.

Baker, K., Harris, P., & O'Brien, J. (1997, January). Data fusion: An appraisal and experimental evaluation. *Journal of the Market Research Society, 39*(1), 225.

Cooke, M., & Buckley, N. (2008). Web 2.0, social networks and the future of market research. *International Journal of Market Research, 50*(2), 267–292.

Fishbein, M., & Ajzen, I. (1975). *Belief, attitude, intention and behavior*. Reading, MA: Addison-Wesley.

Kamakura, W. A., Wedel, M., de Rosa, F., & Mazzon, J. A. (2003, March). Cross-selling through database marketing: A mixed data factor analyzer for data augmentation and prediction. *International Journal of Research in Marketing, 20*(1), 45–65.

Kraus, S. J. (1995, January). Attitudes and the prediction of behavior: A meta-analysis of the empirical literature. *Personality and Social Psychology Bulletin, (21)*1, 58–75.

Lee, E., Hu, M., & Toh, R. (2000, February). Are consumer survey results distorted? Systematic impact of behavioral frequency and duration on survey response errors. *Journal of Marketing Research, 37,* 125–133.

Milne, G. R. (Ed.). (2000, spring). Privacy and ethical issues in database/interactive marketing and public policy (special issue) *Journal of Public Policy and Marketing, (19)*1, 1–6.

Mittal, V., & Kamakura, W. A. (2001, February). Satisfaction, repurchase intent, and repurchase behavior: Investigating the moderating effect of customer characteristics. *Journal of Marketing Research, (38)*1, 131–142.

Murphy, J., Hofacker, C. F., & Bennett, M. (2001, February). Website-generated market-research data. *Cornell Hotel and Restaurant Administration Quarterly, (42)*1, 82–91.

Soong, R., & de Montigny, M. (2001, October). *The anatomy of data fusion*. Paper presented at the Worldwide Readership Research Symposium, Venice, Italy.

CHAPTER 4

The 21st Century Development of Products

Where Customer Guidance Is Taking Us

HOWARD R. MOSKOWITZ

BERT KRIEGER

LINDA ETTINGER LIEBERMAN

Moskowitz Jacobs, Inc.

INTRODUCTION

Product testing enjoys a long history, tracing its roots to many fields. Today's practitioners in market research might believe that it is the world of commercial product testing among consumers that has spawned the methods we use today and that will give rise to tomorrow's new procedures. *Nothing could be further from the truth*. It's worth taking a quick tour through some important books that gave rise to product testing. These books vary in tone, from a book on psychophysical foundations (Stevens, 1975), to a historical treatise on what has happened (Amerine, Pangborn, & Roessler, 1965), and to examples of applications (Lawless & Heymann, 1998; Meilgaard, Civille, & Carr 1999; Moskowitz, 1985).

Historically, product testing began in the food industry, arising out of the corporate need to ensure product quality from the consumer's point of view. Quality in its simplest terms meant sensory enjoyment, at least in the language of consumers. When the product didn't taste right, smell right, look right, feel right, and so forth, the product quality was deemed below par. There were economic consequences to being below par, the worst being consumer rejection.

The earliest practitioners of product testing were bench scientists, typically chemists or product developers. The notion of professional product testing was unknown. Practices

71

were developed by cobbling together some testing methods with inferential statistics. Of course, this was in the 1920s and 1930s, when consumer requirements were less relevant than technical feasibility and the ability to produce enough food.

During the 1940s, the United States Government, especially the Quartermaster Corps, the sustainment, combat service support, and logistics branch of the United States Army began to focus on food acceptance by soldiers. As a result, a great deal of pioneering work occurred at the Quartermaster Corps, then headquartered in Chicago. It would be fair to say that product testing began there, as scales, experiments, and the wholesale application of testing, accepting or rejecting food for the military increasingly became the norm (Meiselman & Schutz, 2003).

In our rapid scan of what happened, we move quickly from the scales of the 1940s to the methods of the 1950s. In the 1950s, the focus was on describing the sensory characteristics of food and measuring differences. We went from an era of scarcity to an era of increasing abundance, from an era of selling what was manufactured to an era of marketing. Product testing focused on acceptance, but also on understanding what one could do with the food to increase consumer acceptance and/or maintain or lower cost of goods. Competition among companies drove the growth of testing. Amerine, Pangborn, and Roessler (1965) provide a good history of these efforts, at least in the technical and trade literature. It is worth the read.

Descriptive analysis focused on expressing the sensory properties of food, typically using an expert panel trained for the purpose, for example, the Flavor Profile (Caul, 1957). Fundamentally, these expert panels veered away from consumers, moving in the direction of testing foods using the panelist as an instrument. Descriptive analysis of this sort continues today, but it has little to do with consumer product testing. Today's zeitgeist appears to want to relate expert profile ratings to consumer perceptions, as companies discover applications for descriptive analysis beyond simple quality control and product matching.

In this era, the other side of the research world was difference testing, a workhorse method in wide use, with a limited practical focus. Difference testing focuses on whether two products differ from each other. Again, the panel is being used as an analytical instrument, not to measure what the consumer wants, but simply to say, "same or different" (O'Mahony, 1995). As one might guess, difference testing is a procedure used primarily to maintain product quality. When changing a product, primarily for cost reasons, the objective is to ensure that consumers *don't* perceive the change.

Obviously, too, difference testing has other applications. For example, we know of a brewer whose test for new product acceptance was that it should taste at least as good as a targeted competitor (as good as or better). And we probably all are familiar with the most famous difference test of all time—The Pepsi Challenge, a blind taste test in which consumers preferred the taste of Pepsi over Coke and which drove an advertising campaign that upset market shares between Pepsi and Coke for half a decade.

PRODUCT TESTING GROWS UP

By the 1970s, product testing had split into different worlds. One world, analytical product testing, remained in the domain of research and development. Panelists for analytical product testing were considered instruments. The focus was on the product, and the goal was to describe it. There were no consumer issues.

The second world involved consumers. Marketing researchers became increasingly involved in the evaluation of products. Without the technical predilections that sensory evaluation enjoyed, marketing researchers focused more on the consumer, less on the expertise. The questions from product testing that needed answers revolved around consumer acceptance as the major concern—was this particular product acceptable? Yet beyond that simple question were a host of other marketing related questions, such as the likelihood that a consumer would buy the product (purchase intent), the degree to which the product fit a positioning concept, the expected frequency of use, and so forth. The marketing researcher's focus was on the product as a key factor in the consumer's world. At the end of the day though, it might be said the product itself was of *less* interest than the person who would buy it and consume it.

A great deal of the growth of product testing in the world of consumer research came about because of financial opportunities. Some of the best researchers in the 1960s through the 1980s were attracted to product testing. Reasons included the fact that corporations were waking up to the need to have superior products, to have products that fit concepts, and the ever-present need to predict share. Such bottom-line business requirements engendered different approaches, ranging from development methods, for example, experimental design to get the product right (Box, Hunter, & Hunter, 1978), to custom product tests and product concept tests (Lawless & Heymann, 1998), and even to market simulation (Mahajan & Wind, 1992). The period of the 1960s to the 1980s marked the heyday of product testing in the consumer/market research industry. Consumer packaged goods were well funded by companies, the economy promoted competition, enough companies were offering their products, and the mood of the corporations and consumers was optimistic. The United States led the charge to develop better methods while the rest of the world ran to catch up as the consumer research industry burgeoned.

As we conclude this short history of product testing, it's worthwhile noting that we stop at the 1990s. It is that decade, the next (called the naughts), and the current decade, which now occupies us, that will set the stage for the future. Of course, as Yogi Berra said so wisely, "Prediction is hard, especially about the future." However, the tools developed in the 1990s and more recently seem sufficiently powerful to be the basis of the future in product testing.

FOUR THEMES SHAPING PRODUCT DEVELOPMENT IN THE 21ST CENTURY

As the decade of the 1990s progressed, we saw the beginning of four trends, which are still with us today and which we expect will dictate the next generation of product testing.

1. *Researchers are evolving*. Research professionals are becoming increasingly comfortable with the notion of looking for patterns. This comfort stands in stark contrast to the tradition of consumer research. For many years, researchers had relatively little statistical training. Most of them were familiar with statistical testing for significance, so-called inferential statistics. Suppliers (vendors) who did product tests executed the studies and highlighted those significant differences in their reports. Statistical testing consisted generally of tests of differences in proportions and sometimes tests of differences between mean scores. In recent years, however, researchers have been continually exposed to the notion

of looking for patterns, rather than looking for statistical differences. As a result, the idea has become tenable that research is the search for patterns, rather than simply the discovery of differences.

2. *Companies demand more from the test*. Whereas in previous years it was important for a company to know that its product scored well versus competition, that knowledge is no longer the only criterion. Over time, companies have become increasingly sophisticated as well. A company must understand the so-called **levers** in the product, the variables that drive acceptance (**drivers**). This understanding can only come about when the researcher systematically varies the characteristics of the product. Sophisticated tools do not drive this modeling, but rather corporate demands for control and understanding of the product.

3. *The definition of product is changing*. In days gone by, the product was the physical essence. Product testing was a more or less defined specialty. There were specific methods, often best practices, for presenting products in a test (only one product for any respondent—pure monadic; sequentially to a respondent—sequential monadic), methods for asking questions (typically preferences, but occasionally scaling), and standard analyses (statistical analysis of differences). Products were well-behaved entities. People knew what to do. Today the notion of the product is far more diversified. Whereas products may be physical things, they also have service components attached. Products may be the physical stimulus, but they are accompanied by the emotional connections related to brand, the quality perceptions of price, and so forth. And of course, the product is the experience (Pine, 1999). So it is not only the physical essence but also the psychosocial attributes and the experience that need to be studied.

4. *Different players are involved in assessing products*. In the world of fast-moving consumer goods, at least two different groups are involved in so-called product testing. One group, market researchers, owes its intellectual heritage to sociologists. Market researchers are interested in how the product will perform in the marketplace. They are interested in sales, share, cannibalization, and so forth. The second group, so-called sensory professionals, focuses on the product itself, from the point of view of the consumer. It's not market share that is of interest to the sensory professional, but rather the sensory nature of the product, those intrinsic factors of the product that drive acceptance. Market researchers typically report to the marketing management, whereas sensory professionals report to research and development or product development management. These are two different corporate groups, each having a different intellectual history and predilections. Each deals with product, albeit from a different perspective.

NEW DIRECTIONS FOR MODERN AND FUTURE PRODUCT DEVELOPMENT RESEARCH

Let's move now beyond traditional product testing to today's leading edge, to borrow from the title of this book. The direction is moving deliberately toward product research rather than product testing: a move away from testing, report cards, and performance toward knowledge, patterns, and strategic direction.

New Direction 1: Segmentation Moves to a More Profound Place

The marketing community typically thinks of segmentation in some grand, overarching way to divide customers into separately targetable groups based on actionable similarities. Indeed, the archives of corporations are filled with countless segmentation studies of proprietary projects, across hundreds of product categories. The goal of this segmentation research is to understand how the attitudes, perceptions, and behaviors of the customer are structured and, of course, whether any new opportunities exist (Wells, 1975). We might very well think of it as trying to understand the mind of the customer.

Given the potential value of a good segmentation analysis, it is not surprising that the market research industry offers broad-spectrum approaches such as values and lifestyle segmentation (VALS; Novak & Macevoy, 1990) and Nielsen PRIZM, a segmentation system that marries demographic and lifestyle data with geographic location to help companies target their customers (Nielsen.com; Wedel & Kamakura, 2000). VALS assigns consumers to different groups based on an extensive questionnaire probing attitude, lifestyle, and personality variables. In contrast, PRIZM is based on the notion that there are inherently different groups within populations and that "birds of a feather flock together," meaning actually live near one another in more or less homogeneous neighborhoods or enclaves. To those using PRIZM, all one needs to know is the customer's ZIP code to get a sense of what people in that geographic location are like. The PRIZM model also works down to the level of the ZIP+4 code (the five digits of the ZIP code, a hyphen, and four more digits that determine a more precise location than the five-digit ZIP code), and even further to the level of census block groups and also postal delivery routes for direct response applications. The PRIZM algorithm uses the entire census of the population and the previously mentioned indicator(s) of place. Via hierarchical cluster analysis, PRIZM produces a model of the United States with 66 distinct clusters. What makes this model so generally useful—albeit not so much for product development—is that because it is based in part on geography (ZIP codes), it can be linked to any other databases similarly identified (e.g., the SMRB annual surveys of product and media consumption, company customer files, etc.). VALS can also be linked to PRIZM.

These general and specific segmentations are nice to have, make interesting reading, as well as enlighten and even entertain us with their clever segment names. The only problem is that they have *little or no relevance to product development*. Cross-tabulating segment membership with responses to products has shown little or no relation. Knowing a person is a member of a PRIZM cluster or a VALS typology doesn't tell us how to create food (or any other product) for that person. There has to be another way.

The origin of a new method of segmentation actually derives from research performed by Engel (1928) in Germany in the early 20th century. Engel published observations that there seemed to be a difference of opinion as to whether high concentrations of sugar were liked or disliked. This might seem to be an academic squabble, appropriate perhaps for a physiology study because it dealt with pure sugar, not yet applicable to food in general, and certainly not to segmentation. That some people could find a taste pleasant and others find the same taste unpleasant was so obvious as to be simply a factoid of nature. The same difference of opinion held true for odors as well. Kenneth (1927) reported that some people found the smell of onion pleasant while others found the same smell unpleasant. (Only the scent of roses seemed to be universally liked.)

Segmentation based on what respondents like or dislike is, by itself, nothing new and certainly not worthy of being identified as the precursor to a new way of segmenting people. However, what is done with the data resulting from that segmentation is what's important. That "what" would have to wait some 40 years, when it would reappear in Stockholm, Sweden at Gosta Ekman's Laboratory of Psychophysics at the University of Stockholm. It's from this work that we got our new segmentation method. Let's look at the steps that Ekman followed (Ekman & Akesson, 1964).

As a psychophysicist, Ekman thought in functional relations between two variables. To Ekman, the interesting question was not whether a product or a test stimulus was liked, but rather as a sensory or physical variable increases, how did liking change, if at all. For instance, when we make a beverage sweeter and instruct respondents to rate liking, how does this rating change as the perception of sweetness (or the level of sweetener) increases? Is the relation linear upward, so that more sweetness covaries with more liking? Or is the relation downward sloping, so that the increased sweetness covaries with a drop in liking. Or is the relation flat? Or finally, does the relation look to be an inverted U shaped curve, suggesting an intermediate optimum level, where liking is highest. Figure 4.1 shows the typical result for liking ratings given the sweetness of a beverage. The same figure has been developed thousands of times as researchers in both academia and in food companies repeated these tests.

If we were to stop when our research resulted in the data shown in the left panel of Figure 4.1, we would still be far ahead. Researchers would learn to create the curves relating

Figure 4.1   Sensory Liking Function for Total Panel and for Individuals

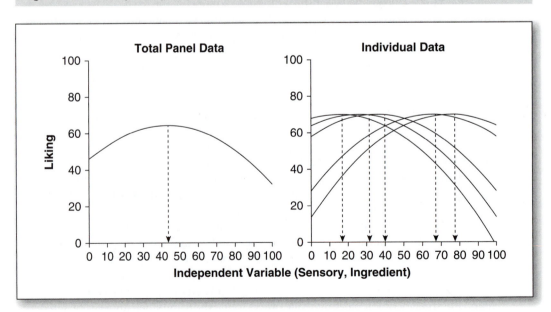

Source: Moskowitz Jacobs, Inc.

sensory level or ingredient as the independent variable to liking as the dependent variable. The developer would then search the curve to find the optimum ingredient or sensory level. For example, in Figure 4.1 (left panel), the curve reaches its optimum when the independent variable is approximately 45. Knowing this optimum level tells the developer the sensory level to aim for as a target, or even the formulation level for the ingredient that will generate the optimum. This approach is still used today, and it represents a significant leap forward in the testing of products. This approach looks for the sensory-liking relation, and it finds the maximum level reached by the liking curve within the range tested, and then looks at the level of the independent variable generating this optimum level.

What happens, though, when we create curves such as the one we see in the left panel of Figure 4.1, but do it on an individual-by-individual basis? We end up with a family of sensory-liking curves, which we see in the right panel of Figure 4.1. (The five individual-respondent curves in Figure 4.1 have been smoothed and idealized.) The truth of the matter is that we end up with a not-so-nice looking family of curves, some look like inverted U-shaped curves, some look like linear going up (more sweetness the better the product), and others look linear going down (less sweetness the better).

We have the liking curve for each individual respondent. Each of these curves has a location on the independent variable (e.g., sweetness) where the curve reaches its peak (within the range tested). What if we want to find the optimum level of sweetness for each person? We could record each individual's optimal level in a table such as Table 4.1.

At the end of this exercise, we are left with a simple matrix of data. *For each person and for each sensory attribute of the product*, we have discovered the sensory level at which the person's liking reaches its maximum. We determine this optimum level by plotting liking as the dependent variable on the y-axis as function of the sensory level on the x-axis. We find the optimum level of liking, as well as the sensory attribute, that generates this optimum level.

Table 4.1 Individual Optimal Levels for a Carbonated, Cherry Vanilla Beverage[*]

	Perceived Sweetness	Perceived Tartness	Perceived Cherry Flavor	Perceived Carbonation
Person 1	45*	23	49	23
Person 2	39	21	55	20
Person 3	55	19	55	18
Person 4	54	30	47	24
Person 5	60	27	50	27

Source: Moskowitz Jacobs, Inc.

*The group rating of sweetness (or tartness or degree of cherry flavor or carbonation, etc.) was on the x-axis and the individuals' rating of liking as on the y-axis is displayed in this table.

Finally, we cluster the people, based on the profile of sensory levels where the person reaches an optimum. *We end up with people who show different optimal sensory profiles.* This clustering generates an entirely new way to divide people, not based on demographics or attitudes, but based on their sensory product preferences.

Although it might seem like a lot of effort, this new way of segmenting respondents (i.e., by revealed sensory preferences) has been used and continues to be used to develop products. Manufacturers continue to look for product opportunities, as they have come to realize it will be very difficult to create new, single-product blockbusters that appeal to everyone but rather the next big opportunities may come from exploiting hitherto unsatisfied consumer *segments*.

This approach, creating products for segments, was first used 30 years ago by Vlasic Pickles in Michigan. The issue there was to create a product that could produce revenue in a world where no one realized or bothered to remember the type of pickle purchased and consumed the last time. People like pickles, but by 1982, the pickle section was full of similar-looking products. Focus groups and tracking studies had revealed that no one really understood the differences between types of pickles. The wall of pickles in the supermarket was just a wall of undifferentiated products, hard to understand and hard to remember. Few respondents appeared to remember the pickle they had purchased. Through product testing, research and development, and marketing, Vlasic created the database necessary to produce the data and graphs for pickles, similar to those shown in Figure 4.1 and Table 4.1.

> The rest is pickle history. The segmentation revealed that a full third of respondents fall into what Vlasic called the High Impact segment. They wanted a strong pickle, one with an intense garlic spice flavor. The problem was that all the marketers had refrained from creating such a bold pickle, simply because it was not good policy to alienate consumers. And many consumers—at least two-thirds—were alienated by overly strong pickles. The remaining third though loved the very strong tasting, high impact pickle. And so product testing to identify sensory segments revealed the opportunity. Afterwards, systematic design and testing of different products identified the optimal formulation for the segment, and marketing and Vlasic introduced the most successful pickle in decades, its Zesty pickle. (Moskowitz & Gofman, 2007, p. 47)

New Direction 2: Product Research Will Be Systematic, Not Haphazard

If we were to hazard a guess about the most critical development for the next decades, the notion of *systematic* would probably emerge. Looking at the way we test products today, we typically find that whoever performs the test is actually confirming the developer's best guesses. Corporate product development teams come up with what they believe to be the most likely candidate or prototype with which to go forward. The prototype may not necessarily be the best; however, from a pragmatic, procedural standpoint, this is the product that will be offered. When challenged to defend the product offering, the developer typically answers that the prototype is the best that can be created given the constraints of low budget, short time, and lack of developer resources.

This best-guess focus affects the way consumer researchers test the product. The typical consumer researcher has become accustomed to testing one or two products, getting diagnostics (e.g., too much versus too little of a characteristic), and then reporting these results back to marketing and to product development. The market researchers recommended suggestions tend to be couched in nontechnical terms, such as, "60% want a stronger flavor," "30% feel the product is too greasy," and so forth. Product developers have frankly been unable to use these results, except in the bluntest way. Developers can identify problems, but their methods do not identify solutions, except in the rarest of cases.

The practicality of testing one's best shot is compelling, if not necessarily productive. This approach is easier and uses fewer resources because it creates one or two prototypes and then executes product tests to determine whether the prototypes satisfy the business criteria (e.g., sufficiently acceptable, perceived to be appropriate or to fit a specific positioning, etc.). Corporations habitually spend as little as possible on product development, perceiving it to be a cost rather than an investment. The consequence of this traditional reluctance has been a spate of less-than-actionable product tests, using such procedures as "JAR" (scales including a variable, "just about right," that provide directional information; Moskowitz, 2004) and "mean drop analyses" that examine *when* mean liking scores decrease with increased levels of an ingredient (Schraidt, 2009).

The unspoken hypothesis underlying these methods is that 1,000 people rating one product is equivalent to 30 people each rating 33 products. The truth is that it *just isn't so*. Classical product tests like these result in learning about the products, but *not* about the people using them. That's a hard lesson, countercultural, and paradigm shifting, all reasons why it's only now, in the year 2011, that we see an interest in moving beyond this kind of testing toward broader learning as a strategic goal of product development research.

Until recently, there has been reluctance on the part of developers to use the principles of experimental design to create many different prototypes (Box et al., 1978). Times are changing caused, in part, by expensive failures that could have been avoided with development homework and more disciplined testing. The principles of experimental design have been with us for the better part of a century, since agronomists began using systematic approaches to identify what improved crops. Those methods, developed in the early part of the 20th century, were codified into methods for laying out different combinations and then analyzing the results by methods such as analysis of variance and regression (SYSTAT, 2008). The application of such methods to product development has been episodic, beginning with work in the chemical industry (Cornell, 1973) and moving only later to the food industry (Gordon, 1965; Moskowitz, Wolfe, & Beck, 1978).

In the food industry, we have learned that experimental designs produce much learning. The systematic variation of prototypes can now be coupled to consumer responses *and* to objective physical measures, such as yield and even cost. The output is a product model showing how the different product factors drive consumer responses. That model becomes a valuable piece of intellectual property, usable for years to guide development, reformulation, discovery of blue ocean opportunities (new segments, new products), and clean labels (fewer "bad" ingredients), generating greater interest in the product, and acceptance of the product on a sensory basis.

Adoption of experimental design methods changes a great deal of product testing. For example, there's use by technical people of small-scale experimental designs, varying one or two ingredients over a modest range, to identify the impact of the ingredients. Most of these small-scale designed experiments are run by sensory analysts in the research and development laboratories of corporations.

In this second decade of this new millennium, much larger experimentally designed product development studies encompassing many variables, varying three to eight different ingredients, are taking place–even though they call for a lot of labor. In some cases, research and development may generate as many as 20 to 60 prototypes. Surprisingly, these experiments are funded by marketing. As already mentioned, these large designs, the data, their models, and the output, containing four to eight or more variables, actually comprise the new intellectual property of a company.

It is relevant to ask why these tests are being performed now because they are not small, tactical studies. The answer is that marketing is charged with the task of coming up with new products. Furthermore, marketing has the funds to invest in a wide, systematic variation of different physical factors of a product, whether this is the amount and concentration of different ingredients, process variables, and so forth. Experimental design dictates the number of prototypes. Testing these prototypes quickly generates a data set comprising, on the one hand, the physical variables under the developer's control and, on the other, the ratings assigned by respondents. These ratings cover acceptance, sensory attributes, and more cognitively complex image attributes. The database also covers objective physical measures, such as nutritional characteristics, as well as the cost of goods.

Table 4.2 displays an example of part of a product database from an experimental design. The top of the table shows the variables under the developer's control. Below the

Table 4.2 Example of a Database for Three Products From an Experimental Design Comprising Many More Prototypes

Prototype (from the design)	A	B	C
Variables under developer control			
Pineapple	3	3	1
Grape	3	2	1
Apple	3	3	1
Fruit Boost	1	1	1
Sweeteners	1	2	1
Carbonation	3	1	2
Cost of Goods	101	102	25

Prototype (from the design)	A	B	C
Average Ratings From Consumers			
Acceptance			
Overall Liking	74	69	64
Segment 1	66	64	70
Segment 2	79	72	60
Attribute Liking			
Appearance	82	81	83
Aroma	73	71	66
Flavor	72	68	65
Sensory Attribute (amount of)			
Darkness	17	18	14
Aroma	61	56	51
Flavor	69	65	58
Amount of Pulp	61	59	52
Cherry Flavor	60	54	51
Grape Flavor	30	30	28
Banana	28	31	24
Citrus Flavor	62	61	54
Sweetness	58	55	55
Tartness	50	50	48
Bubbliness	75	54	70
Aftertaste	56	54	52
Image			
Artificial-Natural	61	52	50
For Breakfast	67	62	59
For Lunch	70	63	60
For Dinner	69	62	59

Source: Moskowitz Jacobs, Inc.

Table 4.3 Example of a Regression Equation for Attributes

Dependent Variable	Liking
Squared Multiple *R*	0.72
Standard Error of Estimate	1.55
Regression Equation	
Constant	64.83
Pineapple	−1.93
Grape	−5.59
Apple	−0.16
Fruit Boost	1.49
Sweetener	3.05
Carbonation	6.05
Pineapple*Pineapple	0.62
Grape*Grape	0.98
Apple*Apple	−0.26
Fruit Boost*Fruit Boost	0.07
Sweetener*Sweetener	0.46
Carbonation*Carbonation	−1.93
Pineapple*Apple	0.13
Pineapple*Fruit Boost	−0.45
Pineapple*Sweetener	−0.83
Pineapple*Carbonation	0.76
Grape*Apple	1.84
Grape*Carbonation	−0.54
Apple*Sweetener	−1.87
Apple*Carbonation	0.55

Source: Moskowitz Jacobs, Inc.

The equation is a simple quadratic equation (polynomial), estimated using standard regression analysis (ordinary least squares).

variables is the cost of goods, which have been obtained from the purchasing department. Following the cost in the table, we see ratings of liking, then the sensory attributes, and finally, image attributes, such as "artificial-natural" and "fit to specific day-parts."

Corporations do not perform extra work for nothing. The extensive efforts required to create a product database such as that shown in Table 4.2, even for 15 to 50 prototypes, will pay out in new business. Based on consumer reactions to these prototypes, the developer and marketer can accomplish many objectives quickly, without much guessing. That capability increases sales and profits.

We now provide an eight-step process to accomplish these objectives

1. Create a *product model* relating the ingredients and their interactions to each of the ratings, whether sensory, liking, or image. Table 4.3 shows an example of a product model, which is really simply a regression equation, based on data like what appears in Table 4.2. (Actually, several different such equations are possible; Table 4.3 shows just one for illustration purposes.) The equations are estimated using standard, off-the-shelf software, such as SYSTAT (2008).

The apparent equation in Table 4.3 should not be cause for alarm. Today's statistical systems perform estimations rapidly, automatically, virtually at the click of a drop-down menu. It is important to remember, however, that the equation summarizes the relation between the product variables under the developer's control and the responses assigned by consumers. Unlike traditional data from product tests, the equation summarizes the relations, so one can use the equation to dial up new products. Traditional product tests don't provide that capability, but that's getting ahead of ourselves.

2. Within this product model, the product developer can incorporate other variables such as nutrition, cost of goods, yield, and so forth. The key thing

to remember is that the product model summarizes the relations between what the developer/manufacturer can do operationally and what the product delivers from the point of view of the consumer. Such a model has significant uses, as we shall see in the following sections.

3. If we were to plot the model and could see in many dimensions (a physical impossibility, but a mathematically simple capability), we might see what is termed a "response surface," such as the one plotted in Figure 4.2. While we can see in only two dimensions, mathematically, there are more dimensions. Two independent variables will suffice to make the point. The model is *idealized*, summarizing the relations within the data collected.

4. Any combination of the two variables in Figure 4.2 leads to an expected rating. When we do this for two variables versus the rating, we are ahead of the game. If we do this for four, five, six, or more variables versus the rating, we are even further ahead. When we create this surface, not for one product alone but for many company's products, we are very far ahead. It becomes possible to manage products for cost, acceptance, and sensory character, as well as rapidly develop new, highly acceptable products with the same formula variables.

Figure 4.2   Response Surface

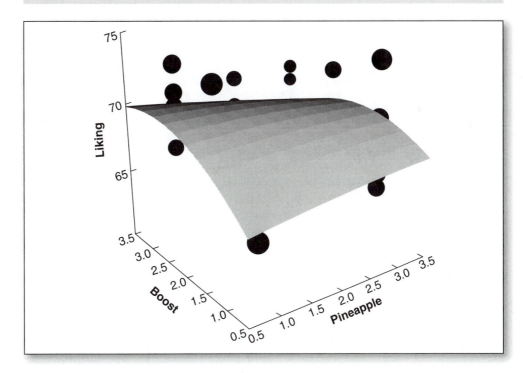

Source: Moskowitz Jacobs, Inc.

This is a plot of liking versus two of the six formulation variables under the developer's control (pineapple flavor and fruit boost). The size of the circles is in proportion to the liking rating achieved by the prototype.

5. The product model is a living, breathing tool. Although it might seem like a lifeless set of equations, they deal with what one might expect for given changes in ingredients and processes. The variables in the product model have an exquisite reality. They are the stuff that the developer uses, levers that can be pulled to make changes. With the product model, the developer can identify optimal levels of ingredients that generate high levels of acceptance. The product model eliminates the need for many traditional product testing, the time-consuming, often costly, often error-prone tests that generate short report cards of product performance and leave the developer wondering what to do. The type of result is shown in Table 4.4, just one set of examples of a general category of problems known as optimization problems (Moskowitz, 2000).

Table 4.4   Optimizations for Different Marketing Goals*

	A	B	C	D	E	F
	Total	Seg1	Seg2	2% cost reduction (<144)	Appropriate for Breakfast	Appropriate for Dinner
Variables (under the developer's control)						
Pineapple	3.0	3.0	2.7	3.0	1.0	3.0
Grape	3.0	3.0	1.0	3.0	3.0	1.0
Apple	3.0	3.0	3.0	3.0	2.6	3.0
Fruit Boost	3.0	1.0	2.3	1.2	3.0	1.5
Sweetener	1.0	1.0	3.0	1.0	3.0	2.3
Carbonation	2.2	1.6	3.0	2.2	1.0	1.0
Estimated Values						
Liking						
Overall	77	76	64	76	73	63
Segment 1	79	80	46	79	75	52
Segment 2	74	65	90	69	71	75
Cost of Goods	189	136	162	144	156	153
Expected Sensory Profile						
Aroma	60	57	60	59	70	61

	A	B	C	D	E	F
	Total	Seg1	Seg2	2% cost reduction (<144)	Appropriate for Breakfast	Appropriate for Dinner
Overall Flavor	82	62	84	63	57	70
Apple	66	65	79	63	61	83
Grape	62	76	70	72	53	68
Pineapple	32	30	31	30	31	32
Fruity	62	65	63	64	62	60
Sweetness	63	54	74	57	60	64
Tartness	48	48	59	47	46	59
Bubbles	71	56	77	61	80	63
Appropriate for Image						
Breakfast	71	69	47	70	83	42
Lunch	85	75	37	79	92	27
Dinner	37	39	61	39	39	68

Source: Moskowitz Jacobs, Inc.

* Different marketing goals (A, B, C, etc.) include designing a product for the total panel, for each of two segments, for a cost reduction, and for different day-parts, respectively. All ingredients remained within the range originally tested.

6. Let us move beyond simply finding the best, either for total panel or for sensory-preference segments. Had we been performing ordinary product testing, the solution shown in Table 4.4 would not have been happened upon. Perhaps, in a lucky world, that corporate developer might have discovered the best area, but more than likely, the typical corporate back-and-forth, iterative approach would have quickly ground to a halt. Corporate politics being what they are, the developer and marketer and, finally, the corporation would have rather quickly settled for some sort of satisficed outcome.

7. Companies are always fine-tuning their products to reduce costs. Much of the work performed in product development laboratories focuses on what's best at a given cost of goods. All too often, the efforts are shooting in the dark, where it's not obvious what variables drive acceptance, although it is clear which variables drive cost. And so, it's natural for developers to reduce the one variable that is most costly (e.g., sweetener in a beverage), hoping that the respondent does not notice or at least finds it as acceptable as possible. With use of large-scale designs and the product model, guesstimates have become outdated,

at least for those professionals in companies wise enough to invest in the product model and systematized learning. (See Table 4.4, Column D.)

General Foods, for example, had a well-known program where one period they would increase the quality, and later they would reduce the cost. The goal was to maintain profitability. The process was given an abbreviation; QI (quality improvement), and CR (cost reduction). When General Foods began to do this work in seriousness, it might take a year or more to get it right, unless of course there was a compelling reason to do it more quickly. Their next generation of product research, using the previous product model, allowed for optimization within the constraints of cost. Author Malcolm Gladwell, who saw this in action, called it "dialing the product," in his speech at the TED 2004 conference in Monterray. This is a nice way to think about how the model can be used. (Gladwell, 2004)

8. As companies move beyond pure product to product as experience, the nature of the product model will change. As they fight for share of market, companies have to ensure that their products stand up to the abuse that they may encounter, for example in storage or in preparation. Thus, preparing a product in a restaurant may subject the product to abusive conditions, such as being held too long before serving, being served at the wrong temperature, and so forth. Companies are starting to recognize that the product model can provide ways to not only identify the optimum formulation upstream, during manufacturing but also to discover the acceptable range of downstream conditions, after the product has been prepared. Experimental design of both formulation and of downstream preparation will create a product model that can be used to maintain product quality throughout the entire chain, from manufacture to preparation to serving.

New Direction 3: Involving the Consumer as a Cocreator in Product Development Research

In recent years, the notion of involving the consumer in the creation of a product has gained acceptance. The process of designing a product need not spring entirely from the fertile mind of a single talented individual or group of individuals in a corporation. It's feasible and even desirable to involve consumers in product design. In fact, for many years cocreation has been done in focus groups, where the developer would bring in a nascent idea and involve group participants in the task of shaping the particulars.

How is cocreation possible in product research? We have already discussed the idea of product modeling, of taking a prospective product, identifying its key variables, and then expanding these variables to create a set of different recipes. Rather than working with one product, we work with a matrix of products. The respondents simply evaluate the different combinations, rating each one on relevant attributes.

For cocreation in product research, we must move beyond having the respondents rate liking to having them act more as a product director. When the respondents rate the product on more cognitively complex attributes, such as "appropriate for a specific day-part," the respondents are now more active in the process of cocreation. The product developer creates the prototypes, and the consumer respondents sense the prototypes. They then judge the prototype in its fit to a specific *mental image*. This combination of developer as *creator of prototypes* and the respondent as *director of prototypes* to fit a specific goal comprises cocreation in the world of product development.

We've gone beyond simply evaluating products on sensory attributes and liking. We can instruct respondents to rate product prototypes on different end-uses. That is, the respondent can move beyond the evaluation of the product per se and begin to think of the particular product as doing a job. Each prototype may be perceived to be doing different kinds of jobs, some prototypes doing the job better while some perform the task less well (Christensen, Cook, & Hall, 2006). With respondents evaluating each prototype on its ability to do multiple jobs, we now have a data matrix that comprises both ingredients/processes as independent variables and ratings of the jobs to be done as dependent variables. The consumer is the judge of how well the prototype does each one.

Thinking of the problem in this fashion, we find ourselves dealing once again with the product model. The only new thing to be added is one column in the database for each job to be done (each end-use). (See, for example, product fitness for a specific day-part in the study shown in Table 4.4.) Product modeling using regression analysis enters once again, creating one more equation, this time relating end-use (job to be done) to the ingredients. From those data, one can develop a series of equations, one equation for each job to be done. By optimizing the product model, the product developer can now study the formulation that the consumer believes can perform a specific job. As before, it's important to impose realistic constraints on the optimization. These constraints ensure that the product does the job and is acceptable and cost effective. Table 4.4 (columns E and F) shows how the approach generates new formulations that fit a day-part, at least in the mind of the consumer respondent.

CONCLUSION

This chapter suggests three quite evolutionary steps in the development of products and in so-called product testing:

1. *Sensory preference segmentation, based on product experience rather than on lifestyle.* The key benefit is the discovery of product opportunities based on different sensory profiles that people find acceptable. Sensory preference segmentation makes the developer's job easy. The focus is on satisfying a group of individuals with demonstrably homogeneous preferences for a particular product.

2. *Systematic rather than haphazard development and testing, leading to a product model.* The key benefit is product design and having the ability to reformulate products more quickly, with far fewer back-and-forth iterations, as well as the ability to identify the likely product formulations for cost reductions.

3. *Consumer cocreation, where developers create the products, consumers respond to the prototypes in fitting consumer needs.* The key benefit is the ability to create new products

to fit new needs, using the same set of ingredients. Even when the ultimate product may need new ingredients, consumer cocreation identifies promising regions far more quickly because development is guided by the product model.

The roots of each of these future dimensions are already in place and, in some cases, quite evolved. It's no longer the case that the field of product testing, whether under the control of sensory analysis or consumer research, lacks the necessary technology. It already exists, is easily deployed, and has proven itself. The big challenge for the field of product development is to win widespread approval and use in the world of business.

Approval and use require cultural change. Today, at the time of this writing (mid-2011), we are witnessing rapid changes in the world of consumer research. One of the barriers to the new product testing has already fallen. Increasingly companies are accepting change in their testing methods—venturing into new worlds, *terra incognita*, that are not circumscribed by inferential statistics and best practices.

The good news is that this brave new world of product research is at hand, simply because it makes good business sense to know one's product in a profound manner.

FURTHER READING

ASTM Committee E18. (1979). Manual on consumer sensory evaluation. In E. E. Schaefer. *Special technical publication 682*. West Conshohocken, PA: American Society for Testing and Materials International.

ASTM Committee E18. (1996). Sensory testing methods. In E. Chambers IV & M. B. Wolf *ASTM manual Series: MNL* (26th ed.), (pp. 38–53). West Conshohocken, PA: American Society for Testing and Materials International.

Chambers, E., & Wolf, M. B. (1996). *Sensory testing methods* (2nd ed.). West Conshohocken, PA: American Society for Testing and Materials International.

Moskowitz, H. R. (1983). *Product testing and sensory evaluation of foods*. Westport, CT: Food & Nutrition Press.

Munoz, A. M., Civille, G. V., & Carr, B. T. (1992). *Sensory evaluation in quality control*. New York, NY: Van Nostrand Reinhold.

O'Mahony, M. (1986). *Sensory evaluation of food*. New York, NY: Marcel Dekker.

CHAPTER 5

Behavioral Economics

A Blueprint for New Aha Moments

CRAWFORD HOLLINGWORTH

The Behavioral Architects

THE WORLD IS GETTING FASTER AND FASTER

The computer revolution that started around 25 years ago propelled the rate of change into its exponential rise. The period of acceleration we're now witnessing can and has strained individuals and entire societies.

In 1970, futurist Alvin Toffler identified the effects of "too much change in too short a period of time" in his book *Future Shock*. He predicted that people exposed to the rapid changes of modern life would suffer from "shattering stress and disorientation." They would be, in effect, "future-shocked." He maintained that the need constantly to adapt to changing situations could lead to feelings of helplessness, despair, depression, uncertainty, insecurity, anxiety, and potentially burnout. He also suggested that when people experience times of rapid change they need "islands of stability." These are the things that do *not* change in your life—sources of security, safe harbors, and anchors against the inevitable storms.

Image 5.1

OUR LIVES HAVE BECOME MUCH MORE COMPLEX AND TIME COMPRESSED

For many people, *faster* has become the modern-day mantra. For some, especially the younger among us, even e-mail isn't fast enough, with people preferring to text or tweet because messages are shorter and faster to compose and send.

We are busier than ever before. Just think of how much we all try to pack into a day, a week, a year! There is a societal expectation that we can and should accomplish a great deal with our time. And since technology allows us to complete our work faster and more efficiently, we do just that. How many of us will take our Blackberry to bed with us tonight? We have lost the ability to switch off. We are connected to our friends and family 24/7 via social networks, such as Facebook, where we can be regularly alerted to the minutiae of other people's lives. The term *24/7 was coined in the late 1980s* and has given its own snappy authority to the concept of a world with the switch forever flicked on. We probably need a new rubric: 60/60/24/7.

Image 5.2

So we're busy, we feel the need to be busy, and our business is compounded by the onslaught of options and variety of *stuff* from which we have to choose. Every day we are bombarded with a plethora of options; from what to eat for breakfast (there are around 387 different types of breakfast cereal sold in the United States, and each family on average purchases 17 different brands) to what kind of Starbucks coffee we will buy. A quick trip to your local supermarket (which will stock around 30,000 products) confirms this. In the fresh produce section, you may have 22 varieties of tomato from which to choose. In the dairy aisle, you must decide whether you want full cream milk, semiskimmed, skimmed, organic full fat, organic semiskimmed, soymilk, almond milk, goat's milk, long-life milk, or calcium enriched milk? Where do you start? Which do you choose? *If we were to consider every single aspect of every single purchase—ethics, food miles, price, flavor, sell/use by date, ingredients, and so on—our shopping trips would consume our days.*

How do we deal with the enormous pressure of choice on our limited cognitive abilities? Simply put, we create rules of thumb or, as they are often called, shortcuts to make dealing with choice simpler and everyday life more manageable. In the dairy context for example, we decide what kind of milk to buy and then, more than likely, we stick to that choice day in day out. We don't reconsider every conceivable milk option each time we need some. That's our milk rule of thumb, if you like. And the lid caps offer us a further shortcut, so we look for a red cap or a blue cap (or whatever), and *that's* how we know we have the right one.

Image 5.3

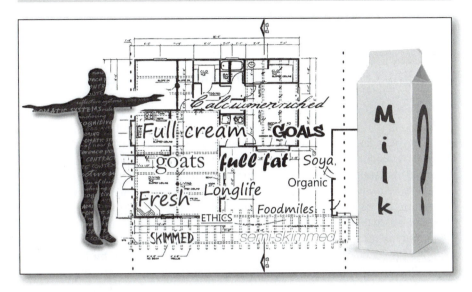

THE DEMISE OF RATIONAL ECONOMIC MAN

In this 24/7 speeding, time-starved, choice-saturated world, we have been quietly witnessing the demise of rational economic man on whom much of our behavioral understanding, marketing, and market research has previously been modeled. The model of rational economic man presumes that man analyzes all the information provided and the incentives offered in an egocentric way as to identify the solution that reflects his best interests. In the world of REM, it is assumed that the provision of new information or incentives will alter behavior by changing minds, and much of modern society is organized around this long-held belief.

Increasingly, however, we see that people do not always respond in this perfectly rational way. We don't have the time and, even if we did, our behavior is often led by our very human, sociable, emotional brains and not by the perfect logic of a computer analyzing each aspect. We are motivated by many contextual factors, be they societal, social norms, habits, moral codes, personality, memory, money, and many more. These factors define how we behave and choose.

While marketing and market researchers have been, at best, considering the impact of this demise, the study of behavioral economics, which has only just begun to be applied to business, has advanced at a stellar pace with significant breakthroughs in our understanding of why people behave as they do, both rationally and irrationally.

For example, behavioral economics studies showing how attitudinal change is not necessarily the Holy Grail, how self-efficacy impacts behavior, how the processes of conscious and unconscious thinking (habits and routines) operate in distinct parts of the brain, and how high emotional connection does not necessarily imply behavioral change have greatly illuminated the complex area of human choice and suggest exciting ways in which this thinking can build on and inform how we currently practice marketing and market research.

BEHAVIORAL CHANGE AND BEHAVIORAL ECONOMICS

As we have seen, making decisions is complex—there are a myriad influences to consider, and to add to the complexity, some of these occur at a subconscious level. In its purest form, behavioral economics combines psychological insights relating to behavior with economic models to try to account for decision making and, in particular, seemingly irrational decision making. (In Dan Ariely's [2009] book, *Predictably Irrational: The Hidden Forces That Shape Our Decisions*, much of the thinking and excitement about behavioral economics is perceived to lie in understanding seemingly irrational behavior.) Over the years, behavioral economics has evolved to challenge the simple assumptions of classical rational self-interested economic man and to seek to explain why various economic predictions have not come true. Analysis of various experiments by Kahneman and Tversky (1979), for example, and for which Kahneman received the Nobel Memorial Prize for Economics in 2002, isolated a whole range of factors, which essentially influence and bias decisions away from those predicted by the classical rational economic model.

In addition to understanding or predicting irrational behavior, behavioral economics also provides architecture for understanding behavior and choice per se; thus, it has broad implications for marketing thinking. What's more, even though the theory is well developed, it hasn't been transferred to the practical world of marketing as yet.

Image 5.4

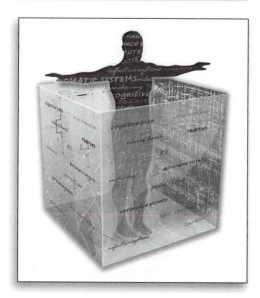

CHOICE ARCHITECTURE— NEW STRUCTURES AND TOOLS

At a very simple level, behavioral economics provides a way of *coding* the way we make choices or the way we behave. This is known as "choice architecture."

Three key umbrella terms define choice architecture in behavioral economics:

1. *Heuristics*: methods used to shortcut the decision-making process when a detailed analysis of all elements is impractical or deemed unnecessary

2. *Anchors*: the fulcrum on which any one decision is based and on which all other relevant information rests or links to

3. *Framing*: the context in which information is presented or ordered (where *re*framing can be a significant manipulator)

Studies have shown how heuristics, anchors, and framing can create biases in our behavior. Most models developed in behavioral economics typically address a particular market anomaly and modify standard neoclassical models by describing decision makers as using heuristics and influenced by framing effects. Much of the research so far has concentrated on social issues such as health (smoking, obesity) and financial issues (savings, pensions).

HEURISTICS—RULES OF THUMB OR SHORTCUTS

Image 5.5

In psychology, heuristics are the simple, efficient rules, hard-coded by evolutionary processes or learned from experiences, which help people to make decisions, come to judgments, and solve problems. We all recognize we are doing this all the time; otherwise, we would be paralyzed by information and choice. In a sense, these shortcuts and rules of thumb are our cheats for everyday life. Interestingly (and challengingly), heuristics operate at both a conscious and subconscious level. Daily, we do stuff without even thinking about it. Our routines are so well rehearsed we need little cognitive effort to carry them out. Over the years, a number of experiments have given us insight into two distinct operating systems in the brain: the reflective or conscious system (controlled, effortful, deductive, and self-aware) versus the automatic or unconscious system (effortless, fast, and uncontrolled). We have developed many habits in our day-to-day lives and these habitual behaviors require little cognitive effort and are hard to break.

Psychologist Kurt Lewin (1947) maintained that breaking a habit required an "emotional stir up" to raise the habit to conscious scrutiny. Lewin's change theory consists of three distinct and vital stages:

1. *Unfreezing* involves finding a method of making it possible for people to let go of an old pattern that was counterproductive in some way.

2. *Moving to a new level* involves a process of change, in thoughts, feelings, behavior, or all three, that is in some way more liberating or more productive.

3. *Refreezing* involves establishing the change as a new habit, so it now becomes the standard operating procedure. Without some process of refreezing, it is easy to backslide into the old ways.

ANCHORS

In decision making, individuals anchor or *rely on*, one specific piece of information, reference point, or value and then adjust from that, overlaying other elements onto the decision-making process, having determined what is the key load-bearing information (or deal maker/breaker).

Companies often use anchors within a marketing strategy, advertising their services as similar to brand X (citing a well-known, well-respected brand or product), but *better*. This is also evident in movie trailers, where references to the previous award-winning movies of the director or actors involved pepper the introductory voiceover: "From the director of *X* (insert name of old movie), comes . . . *Y* (insert name of new movie)!" and "Starring Oscar nominee *Z*" and the like.

The cognitive bias that can occur is the audience's tendency to rely too heavily, or anchor too blindly, on one trait or piece of information when making a decision. For example, when a sample of American citizens was asked how happy they believed Californians to be compared to Midwesterners, Californians were thought to be significantly happier, when, in fact, levels of contentment among Californians and Midwesterners show no significant variation. Respondents had *anchored* their perceptions on the sunnier Californian climate and its likelihood of bringing about a more easygoing lifestyle for its inhabitants, consequently devaluing and underrating the happiness quota for those in the not-so-sunny Midwest (Schkade and Kahneman, 1998).

FRAMING—CONTEXT IS EVERYTHING

How one frames or presents information can have a fundamental impact on how consumers respond to it. Framing also allows people to process information quickly and easily. We are "cognitive misers" by nature (Fiske & Taylor, 2008) and prefer to do as little thinking as possible.

So in South Lanarkshire in Scotland, there are 226 vehicle-activated signs that, instead of telling drivers their speed, show them a smiley or sad face, depending on whether they're under or over the limit. Thanks to these little faces, the number of people exceeding the speed limit in the South Lanarkshire area fell by 53% (South Lanarkshire Council, 2007).

And at a train station in Sweden commuters regularly crammed onto one tiny escalator, despite the wide (empty) staircase next to it. Overnight the staircase was transformed into what looked like a black-and-white piano keyboard, which played notes when walked on—with speakers and in tune. Anyone who walked up the stairs found that they could play notes up or down the piano scale. The minor chore of climbing the stairs had been reframed as a game. It made walking fun, and it reportedly led to a 66% increase in stair use (www.thefuntheory.com).

And the classic ad claim, "More dentists choose Colgate" combines authority framing with the principle that *what other people do matters.*

An aspect of anchoring and framing can also be identified in *social proofs* and *social norms.* In our overconnected speeding world, social proofs or social norms provide important guidelines and anchors. Social and cultural norms are the conventions, implicit assumptions, and social expectations that regulate behavior in communities. They are supported (and created) by governments, social groups, and cultural, moral, and ethical codes.

People derive their understanding of social norms either from observing and emulating the behavior of others, which means behavior can develop and spread rapidly through social networks (becoming the norm) or from environmental clues that provide evidence as to how other people *have* behaved (e.g., litter dropped on the ground, cars parked in no-parking zones, etc.)

We determine what is correct by finding out what others think is correct, and our reliance on others is particularly prevalent in the presence of uncertainty. Thus, a study of energy conservation in California found that social messages about the conservation behavior of their neighbors spurred people to conserve more energy than did any appeals that are traditionally accorded motivational power such as saving money, protecting the environment, or benefiting society (Nolan, Schultz, Cialdini, Goldstein, & Griskevicius, 2008).

A United States study gave cards to hotel guests asking them to reuse bath towels, either to "help save the environment" or appealing to peer influence, as in, "75% of guests who stayed in this room reused their towels." The social norm based message resulted in a 34% increase in towel reusage.

In a day-care center in Israel, a study was carried out to determine whether imposing a fine on parents who arrived late to pick up their children was a useful deterrent.

> Before the fine was introduced, the teachers and parents had a social contract, with social norms about being late. Thus if parents were late they felt guilty and their guilt compelled them to be more prompt in picking up their kids in the future. But once the fine was imposed, the day care center had inadvertently replaced the social norms with market norms. In other words, since they were being fined, they could decide for themselves whether to be late or not, and frequently chose to be late. (Ariely, 2009, pp. 76–77)

Two weeks before Election Day in 2008, Barack Obama's campaign was mobilizing millions of supporters; it was a bit late to start rewriting get-out-the-vote (GOTV) scripts. "But, but, but," deputy field director Mike Moffo wrote to Obama's GOTV operatives nationwide, "What if I told you a world-famous team of genius scientists, psychologists, and economists wrote down the best technique for GOTV scripting?!?! Would you be interested in at least taking a look? Of course you would!!" (Moffo quoted in Grunwald, 2009, para. 1). Moffo then passed along guidelines and a sample script from the consortium of behavioral scientists, a secret advisory group of 29 of the nation's leading behaviorists. The key guideline was a simple message: "A record turnout is expected." That's because studies by psychologist Robert Cialdini and other group members had found that the most powerful motivator for hotel guests to reuse towels, National Park visitors to stay on marked trails, and citizens to votes is the suggestion that *everyone is doing it.* "People want to do what others will do," says Cialdini, author of the best seller *Influence.* "The Obama campaign really got that" (Cialdini quoted in Grunwald, 2009, para. 2).

In *Legally Blonde* (Kidney & Luketic, 2001), Reese Witherspoon's character, Elle Woods, feigns heartbreak in the presence of two other (alpha) women on the pretend basis that the male friend she is with (who is slightly overweight and not a stereotypical jock) has broken up with her. Her behavior causes the women to instantly reevaluate their initial assessment of him and, on the basis of her endorsement, he is suddenly transformed into a highly attractive man.

COMPLICATING CHOICE ARCHITECTURE: SOME BEHAVIORAL BIASES OPERATING IN EVERYDAY LIFE

Image 5.6

Much of the work done in behavioral economics has focused on understanding the behavioral biases (the human tendency to make systematic errors in judgment, knowledge, and reasoning) that heuristics, anchoring, and framing potentially cause, unlocking insights into why people behave as they do, both rationally and irrationally. What follows is a brief description of 15 of the biases we have to understand as marketers, which influence customers in their everyday lives. (These are also summarized in Table 5.1.)

Availability Bias

The availability heuristic occurs because people predict the frequency of an event based on how easily they can imagine it. Consequently, events that have had extensive media coverage can cause people to believe such events are more likely to occur than is actually the case. People are more fearful of plane crashes than car crashes despite car crashes being significantly more likely to occur. By the same token, if individuals have personally experienced something they are more likely to overestimate the likelihood of it happening or to use a past experience as a proof for a similar set of circumstances. So for example, if the swimming pool at the local gym has been closed on successive Monday mornings, word might go around the regular users that the pool is now *always* closed on Monday mornings—the reality is that it's just coincidence.

Authority Bias

Stamp your authority onto something and, if what you are saying and the way you are saying it has confident appeal, people will follow your instructions even against their better judgment, ethics, and feelings (Milgram, 1974).

Thus, Sanka made a commercial for decaffeinated coffee that was very successful and ran for years. It featured an actor who had played a doctor on a medical show extolling the health benefits of the coffee. And in the same vein, an ambulance-chasing ad for legal services used an actor who had played a hard-hitting police detective in a long-running cop show to front the brand.

Diversification Bias

Diversification is a choice heuristic that indicates that when asked to make several choices at once, people tend to diversify more than when they make the same type of decision sequentially. Itamar Simonson, Professor of Consumer Psychology at Stanford University, and his colleagues showed that when people are asked to make a simultaneous choice, for example to choose *now* which of six snacks they will consume over the course of the next three weeks, they tend to express more variety in their proposed menu than when they make an actual sequential choice (e.g., choose once a week which of six snacks to consume that week). It's likely that although people tend to eat the same kind of snacks day to day, week to week, no one wants to be perceived as drone-like in their commitment to food products (Drolet, Luce, & Simonson, 2009).

Commitment Bias

Once an individual has made a definite commitment to someone or something, they are likely to follow through on this commitment. If you want to encourage people to vote in an election, a great way of doing so is to conduct a telephone survey asking people to predict whether they are planning to vote in the forthcoming election. Since it's hard to be seen to throw away a hard-won right to vote by saying they're not planning on voting, most people will answer yes to the question. And having said yes, the voting now becomes a personal commitment (Greenwald, Carnot, Beach, & Young, 1987).

Relatedly, self-contracts are a simple and effective commitment device where, by offering people the opportunity to sign a contract with themselves, they become compelled to commit to a course of action. Two Yale professors, Dean Karlan and Ian Ayres, studied the effects of commitment contracts on quitting smoking and then applied that research to dieting, developing a business around their theories. The website, www.stickk.com motivates people to make changes to their lives by signing contracts: If they fail in their goals, it costs them money. The site has $1.3 million invested and more than 23,000 users, the highest percentage of whom (42%) have commitment contracts for losing weight (Fuller, 2009).

A Danish chain of gyms offers a contract for an introductory three months free membership, with the only caveat that members have to show up each week during the three months for it to remain free. If members fail to attend, they are billed the normal weekly fee (Vigna & Malmendier, 2006). This is predicated on the insight that, once a habit is established, people will continue to go to the gym after the three months. So a short-term free contract will help people to become engaged—the hardest first mile. The reality is, that although people commit to regular attendance and feel great about it, they will, *inevitably*, have to miss some sessions—they get sick, their kids get sick, and so on, so they'll have to pay up, but subsequently, they'll end up making extra effort to attend and blaming themselves for the times they can't. They won't think about canceling their membership; instead, they will intensify their commitment to it.

Default Setting Bias

We are often presented with default options (opt in/opt out) already set and just accept what is presented. This can simply be about inertia or not having the cognitive space to process and consider all options.

Organ donation is a key example of the difference the default option can create. European countries that set up opt-*out* organ donation programs have increased participation from 10 to 20% to around 90%. Germany, which has an explicit consent opt-in policy, achieves only a 12% participation rate, while Austria's opt-out policy is associated with 99.98% participation. In the United Kingdom, (opt-in) participation was at 17% in 2002. (Johnson & Goldstein, 2003).

According to Thaler and Sunstein (2008), we are strongly influenced by defaults set for us by authorities, and they argue in favor of using this bias when designing policy, they call it "libertarian paternalism."

Barack Obama's budget proposal for 2010 included a plan that would automatically enroll workers into personal saving schemes offering an opt-*out* option. In the budget document, it was noted, "Research has shown that the key to saving is to make it automatic and simple. This 'opt out' idea will dramatically increase the savings participation rate of low and middle income workers to around 80%" (Office of Management and Budget, 2009).

Discounting the Future or I Want It Now

This is a very recognizable heuristic for our modern consumption-driven world. It is the simple human tendency to focus on today rather than think about what tomorrow might bring. We often underestimate the importance or relevance of something that might happen in the distant future, and we are happy to postpone unpleasant tasks, even if it means this will make completing the task trickier in the future.

This bias often translates into people choosing short-term gratification over longer-term rewards, leading to issues such as obesity (I'll eat that now and start my diet on Monday) or lack of savings for old age (I'll have that holiday and start my pension contributions after the summer).

Effort Bias

This is where an object's *value* is assigned based on the amount of perceived effort that went into producing the object. A homemade cake can taste more delicious than a shop bought one for this very reason, and money earned for a job well done is worth more than money found in the street.

Endowment Effect

People place a higher value on objects they own than objects that they do not own and can demonstrate this by demanding more to give up an object than they would be willing to pay to acquire it. Although this differs from loss aversion, these two biases can reinforce each other.

In 1980, Richard Thaler (Kahneman, Knetsch, & Thaler, 2011) presented half the students in a class with Cornell University coffee mugs and then allowed them to trade with their less fortunate classmates. Those holding the mugs set their minimum selling prices too high, and those without mugs set their maximum offers too low for many trades to clear. Apparently, briefly owning a coffee mug raised its value to the owner sufficiently to price it beyond the reach of most nonowners. Thaler called this pattern—the fact that people often demand much more to give up an object than they would be willing to pay to acquire it—the endowment effect. Another example of the endowment effect cited by Kahneman, Knetsch and Thaler (2011) concerns a wine-loving economist who purchased some nice Bordeaux wines years ago at low prices. The wines have greatly appreciated in value, so a bottle that cost only $10 when purchased would now fetch $200 at auction. The economist now drinks some of this wine occasionally, but would neither be willing to sell the wine at the auction price nor buy an additional bottle at that price.

Fairness [Do the Right Thing] Bias

Most people are instinctively motivated to 'do the right thing' and by and large this extends to incorporate our preference for things to be fair. We can't help but feel discomforted by incidental inequalities. When we are naturally motivated to 'do the right thing' and we fail to achieve the desired outcome, we feel bad and have a guilty conscience. This is an extremely interesting, heuristic that speaks of modern day citizenship in both local and global contexts. In Will Hutton's (2010) recently published book he called for fairer wages (part of what he called a fairer society) suggesting that the top earner in any company should not earn more than 20 times the salary of the lowest earner.

Gambler's Fallacy (Also Known as the Monte Carlo Fallacy)

The gambler's fallacy is the belief that if deviations from expected behavior are observed in repeated independent trials of random processes, then these deviations are likely to be evened out by other deviations in the future. Consider a series of 20 coin flips that have all landed with the heads side up. Under the gambler's fallacy, a person might predict that the next coin flip is more likely to land with the tails side up. This line of thinking represents an inaccurate understanding of probability because the likelihood of a fair coin turning up heads is always 50%. Each coin flip is an independent event, which means that any and all previous flips have no bearing on future flips.

Greed and Fear Bias

Greed and fear are two of the main emotional motivators of stock market and business behavior and a primary cause of bull and bear markets. According to economist Hersh Shefrin (2000), hope and fear would better describe the alternating excessive expectations of market players. Research studies tend to show that when greed and fear occur they can take primacy over more considered, rational decision making.

Loss Aversion/Avoidance Bias

The overall premise here is that we tend to dislike loss more than we like gain. And we *particularly* dislike losing what we already have, to which we assign a disproportionately higher value. Our loss aversion compels us to put more effort into avoiding loss than to ensuring gain. And so, according to this principle, a message that starts, "You could lose $X each year if you don't insulate your loft" will speak to us more powerfully than one beginning, "You will save $X." In the same way, we are more likely to be influenced by a $5 surcharge than a $5 discount. Studies have found price increases to have twice the effect on customer switching, compared to price decreases (Kahneman & Tversky, 1979).

Reciprocity Bias

Good follows good, and bad follows bad!

When we receive a gift from others, we naturally feel indebted and are more likely to act positively in our future dealings with that person or to comply with a request from them. This works both on a personal and commercial level:

- Waiters who give a piece of candy with the bill get 3.3% larger tips. Waiters who give two pieces get 14.1% larger tips (Strohmetz, Rind, Fisher, & Lynn, 2002)
- A £5 incentive included with a survey produces more responses than the promise of £50 after responding (James & Bolstein, 1992)

While reciprocity is commonly considered primarily a positive action in social norms, it can also operate negatively; with one negative action prompting a reciprocal negative response.

Hot and Cold Zones or Time or Place Inconsistent Preferences

This is where a decision maker's preferences change depending on time or place. Another way of thinking about this and relevant to the research world is hot and cold zones. Economists now recognize that we can prefer one thing in a low stimulus (reflective) context, but in a high-stimulus (tempting) context, we act differently. Table 5.1 summarizes these.

BEHAVIOR ECONOMICS AND ITS APPLICATION TO THE WORLD OF MARKETING

Behavioral economics (BE) provides an interesting architecture for looking at choice per se, and for understanding many of the seemingly irrational behaviors in everyday life. I hope you are beginning to surmise how this new tool kit might apply to marketing and marketing research.

Table 5.1 Summary of Choice Biases

Availability Bias	People predict the frequency of an event based on how easily an example can be brought to mind.
Authority Bias	People value something according to the opinion of a perceived authority figure.
Diversification Bias	People tend to diversify less when they make the same type of decision sequentially.
Commitment Bias	An individual makes a definite commitment to someone or something, they are more likely to follow through on this commitment.
Default Setting Bias	We are often presented with default options (opt in/opt out) already set and just accept what is presented.
Discounting the Future or I Want It Now	It is a simple human trait to focus on today rather than think about what tomorrow might bring.
Effort Bias	The value of an object is assigned based on the amount of perceived effort that went into producing or attaining the object.
Endowment Effect	People place a higher value on objects they own than objects that they do not.
Fairness (Do the Right Thing Bias)	Most people are instinctively motivated to do the right thing.
Gambler's Fallacy (Also Known as the Monte Carlo Fallacy)	The tendency to think that future probabilities are altered by past events, when in reality they are unchanged.
Greed and Fear Bias	When greed and fear occur they can take primacy over more considered, rational decision making.
Loss Aversion/Avoidance Bias	We tend to dislike loss more than we like gain.
Reciprocity Bias	Good follows good, and bad follows bad!
Hot and Cold Zones or Time or Place Inconsistent Preferences	We can prefer one thing in a low stimulus (reflective) context, but in a high-stimulus (tempting) context, we act differently.
Status Quo Bias	In general, people do not like to "rock the boat" and like things to remain the same.

We can see there are myriad variables in play to make us behave in a nonrational way. We use strategies to simplify choice, we don't like change, middle ground is the safest, we neglect probabilities, and in hot and cold contexts we switch preference sets. When evaluating the long term, we tend to discount the future excessively, we tend to think overoptimistically, to be loss averse, and to endow importance to things simply because they grab our attention, to name a few.

"BE finally gets marketing thinking about the single most important topic—the consumer decision" (Chad Wollen, Group Head of Consumer Futures, Vodafone).

If we were being honest, we could say that over the course of the last decade the world of marketing and marketing research has not changed fundamentally. We continue to follow old rules and models, but we become increasingly frustrated when these approaches fail to deliver the aha moments we seek.

Yet, as we have seen, there have been many advances in the behavioral sciences and in our understanding of how people make choices, and *it is time we fully embraced this new learning.*

> Given its obvious importance, this area of study has been dangerously overlooked by marketers so far. . . . We have lazily adopted a model for consumer decision-making whereby brand preference is assumed to translate into purchasing behavior. Why have marketers and agencies not fought back against a left-brained business culture which seems to place human understanding so low on its list of priorities. (Sutherland, 2010, p. 3)

The language and structure provided by behavioral economics are extremely applicable to the world of persuasion. The idea of mapping out the decision-making context to define choice architecture (why someone behaves in one way and not another) is a powerful approach to unlocking penetrating insights into behavior, brand building, and positioning, and it allow us to understand the strategic anchors and executional nudges operating in our markets—both current and potentially future.

Simply put, we will know which of numerous levers within the choice architecture can be pulled to influence behavior. Behavioral economics can provide an empowering way to pinpoint a brand or category's strengths, weaknesses, opportunities, and threats. It has implications for the following:

- How we might think about brands and categories
- What we research and focus on/the questions we ask/or seek to answer
- How we endeavor to understand consumers—methodological approaches
- The metrics we choose to measure
- How we market to consumers

Let's look at how three organizations have leveraged behavioral economics principles to inform strategy and bring about behavior change. The results illustrate the practical application and potential power of behavioral economics to the world of marketing.

We're by no means suggesting everyone throw out the proverbial baby or, to use the words of Jeff Jones of ad agency McKinney,

> It's not about "we used to do it this way and now it's a wholesale change and we're doing it *this* way." These are just new ways of understanding how and why people make decisions. And it's just smart marketing to understand them and use them.

Case Study 1: UK Training Development Agency (TDA) Teacher Recruitment: Best in Class IPA Effectiveness Awards 2010

Qualitative research found the TDA didn't face an attitudinal problem in the recruitment of teachers among potential career changers in that there was no shortage of people who *wanted* to make a career switch and become teachers, but it did face a *behavioral* problem in that potential recruits were failing to convert their interest in teaching into actively training and qualifying as teachers.

Reframing the communication task as a behavioral problem led to a radically different media strategy: from selling teaching (the result) to encouraging people to take the necessary steps to train and qualify as teachers. A series of *behavioral triggers* to nudge career switchers into and along this journey was devised, turning a big decision into a series of small steps—a chunking approach.

The campaign achieved a minimum payback of £101 for every £1 spent, increasing teacher inquiries and applications to record-breaking levels on a smaller spend.

The communication strategy was devised by DDB to act like a behavioral pinball machine. The communication strategy was to nudge people along the journey:

1. **Drip feed** versus **big burst** strategy, as people don't make life decisions in handy campaign cycles.

2. **Using a wider range of media to reach people in more places**, increasing channels from 7 to 15.

3. **Prioritization of media** most likely to get people to do something (e.g., search engines and online job sites).

4. **Ad space was cannily scheduled at times** and in places most likely to capitalise on people feeling dissatisfied with their current careers (also known as the working blues strategy). Ads were placed in Monday-morning commuter newspapers, posters placed on underground and rail platforms, and advertising scheduled for the dark times in January or after the clocks went back in October. TV advertising was maximised between Sunday and Tuesday when people feel least content. They also tapped into places where people time-waste in working hours such as social networking sites.

5. **Real teachers were deliberately featured** in the ads to reassure career switchers that teachers were people like them.

The campaign evaluation showed that every behavioral metric had improved: from web visits, to inquirers, to eligible inquirers, to applications.

(Continued)

(Continued)

Barrier	BE Informed Approach	Link to BE Construct
Scared of the unknown, worried they wouldn't be a good teacher	Help them visualise authentic positive classroom experiences	Anchoring
Easiest thing to do is put off the decision	Communicate frequently across the year	Immediacy bias
Scared about starting over again emotionally and financially	Showcase experiences offsetting fear of losing current status	Loss aversion bias
Too big a leap to make in one go	Break the application process into small steps	Chunking

Case Study 2: Reducing Energy Consumption in a U.S. State: California Energy

The challenge was to reduce energy consumption in California. Previous initiatives based around specific utilities had not been particularly successful, and it was felt that a more holistic campaign was required. Draftfcb won the assignment and took an unconventional approach for an ad agency—they chose to pitch a *behavioral* path rather than a communications path. The proposed plan leveraged a vast range of behavioral economics theories.

Stage 1. The first challenge was to find a *unifying consideration bias* across a diverse range of consumer target groups. Reviewing existing ethnographic research produced a simple but powerful insight—*the dislike of waste*.

Stage 2. The second stage involved consumers *acknowledging* that their behavior was wasting energy in various ways (e.g., they knew that overfilling the kettle wasted energy, yet they continued to do it). This acknowledgement created what Leon Festinger (1957) calls "cognitive dissonance," which creates in the consumer the desire to resolve the dissonance and *change behavior*.

Stage 3. To *resolve the dissonance*, three to five simple ways of reducing personal waste were suggested for people to adopt in their *behavior*. Consumers selected the ways they felt they could adopt and were encouraged to develop action plans to put the ideas into practice.

Stage 4. A *self-contract approach* was used to act as a constant reminder to make a change in behavior more likely to happen. Making the contract public (i.e., telling people what you have committed to) makes behavioral change more likely.

Stage 5. The campaign was then taken to a *local level* and consumers were asked to develop specific action plans to achieve their contracted waste reduction targets. This information was shared within the local community.

In summary, the behavioral path developed by Draftfcb identified a trigger (the dislike of waste), which led to cognitive dissonance, provided a way of reducing this dissonance via action, pushed people to create self-contracts and made these public, and finally asked people locally for action plans to achieve them. Following a behavioral pathway and nudging people at key stages narrowed the gap between attitudinal intention and actual behavior.

Case Study 3: Increasing Sustainable Behaviors— A Behavioral Change Experiment, London Borough of Barnet, U.K.

The challenge for the London Borough of Barnet, (LBB) was to find ways of reducing household carbon consumption.

The pilot involved 700 households over three months. The objectives chosen were those deemed achievable within a short timescale: changing habits (such as switching off power at the socket) and seeking commitment to make a longer-term change in the future (such as changing to a green electricity provider).

The pilot targeted those households who were already environmentally aware and could be encouraged to do more, with the idea that these early adopters could then model green behaviors for the rest of the community.

The experiment was structured in three phases:

Phase 1: Waking People Up to Unsustainable Behaviors

The LBB recruited local volunteers to knock on doors to conduct a baseline study of awareness and habits. This involved, for example, showing people thermal images of the area and installing smart meters where households expressed an interest.

Phase 2: Introducing New Behaviors

This stage involved getting people to sign up to pledges and signposting to useful organizations; free gifts were offered such as energy meters, retrieval cues (e.g., stickers

(Continued)

(Continued)

warning against overfilling the kettle), and posters. The council aimed to make it real for people by using local residents in publicity material and saying that "x number of people had signed up." Other initiatives included an online portal, "Do the green thing," where people were able to post stories and ideas. This proved an inexpensive way to maintain contact, linking people with their peers and encouraging a competitive approach in which people tried to keep up with the Joneses in their green activities.

Phase 3: Refreeze Behaviors

Further contact with households took place to find out whether people had been able to remain faithful to their pledges, checking energy use via the smart meters and giving positive feedback to demonstrate success and label people as green. It also involved a wider opportunity for communication, publicising success stories across the borough.

These case studies show how the principles of behavioral economics can provide a blueprint for behavior and behavioral change. This understanding can inspire communications that

- challenge an existing cognitive bias by confronting current consumer perception;
- change or challenge existing consumer reference points;
- unfreeze a habit or routine; and
- create new heuristics/rules of thumb for navigation.

Or as Thaler and Sunstein (2008) say, it's about creating better choice architecture, which would nudge people toward better decisions.

BRANDS AND CHOICE ARCHITECTURE

Behavioral economics can equally be applied to the world of brands. We want brands to become heuristics, to be rules of thumb, so that they are chosen with little deep rational or emotional evaluation at the time of purchase. We want them to become a habit and enjoy the virtuous circle of habit reinforcing habit.

Many of the world's leading brands have created key elements of the choice architecture in the sector in which they operate. They may have knowingly or unknowingly built a number of heuristics and cognitive biases via their brand values or created anchors (reference points) through both their visual and verbal language. Coca-Cola, for example, has created a powerful emotional connection with their brand and Christmas by building a heuristic for enjoyment and celebration at Christmas time. Activia yogurts have developed a powerful heuristic around stomach health, encapsulated in their tagline "tummy loving care." Similarly, Benecol has become a shortcut for cholesterol reduction. And Amazon might be described as the master builders of choice architecture with their vast array of consumer nudges, "Customers who bought the items in your shopping basket also bought . . ." "Today's recommendations," and "You may also like. . . ." Their customer review system is a particularly good example of how we use shortcuts to aid decision making. How many of us, I wonder, have bought an item on Amazon with five stars that perhaps only one person actually reviewed? In fact, over the years, via consistent brand building, leading brands have shifted much of our decision making into our unconscious by creating shortcuts and potential cognitive biases that benefit them.

This has been demonstrated in experiments looking at blind versus branded product tasting using multiresonance imaging (MRI) of the brain, which have shown how different parts of the brain are active when branded versus unbranded products are presented. The results showed that strong brands activated a network of cortical areas involved in positive emotional processing and associated with self-identification and rewards. The activation pattern was independent of the category of the product or the service being offered. Furthermore, strong brands were processed with less effort on the part of the brain. Weak brands showed higher levels of activation in areas of working memory and negative emotional response.

Brands have also developed rituals or new behaviors to try to reinforce, awaken, or challenge the contextual architecture in which they operate. Pom Wonderful pomegranate juice is a great example of reframing choice architecture as, unlike other similar juices that you might expect to find in the juice aisle, "You can find POM Wonderful Juices in the refrigerated section of the produce department of your local supermarket." Thus, *Pom* works with the operating heuristics for fruit and vegetables (fresh, natural, healthy), while challenging habitual consumer behavior.

And Bank of America's "Keep the Change" service highlights how choice architecture can effectively be reframed to change behavior. Confronted with the challenge of trying to get people to open new accounts, Bank of America, with IDEO, came up with a powerful solution to challenge the consumer status quo bias and create a new *default* heuristic. The IDEO team had discovered that many people would often round up their transactions for speed and convenience. In addition, they found that many women had difficulty saving what money they had. They created a service called "Keep the Change," which rounds up purchases made with the Bank of America Visa debit card to the nearest dollar and transfers the difference from the individual's checking accounts into her savings accounts. Thus, they changed an existing behavior by creating a simple default solution for consumers. In less than one-year post launch, it attracted 2.5 million customers, translating into more than 700,000 new checking accounts and one million new savings accounts for Bank of America.

APPLYING BEHAVIORAL ECONOMICS TO MARKETING

While marketers have embraced behavioral economics in many ways, much of the work has been done intuitively and is still overshadowed by the pervasive influence of rational economic man. What behavioral economics offers is a new framework for exploring and understanding customer behavior. And in a world where we have been trudging down the same paths for many years (and still expecting aha moments), it is exciting to have some new ideas and tools to build advantage. For example, by mapping context we can identify (and create) more directive behavioral actions; we can challenge or create shortcuts or reference points from which people navigate; we can change how a brand is framed, address an existing cognitive bias, raise (unfreeze), and challenge an unconscious belief.

We established earlier that the contexts in which we operate are dynamic spaces full of opportunity and risk. These contextual dynamics continually create new building blocks for new heuristics or anchors. Just look around at heuristics that you might now take for granted, such as fair trade, organic, light, or fat free. Look at all the shortcuts operating at a food retailers' level in the U.K., for example the Basics, Taste the Difference, Healthy Living and Finest ranges. Consider a brand that reframed its product like Nestlé, which put the calories (with the implicit suggestion that calorie content was lower than might have been expected) on the front of Kit Kat packs to encourage consumers to reappraise Kit Kat's relevance or consider it within a wider competitive set.

Image 5.7

Yet how many brand experts and custodians focus on their choice architecture and can define their brand's strengths, weaknesses, opportunities, and threats based on context? Who has seen (or written) brand plans that highlight context definition and context strategy?

A Behavioral Economics Research Tool Kit

We need to consider both how we can incorporate the learning from behavioral economics into our current methodologies as well as how this new thinking provides market research with new ways to explore consumer behavior and the influences on it. For example, we need to challenge the Little Caesar research that is still so widely practiced, the kind of research in which the consumer is presented with lots of ideas and has the power to give a thumbs up or down response, in many (not to say most) cases, completely oblivious to any contextual bias operating in the real world. And we need to design new approaches and new methodologies that unlock the relevant contextual architecture, conscious and unconscious, existing and emerging dynamics across the contextual layers (society, social, situational, and brand/category).

I think we do need some new techniques and maybe a slightly different emphasis. People don't understand and can't necessarily articulate the reasons why they buy things, and that takes you in one of two directions: you concentrate more on studying people's behavior—on what they do rather than what they say they do— or you try to devise techniques that reveal the things people are not conscious of or willing to admit. (Bain, 2010b, para. 21)

Next, we highlight a number of key principles to inform more effective research design and illustrate how these can be applied using case studies and examples of behavioral economics inspired research methodologies.

Principle 1: Consider the Context!

Context is the new king, and as we have seen, it is also a complex multilayered system that involves both micro- and macrofactors as well as conscious and unconscious elements. To aid investigation, we have developed a simple way of structuring and conceptualizing context. Imagine looking at the consumer from different vantage points—from really close and from further away. Think of Googlemaps and the way you can zoom in and out of your target. You need the big picture view of the map to get the general sense of where you are at the beginning and the up-close perspective at the final stage of your journey. This is an analogy for how to think about consumer context—we need to look at context on different levels—from the macro all the way down to the micro.

Image 5.8

This is a working framework whose relevance will depend on the actual brief. For example, sometimes our job will be to identify the impact of the cultural context across markets; at other times, we will need to understand the social context and the different responses of different segments/groups of customers, or the brief will concern the physical situation or immediate competitive context. Often it will be important to consider the contexts at all four levels and how they work together because, as it is said, "Eventually, everything connects" (Charles Eames).

A. Cultural Context—Heuristics, Anchors, and Biases

We are influenced by the society we belong to: our societal values and societal pressures impact the way we think and behave. They create contextual heuristics, anchors, and biases at this macrolevel. Understanding this societal context and the changing dynamics and pressures within it is a great starting point. It is also a perfect starting point for understanding cross-cultural differences in the consumer context that can impact brand positioning and communication.

B. Situational Context—Heuristics, Anchors, and Biases

Where you are, in a store, at a train station, at home, and so on, has a major impact on choice and behavior. We need to understand the contextual differences and biases between these cold to hot behavioral zones.

The growth of online shopping offers a fascinating new context with which to contend. Recent advertising for a U.K. supermarket positioned its online service as essentially removing choice or competitive context with the line, "What if when you shopped all your favorites were in one place," before offering the "favorites already in the basket" solution. This clearly creates an environment in which it is harder to provide cues to disrupt or challenge behavior, unless, like the retailer, you own that context.

C. Social Context—Heuristics, Anchors, and Biases

The social groups we belong to or connect with expose us to social norms and pressure points that impact our behavior and our willingness to change. Most people are impacted by more than one social group, be they friends (and peer groups), work colleagues and clients, or family. Understanding the relative importance of each social group within the choice architecture and potential points of conflict is vital to understand the range of behavioral drivers.

Principle 2: Unearth Potential Biases—Among Customer Decision Makers *and* Among Researchers

When we think about market research, we are often influenced by our cognitive biases. How often are the methodologies we choose based on what we have done before or what procurement we will be benchmarked against? In the time-starved world of marketing and market research, do we have the cognitive space to consider new approaches? We need to confront our internal rules of thumb and our cognitive biases, assessing the potential biases at play.

Principle 3: Reframe Research Designs Around Behavior (Versus Attitudes)

BE reminds us that many research briefs and approaches are not optimized to understand consumer behavior. At every stage of the process, from the writing of the brief to research design and delivery, BE provides opportunities for fresh eyes on existing approaches, as well as new methodologies.

Reframing the research brief. Most research briefs are focused on understanding *why* consumers are doing something. BE suggests that there should be more focus on the actual behavior rather than a postrationalization of it.

Reframe methodology. Use more qualitative behavioral techniques, such as cultural analysis, ethnography, observation, and so on.

Reframe recruitment. Typically, respondents are recruited on brand preference or attitudes, but these may not be as important as *actual behavior.* Contrasting different *behavioral* groups may be more useful than contrasting different *attitudinal* groups.

Reframing questionnaire structure. What's the most relevant way to frame the consumer choice? Often, it will be more relevant to focus on the category first and then the brand.

Reframe question writing/discussion guides. This allows us to understand specific behaviors (versus attitudes). This would involve focusing on more "what" "when" "where" "how" questions rather than so many "why" questions.

Principle 4: Harness the Power of Deep Observation

Research has a tendency to concentrate on understanding what consumers think and why. Too often, we assume that consumers can pinpoint and describe their motivations, when, in fact, this is not the case. Observational research is an increasingly widely used technique, but it is often used at a superficial level, with not enough focus on what the researcher should be looking for. Many elements of choice architecture will be unconscious and unrecognized by consumers. BE-inspired observation should be focusing on how behavior is linked to the context and relevant heuristics and anchors that operate within it. We should also employ other experts such as social psychologists to unlock insight into specific behavior. This will yield deeper, more powerful behavioral insights to act on.

Principle 5: Be Open to Experimentation

If "an experiment is an interesting event combined with insightful observation," (Jones quoted in Balik, 2010, p. 24), then we need to be more open to research that does not necessarily have a clear end point. There is an opportunity to think of research as a series of iterative consumer experiments, each designed to explore a different hypothesis.

Obviously, experiments that simulate a real-life context are difficult to create (as are experiments using MRI scans to look at brain function and stimulus). So we need to conceptualize experiments as being interesting, relevant events that are staged and then observed, bringing fresh eyes and BE constructs to bear.

"The huge challenge is taking insight creation out of the proverbial laboratory. . . . How do we deploy the full range of methodologies in new places and so understand the consumer in their natural habitat" (Jones quoted in Balik, 2010, p. 24).

The following case studies illustrate how these five *new* principles of research design can be applied to yield fresh insights.

BE MARKET RESEARCH CASE STUDIES

BE Research Case Study 1: Final Mile—Improving Safety on the Indian Railways

The Challenge

How to reduce the high number of deaths on the Indian Railways.

Final Mile Consulting operates on the philosophy that irrationality in human behavior is best explained by cognitive neurology and behavioral economics. The task of primary research is, hence, not to explain behavior but to record and decode patterns in behavior to find ways to influence behavior in different contexts.

Current research methods assume that consumers know the reasons for their behavior, and through intelligent inquiry, we can unearth those reasons. We know from advances in cognitive neurology that this is not true. Of all human cognitive processes, 95% are beyond the realm of conscious recall. People say what is easy to articulate and what sounds rationally correct to explain their behavior. It is impossible for a person crossing railway tracks to admit that they perform this dangerous act because of overconfidence wired in their brain. Even in life-threatening situations, people find it difficult to change behavior in ways that are beneficial to them. Nor would it be possible for them to articulate that there are deficiencies in visual processing that prevent them from judging the speed of an oncoming train.

Imperative in any approach is rapid experimentation to validate hypotheses generated during research and subsequent analysis.

Research Approach

The approach used *deep observation* and *cognitive neurology* to explain and modify human behavior, working with irrationality rather than trying to fight it.

Observation and open-ended discussion were used as techniques for developing behavior-altering hypotheses. Observations were done at the point of action and discussions carried out in a "hot" state, with people whose behavior had just been observed. Observation of current behavior is a time-intensive and rigorous process. It requires being at the point of action for hours, and observing and recording behavior. Manuals, time sheets, photographs, and video recordings were used. Decoding patterns in behavior and understanding the emotions surrounding the behavior were critical.

Research techniques included method acting to help unearth the emotions and mental models around observed behaviors. For example, to unearth insights around crossing railway tracks, the team spent hours at the tracks, spent time with people living by the tracks, and crossed the tracks hundreds of times over a significant period.

Conversations were initiated through an open-ended discussion guide with people in a hot state. The idea of these conversations was to understand the conscious processing behind the action and not to decipher the unconscious aspects of decision making. The two key problems identified were (1) the overconfidence in their capacity to cross the track safely and (2) deficiencies in visual processing impairing judgments about the speed of oncoming trains.

Traditional approaches have always tried to inform people about the danger of crossing the track. The most commonly used signs say, "DANGER" and/or have the image of a skull and crossbones, which speak directly to the rational side of the person. However, when these signs were shown to people, Final Mile realized that they evoked no emotion since they required conscious processing.

The approach adopted was to design a warning for the unconscious mind and to tap directly into emotional memories related to fear. An artist was used to evoke the helpless fear of a person about to be hit by a train. This stimulus created the same emotions in the observers since it enabled them to immediately see themselves in this position.

To address visual processing deficiencies, Final Mile drew on theory hypothesized by Leibowitz that the speed of larger objects (like trains) is underestimated by the observer.

Final Mile painted alternate sets of railway ties in fluorescent yellow—five painted, five unpainted, and so on—to tackle what is known as the Leibowitz Hypothesis. As laid out in a 1985 issue of American Scientist by experimental psychologist Herschel W. Leibowitz, the hypothesis found that we frequently underestimate the speed at which large objects move. Leibowitz first observed this with aircraft, and in 2003, a pair of scientists proved the hypothesis for trains. "The misperception happens because the brain has no frame of reference, no way to evaluate roughly how fast a train is moving," said Satish Krishnamurthy, a Final Mile behavior architect. But with the new paint job, Krishnamurthy said, "The mind now has a way to gauge the train's speed, by observing how fast it traverses these ties." (Agrawal, 2011, para. 11)

(Continued)

(Continued)

This leads to people making fatal judgments about their ability to cross the tracks before the train reaches them. The solution was to create speed reference points in the form of yellow lines across the tracks. The speed of these lines disappearing under the train gave a speed reference without the observer being consciously aware of it.

The Results

Every minute, 25 people cross the railway tracks, rising to 45 during rush hour. From June to December, in 2009, there were 23 deaths at Wadala junction in Mumbai. From December 2009, after the new safety methods were implemented, there were only nine deaths. The number of deaths during the day has dropped to around 70% (Agrawal, 2011).

Image 5.9

Source: Reprinted with permission © Final Mile Consulting.

BE Research Case Study 2: Reframing Brand Health—U.K. Television Broadcaster

The Challenge

Traditional measures of brand health tend to rely on single measures of brand performance, derived from a small number of abstract questions measuring variables such as consideration (e.g., via a brand preference measure) or commitment (e.g., via a net promoter measure). In broadcast television, such measures may not explain changes in viewing patterns and, in the case of this particular client, were found to move independent of viewing patterns over an extended period.

Television is characterized by a very large number of category decisions—80 million TV viewing decisions in the U.K. in a month. Many of these decisions are habitual in nature, as viewers tend to tune into their favorite channels and programs. Teasing apart habitual behavior from more considered behavior and separating out the behaviors of loyal channel viewers from more marginal viewers are critical to inform television marketing.

Informed by an understanding of behavioral economics and, in particular, the need to ground the research in the context of television *choice architecture*, the brand health tracker was redesigned by international research agency, 2CV. Brand health questions were, for the first time, framed in the context of *category decisions*. The start point was the numerous buying decisions or, in this case, *viewing decisions* that consumers make within the category:

Seventeen discrete category needs for broadcast entertainment were introduced as proxies for the range of decisions within the category.

The extent to which these needs were important to the prospective viewer was established.

The association between broadcasting brands and each of the category needs was measured.

A weighted composite brand health score was derived, taking into account the salience of each of the category needs.

The Results

The BE informed approach to measuring brand health has significant advantages over previous approaches, most critically the ability to predict consumer viewing behavior.

(Continued)

(Continued)

The approach successfully proved a link between meeting consumer category needs, brand health, and TV viewing share. Particularly useful was the fact that habitual viewing behavior could be teased out (in particular the heavy viewing of channel loyalists), enabling the viewing patterns and perceptions of the more marginal viewer to be isolated. These more marginal consumers are critical targets for marketing as nudging and changing their behavior will disproportionately drive viewing share.

BE INFORMED RESEARCH METHODOLOGIES: THOUGHT STARTERS

The following qualitative methodologies are a starting point for thinking about how BE can shed new light on existing approaches, as well as help us think about fresh ideas. Some of the methods listed are variations on a well-known theme, while others are perhaps more radical. As always, it is important to remember that methodology is not the end in and of itself; there is no substitute for analytical rigor and thinking. However, research recommendations that are framed within a powerful scientific theory, such as BE, are more likely to generate richer, behavioral insights and, therefore, have more potential impact and carry more weight than superficial research observations.

BE will help us navigate between simple solutions which try to understand the consumer in such an abstract way they offer nothing grounded in the real world, and an attitude of let's give up, it's all too complicated. BE makes the paradoxical and contradictory world of the consumer available to be understood if we look long and hard enough. . . . BE is all about getting research out of a project based mentality, and getting it to think about how one creates platforms for learning . . . grounded understanding that should inform every marketing decision. (Chad Wollen, Group Head of Consumer Futures, Vodafone)

Reverse Shopping

Traditional accompanied shopping techniques potentially interfere with consumer decision making by interrupting the flow of shopping or affording only a rational interpretation of purchase drivers. During **reverse shopping**, the interviewer silently observes consumers going about their shopping to highlight moments when behaviors need to be further explored. After the shop, the consumer reverses the shopping process, putting products back on the shelf and contextual drivers and purchase heuristics are explored in depth by the interviewer. Rather than questioning the consumers as to why they have behaved in a particular way, the researcher simply makes observations as to the observed behavior, which are then followed up during discussion with the consumer.

Making and Breaking Habits: Deprivation and Forced Choices

This is a three-stage methodology to bring to the surface subliminal patterns of consumer behavior to understand how they can be altered or reinforced. The first stage involves understanding the impact of loss aversion by asking the consumer to consider life without a given product or service. The second stage involves a classic deprivation diary exercise whereby the consumer records their behavior and feelings in response to the loss. The results of Stages 1 and 2 are compared and contrasted to explore conscious and unconscious drivers of behavior. The third and final stage forces alternative choices to explore the strengths and weaknesses of competitive offers. This approach generates insights into the triggers required to create behavior change by understanding the impact of unfreezing current behavior.

Expert Eyes

This method leverages the contrasting perspectives particular individuals can bring to a problem to shed new light on potential interpretations. This approach uses three to four experts with different types of relationships with the category/brand/research question to explore the different responses and perceptions. The ideal would be to have behavioral economists, social psychologists, researchers, and consumers all observing and decoding behavior together (Totman, 2010).

In the Moment

Using mobile and digital technology to capture consumers' emotional and behavioral responses *in the moment* is an intimate methodology enabling consumers to express gut reactions and unarticulated feelings—elevating the unconscious. Traditional research only captures "cold" responses from consumers. "In the moment" creates contextual disruption at the moment of purchase or consumption. This generates richer, deeper *contextual insights* (e.g., in hot versus cold moments).

Social Interaction and Observation: The Power of We

BE identifies social norms as one of the key influences in real behavior—beliefs about how other people might behave based on interaction and observation or what other people think should be done. These norms operate below the level of conscious deliberation and are not accessible by direct questioning. This procedure makes use of the fact that people are embedded in social networks.

Participants are given the task of generating their discussions, pre- or postinterview or group session. They take an aspect of a problem/question out to their social network and experience themselves what the hidden norms might be. This puts the respondent in control of their context. They are asked to invite others they think might be interested or perhaps join a discussion of their choice, recognizing the role of social norms and pressure points on behavior. They may be asked to observe the behavior of others in this context and report on it.

CONCLUSION

While there is some way to go methodologically, it is clear that this new learning, this new behavioral economics architecture, *can provide penetrating insights into consumer behavior and deliver the new aha moments we seek*. It has implications for what we research and focus on, implications for how we seek to understand consumers, implications for how we market to consumers, and implications for the metrics we employ.

There is a long road ahead and, in my view, the best way to tackle the challenges is for client, agencies and researchers to work together using the same frameworks. Only then will BE thinking make a real difference to what we do. (Gordon, 2010, p. 39)

FURTHER READING

Benartzi, S., & Thaler, R. (2001). Naive diversification strategies in defined contribution saving plans. *American Economic Review*, (91), 79–98.

Camerer, C., & Loewenstein, G. (2004). Behavioral economics: Past, present, future. In C. Camerer, G. Loewenstein, & M. Rabin (Eds.), *Advances in behavioral economics*, (pp. 3–51). Princeton, NJ: Princeton University Press.

Carroll, J. S. (1978). The effect of imagining an event on expectations for the event: An interpretation in terms of the availability heuristic. *Journal of Experimental Social Psychology, 14*, 88–96.

Cialdini, R. (1993). *Influence: Science and practice*. New York, NY: HarperCollins.

Combs, B., & Slovic, P. (1979). Newspaper coverage of causes of death. *Journalism Quarterly, 56*, 837–843.

Earls, M. (2009). *Herd: How to change mass behavior by harnessing our true nature*. New York, NY: John Wiley & Sons.

Earls, M., & Bentley, A. (2009, April). How ideas spread: From me to we marketing. Applying Darwin's theories to marketing and market research. *Research World, 8,* 12.

Schwartz, B. (2003). *The paradox of choice: Why more is less*. New York, NY: HarperCollins.

Sechrist, G. B., & Stangor, C. (2001). Perceived consensus influences intergroup behavior and stereotype accessibility. *Journal of Personality and Social Psychology, 80*, 645–654.

Staw, B. M. (1976). Knee-deep in the big muddy: A study of escalating commitment to a chosen course of action. *Organizational Behavior and Human Performance, 16*(1), 27–44.

Tversky, A., & Kahneman, D. (1981). The framing of decisions and the psychology of choice. *Science: New Series, 211*, (4481), 453–458.

Tversky, A., & Kahneman, D. (1986). Rational choice and the framing of decisioms. *Journal of Business, 59*, 251–278.

Wilczek, F. (2006, Sept/Oct). Archaeopteryx looks up. Speculations on the future of human Evolution. *New York Academy of Sciences Update*. Retrieved from http://www.nyas.org/publications/update Unbound.asp?updateID=76.

CHAPTER 6

State-of-the-Science Market Segmentation

Making Results Actionable for Marketers

KEVIN CLANCY

AMI BOWEN

Copernicus, Inc.

INTRODUCTION

In a seminal article in the *Harvard Business Review* in 1964, Daniel Yankelovich introduced the idea of going beyond demographics for dividing buyers into groups. He argued that "once you discover the most useful ways of segmenting a market, you have produced the beginnings of sound marketing strategy" (Yankelovich, 1964, p. 83). While we wholeheartedly concur with his thinking, we just might have bolded, italicized, all-capped—whatever the HBR's standard convention was at the time for heavily emphasizing a point—to draw attention to the phrase "most useful." Here we are, 50 years later, and the usability and actionability of results is a major issue.

Take the case of a popular cable television channel Kevin spoke with recently. According to top management, the company was interested in an audience segmentation study to see what it could do to expand its viewership. While having the conversation, Kevin noticed a thick binder—what appeared to be a segmentation report by a well-known consulting firm—on the bookshelf right behind the CEO's head. At an appropriate point, Kevin said, "Have you ever done one of these before? There appears to be a strategy study right behind you."

"Yes, we did, but it wasn't very helpful," the CMO reported.

"Why wasn't it helpful?" Kevin asked.

"We couldn't make heads or tails of the results!" The CEO and CMO exclaimed in unison. "We couldn't use the results to make any decisions that we needed to make. We couldn't even use it to just tell us where we should focus our marketing efforts" (Clancy, Krieg, & Gamse, 2006, p. 18).

We hear this complaint too frequently.

In fact, according to Ron Park (2008), senior director at database marketing firm Merkle, today many marketers "connect segmentation with a negative past experience in which the solution ultimately disappointed" (p. 2). It's gotten to the point that "in some companies, the word 'segmentation' is actually taboo, where past horror stories involving failed strategies make marketers shun any resurfacing of the idea" (p. 2). As an illustration, one of our clients has had so many bad experiences over the years with segmentation studies that marketers at the company now only talk about market structure and alternative taxonomies.

Following up on his original thought, Yankelovich, this time with coauthor David Meer, wrote in a recent *Harvard Business Review* piece, "The idea was to broaden the use of segmentation so that it could inform not just advertising, but also product innovation, pricing, choice of distribution channels, and the like. Yet today's segmentations do very little of this" (Yankelovich & Meer, 2006, p. 124). To our way of thinking, the litmus test of a truly state-of-the-science market segmentation needs to be as much about the relevance and applicability of the outcome to fundamental strategic decisions like these as much as the complexity of the algorithm or analytical technique used to sort buyers into groups.

It's important to think of state-of-the-science market segmentation as a **strategic research process** rather than a one-off data collection and group-and-sort exercise. A process that will produce results useful, actionable, and applicable to different marketing, operational, and business decisions for the *longer term* starts with an understanding of exactly who in the company plans to use the segmentation and how they plan (or hope) to use them.

BRING THE WHOLE TEAM TOGETHER

It's just not enough, says Ron Park, "to assume that a 'better understanding' of customers will yield results" (Park, 2008, p. 3) that can guide a business on a variety of issues. In an up-front meeting, you need to gather representatives—from all branches of the organization—who (if all goes as planned) will use the segmentation to ensure that the results will address as many collective needs as possible.

The conventional up-front meeting includes a very narrow set of people, usually a marketing manager—often one with limited responsibilities in functional areas—and a marketing researcher. The discussion kicks-off with which methodology to use. It's not typically an open forum aimed at defining the needs of all potential end-users and/or understanding how they might apply the results.

Rarely do we find representatives from research and development; pricing; the sales force; the ad agency, media buyers, and planners, or digital gurus or social media mavens in the same room. Consequently, the segmentation study becomes immediately paralyzed

Figure 6.1 A State-of-the-Science Market Segmentation Process

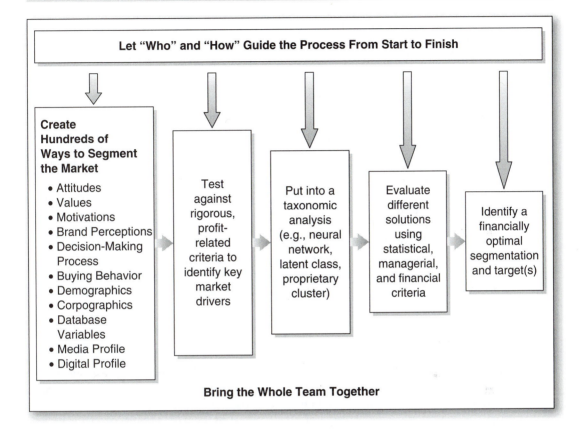

by the lack of involvement of different functions in the organization. By definition, the results will suffer from serious constraints in generalizability and actionability across the organization.

Let's face it, market segmentation work can suck up a big chunk of time and budget dollars. It's the largest deep-dive strategic study a marketing manager will undertake in any three-year period. To make sure it's going to be marketing money well spent, taking a step back and thinking through the who, what, and how will drive state-of-the-science segmentation forward.

As a real-world example, we asked Air Products Corporation to convene a cross-functional team of 18 different people from across the organization to help plan a major strategy study. Representatives from marketing management, sales management, product development, pricing, logistics, and research and development—in other words, any area that touched the customer in some way—all joined the meeting. A common story in any large organization, some of the people had never even met one another—never mind spent time thinking about practical applications of research results in the day-to-day operations of different areas—before we all came together.

We started the first of a series of half-day sessions by explaining our two overriding objectives:

1. *To set the scope of the final results.* In consumer research, in which large companies will use sophisticated media plans or database modeling, a company can afford to entertain many variables. In business to business (B2B) marketing, however, the ultimate use of the segmentation will be fairly straightforward—by salespeople in the field or for searching business databases.

2. *To establish parameters for the research.* What kind of questions do you need to ask? What databases do you need to link to? For media planners, for instance, you can marry a segmentation to a syndicated media database, such as MRI and SMRB, to provide rich insights into the media exposure patterns of the different segments. If your media plans might include digital options, it might not be such a bad idea to find out more about digital media habits. Or for the sales force, you can integrate information from established customer accounts, third-party, and/or block-level census databases.

With that out of the way, we asked the members of the group to write questions that a strategy study would need to answer to make the results useful to them. Further discussions ensued about the possibilities and likelihood of answering the different questions, and by the fourth session, a study design and questionnaire outline began to emerge.

YOU REAP WHAT YOU SOW

With the discussions and decisions made during the up-front planning sessions at Air Products in mind, a technical research team comprised of research whizzes inside the organization and outside consultants gathered to discuss what segmentation approaches to use to get the questions answered. Very important, we asked them to hypothesize *all* the different ways that we could segment the market. We wanted to get anything and everything—demographics, corpographics, decision-making power, influence, attitudes, database variables, needs, media habits, buying behavior, brand perceptions, and so on—potentially relevant and related to profitability out on the table.

That many of the folks in the room had not done this level and extent of hypothesizing before doing segmentation research didn't surprise us too much.

Remember our earlier comment about the typical upfront meeting—a marketing manager and marketing research talking about which methodology (also known as model, algorithm, procedure, or approach) to use? This conversation usually involves selecting a preprescribed list of variables, troublingly without a lick of evidence that they will deliver the best segmentation solution. Because the *a priori* segmentation drives the data collected, by definition, the results suffer from serious contraints in useability and applicability to key decisions.

Consider the case of the CMO of a marketing powerhouse—top in its industry—who asked us to help explain the sputtering performance of one of its flagship brands. The executive explained, "We were doing well until last year when we decided to restructure all of our marketing efforts (advertising, product design, promotion, channel choice, pricing, and so on) based on the results of a new psychographic segmentation."

Curious, we asked about how the segmentation research was designed and executed. The CMO explained that the company brought in a psychology professor from a local university who developed a psychographic battery of 46 questions (e.g., "I always like to be surrounded by a lot of people," versus "I consider myself to be a loner;" "I am an extroverted, garrulous person," versus "I tend to be a reticent person with not much to say;" "In any group activity, I always find myself in a leadership position," versus "I'm much more of a follower than a leader"). The battery was administered to 1,000 people, ages 18 years or older, over the Internet. The professor next analyzed the data and clustered respondents into groups based on their answers.

But why did the company opt for a psychographic approach orginally? And why this specific set of personality dimensions? Was there something to suggest it would work better than what they had used up to that point to segment the market?

As it turned out, the CEO had read something or other about the power of personality and gave the idea to the CMO. Previously, they'd been using a mix of demographics and occasions. To the CMO's knowledge, no serious thinking or analysis was undertaken to determine whether psychographics might be a more useful, practical, or helpful way of segmenting that market. The items used to delineate and define the groups were of unknown reliability and validity at predicting (among other things) behavior or purchase intent in the category. No attempt was made to evaluate each respondent or cluster in potential profitability or if there would be a way to connect groups delineated by psychographic characteristics to existing databases. Yet standing orders were to develop marketing plans and programs against the five resulting buyer segments.

We did some *ex post facto* analyses and eventually discovered that few of the psychographic items had anything to do with behavior (never mind profitability) in the category, and the five segments were perfectly flat in product motivations, problems, demographics, media exposure patterns, and anything else the marketing folks in the organization might use for communications, distribution, or innovation decisions. And when we did try to find the groups in databases, it was impossible; they were all the same (Clancy, Krieg, & Gamse, 2006, p. 20).

By no means, do we intend to pick on psychographics. Although many of the popular approaches to market segmentation today appear superficially appealing, when you get down to it, they are not particularly revealing on more than one or two critical issues—issues that may not have anything to do with the information needs of the organization. We've pulled together some of the pros and cons of popular conventional approaches marketers we've worked with have offered based on their experiences. Disturbingly—given the frequency with which many of these models get used—the cons often outweigh the pros.

Buyer Needs Segmentation

What It's Good For

- Generating new product ideas
- Providing some insights for advertising and other marcom content and copy

Some Pros

- Easy to do
- Intellectually interesting
- Engaging consensus-building group exercise to name groups

Some Cons

- Needs are often weakly related to behavior
- Basic needs (i.e., "tastes great" in a soda or "on-time delivery" for a B2B component manufacturer) are not the same as problems
- Impossible to find in databases

Lifestyle Segmentation

What It's Good For

- Providing some insights for advertising and other marcom copy and content

Some Pros

- Interesting and fun to work with
- Easy for everyone in the organization to understand
- Exciting and engaging exercise to name groups

Some Cons

- Lifestyles rarely predict brand choice
- Few insights into the unique problems of each segment that a marketer might solve
- Impossible to find in databases

Demographic Segmentation

What It's Good For

- Guiding the media plan
- Helping creative agencies understand how to bring the segments to life

Some Pros

- Easy to find in databases
- Easy for everyone in the organization to understand
- Have distinct media preferences and habits

Some Cons

- Not predictive of behavior
- Segments have similar brand preferences and behavior patterns
- Few insights into the unique problems of each segment that a marketer might solve

Behavioral Segmentation

What It's Good for

- Guiding the media plan
- Helping the sales force find the segments in its database

Some Pros

- Straightforward
- Easy for everyone in the organization to understand
- Easy to find in databases

Some Cons

- The heaviest users are often also the most price conscious
- Few insights into the unique problems of each segment that a marketer might solve
- The segments look the same in differentiating features, such as demographics, media exposure patterns, and brand preferences (Clancy & Krieg, 2000, p. 98)

TAKE YOUR MOTHER'S ADVICE

The plain truth is we just don't know in any given market what will be related to profitability and desirable, brand-positive behaviors until we talk to current and prospective customers, collect data, and do analysis. Yes, it's human nature to want to select a certain set of variables—be they psychographics, attitudes, demographics, or behaviors—ahead of time so one feels more in control of the final outcome. Particularly if the results sound as though they'll be cool and fun and, therefore, in theory, easier to shop around the company and show the CEO, or, as is often the case in B2B settings, easier to implement, why not just go ahead and pick one set as soon as possible?

When it comes to doing state-of-the-science market segmentation, however, if your mother ever told you, "don't put all your eggs in one basket," take her advice. Why bet only on psychographics or any other exclusive set of variables as the key predictors of behavior in the *absence of any evidence* that they are—investing significant time, money, and brand equity, not to mention personal credibility—in a market segmentation when you don't have to?

When all is said and done, you could easily have 250 independent or predictor variables from a typical in-depth interview with a consumer or B2B buyer. Those often consist of 15 to 20 demographics, 40 to 50 attitudes, 20 to 40 behaviors, 30 to 50 motivations to buy the brand and in the category in general, 20 to 30 media habits, and numerous database variables. Some of those are relatively simple variables, such as gender, age, marital status, and purchasing behavior. Others are more complicated, such as relative income, the subject's income relative to households in the same ZIP code, block, or age group. Sometimes, very complex variables are created, such as household income per capita compared with that of close friends and relatives. Factor analysis can reduce the large quantity of the variables; it can take the 150 and find the things they have in common to reduce the list to 30 or 40 dimensions or individual items.

A friendly reminder here, though, to stay razor-focused on what decisions you want the segmentation to help you make—the parameters of the research we talked about establishing at the outset of the research process—when selecting the variables to include. Medical-equipment supplier Hill-Rom, for instance, wanted to restructure its increasingly complex sales organization to reduce the cost of sales, which had steadily increased year after year unchecked. It also wanted to better support the company's plan for growth primarily through innovation. Management made sure to include variables in the segmentation research, such as primary decision makers, replacement cycles, and purchase behaviors that could help the sales organization. At the same time, it also considered customer needs and problems, product preferences, and primary purchase drivers that could help direct innovation efforts (Waaser, Dahnehe, Pekkarinen, & Weissel, 2004, pp. 2–3).

If you want a segmentation to guide digital and social media decisions, you need to capture how high-value targets behave in a digital envirnoment. How do they use digital and social media throughout the pre- and postpurchase process? How do they like to interact with a brand within different digital and social communications channels?

We've come across many different typologies that depict digital media usage and engagement. The one we use most frequently comes from our sister firm Carat and is depicted in Figure 6.2.

Figure 6.2   Digital Medial Usage

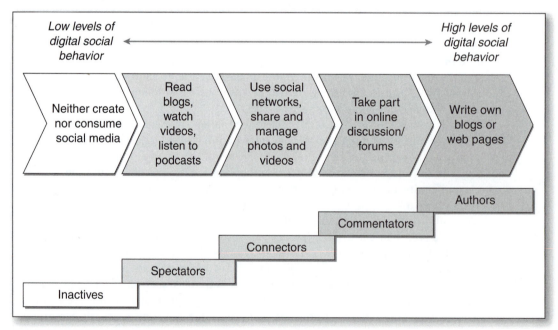

Source: Carat.

Just as you should ask and answer the same questions used in the database resources media planners regularly access—Simmons, MRI, Nielsen, @Plan, Compete Inc.—to develop direct links, you should do the same with a digital typology.

As Phil Kotler (2004), the dean of American marketing professors, writes in *Ten Deadly Marketing Sins*, "The first commandment of marketing is to segment the market, choose the best segment, and develop a strong position in each chosen segment" (p. 15). Determining all the potential ways to segment a market makes for a step in the right direction, yet if the ultimate end-goal of a market segmentation exercise is to decide about which group(s) to target, you need a full sense of the financial implications of your decision.

SHOW ME THE MONEY

Interestingly, Larry Selden and Geoffrey Colvin (2003) maintain that "a surprisingly large percentage of executives we've talked to believe their companies have no unprofitable customers, which is virtually never true. When asked to name their most profitable and least profitable customers, most executives name the wrong ones or simply have no clue" (p. 1). Having a sense of the economic value of different market segments would help marketers on numerous fronts when it comes to maximizing the return on investment (ROI) of their budget dollars.

Today, assessing the value of individual customers requires a profitability equation balanced with financial and, very important, nonfinancial inputs. Besides revenue measures, such as lifetime value, current spending in the category in dollars, current brand share, behavior and prices paid in different channels, and brand switching history/potential, several other characteristics make one customer more valuable than another because they're easier to get and keep, as well as engage as comarketers.

What we call "proxies for profitability" could include the following:

Level of satisfaction. One popular idea circulating in business these days is to "flip the funnel" and focus on the customers who're currently happy with a brand. Certainly, customers who express a high level of satisfaction have a lower likelihood of switching, a higher likelihood of repeat purchases, and a greater chance they'll enhance marketing activities. Marketers also don't have to invest significant resources in reversing their negative opinions or undoing its potentially damaging effects. Just ask the folks at Dell about Ihatedell.org.

An important addendum to this notion, though, is to take advantage of any unhappiness current and prospective customers have with the competitive brands they may use. Given the right incentive, they might bring their business over to another brand.

Price insensitivity. Unless you're Walmart and want to grab share among the folks who put price above all other brand considerations, price *in*sensitivity is another important indication of a buyer's value to a brand and is particularly relevant these days. Interestingly, our research suggests that price is the primary consideration for only 15 to 35% of buyers in most product and service categories. We'd agree that price very likely does become a *more* important consideration as household and corporate budgets get tighter. That doesn't necessarily mean it becomes the *most* important consideration, however. Price insensitives are the folks that marketers want to find.

Mickey Drexler, CEO of retailer J.Crew, for example, looked for the customers willing to pay more for well-made clothing and increased revenues 107% his first five years in charge (Gaudoin, 2010, p. 1).

Magnitude of problems. As we said earlier, needs are not the same as problems. A problem is something that a buyer says is important—"processes claims quickly" for an insurance company—but no brand or company adequately addresses. The bigger the problem a brand can solve, the bigger the market response. In the early days of Internet surfing, AOL went after people interested in getting on the web, but felt afraid of doing it on themselves. More than 30 million people over several continents signed up for AOL's service and the *USA Today* (2007) put it at Number 4 in its ranking of the events that shaped the first 25 years of the web.

Interest in new products and services. Introducing new products and services—in good times and in bad—can generate the kind of organic growth companies crave. So why not ensure that new products and services *will* generate bottom-line growth by narrowing in on the customers most interested in considering the latest offerings from a brand or company? Apple's pretty much got this one down.

Brand advocacy. Brand advocates typically makeup about 5 to 10% of a customer base, but what they lack in numbers, they make up for in influence among their peers and love for the brand. The greater the level of influence a buyer has among their social networks, the more a brand's marketing ROI will benefit. Customers who do some of the work for a brand because they're more likely to spread the word to family and friends online and off about a product/service they found that really works are like money in the bank.

For instance, one restaurant chain we worked with found that while the brand advocates visited the stores the same number of times in an average month as the frequent users, they introduced the brand to other people in their social networks *three times* as much.

Social connectvity on the web. Because of the speed and number of tools available to spread information about product and services online, word-of-mouth activity is even more important to capture in a digital environment. The more active and engaged a customer is with different social media, the more valuable they can be to a brand.

For instance, Ford picked out 100 twenty-something YouTube storytellers who'd developed a fan community of their own and gave them a Fiesta for six months. Each month they shared their experiences with their communities via YouTube, Flickr, Facebook, and Twitter. Ford received 50,000 requests for information on Fiesta—almost entirely from new-to-Ford customers—and sold 10,000 units in the first six days of sales (McCracken, 2010, p. 1).

Marketers have understandable concerns about divining future customer behavior based only on what they have done in the past. We strongly recommend you employ financial and nonfinancial measures to assess potential economic value (profitability) that give you the ability to get a sense of not only who buys what, how much, and how often *currently* but also what they have the *potential* to do if marketed to in a manner tailored to their needs, interests, media habits, and so on.

WHERE THE RUBBER MEETS THE ROAD

This brings us to the next task: using the data collected in a large-scale quantitative survey to determine what variables are *most predictive* of a customer's—whether a person or a company—economic value (profitability).

The rubber really meets the road when you take all the different ways to segment the market you came up with and test their relationship to proxies for profitability. Depending on the scope of the results you set at the beginning, you could entertain a small or large set of predictor variables. In B2B, if you want the sales force to use the segmentation in the field, you need a more straightforward segmentation and, therefore, smaller set. In business to consumers (B2C), where you might have a communications plan with traditional and digital elements in media and distribution channel environments, you can afford to entertain a larger set.

Lafarge, one of the largest diversified suppliers of construction materials in North America, for example, wanted to segment its B2B base of customers to enable its sales force to quickly identify which package of products and services to offer to increase the likelihood and profitability of a sale. In that case, a complex algorithm with multiple variables would have gone over about as well as a pregnant pole-vaulter. The segmentation criteria had to be easy and few enough for the sales force to identify, assess, and react to quickly in the field. So limiting solutions to only a handful of variables was realistic (Braselton & Blair, 2007, pp. 14–17).

At this point, you can group buyers into segments based on their answers to the set of 5 to 25 variables. The company can use different statistical methods here, such as cluster analyses, latent class analysis, and neural networks.

Finally, test again looking at numerous segmentation schemes. Apply the managerial, statistical, and financial criteria you worked out up front when you set the scope of the results and parameters of the research to evaluate different solutions. Will the sales force be able to use them? How about traditional and digital media planners and website managers? Do they answer the questions important to all the constituencies need to serve? Are they interested in new products and services? Are there different brand preferences, different consumption levels, different channels, different media profiles, and—very important— different levels of potential profitability? Which is more or less easy to implement?

There's one more hurdle the segmentation solution that comes out of this process needs to overcome: Does it tell you which group or groups to target?

Our definition of the best target includes the following:

- A segment sufficient in size to merit disproportionate attention (e.g., 10–30%)
- A segment with economic value or potential profitability to the company considerably greater than its size (e.g., 50–70%)

- A segment growing—not shrinking—in size
- A segment with different demographics/corpographics making it differentially reachable with media, by salespeople, via channels, via content, and so on
- A segment whose problems/needs/wants distinctly differ from other segments

At the end of the day, the ultimate segmentation solution you select should deliver a set of segments that provide a clear understanding of (1) which group or groups represent the best target, (2) what distinct needs they have that can be addressed and marketed to, and (3) how to find and reach them. If the results of a segmentation exercise are a mystery to marketers, the sales force, communications planners, agencies, research and development, operations, and any other critical parties, it won't pass the litmus test for a state-of-the-science segmentation.

STATE-OF-THE-SCIENCE SEGMENTATION: A PROCESS YOU CAN BELIEVE IN

Following a process like the one we've described will give you segments—and, very important, a target—that differ in demographics because you have used key demographics to form the segments. You know the segments will be different in needs/wants because you have used them to form the segments. And you know the segments will be different in brand preference and consumption—and one segment will be considerably better than all the others on these—because you selected only those demographics, attitudes, and behaviors that relate to those issues.

The results will provide a detailed, well-balanced picture of the current and prospective buyers in different groups. It will tell you more about them than just their gender or age, their attitudes, or their needs—it gives you all these things and more.

It will define groups that are very different in their economic value to a firm and in their traditional and digital media habits. There should be clear guidance you can use to develop an engaging messaging strategy and/or breakthrough new products. There should be specifics media planners and/or the sales force can use to formulate plans.

In others words, it can be widely used across a marketing organization to drive strategy and marketing programs—exactly where most conventional approaches fall short.

Here, we'd like to introduce the case of a financial services firm that asked us for help figuring out which one of the numerous segmentation schemes it had would be the best to give it clear guidance across a spectrum of decision areas, sales, and marketing issues. No small task, as it turned out; the firm had 11 different segmentation approaches it or its ad agency applied, ranging from affinity groups to tenure as a customer with the firm, from attitudes to basic demographics.

In and of themselves, all the different schemes had some good points. Senior management at the company, for instance, was not entirely convinced that another scheme would perform any better than the demographic-based segmentation it had used for a decade. It could easily find demographic groups in databases, not to mention the marketing and sales organization readily comprehended the demographic-based distinctions between the groups. Yet even senior management had to admit the demographic groups didn't differ on the company's internal measure of economic value—they all looked about the same.

Demographics also didn't help when it came to giving the firm's ad agency messaging direction. Instead, the agency had come up with groups based on attitudes and used them to develop a campaign. Attitudes, however, proved no better than demographics at predicting responsiveness to new product offerings—not particularly well. Nor did they make it any easier to distinguish which group or groups the firm should focus on because of their higher economic value. What's more, the sales team couldn't really use attitudes to qualify a prospect in the field as belonging to one segment or another.

For different kinds of marketing and sales efforts, the organization used affinity groups, channel preferences, and tenure with the company, among other one-variable-set approaches, to guide messaging development and program execution. As one example, for several years running, the marketing department ran a major direct-mail campaign to different alumni groups. None of the one-variable-set approaches considered things like category usage, current value to the firm, or openness to the brand to improve program efficiency. They weren't at all insightful when it came to new product development either.

To demonstrate for skeptical senior management that a state-of-the-science market segmentation would better distinguish the high-value targets from the low-value ones and, very important, simultaneously improve effectiveness and efficiency, we compared the 12 segmentations—state-of-the-science plus the 11 others already in use—on five items management selected as the criteria for picking a winner:

1. The firm's internal measure of economic value

2. Openness to new products

3. Unique needs/benefits

4. Demographics in key databases

5. Attitudes

Because it had been created with all of these criteria in mind from the start, the state-of-the-science solution beat all the other possibilities hands down. It did as good or better than management's favorite demographic segmentation when it came to finding people in databases, with the added bonus of identifying the high-value groups. It painted as good a picture as the agency's segmentation as far as distinct sets of attitudes, but it also brought out differing levels of interest in and receptivity to new products from the company. It gave a much more comprehensive look at the unique needs and benefits each group had than the various one-variable sets, such as affinity groups, did.

Not only did this point-by-point comparison win over senior management but also it also made it clear to the proponents of each of the existing solutions that applying the results of the state-of-the-science market segmentation to make decisions, developing an overall marketing strategy, implementing plans, and launching campaigns and programs would not prove an exercise in frustration for anyone.

BRINGING IT ALL TOGETHER

On that note, we're firm believers that terrifically successful marketing campaigns and new products come from the combination of great marketing strategy and great execution of that strategy. Think of market segmentation as the foundation on which marketing strategy *and the execution of that strategy* is built. Doing a state-of-the-science market segmentation exercise makes it possible for marketers to do both, as Mobil, now ExxonMobil, discovered when it sought options for its failing service station business in the mid-1990s.

The results of the market segmentation work Mobil undertook using the approach we've outlined in this chapter formed the basis of one of the most exciting marketing strategies ever launched—the Mobil "Friendly Serve" campaign.

Mobil found five distinct consumer groups, all roughly the same size numericly, but with vastly different shares of potential profitability. Representing 38% of the population and 77% of potential profitability, car buffs and loyalists were clearly the financially optimal market segments.

Once Mobil knew the groups that made the most financial sense to focus on, it knew the customers it needed to talk to, where to find them, and how to communicate with them in which media, about which products, and at what price.

The results demonstrated that customers in the target group wanted friendliness, cleanliness, safety, and speed, but they didn't feel they got any of these things from service station brands. It knew it could adopt a pricing strategy that was neither low nor premium. It began to reconfigure participating stations—doing things like putting fresh flowers in the

Figure 6.3 Car Buffs Represent 20% of the Population and Account for 45% of the Potential Profitability

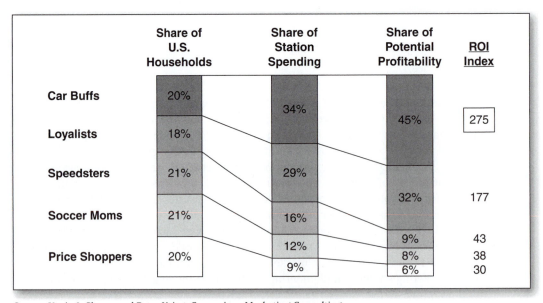

Source: Kevin J. Clancy and Peter Krieg, Copernicus Marketing Consulting.

restroom a standard operating procedure—to address the target segments key needs. It introduced Speed Pass technology to make it possible for target customers to get in and out of the station more quickly (Clancy & Krieg, 2000, pp. 91–93).

Stations embracing the program enjoyed 30%+ sales growth, and Friendly Serve contributed to $2 billion in new revenue. Inventors of the Balanced Scorecard, Robert Kaplan and David Norton (2000) maintain that ExxonMobil at the time of Friendly Serve's implementation remains perhaps their "best example of putting the five principles of a Strategy-Focused Organization into practice" (p. 1)

Jumping industries, Constellation Wines U.S., part of the largest beer, wine, and spirits maker in the world, wanted to capitalize on rapidly increasing consumer interest in wine at the turn of the millenium and grow its market share. The firm needed a plan to engage its B2B customers—liquor stores, restaurants, and bars—to help move its products and secure additional shelf space. It dubbed the effort "Project Genome" and launched one of the largest consumer research studies ever undertaken in the wine industry.

The firm focused on premium wine consumers and the resulting analysis produced richly descriptive profiles of six market segments. Constellation, in turn, appended the segments with ZIP code information, so for any retail or restaurant location, it could offer a customized profile of the relative mix of customer types that frequent it.

The market segmentation work included a classification of all premium brands—not just its own, but also its competitors'—by segment, so it could evaluate an account's product assortment. The segment profiles included preferences for the promotions, displays, and featured products, enabling Constellation to determine whether a retailer adequately addressed the needs of customers in a particular trading area. The company's sales force arrived at an account armed with a customized profile of the relative mix of customer types to make product mix and merchandising suggestions and could demonstrate to the account how to most effectively inspire purchases and enhance shopper experience.

As the division's President and CEO, José Fernandez explained at a press conference, "Everybody wins with this sort of segmentation research. Our retail and on-premise partners will now have even better insights into their customers and that can only lead to increased sales and more satisfied consumers" (Clancy, Krieg, & Gamse, 2006, p. 43).

A state-of-the-science market segmentation smooths the transition from research report to action steps. An auto parts manufacturing firm we worked with wanted to update its online efforts based on the insights it gathered about the digital behaviors and preferences of the segments. It collected data on if, how, when, and what customers researched online in the specific product category, as well as the underlying motivations for doing the research (i.e., finding the right product for them versus ensuring they don't get taken for a ride) and desired features in a website. It turned over to its digital agency a detailed profile that could direct content development and user experience with search marketing.

In addition, it also overlaid the digital typology we talked about previously onto its key target segment to provide direction about other digital and social programs. Key targets were primarily "connectors," using social networks to share information with friends and family, and "commentators," taking part in online discussions/forums. The digital agency could use this breakdown coupled with an understanding of the needs and attitudes unique to the target to craft social media promotions and programs.

Figure 6.4   The Six Key Premium Wine Consumer Segments

ENTHUSIAST: 12%

"So much variety to try. I like to look at labels but I also like to look at Wine Spectator. I really like to entertain, tasting wine with friends. It's the best experience."

Key differentiating need
Enthusiasts are passionate about the entire wine experience — from researching what to buy to sharing it with friends and family.

IMAGE SEEKER: 20%

"I'm not sure about wine, but know a bit. When I'm not sure what I want, I typically go for the one that's more expensive."

Key differentiating need
Image Seekers need to feel sophisticated and fun, adventurous and trendy.

SAVVY SHOPPER: 15%

"I love to shop for wine, to see what's on sale or in a bargain bin. I usually have two or four bottles of wine on hand and when I get down to two, I'll go buy more."

Key differentiating need
Savvy Shoppers are looking for a great wine at a great value.

TRADITIONALIST: 16%

"I was raised on traditional values. When I'm shopping for wine, I end up buying the tried and true because I know I enjoy it and can count on it."

Key differentiating need
Traditionalists need to feel that their wine is made by a well-known winery that's been around for a long time.

SATISFIED SIPPER: 14%

"I don't care where the wines come from, and I don't know why anybody would. I always buy the same brand and I'm happy with that. When I go to a restaurant, I always order the house white zinfandel."

Key differentiating need
Satisfied Sippers want a sensible choice they can feel comfortable serving to family and friends.

OVERWHELMED: 23%

'There are so many wines on the shelves; it's so confusing. First I try to read the labels, then I call someone who works there to help."

Key differentiating need
Overwhelmed want good shelf description and/or recommendation by retail and wait staff.

Source: Project Genome by Constellation Bands.

Figure 6.5 Author, Commentators, Connectors, and Spectators

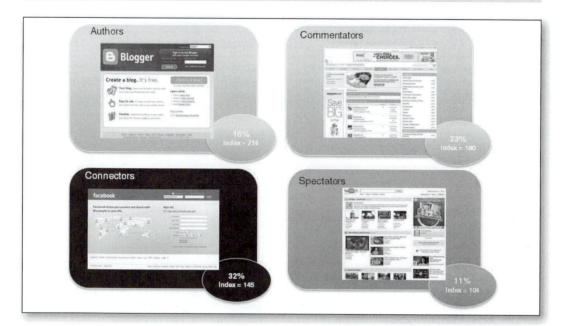

Let's take it as a given that in every product or service category—even those as seemingly commoditized as gas stations, liquor stores, and auto parts—it's possible to segment customers and reveal very profitable target groups. As these cases demonstrate, getting a market segmentation up to state-of-the-science standards dramatically improves the ability of a business to build strategies and plans that change a brand's trajectory.

THE PROFIT-FOCUSED PAYOFF

In the age of marketing accountability where CEOs and CFOs want proof down to the penny that marketing's working as efficiently as possible, minimizing costs is as critical as maximizing revenues. With accountability in mind, Figure 6.6 shows the marketing costs per acquired customer in a range of product categories, from a domestic luxury car manufacturer to social networking site to a credit card and subscription-based data provider.

Figure 6.6 reveals the marketing costs per customer under four conditions. Since the figures are based on a small number of marketers in each product category, they should be read with caution—think of them as illustrative rather than definitive. The first column represents the cost per customer in an undifferentiated market situation where, for example, the marketer is going after all households or all small businesses.

The second column represents cases where the marketer has narrowed focus to all known prospects in the product/service category; for example, all people who plan on buying mobile

Figure 6.6   Acquisition Costs for Different Targets

	Undifferentiated Market	All Prospects	A Good Target	An Optimal Target
Domestic Luxury Cars	$1,350+	$439	$203	$134
Credit Cards	$450+	$246	$189	$66
Social Networking Site	$108+	$85	$39	$11
Mobile Phone Service Provider	$675+	$494	$209	$112
Private Banking	$67,500+	$16,335	$8,505	$4,725
Subscription-Based Data Provider	$1,350+	$869	$482	$292
Utilities	$1,080+	$563	$178	$101

phone services in the next three months, all people owning or considering applying for a credit card, all companies planning IT purchases in the next two years, and so on.

The third column represents buyers who would be considered a good target. Not an exceptional or optimal, but a *good* target. It might be people under the age of 35 who like to connect with friends on social networks and like to share music and entertainment news. These might be people who buy new cars and whose current car is more than three years old. It might be people who carry only one major credit card and are unhappy with the current vendor. It might be CIOs of North American companies with budgets of $500K+ a year.

The final column represents the acquisition costs per customer among people who are considered to be a financially optimal market target.

As you move from left to right, note that marketing costs drop rapidly and the optimal target across all industries requires half the resources to reach and impact as a good target, and a fraction of an undifferentiated, let's cast-a-wide-net-and-see-what-we-drag-in marketing effort. Clearly, finding the best target for your business and brand has positives on both sides of the balance sheet. Especially these days, a segmentation that tells a marketer where to direct resources to generate the biggest return is worth its weight in gold.

Unfortunately, even major companies—some of them supposedly the best marketers in America—routinely earn D grades (scores in the 60s) in marketing audits on the most basic of marketing decisions: Who do we target? Given that the conventional segmentation models marketers most frequently apply aren't often predictive of brand-positive behavior or proxies for profitability, these results don't exactly shock us. The conversation about doing a market segmentation exercise should not begin and end with what approach to try next, but rather what will get at the questions the organization needs to answer to improve marketing performance and significantly contribute to the bottom-line growth better than what they've got now.

Setting the scope of the segmentation and parameters for the research *before* collecting any data forces marketing management to really consider which of the company's strategic decisions would benefit from the guidance of a segmentation. It puts some structure around what profile information the ultimate segmentation solution needs to include so crucial parties can understand and work against it.

Forget about preset lists of variables, and throw everything into the mix to identify those most predictive of value. Luck favors the prepared, and establishing the financial and non-financial measures of profitability to include in the research—again, before data collection begins—ensures that results will reflect the economic value of different segments. After all, no one wants to waste time and energy trying to reach and impact customers with little or no economic value to a firm.

When evaluating different solutions, go back to the business and managerial criteria set at the outset of the process to make sure the evolution from report to real-world plans and programs moves as quickly and painlessly as possible for the organization.

If marketing management wants to know why a segmentation no longer meets their needs—or fell far short of them in the first place—they can start by asking the following seven questions:

1. Have our targets changed in the last few years? Are we seeking the same targets we always went after?

2. For each of our core businesses or brands, how do we describe—in detail—the market target?

3. Have we segmented each market in which we operate to identify and describe the most profitable market targets to pursue?

4. What was our rationale for selecting these targets? What process did we use to find them?

5. Can we prove our targets are profitable? Can we show that they have made money for us in the past, or will make money in the future?

6. Would another target or targets be more profitable?

7. Do all functional areas of the marketing organization have information about the target relevant to their activities?

Answers that paint an uncertain, unclear, or mixed picture about profitability and useability at the very least warrant a closer look.

Our consultants and researchers are often asked about the future of market segmentation research. Particularly now, when some in the research profession say it's no longer necessary to marketers to have a segmentation—it's based on past behavior, not real-time information. Customer needs and the way they like to be communicated with are in a constant state of flux. All reasons to believe in a state-of-the-science market segmentation—one based on a comprehensive definition of economic value, as we discussed, that tells you not who bought the brand today but to see who might buy it tomorrow.

That said, certainly, there's a big opportunity where it comes to keeping a segmentation fresh and relevant on an ongoing basis. Tying in tracking research, for example, to monitor shifts, advances, setbacks, and the like within the different segments could signal to marketing management that adjustments might be necessary. As marketing mix-modeling technology continues to advance, marketers will be able to change not just the tactical elements of a plan—GRP allocation to different media for example—but strategic elements as well. Marketers will be able to experiment with different target groups and get real-time results, opening the potential to more dynamic market segmentation.

Nevertheless, the original and true purpose of a market segmentation exercise remains "discovering customers whose behavior can be changed or whose needs are not being met" (Yankelovich & Meer, 2006) and using these insights to decide who to target and how to reach and impact them. In the near term, bringing current approaches to state-of-the-science standards of actionability help this important marketing research tool fulfill its full, powerful potential to drive strategy and successful execution of the strategy.

FURTHER READING

Christensen, C. M., Cook, S., & Hall, T. (2005, December). Marketing malpractice: The cause and the cure. *Harvard Business Review, 83*(12), 74–83.

Clancy, K., & Kreig, P. (2007). *Your gut is still not smarter than your head: How disciplined, fact-based marketing can drive extraordinary growth and profits.* New York, NY: John Wiley & Sons.

Marketing Accountability

Understanding Performance and Drivers of Brand Success

WILLIAM PINK

PHILIP HERR

DOROTHY FITCH

Millward Brown

INTRODUCTION

Understanding the impact that marketing investment has on brands has been a challenge to advertisers ever since advertising began. Over the years, marketers and researchers have approached this issue in a variety of ways, some direct and specific, others oblique and inferential. Three approaches—continuous advertising tracking; market modeling; and the most recent addition, cross media research—are the anchor points in contemporary investment impact evaluation.

In recent decades, the most widely accepted and commonly used approach has been market modeling, an econometric approach that uses multiple regression analysis to tease out the causal relationship of marketing investments on sales. Over the past 20 years, as computing power increased and its attendant cost fell, this approach became a market research staple, firmly entrenched in the arsenal of consumer packaged goods (CPG) manufacturers—and more recently, in non-CPG categories (Leefling & Hunneman, 2010)—in their ongoing evaluation of the return on their marketing investments.

By analyzing the patterns of sales in juxtaposition with the timing of advertising and activities, such as price reductions and coupons, market modeling explains the return on investment (ROI) for each type of activity and identifies the activity that will deliver the greatest incremental sales for the next dollar spent.

But market modeling can no longer be regarded as the complete solution, even if it had become the primary method for market measurement. The marketing paradigm has changed, and research needs have changed with it. The media environment is vastly different than it was just 10 years ago. TV is no longer the preeminent mass medium it once was; its reach accumulates much more slowly and requires more individual buys. Media choices have exploded along with the choices within any one medium—consider all the options available just within TV and online, let alone in-store and out-of-home channels.

Consumers, faced with a deluge of information from all sources, including advertisers, are increasingly exercising the power they have to control their media exposure. They fast-forward. They leave the room. They change the channel. They switch radio stations. They turn the page. They develop tunnel vision on web pages. As people choose to avoid commercial messages, the result is a leveling of the playing field for brands.

Not only has the marketing macroenvironment changed but marketers, brand managers, and researchers have changed as well, particularly in their appreciation of brands and their understanding of the way brand value is created. They know that a brand is not built in a day or a week or over the course of one marketing campaign; the strongest and most familiar brands have been around for years, decades, even centuries. Like a pearl in an oyster, a brand's equity accrues over time with successive layers.

For all of these reasons, market modeling is not sufficient as the only tool. It is an important and valuable tool, but by itself, it cannot provide answers to all the critical ROI questions—because the questions have also changed. Because of all the changes in the marketing environment and our increased understanding, we now ask more sophisticated questions. We still need information to inform the allocation of future marketing dollars, but instead of asking, "Which will lead to more sales: a price reduction or a coupon drop?" we now ask, "In the long-term, would the brand be better served by short-term promotions or brand-building advertising?"

We still need to allocate funds strategically, in light of a brand's strengths and vulnerabilities, but instead of asking, "How much revenue will I get six weeks after that flight of advertising?" we ask, "How will this campaign support my base sales?" and "What marketing activities are supporting my brand over the long term?"

We still need to understand the effectiveness and efficiency of our advertising, but we can no longer simply ask, "How many people are responding to our TV ads?" Instead, we ask, "How does the communication of my messages vary across media? And how are these media working together?"

APPROACHES TO MARKETING ACCOUNTABILITY

In addressing the state-of-the-art philosophies and approaches, this chapter will highlight the advantages offered by many different research techniques because no single approach can answer all marketing accountability questions. To address the information needs of today's advertisers, to understand time-based returns on marketing investment, and to understand the influence of today's rapidly evolving media environment, we need many approaches. So our explanation of methods of measuring marketing ROI will break down the question, "What did I get for my marketing investment?" into three broad pieces:

1. What marketing activities are driving my sales, and by how much? To answer this question, we apply market modeling, primarily for understanding short-term contributions, but also for understanding some long-term effects.

2. What marketing activities are supporting my brand's equity over the long term? To answer this question, we turn to tracking studies to understand the effect of all marketing communications. We also use metrics derived from tracking measures to monitor the status of a brand's equity on an ongoing basis.

   (Invariably, within the area of digital planning there would be a unique analysis describing the performance of campaign effectiveness totally within the digital footprint—portal to portal, portal to search engine, banner to flash, and so on—as opposed to comparing digital to TV or print. This would warrant a dedicated chapter.)

3. Which media drive brand metrics, and how do various media work together? To answer these, and other media-related questions, we use cross-media measurement to identify the unique contribution of individual media as well as synergies across media.

WHAT MARKETING ACTIVITIES ARE DRIVING MY SALES, AND BY HOW MUCH?

Understanding the Performance of Marketing in the Short Term

As described at the outset, the most conventional approach to assessing the short-term response to marketing is the use of market modeling. This approach answers the question: "What marketing activities are driving my sales, and to what degree?"

Market modeling breaks brand sales into two components: short-term incremental sales and long-term base sales. Short-term sales (those that occur between two weeks and six months after advertising) are attributed to recent marketing activities and broader macro-economic factors such as seasonality, unemployment, prevailing interest rates, and so on.

As brands mature, baseline sales become an increasingly large proportion of total sales. These long-term sales (six months to two years) can be thought of as the payoff for years of investment in product formulation and improvements, maintaining distribution and shelf presence, advertising and communications, trial mechanisms, price promotions, and other marketing vehicles.

In Figure 7.1, the blue area represents baseline sales. These sales would have occurred independent of marketing activities and other factors, including the seasonal component represented by the yellow area. Multivariate econometrics enable us to statistically quantify the incremental sales generated by each type of marketing activity.

Figure 7.1   Decomposition of Sales

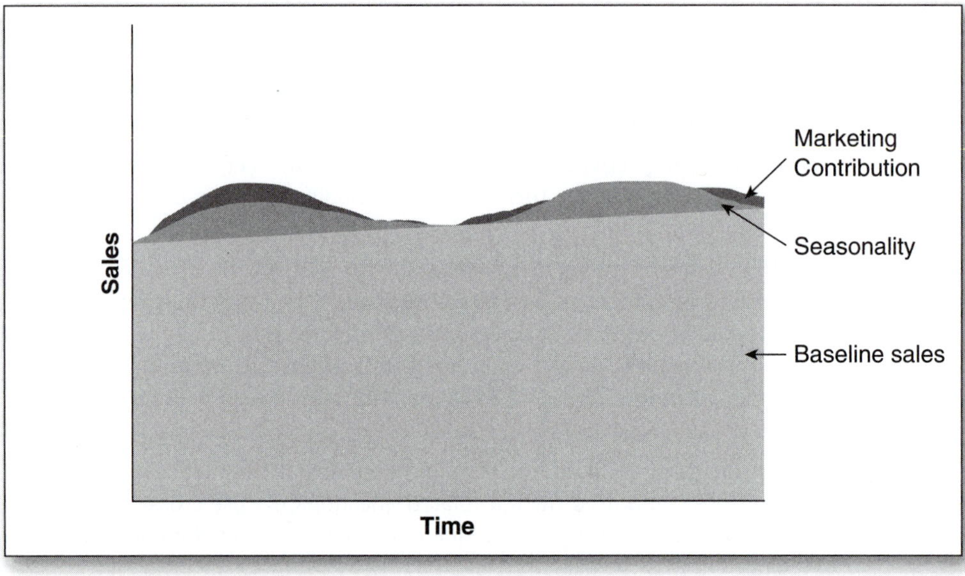

Analytic Approaches

There are many different analytic approaches to modeling short-term response, but two broad approaches are important to us in this chapter. The first type, the **dynamic linear model** provides an accurate and sensitive read of media elasticities for planning media strategy, typically, at a national level. The second type, the **general linear model** (GLM) is particularly good at teasing out below-the-line activities at varying levels of granularity—from region, to state, to store level. The advantage of dynamic models is that they offer time-varying components while GLM models allow for fixed and random effects (Leeflang et al., 2008).

Dynamic Linear Models

Because it allows factors to vary over time, the dynamic linear model makes it possible to have more accurate control for seasonality and economic factors at the category level. If the data available for modeling is weekly, a dynamic model will reestimate the contribution of each marketing activity on sales for every week in the data set, while a static model will make one estimate for each activity over the entire period of the model. We believe that this time-varying approach more closely reflects how advertising works because it allows the estimate of contribution to evolve over time.

Thus, when a dynamic model estimates the contribution of recent advertising to short-term sales, the recent past has a bigger influence than the more distant past. That is, last week's advertising will have a bigger effect than advertising from two months ago, while advertising from two months ago will have a bigger effect than advertising from six months ago.

Another attractive feature of dynamic models is that they allow us to estimate changes in base sales. This ability is an important prerequisite for assessing long-term ROI, which is discussed later in this chapter.

General Linear Models

As stated previously, a GLM allows for both fixed and random effects. This feature makes it especially powerful at teasing out below-the-line activities at varying levels of granularity—from region, to state, to store level. If we were modeling a situation that had a national advertising campaign supplemented with regional promotions, the general linear model would set the national advertising campaign as a fixed effect. Since the advertising is delivered at the same time and weight across regions, the estimate of its impact would be constant. The regional promotions, however, would need to vary since they are delivered at different levels and times; thus, the model would allow varying promotional effects by region. If you take this framework out to the store level, you can see how much variation the GLM approach can handle.

Tradeoffs Between Analytic Approaches

Clearly, choosing one approach over the other involves a tradeoff. The time-varying component of dynamic modeling enables it to yield a better measure of marketing contributions at a global level, especially when campaigns are changing in either messaging or media delivery. GLM models lack this flexibility, but are particularly useful for drilling down to more granular actions that vary at the store level, such as pricing or promotions. In some cases, we find a happy medium and create groups or clusters of stores or regions that show similar response patterns, and then run dynamic models within those groupings.

Irrespective of the approach (dynamic or GLM), inputs to the model invariably include marketing and media activities, macroeconomic variables, quantification of intangibles, such as word of mouth, online chatter, search activities, and so on. Some of the independent variables (inputs) to market modeling are the common currency of media planners: gross ratings points (GRPs) for TV and radio and, where available, magazines. More often, print media are defined by impressions or exposures (the number of people exposed to the issue). Outdoor metrics and online display ads are likewise usually defined as impressions, though online advertising can also be measured by clicks—the number of people clicking a banner or display ad. Newer measures include online conversations, described in their volume and tone: positive, neutral, or negative. Publicity is typically described in a similar manner, and sometimes, it is qualified by the stature of the source and whether it is online or off-line. Macroeconomic variables such as unemployment, inflation, or consumer sentiment are also frequently included, and factors such as weather might even be taken into account.

Model outputs include contributions, elasticities, and the ROI for each marketing variable, as well as overall plan optimization. Marketers can use these outputs to forecast business performance, reallocate resources, and plan for the impact of factors beyond their control (such as inflation) that have an important impact on the business. Or they can create scorecards to evaluate and compare different approaches—campaigns, media allocations, or complete marketing communications plans.

WHAT MARKETING ACTIVITIES ARE SUPPORTING MY BRAND LONG TERM?

Decomposing Base-Level Equity

Baseline sales were once thought of as the residual, left over when all else that could be accounted for had been accounted for. However, the short-term effects of marketing usually account for only 25% to 40% of sales (with as much as 50% noted in a few cases). The percentage that can attributed solely to advertising is smaller still—the estimates range from study to study from a high of 25% to a low of 1% overall (Ataman, van Heerde, & Mela, 2009). So since the majority of sales—60% to 75%—fall into the category of what we call baseline sales, we now recognize the base level of sales as a starting point for another level of analysis. Given that base sales come from consumers who will buy your brand whether it is advertised or promoted, these sales are a barometer of a brand's equity, which we know how to measure. Consumers' predispositions to buy a brand are built on the aggregation of positive perceptions built over time by marketing and brand experience. Positive brand experiences will enhance equity (and ultimately base sales), while negative publicity, declines in product quality, or loss of distribution will erode equity (and ultimately base sales).

The dynamic linear models described in the previous section will reestimate the level of base sales each week. This is a unique benefit of that approach, one that is particularly important for mature brands because once brand equity is established in the early years of a brand's life, it tends to evolve slowly over a long time.

Figure 7.2 Decomposition of Baseline Sales

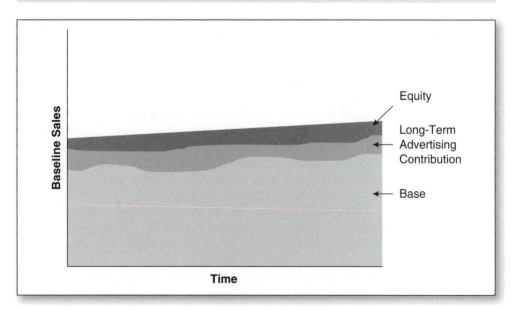

To detect the changes in brand equity that are hidden in the baseline, and to understand what factors are driving these changes, we combine the dynamic modeling technique with inputs from tracking studies. This type of analysis starts by setting weekly base sales as the dependent variable and uses perceptual measures from tracking as independent (explanatory) variables. Measures such as saliency, image, overall brand opinions, and usage or consideration are among those that would normally be included. Typically drawn from continuous tracking studies, these inputs represent the proportion of a sample audience's recall of advertising for the brand, changes in levels of brand association on a predetermined list of image attributes, and levels on stated outcome measures, such as claimed purchase behavior or intent.

We use the same media activities in this model as we did in the original market model, but here we are not looking for their incremental effects on sales. Rather, in this second phase, we see how these same activities affect long-term sales through their impact on consumer equity metrics. Because these effects are indirect and short-term effects have been removed, this technique does not double-count media effects. Rather, it provides a more accurate assessment of marketing contributions by looking at direct and indirect effects on sales.

The output from this analysis usually pinpoints a key measure, such as "trust," "perceived superiority," or "emotional closeness" as being critical to driving brand equity. Once such a dimension has been defined it, in turn, becomes the dependent variable for the final stage of the analysis, which is a path (or structural equation) model.

We use path modeling because many variables have an influence on a consumer's ultimate decision to purchase a brand, and we can seldom describe these influences in a straight line. The path model describes the perceptions and interim behaviors that drive sales in a way that shows the interrelationships among them. Path analysis is a multivariate statistical technique that differs from regression analysis in several ways. First, it is a multiple equation model that allows for multiple dependent variables. It enables us to identify direct effects (variable *A* drives variable *B*) as well as indirect effects (variable *A* drives variable *X*, which in turn drives variable *B*). The implications of direct and indirect effects can be quite important, possibly leading to a different resource allocation decision based on where the total combined influence is likely to be most impactful.

The process involves several iterations until the path of best fit is found based on the empirical evidence. In the end, we can visually represent the relationships between media awareness, brand awareness, brand imagery, and consideration, and we can draw causal inferences about the contribution of each variable at each stage of the model.

In one instance, we found that a tracking measure, designated here as "equity," was found to be a key driver of sales. Once we knew that equity was a key driver of sales, we were able to drill down via path analysis to understand what drives equity. In this example, shown in Figure 7.3, we have a path in which advertising drives ad awareness, which in turn drives statements related to trust, expertise, empathy, and a realistic view of the female customers, which ultimately leads to equity. It is important to note that we find both rational and emotional statements in this path, and a rational statement leads to an emotional one: a brand being recommended by experts (rational) evokes trust in the brand (emotional) as well as a sense that the brand understands women (emotional). Because we have observed that equity is invariably driven by both rational and emotional

Figure 7.3 Path Model: From Path Spend to Equity

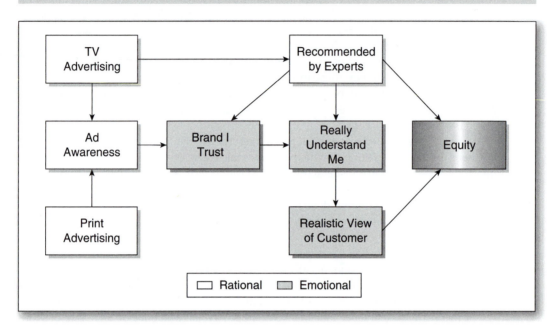

messages, we recommend that clients adopt a strategic philosophy wherein rational benefits are laddered to emotional benefits.

These types of analyses lend themselves to the development of simulators, which enable us to understand how baseline sales will change because of changes in equity. For example, a 10% improvement in equity would lead to a 2.4% increase in base sales.

What if I don't have a Long Time Series Data Set of Brand Equity Metrics?

The analysis just described, which links tracking measures to base sales, is one way of recognizing and measuring carryover and/or indirect effects of advertising—the degree to which an activity generates sales in both the short and the long term. The knowledge gained from these analyses can be invaluable for strategic planning. But one limitation of such an analysis of long-term sales is that the results are not always ready to apply in time for decision making. Sometimes investment decisions must be made without the luxury of time to observe the unfolding of long-term effects across multiple years of data.

An alternative approach that decision makers can adopt when faced with this problem is to leverage what is already known about their brand and their category, both from existing normative findings and point-in-time strategic research. Importantly, the variance that underlies all of these analyses moves from time-series to respondent level. Rather than viewing changes over time, we now observe them from respondent to respondent. This makes the analysis more granular, enabling us to link sales or other outcomes at the consumer level either through recontact surveys, sampling from databases, or surrogate metrics. Once identified, these metrics should be tracked on an ongoing basis and can be linked to sales effects when sufficient data has been accumulated. Decisions can then be based on the movements observed in these measures (Srinivasan, VanHuele, & Pauwels, 2010).

WHICH MEDIA DRIVE BRAND METRICS, AND HOW DO VARIOUS MEDIA WORK TOGETHER?

Cross Media Analysis

As suggested in the previous section, market modeling has its limitations even for mature brands. Accumulating the requisite amount of data takes a significant amount of time, and then that large amount of data must be aggregated and analyzed. Thus, market modeling cannot provide a quick read on new campaign launches to help brands reallocate marketing investments. (We briefly discuss this concept of on-the-fly optimization at the end of the chapter.) Nor, for that matter, is market modeling particularly good at reading the effects of low-reach media. But what if a low-reach or heavily targeted medium, such as digital advertising, is having a big effect on the small number of consumers it reaches? This significant effect would be masked in a market model, in which a large number of consumers must be reached for an effect to be identified.

As media dollars have shifted from TV, print, and radio to digital and other media forms, it has become more important to understand how media are working both uniquely and synergistically. A unique effect is the distinct role of one medium when all others are controlled for; a synergistic effect is the interaction of multiple media when unique effects are controlled for. Meta-analyses of our tracking studies have uncovered the media multiplier effect, where activities in a secondary medium—for example, radio or magazine—are able to evoke memories of the brand initially generated by TV. These secondary effects extend reach and frequency and add a magnifying effect by surrounding the consumer with multiple messages (Fitch & Herr, 2002).

Because market modeling is based on estimated relationships and does not use an integrated consumer-level dataset, it cannot do a very good job of identifying synergies. Cross-media research and analysis is designed to fill the gaps. It is a very quick and very deep analysis of the effectiveness and efficiency of a specific campaign. Unlike market modeling, it is not geared around behavioral outcomes like sales; rather, it focuses on how the campaign moved brand metrics (such as awareness or purchase intent). Cross media is explicitly designed to measure the degree to which marketing activities are working both uniquely and synergistically to drive brand outcomes and to do so at the most granular level (an individual person).

So how does it work? In preparing for a cross-media analysis, we collect standard brand metrics, but we also collect data on media consumption and brand predisposition. These two sets of variables are vital.

In the media consumption section, we ask respondents about their media habits pertinent to the specific media used in the campaign to evaluate their opportunity to read, see, hear, or experience the individual executions. We do not ask about specific ads; we just want to be able to determine whether someone has a chance to be exposed to an ad in a particular medium. For example, for magazines, we ask about frequency of reading each magazine in the plan (getting down to individual covers if necessary). We then take this information and incorporate the timing of the interview relative to the timing of the advertising in that magazine, the number of weeks the ad ran in that magazine, accumulation curves as appropriate for weekly or monthly ads, and decay rates to derive an estimated opportunity for that respondent to be exposed to the ad in that magazine. We repeat for all magazines, and ultimately, we derive total opportunity to be exposed to magazine advertising in the campaign for each respondent. Once completed for all media, we have a single-source respondent-level data file for analysis. This dataset contains enough granularity to get at the unique and synergistic media effects referenced earlier.

Next, we focus on brand predisposition. Before we can evaluate the effect of new advertising, we need to understand how different groups of consumers already feel about the brand. This is especially important when dealing with mature brands. We must use the right set of benchmarks. Planners and strategists are purposefully selecting the media that are most likely to reach the consumers that are open to their messages, and while this is a smart decision, it makes our job more complicated. As researchers, it is our task to control for consumer predisposition when evaluating campaign effectiveness.

We typically look at brand consideration data collected before the launch of each new campaign. Because we captured media consumption per person, we could estimate the number of media each respondent would have been exposed to had they had been interviewed during the campaign. We observe that as the number of media increases, brand consideration rises. Therefore, we can't simply lump all respondents together into one control group. If we don't account for the different levels of preexisting consideration, we may misrepresent the performance of the campaign.

What predisposition means is distinct across categories, but we look for metrics that are unlikely to move as a function of the campaign. Information on demographics and media consumption can be helpful, but they are not always sufficient. Usually, we need to look at category involvement, existing usage patterns, or attitudinal segmentation to help control for these effects.

Dereached Cross-Media Analyses

The objective of dereached cross-media analysis is to evaluate the unique and combined contribution of each medium for one touch. This approach puts all media on a level playing field because the number of consumers touched (i.e., the reach of the media) is irrelevant to the contribution assessment. After we determine the impact of exposure, we then go one step further and look at the impact of frequency, per medium, on changing brand metrics.

To begin, we interview consumers prior to the campaign launch, and we create groups of individuals that represent the different media possibilities: those who would have seen the campaign only on TV, those who would have been exposed via both TV and online, and so on across the relevant media combinations. Then we continue interviewing consumers at the launch and throughout the initial months of the campaign. We then repeat the grouping analysis. This allows us to compare similar groups of respondents to see how much brand metrics have moved (if they've moved at all) from the campaign. However, the analytics go beyond simply slicing and dicing, as we need to weight the data to account for the effects of demographics and brand predisposition.

The data shown in Table 7.1 shows the results of the approach. In this campaign, the advertiser only employed TV and online. We can see the benchmarks for the TV-only group and the group exposed to both TV and online, and we can see the delta (Δ) or incremental gain on each metric for those groups. Exposure to all media benefited communication awareness and sponsorship association, but not brand awareness. Brand favorability was improved by exposure to TV, but not the combination of TV and online. (The high baseline level of favorability for the TV-and-online group explains this seemingly counterintuitive finding.)

Table 7.1 Impact of TV Versus TV + Online to Key Brand Measures

	TV Only (A)		TV + Online (B)	
	Ctrl (%)	Δ	Ctrl (%)	Δ
Brand Awareness	60	NS	66	NS
Communication Awareness	47	+5.6*	67	+5.9*
Sponsorship Association	33	+8.8*	38	+14.4*
Brand Favorability	67	+4.6*	78	NS

Based on the delivery of these two media, we could create readable groupings of TV-only consumers and TV-and-online consumers. Because the unique reach of online is so low, we could not find enough respondents for an online-only group. Although we can remove reach from our contribution assessment, it still matters in what media we can read uniquely.

To build on this initial learning, we look to understand the *rate* at which brand metrics are increasing (or not) as a function of increasing frequency of exposure. To do this, we build multiple regression models within our exposure groupings. This allows us to see if different levels of frequency produce different response curves. We then combine this information across groups to understand the overall relationship between frequency of exposure to a medium and brand response. In general, we find that when it comes to generating awareness, the marginal effects of TV and print are greater than those of online and that these effects occur at lower levels of frequency. However, the effect of online advertising on generating awareness continues to grow with increased frequency while TV and print show diminishing returns. This is driven by the qualitative differences between the media. Print must be actively consumed; readers are engaged with the content and, if they choose to attend to it at all, with the advertising. But once readers have taken in a print ad, they are likely to skip over it the next time they see it. TV, by contrast, is a passive medium, and during the ad breaks, the commercials will wash over viewers unless they take active steps to avoid them (e.g., change the channel or leave the room).

Online is the anomaly: Despite highly targeted campaigns, viewers actively avoid messages, and the marginal contribution per exposure is very low. Consequently, it requires far higher levels of frequency to create an impact. The reciprocal benefit is that online advertising can continue to add marginal contributions to awareness at frequency levels 10 to 20 times those of print or TV.

Reach-Based Cross-Media Analysis

The output in reach-based cross-media analysis is very similar in look and feel to the output generated from market modeling. The analysis creates an estimate of the base level per brand metric, which is the estimated level of what the brand metric would be in the absence of the campaign. After calculating the incremental (above base) growth in each brand metric as a function of the campaign, we decompose that lift into the portions attributable to each medium. Last, we relate the media effects with spend levels to understand the relative efficiencies of the various media.

As in the dereached analysis, we feed media exposure and predisposition factors into the analytic engine. However, the models are not run within exposure groups, but against the whole sample simultaneously. This total-sample approach factors reach back into the process. Media with very low exposure levels are unlikely to emerge as significant; invariably,

Figure 7.4 The Marginal Effects of TV and Print to Awareness

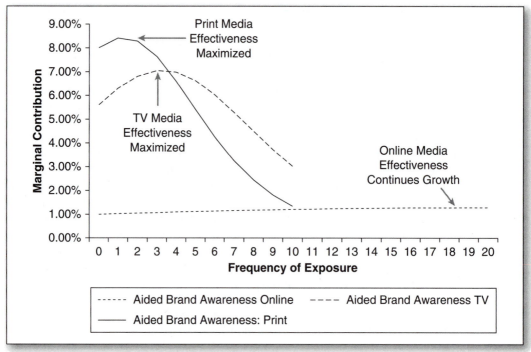

their effects will be swamped by those of the big-reach media. But since the question in a reach-based analysis is *not* the value of one touch of each medium, but what drives brand success across the campaign, this approach will yield a fair assessment of what is driving the brand overall. Broad-reach media vehicles are going to be more important to the total since they touch more consumers.

In addition, because we are looking at the total sample, we have the benefit of large base sizes, which enable us to try other modeling approaches. We use the same structural equation models we described earlier in the long-term sales section, but for this analysis, we use respondent-level data instead of aggregated time-series data. Campaign variables are represented by respondent-level estimates of exposure to each medium instead of aggregated media weight.

As stated earlier, the implications of having both direct and indirect effects can be quite important for campaign evaluation, and it may lead to different resource allocation decisions. For example, assume we are analyzing a campaign in a category with a very long purchase cycle, such as banking. We would expect that exposure to the campaign might have a direct impact on consumer perceptions of the brand based on the creative content. However, exposure to that one campaign is unlikely to change consumers' intent to renew (or shift) their savings and checking accounts. This type of behavior tends to be considered over the long term, and if we model intent to renew directly as a function of exposure, we are unlikely to find much of a relationship. But a path model may suggest that exposure to the campaign has a direct impact on brand perceptions, which, in turn, impact intent. Establishing the linkage in this way highlights the indirect effect of the campaign on intent to renew via perceptions, which would otherwise not be seen.

By juxtaposing the contribution to awareness by medium against the cost per point of gained awareness, we can create an ROI analysis that is expressed as a percentage gain in awareness per $1 million spent. The inherent risk in this analysis is that larger brands will invariably grow less (having a much higher baseline) and, consequently, be seen as inefficient.

One Final Thought: Is On-The-Fly Optimization Possible via Cross-Media Research?

On-the-fly optimization is an interesting construct, which, if deployed successfully, can allow for both accountability and tactical course correction. The idea is to optimize the media plan as quickly as possible, to reduce waste, and to revise media allocations that are not working as expected.

However, because of how different media effects unfold, many media plans do not lend themselves to this approach, and the on-the-fly approach comes with its own set of trade-offs. For example, if monthly magazines are in the plan, we need a longer lead-time to read their effects because of the slow accumulation of readership of these magazines. TV can certainly be measured at an early stage, but when we take a quick read on TV effects, we are forgoing the opportunity to test for the presence (or absence) of diminishing returns. Internet effects can be measured and optimized the fastest, but we know that online benefits from increased frequency, and time is needed for online frequency to accumulate. Finally, initial synergies between Internet and TV can only be read quickly if we have a sufficient sample of respondents exposed to both media.

So if it is imperative to be able to use on-the-fly optimization, the media plan must be designed with the research plan in mind. This may not make strategic sense. Nor would it allow for an understanding of the effects of media sequencing.

CONCLUSION

As stated in the outset of the chapter, all of the approaches reviewed enable an evaluation of the drivers of brand success. Each, however, looks at a different component of the puzzle. All the solutions are necessary for a complete evaluation of marketing accountability, yet often marketers are confused about how to fit these pieces together. We advise the use of a three-step process.

First, before launching a new campaign, use market modeling to evaluate the historical effectiveness and efficiency of media investments on short-term sales effects. Then, take the analysis further by looking at the drivers of long-term ROI, tying these to baseline sales in the mix model. The results can be benchmarked against norms and used to set spending guidelines and goals. If the brand has a portfolio of products, the models will provide understanding of how advertising for each product halos (or not) across the portfolio. However, for any subsequent launches, this analysis will *not* provide guidance about the effects of media that have not been used before, nor historical media at weights or flighting patterns very distinct from what has been done in the past. Neither will it inform understanding of the effects of campaigns that incorporate new messages.

The second step is to use cross-media research to quickly and accurately evaluate the impact of a new campaign. The cross-media research will identify media synergies, provide guidance on how to improve the campaign moving forward, and inform planning for the next campaign. It will not, however, provide a comprehensive assessment of competitive effects, nor will it enable an understanding of time-series trends over long times. Finite questionnaire space will also likely limit the ability to read halo effects.

The third step is to measure launch returns against sales by updating the market models and long-term ROI work. These models can leverage the information provided by the cross-media research. For example, if the cross-media research showed that, at high levels of frequency, online exposure has a large effect on consideration, then the market modelers can build this into their analyses. And because the short- and long-term ROI work is time-series based, we can now see whether any course corrections recommended by the cross-media research achieved the desired effects.

This process helps us integrate the tools we have to evaluate the drivers of brand success. As noted, each tool can do two things: enable evaluation of a campaign and inform future planning decisions. It should be cautioned, however, that although it is tempting to generalize from any one analysis of marketing accountability, it takes an extensive body of knowledge to extrapolate what works and doesn't work for any particular brand. A media plan with different weights, online sites, or TV programs might produce different results, as might creative plans that are better branded, more relevant, or more engaging. Sweeping generalizations from any single campaign evaluation should be avoided; this work is not designed to set hard and fast rules of media planning. Instead, it evaluates the past to help inform future decisions, providing guidance for judgment. Our tools are better than ever at explaining the past, but in our fast-changing world, the ability to predict what will happen next is very difficult.

An example will help make this point. A large communications client was about to launch a new campaign in support of a well-established sport they air on their network. The client had several questions: Was the new campaign working to support incremental tune-in to the sport? If it was, which media were working together to drive the incremental effects? Assuming the campaign was working, how much should be invested in each of the media throughout the season?

Cross media addressed the first two questions. The third question required market modeling because the impact of historical marketing investment, seasonality, and other influences needed to be factored into recommendations. Using both analyses, the delivery of the campaign was optimized for the second half of the season.

FUTURE CHALLENGES FOR ROI

Marketers are increasingly relying on accountability measures to manage their businesses. Trust marketing is gone for all but the least-sophisticated advertiser. Nevertheless, as indicated in this chapter, the tools are evolving and will continue to evolve as new marketing tactics and measurement options continue to emerge. There are clear trends pushing forward in ROI, each one offering the potential for a better understanding while bringing forth new measurement challenges.

First, data are being disaggregated at a pace never seen before, and in its disaggregated form, the data shows patterns that were simply unavailable for analysis before. For example, for given households, we can look at exposure to advertising via set top box recordings: whether they fast-forwarded; how much of the ad was consumed and how often, and so on. And let's assume, for those same households, we have shopping data from sources such as loyalty card membership or credit card purchases. In traditional market modeling, we would look at aggregated samples of these variables and estimate the effects of exposure to the TV ads on shopping from the model. However, using disaggregated data, we need to make far fewer assumptions. Therefore, we can understand advertising effects much more cleanly on shopping.

Second, the race is on to integrate the disaggregated data. Set top box exposure to TV ads, digital tagging of online exposures, online search and shopping behaviors, off-line sales, and survey-based measures of attitudes to brands are typically collected and housed in disparate data sources. The analytic potential of integrating these data sets is huge, but so is the complexity of integration. Integration requires massive data storage capacity (as promised in cloud computing technology), common ID variables and data structures, overlapping membership in each data set (or fusion-modeling techniques to bring it all together), and a well-defined, understood, and enforced privacy policy to protect consumers.

In addition, new technologies have built data sources that never existed before. Take social media sites, such as Facebook or LinkedIn, which facilitate ongoing dialogue that takes place among consumers. Marketers can use these platforms to passively observe consumer sentiment and behaviors, or they can actively participate in the dialogue and measure the subsequent consumer reaction. There has never been a technology that enabled nearly instantaneous dialogue between brands and consumers that was simultaneously measurable. In the past, direct mail was often highlighted as a great tactic for tightly targeting a consumer segment and easily measuring response to offers. But social media goes much further, enabling constant learning of sentiments to feed improved targeting. In effect, social media enables the kind of learning relationships that customer relationship management (CRM) advocates have always sought at a one-to-one level with consumers.

Putting that back into a future-of-ROI perspective, the challenges again lie in integration: in integrating the social media data and insights with the research and findings from more traditional media sources and analyses to answer new questions, such as, "Is my off-line advertising driving buzz online?" and "How effective are my magazine ads at driving search behaviors?" and "Is a consumer who interacts with my brand's Facebook page more likely to consider my brand on a future visit to a bricks-and-mortar store?"

Still other questions are developing for researchers. Should the same value be assigned to a blog post, or a "like" on Facebook, as is currently placed on a commercial exposure? Are we to develop ad equivalents for a two-way medium? In all likelihood, the answer to these questions is likely to be no because the value of a conversation exceeds that of a one-way push message, but from a planning perspective, this is what marketers are looking for as they wrestle with where to allocate marketing budget.

FURTHER READING

Ataman, B., van Heerde, H., & Mela, C. (2008). Building brands. *Marketing Science, 27*(6), 1036–1054.

Dyson, P., & Weaver, K. (2006, February). Advertising's greatest hits: Profitability and brand value. *Admap Magazine,* (469).

Ephron, E., & Pollak, G. (2003). The curse of Lord Leverhulme. *Admap Magazine* (441).

Frühwirth-Schnatter, S. (1994). Data augmentation and dynamic linear models. *Journal of Time Series Analysis, 15*(2), 183–202.

Hamilton, J. (1994). *Time series analysis.* Princeton, NJ: Princeton University Press.

Hanssens, D., Parsons, L., & Schultz, R. (2001). *Market response models: Econometric and tie series analysis* (2nd ed.). Boston, MA: Kluwer Academic Press.

Harvey, A. (1994). *Forecasting, structural time series models and the Kalman filter.* Cambridge, MA: Cambridge University Press.

Hendry, D. (1995). *Dynamic econometrics.* New York: Oxford University Press.

Jedidi, K., Mela, C., Gupta, S. (1998). *Managing advertising and promotion for long-run profitability.* Cambridge, MA: MSI Technical Working Paper, Report No. 98–132.

LaPointe, P. (2005). *Marketing by the dashboard light.* New York, NY: Association of National Advertisers Press.

Pole, A., West, M., & Harrison, P. (1994) *Applied Bayesian forecasting and time series analysis.* New York, NY: Chapman-Hall.

Robinson, N., McWilliams, H., Bullinger, F., Schouest, C., & Duckworth, S. (2008). *Dove—Dove's big ideal: From real curves to growth curves.* New York, NY: IPA Effectiveness Awards.

Tellis, G. (2006). Marketing mix. In Grover, R., & Vriens, M. (Eds.). (2006). *Handbook of marketing research.* Thousand Oaks, CA: Sage.

PART III

Qualitative Marketing Research

CHAPTER 8

Taking Qualitative Research to the Next Level

JUDY LANGER

Langer Qualitative

SHARON DIMOLDENBERG

GfK NOP

INTRODUCTION

Used for decades by marketers, politicians, and government, qualitative research methods have changed dramatically in the last decade—and the changes aren't finished yet. We write from the pragmatic perspective of marketing and public opinion practitioners based in the United States and the United Kingdom. Our experience goes back to the early 1970s in one case and to the early 1980s in the other. Overall, we believe that the changes are positive ones, while we also find continuing value in some long-standing approaches.

Qualitative research (QLR) in the business world has matured, expanded, and diversified over the last decade. Methodologies today are a mix of new, old, and renewed, of high tech and high touch. And the idea of mixing has taken hold with hybrid studies employing a range of methods.

The desire to get closer to the customer, to understand consumers more deeply, drives the push to new approaches. Several shifts are taking place, although it should be emphasized that they have not fully taken over, and, indeed, may never do so:

- From in-person interviews as the dominant method to include online and digital
- From relying on what people *say* they think, feel and do to greater exploration of what they *really* believe, feel and do

- From sole reliance on words to greater use of visual imagery and metaphor, fitting in with the findings of neuroscience
- From high touch with minimal/low-key use of technology (to record interviews, show commercials) to front-and-center use of technology at all stages of research (participant recruiting, interviewing, exercises, observation, analysis, etc.)
- From almost exclusive use of focus groups to a wider range of methods and hybrid approaches mixing methods
- From interviews in research facilities to interviewing and observing in natural environments
- From the moderator/respondent relationship to peer and participant
- From client-prepared ideas and materials to cocreation with participants and user-generated content

A number of real-world factors are also motivating changes:

- Clients' demand for faster, cheaper, better research methods
- A more competitive marketing research environment that encourages supplier firms to introduce and promote new techniques
- Desire of both clients and qualitative research consultants (QRCs) to avoid travel hassles and expense
- The quest for innovation and novelty on all sides

Sorting out what's new for its own sake and what truly takes qualitative research to the next level is a challenge.

One of the major trends in qualitative research is the resurgence and modernization of ethnography, the push to observe behavior in natural environments. (Chapter 9 covers this subject in depth.) We will only say here that the term "ethnography" has become a buzzword in the market research industry. It is used (or misused) today to describe almost any kind of research outside a one-way mirror fieldwork facility. While we view ethnography as an important qualitative tool, it is still one of many approaches that should be considered and not the end-all.

CHANGES IN TRADITIONAL QUALITATIVE RESEARCH METHODOLOGIES

The dominance of in-person focus groups in market research started back in the 1950s and continued through the end of the century. For many clients, focus groups were virtually synonymous with qualitative research, the only form of QLR they knew of. This trend both benefited QRCs by giving them business and frustrated them when they believed other qualitative methods were better suited to a study's objectives.

In the United States, an important reason for focus groups' popularity was that clients could observe discussions from behind one-way mirrors at fieldwork facilities. Being able to watch the discussions firsthand created a sense of immediacy for clients while also giving them more control of the research process. Slower to catch on in the United Kingdom, viewing studios eventually became as popular as in the United States.

Today, in-person focus groups remain the major qualitative method in our countries and many others as well, but their share of market has dropped significantly. The expansion of qualitative methods is likely to continue because some have demonstrated their value and because of the reasons described earlier. So-called traditional focus groups have come under fire and remain an easy target for researchers promoting new alternative approaches (often new just in their names). Claims that insights gained from a new approach would never have been learned through a focus group study should be questioned, we believe, if not supported by side-by-side comparison studies. (American men's fascination with the "macho job of backyard barbecuing," for instance, was evident in focus groups we conducted, not just in ethnography.)

The decline in the popularity of focus groups also partly stems from several valid issues, including the following:

- The field has attracted a number of mediocre moderators with little training and experience. Often focus groups are run poorly, with moderators mechanically marching through the topic guides, not probing well, not managing group dynamics effectively, such as by allowing some respondents to dominate by talking too much and swaying others.
- Many clients feel moderating focus groups is easy because it can (and should) look that way and that they can save money doing the job themselves. However, they tend to ignore the fact that they might be biased rather than objective in their perspectives on their company/brand.
- Journalists and other commentators, in some cases, dispute the validity and relevance of focus groups as a technique to gather opinions and understand motivations (Gladwell, 2006).

Despite the criticisms, the traditional focus group is still used by many clients and QRCs. Group interaction, if properly guided, can generate more insights and ideas as respondents' comments build on one another, bringing out revealing truths. There are practical advantages of focus groups, too, in time, convenience, and cost-per-interview over depth interviews. The typical focus group format (one-and-a-half to two-hours long, 6 to 10 respondents, held in a one-way mirror facility) is increasingly being used flexibly with a greater variety of creative technique approaches, which we discuss next.

The in-person depth interview, long an unsung staple of QLR, has grown more popular as well. Some researchers claim it is the only way to interview because respondents have more time to talk and there is no group bias. Others, like us, say that both methods have value, depending on the study purpose. Depth interviews are, we believe, the best approach in some cases: to learn more about individuals, such as the details of their history and their decision-making process; to interview executives/professionals, who tend to be highly competitive in groups; and to probe responses to new stimuli, such as packaging and advertising, where respondents do not have formed opinions. The argument that sensitive topics must be probed in individual interviews, however, is debatable; in our experience, people may in fact open up more when they are in a group of peers who experience the same problems and issues.

Qualitative interviews by phone, around for a long time, are also being updated. Long used for studies with busy executives, professionals, and other hard-to-reach people, phone depths are commonplace now in consumer studies as well. A variation is the "telesession," a focus group by phone. Enhanced by use of the Internet, these sessions can be observed by clients, who can communicate privately with one another and the moderator on a secure website. While not providing the body language element of webcam focus groups (described later), telesessions do provide respondents' tone of voice, an important cue to emotions. We find this method less satisfying than in-person and webcam alternatives but, nevertheless, worth considering when respondents are geographically dispersed. For example, in a study of rural landowners participating in a particular program, many of whom did not have high-speed Internet access, a phone group was the best option available.

VARIATIONS IN TRADITIONAL QUALITATIVE RESEARCH

Greater flexibility and creativity are transforming both in-person focus groups and depth interviews, as many elements can be modified to suit the study objectives. The benefits and challenges of these methods as we see them are outlined here:

- Length of group—extended sessions of four+ hours, often called workshops.
    - o *Approach.* Creativity exercises, projectives, and other exercises to probe beyond superficial thoughts and ideas; breakout subgroups for deeper discussions or brainstorming; multiple moderators.
    - o *Benefits/claims.* Greater depth versus the rush to get through topic materials in the standard time frame.
    - o *Challenges.* More effort to vary format and pace to keep participants engaged; recruiting can be more difficult; more expensive.
- Smaller group sizes—dyads (two respondents), triads (three) and mini-group (four to six)
    - o *Approaches.* Friendship circles conducted with friends, family, or coworkers; sessions with strangers, similar to regular focus groups.
    - o *Benefits/claims.* More opportunity to probe individuals in depth; "girlfriend groups" and other groups of people in established relationships can be more open with one another; in employee satisfaction studies, some researchers contend that coworkers open up more with friends they trust rather than in larger groups or even in one-on-ones with an interviewer.
    - o *Challenges.* Stimulating dynamic interaction can be difficult, with respondents answering one by one; friends/family members have established hierarchies and may not want reveal certain information.
- Larger/super group size—25 to 100+ participants
    - o *Approach.* Held in large fieldwork facility rooms or auditoriums; often two or more co-moderators; clients often participate; several types of super groups are conducted.
        - a. Dial-test sessions—using handheld devices (described later), respondents vote on materials (advertising, packaging designs, etc.), then are divided into subgroups (e.g., concept lovers and haters) for qualitative probing

  b. Brainstorming sessions—to generate and build creative ideas

  c. Talk-show style focus group—the moderator asks selected respondents to stand up and speak out

  ○ *Benefits/claims.* Dial tests provide numbers on respondent reactions, combined with the opportunity to select relevant target consumers for probes; greater creativity in ideation/brainstorming; talk-show style groups provide vivid sound-bite videos.

  ○ *Challenges.* Difficult logistics, problems of keeping respondents/clients engaged, only a few participants get to speak in the large groups.

- Venue—groups and depth interviews held in a variety of settings outside research facilities

  ○ *Approaches.*

  a. In-context interviews conducted where the behavior studied actually takes place—in the respondent's home or office, as shop-alongs in stores, or drive-alongs in the respondent's vehicle. This is not ethnographic research in the sense of observing the actual behavior; for example, a respondent might talk about cleaning in the bathroom, showing some of the steps taken without going through the whole process.

  b. Other venues where people are used to spending their time, such as coffee shops, bars, and restaurants or places that are specially set up for the interviews, such as hotel conference rooms.

    ○ *Benefits/claims.* More natural/real-life settings create a comfortable environment that encourage candor versus a focus group facility with a conference table and one-way mirror, which some call sterile and intimidating

    ○ *Challenges.* In some venues, video- and audio-taping have unwanted background noise, lack of privacy in public areas, need to rent adjacent room for closed-circuit viewing, more travel time and expense for the moderator and observers; limited number of clients can observe in person; logistics of providing refreshments (not in the bars or restaurants, of course). The same results might be obtained with greater convenience in facilities with alternative set-ups that are informal and similar to real-life ones, such as in living rooms, dens, or kitchens.

- Pre-interview exercises

  ○ *Approach.* Homework assignments expand the scope of many projects. In addition to direct question-and-answer elements, exercises can include private journals, video diaries, photographs of meaningful moments, shopping visits, online work, collages, product trial, and product deprivation (living without a favorite item/habit for a while). Increasingly, assignments are completed online; digital images can also be sent by e-mail or printed at a research facility directly from the respondent's cell phone or memory card.

  ○ *Benefits/claims.* Homework helps greatly in warm-up to the discussion, especially difficult or broad topics (happiness and humor, for example);

heightens participants' self-awareness about topics, such as triggers to eating; provides a lot more information, particularly difficult-to-recall types like a pantry or a closet inventory, steps in meal preparation from start to finish; saves time in the interview by having collages and other projectives done in advance; done online, pre-work can be reviewed and used as a springboard for deeper probing in the actual interview.
  - o *Challenges*. Higher respondent incentives; difficulty recruiting if tasks are seen as silly, uninteresting or overly time-consuming; more research analysis time, which also results in higher costs.
- Client involvement
  - o *Approach*. Dialogue or collaboration of clients with the participants, guided by a facilitator.
  - o *Benefits/claims*. Clients become actively and directly involved, working with and learning from participants rather than passively observing them from behind a one-way mirror; participants have the opportunity to question marketers and designers about their products and services. In an online bulletin board, when readers communicated directly with a decorating magazine's editors, they brought up new points, such as asking if the home photographs are staged because they looked so perfect.
  - o *Challenges*. Ground rules need to be set so clients do not try to sell the benefits of their products to respondents, dominate the conversation, or use marketing jargon; they need control their body language to avoid their reactions showing through.
  - o *Approach example*. An advisory group of specially recruited top-level customers or prospects, such as high-net-worth individuals, periodically meets with the client over the course of a year. The goal is for clients to gain greater understanding of what their customers want and need from them. Participants may be given VIP treatment, such as dinners at exclusive restaurants and box seats at sporting events. While this can be exciting and flattering to respondents, the pampering may inhibit their honesty and frankness.

NEW APPROACHES IN QUALITATIVE RESEARCH

A variety of new qualitative approaches being adopted or experimented are discussed next.

Deliberative Groups

A relatively new type of public opinion research has extended the reach of market research. Variously known as deliberative research, forums, Deliberative Polling, citizens' juries, town meetings, 21st century meetings and public engagement, this approach incorporates an alternative form of qualitative research. Often involving another variant on focus groups, it is generally used to tackle social, environmental, and political issues.

Because people's initial reactions to new ideas often reflect a lack of knowledge, the aim of the approach is to give respondents the time, capability, and information to consider an issue fully. Deliberative groups allow respondents to go beyond those first feelings to explore a topic in light of new and/or fuller information, after which they are given additional time to discuss and consider the subject. The process also helps the sponsor to understand trigger points at which opinions can change based on different arguments.

Sessions may be quite small, involving as few as eight participants, or very large with as many as 1,000 people; the larger sessions incorporate a mix of qualitative and quantitative research techniques. Decisions on sample size depend, of course, on the research objective: a smaller sample is appropriate if the sponsor's goal is limited to a particular target group, and a robust sample may be needed if the results will have an impact on the population as a whole.

In deliberative research, participants are exposed to stimulus and information from a balanced range of sources. The information might include the constraints within which the client is operating, challenges the client faces, and reasons for and against a particular solution or action. Findings are positioned as "the likely opinion of the public as a whole *if* they are given time and space to understand the issue." In the United Kingdom, for example, deliberative research has been used extensively by the government in recent years to understand opinion relating to various policy decisions, including human organ donation and the future of nuclear power (Wood, Parry, Breeze, & Wormald, 2009).

Deliberative plenary sessions often involve participants voting on issues, typically using handheld voting machines (discussed later). Participants may first debate the issues and vote; then they receive additional information from experts on the issues, ask questions, and receive client feedback before recasting their votes. Reasons for and against a particular solution or course of action might be discussed further and new votes taken. Some deliberative sessions divide large numbers of participants into breakout groups, especially when issues are more complex, for more in-depth discussions.

Deliberative research seems likely to grow in democratic societies since "we live in an age of democratic experimentation," as James Fishkin (2009, p. 1) points out. Besides the topics mentioned previously, the approach has been used by government or quasi-government agencies for understanding opinion dynamics on energy policy, transport issues, and on changing social, health, and welfare policy. The method is also clearly appropriate for corporate issues affecting people's lives or the environment, such as genetically modified food or deep-water mining of oil and gas.

Researchers must ensure that the deliberative process meets certain criteria. Fishkin (2009) identifies five indicators of quality:

1. *Information*—the extent to which participants are given access to accurate information they believe is relevant to the issue

2. *Substantive balance*—the extent to which arguments offered by one side or from one perspective are answered by considerations from other perspectives

3. *Diversity*—the extent to which the major positions in the public are represented by participants in the discussion

4. *Conscientiousness*—the extent to which participants sincerely weigh the merits of the argument

5. *Equal consideration*—the extent to which arguments offered by all participants are considered on their merits, regardless of which participants offer them

THE RISE OF ONLINE QUALITATIVE RESEARCH

It probably is not surprising that the Internet, a daily staple of many people's lives today, has come to qualitative research. Much QLR today takes place online, but until recently, the primary use of high-tech methods was largely limited to website usability tests, in which participants were asked to navigate and critique sites.

From the beginning, certain practical advantages of online qualitative research have been obvious: people can participate across geographic boundaries; no travel is needed by participants, moderator, or clients; busy and hard-to-reach people are more able and willing to participate because of the convenience.

Adoption of online methods beyond high-tech issues was relatively slow, however, because of doubts about quality. In essence, many QRCs and clients wondered if online qualitative research is true qualitative. They questioned if they would have to give up what they value from the in-person qualitative experience. Questions raised include the following:

- What assurance is there that participants are the intended target respondents and who they say they are rather than fakers at a keyboard?
- Is the research dynamic the same when people are online rather than sitting together face-to-face in a room?
- Aren't body language and tone of voice—important cues to emotion—lost when people interact only by typing?
- How can moderators probe effectively when live discussions move so quickly?
- Is online research only useful for tech-savvy researchers and respondents comfortable expressing their attitudes in an online forum?
- How can the security of the discussion and materials be ensured?

When online qualitative research was introduced in the mid-1990s, it consisted of fast-paced live chats that relied solely on text and slow, unreliable Internet access. Disappointment in these early platforms kept some researchers and clients from using online qualitative again, and deep distrust kept others from even trying it. Real-world issues played a part, too, as highly labor-intensive online qualitative was neither the bargain many clients expected compared to in-person focus groups nor the profitable convenience researchers hoped for.

Driving the dramatic growth in online qualitative research are two important changes that occurred: growth of online penetration and improvement in the online research tools. As Thomas Friedman (2006) points out, the dramatic rise of online communication has caused the world to become flat, so our markets are no longer geographically limited. While only a small minority of people was online in our countries a decade ago, penetration has spread across most demographic segments; researchers and clients have become increasingly comfortable about interacting with almost any type of consumer in almost all environments.

There are a growing number of online methods, but they vary on three key dimensions:

- When—live/real-time or asynchronous (meaning that respondents come online at times convenient for them)
- Participant number—one-on-one or in a group
- Medium—text only, video, audio

Whatever online method is used, they share several features. The sites are password-protected so only permitted participants, moderators, and observers can participate. Questioning approaches and topics can be modified as desired during the course of the discussion. Text-based online methods in which participants type their answers (rather than speaking on video) have the advantage of instantaneous transcripts. Good online recruiting for qualitative studies always includes telephone interviewing or confirmation, which aids in checking on respondent veracity.

The more common online qualitative methods of interviewing are the following:

- Bulletin boards (asynchronous group)—a widely used technique that allows for extended discussions; benefits include more time to cover broad subject matter, rich responses since participants are not rushed to answer, opportunity to give participants a variety of exercises/tasks during a study. The variables of the board can be modified depending on the study objectives.

  A typical format and alternatives are the following:

  o Size—17 to 20 active participants, about double the number in an in-person group; boards have been conducted with up to 80 participants.
  o Duration—usually three to six days; some are just one day while others go for months, a year, or even longer.
  o Participation frequency—participants are asked to come onto the board once or twice a day for shorter boards, less often for longer ones; they answer questions, see new assignments, and read and respond to other participants' posts.
  o Posts—primarily text-based, along with user-generated videos, photos, and links to websites.
  o Other features—a whiteboard for showing materials in either static or video form; close-ended polling questions, with follow-up probes on reasons why and comments.
  o Challenges—probing and stimulating respondent interaction are harder than in face-to-face interviews; clients sometimes are difficult to engage, not paying attention while the study is going on, in contrast with in-person groups that they typically attend.

A few examples of bulletin boards we have conducted, either as a standalone method or as part of a larger study, include the following:

- o *Legal website.* Step 1: In-person focus groups in the client's home market, used to explore attitudes and use concerning websites for attorneys, including prototype designs for the client's site. Step 2: After refining the topic guide and materials, a three-day online bulletin board was conducted with attorneys around the United States. Hypotheses developed in the first phase were confirmed, without the travel time and expense of in-person interviews.
- o *Automotive study.* Step 1: A three-day bulletin board conducted with target customers considering a new vehicle and fitting the psychographic segment, conducted with private answers (respondents didn't see what others posted); discussions covered their lifestyles, values, media behavior, and, to a lesser extent, thoughts about vehicle purchase. Step 2: The most articulate respondents were selected for in-home interviews and drive-alongs by ethnographers.
- o *Women's happiness study.* Using online bulletin boards prior to focus groups, respondents explored this wide-ranging topic by describing recent happy and unhappy moments. This helped to serve as a warm-up to the discussion and gave the moderator valuable information to probe.
- o *Business-to-business new concepts.* A three-day bulletin board with decision makers explored 17 concepts with both close-ended ratings and open-ended discussion. That large number of ideas could not have been crammed into an in-person focus group but worked well on the board.

- Live focus groups—The key benefit is quick feedback on hot issues, such as an advertising campaign.

  A typical format and alternatives include the following:

  - o Size—6 to 15 respondents; usually 6 to 8, the same as an in-person group.
  - o Duration—60- to 90-minutes long, the same or somewhat shorter than in-person groups; some go for two hours, but many researchers find it difficult to engage respondents on their keyboards for this long.
  - o Posts—primarily text-based.
  - o Challenges—these fast-paced discussions demand greater moderator multitasking than other online methods: simultaneously reading participant responses on the computer screen, choosing questions from the preloaded topic guide, writing new questions and probes, reading and digesting client comments; participants' responses tend to be shorter and more superficial.

- Live webcam interviews—either individual or group—Benefits include participants can be seen and heard by researchers/clients, and they can see and hear the moderator—contributing to rapport and ability to pick up on emotions; conversation is more natural, closer to in-person interviews; cameras can video participants in their environment; sessions are easily recorded.

  A typical format and alternatives include the following:

  - o Size—individual depth interview; group of four to six respondents.
  - o Duration—one to two hours.

- o Equipment—if participants do not have a webcam, one can be sent to them and serve as part of their incentive.
  - o Communication—little or no typing, except for poll questions and other exercises.
  - o Other features—in website usability studies, the moderator can share participants' computer screen (with their permission), see, and record their movements.
  - o Challenges—the slight time lag between sound and image is somewhat disconcerting at first; views of participants are headshots, not showing the rest of their body language; facial expressions cannot be seen as clearly as in person. (Plus, moderators may find seeing themselves on screen unnerving; a cover-up Post-It note helps.)
- Market research online communities (MROCs)—Another increasingly popular tool, these are communities of interest over long periods. Benefits include the ability to conduct multiple types of research projects with a continuing group of people who have like-minded interests. This saves recruiting time and costs, provides a high level of participant involvement, and allows subgroups to be put together quickly to probe relevant segments.

Types

a. Proprietary panels are sponsored under a company/brand name, conducted with target groups based on demographics, product use, or brand loyalty; the client's goal may be building loyalty as much as or more than research.

b. Research company panels without overt sponsorship focus on specific products, conditions/situations, or target audiences (e.g., people with diabetes, mothers of young children).

- o Size—a wide range, from 30 to hundreds of participants.
- o Duration—from six to eight weeks, up to a year or more. Some sponsors have found that participants protest when they announce the community is ending.
- o Engagement—varied activities include forums, blogs, photo-sharing, video diaries, and targeted surveys where respondents are selected based on demographics, attitudes, or product usage; these are sometimes combined with local in-person focus groups for product usage or in-depth discussions.
- o Uses—iterative building of concepts, where the client listens to consumer needs and wishes, then constructs and explores concepts for tweaking based on consumer feedback; product testing; discussion of sensitive subjects, such as health or financial issues.
- o Challenges—maintaining member involvement requires sufficient financial and/or other incentives to motivate continued interest (discounts, sponsor products, reports on the research's impact, etc.); participants may become too experienced and savvy about market research, may try to please a known sponsor; the borderline between qualitative research and marketing may not be sufficiently clear; misuse by some clients who treat this qualitative feedback as a substitute for quantitative research.

Evolving Online Approaches

Online platforms have greatly improved from their early days. Far more sophisticated and interactive, this form of qualitative is now closer to the face-to-face experience. These advances include the following:

- Easier use by moderators, participants, and clients. Virtually anyone who knows how to use e-mail and has high-speed Internet access now can be involved with just a little instruction.
- More effective probing and follow-up methods. These allow for greater, deeper responses. E-mails can be sent directly from the discussion to individuals or the group; mandatory questions have to be answered before a respondent can move on; participants immediately see what questions and exercises they have not responded to yet.
- Respondent profiles (demographic and usage characteristics) visible to the moderator and clients, along with their photos or avatars.
- Webcam technology in real-time/live interviews, as mentioned, bring in the key element of body language sorely missed in text-only online qualitative.
- Greater incorporation of visual media. Participants can upload photographs and video that they create, or choose from their files or the Internet.
- Better tools for tagging comments, coding them, and highlighting relevant verbatim for analysis.
- Graphic tools for marking up stimuli. Rather than responding to materials like ads and packaging designs only through words, participants can use a variety of visual methods, such as color-coded icons, arrows to point, color highlighters, circling elements, and so forth.
- Projective question templates. The purpose of projectives is to get beyond more rational responses to a deeper emotional level. Widely used in face-to-face qualitative research, these are now easier to do online. Some examples include the following:
  - Perceptual grids—a two-by-two axis or quadrant chart (e.g., high to low price, modern to old-fashioned) on which respondents can place logos of different brands and then discuss their choices.
  - Photo sorts—drawings or photographs that respondents can divide into groupings they feel represent types of different brands, products, or users.
  - Laddering—a form participants fill in that starts with a product attribute and moves up to true emotional end-benefits.
  - Mind map—a diagram of thoughts starting with a keyword at the center, with branches for different images and feelings it evokes.
  - Collaging—using the respondent's pictures or ones supplied for the research to create a collage showing their perceptions and feelings about a subject, such as their lifestyle, images of different brands, product experiences.
  - Easier blogging and journaling—rather than a question-and-answer approach, participants record their thoughts and experiences about a topic (similar to a diary, for example), along with images and other self-generated content.

Researchers are discovering that online qualitative cannot only do much of what in-person qualitative does but that it also can do what in-person can't do at all or can't do conveniently. Here are a few examples:

- Providing anonymity through respondent screen names (without their pictures) encourages greater candor, prevents participants from making judgments based on gender and ethnicity indicated by their names. The moderators too can choose not to reveal their characteristics.
- Obtaining in-depth individual private/masked responses before group discussion to control group bias.
- Shifting group composition during the study. A group can be divided into subgroups for deeper probing of like-minded respondents; conversely, separate homogeneous groups can be combined for productive or provocative dialogue.
- Giving clients and observers the opportunity to talk with one another and send the moderator questioning suggestions, without disrupting the flow of conversation. (In contrast, clients notes sent into a facility conference room during a focus group throw off the moderator and participants.)
- Easier follow-up with respondents after the research has officially ended to explore further changes in stimuli, probe more deeply, and so on.

SOCIAL MEDIA AS A QUALITATIVE RESEARCH TOOL

The rise of social media is having growing impact on qualitative research, just as it is on survey research. Sites like Facebook, LinkedIn, and Craigslist are used by some fieldwork companies to recruit respondents for qualitative studies. This raises some concerns, however, including are the same people recruited repeatedly; do field services state too directly exactly what kind of people they seek, making it all too easy for prospective respondents to cheat ("Yes, I'm that age, and I use the brand that often"); are respondents honest about their demographics and product usage behaviors? On the other side, use of social media to verify respondent information is seen as helpful (e.g., checking that a person really is a company vice president). Professional organizations like the Qualitative Research Consultants Association (QRCA) are working on developing best practice recruitment guidelines.

Perhaps more important, social media are also being used and analyzed as actual research content. Listening to the free-form unmoderated discussions is considered by some a way of gaining greater understanding of consumer opinions and behavior. Proponents claim that social media conversation is organic and natural—unprovoked, unbiased statements from real people—while they contend that interviewing has an inherent bias. A number of client organizations and research companies now conduct Internet monitoring to collect and analyze data. **Web mining** pulls together thousands or even millions of real-time comments about brands, companies, medical conditions, and so on. Quantitative charts and counts can be shown on keyword searches, for example, for a product category, the client's brand, and its competitors. Going further, sophisticated software tools provide text or sentiment analysis, in which positive, negative, and neutral comments can be tallied.

At this time, the debate is whether such social media analysis will replace traditional market research or supplement it. The number of people observed in social media is, of course, much larger than any individual qualitative study or, for that matter, many quantitative ones. However, there are serious questions about how representative these self-selected posters might be. Although some may be representative of emerging trends, others might be plants promoting particular brands or bashing competitors. Privacy concerns also arise about research companies/clients who break into websites to mine the comments and about companies/social media sites that leak or sell personal data.

Analysis is also an issue. In computerized sentiment analysis, sarcastic remarks or the use of metaphors are open to misinterpretation. For example, a *New York Times* article said that a website gave a negative score to a tweet stating that *Julie and Julia*, the movie about Julia Childs and another cook, "was truly delightful" and that "we all felt very hungry afterward." "Hungry," in this case, was viewed as a negative. (Programmers are working on this problem.)

Some qualitative researchers argue that the social media data do not "speak for themselves," but need interpretation—and that qualitative researchers, in fact, may be the best people to analyze the information. Social media can be a good precursor to primary research, generating hypotheses to explore in qualitative research and test in surveys.

Other Qualitative Approaches

- Immersion Depths

  This individual qualitative approach integrates blogging, diaries, and still or video photo journals over extended periods. Respondents can participate directly from their mobile phone or smartphone in addition to their computer. Benefits include participant engagement in interesting activities and exercises, in-the-moment responses versus recalled ones, providing a real-time view of people's lives and behavior.

- Self-Recorded Diaries

  Participants receive an unloaded audio/video device or are directed to a website where they respond to preset questions in their environment. Proponents believe this contributes to greater participant comfort and candor, along with vivid video. Because the interview is self-recorded, there is no moderator to pay—or to probe responses at the time.

- Hybrid Research

  The hybrid research trend has led to the mixing of approaches:

  ○ *Multiple online techniques*—studies combine bulletin boards, live webcam groups, and/or social network interaction.

o *Online with off-line methods*—phone interviews, in-person focus groups, or one-on-ones, home visits, shop-alongs, and so on. In the case of extended online research, in-person and phone methods enable researchers to get to know individuals better, probe certain issues, give respondents the opportunity to bond with one another, and try out products. Other times, the online component may be secondary (such as the homework before an in-person focus group mentioned earlier).

o *Online qualitative with online surveys*—one format, for example, entails live groups with several hundred respondents who answer both close-ended and open-ended questions. In others, respondents in large-scale surveys are selected based on their answers and invited to participate in a follow-up bulletin board or individual online interview to probe the reasons for their views.

MOBILE QUALITATIVE RESEARCH

Since smartphones are carried just about all the time by many people today, mobile qualitative research enables them to participate from almost anywhere. Respondents can share information with the researchers about what they are doing, thinking, feeling, or observing in the moment. This enables researchers to learn about people's behavior and experiences in real time, rather than relying retrospectively on the respondent's memory. Mobile qualitative also fits with the trend of involving participants more in the research process, offering them a way to give feedback easily and on their terms. Smartphone apps are being used by a number of research companies to enable research participants to log on to their platforms.

A few examples of real-time information that can be collected more accurately this way include the following:

- When and why one particular credit card is used over another at the point of purchase
- Why certain foods are eaten in different places at various times of day
- How a store shelf-talker/merchandising or promotion grabbed attention and motivated purchase of a certain brand or product

Mobile research has many other benefits as well, including the following:

- Responses can be audio- and/or video-recorded.
- It provides convenience for respondents, who can use smartphones in their downtime.
- Built-in cameras provide a great tool for providing quick and powerful visual responses. For example, respondents can record store environments where it is either easy or difficult to locate the product they seek.

- GPS enables the smartphone to track the user's movements. In the future, a profile of locations the user has visited may be collected and analyzed. (We are still at the stage of assessing the possible applications and the regulatory and ethical issues entailed. But watch this space—we predict location tagging will have a significant impact on research in the future.)

Today's smartphones also have some limitations, including the following:

- Limited battery life can be a concern making some respondents wary of online research as an unnecessary drain.
- Reliable network coverage does not exist everywhere.
- Using the mobile Internet can be expensive depending on the respondent's particular phone plan. Since there is no way currently to call so that research companies can pay expenses at the time of usage, the costs should be factored into study incentives.
- Many respondents find it easier and more convenient to input large amounts of text on a computer, rather than typing with their thumbs. Since text responses are often quite brief, researchers can probe further through using other methods. Smartphones with larger keyboards will probably help to alleviate this problem. Audio voice mail also gives participants an easy way to respond fully.

As mobile devices for Internet access, communication, and picture-taking evolve, it is very likely that this form of qualitative research has a good future.

HANDHELD VOTING SYSTEMS

These devices provide instant tabulations of responses in qualitative research sessions. Although the technology has been around for at least a decade, it has had relatively little impact since many qualitative researchers resist the idea of vote counting. Nevertheless, it seems likely that the systems will become more prevalent as there are a number of benefits:

- Collecting individual opinions prior to group discussion. In qualitative projects with a large number of participants, such as deliberative research previously discussed, this enables the moderator to gauge opinion overall without group bias and to focus immediately on areas of greatest interest.
- Providing a check on how well advertising messages, concepts, designs, and other material communicate. Where problems are noted, attitudes can be probed right away.
- Allowing the screening of best ideas for fine-tuning. Strong ideas can be further strengthened and negatives associated with weaker ones can be addressed.
- Like-minded respondents can be immediately identified and chosen for subgroup discussions.
- Engaging participants. As they can instantly be shown the results, respondents usually find it interesting and fun to vote. This, in turn, sparks greater involvement as respondents become encouraged to compare their feelings to those of others. (Teenagers, notoriously difficult to interview, enjoy the process.)

Despite the positives, concerns about the use of voting handsets remain. Some researchers question whether voting with its numbers and percentages is ever appropriate in a qualitative study. Others fear clients may mistake the voting as indicative of what quantitative research would show, leading them to make poor decisions. The responsibility remains with the researcher to ensure that results are not misrepresented or misinterpreted, by stressing that the goal is to simply provide an additional tool for gaining qualitative insights.

SEMIOTIC ANALYSIS

Another development attracting attention is the rise of semiotics. Long championed by a group of leading qualitative researchers in the United Kingdom, led by Virginia Valentine, semiotics examines consumer culture to understand what is shaping and directing consumer impressions of brands. This stands in contrast to qualitative research that has traditionally understood needs by talking directly and actively to consumers.

Semiotics recognizes that brands, products, advertising, packaging, websites, and other forms of communication send messages that people unconsciously absorb and that become part of shared meanings existing in everyday culture. For example, in a print advertisement for glassware featuring the image of a woman wearing a diamond necklace, the jewelry signals a chic and expensive brand.

Semioticians are trained in decoding messages presented to those viewing stimuli (an advertisement, packaging, etc.). The messages—variously referred to as codes, signs, signals, and signifiers—are relayed via elements that include pictures, words, styling, body language, colors, objects, smells, texture, text, and narrative.

Overall, semiotic interpretation can provide fresh angles on why consumers react to messages the way they do, as well as identify important messages that may go unspoken. The analysis can also be used to help create, improve, or modify such things as packaging designs and advertising messages for possible follow-up qualitative research. Susan Bell, a semiotic researcher in Australia, cites an example of how semiotics aids in developing stimulus material:

> The research team carefully and rigorously deconstructed cereal packaging to identify relevant codes and signifiers. Signifiers of sensory experience included words such as "sweet" and "crunchy." Visual images were also coded, such as a bowl of milk; graphic shapes such as swooshes; as well as formal logos and symbols including the brand name. The analysis showed that some cereal packages seemed to denote only intrinsic sensory attributes, such as crunchiness, while others used a greater variety of codes to potentially connote extrinsic sensory qualities, such as "freshness." This led to the development of new stimulus material for both the product and package development that were then evaluated in focus groups and in-depth interviews. (personal communication)

QUALITATIVE RESEARCH ANALYTIC APPROACHES

Qualitative research has to work harder today to meet researchers and clients' expectations and to provide deeper understanding and interpretation. For results to come alive, qualitative researchers should go beyond simply submitting reports.

The demand today is to derive even greater insight from the information that is captured—working harder to understand subtopics, subgroups, underlying themes, as well as presenting results in an engaging manner. A strong imperative of 21st century qualitative is to make sense of the reams of unstructured data elicited in studies. Longer field periods, larger numbers of participants, additional participant tasks can result in a predicament for researchers: how to make sense of the wonderfully rich information we collect.

Fortunately, the tools for qualitative analysis have also expanded, opening possibilities of going deeper and presenting qualitative data in more interesting, accessible ways. Statistical-text analysis software programs have been commonplace in academic environments for more than a decade, but only recently have they had an impact in commercial market research. These programs present an obvious way to deal with the huge amounts of unstructured text on the Internet, and they are receiving increased recognition as a way of enriching qualitative analysis.

Before discussing the new tools, let's consider the processes and skills required for perceptive, thorough qualitative analysis. Traditionally, qualitative researchers have used a combination of approaches to grasp patterns and meaning. These include their top-of-mind impressions, detailed review and hand-coding of transcripts, listening to interview recordings, pragmatic interpretation of respondent comments, and looking for tendencies and patterns of response instead of taking respondent explanations at face value. At its core, the process entails intuition nurtured by years of experience.

Going forward, keen observation skills and experience will continue to be critically important. But more and more, an understanding of psychology, sociology, anthropology, and the value of social networks will also be crucial. We are quickly reaching the time where our success will be judged on our ability to integrate fragmentary pieces of dialogue, language, and actions from seemingly disparate sources into meaningful insights.

To aid in all of this, the use of computerized assistance, long anathema to some qualitative researchers, should not be feared. It will not take away from the skills and craft of our work because *we* are still the ones who do the analytic thinking and interpretation. What the software does is to sort verbatim responses by easily tying respondents' comments to their characteristics, pointing out who says what about what. Researchers can revisit and apply different filters to sort the data and comments and, using their experience, interpret what is meaningful and what is not. Ultimately, it is still the researcher who will bring the microperspective of differing subgroups into their analysis, thus, providing a bigger-picture understanding of the whole.

There are other compelling reasons to consider qualitative analysis software:

- It simplifies keyword searching by identifying incidence and patterns of words and phrases.
- It is easy to import documents and image file formats, thus, adding further content for consideration.

- The actual process of inputting, coding, and annotating data is far easier than it was several years back.
- In large projects, the software enables researchers to work independently using a master analysis template, then merging their analyses into one document. This ensures that information is analyzed in a reliable and consistent way.
- Reports and presentations are simpler to prepare. Users can make scratchpad notes on their light bulb moments of insight, then export these along with relevant verbatims into Microsoft Word or PowerPoint documents.
- The very act of coding and annotating information provides a transparent audit trail of the research analysis process. If required by the client, this demonstrates the study's robustness and credibility.
- Statistical and visualization tools, such as pie and bar charts, mind maps and process diagrams can be generated. These provide a powerful battery of tools to add to the qualitative researcher's kit.

With all the advantages of the analysis software, there are caveats too:

- The analysis framework into which the information is inputted has to be carefully constructed. Typically, the software framework follows the study's topic guide structure and incorporates relevant sample characteristics used in recruiting respondents, such as demographics, key attitudes, and usage behavior. Sometimes, though, it may be more appropriate to turn the topic guide on its head and analyze based what is learned and new hypotheses.
- Projects with relatively few interviews may not lend themselves to software analysis as inputting the information may not be worth the effort.
- While the software is intuitive, some training is required to use the program to its fullest. This means that initial projects will go more slowly.
- There are costs involved in purchasing the software, typically involving an annual license fee.

There are various software tools available, with the popular Microsoft Office Excel the most basic. More sophisticated packages currently available include QSRs' NVivo and XSight, Provalis Research's QDA Miner, and NatCen's FrameWork.

Analytic Case Histories

A few case studies conducted by GfK NOP show the added value of the software.

Case Study 1: Reporting Speed

The client, a leader in the technology market, studied the views of 15 senior IT and business decision makers concerning the future of telecommunications. Participants in the research formed a leading-edge panel that engaged bimonthly for more than a year. The research, which involved respondents in both face-to-face interviews and online bulletin boards, was structured to build knowledge and enable the client to act rapidly on emerging ideas.

Although the sample size was small, the task of processing the amount of data generated by the online boards was challenging; the final output of all the boards ran to several hundred pages of intensely detailed responses. Additionally, the client required a topline report two days after the end of each phase of fieldwork to develop new ideas that could be fed back to the panel for further discussion.

Analysis of transcripts using the XSight software, done immediately after each bulletin board, meant that the reporting process gained insight, speed, and efficiency. The clients learned what product features were wanted by different customer types, and they could ask the researchers to test hypotheses by revisiting the information in the next panel.

Case Study 2: Long-Term Usefulness

A major transport provider regularly researched its employees on a broad range of workplace issues, such as equality and diversity, company communications, and attitudes to changing work practices. Employees were drawn from various company groups encompassing different operational functions and job levels.

Over a two-year period more than 20 individual qualitative projects were undertaken with 700+ face-to-face depth interviews and 40+ focus groups in total, a massive amount of information. Using XSight, a comprehensive, searchable database was created that the research team could continually update and access. Data mining enabled the researchers to identify and track employee trends as they emerged; the information became the basis for generating and testing new hypotheses. In some cases, the information eliminated the need for the client to commission further research.

Case Study 3: Reporting Credibility

The client was a government regulator undertaking a high-profile consultation process with international opinion leaders, entrepreneurs, and academics. A four-week online bulletin board generated complex data with many subtopics. The client required a rigorous, robust analytic process along with an auditable record of analysis and reporting should the study ever be subjected to a freedom of information request. Using the XSight software, researchers were able to provide a structured approach to the analysis and a demonstrable record of how the project evolved.

Word Cloud Software

As detailed text analysis becomes more commonplace in the social media landscape, so does the visual presentation of results. Thus, we are seeing an increasing use of word clouds as a way of presenting qualitative data in a visual and engaging manner.

Wordle and Tagxedo are some of the online applications that convert word frequency counts from simple lists to user-friendly graphics and pictures that incorporate words and phrases. Such software can also show different colors and type sizes to demonstrate the relative frequency of words or phrases. For observers, the images are easy to grasp.

The extent to which these word clouds offer truly meaningful insight is debatable, however. Conversations that take place in qualitative research are not disconnected utterances of individuals. Instead, they are dialogues with people responding to and often relying on what other participants say. There is a natural tendency for participants to mirror the language of fellow speakers, so the range of words is often limited. As a result, a word cloud of a focus group discussion may only provide a rudimentary form of analysis.

Overtime, text-analysis programs, such as Wordles, may prompt researchers to explore linguistic analysis, such as critical discourse analysis (CDA), which examines the connections between language, text, and talk.

As text analysis develops and software options become more prevalent, qualitative researchers will undoubtedly come to view technology as a supplementary tool for obtaining deeper insights. Additionally, the growth of cloud computing will make the software platforms even quicker and easier to assess. Such software will become less expensive and, thus, more attractive to researchers who need it only occasionally.

ANALYTIC TOOLS DOWN THE ROAD

Looking to the future, we can expect to see analysis tools currently used in criminal investigation begin to filter into the qualitative kitbag. These techniques represent a major departure from the question-and-answer interviewing approach. One example is facial analysis or facial coding. Kinesics—facial expressions, postures, and gestures—plays a large role in revealing the emotions of respondents. Paul Ekman (2004), former professor of psychology in the Department of Psychiatry at the University of California, San Francisco, developed the Facial Action Coding System (FACS) to taxonomize every human facial expression.

Some qualitative researchers already use video to record the critical moment when the respondent sees and/or hears an advertisement, proposition, logo, or other communications material to capture micro-expressions, fleeting facial expressions, such as eye movements and pleasure expressions that become evident in the eyes, mouth, or movements of the head. This allows the researcher to identify signs of instantaneous engagement, as well as positive and negative reactions. Primarily used in communication testing, nonverbal results are likely to become popular, especially when combined with verbal responses, as a means of retrospective analysis.

Another technology borrowed from police interrogation techniques is layered voice analysis (LVA). Originally designed for security purposes, LVA technology identifies a respondent's state of mind by analyzing key vocal properties in his or her speech. These reveal a range of emotions, including anger, happiness, sadness, stress, concentration, excitement, confusion, hesitation, anticipation, and embarrassment. Still in its infancy in usage in the commercial environment, LVA appears most relevant to face-to-face, telephone, or online webcam interviewing. By uncovering underlying emotions, which may not match respondent comments, the technology alerts the moderator to areas for probing during an interview or, retrospectively, aids in judging the reliability of the respondent's statements during the analysis.

Akin to a lie detector test, this technology introduces a number of ethical considerations for the researcher. Because it is nonintrusive, relying on speech patterns and vocal parameters, respondents will not be aware of its usage unless they are told in advance. The introduction of the technology, therefore, needs to be carefully positioned to both clients and respondents if it is to find favor in the commercial world of market research.

CONCLUSION

Approaches to qualitative research are rapidly changing to meet the many challenges involved in understanding consumer attitudes and behavior. Technology advances will be just one of the forces motivating continuing change, along with the drive for deeper insight, engagement, and dramatic presentation. Qualitative researchers will be strongly challenged to master many of the new approaches outlined in this chapter. But just as websites have not totally replaced physical brick-and-mortar stores, and online meetings and networking have not totally replaced in-person ones, we are confident that live in-person interviewing, be it focus groups or one-on-ones, will continue to play a strong role in the future of qualitative research. The mix of new and old and renewed methods, of high tech and high touch, will be with us for a long time.

FURTHER READING

Berkman, R. (2008).*The art of strategic listening: Finding market intelligence through blogs and other social media.* Ithaca, NY: Paramount.

Ekman, P., & Friesen, W. V. (2003). *Unmasking the face: A guide to recognizing emotions from facial expressions.* Cambridge, Ma: Malor Books.

Langer, J. (2000). *The mirrored window: Focus groups from a moderator's point of view.* Ithaca, NY: Paramount.

Morais, R. J. (2010). *Refocusing focus groups: A practical guide.* Ithaca, NY: Paramount.

Wodak, R., & Meyer, M. (Eds.). (2004). *Methods of critical discourse analysis.* London, UK: Sage.

Consumer Anthropology as a Framework for the Use of Ethnography in Market Research

JAMIE L. GORDON

Northstar Research Partners

LARRY R. IRONS

Customer Clues, LLC

INTRODUCTION

This chapter introduces marketers and market researchers to a holistic, human culture-centric practice of research for marketing. We discuss the evolution of consumer anthropology, including emerging practices of ethnographic research as it adapts to a changing world. Specifically, we examine changes in the overall understanding of consumer needs that result from macroforces in global and regional markets.

We propose that these changes produce an imperative for marketers to understand the context of consumer culture so that marketing research can rapidly generate actionable findings. Context helps us give meaning to consumer behavior, framing it in the influence of environmental and social factors. The greater the understanding of context and the stronger the collaboration between consumers and marketers, the more likely an increasing return on investment (ROI) results. This is the central philosophy of consumer anthropology as we discuss it here.

Additionally, within the framework of consumer anthropology, we discuss several unique approaches to ethnography useful in generating a deeper understanding of the collective consumer culture. Some perspectives put forward in this chapter come from data collected in social networks and online discussion forums from active practitioners in consumer anthropology and related fields. This approach was deliberate on our part and followed to demonstrate the evolution of consumer anthropology and its role in shaping best practices.

Although we do not try to give a complete history and compendium here, we draw from several authors who do. Nor do we seek to reinvent any wheels with this discussion. Rather, we illuminate the direction of progress and aim to inspire the evolution of ethnographic practice by discussing its challenges and benefits.

To summarize our overall points, we cite concrete examples and discuss several key practitioners who are innovative in how they bring technology to the practice of ethnography. We also specifically focus on the research and brand strategy used in the development of Levi Strauss' new-to-the-world apparel brand, dENiZEN.

THE NEED FOR A NEW WAY

In their recent book, *What's Your Story?* Ryan Matthews and Watts Wacker (2008) offer a basic insight into the changing relationship between brands and the cultural experience of consumers. Specifically, they note that a key challenge currently faced by brands results from a sociocultural transformation they refer to as "The Abolition of Context." The term refers to a generalized inability of people and institutions to "find commonly agreed-upon reference points" (p. 42).

The importance of context to brands results from the forces that create markets for products across people characterized by increasingly diverse cultural practices, fragmented identities, subcultures, and affinities with fewer common, overarching reference points (Kjeldgaard & Askegaard, 2004).

Consequently, consumers increasingly improvise the way they use products, constructing meaning around those products independent of a brand's official story. That is, irrespective of the manner in which a marketer might position its brand(s) is the reality of how consumer's perceive, interact with, and communicate about the brand. Based on differences in culture, these perceptions and uses often differ from the ideal that the marketer envisions.

Matthews and Wacker (2008) attribute the pace of this transformation to communication patterns afforded by the Internet. They assert that the Internet "made it possible to be an expert on anything but also impossible to have certitude about any individual authority" (p. 43). Additionally, development of social media as part of Web 2.0 technologies provides consumers with the ability to produce media and share it across locales, regions, and nation states, amplifying the communication patterns supported by the Internet.

Sunderland and Denny (2007), in *Doing Anthropology in Consumer Research*, remind us that culture "points to symbolic meanings and practices constituted by humans which, in turn, are the organizing matrices of ongoing human activity and meaning making" (p. 49). Thus, it is important for practitioners of consumer research to remember that culture is in flux by virtue of the fact that humans play an active role in both creating and sustaining the context in which they act.

Communication technology definitely plays a role in speeding up this process of cultural change. As such, it is imperative to understand the evolving nature of change and the factors that are relevant when developing strategies for brands and products.

WHAT IS CONSUMER ANTHROPOLOGY?

Consumer anthropology is an umbrella term used here to describe a robust set of insight generation techniques based on consumer cultures, actions, attitudes, and values. When we practice consumer anthropology, the world is our data set, not just what comes out of consumers' mouths. It is an exercise in understanding context through passive observation and as well as through active researcher-generated data-collection methods. This includes the use of immersion techniques, cultural probes, ethnographic photo and video diaries, exercises, narrative creation, in-depth interviews, focus groups, and other methodologies.

Consumer anthropology uses ethnographic approaches; those focused on gathering facts generated by social mores and behaviors. The goal is to explore the culture that surrounds and shapes consumer lifestyles and their relationships with brands and products. It is an exercise in understanding the context and culture of both the consumer and the marketing organization itself.

Explicitly recognizing this dual nature of the collaboration allows consumer anthropology to develop approaches and deliver results on which marketers can more quickly and effectively act.

Ethnographers do not aim to get to know consumers personally or to get into their heads and hearts. Although this level of psychological understanding can be a byproduct of ethnography, it is important to recognize that the goal is in understanding the context of individual action. As Gavin Johnston (2009), Chief Anthropologist for Two West Interactive, observes, "Ethnographers sample settings and interactions as much as individual people. The individual is rarely the unit of analysis" (para. 11).

THE CULTURE DIVIDE

Situations and behaviors often fail to translate across cultural contexts (Cohen, 2007; Shweder, 1997). Consumer anthropology recognizes this limitation in studies that assume psychological universals, focusing instead on the way consumers engage in sociocultural practices in their behavior and the way they express themselves. The role played by macroforces in shaping sociocultural practices is important.

The following figure provides an overview of consumer anthropology as it relates to marketing research. Consumer culture is viewed in a broad spectrum and works to inspire innovation or transformation in products and services.

Figure 9.1 emphasizes the collaborative nature of cultural trends, brands, and product creation. Consumers are not static receivers or creators. Rather, they exist in a context influenced by macroforces of the world and the cultural realities that shape their social relations. As humans, we are consumers, but we are also part of a cultural collective influencing and engaging with cultural trends. The result of this interplay is a brand and product space.

Understanding the way consumers create meaning in their use of products and services, as well as in the way they create, conceive, and adopt trends, will lead forward-leaning marketers in the development new products or strategies. Answering questions relating to

Figure 9.1 Consumer Anthropology and Marketing Research

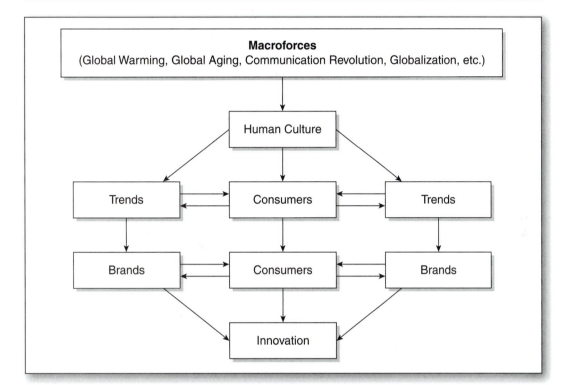

the consumer experience helps researchers color in the full context—thus, adding greatly to sketchy answers that often result when approaching the situation on a purely tactical basis. The resulting insight will invariably lead to distinct and pronounced brand and product differentiation and with it a stronger competitive advantage.

Whether it is Samsung's interest in understanding the meaning of "ruggedness" among cell-phone consumers in the United States (Lextant, 2008) or Sunderland and Denny's (2007) multisited exploration of the sociocultural meaning of emotions, such as "boredom" for teenagers. Or Pink's (2009) research for Unilever on the meanings of the sensory qualities of "household" laundry; it is this engagement of people in sociocultural practices that produce meaningful context and that is a guiding principle when practicing ethnography.

CHANGING STAKEHOLDER RELATIONSHIPS

As global forces shape markets, the practice of anthropology applied to consumer experience is undergoing transformation (Marcus, 2002; Sunderland & Denny, 2007). Ethnography, the key methodological approach to anthropological study has changed over the past couple decades. It changed from emphasizing a focused, place-specific field investigation, often lasting a year or longer, to a research practice involving multisited (Marcus, 1995), multimodal (Pink, 2004, 2009), and multiple vantage points when seeking to analyze change in cultural practices within and across societies.

Further, when using ethnography or any other anthropological method, the professional researcher needs to understand what they are *not* doing as well as what they are doing. At a basic level, this means that ethnographers do not gather data as much as produce data. It also means that there is an imperative placed on the marketers themselves to understand the approach to question what it can and cannot answer.

Ethnographers do not only observe and listen. They inquire, elicit, clarify, and report. Consider the following analogy offered by Sunderland and Denny (2007), "Focus groups, usually the perennial whipping post, are no more superficial (as in false) than an ethnography grounded by a belief that observation (behavior) is truer than talk" (p. 54).

In other words, the ethnographer and marketer need to understand the context in which people say and do things. Emphasizing just one or the other, saying or doing, is not sufficient. Making a sociocultural practice visible that previously was unrecognized, or invisible, often means recognizing what did not occur in a setting or was not said.

In ethnography, "just do it" is not a sufficient practice. Rather, tying cultural understanding to insights gained from asking questions should be part of the model. In fact, many initial efforts to crowdsource ethnography using Web 2.0 technology, as we discuss later, relied on the fallacious assumption that only recording observations of others' actions was sufficient.

You cannot know what you are doing if you do not understand what your research fails to do. The point, as Marcus (2007) noted, is that all anthropological research remains incomplete and a work in progress. This doesn't mean that at any one time it fails to inform sufficiently enough to act on the insights gained. Rather, as Denny (2002) notes, it represents "a different set of assumptions about who consumers are, how they are evolving, and their relationship with brands and products" (p. 152).

As the speed of business has accelerated dramatically over the past decades, we see that ethnographic research in the business world is increasingly compressed into shorter time spans (Cefkin, 2010; Lassiter, 2005). Consumer anthropology is a research paradigm rooted in the concept that the correct way to find the answers is always evolving, and at any time, it is relevant. Therefore, the best approach is in carefully and continually scrutinizing the sociocultural realities of the consumer as well as the sociocultural reality of the marketer. Then using the information when it most strongly needed.

ADDRESSING LIMITATIONS OF SILOED TRADITIONAL APPROACHES

At the core of our argument for increased use of anthropological approaches is the desire to compensate for the limitations faced when clients use siloed approaches to gather insights, such as exclusive use of custom quantitative or qualitative studies. These approaches to generating research solutions have several risks.

First, traditional quantitative and qualitative studies are very useful for helping develop models that seek to predict consumer behavior and for uncovering surface-level attitudes that consumers hold toward brands or products. Such approaches, though, can be limited in the depth and breadth of strategic insight they produce (Boston Consulting Group, 2009).

There is no opportunity to identify patterns and differentiate between what consumers say and what they actually do, nor is there an ability to understand the impetus for those actions and the cultural influences explaining why certain patterns exist. Ethnography is a methodology of discovery that seeks to compensate for the limitations inherent in traditional qualitative and quantitative research.

Specifically, if marketers rely exclusively for insight development on what consumers say in a response-based setting, such as focus groups or surveys, they risk missing bigger pieces of the puzzle and leaving holes in the efficacy of their final solution. Consumer anthropology is most effective when it uses ethnographic methods to translate between attitudes consumers hold toward brands or products versus a potential disconnect in the way the marketer is attempting to motivate consumers to use its brands or products (Denny, 2002, pp. 156–157). In focusing on the lived experience of research participants, we gain insight into patterns of behavior that allow ethnographers to recognize unspoken assumptions, making the invisible visible to both the participants themselves as well as the marketer.

Second, by the time a research report and its implications reach the marketer who must act, the insights can be outdated. This is largely because of the rapid pace of change in consumer culture made inevitable by the speed of communication, changing tastes, and the proliferation of marketers who are hoping to provide new solutions for emerging demands. As a result, marketers who effectively act on consumer insights must not only understand consumer culture but also have a firm grasp on how their company executes marketing solutions. To effectively practice consumer anthropology, empathizing with the consumer is just the first step. If the marketer's culture prevents it from adopting innovation strategies, the whole exercise is futile.

COLLABORATING ACROSS ROLES IN THE STRATEGIC PROCESS

Precisely because of the fluid nature of consumer culture, the creation of understanding is not static. There is no single, designated point within a process where consumer understanding most effectively translates to best practice. Rather, consumer anthropology is a fluid paradigm that applies throughout the innovation process, involving an effort to continually apply cultural context to give brands and products a competitive advantage.

It is, thus, imperative that we consider the context of work on the brand and product as a critical part of the innovation process. When we look at traditional stage-gate processes for innovation, brand strategy, or product development (Figure 9.2), we often see several phases of work.

Consumer anthropology assumes a need exists for critical understanding of context at every phase of the strategic process. In some cases, understanding lies within the client organization; in others, it lies outside—in the world at large, among target consumers and prospects.

Figure 9.2 Traditional Stage-Gate Process for Innovation

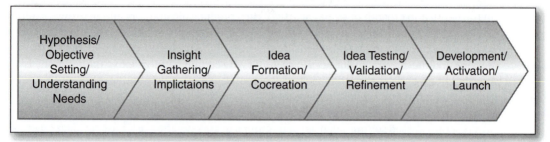

Source: Consumer Anthropology Northstar Research Partners.

A basic understanding of cultural realities starts with observing macroforces. The insight-gathering phase is usually where the heavy lifting occurs. Insight gathering means facilitating all kinds of research to help understand the size of an opportunity, the behavioral and cultural realities of the target, and emerging ideas for growth.

Indeed, consumer anthropology can make a big impact in generating insights and ideas. The problem is that often such insights are reduced to a list of bullet points in a PowerPoint presentation, and the result is little marketer interest or action. Suffice to say, insights and implications produced in the understanding of cultural context, must be properly presented by the researcher, and effectively processed by the marketer to drive innovation.

Words on a page do not create momentum (WhatIF, 2002). Rather, a key requirement for innovation for any level of strategic development requires creating deliverables that inject realism and provide stimulus that inspires those having to take action. Therefore, creating meaning-laden deliverables assists the marketer in translating the language of consumers into the language of their industry, allowing increased effectiveness in the way consumer insights are implemented (Boston Consulting Group, 2009).

There are many ways to bring insight to life. One of the most important is for marketers to create immersive journeys for their cross-functional teams, such as curated field trips designed to create experiences that develop empathy for the consumer and stimulate ideas (Patnaiak & Mortensen, 2009). In addition, videos and narratives are useful in conveying insight stories, rather than using traditional presentations.

ROLE OF THE MARKETER AS A PART OF THE JOURNEY

We have stressed one of the most crucial components for the effective use of ethnography is in optimizing the roles of both the researcher and marketer. Flexibility and collaboration between those two is essential.

At the core of this is creation of experiences that allow both researcher and marketer to understand the contexts studied so all participate in data production. No member of the team should merely be a receiver of data.

As Sunderland and Denny (2007) point out, "There is on-the-ground reality of engagement, curiosity, fascination and commitment to the research goals" (p. 32) that comes from the immersive nature of ethnographic research. The marketer can participate by reviewing and suggesting specific questions for consumers to address in using diaries, making videos, or taking photographs that relate to the issues at hand.

Marketers can also join fieldwork journeys as recorders and observers, thereby increasing their understanding of the consumer's culture and enjoying the insights that emerge.

When marketers actively engage in the research process, the resulting benefit is information generated from multiple vantage points. Although the client team may occupy the same space and hear the same conversations, each individual experiences that moment differently, and as a result, the insights generated increase dramatically.

In essence, marketers participating in fieldwork are certainly likely to contribute to the resulting strategies, meaning that once analysis takes place and insights develop, there is momentum to take action. Because of the connection that develops between the consumer context and the marketer's culture, innovation is far more likely an outcome than simple incremental improvement.

COMMUNICATING CONSUMER CONTEXT THROUGH ETHNOGRAPHY DELIVERABLES

The most important goal in presenting ethnography insights is ensuring that the deliverables exude context. Whether metaphorically or literally, conveying the research experience through the deliverables is the optimal way to communicate an understanding of context that supports the consumer insights generated. Presenting the voice of the consumer, as well as painting a picture of their world the way they see it, is far more impactful than a report full of analytical narrative and bullet points.

Although the use of photographs can help communicate context, especially when accompanied by storytelling that turns data into narrative, video has become a popular form of illustration when presenting ethnography research. One simply cannot capture and accurately report on context without visual representation (Banks, 2001; Pink, 2005). Simply stated, we feel video recording has a significant impact in driving home understanding and insight, and it is an important tool for effectively telling the story and motivating action, as, if properly used, it can provide a cultural narrative that might not jump off the page with words alone.

WEB 2.0 TECHNOLOGY AND CULTURE IN DATA PRODUCTION

Advances in communication technology accelerated our ability to seed and assist in generating knowledge and ideas and in improving business practice. Besides the benefit of getting business done, the Internet has also provided new platforms for heterogeneous populations to share a consumer culture.

Clearly, the web has provided new ways for consumers to connect with brands and other consumers. However, those new ways of connecting are amplified by the fact that, today, consumers in many developed societies typically carry smart phones as they go about their everyday lives. As a result, consumers are able, if so motivated, to record their experiences with a brand, products, or service as they occur by sharing photographs, audio, or video recordings on the go.

And Web 2.0 provides a new kind of communications architecture. Previously, brands most often spoke at consumer audiences, who possessed little ability to respond until social software came along. Now, consumers produce stories about their shopping and usage experiences, index their stories with tags, and share those stories using social networks, online communities, blogs, or directly to researchers.

When we consider mobility as part of a ubiquitous computing environment made possible by Web 2.0, there are far fewer restrictions between space and place. That is, marketers must understand that the creation and conveyance of what the consumer is experiencing at the time it occurs allows conceptualization of brand, product, and marketing strategies from a whole new, and far more reliable, vantage point.

Now, rather than merely observing behavior or asking questions in surveys, we can engage in dialogue with consumers by using Web 2.0 and other technologies to more intimately engage the consumer. These real-time ethnographic approaches will certainly provide more profound consumer insights.

Taking advantage of increased access to experiences "in the moment" provides consumer anthropology and marketers new data streams to use in developing actionable insights into brands and products.

CONSUMER ANTHROPOLOGY AND DATA STREAMS

Many people assume that engaging in ethnographic research only means participant observation. However, participant observation is merely one method for uncovering ethnographic insights. As Sunderland and Denny (2007) note,

> Ethnography is not a method per se, but rather a collection of methods. What seems most accurate about ethnography as a mode of discovery is that it must be viewed through, the culture, and that the manner of achieving this view is highly flexible. (p. 50)

Thus, the specifics of a research technique, whether it involves primary or secondary data, matter less than its application. Sunderland and Denny (2007) contend that the methodologies employed, whether participant observation, focus groups, in-depth interviews, diaries (online or off-line), village censuses, surveys, or maps, "are not 'ethnographic' per se, but . . . are made so by the framing of the task" (p. 52). In other words, the entirety of the research approaches used make a project ethnographic, the way they combine to provide understanding and meaning of sociocultural practices is ultimately what is important.

INFORMANTS AND COLLABORATION IN ETHNOGRAPHY

In ethnography, we traditionally refer to the people involved in a research study as informants. Ethnographers select informants with a view to their access to information or knowledge as well as their social standing, community or organizational position, or their understanding of cultural practices. As Bernard (2000, p. 346) noted, traditionally, informants serve a consulting role in the research process and, in exceptional circumstances, actually create ethnographic content. Lassiter (2005) classified this sort of engagement with people as collaborative ethnography.

As discussed, collaboration at minimum plays a dual role between the researcher and marketer and between the researcher and consumers. In multisited fieldwork, collaboration can become more complex as any number of ethnographers, consumers, and research team members become involved with learning taking place at various times and places.

As such, there are several reasons for emphasizing the importance of collaboration when engaging a number of participants in ethnographic study. The most basic reason is that developing ethnographic insight requires engagement with people willing, interested, and able to share their experiences and to work together toward the most productive end.

Fortunately, traditional ethnographic practice is quickly evolving, as technology now allows researchers to elicit information from many sources. Time, space, or number of participants is far less a factor than in the past, and the resulting output provides a much wider view of consumer culture.

Even with this, a most serious question is whether doing ethnography through digital means makes the process of social observation straightforward enough so that useful information, insight, and even surprise can be observed (Shweder, 1997).

We think the answer to this question is a resounding *yes*. However, it is a mistake to assume that most people possess the observational skills, technical competence, creativity, and analytic inclination to engage in ethnographic research online without structured collaboration with a skilled ethnographer.

PRODUCING DATA IN THE FIELD

Regardless of how the results of ethnographic research are used, key questions relate to who produces the data and how they produce it. Regarding who produces the data, the sample of people, can include any of the following:

- Passionate or leading edge/fringe consumers
- Mainstream consumers
- Cultural/category experts
- Professional marketers

And irrespective of who might be producing data, the following techniques are useful:

- *Response-based group discussions* (among strangers, friends, or peer groups). This type of data collection is best used to gain input on new topics and to develop hypotheses.

- *Response-based one-on-one discussions.* This works to get a deeper look at attitudes, values, motivations, and behaviors and identify patterns of reactions and actions.
- *Ethnographic immersion.* This is done one-on-one or among a family or subculture group lasting half of a day to several days.
- *Narrative creation.* Asking consumers to write stories will provide context and language that describe how they relate to a brand, product, or category. The trick here is to use this tool with the right target consumers—obviously, creative types often are better at constructing narratives.
- *Ethnographic photos, video diaries, or journals.* Consumer-generated photography or videography of their lives that often include stories or narrative will add further texture and insight.
- *Metaphor elicitation.* Having participants create collages of words, pictures, and other imagery around a specific topic helps participants think more critically and abstractly. Usually assigned as homework, collages are an interesting way to identify cultural patterns.

Doing ethnographic research by digital means is sometimes a single step in a larger research process. It is particularly useful in screening people and then selecting those who have the ability and willingness to collaborate online. This includes the following:

- Filtering to select participants for face-to-face, immersive fieldwork
- Selecting the best participants for ideation or cocreation workshops
- Selecting participants who are comfortable in collaborative activities
- Generation of participants who have a particular lifestyle that is relevant to the project
- Generating digital ethnographic data via photos or metaphor-elicitation using Web 2.0 tools

CUSTOMIZING RESEARCH DESIGN FOR THE NEW WAY

Customizing an approach is often critical to the marketer in understanding the ethnography that surrounds their brands and products.

Kearon and Earls (2009) of Brainjuicer offered an exemplary approach for a research strategy supporting the use of mass ethnography. Labeled "Me-To-We Research," the strategy drew inspiration from the underlying idea that humans are unreliable observers of their motivations for how they act, yet reliable in their observations of the motivations underlying the conduct of other people. Leaving aside questions about the underlying assumption, the Brainjuicer attempt to crowdsource ethnography yielded several key insights into digital research design.

One of the most relevant questions related to the lessons learned of the Brainjuicer (Kearon & Earls, 2009) study is whether mass or citizen ethnographers can overcome technological hurdles to capture behavior. Early indications are that collaborators work more effectively with structured interaction as opposed to receiving general instructions in how to record an activity and communicate it to an ethnographic researcher. This insight is increasingly important to understanding what can be expected of participants, particularly when complex technology-based approaches to generating ethnographic data are being considered. In other words, don't expect magic without providing strong guidance to participants as they involve themselves in a study.

ETHNOGRAPHIC APPS FOR SMART PHONES

At least two applications, Ethos (by Everyday Lives) and Revelation Mobile (by Revelation), now make it easier to record observations on select smart phones (e.g., iPhones, Blackberries, etc.). Rather than review specific design details of the apps, we provide an overview of the best practices emerging from public reports of their early use, and we note differences in their overall development.

Ethos

Siamack Salari (2009) of the consumer ethnography firm, Everyday Lives International, made a bit of history over the past year by developing an iPhone application—the Ethos app for collecting ethnographic data from collaborators. The initial inspiration for developing the application came from Salari's interest in developing ethnographic panels, along the lines of Brainjuicer's mass ethnography concept. His intent was to use participants for immersive ethnographic fieldwork for use by his company (Salari, 2008).

Ethos is now available in two versions, one for professional ethnographers and one for consumers. Both run on smart phones (iPhone and Blackberry). Both versions interact with a web server application for managing projects.

After fielding the Ethos app, Everyday Lives developed a web server application allowing ethnographic teams to manage the data. Initially, Ethos' design was project driven in that before recording an experience with photography or video, or annotating with text, the user needed to enter project specific information. As the Ethos development team began designing the consumer version, it changed strategy to an experience-driven design. Users could now record experiences without thinking about project criteria, such as client, themes, researcher, tags, followers, and so forth. Researchers and consumers could add project specific information after recording the experience.

Key points of learning from the Ethos application include the following (Salari, 2010):

1. Recruiting and preparing participants for ethnographic research where they will need to use an app on a smart phone takes as much time as any ordinary ethnographic project.

2. Do not assume that ownership of a smart device means tech-savvy people; therefore, be careful who is recruited to participate.

3. Just because consumers own an iPhone doesn't mean they've ever downloaded an app; therefore, be sure to recruit people who can navigate to the appropriate app.

Further, people need examples of what is expected from them when using an app, such as short videos to serve as templates.

4. Ethnographic diaries, including written, visual, video, or audio input, are best managed by the Ethos app, and are a preferred research technique.

5. Diary output from consumers can be interpreted for what is shown and why it is shown.

Revelation Mobile

Revelation Project started as a hosted web-service platform for qualitative research built to support Web 2.0. Revelation released its iPhone app, Revelation Mobile, in the summer of 2010. Revelation Project allows researchers to create diaries, assign photo exercises, ask questions, present stimuli, engage participants in online group discussions, and probe participants on their responses. Nevertheless, Revelation Mobile currently supports only a limited subset of those research techniques including diary-based activities, photo uploads, and open- and close-ended answers from research participants. As Revelation Mobile's design is refined, it promises comparable functionality to that in the Ethos app.

Finally, August (2010) summarizes the importance of mobile apps for qualitative research as follows, "Mobile is the killer app for immediacy, but it is weak in expression, therefore, great for your retail diaries, but not so hot for your metaphor elicitation exercises" (para. 9).

Whether August's (2010) assessment of Mobile's limitations in supporting metaphor elicitation results from the current capabilities of the Revelation Mobile application remains an open issue in our mind. Revelation Mobile is, at present, a participant-only application. Unlike Ethos, Revelation Mobile does not allow moderators to interact with participants. Metaphor elicitation, as we noted previously, involves participants creating visual collages to represent a feeling or thought. Researchers then ask probing questions to understand the connections participants make between the visualization and a product or brand experience.

Nevertheless, even the limited functionality of the current Revelation Mobile design allows research participants to tell their stories with words and photos created in the moment of experience.

Best Practice Case Study: Levi Strauss and Company Launch dENiZEN Brand Based on Consumer Anthropology Applied to Brand Development

A new-to-the world apparel brand, dENiZEN's development is rooted in consumer anthropology. Following the vision of Michael Perman, who then was leading market research for the development of the dENiZEN brand at Levi Strauss and Company, Trend Influence, a brand and product innovation consultancy that bases its processes in the fundamentals of consumer anthropology, designed, fielded, and delivered the project. The lead author of this chapter participated as the lead member of the research team.

The project was guided by a previously completed segmentation study that revealed a market opportunity among an emerging consumer group for which LS&Co. had no meaningful offering.

The objective of this qualitative research was to develop a deep understanding of attitudes, behaviors, and unmet needs of this consumer target. The research took place in five countries and was undertaken to inform how LS&Co. could create a relevant product offering that would resonate among emerging, middle-class, young-adult consumers. This was accomplished through an anthropological research approach that included lifestyle immersion as well as group dialogue and individual ethnographic and observational tactics.

The design of the study was rooted in development of several key objectives for understanding this particular emerging, middle-class consumer target. The topics for understanding that framed the work included culturally driven definitions for the following: "admiration," "achievement," "passions," "upgrading behavior" (to brand names), the role of retail, and the role of jeans.

To produce the data that would define the brand, several tactics were deployed to construct a holistic anthropological approach. The process began with expert interviews, conversations with cultural experts in the apparel, youth, and emerging middle-class spaces that helped us frame the questions we would seek to answer in the consumer fieldwork. In addition, local experts produced brand landscape documents that illustrated which brands resonated most with the selected consumer targets in that market.

Consumer work began with homework: "about me" collages where the young-adult consumers were asked to give a visual representation of who they are and how they present themselves to the world. Both the metaphors presented in those collages as well as the ways in which the collages were constructed (digital, using artifacts, using personal pictures versus magazine images, etc.) provided insight and helped develop universal themes that connected them as attitudes, values, and beliefs.

Focus-group discussions were then held in target relevant venues to gain a surface understanding of the key factors that influence their points of view on the research objectives. From those groups, "iconic" members of the consumer target were selected to provide immersive tours of their life: their home environments, school, work, play, retail, and the places where they hang out and interact with others. Additionally, local "sherpas" were hired to give us the lay of the retail and lifestyle venue landscape as it related to the targets. This helped the team to not only understand how retail environment and the product itself appealed to the consumer but also how consumers interacted with each.

Key to the success of this research was not only the tools and participants selected but the markets. In each country where the research was conducted, three different levels of market maturity were selected based on levels of economic development. This allowed the team to understand how shifts from traditional to more modern culture were occurring from market to market; which attitudes, values, and trends migrated from places; and how they were transmitted.

Data were captured using several tools: consumer-generated data (collages), videography, still photography, and good old-fashioned note taking. Field teams uploaded blogs with key themes from each day of work to share with the global project team, as everyone collaborated on insights and refined tactics in real-time. Video was also uploaded daily to allow those who could not travel to experience the fieldwork firsthand.

Post fieldwork workshops enabled analysis as well as more inclusive interaction between the agency and client. This lead to a synthesis of consumer insights that were deemed truly relevant and actionable by the client organization.

The deliverables for this stage of work took the physical form of a coffee-table book that used photography and narrative and organized insights in the following ways:

- Commonalities—high-level concepts that were universal with the target at a transnational level were conceptualized and developed into a cohesive global brand platform.
- Unique national characteristics—insights revealed how the brand could be designed to increase relevance of product, retail, marketing, design and brand platforms that resonated on a local level.

Video deliverables were also used to show context and drive empathy with the consumer target.

The brand was developed and tested, and product, retail, and marketing programs were also developed and tested for the launch of dENiZEN in September/October, 2010, in China.

The resulting brand, and all the elements therein (product, retail, marketing) were based on deep unifying insights that were emotionally and culturally relevant. The brand value proposition reflected research insights and was defined with a tag line, "Outfitter for a Brighter Future."

The emerging brand differentiates itself as a "modern, affordable jeanswear product built for life," designed to symbolize values that match the attitudes of its target: "for 24-hour living," "clever," "made well," "globally aware but locally dialed in," and "focused on the promise of tomorrow."

Also built in to the strategy for dENiZEN is the concept of cocreation, an implication based on the desire for this target to have a hand in creating the culture that they adopt and pass on. In an equally inspired marketing move, the Denizen brand team plans to continue incorporating anthropological insight into the ongoing development of their brand. The following copy announcing the dENiZEN launch taken from their consumer-facing website (Levi Strauss & Co., 2010) explains the brand and its philosophical approach:

> "This is the birth of a new history for Levi Strauss & Co. in Asia," said Aaron Boey, president, Levi Strauss & Co. Asia Pacific Division. "The dENiZEN ™ brand will offer our consumers what they have been looking for—stylish, well-made and comfortable clothes from a company they trust. With our 137 years of denim heritage and recognized jeans leadership in Asia, Levi Strauss & Co. is strongly positioned to meet this need among emerging middle class consumers in Asia."
>
> The dENiZEN ™ brand is designed for 18 to 28-year-olds who seek high-quality jeanswear and other fashion essentials at affordable prices. The product collection—including a variety of jeans, tops and accessories—complements active lifestyles and empowers consumers to express their aspirations, individuality and attitudes.
>
> "The dENiZEN ™ brand is made for a new generation of young people who are motivated and forward-looking," said Terence Tsang, senior vice president, dENiZEN ™ brand, Levi Strauss & Co. "It offers an updated twist on classic

essentials, encouraging consumers to create their own style and find their own voice. With the dENiZEN ™ collection, we present quality jeans that are fit for everybody."

To represent this new generation of consumers who inspired the development of the dENiZEN ™ brand, the company is also introducing dENiZEN ™10, an innovative and unique pan-Asian social media project involving real people with unique personalities and individual voices.

The dENiZEN ™ brand selected ten individuals from across the region—China, Hong Kong, Singapore, Korea and India—to capture the mood of Asia Rising. These ten people represent the spirit of the dENiZEN™ brand. They are optimistic global citizens passionately pursuing their dreams.

The dENiZEN ™10 will spend 100 days sharing their experiences and response to the new brand on social media channels—as well as their thoughts on various life themes that speak to the new generation.

Approximately 50 dENiZEN ™ retail stores will open their doors to shoppers by the end of 2010 across China, Korea and Singapore.

CONCLUSION

In the coming years, we are confident the use of ethnographic tools will continue to evolve. Consumer anthropology is not just a practice but also a mindset. It encompasses a paradigm whose mantra is first to seek to understand. In an era of consumer culture where brands are no longer relevant by simply being ubiquitous, but earn their relevance by being empathetic to human and cultural needs, the ethnographic approach to finding meaning is critical.

For the researchers who embrace this, the world is their data set. As technology and speed of cultural transformation continues, more ways to view cultural meaning and influence will emerge. The 21st century calls for practitioners who are skilled in pattern recognition from a both depth and breadth of data point of view. We have no doubt that ethnographic approaches combined with those that incorporate more traditional quantitative and qualitative research will round out a fuller picture of consumer cultures in which brand and products must compete.

Rather than forever remain considered a leading-edge practice, it is our prediction that the story of consumer anthropology as a guidepost for research and strategy foretells an increasingly mainstream practice. There is no doubt that ethnography can improve the process of innovation and allow businesses to more strongly cater to the many consumer cultures in which brands and products must compete.

FURTHER READING

Books

Geertz, C. (1973). *The interpretation of cultures*. New York, NY: Basic Books.

Hertzfeld, M. (1987). *Anthropology through the looking-Glass*. New York, NY: Cambridge University Press.

Kahl, S. J. (2009). *Dominant use: How customers influence the evolution of new products*. Capital Ideas: Selected Papers on Organizations and Markets. Retrieved from, http://www.chicagobooth.edu/capideas/oct09/4.aspx.

McGuigan, J. (1997). *Cultural methodologies*. Thousand Oaks, CA: Sage.

Morville, P. (2005). *Ambient findability*. Sebastopol, California: O'Reilly Media.

Pink, D. (2005). *A whole new mind*. New York, NY: Riverhead Books.

Postrel, V. (2003). *The substance of style*. New York, NY: HarperCollins.

Serota, L., & Rockwell, D. (2010, March/April). An introduction to casual data, and how it's changing everything. *Interactions*, 43–47.

Van Leeuwen, T., & Jewitt, C. (2001). *Handbook of visual analysis*. Thousand Oaks, CA: Sage.

Internet Sources

Anthrodesign Group on Yahoo http://tech.groups.yahoo.com/group/anthrodesign/

Consumer Anthropology Group on LinkedIn http://www.linkedin.com/groups?mostPopular=&gid=2310074&trk=myg_ugrp_ovr

Ethnosnacker Group on LinkedIn http://www.linkedin.com/groups?mostPopular=&gid=129888&trk=myg_ugrp_ovr

ESP-Challenge 15. (2010). *The ethnographic sampling project* (September). Retrieved from http://ethnosampro.posterous.com/

Diving Deep

Using ZMET to Unearth Insights About Unconscious Consumer Thinking

JOSEPH PLUMMER

Columbia University and Olson Zaltman Associates

JAMES FORR

Olson Zaltman Associates

KATJA BRESSETTE

Olson Zaltman Associates

DEEP CONSUMER INSIGHTS LEAD TO CO-OWNERSHIP OF BRANDS

Faced with expanding brand competition and shrinking duration of product uniqueness, marketers have turned to creating brand meaning and brand-consumer relationships to stimulate brand demand. Consumers have become more selective about media, messages, brand dialogue, and brand relationships (Cook & Plummer, 2007).

Since 2000, Internet penetration has grown significantly, so that in many ways its reach is now comparable to that of television and radio, the major mass media of the 20th century. The increase in consumers' use of the Internet has provided them with needed information that is often not provided by the brands themselves. Additionally, people are using technology and media of all kinds outside the home. Globally, there are more than four-billion mobile phones in use, far exceeding available television sets and computers. All this technology has not only empowered people but also has opened many new ways of listening to and learn about consumer actions and conversations (with permission, of course) to gain consumer insight.

Expanding on the need to listen and understand, Marc Gobe, the founder of Emotional Branding, said at a November 2009, Women Worldwide in Advertising CEO Summit, "It is time to reconsider how we connect with women and the types of messages we want to send them. The tendency is for brands to talk *at* people, to be pushing information, and they forget to listen to what people want."

Today, people are able to find information on themselves, when they want it rather, than waiting for it to be programmed, timed, and delivered to them on the schedules of brands and media owners. ComScore recently reported that 123 million Americans searched a newspaper website in May 2010. The *New York Times* led the category with more than 32 million visitors. The print circulation of the *Times* is about four million (Audit Bureau of Circulation, 2010).

Great brands seem to understand this sea change in media technology and the growing empowerment of consumers. They permit their customers to be *co-owners of the brand*. When consumers are co-owners, they don't simply show a preference for a brand or its products; instead, they feel a powerful sense of kinship with the brand. It is a sense that the brand is "my brand."

Brands that foster co-ownership connect emotionally and fit into the lives and aspirations of their customers instead of asking their customers to conform to the business goals of the brand. Enabling customers to be co-owners of the brand, as Apple does, for example, by creating a cadre of "brand ambassadors," creates a competitive advantage because it is a multiplier of a company's media spend (Apple is outspent by its competitors three-to-one). When customers feel like co-owners of the brand, they develop powerful emotional brand loyalty over time. Apple's case creates a potential market for new products. It is common to find people owning iPods, iPhones, MacBooks, and a new iPad.

Great brands like Apple are relentless in their quest for deep consumer insights. When consumers make purchases, they do not focus solely on product attributes; rather, people purchase products whose attributes activate salient emotional responses (Gutman, 1982; Reynolds & Craddock, 1988; Walker & Olson, 1991). Thus, it is critical for marketers to understand the goals, personal values, feelings, and emotions that influence consumer choice and preference, often unconsciously (Christensen & Olson, 2002). These deep insights about people and their world is a priceless intangible asset in today's business environment. These brands leverage that insight by developing marketing communication that enables consumers to cocreate meaning, and, thus, make the brands their own. Deep insight comes from what Gerald and Lindsay Zaltman (2008) in their book *Marketing Metaphoria* call "workable knowledge" and "workable wondering."

> In our work we have come to refer to the process of thinking deeply as workable wondering. Workable wondering involved the use of empirical, rigorous, and relevant information, also called workable knowledge, to challenge assumptions and to engage in disciplined imagination. It means more than collecting information. It means thinking deeply about the consumer insights that have surfaced. (Zaltman & Zaltman, 2008, p. 10)

Great brands take these deep insights and use them as a framework for all their actions. Most soft drinks offer a specific type of refreshment for the body; Coca-Cola goes beyond this to offer refreshment of the spirit.

Most technology brands extol their internal power on extra features, but Apple shares the magic of sight, sound, and touch.

Most hybrid cars focus on high mpg or low emissions, but Prius had the insight that people who care deeply about saving the planet want others to know they care, so Prius offered them a unique, recognizable shape and communication of a shared commitment to our planet.

In this chapter, we discuss a cutting-edge market research tool called the Zaltman Metaphor Elicitation Technique (ZMET), which can help unearth deep insights from consumers. We will begin by discussing the science behind ZMET, including the relevant theories of the mind and the importance of metaphor in human thought and communication. Next, we will present an examination of how this methodology developed, followed by a detailed explanation of how ZMET interviews are conducted and how the data are analyzed. Finally, we will present a short case study that illustrates how one company used ZMET insights to create a more powerful and emotionally resonant brand image.

DIVING DEEP FOR INSIGHTS

For a long time, academics and marketers assumed that consumers could explain exactly what they were thinking—that what people said was what they meant. They believed in the power of consciousness, of the rational mind; however, insights and discoveries in cognitive neuroscience, linguistics, psychology, and related academic fields indicate that the subconscious is much more powerful than previously thought. Consumers cannot tell us what they really want because, for the most part, they are not fully aware of what they want.

Why is that the case? What makes the unconscious so powerful and so important?

The first reason is that the vast majority of human thought and emotion takes place below the level of awareness. Tor Norretranders (1999) details the extensive unconscious processing of information in his book *The User Illusion: Cutting Consciousness Down to Size*. The bandwidth of information intake through our senses has been measured by neuropsychologists since the 1950s. The amount of information we take in per second is about 12 million bits of information. Our conscious mind is capable of processing a maximum of 40 bits per second, or less than one thousandth of 1% of the information we absorb (Norretranders, 1999). This explains why, when asked directly, consumers will provide answers that may be incomplete at best and quite misleading at worst. The reasons for our behaviors and preferences are largely unknown to our conscious mind.

However, researchers can unlock those secrets by unearthing and understanding the metaphors people use when thinking about a topic. Metaphors are everywhere. In the English language, we use an average of five or six metaphors per minute in everyday speech (Gibbs, 1992), even though we are usually unaware of the metaphoric nature of those expressions as they are escaping our lips. Metaphors are more than just rhetorical flourishes. Our conceptual system is largely metaphorical (Lakoff & Johnson, 1980), which suggests metaphor does not occur primarily in language but in thought (Kövecses, 2006), and thereby, it helps us to understand meaning and make sense of the world.

Metaphor, like much of human thought, is based on embodied human experiences (Clark, 1997; Lakoff & Johnson, 1980). For example, think about the idea of loneliness when feeling cold. Social psychologist Chen-Bo Zhong explains how people use temperature metaphors ("icy stares," "cold shoulder," "being left in the cold") to describe acts of social rejection while also literally experiencing rejection and loneliness as physical coldness (Zhong, as cited in Lehrer, 2008). This physical experience gives us the conceptual metaphor, "Loneliness is cold." We don't have to learn a metaphor; our mind triggers it automatically and unconsciously.

This intimate relationship between our bodies and our minds gives us a foundational set of metaphors that is common to all of us, regardless of sex, ethnicity, country of origin, or socioeconomic status. As Kövecses (2006, p. 14) argues, "Universal primary experiences produce universal primary metaphors." We will refer to these kinds of universal primary metaphors as deep metaphors. Deep metaphors are schemas that are typically unconscious (Shore, 1996; Zaltman, 1997, 2003) but that human beings use to make sense of all domains of life, and they help us structure the massive amount of information flooding our senses at any given moment.

Deep metaphors come to us through our earliest physical experiences. For example, as infants we learn to sit upright. Then, eventually, we learn how to crawl, walk, and run. All of these motor activities require that we maintain our sense of equilibrium. We quickly learn the positive consequences of maintaining our balance and, conversely, the negative ramifications of failing to maintain our balance. Thus, balance becomes a deep metaphor that we use unconsciously to structure how we think about other, more abstract concepts. For example, in the English language we use the balance metaphor to understand, among other things, crime and punishment (the *scales* of justice), goals and priorities (work-life *balance*), human relationships (marriage is a *give-and-take*), and personalities and emotions (Maryann is *steady* and *levelheaded*, but her friend seems unstable). Figure 10.1 identifies several common deep metaphors along with brief explanations.

Marketers are well advised to pay attention to how consumers express these deep metaphors because those expressions reflect the emotions and meanings attached to a given experience, person, brand, or situation. For example, when we spoke with men about why they buy diamonds for their wives or partners, we heard statements such as the following:

"I want her to remember that I have been with her every step of the way."

"Different pieces of jewelry are markers of milestones in our relationship."

"That ring will be with us as we are going through life together."

These phrases are expressions of the deep metaphors of journey and connection. The journey of love, with its specific milestones, leads to a closer and closer bond. For years, DeBeers had used a slogan that tapped into these deep metaphors, "A Diamond is Forever." That tagline helped frame a diamond as a symbol that a couple's love will last forever (or at least until death do them part). However, based on this new research, DeBeers has taken

Figure 10.1   Selected Deep Metaphors and Their Common Expressions

Deep Metaphors	How Deep Metaphors Are Expressed
BALANCE	References to equilibrium, stability, equalize, or compensate; including both sides; equivalence of scales, teeter-totter, balance beam; references to reciprocity—give and take; references to "stable" emotional states such as calm, relaxed, serene; feeling "right" with the world
RESOURCE	References to having/getting the requisite knowledge, energy, tools, or materials to accomplish some task; having or getting help and assistance from others
CONNECTION	References to connecting to things or people; making an association; references to linking or attaching; to be a part of; to not be isolated from; liking or loving someone or something; references to getting in touch with yourself; find your true self
CONTAINER	References to being in (or out) of a place (house, room); references to keeping or storing; references to "in" and "out;" keeping things out as well as in; being wrapped up or out in open
JOURNEY	References to taking a trip; following a path, choosing a direction; getting there; the journey of life
TRANSFORMATION	References to changing from one state to another—physical or emotional; becoming something or someone else; references to evolving, maturing, growing

those two deep metaphors in a fresh direction with the creation of the Journey Diamond (and the accompanying tagline, "With every step love grows") to suggest that the connection between a couple grows stronger over time, that there are milestones along the way, and that those various milestones should be celebrated with new and different size diamonds. Although this new product and the messaging that supports it are grounded in the traditional deep metaphors of journey and connection, the company is expressing those ideas differently than it has in the past. This updated way of talking about journey and connection bundles and conveys all the information and emotional content associated with the new product.

An analysis of how consumers use deep metaphors will reveal insight into the emotions that are relevant to a given topic. Emotion is critical to how humans think, behave, and interpret the world, but often, these emotions are hidden from the conscious mind and are almost always very hard to express. Looking at the old paradigm of "think—feel—do," we can easily see how much value both academics and marketers traditionally have put on the rational mind, the cognitive abilities of consumers. The thinking is that if you make a logical argument that appeals to reason, people will make good, rational decisions.

However, this model, still prevalent in marketing today, has been proven incorrect by research in cognitive neuroscience and other fields. Neuroscientist Antonio Damasio (2000) outlines this in detail in his book *Descartes' Error*. At a basic level, the sensory cortices detect and categorize a stimulus, which can lead to an immediate body response based on an emotion such as fear, (e.g. moving quickly to hide from a predator or showing anger toward a rival). But it does not stop here. The next step is the feeling of that emotion, which is the conscious recognition of the emotion. This feeling then triggers additional cognitive processes such as planning ahead, generalizing knowledge, or consciously exploring different strategies for dealing with a situation or person (Damasio, 2000, pp. 131–133).

Without emotion, we cannot function as human beings—whether in a personal, business, or other setting. Joseph LeDoux (1998) writes in his book *The Emotional Brain* that emotions are biological functions of the nervous system. They occur because of certain external or internal stimuli, and we have little control over those emotional reactions. LeDoux notes, "The brain accomplishes its behavioral goals without robust awareness" (p. 12). Only when they rise to conscious awareness as feelings do we really notice them, and that is well after our bodies have already reacted to a situation or a stimulus. In other words, only the *outcome* of emotional processing (and cognitive processing, for that matter) enters awareness and occupies the conscious mind.

Equally important is the close and inseparable relationship between emotion and reason. In fact, healthy decision making without emotion is impossible. Damasio (2000) has documented this in his work with patients whose emotional centers (such as the prefrontal cortex) are injured but who have otherwise intact brains (pp. 34–38). Because of their injuries, these people could not make wise choices. In some cases, they could not make even the most basic decisions. They also often undergo dramatic personality changes that render a person "unable to reason and decide in ways conducive to the maintenance and betterment of himself and his family, no longer capable of succeeding as an independent human being" (Damasio, 2000, p. 38).

Unfortunately, humans have difficulties explaining their emotions fully. Our verbal language is often inadequate, and the conscious mind tends to jump in and rationalize. To dive deep, marketers need to bypass the conscious mind so they can uncover the emotional framework and associations underlying attitudes about brands, products, and decision-making processes. Understanding and exploring metaphoric representations is one way to do so. Another related technique is the use of images. We all know the expression "a picture is worth a thousand words." There is much more truth in that cliché than we might realize. Pictures are not just an incredibly efficient way to express information, feelings, and memories. Actually, humans literally think in images—to be precise, we think in neural activations, which are mostly in the form of images, not words.

Damasio (2000) explains that having a mind essentially means being able to form these neural representations, manipulate them in a process called thought, and eventually be able to use them to impact behavior by planning, predicting the future, and choosing a course of action. These neural representations can take a variety of forms. Critically, our words are not our thoughts, although verbal and other forms of language are instrumental in expressing and even shaping thought. Consider, for instance, how much longer it takes to explain a thought than to think it.

To demonstrate this, try to describe, in words, exactly what Angelina Jolie looks like. You almost certainly could not fully describe her physical features, such as her eyebrows, her eyes, her nose, her lips, and the shape of her face in a way that would make her instantly recognizable to someone who had never seen her. However, when you think about Angelina Jolie, a very clear image probably comes to mind immediately—maybe a memory of a movie scene with her or a photograph her doing humanitarian work or her being involved in some kind of scandal. And so it is with our thoughts and feelings about brands, products, or companies that we try as best we can to put those mental representations into words, but our initial reactions and associations are not verbal. They are in our heads. Therefore, it is essential to uncover those mental images and associations using metaphors and other forms of imagery, rather than just relying on people's words.

HISTORICAL ROOTS OF ZMET

ZMET is a multidisciplinary approach developed by Dr. Gerald Zaltman (then a professor at the University of Pittsburgh and later at the Harvard Business School) in 1991 to help organizations understand consumers' unconscious emotional needs (Zaltman, 1997; Zaltman & Coulter, 1995). With that knowledge in hand, managers are empowered to develop products and services that satisfy unspoken demands, and ad agencies and marketers have the tools with which to develop communications that frame brands in ways that resonate with consumers' unconscious mental models and, thus, highlight the personal relevance of those brands.

ZMET arose from several ideas that coalesced in Zaltman's mind. He had been thinking about a paradox of advertising research, specifically that research output generally took the form of numbers rather than imagery and, thus, the research output did not resemble the way in which ads are created. Simultaneously, Zaltman developed an interest in photography and had become particularly captivated with how a single photograph can provide deep insight into the thoughts and emotions of the photographer. Finally, he had become interested in the work of researchers Melanie Wallendorf, Russell Belk, and others who were using photography and videotape to document the importance of various material possessions in consumers' lives. Laddering techniques, which are an integral part of ZMET, had played a role in some of Zaltman's previous research. **Laddering** is a technique in which consumers are asked to describe the functional benefit of a product feature, the psychosocial benefit of that functional benefit, and then the emotional outcome of the psychosocial benefit. The end-result is a means-end chain that illustrates a product's emotional salience (Reynolds & Gutman, 1988). Zaltman had used laddering in combination with the repertory grid technique, in which a respondent is asked to describe how any two constructs or ideas are similar to one another, yet different from a third idea or construct, in how that person thinks or feels about a topic (Fransella, Bell, & Bannister, 2003). Thus, ZMET stemmed in part from a convergence of established research methodologies.

Zaltman, who had long been interested in how humans use metaphors to construct theories and reveal their sense of their worlds, developed ZMET so that consumers could harness the power of imagery (in essence, visual metaphors) to express in their thoughts and feelings about a variety of topics. His methodology also incorporates elements of psychodrama, art therapy, and dance therapy to elicit other kinds of nonvisual metaphors that can shed light on additional aspects of consumer thought. Zaltman considers ZMET an improvement over laddering because his methodology incorporates metaphors, which are central to consumer thinking, and because the interview process enables researchers to explore more deeply the meaning of key ideas and their nonhierarchical associations.

The methodology continues to evolve. Zaltman has created a modified form of ZMET that is geared toward eliciting consumer reactions to advertising and other communication stimuli. ZMET also has been used in conjunction with the Implicit Association Test (IAT), a computer-based reaction-time test that measures how strongly different concepts are associated at an unconscious level (a battery of sample tests is accessible at https://implicit.harvard.edu/implicit/demo). IAT is designed to measure people's most privately held thoughts and feelings including those they may explicitly reject because of conflicting personal belief systems or those beliefs that are simply below the level of conscious awareness (Greenwald, McGhee, & Schwartz, 1998; Greenwald, Poehlman, Uhlmann, & Banaji, 2009; Nosek, 2005; Nosek et al., 2007). A standard ZMET project, for example, could reveal the deep emotions associated with a product experience while a follow-up IAT study could provide quantitative insights into the pervasiveness and relative strength of those deep ideas within a larger population. Zaltman also anticipates increased opportunities to use ZMET in conjunction with eye-tracking software and methodologies that incorporate biometric measures, such as respiration, heart rate, and skin conductance.

ZMET METHODOLOGY

ZMET interviews are one-on-one discussions between a respondent and a trained interviewer. The one-on-one format is designed to overcome the shortcomings of focus groups that, because of issues related to social dominance, groupthink, and minimal time to explore an individual participant's thinking, are ill-suited to providing deep insight into the emotional landscape of people's thoughts (Hauser & Griffin, 1993; Rubin & Rubin, 1995; Zaltman, 1997). ZMET interviews last between 90 minutes and two hours and, typically, take place in a market research facility.

At the outset of a ZMET project, the research team and client must come to agreement on two fundamental questions: (1) Who should we interview? (2) What do we interview them about? As for the first issue, the guidelines for respondent recruitment can vary dramatically from project to project, depending on client objectives. One consistent rule of thumb is that 12 to 15 interviews per segment are sufficient for understanding the overall mental model for that segment. This is a smaller sample size than is typical for focus group research; however, one-on-one interviews can be dramatically more productive and efficient in uncovering a large number of ideas—and the connections between those ideas— than focus groups (Hauser & Griffin, 1993).

Regarding the second issue, part of the upfront work in a ZMET project is the development of the ZMET question, which is the assignment sent to respondents about a week before their interview. Respondents are asked to think about a topic, and then bring to the interview between five and eight images that represent their thoughts and feelings about that subject. The discussion topics typically are broad and open-ended (e.g., "Your thoughts and feelings about the current economy," "Your thoughts and feelings about caring for your child," or "Your thoughts and feelings about Brand X")

Respondents frequently copy these images from the web or clip them from magazines or newspapers, but occasionally, participants are inspired to take photos or draw pictures especially for the research. The source of the images, though, is less important than the meanings the images are intended to convey.

The ZMET interview employs traditional laddering techniques described earlier to understand how functional consequences lead to emotional outcomes. For example, in 2008 research into how the declining United States economy was affecting Americans' lives, one respondent collected an image of a gasoline pump, which led to the following exchange.

> Q: How does this picture of a gas pump relate to your thoughts and feelings about the current economy and how it affects your life?
>
> A: I remember when gas was 99 cents a gallon. Now, I think I have seen where it was $4.09. I have to spend a lot of money just to drive my car.
>
> Q: How does spending a lot of money to drive your car affect you?
>
> A: It affects me quite a bit because my mom lives in Kentucky, and I haven't seen her in three years because I can't spend four dollars a gallon going to visit somebody.
>
> Q: How does it make you feel that you haven't been able to see your mom in three years?
>
> A: Upset. Depressed. We have a pretty close relationship. But I'm sure there are lots of people that aren't going to have a vacation this year because of the economy.
>
> Q: What's wrong with not being able to take a vacation this year because of the economy?
>
> A: That means the American way of life isn't there anymore.
>
> Q: What happens when the American way of life isn't there anymore?
>
> A: That's taking away your happiness. That means your freedoms are tightening up, and that's what America is all about—freedom.

In this example, laddering techniques uncovered the deeper emotional consequences of higher gas prices. The consequences are not only personal (a sadness that he is unable to spend time with his mother) but also societal (a fear that higher gas prices are limiting his freedom and, thus, profoundly changing what it means to be an American).

The ZMET interview also includes probes designed to elicit metaphors from respondents, and to encourage them to elaborate on those metaphors, often in vivid ways. In this example from the economy study, skillful metaphor probing helped a participant vividly describe the helplessness and fear she was feeling in the face of increasing unemployment rates and a plummeting stock market.

A: This is a picture of a little boy in a soldier's uniform. I'm like this kid, like a kid on a battlefield.

Q: Imagine yourself as that kid on the battlefield. How are you feeling?

A: Unprepared, unequipped. Like, why am I here? I'm scared.

Q: How does that scared feeling relate to your thoughts and feelings about the economy and its impact on your life?

A: I can't help being part of the economy living here. But I look around and say, "I don't want to fight. I don't want to do this. This isn't my problem, but I've got to fight." And it's really difficult for me to win.

Q: What are your weapons on the battlefield?

A: I don't have any. There are others who are much more powerful than I am. I'm not a big fan of banks. They are all kind of big, ominous, and evil. Sort of like Frankenstein. And that's who I'm battling.

Q: In your mind's eye, what does the battlefield look like?

A: Organized chaos. Just a chaotic frenzy of adrenaline and energy. It's not like there are just two sides on the battlefield. It's everyone for themselves.

Q: What are you fighting for?

A: Survival.

Additional steps include a vignette step, in which respondents are asked to personify key ideas or stakeholders and to create a story around those characters (for example, in the economy study, participants created a story with three characters: themselves, their money, and the U.S. economy). The sensory step asks respondents to describe their thoughts and feelings about the topic using sensory modalities other than sight (e.g., "What sound, touch, and taste would represent your thoughts and feelings about the U.S. economy and its effect on your life").

Then in the final 30 minutes of the interview, in a step that borrows from art therapy, respondents are joined by a graphic artist who helps them create a summary digital image—a visual representation of all the key ideas discussed during the interview. Participants use a subset of the pictures they brought to the interview to create the image using Adobe Photoshop software. The graphic artist acts as the hands, taking care of the technical aspects of the image creation while the respondent supplies the ideas. Image 10.1

shows a representative digital image from the economy research.

- "A welcome to Las Vegas sign represents the gamble that some investment banks take, the risk they take on to stretch their profit."
- "There's a giant fire and smoke-filled sky with firefighters carrying a large fire extinguisher to put it out. This represents growing distress in financial markets and the global economy. Although there are several people trying to put it out, it just keeps growing. There's nothing they can do."
- "There's Uncle Sam with an upside-down oil rig dumping coins into the hat. I work at an oil/gas company, and there's less demand for my services. So my wages are being cut and the job is not as steady."
- "The overall image is frightening. This very powerful fire, and all these small firefighters, they look as if they stand no chance. All the economies around the world coming together to try to take on this big, powerful crisis and it just seems uncertain whether or not we'll be able to put it out."

Image 10.1 A Digital Image From a ZMET Study of the U.S. Economy

All interviews are transcribed, with a typical interview spanning 15 to 25 single-spaced pages.

ZMET ANALYSIS

A key output of the analysis of ZMET interviews is identifying the constellation of deep metaphors that structure participants' thinking about the topic (Zaltman, 1997, 2003). It also is important for the analysis team to focus on how participants express the key deep metaphors because a deep metaphor can assume many different forms. Consider, for example, the deep metaphor of journey. Not all journeys are the same. For one person, the process of completing a project might be smooth sailing. For another, however, it might be a rocky road filled with pitfalls. Similarly, containers can be warm and protective (like a mother's womb) or restrictive and confining (like a prison).

For example, in the economy research many participants conceptualized the effects of the economic downturn with the deep metaphor of force. They collected images of hurricanes, tornadoes, and explosions to represent their feeling that the economy had spiraled out of control and was in danger of destroying both their individual financial security and, more broadly, the American way of life.

However, at a thematic level, people of different political persuasions tended to describe the Force slightly differently. Voters who planned to vote for Democrat Barack Obama in the 2008 presidential election described the economy as a violent, malicious, hostile enemy that needed to be controlled or tamed.

> "I am not a fan of international banking and all these things that are **big, ominous, and evil** to me. Free marketers see the economy as something that self-regulates [but] those people are finding they created something out of control, **like Frankenstein**."

On the other hand, respondents who pledged their support to Republican presidential candidate John McCain described the economy not as something inherently evil, but as a victim of bad decisions by individuals and the government. This segment felt like the economy needed to be repaired rather than controlled.

> "They gave us a $600 tax break, but in order to do that, we borrowed $90 billion from China. That's **crushing the economy**."

> "If somebody is going to be borrowing money irresponsibly and the economy goes in the tank, the rest of us have to **pick up the pieces**. Right now those pieces are huge and heavy."

As was evident in this study, differences in the deep metaphors people employ, and even differences in how those deep metaphors are expressed, can reveal the presence of important psychological segments that marketers might find important to attend to. Frequently, these psychological segments transcend traditional demographic divisions like race, ethnicity, gender, or income. The result of the analysis is, in essence, a psychological profile of the consumer segment, with insight into how the product, service, or experience in question affects consumers' lives at an unconscious emotional level.

The analysis team also uses these insights as inspiration for strategic or tactical recommendations. For example, although voters described the economic downturn as a devastating force that was laying waste to the American Dream, policymakers often used metaphors that depicted the economy as a mechanical system in need of repair. These are two very different and not altogether congruent metaphors. Engines, in the hands of a competent mechanic, can be repaired or overhauled relatively easily. However, recovering from a bomb blast or a tornado (which were among the metaphors voters used to describe the force of the economic collapse) is a protracted, difficult, and sometimes unpredictable process. Were we using this research to advise President Obama, we might have suggested that he scrap the term "economic stimulus," which implies a set of actions that would lead to immediate improvements, and substitute a term such as, "economic rehabilitation plan," which suggests a steady but longer-term return to normal.

CASE STUDY: CISCO

The Company

Cisco, a major supplier of networking equipment and network management for the Internet, is one of the world's largest technology corporations with annual sales in 2010 of more than $40 billion. Its primary business is in the routers, switchers, and software used to manage data, voice, and video traffic on the Internet. The company was started in 1984 at Stanford University by a husband-wife team and their colleagues. Cisco Systems went public in 1990 after creating a large business primarily with the United States government, aerospace industry, and major universities. In 1999, Cisco Systems launched a new business bringing high-speed Internet access to the consumer market. This expansion advanced further in 2000, when Cisco bought Cerent, a fiber-optic network equipment maker, for $7 billion.

The Challenge

In 2005, Cisco Systems prepared to undertake a major rebranding effort. It was management's belief that while people recognized the Cisco Systems name, few consumers understood exactly what Cisco provided, and the company had little or no emotional bond with customers or employees. It was a company with brains and brawn but uncertainty about its heart. The company believed its customers viewed their relationship with Cisco in expertise and functional benefits of high-speed network connection but that they lacked any emotional loyalty to the company.

The Research

One of the critical elements, therefore, in the rebranding effort was to understand the emotional needs that Cisco Systems' hardware helped people to meet. The company's new identity would center on these deeper customer needs, rather than technology for technology's sake. To develop an understanding of this emotional territory, Cisco hired Olson Zaltman Associates to conduct a ZMET research study with business customers and consumers across the United States to better understand the feelings, perceptions, and meanings people had regarding Cisco Systems.

The sample consisted of 36 people, evenly divided across three segments. The consumer segment consisted of people ages 18 to 60 who had high-speed Internet access and were responsible for household decisions about technology purchases. Other segments were business managers (who worked in a business management function) and technology Managers (who worked in IT departments). These were drawn from a mix of companies ranging from small firms with at least 20 employees to large corporations employing 5,000 or more. All managers were involved with the decision-making process for computer equipment, and all used Cisco's products as part of their IT networks.

The ZMET interviews took place in Chicago, IL, Los Angeles, CA, and San Jose, CA. Each interview lasted approximately two hours. The respondents brought six to eight pictures that they selected to represent their thoughts and feelings about Cisco Systems. The three segments were analyzed separately to determine if there were any major perceptual and meaning differences among these key stakeholder groups. Few such differences emerged in the key deep metaphors and other insights.

The Insights

Cisco management's main concern was the lack of a strong emotional connection between the company and its customers. A key learning, however, was that this hypothesis was false. Participants appreciated that Cisco helped them fulfill many important emotional needs. Customers brought in pictures that included bridges, rowing teams, handshakes, interconnected artwork, maps with roads or lines of longitude and latitude, and families coming together—all images that symbolized the deep metaphor of connection. Cisco's technology makes it possible for people to connect with friends and family, colleagues, and even information and enjoy the emotional benefits (e.g., love, belonging, and success) that result from those connections. Image 10.2 is a digital image created by a customer that illustrates connection.

Image 10.2 A Consumer Digital Image Expressing Thoughts and Feelings About Cisco

The respondent explained the circled part of this collage:

> The image of the people having dinner around the table represented community and the idea that Cisco enables communication, sharing ideas and knowledge. The people are walking over the bridge. The bridge expands the world and opens up new frontiers for tomorrow.

Although Cisco was already linked in consumers' unconscious minds with connection, management recognized it had not been leveraging that powerful idea as strongly as it could have been in existing branding and communications efforts. Indeed, it hadn't even been aware that consumers made these associations in their minds. Cisco believed the next step was to talk more explicitly about its role in helping consumers connect to critical information and to important people in their lives. In their book *Marketing Metaphoria*, Gerald and Lindsay Zaltman (Zaltman & Zaltman, 2008) discuss how connection became the inspiration for the new Cisco branding and advertising worldwide:

> One person commented, "I see the image of a spine because I feel that Cisco is the internet backbone. It holds everything together." Another noted, "Cisco is a bridge from where you are to somewhere else. It is a vital link."

Conversely, the threat of disconnection led to feelings of isolation, anxiety, and fear. . . . When a company owns a Deep Metaphor, this creates archetypes. One archetype here was Cisco as a father archetype: Fathers provide connections for their children, helping to socialize them and prepare them for a life and career in a world with many other people. (p. 134)

Armed with these insights from ZMET, Cisco and its branding partners created a new theme for the company, "welcome to the human network," which emphasizes the kinds of emotional connections that Cisco's products can facilitate (Image 10.3).

Cisco also tweaked its corporate logo to make itself more personable and less distant. It retained the image of a bridge (a nearly universal symbol of connection), but humanized the bridge by removing it from the box and giving it a rounder, friendlier appearance. It also removed "systems" from the company name and made the font rounder and friendlier, as shown in Image 10.4.

Image 10.3   Cisco Advertising

The Results

Cisco management was quite pleased with the results of the rebranding effort after one year in the marketplace. All the indicators were positive, including a 9% increase in brand value as measured by Interbrand (about a $2 billion improvement). Their ranking among the most respected companies, as measured by *Barron's*, improved from 30th place in 2006 to 9th in 2007. Important, the perception of Cisco as a technology leader among customers in their tracking study showed an 80% improvement in just one year. It seems that by highlighting the emotional benefit of connection (human) and strengthening their association with the Internet (network) and developing a warmer personality (welcome), Cisco strengthened perceptions of technological expertise.

Image 10.4   Evolution of the Cisco Logo

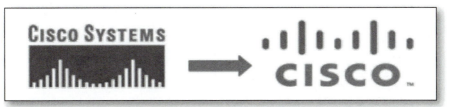

Source: http://www.olsonzaltman.com/downloads/ZMET_Study_on_the_US_Economy.pdf.

CONCLUSION

We hope that with the insights about the situation in the marketplace with its changing media landscape and increasing consumer power, the insights about the human mind and how it functions, as well as the knowledge of a methodology that dives deeper to create more effective strategies, we have brought home the importance of adopting the new paradigm that the subconscious matters. It matters in understanding consumers on a deeper and more meaningful level, and it matters for reaching them in a way that is emotionally engaging, taps into existing psychological frameworks, and/or creates new and powerful ways of thinking. In all of this, we should not forget that we are humans, too, and the same principles apply to our minds. We are aware of only a tiny sliver of our thinking. How many great ideas for brands, products, and innovative communication lurk in the depths of marketers' minds? If we try to apply some of these principles (such as the use of imagery, of metaphor, of the importance of emotion) to ourselves, to our work, and to our approaches to issues, the possibilities are endless.

We hope this chapter has inspired you to rethink consumer research but maybe also your approaches to uncovering your hidden thoughts, attitudes, and mental frames.

FURTHER READING

Hansen, F., & Christensen, S. R. (2007). *Emotions, advertising, and consumer choice.* Copenhagen, Denmark: Copenhagen Business School Press.

Lehrer, J. (2009). *How we decide.* New York, NY: Houghton Mifflin.

CHAPTER 11

Crowdsourcing and Consumer Insights

ROBIN PENTECOST

Griffith University, Australia

MARK T. SPENCE

Bond University, Australia

INTRODUCTION

Wired magazine introduced crowdsourcing to our lexicon in "The Rise of Crowdsourcing" (June 14, 2006). Jeff Howe, the writer of the article, defined crowdsourcing in a separate 2006 blog as "the act of a company or institution taking a function once performed by employees and outsourcing it to an undefined (and generally large) network of people in the form of an open call" (Howe, 2006a, p. 5). The job to be performed is to resolve, or take steps toward resolving, a problem of a technical, creative, economic, or informational nature.

Unlike outsourcing, where predefined people/groups perform the work outside the organization, "The crucial prerequisite for crowdsourcing is the use of an open call format and the large network of potential labourers" (Howe, 2006a, p. 5). Anjali Ramachaandran (2010), appealing to crowds to provide input, compiled a list of 150 crowdsourcing websites—and no doubt that list is already far out of date.

A driving force behind crowdsourcing is the belief, popularized in books such as *Macrowikinomics* (Tapscott & Williams, 2010), that tinkering with contemporary business models is no longer a viable long-term strategy. Consider Larry Huston and Nabil Sakkab, Procter & Gamble's Research and Innovation Vice Presidents who comment, "By 2000, it was clear to us that our invent-it-ourselves model was not capable of sustaining high levels of topline growth. The explosion of new technologies was putting ever more pressure on our innovation budgets" (Huston & Sakkab, 2006, p. 60). P&G is but one example of a firm that regularly appeals to crowds to curb the rising cost of corporate research. It is, therefore, not surprising that a process so rich in potential has attracted much interest, both from practitioners and academics.

DEFINING CROWDSOURCING

In light of the explosion of applications, what precisely *is* crowdsourcing is being revisited, with some of the early sages calling for a narrowing of the definition to distinguish it from concepts, such as collective invention (Allen, 1983), collaborative innovation (Tapscott & Williams, 2006, 2010) or commons-based peer production—free or open-source software are good examples of the latter (Benkler & Nissenbaum, 2006). Some narrowing of the definition is warranted. For example, crowdsourcing is coordinated by an organization that takes some level of ownership over the solutions, unlike open-source software. However, we caution against narrowing the definition too much for two reasons: (1) conceptual and (2) operational.

Conceptually, like others, we view crowdsourcing as a verb not a noun, whose ultimate aim is for an organization to learn from crowds. However, relevant problem-solving insights from crowds can be gleaned without individuals responding to an open call, a key element in Howe's (2006a) definition. For example, monitoring foot traffic flow within a retail establishment, as Path Intelligence, a UK-based firm, does by tracking mobile phones, is used by the more sophisticated stores to improve store layout. This is just one example where much can be learned from observing crowds, with or without their knowledge.

Operationally, the predominant view is that crowdsourcing is "enabled only through the technology of the web," as it is a "creative mode of interactivity, not merely a medium between messages and people" (Brabham, 2008, p. 87). The web is certainly an efficient means for interactive communication. To use Williamson's (1979) Nobel Prize winning parlance, the web has vastly lowered *transaction-costs*: Firms used to vertically integrate because it was more cost efficient to hire employees than to "employ" people on an as-needed basis—the latter required too many transactions. The web has made it much easier and cheaper to interface with individuals outside the firm, thereby, allowing firms to trim their permanent labor force to become more market-mediated rather than vertically integrated. Although the web is an efficient communication medium, interactivity is, by no means, limited to that mode.

With this as a backdrop, we advance the following definition of crowdsourcing. Crowdsourcing is a coordinated effort initiated by an organization to solve a problem once performed by employees by either actively engaging a large, initially anonymous community of individuals, or passively observing a relevant group of individuals to learn from their behavior as an input toward problem resolution.

Crowdsourcing and Problem Structure

Whether actively engaging or passively observing a crowd, the problems best suited for crowdsourcing are those that are classified as *ill structured*. To elaborate, problems can be thought of as consisting of three elements: (1) inputs available to the problem solver, (2) the goal or goals (outputs) to which the problem solver is striving, and (3) the allowable rules to get from the inputs to the outputs (Spence & Brucks, 1997). In some cases, all three elements are clearly defined, hence the problem would be considered well structured. Processing accounts receivable would be a good example, and one that would not benefit from accessing crowds. On the other end of the structuredness spectrum are new product planning and research and development efforts.

Consider new product development. At an abstract level, the goal is straightforward: develop a successful product. However, operationally most new products fail for the simple reason that there is no set methodology to ensure that a successful goal or outcome will be achieved. A clothes manufacturer could design several lines of clothing, some of which sell well and others fail. Minimizing the latter has obvious advantages. A means to do so is to have your target audience participate in the product development process, as some of the forthcoming examples will illustrate.

Research and development is another example of a problem where one or more of the inputs, goals, or allowable rules to get from inputs to goals are ambiguous or poorly defined, hence opening the problem to a large number of problem solvers has advantages. Like ant colonies, which are widely considered extremely efficient at resolving the proverbial travelling salesperson problem—in their case, determining the shortest path to food, bringing masses to bear on the problem can yield an efficient solution, but it is not a guarantee for so doing. Many would-be problem solvers will head in the wrong direction, arguably wasting their time as well as the firm's time collecting and processing their opinions.

THE WISDOM OF CROWDS

Organizations are now turning to new ways of connecting to brainpower outside the company to ward off rising costs. Take, for instance, a problem posted by Colgate-Palmolive, which had stumped their in-house researchers. The packaged goods company needed a way to inject fluoride powder into a toothpaste tube without it dispersing into the surrounding air. Ed, who has a master's degree in particle physics, knew he had a solution by the time he had finished reading the challenge: impart an electric charge to the powder while grounding the tube. The positively charged fluoride particles would be attracted to the tube without any significant dispersion. Ed earned $25,000 for his efforts. Paying Colgate-Palmolive's research and development staff to produce the same solution could have cost many times that amount (Howe, 2006b).

Crowdsourcing has huge potential, but rightfully, it has its critics. Wikipedia's cofounder, Jimmy Wales, is one: "I find the term 'crowdsourcing' incredibly irritating. Any company that thinks it's going to build a site by outsourcing all the work to its users not only disrespects the users but also completely misunderstands what it should be doing. Your job is to provide a structure for your users to collaborate, and that takes a lot of work" (Wales quoted in McNichol, 2007, para. 1).

We would add that crowdsourcing is a means to learn from crowds, which might not lead to wisdom. An aggregated group response may be inappropriate. For example, the herd mentality in financial decision making is suboptimal for individuals as well as the collective; yet unearthing the follow-the-pack tendency (purchasing stocks or houses when prices are rising rapidly) has clear, practical importance to policy planners.

Another example of suboptimal decision making can be found in the children's cable television network Nickelodeon. In the early 1990s, this network setup one of the world's first consumer product testing panels over a computer network where children could react to new children's shows. Nickelodeon researchers concede that using such a research technique is not perfect. Reactions from such an age-group are best revealed by their body language rather than their spoken and written English skills, which are often monosyllabic. To compensate for this, Nickelodeon continues to use traditional research (Churchill, 1995).

Google has reportedly compiled a "Google Price Index" based on consumers' e-shopping data it has on file. Is such information a leading indicator of economic activity, or is it too late to be of strategic benefit? Google has not released the index publicly. The White House has also undertaken crowdsourcing initiatives—constituents can provide input to policies up for discussion (www.whitehouse2.org). However, some caution is advised: such a path to policy making could lead to populist politics.

These last examples suggest that appealing to the masses may be suboptimal. Henry Ford reportedly quipped that had he listened to the masses, he would have developed a better horse-drawn buggy. Henry Adams was similarly damning, "There is no such thing as an underestimate of average intelligence."

Despite these examples that challenge the benefits of crowdsourcing, there is a burgeoning number of successful applications, some wildly so. The producers of the TV hit *American Idol* and its many variants may not have realized they were on the cutting-edge of a broadcasting application predicated on crowdsourcing, where the masses provide both the talent and are the judges. And then there is Wikipedia, a fabulous ongoing exemplar that now contains 14 million articles in various languages (and includes pages dedicated to describing crowdsourcing).

The broader definition of crowdsourcing advanced herein is compatible with a legion of real-world examples, many of which predated the existence of the term. For example, compiling input from independent hobbyists on topics as varied as weather observations and bird migrations has been used for years, as has the recognition that averaging a series of forecasts by independent judges typically proves to yield a much better prediction than any of the individual judges (and outperforms any individual over repeated trials).

Dimensions of Crowdsourcing

A series of exemplars will be presented that can be classified as *active* or *passive* crowdsourcing. In the former case, active participation is in response to an open call, a key component of the Howe's (2006a) definition. An organization is, therefore, *actively* endeavoring to source a heterogeneous crowd of individuals to address an immediate issue.

It is reasonable to assume that active crowdsourcing applications will continue to grow as long as the benefit to cost ratio remains favorable for both the organization initiating the effort as well as for the crowd being appealed to. However, in light of the rush of firms entering into this domain, including the plethora of independent web-based firms willing to organize and manage crowdsourcing initiatives, it is reasonable to assume that the number of crowdsourcing initiatives (supply) will outpace the willingness to participate (demand), hence a wash of some of the players should be expected, reminiscent of the late-1990s dot.com crash.

The potential for *passive* applications of crowdsourcing is huge, just as marketers are finding with data mining. (A Google search on "crowdsensing" is returning an increasing number of hits, although crowdsensing is not [yet] defined in Wikipedia. We view crowdsensing as the passive component of crowdsourcing.) Previously, we mentioned monitoring foot traffic flow in retail stores. Another nice example of passive crowdsourcing that far predated the term is provided by Churchill (1995). William Benton, one of the cofounders of the Benton and Boles advertising agency, was walking in Chicago on a hot summer's day when he happened to hear the radios from the open apartment windows. He noted that 21 of the 23 radios were tuned to Amos and Andy, a leading comedy program in 1929. Once back at his firm, he suggested to one of his clients, Pepsodent Toothpaste, that they advertise during this program; they did and sales of Pepsodent took-off (Cornish, 1981). In these examples, participation was neither actively sought nor was user input web-enabled, yet what was learned had obvious benefits.

A passive, web-enabled approach to crowdsourcing has been adopted by the Richmond, Virginia, police department. They estimate they save $15,000 in overtime pay by monitoring social network sites like Facebook and MySpace to determine where rowdy festivities are likely to be (*The Economist*, 2010), hence police can be sent straight to high-probability problem areas.

Amazon also does passive, web-enabled crowdsourcing. Founded in customer relationship marketing, Amazon uses statistical software to monitor the page viewing and purchase profile of its customers. By collating this data, the company can send a customized newsletter based on what products a customer has been viewing and matching that to products purchased by others with similar viewing habits. If the customer had been reviewing DVDs, the customer might receive a newsletter profiling DVD specials of a similar genre. E-tailers use cookies to passively monitor the behavior of their customers (Wilson, Johns, Miller, & Pentecost, 2010); and, as noted earlier, Google is exploring value in the massive amounts of user data to which it has access.

Figure 11.1 shows a framework for classifying applications, separating them on the dimensions *operational* (web-enabled versus not web-enabled) and *conceptual* (active versus passive). An example for each of the four cells is presented, some of which have been mentioned, others to be discussed.

Figure 11.1   A Framework for Categorizing Crowdsourcing Applications

	Web-enabled	Web not necessary
Active participation	iStockphoto	Tracking bird migrations
Passive observation	Richmond police	In-store shopper traffic flow

Source: Based upon the Boudreau, and Lakhani, (2009). "How to manage outside innovation", *Sloan Management Review,* Vol. 50 (4).

Currently, most action for participants and debate with respect to efficacy exists in the top-left cell, active and web-enabled. Most of the remainder of this chapter will focus on this quadrant; however, readers should recall that in the 1990s most start-up applications in the dot.com world were in business-to-consumer applications (B2C), not business-to-business (B2B) applications where the most revenue is being made today. If readers accept the broader definition of crowdsourcing advanced herein, anticipate much growth in activity in the other three quadrants.

Crowdsourcing is a hot topic, and not surprisingly, researchers are turning to crowds to advance and fine-tune a definition that may not coincide with ours. Regardless of what definition ultimately emerges, our purpose is to expose readers to what can be learned from crowds, actively or passively, thereby enlightening readers to a technique that can directly benefit their organization.

If one rigidly conforms to the opinion that crowdsourcing is only in response to an open call and is web enabled, as advanced by Howe (2006a, 2006c) and Brabham (2008), respectively, some of this review will be tangential—but, we hope, nevertheless, interesting.

A HISTORICAL PERSPECTIVE ON CROWDSOURCING

"I not only use all the brains that I have, but all that I can borrow."

Former U.S. President Woodrow Wilson

A decade before the word crowdsourcing existed, Pierre Lévy (1997) proposed a vision of societies living in a state of collective wisdom. In an effort to understand the implications of the interaction of mankind and modern communications technology, he stated, "What then will our new communication tools be used for? The most socially useful goal will no doubt be to supply ourselves with the instruments for sharing our mental abilities in the construction of a collective intellect of imagination" (p. 9).

The author's focus was on democracy, ethics, arts, and spirituality, rather than the more prosaic world of commercialism (Brabham, 2008; Jenkins, 2006); nevertheless, the underlying intention of crowdsourcing is the same: encouraging and embracing collective thought to better the performance of both for-profit and not-for-profit organizations. But what theory, if any, underlies this new approach to decision making within the commodity culture and what does this mean for an organization?

The resource-based view (RBV), strategic-management perspective of the firm is relevant. A basic premise of RBV is the assumption that intellectual effort/skill possessed by a firm is a source of sustainable competitive advantage (Wernerfelt, 1984, 1989). RBV encourages knowledge sharing because alliances gain access to other valuable resources (Connell & Voola, 2007; Das & Teng, 2000), including serendipitous discoveries.

At the heart of the RBV theory, as viewed by Connell and Voola (2007), is heterogeneity. In crowdsourcing, the resources the company has access to (the problem solvers) are not only exogenous to the firm but also highly heterogeneous. Although they may be itinerant across firms, a competitive advantage can be derived by the company using these resources to obtain or maintain a dominant or growing position in their respective markets (Hamel & Prahalad, 1994; Spanos, Zaralis, G., & Lioukas, 2003).

A commonly accepted and efficient means to access heterogeneous and, at least, initially, anonymous individuals is via the web. The advantage of this ever-growing communication tool is that it provides a technology capable of aggregating many dissimilar, autonomous ideas, and if desired, without the dangers of excessive communication and compromise (Surowiecki, 2004). Looking at the social aspect of this new technology, Lévy (1997) alluded to this harnessing of power when he stated, "But cyberspace refers less to the new media of information transmission than to original modes of creation and navigation within knowledge, and the social relations they bring about. . . . It is designed to interconnect and provide an interface for the various methods of creation, recording, communication, and simulation" (p. 118–119).

As Brabham (2008) asserts, "The web provides the means for individuals around the globe to commune in a single environment" (p. 81). Don Tapscott and Anthony Williams (2006), authors of *Wikinomics: How Mass Collaboration Changes Everything* would agree. Initially, their focus was on how firms can embrace technology to "breathe new life into their enterprises." More recent, their purview has broadened.

In Anthony Williams's blog announcing the release of the 2010 sequel, *Macrowikinomics: Rebooting Business and the World*, he comments,

> In this new age of networked intelligence, businesses and communities are bypassing crumbling institutions. . . . In every corner of the globe, businesses, organizations, and individuals alike are using mass collaboration to revolutionize not only the way we work, but how we live, learn, create, and care for each other. (para. 2/3)

Don Tapscott, in an interview with the Economist (Economist Magazine, 2010), expressed reservation with the term crowdsourcing in reference to collaborative innovation because the latter is directed to appropriately qualified individuals, not an amorphous crowd. If one can accept that there can be, for example, a crowd of biochemists, his concern becomes one of semantics.

Surowiecki (2004), in his book *The Wisdom of Crowds*, examines such wisdom at work. Assessing empirical investigations differing from estimating the weight of an ox to sports betting spreads, he found synergistic effects from the crowd in that given the right conditions, groups were found to be remarkably intelligent and often smarter than the brightest people in them. Thus, organizations should think of the web as more than just a communication medium but as an open-design technique (Terranova, 2004); problem solvers should be perceived as creating and innovating *within* a communications medium, rather than witnesses to it (Brabham, 2008).

The web does facilitate the exchange of diverse opinions within the community and can expeditiously aggregate this diversity of thought. Nevertheless, the web is not essential; *the web is a communication technology, not a problem-solving methodology*, as is crowdsourcing. Furthermore, the distinction between communication technologies such as the web and the mobile phone is blurring.

In the developing world, fewer than 20% of people have access to the Internet, yet more than half have a mobile phone. Thus, in response to postelection rioting in Kenya, a concerned citizen launched Ushahidi.com, where private individuals can send content via their mobile phones about violence and crises within their area that are, in turn, used to generate maps of where such events are occurring, as has been done in Gaza and Haiti. Estonians responded to a government call to GPS illegal dumpsites, with 10,000 sites reported. And Nathan Eagle, a scientist at MIT, rolled-out txteagle, where the 2 billion people in developing countries, who own mobile phones, can earn small amounts of money by, for example, texting local price information or completing surveys. Such applications are limited only by one's imagination.

MORE EXAMPLES OF WEB-ENABLED APPLICATIONS

Goldcorp, a Canadian gold mining company, provides an example of web-enabled active crowdsourcing. In March of 2000, it developed the Goldcorp Challenge in which geologic data from their Red Lake Mine was examined by participants from around the world. Offering more than $500,000 in prize money, these examiners were encouraged to submit proposals identifying potential targets of where the next 6-million ounces of gold could be found.

More than 1,400 online prospectors from 51 countries registered as challenge participants, with many proposals not only confirming Goldcorp's suspected deposits but also identifying several new ones (Brabham, 2008; Goldcorp Challenge Winners, 2001).

Who received the prize money and how much was dispersed is unknown to the authors; but the 6-million ounce targeted has a street value of around $7.5 billion. This is a nice and mutually profitable example of how crowdsourcing drove research and development, a classic example of an ill-structured problem. It is possible that the firm did not even know if the 6-million ounce goal was achievable, let alone how to get to the goal.

At present, commercial applications that appear to be burgeoning on the Internet are more banal and user-friendly, where the output from the decision-making effort is intended for mass consumption. Hence, sourcing the masses for their opinions has obvious benefits.

Take, for instance, Threadless (threadless.com), a web-based T-shirt company. The central core of their delivery of superior value is the use of an ongoing T-shirt design competition. Any interested individual can upload their new design for a shirt that conforms to the given guidelines and then wait two weeks while votes are counted on their design. Top-scoring designs are then selected by the Threadless staff, and the winners receive $1,500 in cash and $500 in T-shirts and gift certificates. The benefit to Threadless is that the amount paid for the design is low while the sales for the T-shirts (valued at $10 to $15) can exceed $60,000 per month. This turnover is achieved by a firm with only 20 employees (Brabham, 2008; Howe, 2006c).

But new product development and research and development is not always the objective. Sometimes the "what is" already exists; instead, what interests the organization is making sense of their current offering and reacting to the manner in which the consumer behaves when making decisions about the company, its marketing programs, and its products.

An example of this is Apple's iPhone. At its launch, the iPhone had just a few internally designed software applications and executives claimed that they had no plans to allow others to create new features and applications. However, outside innovators figured out how to hack into the iPhone to create missing applications. In a matter of months, this community had written more than 100 applications.

Executives at Apple decided not to squash this unauthorized external innovation, but instead, they helped it evolve by implementing a formal third-party development program. Besides facilitating access to the technology through the establishment of tools and interfaces that the outside innovators should use, Apple defined a set of licensing terms and a revenue-sharing plan through its iTunes Store.

The overall result of this change in management philosophy was the transformation of the external innovators into a centralized marketplace—a win-win solution, but under Apple's control. However, unlike outsourcing, Apple does not select the individuals/groups that provide the applications, and at its inception, participation was not in response to an open call.

CROWDSOURCING AS A UNIQUE RESEARCH TOOL

Broadly speaking, crowdsourcing can be thought of as an applied approach to market research. The intention is to solve a business problem or at least gain insights relevant to problem resolution. There are, of course, clear points of differentiation. First, market research is "undertaken to assist decision making and problem solving in marketing" (Wilson et al., 2010, p. 4), whereas crowdsourcing is not limited to addressing marketing problems as many of the aforementioned examples illustrated.

Second, in traditional research, care must be taken to ensure the anonymity or confidentiality of participants (Wilson et al., 2010). Crowdsourcing is quite different. By responding to an open call, the individuals may very well want their contact details to be kept so that they can receive any gratuity, if applicable. In some cases, the winner may be offered the opportunity to promote the product or him- or herself. For example, being publicly acknowledged as the solver of a scientific problem or, in the case of Threadless, being offered the opportunity to be product endorsers by uploading photos of them wearing their designs.

A third difference is in the area of research design, especially as applied to experiments. At a simple level, experimentation involves the comparison of groups or individuals who have been differentially exposed to changes in their environment and involves a three-stage process: (1) develop a hypothesis, (2) modify something in the given situation, and (3) compare outcomes with and without the modification. This does not exist with crowdsourcing.

Take, for example, the 2006 Doritos "Crash the Super Bowl" contest. Similar to Threadless, this contest involved asking people to create television ads promoting its chip brand, and then upload these ads to a Doritos website. The public was then asked to vote on five finalists chosen by the company, with the winning commercial aired during the 2007 Super Bowl broadcast, a coveted and expensive advertising period. All the finalists received $10,000 as well as a trip to Miami for a private Super Bowl party and, in due course, all five finalist commercials aired on television.

Via mass trial in countless directions by content providers, a good solution was achieved—as perceived by the masses, albeit facilitated by the company in screening submissions and providing software tools to assist in ad creation. In the Doritos example, there was no hypothesis generation nor were ads *a priori* manipulated. The research process was not an experiment; both the advertisements generated as well as the people participating in the research were not under the firm's control.

This then leads to a fourth difference—people involved in active crowdsourcing are contributing to problem resolution, not subjects as found in traditional research. Consider iStockphoto, a web-based company that sells stock photography, animations, and video clips. To become a photographer for this company one only has to fill out an online form and submit proof of identification along with three photographs. If the photos are judged technically sound by the iStockphoto staff, the photographer can then be admitted as a stock photographer onto their website. Thus, anyone able to operate a camera can potentially earn money as a stock photographer.

Revenue for the photographer comes from clients seeking stock images for use on their websites, brochures, business presentations, and so on. These clients purchase credits ($1 per credit) and buy the stock images they want. Photographs can be purchased, royalty-free, for between one and five credits, with high-resolution photographs, oversized images, and some longer video clips costing as many as 50 credits. For their effort, stock photographers receive 20% of the purchase price anytime one of their images is downloaded (Brabham, 2008).

It should be noted that this crowdsourcing application significantly undermined a source of revenue for professional photographers and no doubt will put many out of business. It is an example of what Schumpeter (see McGraw, 2007) called "creative destruction," and it shows how a nimble competitor can benefit by harnessing the power of a crowd.

HOW, WHEN, AND WHERE TO USE CROWDSOURCING

Unless an organization knows how to use and control crowds, problems will almost certainly arise. Companies have struggled with precisely how to open product development to the external world, as well as how to motivate and manage outside idea generation and problem solving.

Organizations considering using the power of crowdsourcing need to reflect on the dynamics of problem-solving communities. Boudreau and Lakhani (2009), researching management of external innovation, propose two general categories: (1) those that tend to be governed by arm's-length, contractually oriented relationships and (2) communities typically consisting of more informal interactions.

Because the dynamics are so dramatic, companies need to consider carefully which approach makes the best sense for their research objectives. Specifically, the following needs to be considered: (1) the type of issue that will be shifted to crowdsourced problem solvers, (2) how to motivate participants, and (3) how to control the crowd, which affects the nature of the business model platform.

Types of Crowdsourcing Problems

Opening a problem to external participants first depends up the degree of information and knowledge contained within the organization. Should the technology and consumer preferences regarding a product be well understood, then the company can simply conduct internal development or engage in traditional outsourced contracting for that work (Pisano & Verganti, 2008). In these situations, the problem is well structured.

In contrast, should the technology, design, and innovation approaches be less established, are yet to be established, and/or when customer needs are poorly understood—characteristics of an ill-structured problem—then opening the task to the external world becomes more viable. For a variety of reasons, some organizations may lack the ability to crowdsource, as it requires both expertise and some technology that a company may not possess. In these instances, a company can outsource to a firm that specializes in crowdsourcing, such as InnoCentive or IdeaConnection.

Whether a firm conducts crowdsourcing in-house or outsources the crowdsourcing task, the basic question remains: What is the best way to tap the external resource? Some problems are best solved through cumulative effort—these are conjunctive problems. The end-state is best achieved when many individuals are afforded the opportunity to provide incremental contributions, as is the case with Wikipedia. Anyone can contribute to Wikipedia, which does expose the site to vandalism. However, studies suggest that errors tend to be correctly quickly. If problem solving benefits from cumulative knowledge, well-managed communities will have knowledge-sharing and dissemination mechanisms designed into them (Baldwin & Clark, 2006). Common norms can then converge based on a culture of sharing and cooperation, broad agreement on a technology paradigm, and common technical jargon supporting such productive collaboration (Boudreau & Lakhani, 2009; O'Mahony & Ferraro, 2007).

Other problems are disjunctive. The objective is the single-best solution, where in competitive environments it is preferred to control intragroup communication, as were the cases involving T-shirt designs or advertisements. Disjunctive problems are best solved by obtaining a broad range of technical approaches or customer groups (Boudreau, Lacetera, & Lakhani, 2008), the ant colony metaphor, if you will. To encourage trial and foster diversity, a competitive aspect to problem solving must be encouraged. An environment must be created where problem solvers can protect their proprietary interests as they engage in their work. Should their efforts be successful, the benefits will accrue to them as individuals. Participants must therefore be incentivized to differentiate, to search for novel solutions, and to protect rather than share their knowledge with others in the crowdsourced community.

Motivating the Crowd

What motivates participation in these communities in the first place? Tapscott and Williams (2006, p. 70) comment, "People participate in peer production communities for a wide range of intrinsic and self-interested reasons. They feel passionate about their particular area of expertise and revel in creating something new or better." As a simple guide, a competitive disjunctive problem-solving environment tends to best be motivated by extrinsic rewards, while the more collaborative conjunctive problem-solving environment benefits from intrinsic rewards. The choice of motivation will affect the type and number of external problem solvers who participate, as well as the level of effort and investment they devote to the problem resolution process (Belenzon & Schankerman, 2008).

For instance, communities that require mechanisms to facilitate and encourage knowledge exchange and interactions among members can engender a culture of sharing and learning, a sense of affiliation (as well as identity and status), a norm of reciprocity (and other norms regarding conduct, participation, work quality, and effort), and even personal relationships among the participants (Lakhani & von Hippel, 2003). For such a community, their motivation may be purely intrinsic (Deci, Koestner, & Ryan, 1999), as may be found in the community involved in solving the initial iPhone applications problem.

In contrast, the simplest form of extrinsic motivation is financial, for both the organization and the solver. For example, third-party problem solvers who develop software for the Nintendo Wii platform are driven by the potential profits of their efforts. In the medical device industry, established companies rely on physicians (product users) for working prototypes of new products or for concrete suggestions for improvements to existing products and treatments.

Controlling the Crowd

Whatever the company's issue, the decision to open it to external problem solvers means that the company must decide on the degree of control over the flow of communication—that is, from whom to whom. To achieve this, the organization must decide on the best business model or platform to run the research. This issue is particularly important, as it determines who controls the direction of problem resolution as well as the end-customer relationship (and, conversely, how much autonomy is enjoyed by the problem solvers).

Boudreau and Lakhani (2009) advance three business models: integrator, product, and two-sided. In the **integrator** model, the organization is wedged between the problem solvers and customers. In this model, the organization has a high degree of control as it mediates the information between the problem solvers and ultimate customer.

Take for instance, the now-active problem-solving undertaken by Apple and its iPhone. By inserting itself between iPhone software developers and consumers, Apple is able to monitor and directly control transactions with customers. This also places the company in a position to shape development by vetoing applications that it considers undesirable. Apple could go even further by assuming outright possession of externally developed solutions by dictating technical specifications while directly integrating software into the iPhone, thus, acting as a systems integrator, Apple's original strategy (Hobday, Davies, & Prencipe, 2005).

Another integrator example within the scientific community is InnoCentive.com. This Massachusetts-based research center enables scientists to receive professional recognition and financial award for solving research and development challenges, and simultaneously, enables seeker companies (those using the research center for solution to their problems) to tap into the talents of a global scientific community. After posting difficult research and development challenges to the problem solvers, these solvers can then submit solutions through the web. The solvers and their solutions, which go under review by the seeker, remain anonymous during this open phase. If a solution based on the theoretical and methodological proposal meets the technical requirements for the challenge, the seeker company then awards a predetermined cash prize to the problem solver. The submission of these solutions is simple, requiring only the uploading of a word document (Brabham, 2008).

Less control is exerted in the **product** and **two-sided** business models. In both these models, the problem solvers can communicate directly with the end customer, thus, reducing the degree of control for the organization initiating the open call.

Take, for instance, medical device companies and physicians in the product business model. The physician takes the currently developed product, and after a period using the product, the physician makes suggestions for further improvements. In such a case, the physician is moderating the organization/end-user relationship. A similar principle applies in the two-sided model; however, in this model, the organization moderates the problem solver/end-user relationship.

Again, using the medical device company and physician scenario, the physicians may come up with a solution to a problem given to him by the medical device organization after consultation with their patients. In this case, a solution is given to the medical device company, which, in turn, develops the appropriate product for the marketplace in general. In both cases, to exert some control, various rules and regulations are stipulated as a condition for participation in the crowdsourced community.

The process behind decision making when conducting crowdsourcing is given in Figure 11.2.

ETHICAL AND PRACTICAL CONSIDERATIONS

Many ethical and practical factors need to be considered when crowdsourcing. Ethical considerations include the following:

- *Abide by ethical rules of information collection.* If participation is in response to an open call, as in active crowdsourcing, one must still be clear about whether participation is anonymous (participants cannot be identified), confidential (participants could be identified, but identification details have been removed), or neither (a precondition for remunerating participants).
- *Protecting workers rights.* Complaints about having work unfairly rejected and, hence, not compensated are already surfacing and, no doubt, will escalate. And even if compensated, how does a firm fairly divide compensation for collaborative work? Or how should fair remuneration be determined for an "almost perfect solution," but one requiring further work?
- *Determining a fair means to extrinsically motivate participants.* In many active crowdsourcing situations, remuneration is low, often just a few dollars. In light of the low compensation, it should not be surprising that many participants come from low-income countries. Diakopoulos (2009) reports that with respect to Amazon's Mechanical Turk, "22 percent are using the site from India, where $1 to $3 an hour translates to considerably more money." This also suggests that many crowdsourced participants not residing in low-income countries are hobbyists, as is true in the open-source domain.

Figure 11.2 Crowdsourcing: The Decision Making Process

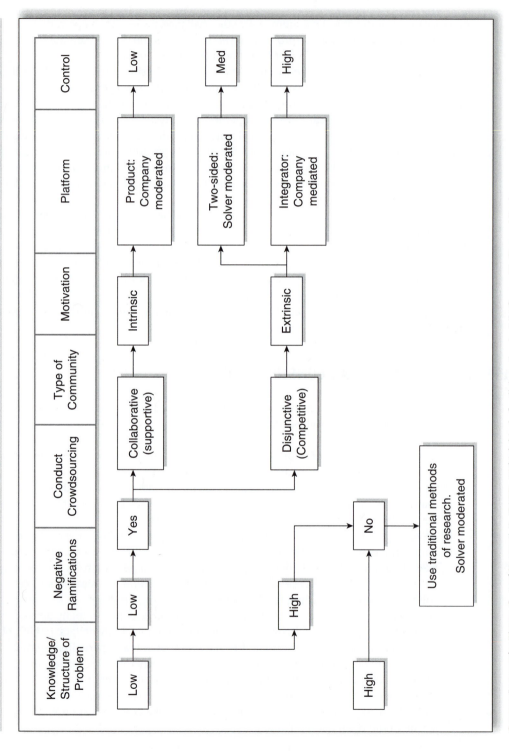

Source: Concept by Pisano G., and Verganti, R. (2008). "Which kind of collaboration is right for you?", *Harvard Business.*

Practical issues abound:

- *Keeping benefits to costs favorable.* As Brabham (2008) notes, "The intellectual labor the crowd performs is worth a lot more than winning solutions are paid" (p. 83). We would caution it is has the *potential* to be worth more, but is no guarantee. An open call may generate tens of thousands of responses, all of which need some level of screening.
- Because crowdsourcing is at the early growth stage in its product life cycle, there is much enthusiasm for this problem-resolution approach and many firms jumping into the domain, whether executed in-house or using independent providers. Like the 1990s dot.com crash, an increasing number of crowdsourced initiatives will fall short of expectations. A washout of independent providers should be assumed. For any combination of the issues listed later, the benefits to crowdsourcing may very well not exceed the costs.
- *Finding the diamond in the grass.* Some speculate that the "junk" in response to an open call constitutes more than 90% of the input; hence locating the diamond can be problematic and take expertise. In fact, research by eMarketer found more than 82 million people in the United States alone created content online (termed "content creators") during 2008, a number expected to grow to nearly 115 million by 2013 (Ostrow, 2009).
- Admittedly, much of this content would have no relevance to crowdsourcing; however, an open call may very well result in a tsunami of feedback. Facebook reportedly has 2.5 billion photos posted on their site each month, a volume that would overwhelm iStockphoto if directed to their site instead.
- *Exposure to competition.* The mere act of making an open call alerts competitors to possible actions that the firm intends or is considering. It also sheds insights into a firm's internal capabilities.
- *Mitigating groupthink.* The intentions of crowdsourcing are to attract or observe heterogeneous individuals. Some would take this to the extreme, arguing for diversity "in terms of gender, sexuality, race, nationality, economic class, (dis)ability, religion, etc." (Brabham, 2008). Arguably, the problem to be solved is simply not relevant or appropriate for such a variety of participants; nevertheless, one must endeavor to attract a crowd that will not merely echo management's opinion.
- *Unintentionally limiting creativity.* Just as some criticize the marketing concept because it tends to encourage firms to focus on evolving products in response to customer feedback rather than encouraging firms to think out of the box with possibly "creative destruction" implications, crowdsourcing is also likely to yield variations to the existing theme. If a crowd is asked to provide input to flavors for coffee, as Starbucks has done, the firm will get exactly that: No one will propose a radically different caffeinated beverage.
- *Loss of control.* Though companies may control the process, how they do so affects their ability to control the crowd. For example, in 2007, Chevrolet intended visitors to create customized ads with the stock video clips and text generator it provided, then to circulate the ads around the web virally. However, visitors took

the opportunity to create commercials deriding anything from Bush's environmental policy to the American automotive industry at large (Bosman, 2006). This illustrates two points: (1) Consumers will not always play along with what companies want them to do, and (2) if whoever is in charge loses control of the crowd, things can turn bad.

CONCLUSION

Social networking has transformed not only the way individuals interact with each other, but it is also a driving force behind a paradigm shift for how companies can harness the power of crowds to solve ill-structured problems. Based in the philosophy that knowledge sharing gains access to other valuable resources and discoveries (Connell & Voola, 2007; Das & Teng, 2000), crowdsourcing can help a company gain competitive advantages in their respective markets (Hamel & Prahalad, 1994; Spanos et al., 2003; Tascott & Williams, 2006, 2010).

In developing a crowdsourcing strategy, executives will have to reconcile the tensions that emerge in trying to define precisely *how* to open problem resolution to the external world. In addressing the three basic issues of (1) what's the level of problem knowledge, (2) how best to motivate external innovators, and (3) what's the best business model, it may be appropriate to apply a *mixed* approach. That is, determine how the principles of crowdsourcing described previously might apply to individual groups of problem solvers, and then construct an appropriate business model and strategy accordingly.

For example, Microsoft has traditionally been hostile to open-source models, but now it realizes that important innovations can be developed in conjunction with a crowdsourced community. To assist this, the company has now defined executive responsibilities for such a strategy, and established staff to assist with development and exchanges of outbound and inbound crowdsourced software. Microsoft's SharePoint is a nice illustration. This server product combines outsourced market-based competitors working on certain elements while a crowdsourced community addresses others (Boudreau & Lakhani, 2009).

TopCoder.com uses a **nested** strategy. This site hosts competitions that connect talented programmers with companies that need software modules developed. Initially motivated by extrinsic rewards, software developers compete fiercely to win prize money associated with particular modules. However, after the competition is over, community members may move to a more collaborative model in which members actively teach one another the ins and outs of various successful approaches that can be used to solve tough programming problems.

This can lead to conflicts between competitive extrinsically motivated markets and collaborative intrinsically motivated communities; hence, mixed and nested approaches can come with potential costs and considerable risks, and they should be deployed with caution and appropriate attention to governing mechanisms (Boudreau & Lakhani, 2009).

A crucial thing to remember is that managers must develop a strategy that makes sense for their particular problem. The key take-away is that a company should develop a research strategy that, at a given time, matches its knowledge of the problem to be solved, the type of crowdsourcing required, the motivations of the problems solvers, and then define its business model. In other words, a company needs to tailor its particular crowd-sourcing approach to the context of its specific business problem. For organizations uncomfortable with answering these issues, many web-based independent providers will assist. If a company is embarking on their first crowdsourcing effort, this is probably a wise choice.

Whether one uses an outsourced specialist firm for crowdsourcing or performs the function in-house, management needs to be cognizant of potential negative ramifications. Consider organizations that possess a highly polarized brand image. Global brands like Nike or McDonalds, or NGOs like Greenpeace should take into account the likelihood that their image is polarized. Although many individuals happily support such major international brands, others see such organizations as exploitive or obstructive. If afforded the opportu-nity to deride the brand, malcontents may seize the moment, as Chevrolet found out to their embarrassment.

Thus, crowdsourcing, like market research, is predicated on carefully defining the prob-lem (including potential negative ramifications), and then designing a set of mechanisms (a research methodology) to govern, shape, direct and possibly constrain the problem solv-ers. Crowdsourcing is not about blindly going to problems solvers and hoping for the best; if so, the firm should brace them self for "garbage out, garbage in."

FURTHER READING

Lakhani, K., & Wolf, R. (2005). Why hackers do what they do: Understanding motivation and effort in free/open source software projects, In J. Feller, B. Fitzgerald, S. A. Hissam, & K. R. Lakhani (Eds.), *Perspectives on free and open source software*. Cambridge, MA: MIT Press.

West, J., & Lakhani, K. (2008). Getting clear about communities in open innovation. *Industry and Innovation, 15*(2), 223–231.

PART IV

Customer Motivation

CHAPTER 12

Understanding Consumer Emotions

How Market Research Helps Marketers Engage With Consumers

ALASTAIR GORDON

Gordon & McCallum Consultants

INTRODUCTION

We are emotional animals. Contrary to earlier theorists who defined humans by the size of our frontal cortex and ability to think rationally, today's academics view the way we process and use emotions as the essential core defining our humanity. Prominent neuroscientist Ray Dolan (2002) points out,

> The importance of emotion to the variety of human experience is evident in that what we notice and remember is not the mundane but events that evoke feelings of joy, sorrow, pleasure, and pain. . . . More than any other species, we are beneficiaries and victims of a wealth of emotional experience. (p. 1191)

The implications of this are vital to 21st century marketing and research. Most practitioners now realize effective measurement and analysis of emotions are key in understanding customer marketplaces. Emotion and branding has become a hot topic with prominent branding gurus like Martin Lindstrom (2008) making strong claims on their links. As he says in his book *Buyology,* "Emotions are the way in which brands encode things of value, and a brand that engages us emotionally—think Apple, Harley-Davidson and L'Oreal just for starters—will win every time" (p. 27).

A strong proponent of the use of neuroscience-based techniques to understand consumers; Lindstrom (2008) has helped give this subject deserved exposure. Unfortunately, such books have sometimes oversimplified discussion of the role of emotion in marketing. Too often, discussion seems to focus on the powerful emotions (love, excitement, and energy) that pull people toward the big brands like Apple. Too little is said about the lower-level emotional responses (familiarity, trust, and safety) that quietly engender habit and keep people from even considering alternatives. *However, emotion is as important a reason for habitual autopilot purchase of Kraft Philadelphia Cream Cheese as it is for the biker who actively chooses a Harley over a Yamaha.*

Researchers discussing this topic need to remember the obviously emotionally charged brands *don't* always win. Microsoft still attracts many sales against Apple; Yamaha is not dead in the water in the superbike market, and L'Oreal has strong competition in most of its categories. Yes, emotion plays a major part in making brands like these great, but big emotions repel some just as they attract others. Brands that carve a highly defined emotional positioning also open opportunities for alternatives among consumers who find their particular emotive messages do not resonate.

Another problem with the hype surrounding this topic is the implication that overtly emotional factors drive *all* consumer choice. This is obviously flawed. A big story in CPG marketing in recent times is the rise of store brands. In many European countries, these now account for 20% to 40% of modern trade CPG sales (Hale, 2010). Store brands' rise provides three useful reminders:

1. Price and value play a part in decision making and *can* override the effect of brand imagery.

2. Some categories are less susceptible to emotional marketing than others.

3. Consumers have to weigh direct emotional attraction (as evoked by packaging or advertising) with diffuse, but even more powerful emotional motivations (such as doing the right thing for the family).

The reality is that the links between emotion and marketing are often subtle. Paper towels, for instance, are a low-involvement category where differentiation by brand personality is clearly helpful (given small functional differences), but emotive response to paper towels is arguably lower level and subtler than a Smartphone. An in-store display ad for a paper towel brand *can* be improved by adding emotional content, but finding triggers linking a paper towel to a consumer's emotional needs is far from obvious.

Emotions then *are* powerful and *do* drive many consumer behaviors. As such, researchers are now working on how we apply this fact across the total spectrum of marketing issues—finding better ways of uncovering emotional response in people's everyday lives and typical choice decisions.

In this chapter, we'll first consider what is really meant by "emotion," and why it matters to marketers. We'll then look at what researchers are doing to solve the issue and what we should do next!

WHY UNDERSTANDING EMOTIONS IS IMPORTANT TO DEVELOPING MARKETING STRATEGIES

Figure 12.1   Are We Wired to Be Negative?

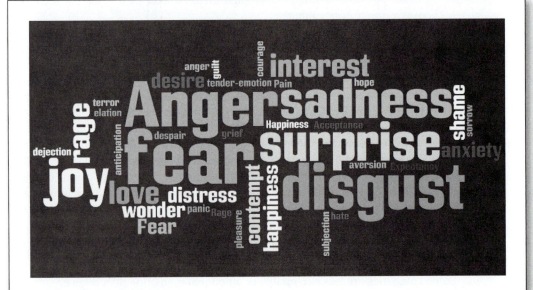

The extent that emotions are innate and/or universal is widely debated. Dr. Paul Ekman (2004) has studied how certain facial expressions seem to be evoked automatically and represent specific emotions. He identifies anger, disgust, fear, joy, sadness, and surprise as core and sees these as biologically determined (not by culture or up-bringing), and this view is gaining acceptance. Some have recognised more elaborate trees of primary, secondary, and even tertiary emotions. For instance, Art Katz (2010), a marketing consultant and author of *Building Your Own Brand Foundation,* has worked with Ekman to build a model of 29 emotions he calls *Emotives.* Such detailed descriptions of emotional language are helpful in categorizing the emotions consumers have toward companies and brands.

Notably, most agreed descriptors of key emotions are negative. The Wordle or word cloud presented here is based on the main emotions listed by nine prominent academics that have published on the subject. Essentially, the size of the words reflects the frequency of academics describing the emotion as key/fundamental. Not only does this list show which emotions are most consistently seen as innately important, it also implies we are more nuanced in expressing negative than positive emotions. (If you are interested in understanding Wordle graphics, visit www.wordle.net to create your word cloud.)

This has repercussions for what emotions we measure. Marketers who have focussed on measuring the "upside" reaction to products or services (top-box liking scores, etc.) may need to examine the "dark-side" of reaction with more care.

Source: Author created with the use of wordle.net.

The word emotion itself is emotionally loaded, often abused, and certainly overused. In daily conversation, it is applied to almost anything we *feel, but can't describe* or regarded as simply the antithesis of reason. Yet there is increasing evidence emotions are not necessarily irrational and are more than just unconscious, uncontrollable drivers unconnected to the rest of our cognitive processes. To use the concept in marketing research, we need to define it.

Alas, academics disagree wildly on the definition of emotion, or even how humans use emotions. Partly, this is because we are still at an early stage of understanding exactly how the brain works. Advances in cognitive psychology, neuroscience research using fMRI (functional magnetic resonance imaging), and similar technologies are transforming our view of the mind and how it works. It's an exciting, but confusing, time. Nevertheless, some key aspects seem to be becoming clear.

- Emotions are more than just influences; we *use* them (consciously or unconsciously) to actively make decisions to decide, for instance, which people to talk to at a party, or whether to prefer McDonalds to Burger King.
- Emotions are mentally efficient; they are automatic responses to events in our environment, and at some level (microfacial expression, brain patterns, etc.) they are difficult to suppress or disguise.
- Much emotional response is biologically hardwired. Core emotions occur across cultures and are expressed (in facial expressions, etc.) in remarkably similar ways. See Figure 12.1 for more on these universal emotions. This is good news for global marketers, as it makes measuring and adapting emotional material seem much more feasible. (Caution is needed though: Anger, surprise, and joy may fire the same neural pathways across cultures, but that doesn't imply an ad that evokes joy in the United States will create the same response in China.)

However, emotions aren't merely a quick way to decide what we should like. Researchers believe emotional response plays a strong part in the formation of memories and in the development of habits. Emotions help us decide what brands and products to notice, and by encoding some into our memory as preferred, *emotions may drive habitual autopilot purchases even when the initial emotional stimuli for preferring a brand is long forgotten.*

So emotional marketing is *not* just about a well-crafted ad eliciting warm feelings about a brand or a new smell or taste setting off an automatic must-try response. Emotional response helps us decide what to ignore. Shoppers, who rush around the supermarket doing a week's shopping in 40 minutes, manage that because they are emotionally predisposed to favor certain brands and can grab them automatically. Even when the in-store environment forces consideration of alternatives (perhaps their brand is out of stock or a big promotion brings a forgotten brand to mind), emotions evoked by color, style, or pricing level automatically come into play and allow rapid choice.

Suffice it to say, without emotion we'd have to rationally consider every possible feature and variant—we'd never get out of the store!

Emotions, then, help leading brands be bought without thought. And language and visual imagery can be used to evoke emotions and grab attention. Stephen Pinker (2007) in *The Stuff of Thought* shows understanding of words is automatic and those with strong emotional connotations act as hooks to distract and grab our attention.

Taboo words are particularly effective in this. As Pinker (2007) points out: "A speaker or writer can use a taboo word to evoke an emotional response in an audience quite against their wishes" (p. 333). It's not just stand-up comedians who take advantage of this. The British clothing chain, French Connection (UK), branded itself FCUK grabbing huge attention with edgy ads using taglines like, *"FCUK Fashion."* (Interestingly, as the brand evolved and targeted a wider market the "FCUK" branding has been deemphasized.) Similarly, a budget airline, Asia Air, advertised cheap fares to a popular holiday destination, Phuket in Thailand (pronounced in fact, "Foo-Ket") with billboards proclaiming, "Cheap Enough to Say, Phuket, I'll Go!"

However, although emotions can force us to pay attention almost against our will, they are not quite the drivers of irrational decisions, as we once thought. Recent years have seen a major expansion in our knowledge of human decision making based on experiments in the areas of neuroscience (e.g., direct study of brain activity in response to stimuli—we'll discuss the techniques used later in this chapter) and cognitive psychology (the study of our internal mental processes including how memory, perception, and learning happen). Such research has thrown into doubt the traditional concept of emotionally based decision making being ineffective, or suboptimal, compared to more rational processes. That is, research is showing that in many contexts decisions based on intuitive and emotional criteria work better than those that are the result of longer, rational deliberation. Gerd Gigerenzer (2007) of the Max Planck Institute has written extensively on this. (His work was a key inspiration for Malcolm Gladwell's popular book *The Tipping Point*.) Gigerenzer shows how simple rules of thumb (heuristics) are used to make thousands of choices every day. Although often based on emotional criteria, these still turn out to be accurate and efficient ways of making a reasonable choice. Applied to buying behavior, this means that not only is emotional response fast but also it's an efficient mechanism to make *correct* (or at least reasonable) decisions between many similar products.

For marketing, the most powerful of these heuristics is the recognition heuristic, the finding *we have a strong, innate tendency to pick the familiar.* Recognition of a brand tends to evoke positive emotions (happiness, attachment, and so on), and this is often enough to trigger a buying response with minimal thought. For researchers, this helps explain why brand last bought remains in most categories a good predictor of next purchase, and why (contrary to some writing on emotional branding) evaluating advertising effectiveness on brand recall and recognition remains important. *Recognition and the emotional content of brands are intimately linked; familiarity triggers its own sort of emotional response.*

My favorite example of both the emotional power of familiarity, and the way words can evoke unexpected responses occurred when Lipton's Tea in Australia changed the name of their main brand (with a long heritage in the market) from "Lipton's Tea" to "Lipton's *Black* Tea." This was part of a strategy to improve appeal to younger tea drinkers and create differentiation from newer, flanker products (flavored teas). The change wasn't treated as a big deal with mass advertising; changes were confined to the name and a few minor alterations to the package.

Result? Sales plummeted, almost overnight. Brand consideration dropped from 82% to 69%. Not due to any obvious connotations of the word "black" itself, but rather the confusion it caused. Consumers noticed and started *thinking* about the brand. They fretted over whether it was the same Lipton's they'd always bought and whether its flavor was altered. Autopilot choice was disrupted and another common heuristic kicked in: the risk-avoidance rule.

That is, consumers reached for the second brand on their mental list. In the event, Lipton's and their agency (JWT) responded swiftly and turned a problem into an advantage: they acknowledged the error and quickly launched a witty campaign, ultimately reversing the slump and even raising sales. This case shows how a seemingly innocuous change in packaging can trigger an emotional response with major consequences.

Once again, discussion of heuristics raises the question of how emotional and rational choice processes interact. It's a question that causes heated debate among marketers and cognitive theorists alike. Some theorists feel that the process involves two steps. In the first stage, we use automatic, simple—often emotionally based—choice criteria (does it smell nice, is it familiar, etc.). If the choice to be made is relatively unimportant to us (e.g., in low-involvement categories), then the first stage may be enough, and we just grab the brand that seems best with little conscious thought. If the choice is more important though, then this model suggest the first stage emotional or nutritive choice still applies, but only to define our consideration set by eliminating brands or products that really do not appeal at all. In this latter case, we then go to Stage 2 and involve the frontal cortex, making a final choice using more rational criteria.

The problem with this model is that it doesn't fit my experience as a researcher. In working on categories like mobile phones, for example, I've seen numerous examples of consumers screening brands and models on reasonably functional criteria, such as size of screens or price range, then making a final choice based on highly emotional factors like status or a general perception of coolness. Similarly, work I've done on low-involvement categories showed a huge mix of rational and emotional criteria working at the early stages of choice (for instance, in one study of paper towel choice, we found one group of people who vetoed a range of brands for the good reason they did not fit on their paper towel holders and another group whose core choice criteria was a strong viewpoint on what patterns were cutest).

More recent, a group of cognitive psychologists have argued for a parallel model of information processing. That we use heuristics and simple criteria, especially emotion-based ones, all the time and in all of our decision making, but under certain circumstances (if the decision is an important one, someone else we know cares, or simply some stimulus that makes us consider the issue in more depth), our rational decision-making apparatus is called in to play. From the perspective of these academics, emotional criteria don't switch off when the rational brain kicks in—it may be more a dialogue or debate between the two. Or even, as recent research suggests is common, a matter of the rational brain providing narrative and story to justify an emotive prejudice (Gilovich & Griffin, 2002).

Whatever the model, it's clear that the old-school dichotomy, where customers making some decisions rationally and others emotionally, is dead in the water. Emotional triggers play a part in *most* purchase decisions, whether in so-called low-involvement categories or high-involvement ones, and our brains seem perfectly capable of adjusting or modifying these emotive inputs.

How emotions fit into our decision-making processes is at the heart of why emotion matters to marketers, and it is at the core of many of the most exciting new developments in research.

HOW MARKETERS USE EMOTIONAL RESPONSES

So what should marketers be trying to do with emotions? In my view, there are seven key ways emotional response can help (or hinder) marketing:

1. *Emotions act as triggers and create change.* Strong emotional response is more likely to create a moment of change for consumers than any rational evaluation of benefits. Marketing is becoming increasingly granular as point of sales and guerrilla marketing tactics supplant topline advertising. Understanding and describing precise emotional tipping points is vital.

2. *Emotions reinforce and drive improvements in brand equity.* Brands building longer-term emotional connections with consumers enjoy higher levels of loyalty and improve their ability to charge a price premium.

3. *Emotions facilitate brand buzz and communication.* People like to talk, Tweet, share, and recommend brands that evoke strong emotional reactions. In an increasingly connected world, this is an important virtue (or potentially a major problem).

4. *Emotions are essential building blocks around which a brand can define itself.* The bedrock of a brand's personality, a key component in most major brands efforts to present a coherent and attractive image to consumers, is the emotional connection between the brand and the customer.

5. *Emotions are navigators through an increasingly cluttered world of brands and media.* As noted previously, emotions save us thinking in-depth about every possible choice we are faced with, providing an instantaneous mechanism for choice. They reinforce habit, hence, the leading-brand advantage.

6. *Emotions can be used to define psychographic and similar segmentations.* By defining consumers in the similarity of their emotional outlook on life or emotive response to a product category, advertisers have often been able to craft more effective campaigns than by relying on traditional demographic segmentation.

7. *Emotions can help lower the cost and failure rate of new product development.* New products are more likely to fail than succeed. Accurate reading of emotional response to a product or service reduces this risk. More sophisticated methods of evaluating emotional reaction to sensory stimuli (taste, tactile characteristics, aroma, etc.) open better, faster ways of screening concepts. Neuroscience can also reveal how branding triggers emotional responses that override purely sensory reactions. Research suggests if Coke had access to neuroscience on how the emotions of their brand impacted choice, they might have avoided the whole New Coke debacle as they could have better judged the value of brand heritage versus taste (McClure, Jian Li, Tomlin, Cypert, & Montague, 2004).

These are seven important ways that understanding emotion can improve marketing and drive sales. Later, we will consider what kinds of emotional research best support these different objectives.

Emotional response also impacts business in less-direct ways. One area is *brand valuation,* where companies. such as Brand Finance and Interbrand, assign dollar values to brands. Brand Finance claims its research shows, "62% of the world's business is now intangible. This represents $19.5 trillion of $31.6 trillion global market value. Intangibles include the value of brand goodwill, customer relationships, talent and similar soft assets" (Brand Finance, n.d.). Emotional attachment to brands and services clearly matter in assessing these.

Nowadays, Nike is defined by brand persona, not its shoes. Apple, of course, has built a strong emotional connection with consumers by attaching to its brand a strong feeling of belonging. Similarly, companies such as Google enjoy an advantage in attracting talent because their image encourages the best people to work for them.

If emotional response to brands, products, and companies affects all areas of business, from in-store purchase to share market valuation, then it needs to be evaluated carefully. In the past though, market research has been of limited help because our measures of emotion have lacked precision and detail.

This is changing. It's now conceivable that emotional branding measures will evolve so a genuine currency for brand emotion can be created. Senior managers may one day await the monthly statistic on emotion value with the anticipation and trepidation currently given to IMS or Nielsen measures of market share and sales.

MARKET RESEARCH AND MEASURING EMOTION: DON'T WRITE OFF THE SURVEY YET

As the science of the mind is increasingly applied to business issues, the research industry's ability to measure unconscious emotion and motivations has been critiqued. As far back as 1998, David Wolfe wrote, "If your job depends on market research, prepare for a shock. New discoveries in brain science . . . are rewriting the conventional wisdom about consumer behavior. Conventional marketing research depends on the assumption that people can accurately report their values, needs, and motivations. But many scientists no longer believe this. 'We have reason to doubt that full awareness of our motives, drives, and other mental activities may be possible,' says neurologist Richard Restak" (Restak, as quoted in Wolfe, 1998, p. 24).

This characterization was a bit thin then and looks quite dated today. Even in 1998, many researchers were aware of limits of relying on purely rational questions to explain consumers' deeper motivations. Global players like Unilever were already using techniques like Peter Cooper's Extended Creativity Groups to delve into the consumer psyche, or models such as Heylen's Impsys to create emotion-based segmentations.

Nor is conventional research as useless as implied previously. Restak (Wolfe, 1998) is correct, and people can't achieve *full* awareness of *all* their motives and drivers, but they *can* reveal quite a lot. True, a questionnaire or group focusing only on direct questions about obvious product/service features will miss emotional drivers and invite a rationalized or socially desirable response. Asked to rank a range of features desired in a car, many will put safety at the top, even though it's seldom decisive when it comes to purchase. The emotion

Figure 12.2   Better Emotional Responses From Traditional Research

Many texts deal with basic questionnaire design and how to run focus groups. Here are five things they talk about less but which can help any study get more in-depth emotional content.

1. *Ask about the key topic in several ways.* Different people respond differently to different kinds of questions. Triangulate on the key objective and get a wider variety of feedback by mixing up questions types in surveys. In groups, mix collage with role-play and other exercises—don't just sit and talk!

2. *Help people feel OK about discussing sensitive subjects.* How a moderator frames a group is key to getting emotional response. Initial, nonthreatening warm-up time is important, as are exercises that let people express feelings indirectly. In questionnaires, try using projective questions asking people indirectly about how they think others would view the subject.

3. *Give people time to tell a story and listen.* It takes time before people start talking emotionally. It's more important to cover the key topics well than to than to tick off the boxes on every subject in the discussion guide. In online surveys, add a story question at the end: "Tell me your most happy memory of driving in your Ford." A simple question like this can yield a lot of emotion.

4. *Don't rate everything on five-point scales.* Standard scales provide reliable, replicable answers. However, when it comes to emotion, they are often not discriminating and encourage rationalization. Forcing people to rate every possible attribute encourages feelings on areas that in reality they don't care about. Make sure you give respondents the chance to decide for themselves what matters. Try using visual scales as alternatives when emotional feedback is key.

5. *Don't take emotional feedback at face value.* Manufacturers spend hours thinking about many feelings that might apply to their brands. Consumers *don't*. They combine emotions into broader feelings about "trust," "sadness," etc. Look for underlying patterns to group emotions (using statistical techniques like factor analysis). In groups, topline emotions gauged through the two-way mirror can be a poor indicator of what's going on. Take time to analyze transcripts and videos, consider body language, and what people *did not* say, not just their surface level response.

matters in car purchase can be clearly seen in the emotive positioning adopted by many of the most expensive marques (e.g., BMW is "The Ultimate Driving Machine," and with Porsche, "There is No Substitute").

But this is a failing of the questions asked and the topics covered, not the method. Properly designed and analyzed surveys and carefully conducted qualitative research can yield good emotional feedback and marketers need not always search for new techniques to get useful information.

My experience of studying consumer markets around the globe and in categories from toilet paper to luxury cars indicates people are usually capable of describing and ranking brands on basic emotional or values criteria (e.g., describing brands in relation to words with established emotional connotations, such as "trust," "joy," etc.). Usually, this results in a fair emotional profile of the brand and an ability to map key differences between brands. For many marketing purposes, this is a good first step in understanding the strong and weak emotional connections consumers have with brands.

EMOTIONS AND EMERGING MARKET TRENDS

Although standard survey questions and qualitative research provide useful information on emotional response *if used properly* (see Figure 12.2), they have limitations. Beyond the obvious issue of rationalization of answers, these include the following:

- *Relying on recall.* Emotions are complex and fleeting. It's easy to forget what I was feeling when I bought my car three months ago and even harder to articulate what I do recall.
- *Problems dealing with rapidity of emotional change.* I can give a reasonable overall approximation of my reaction to a new Sprite ad, but research shows my reaction is likely to vary almost frame by frame, so my response in the first 10 seconds may be very different from my overall reaction.
- *Not real-time.* Traditional methods of gauging emotional reaction often require recoding, reanalysis, and interpretation. But the pace of change in modern markets means service delivery, management of promotional events, or public relations all have to be extremely responsive. You want to know what they feel, right now.
- *Lack of nuance.* Emotions, especially on everyday subjects, such as purchasing a brand of frozen peas or visits to a specific website, aren't subjects we articulate well. Words are often inadequate to convey mixed and subtle reactions. Forced to describe or rate our emotional response, we may focus on a recent easy-to-describe experience, which only partially describes our emotional picture of a brand.
- *Lack of depth.* Ask in a standard manner why I bought Pantene shampoo on my last shopping trip, and I'll probably focus on "quality" or maybe "it was on promotion." Probe again and you may find I think Pantene has a more "up-market image," or "I like its fragrance." But you probably won't get much depth on social influences (e.g., balancing my wife's choice with mine), which particular sensory experiences *most* impacted my choice, or how the emotions evoked by Pantene's advertising fit into a wider picture of my personality and motivations.

Fortunately, newer research methods becoming available are providing answers to some of these problems.

Less fortunately, it seems almost every marketing researcher is jumping on the emotion bandwagon. A Google search on "emotion and marketing research" yields thousands of hits, the first few pages dominated by agencies offering unique and best practice approaches. These range from enhanced qualitative techniques, through online projective methods to in-depth MRI scanning. No wonder research clients become confused by the profusion of claim and counterclaim.

In the balance of this chapter, we'll examine what is *most* important about the new developments, and how users of research should assess which to use for particular purposes.

To do this, it helps to think of emotion research as being composed of three buckets:

1. *Frameworks, models and theories f*or understanding the role of emotion in marketing. These help describe what emotional values a brand has to deliver against and how well it is doing on those.

2. *Methods and tools* for enhancing self-reported emotional response. These add accuracy and efficiency in how we get people to reveal their deeper motivations.

3. *Technologies* enabling direct (passive) recording of emotional response, without the consumer necessarily being asked any direct questions at all. These hold out the promise of direct and scientific measurement.

Most research services combine two or three of these buckets: a framework about how emotions impact consumers and tools to assess emotional response within their system. But some focus on the framework or model and others on the interview approach or technology. So we can reasonably look at examples within each bucket. Note: I am picking examples based on their being typical of a type and do not endorse any of them over other alternatives.

FRAMING EMOTION: GETTING TO THE BIG PICTURE

Recently, I heard the CEO of a bed manufacturing company describe her task, in the face of imports of low-cost beds, as no longer to sell beds, but to sell their brand's contribution to a total sleep experience. They want to move from selling functional aspects of beds (frames and springs) to wooing consumers with a total package of emotions and benefits promising a better sleep experience. Helping clients with complex challenges requires examination of a wide range of emotional and rational drivers and thought applied to how they interrelate.

This requires looking beyond the immediate trigger role of emotions and analyzing them in the context of other choice drivers. Real-life involves practical limits (budget), considering the views of others, and buying in places where competitive messages simultaneously target our emotions.

Consider buying a car. New research techniques allow researchers to test your response to various models and get a direct read on your *real* (subconscious) preference. But outside the lab, when you set out to purchase, you're exposed to multiple ads and articles, plus the opinions of friends, partners, and children. Looking a car over, you'll see details that modify your initial preference (hey, look at that cool rear-view camera) or uncover rational factors that matter (Grandma will have trouble stepping up into this). Then a salesperson comes along and sows doubts about your choice. Between your initial overall emotional preference and final decision, there is much room for slippage.

This welter of emotional influences implies effective brand building and requires us to relate immediate emotional response to broader motivations. This means packaging emotions, and researchers are doing this in several ways. Here are some:

Brand resonance and similar frameworks are used by marketing academics, such as Kevin Keller (Kotler & Keller, 2006), to facilitate brand management. They see emotional inputs as impacting brands in a layered manner, by first helping grab attention, then by developing favorable brand associations, then by provoking positive active reactions, and finally in developing brand loyalty. Such integrated models believe emotional drivers need to combine with rational ones to create deeper brand relationships. Positive emotional imagery needs to be combined with useful performance attributes for instance.

A related brand management concept involves **brand personality**, a way for brands to develop and maintain emotionally engaging personas that resonate with consumers' personalities and aspirations. A brand's personality provides a basis for thinking about all the places a brand touches a consumer's life and how emotional marketing can trigger reactions at each point.

In *MORE Guerilla Marketing Research*, Robert Kaden and Gerald Linda (2009), two of the coeditors of this book note, brand personality

> is a function of every public contact made by a brand: the corporate logo, advertising, public relations, packaging, website, name, sales force appearance and behavior, customer service, office décor, building architecture and certainly the design and performance of the product or service being sold. (p. 180)

They go on to show integrated approaches using emotional triggers to grab attention and engage customers at each of these touch points to build coherent brand personalities. By examining brands like Caterpillar, they also make it clear the usefulness of evoking emotion to build brand personas is not confined to mass market, heavily advertised brands.

Other approaches to creating useful frameworks for emotional research have focused on identifying deeper motivations seen as underpinning specific emotional responses.

Needscope (marketed by TNS around the world) summarizes human emotions into archetypes—instinctual patterns of emotive behavior, which they believe are universal. Needscope argues these archetypes relate to and help drive broader consumer needs states. Some of these are accessible and easy to understand functional needs, but others are deeply buried emotional desires. By employing projective techniques (based on proprietary photosets and collages) to get consumers to reveal their underlying motivations and brand perceptions, Needscope attempts to describe and map brands in relation to the most relevant psychological drivers for a particular market.

These are shown on a Needscope map, such as the Figure 12.3.

Maps like this provide a psychological segmentation of a market in contrast to standard demographic or usage ones, aiming to show a brand's degree of emotional differentiation and to reveal the extent of alignment with the emotive needs of consumers in the category. In this map for instance, the segment names are a shorthand, describing the psychological

Figure 12.3   Needscope's Emotion-Determined Consumer Categories

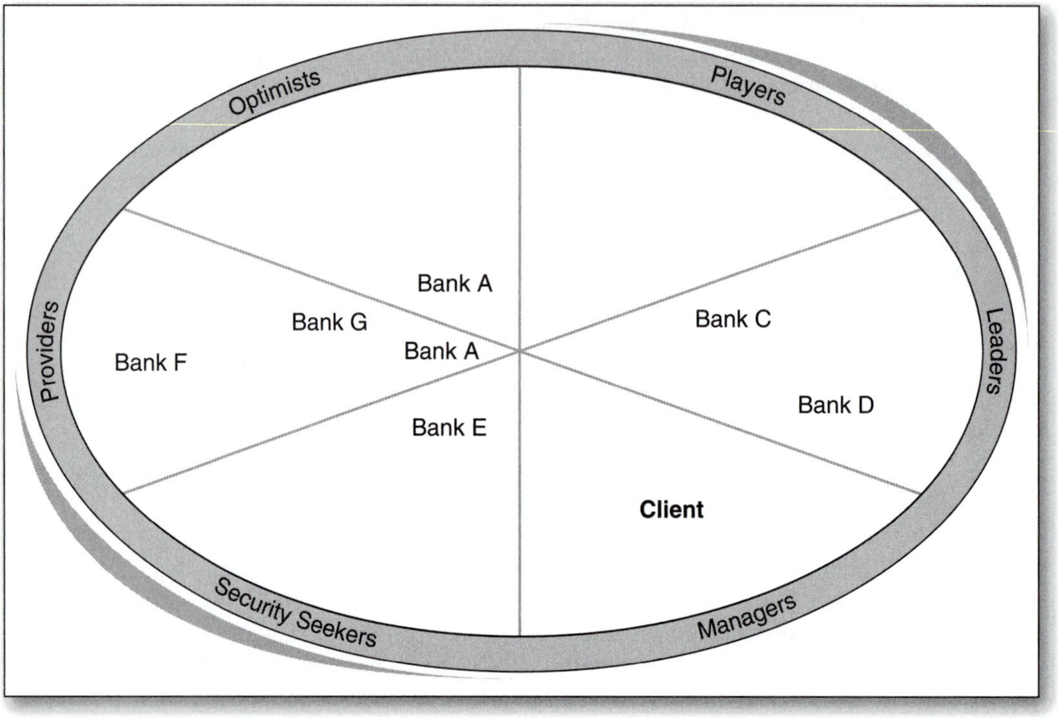

Source: NeedScope.

drivers that underpin them. Thus, security seekers, self-evidently, are risk-averse and looking primarily for financial security. Managers, who the map shows as most associated with the client brand, are driven by a need to be in control, have the right tools and information to make their money work for them, and have a longer-term focus versus other segments (such as the optimists). Not only can such maps help clients think about how and whether they should reposition their brands but, clearly, each of these needs states imply that differing products, servicing, and advertising might appeal to each segment.

Although needs-based models have come from some criticism in recent years, they are widely used by major companies across the globe and still represent one of the most coherent attempts to manage brands in emotional terms (Wilson & Calder, 2006).

Finally, in this area, several researchers are focusing on the exact role of emotions in purchase choice (e.g., how emotions interact with price range and social influences) and in synthesizing these into category relationship frameworks. Such work is influenced by the academic work on emotion's role in information processing and the creation of habits noted earlier (one such system was created by a team at Nielsen, led by the author, and is marketed as DeltaQual).

Clearly, then, as marketers increasingly attempt to integrate strategic and tactical marketing, more sophisticated frameworks for understanding how emotion impacts all stages of the consumer purchase funnel will become more important (Neale, 2008).

BETTER TOOLS FOR MEASURING EMOTIONS

A major argument against conventional research's capacity to understand emotional response is that the very tools and techniques used are predicated on a rational model of information gathering. Precisely defined wordings and rigid ratings scales force respondents to engage their rational brain and attempt to categorize and rank what are generally considered intrinsically soft and ill-defined phenomena and feelings. It's as if Mr. Spock were sent to evaluate Barney, the dinosaur.

Many researchers have reacted against this, and try to create techniques to evoke emotions more directly without being compromised by the way the brain processes language. BrainJuicer (a United Kingdom company) uses a method called FaceTrace, which captures response to pictures of faces rather than points on a scale. The faces represent Ekman's (2004) key human emotions.

BrainJuicer asserts measures like this provide more accurate assessments of the feeling response. For instance, they also claim to predict ad effectiveness better than conventional measures such as persuasion or brand linkage. They

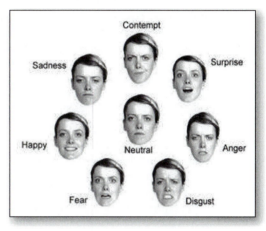

Figure 12.4   BrainJuicer Emotional Response Cues

Source: Reprinted with permission © BrainJuicer 2006.

believe traditional measures actually "actively discriminate against highly effective ads" making the use of alternatives even more essential. Moreover, BrainJuicer suggests their measure, which is rooted in the universality of emotional expression in humans, is actually more culturally transferable than semantic scales, which are subject to cultural and linguistic biases (Wood, 2010).

Other companies have taken up the idea of using images to better tap into emotions. Conquest Research has developed an approach called Metaphorix, using visual metaphors. Respondents see an animated picture based scenario "representing a metaphor associated with an emotion—for example, proximity/closeness as a metaphor for intimacy" (Penn, 2008, p. 10). They are asked (for instance) to move a cartoon figure representing themselves along a sofa to be closer or further away from a picture of the brand or product being investigated. Like BrainJuicer, Conquest believes their system predicts *real* brand preference much better than conventional measures.

Online interviewing and devices like the iPad makes the use of such techniques far more feasible than they used to be. Many respondents find these approaches engaging (an advantage given declining survey response rates), and the companies using them are gaining acceptance from major clients. However, these measures are not without controversy and have been criticized for issues of consistency, reproducibility, and cultural transference. Now, the industry is divided on their role, and I would certainly agree that some care is appropriate in the use and analysis of results from these question types.

Nevertheless, my overall experience is that they markedly improve discrimination between respondents and give more nuanced and useful data on soft subjects like emotions. Expect to see such questions become a regular part of most researchers' toolboxes in the future.

But some researchers feel it isn't the questions we've gotten wrong. *They take issue with the whole idea of independent researchers asking a random selection of strangers a bunch of preset questions on an irregular basis.* "Who really reveals their innermost feelings in a 15-minute structured interview?" they ask. People only reveal emotions, so goes the argument, if you engage with them and develop a relationship that encourages dialogue. Companies such as Communiscape in the United States and Verve in the United Kingdom use specialist customer advisory panels and online communities that aim to let their clients engage directly with customers on an ongoing basis.

Compared to traditional customer advisory/test panels, these new communities are typically both longer lasting and larger (usually more than 200 people and often many thousands). Moreover, unlike traditional consumer panels, these are not intended to simply track survey responses, *but to provide an ongoing 24/7 forum for a dialogue and conversation between client and customer.* The aim is to provide marketers with on-tap access to spontaneous feedback from customers—clients can dip into the panel to generate quick responses to new ideas, public-relations events, or possible product concepts. All this is made possible because of the development of sophisticated software tools that enable free-flowing interaction between client, customer, and researcher.

In this model, the researcher's job is much more about facilitating and interpreting a conversation than structuring and analyzing a questionnaire. This approach is not only used to get richer customer feedback but it also ventures into areas where research support has been limited in the past. One such example is cocreation, where panelists help marketers develop and refine marketing materials. This is an area where traditional customer advisory panels have been widely used in the past, but the new communities offer much bigger panels, faster speed of response, geographic diversity, and an opportunity for independent exchange of ideas among participants—all of which promise new opportunities for collecting emotional response. It's an interesting approach, and some major banks and telecom clients are already using such panels to redefine customer engagement

For emotion research. generally, the use of online communities and customer panels provides several key advantages: Their always-on nature allows the collection of much response information that can be mined for emotional content. Also, because they provide for interactive spontaneous feedback, they are likely to increase the chance of picking up unguarded comments. Perhaps most important, they offer easier means for studying emotional issues not covered well in one-off studies, for instance the role of social influences or changes in emotional response over time. This also means they could be useful in helping us understand how short-term triggers (e.g., an attractive promotion or an ad with great visuals) impact customers' long-term emotional relationships with a brand. Eventually, these panels are likely to incorporate many of the new emotional feedback tools noted here to examine these issues, making the use of such communities in more strategic areas, such as brand building, more enticing.

NEUROSCIENCE AND NEUROMARKETING: ADDING SCIENCE OR HYPE

It's still a very tiny proportion of all market research, but research using techniques borrowed from neuroscience has grabbed much attention. Essentially, these aim to bypass all the problems of self-reported emotions by doing away with direct questioning and relying on passive methods to collect emotional response.

If some stimulus provokes an emotional response—and most things do—this sets off rapid and subconscious physiological and mental activity. See a sad image of a baby in distress and specific neurons in the brain will fire, small muscles in your face will contract causing an unconscious change in your expression, and minor changes in skin temperature or blood pressure are likely.

Research shows none of these reactions are easily avoidable. After a few seconds, your frontal cortex may kick in and reinterpret the picture as "maudlin, not sad" and reset your face from "sad" to "sneer," but if—before that happens—we can somehow measure your immediate response, we have an insight into your feelings at a level even you may not be aware of.

This is made feasible by new technologies coming to the fore in the last decade. It would take a whole book (or a good chapter such as the one in this book) to sum up all the exciting new systems coming on-stream, much less to tackle their competing claims for efficacy. Broadly though, they break down into two groups:

- Autonomic measures
    - Facial expression measurement (techniques assessing changes in microexpressions)
    - Electrodermal reaction (changes in electrical properties of the skin)
    - Eye-tracking systems
- Brain imaging
    - EEG (Electroencephalography: records electrical activity along the scalp produced by firing of neurons within the brain)
    - fMRI/MRI (functional magnetic resonance imaging, a variant of MRI brain-scanning common in hospitals. Measures changes in blood flow associated with neural activity in specific areas of the brain.)

Figure 12.5 People Wearing EmSense's EmBan EEG Measurement Devices

Source: EmSense Corporation.

In rough terms, the autonomic measures are usually less direct and precise in their ability to measure emotional response, while brain-imaging techniques tend to be more intrusive, costly, and difficult to use with bigger samples. (However, effort is being put into improving the accuracy of the autonomic measures while others try to reduce the cost and intrusive nature of the brain imaging methods)

So how do these methods work and what are they good for? They often work on an experimental model, rather than a classic sample-survey approach. A small sample is tested, given, or shown a stimuli, and reactions are recorded. For this reason, they are often used as substitutes for classic advertising, concept, or product tests. Here their directness and ability to get below conscious rational responses potentially have impressive advantages. A United States company, NueroFocus (a subsidiary of the Nielsen Company) claims their use of EEG and complementary methods means their ad effectiveness testing systems

> Provides detailed, second-by-second responses to these questions, including highly actionable insights into the effectiveness of your advertising. Great advertising strikes a responsive chord with consumers where it matters most: the subconscious. Only neurological testing can make the "deep dive" required to access that level of the brain and discover how it responds to all forms of advertising, in every medium. (NeuroFocus, 2011, para. 2)

The concept of measuring which emotional responses are switched into long-term memory is a particular advantage of brain-imaging-based systems, and over time, they may help us work out what kinds of stimuli most contribute to loyal, habitual buying behaviors.

Another company, Swiss-based, nViso is experimenting with recording emotional response by using intelligent software systems with webcams to analyze changes in facial microexpressions, translating these into measures of specific emotions. This allows a very nonintrusive approach to measuring advertising and similar stimuli, and it lets clients and the agency receive live second-by-second feedback. Figure 12.6 shows a respondent in a nViso test watching an ad while the emotions she felt are recorded on a second-by-second basis.

The potential of systems such as this to provide richer, more granular feedback on emotional response is clear. They provide direct feedback on exactly which frame of a commercial or storyboard is evoking what emotion, in terms those who create advertising can understand and respond.

The use of neuroscience-inspired technology is not confined to communications or product testing. Neurofocus carries out work on brand imagery development while another company, EmSense, employs neuroscience techniques (via their mobile EEG devices) to tackle key retail issues, such as understanding shoppers' journeys around the store, staff interaction experiences, and the effectiveness of point-of-sales materials.

As with any new methods, there are naturally debates about accuracy and effectiveness. Marketers wanting to use these techniques would be well advised to do some careful assessment or get independent advice. But the real issue is their air of scientific certainty can blind us to their limitations. Neuroscience may be better at telling us *what* people are

Figure 12.6   nViso in Action

Source: nViso.

feeling in response to stimuli, but there is still room for debate on the issues of *why* and *how* the feelings will translate into real-life behavior.

It is vital to remember neuroscience tests are subject to many of the same limitations as other research. In a recent article, marketing academic Caroline Yoon and colleagues (Yoon Gonzalez, & Bettman, 2009) noted many problems in using fMRI for marketing research derived from interpretation difficulties arising because the research was not planned carefully enough. If people aren't exposed to an appropriate range of packages or you don't test a sufficient range of consumers, an advanced neuroscience test is not going to be any more predictive than a conventional packaging test.

Yoon et al. (2009) also argue fMRI should not be used as a stand-alone methodology and researchers should "seek convergent validity" by linking fMRI data to other measures such as self-reported purchase behavior, reaction time, or eye tracking data. Professionals directly involved in the field have also made this point. Graham Page, Executive Vice President for Millward Brown's Global Neuroscience Practice, notes, "Hype means it is very easy to get carried away with exaggerated claims [for neuroscience]. The results don't stand on their own: you have to combine this with something else" (Bain, 2010a, para. 6).

I couldn't agree more. Neuroscience methods have huge potential, but they are not the whole answer. They represent an increasingly powerful tool, however, and researchers should keep a close eye on this rapidly evolving area.

DECIDING ON THE BEST EMOTIONAL MEASURES FOR THE SITUATION

I've necessarily left out many good examples—notably clever new developments in qualitative, online qualitative, and the role of social media research in analyzing self-revealed emotion on places like Twitter. But we've seen something of the range of current effort: From dialoguing with customer panels though to neuroscience experiments, there are rapid developments everywhere.

However, so many, vastly different, approaches means it can be hard to work out how to best to approach researching the subject. Unfortunately, given the rapidity of advances in theory and technology, this confusion is only likely to worsen. Currently, despite much hype, there is no silver-bullet approach, no one method that will tell you all you need to know. As with marketing research on any subject, it's about prioritizing what you really need to know and then picking methods and vendors to fit those objectives.

The good news is there are advantages in most current approaches, and few will give really bad or wrong information—mostly, it's a matter of depth and coverage. Here's what we tell Gordon & McCallum clients:

1. *Know the basic facts before doing in-depth studies on emotions* (usage, demographics, lifestyle, etc.). Emotional engagement with a service or product varies markedly with usage, for instance. Consider how a frequent user of Facebook might react to changes in the interface or service offered versus a person who dips into the service occasionally. A study of the emotional needs of Facebook users must be able to define and sample those most involved—or it could easily mislead.

2. *Do individuals or group-think drive your category/service?* Some categories almost demand that consumers compromise personal desires to fit in with others, buying the family car, for instance. Movies offer another clear example. A recent study noted, "Group think is critical to the movie decision process. In choosing a movie, the fact that someone else wanted to see it was equally important to the story [in deciding which one to see]" (Paddison, 2010, p. 54). Were you to measure the emotional motivations of teenage males and females separately, you might find very different drivers of movie preference, neither of which was relevant to the movie they eventually decided to see together! Group think doesn't invalidate the usefulness of finding out about emotional influences (willingness to compromise will be highly associated with personality, for instance), but it should influence study design (measure the full range of influencers) and careful analysis of how and when people trade their preferences for those of others.

3. *What are the limits on your actions?* Budget, the marketing levers you can address, global constraints, and so on? A regional manager of a large brand may have limited capacity to change a brand's core values. They might be better putting budget into studying emotional response to promotions or tactical marketing.

4. *What else should you measure?* Emotion is a key driver of consumer behavior, but it is *not* the only driver! Do you need to measure salience (how easy it is for consumers to evoke the brand in a purchase setting), and performance (product or service delivery) alongside emotional attachment (Kotler & Keller, 2006)? It's often sensible to obtain measures of a brand's emotional content *in the same study* as you measure these other factors. This allows comparison of the

impact of functional, pricing, and emotion data and better segmentation (finding out if heavy users have the same emotive drivers as light users for instance). If you need to review emotion alongside other factors and don't want to do multiple studies, you'll probably be better off using the breadth of questioning possible with more traditional survey or panel approaches.

As well as checking off the points mentioned previously, before undertaking research, it's vital to consider the *business reasons* for wanting to understand emotions. Figure 12.7 shows a few of the most common, organized from the more granular to the broader and more strategic

Figure 12.7   Common Reasons to Research Emotions

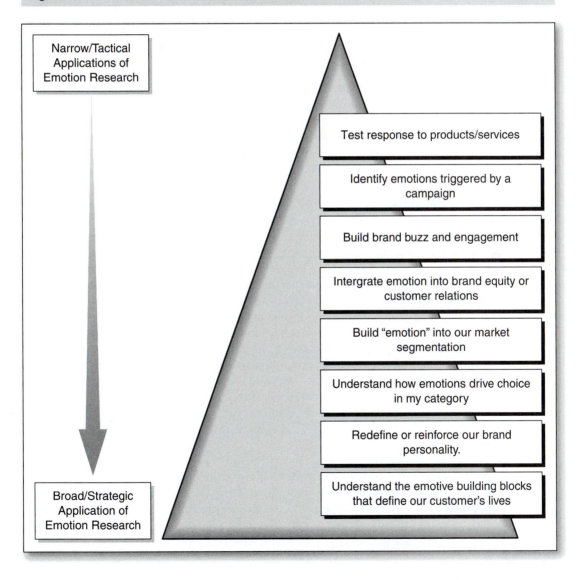

Narrow/Tactical Applications of Emotion Research

Test response to products/services

Identify emotions triggered by a campaign

Build brand buzz and engagement

Intergrate emotion into brand equity or customer relations

Build "emotion" into our market segmentation

Understand how emotions drive choice in my category

Redefine or reinforce our brand personality.

Understand the emotive building blocks that define our customer's lives

Broad/Strategic Application of Emotion Research

The task for researchers is to match methods to objectives. Broader and more strategic objectives (redefining basic brand identity, for instance) imply research approaches covering a wider sample of consumers and providing analysis of the way emotions interact. A framework, such as those discussed in the first bucket, discussed previously, in other words. If your questions are more middling (e.g., building more integrated marketing campaigns), it's necessary to supplement feedback on emotions with other information. This may mean improving your emotional feedback from surveys or panels rather than going to new approaches, the second bucket, in other words. When objectives get more specific and more precise, such as feedback on particular marketing communications, concepts, or products, then neuroscience techniques might be considered, perhaps in combination with some other methods.

This framework is general and (given the pace of development) also likely to date fast. It's also controversial because, on the one hand, many traditional ad-testing agencies will argue their feedback has many advantages over neuroscience approaches, and, on the other hand, neuroscience companies can design research programs looking at broader issues, such as brand identity. Still, the general principle remains—think about your objectives, then think about method, and if a particular research approach offers a solution that seems more or less suited to your aim, then you'll know to ask some hard questions.

The many new approaches to measuring emotion open a realistic prospect of designing such programs. We can now assess emotion in faster, more accurate, and cost-effective ways than we could have dreamed possible a decade ago.

TAKING IT FROM HERE

The next decade will be equally exciting. Not only will we see more sophisticated technology and science brought to bear but practitioners will start moving away from arguing which method is best and begin integrating the various techniques into comprehensive solutions.

One of the big missions for researchers in the next decade involves the collection and analysis of longitudinal information on how consumers integrate short-term reactions to brands into long-term brand equity or category relationships. Now, we are getting better at understanding how to maximize the emotional pull of an in-store promotion or how to develop more engaging advertising. But, despite this, in categories such as carbonated soft-drink, beer, and others—where emotional, motivational, and sensory reactions have been researched almost *ad nauseum*—we don't see any huge increase in brand loyalty or category usage (in fact, in many markets we are seeing the reverse in such categories). How the emotional responses that drive short-term purchase interact with those that are associated with long-term loyalty will be an issue researchers will increasingly be asked to tackle.

Hopefully, though, the new tools and thinking we have reviewed in this chapter will mean researchers will be able to provide clients with increasingly detailed advice on how to engage with customers at every level of marketing. Most crucial, as we learn to better interpret the softer side of consumer life, the advice research professionals can offer marketers will paradoxically become harder and more precise and, hence, more actionable.

As I argued earlier, it is possible—even likely—that these more accurate and granular measures of emotional engagement will become as vital as today's measures of market share or TV ratings. Emotional understanding will, thus, become an essential tool in improving the strategic partnership between marketing and research.

FURTHER READING

Bagozzi, R. P., Gopinath, M., & Nyer, U. (1999, spring). The role of emotions in marketing. *Journal of the Academy of Marketing Science, 27*(2), 184–206.

Damasio, A. (2009). *The feeling of what happens: Body and emotion in the making of consciousness.* Orlando, FL: Harcourt.

Fiske, S. T., Gilbert, D. T., & Lindzey, G. (Eds.). (2010). *Handbook of social psychology* (5th ed., Vol. 1 & 2). New York, NY: Wiley.

Gigerenzer, G., & Todd, P. M., & the ABC Research Group. (1999). *Simple heuristics that make us smart.* New York, NY: Oxford University Press.

Roberts, K. (2005). *Lovemarks: The future beyond brands* (Expanded ed.). New York, NY: Power House Books.

Sorensen, J. (2008). *Measuring emotions in a consumer decision-making context: Approaching or avoiding.* Retrieved from, www.business.aau.dk/wp/08-20.pdf,

Vohs, K. D., Baumeister, R. F., & Loewenstein, G. (2007). *Do emotions help or hurt decision making? A hedgefoxian perspective.* New York: NY: Russell Sage Foundation.

Neuroimaging and Marketing Research

Hook Up, Love Affair, or Happy Marriage?

SEAN GREEN

NEIL HOLBERT

University at Buffalo, The State University of New York

INTRODUCTION

Neuroimaging is the process of creating a picture of the structure or activity of the brain by using techniques that measure its chemical, electric, or magnetic properties. A key goal of neuromarketing is to use neuroimaging techniques to see what parts of the brain are activated when the consumer is exposed to stimuli, such as ads or packages; observing the data (which could be brain waves or the results of a brain scan), taking note of what such reactions can tell us about the consumer's intentions; and then using this information to try to improve on our offerings in the marketplace.

Neuroimaging represents a relatively recent new set of tools that promise to help marketing researchers solve one of the most intractable of problems. When respondents are asked questions, we cannot be sure the answers they provide are either true or accurate. Respondents misremember, they forget, they lie, they don't even know about deep motivations for their behavior. All answers are intermediated by conscious and subconscious processes unknown and unknowable to researchers.

So for many years now, an ideal form of data has been sought, data that are unsullied by respondent-induced errors and biases. The mind and body of the respondent would produce this data automatically without being mediated by spoken or written answers. Earlier examples include pupilometrics, use of lie detectors, analysis of voice pitch, and many others. Over time, these all foundered because, while responses to stimuli could readily be discerned, their consistent interpretation was missing—perhaps most particularly, their valence—whether something was liked or disliked. Enter neuroimaging, borrowed from medical research, which not only produces automatic, unmediated responses but, according to its several practitioners, also allows clear interpretations of what the data mean.

A HISTORY OF PUBLIC SKEPTICISM ABOUT MARKETING RESEARCH

Neuroimaging techniques have led to much discussion and some controversy. Is neuroimaging invasive? Is it a form of brainwashing, taking away the consumer's autonomy? Is it valid, or is it just gimmicky and the latest in a line of fads that have come and gone, such as voice-pitch change analysis and the supposed use of subliminal imagery?

Marketing research inevitably gets involved with three spheres of influence: business, science, and the customer. *Business* because we do research to help marketers make money by selling things that people want; *science* because researchers take seriously the notions of dispassion and objectivity that discipline demands; and the *customer* because whether literally consumer in household or businessperson, that's who marketers target. (As a practical matter, almost all the applications to date have been with consumers rather than business-to-business [B2B] buyers, so we will refer to consumers hereon.)

So neuroimaging is inevitably entangled with these three spheres, involving issues of how far business should go using the tools of *science* when trying to look into the consumer's head.

There is a history of concern about the interaction and intersection of these three spheres. The question could be posed, should science and its tools be used in the service of business through the instrumentality of consumer marketing research? This would include tools and techniques drawn from the psychology lab, and now routinely used, such as galvanic skin reaction (GSR), eye-movement, tachistoscopes, and, most recent, neuroimaging.

This history goes back to when the profession first used psychology and its tools and techniques to try to look into consumers' heads—without instruments at all. (Just as a reminder, the most commonly used research tool of them all, the focus group, actually derives from the group therapy techniques of psychology.) Ever since Vance Packard's 1957 book, *The Hidden Persuaders,* was published, talking about depth interviews and similar techniques that marketers were using to tap into the consumer's unconscious, some have wondered if there was something insidious in this. Might researchers be learning things from these depth interviews that could lead to marketing practices harmful to society?

For example, Hodgson (2003), while holding that persuasion, of course, came from forces deeper and subtler than just advertising, noted that Packard's book,

> Painted a grim picture. The post-World War II vision of a prosperous world, in which genuine human needs were to be met by a strong, efficient, and growing economy, was shattered. Packard alleged that, instead of serving human needs, the

big corporations were manipulating our very wants and desires, using everything from subliminal messages to the exploitation of sexual images. (p. 159)

The picture has changed since the postwar days, with reality television and Internet social networking replacing the staged, one-way communication that emerged in monochrome from the wood-paneled boxes in past decades. The 21st century is eroding the distinction between the constructed virtual world that we perceive through our electronic devices and the real world that we physically inhabit. The immediacy and pervasiveness of these new forms of communication lend them an air of truth, as evident in the term "reality TV" itself. The fusion of the real and the virtual, it seems, aspires to become a "reality" that is somehow more real than the ordinary reality that it is replacing. Marketing has adapted to the changing medium, with guerrilla marketing and viral marketing entering the commercial sphere.

Neuroimaging techniques, which (as noted) try to read what happens in the brain when it's exposed to advertising and promotion stimuli, are themselves a fusion of the virtual and the real. The peaks and valleys of an EEG recording or the patterns of color in a functional MRI scan are mathematical or statistical constructs—as real as a pie chart—but they offer us a glimpse inside the human brain, a chance to see a facet of reality that would otherwise be beyond our reach. This raises the question, If we use neuroimaging techniques to improve marketing, hence the term neuromarketing, are we using technology to augment our reality or are we putting our trust in an artificial and potentially misleading surrogate reality?

To further complicate matters, if we return to Packard's (1957) original concern and update it to the 21st century world of spybots and identity theft, the issue of privacy remains paramount; only now, the question is not just whether marketers may enter our living rooms, but whether marketers may cross the threshold of our skulls to predict the reactions of and, therefore, control the mind within.

Fugate notes that neuromarketing

uses clinical information about brain functions and mechanisms to help explain what is happening inside . . . the 'black box' (that is) so prevalent in many explanations of consumer behavior. . . . If neuromarketers can 'use science to locate consumers' 'buy' buttons, then we have gotten closer to opening the 'black box' of the consumer's mind. (Fugate cited in Moore, 2005, p. 12)

When we study communication, we know indeed that the black box, that threshold between sender and receiver, is full of mystery. Could neuroimaging help unlock that box and stimulate successful communication? And, equally important, is there not the implied worry of should we be doing this not in the service of healing, where the neuroscience tools were first employed, but of selling?

WHY NEUROIMAGING?

Why do we *need* neuroimaging techniques at all? Simply put, in marketing research, we can get answers by asking questions or by *not* asking questions.

Researchers have historically done most of their work by asking questions. They devise questionnaires, short and long, in quantitative research using a variety of ways: personal, mail, telephone, fax, in-media, and online. And in qualitative research, they devise fluid and thoughtful outline-guides to guide discussions in person around tables or one-on-one, or even online.

Quite bluntly, the selection of samples (probability or purposeful), the writing of questioning instruments, and the specifications for analyzing and interpreting them is what researchers get paid for and what they take glory in it.

But what if the answers to those questions are wrong? What if respondents are bored by 25-minute surveys on the minutiae of their laundry habits and don't really pay attention to the questions? What if people get in a yea-saying mode (and give positive answers because they figure that's what is wanted); or in a I'm-not-a-dummy mode (and give answers, any answers, to questions they really don't know anything about); or they just forget or misremember; or, toughest to handle of all, what if they get into a defensive-ego mode (where they decide that what they say about themselves is more important than anything they say about the matter being researched)?

All of this is possible in the realm of questioning, and can lead us astray. Therefore, marketing researchers also use non-question-asking methods. Non-question-asking techniques can, broadly, include *observation* (seeing what people *do*, rather than what they *say*), including ideas from *ethnography* (what they do in a specific cultural context); *diary* research (don't test people's memories—ask them instead to record what they do as they go along); *mystery shopping* (our interviewers pretend to be shoppers); *garbology* (what do people throw out?); psychomechanical methods, where we use devices like *eye-tracking* machines (to see what parts of stimuli catch the respondent's eye first, the trajectory that the eye follows, and the time spent on each element of the scene); and *tachistoscopes* and computer displays that shed light on stimuli for various times to see how the participants react to brief glimpses of a display element.

While their responses may sometimes mislead or confuse us, in all of these techniques, respondents cannot really lie.

That's why we use them; it is good for us and also good for consumers, from whom we are getting information that can ultimately lead to products, services, and issues that we hope will fill their needs.

And now there's neuroimaging, where we (literally or figuratively) attach wires to people's heads and see what happens to their brains when they exposed to stimuli or we put their heads in scanners to pick up the telltale radiation or fluctuations in magnetic force that accompanies their thoughts, emotions, and decisions.

In past decades, researchers have been able to use psychophysical and physiological methods to obtain general information about a consumer's alertness (Krugman, 1971) emotional reaction to advertising, or attention to particular elements of an ad. However, the ability to observe neural correlates of the decision process itself provides a new and conceptually different sort of information to marketing researchers. The possibility is that a researcher might be able to say to a respondent, "Your verbal responses say that you don't like the product, but your brain says that you do."

Furthermore, neuroimaging might often provide insights not only into the consumer's decision but also into how and why the consumer arrived at it. For example, neuroscientists can point to brain areas that are associated with reward, emotional influences on decision making, and evaluation of a product's status or quality.

If marketers can follow the trail of neural breadcrumbs that leads from observing an ad, perceiving its contents, responding emotionally and cognitively, and finally making the decision to buy, then this gives marketers the power to fine-tune their promotion so the consumer not only buys the product in the end but also buys it for an understood reason—as part of a long-term marketing strategy.

And this promise has never been offered before by a research tool.

THE MOST COMMON NEUROIMAGING TECHNIQUES

Electroencephalography (EEG)

EEG involves using electrodes to measure changes in the electric potential at the scalp that result from the electric activity of neurons in the brain. Typically, these changes are very small—millionths of a volt—so finding them is like detecting the ripples from a stone dropped into a pond. Like a ripple in water, the effects of neurons' electric activity diminish with distance, so the electrode will be most sensitive to activity on the surface of the brain near the electrode. However, the electric potential is determined not only by sources of electric activity on or directly underneath a particular scalp location but also by electric activity throughout the brain, in the rest of the body, or electric appliances. To cancel the effects of irrelevant sources, EEG measurements are, typically, taken in a shielded location, and measurements at the scalp are often expressed relative to reference electrodes located at other locations, such as the earlobes. (Luck, 2005)

Because EEG measures the electric field at the scalp rather than inside the brain itself, EEG data cannot determine the location of the activity within the brain, although mathematical models can narrow down the possibilities. EEG has a considerable advantage in that the apparatus required for the technique can, as shown in Figure 13.1, be worn unobtrusively as a helmet or a headband, allowing researchers to record the brain activity of consumers as they shop in a realistic setting (e.g., EmSense: http://www.mrweb .com/drno/news11805.htm, see Appendix 13.1), although as noted earlier, extraneous electric activity in real-world locations could interfere with EEG recording. As an additional advantage, electric field disturbances at the scalp occur simultaneously with the neural activity that generated them, giving EEG the ability to reveal the precise timing of the neurons' electric activity.

In general, EEG signals are commonly analyzed in the fields of neuroscience and experimental psychology in two ways.

1. *Brain waves.* Synchronized activity among many neurons can produce periodic oscillations (brain waves) on EEG recordings. They can provide an estimate of a participant's mental involvement with an advertisement (Krugman, 1971) and correlate with marketing-relevant processes like memory (Klimesch, 1999) and attention (Womelsdorf & Fries, 2007). Brain waves are classified by their frequency, and studies that measure brain waves often

Figure 13.1   An EmSense Headband In Use

Source: Image courtesy of EmSense Corporation.

use mathematical analyses to measure the power in each of the important frequency bands (alpha, beta, gamma, delta, and theta).

Researchers (Hanson, 1981; Rothschild & Hyun, 1990; Rothschild, Hyun, Reeves, Thorson, & Goldstein, 1988) have investigated lateralization (right versus left hemisphere differences) in alpha wave activity as an indicator of consumer responses to advertising. Note that alpha activity is associated with rest; so paradoxically, the side with the greatest alpha "activity," in this context, may be the least active in the conventional sense. Rothschild and Hyun (1990) found that participants were more likely to remember the content of video advertisements when they experienced reductions in alpha activity in visual areas of the brain (the occipital lobe), first in the right hemisphere and then in the left hemisphere, as participants viewed that particular content. The authors attributed this effect to initial (right-hemisphere) vigilance followed by subsequent (left-hemisphere) analysis of advertisement content. Although EEG data can be interpreted in different ways (as the authors themselves note), changes in lateralized alpha activity could be useful in practice if they correlate with consumer recall and purchasing decisions.

Another potential application of EEG activity to marketing is the differences in activity in the left and right frontal lobes, measured as a reduction in alpha wave power, as Coan and Allen (2004) describe. Studies have linked left frontal activity with approach behaviors (e.g., happiness, but also including aggression) and right frontal activity with withdrawal (e.g., fear, anxiety). Although frontal lobe asymmetry has, not to our knowledge, been employed as a marketing tool, in principle, the ability to distinguish between *approach* (happiness: "I want to acquire Brand A," or anger: "I want to fling Brand A out the window") and *withdrawal* (such as "Brand A disgusts me") could be quite useful in weighing the success of a marketing campaign.

2. *Event related potentials (ERPs)* are changes in the EEG recording that occur immediately (usually less than a second) after a particular event, such as viewing an image. By presenting a stimulus many times and averaging together recordings of these presentations, the ERP technique aims to cancel the effects of brain activity that is not related to the event (including the brain waves mentioned earlier). Computing an ERP, typically, involves making tens or hundreds of recordings and averaging them together. Many studies in the neuroscience literature are devoted to identifying the ERP components (changes in electric activity that contribute to peaks and valleys in an ERP graph) that correspond to mental processes, an endeavor whimsically called ERPology (Luck, 2005). Once the ERP components are well characterized, these various components can be applied to a range of fields, including marketing. For an illustration of how ERP data are presented in the scientific literature, see Figure 13.2, which shows electric potentials while performing a task that demands attention after having heard positive, negative, or neutral expressions. Martin-Loeches, Sel, Jiménez, and Castellanos (2009) have used software (LORETA) to identify and display the likely location of electric activity.

One example of a recent application of ERP to marketing is Ma, Wang, Shu, and Dai, (2008) use of the "oddball paradigm" to study brand extension. Infrequent, task relevant stimuli (i.e., oddballs) tend to produce a stronger P300 component. Ma et al., presented participants with a beverage brand name followed by either a beverage name (congruent condition) compared with a nonbeverage product name (incongruent product) and asked participants to evaluate whether the brand name was suitable for the product. The authors found a stronger and more widespread P300 in the congruent condition and suggest that the larger P300s resulted from similarity between the brand name and the product. Consequently, they contend, the P300 could be used to measure "consumers' attitude toward intended brand extension" (p. 16). We would note that a variety of stimuli can give rise to a P300. In applying this sort of research to a marketing decision, it would be important (a) to verify that the observed ERP components are actually triggered by the product characteristic that you are interested in (e.g., brand extension) and (b) to ensure that differences in the observed ERP actually translate into differences in consumer behavior.

Magnetoencephalography (MEG)

MEG measures slight changes in the magnetic field on the scalp that occur because of neural activity in the brain. MEG has an advantage over EEG in that it is less susceptible to distortions introduced by the skull. However, the device itself is quite expensive, and the detectors for magnetic activity, superconducting quantum interference devices (SQUIDs), must be kept at a very low temperature to function. As a result, the MEG

Figure 13.2   Data From a Recent ERP Study (Martin-Loeches et al., 2009)

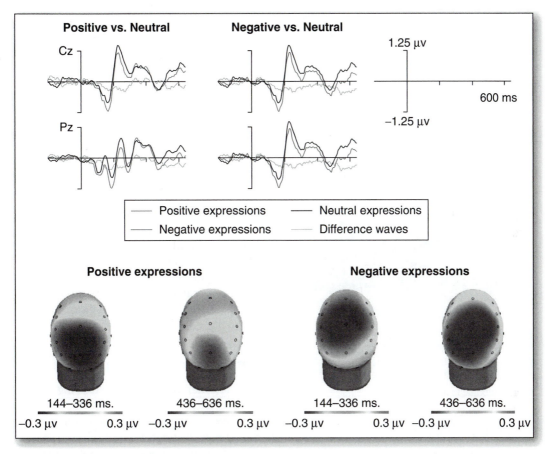

Source: Martin-Loeches et al., 2009. Reproduced in accordance with Creative Commons Attribution License.

Top: Event related potentials (ERPs) taken from two scalp locations (Cz and Pz) recorded while a participant performs a task that requires visual and spatial attention. The participant had recently heard a positive expression (e.g., "You're the best") or a negative expression (e.g., "You're a loser").

Bottom: Estimated location of electrical potentials in the head using a mathematical technique (LORETA).

apparatus is not portable like the electrode caps used for EEG (as shown in Figure 13.3). (See Ioannides, 2006 for more information.)

Functional Magnetic Resonance Imaging (fMRI)

As an indirect indicator of brain activity, fMRI measures changes in blood oxygenation. Nerve impulses themselves do not directly produce a change in blood oxygenation level.

Figure 13.3 MEG Scanner

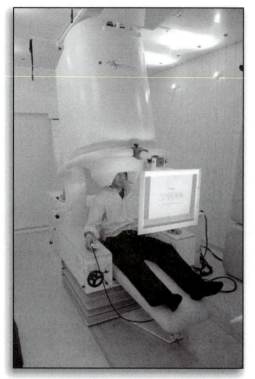

Source: National Institute of Health.

Figure 13.4 fMRI Scanner

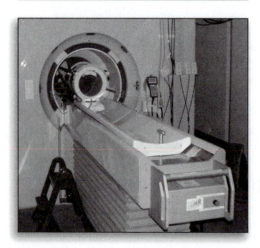

Source: Wikimedia Commons Semiconscious.

Rather, the increased metabolic rate (use of sugar and oxygen) because of neural activity leads to more blood flow to more active brain areas. Changes in blood flow, typically, lag behind increased electric activity by a second or two and can last for several seconds or more (Buckner, 1998). This means that while it is possible, using fMRI, to know *where* neural electric activity occurred within a millimeter (Ioannides, 2006), it is impossible to tell precisely *when* the activity occurred. Conceptually, this is something like measuring consumer demand by monitoring the industrial and commercial activity—factory output, shipping, and so on—that goes into meeting that demand. An fMRI is considerably more expensive than an EEG, and it requires the participant's head to be immobilized in a scanner (See Figure 13.4). An advantage of fMRI is that the radio waves that the fMRI scanner detects pass through the skull in a straight line without being distorted. This allows researchers to calculate the three-dimensional location of changes in blood oxygenation level (Senior, Smyth, Cooke, Shaw, & Peel, 2007).

Positron Emission Tomography (PET)

PET is another method of measuring neural metabolic activity. Unlike EEG, MEG, or fMRI, PET scans involve exposing the brain to radioactivity, which in clinical settings, typically, comes from a radioactive form of fluorodeoxyglucose, a chemical that resembles sugar and is taken up into neurons but not metabolized like glucose (Muehllehner & Karp, 2006). PET measures the buildup of radioactive chemicals within active neurons, and these chemicals, typically, remain in the cell after the activity has subsided. As a result, PET does not give an accurate indication of when the neurons were most active.

Transcranial Magnetic Stimulation (TMS)

Although transcranial magnetic stimulation (TMS) is not strictly speaking a neuroimaging technique, the usefulness of the technology in neuroscience makes it likely that neuromarketing will use it as well. TMS involves magnetic pulses delivered by a coil placed against the head. Magnetic stimulation can trigger neural activity in the brain areas under the coil. If these pulses are administered repeatedly, this disrupts normal function, creating what is called a virtual lesion (Senior et al., 2007), which temporarily impairs the participant in ways that can be informative about what that particular brain area does. This line of research differs from the other techniques that we have discussed in that marketing researchers do not deliberately impair their respondents before making their observations. However, neuromarketers may wish to use TMS data in developing marketing practices. We should note in passing that the application of TMS to marketing, that is, deliberately impairing the brains of respondents, might strike the public as ominous. The role that TMS plays in future neuromarketing research is not yet clear, but it is likely to be more controversial than the other techniques.

THE MARKETING-NEUROSCIENCE RELATIONSHIP

With the neuroimaging toolkit in mind, we turn to a central question of the marketing-neuroscience relationship. What does neuroscience have to offer by way of a dowry? Are neuroimaging techniques really windows into the mind? As Alfred Korzybski once said, "The map is not the territory" (Korzybski, 1948, p. xvii). Just as consumers cannot be reduced to the pie charts and bar graphs of a marketing researcher's PowerPoint presentation, the entrancing images of an fMRI or PET scan are not snapshots of the mind itself. To put it another way, we may have taken the black box and painted it every color of the rainbow, but figuring out its secrets may be as challenging as ever.

Paradoxically, as marketing researchers are becoming increasingly aware of the potential of neuroimaging, a backlash—or at least a cautionary tug on the reins—has been building against the potential for erroneous or misleading interpretations of neuroimaging data. Some questions have risen in academia (Klein, 2010; Miller, 2008; Poldrack, 2006) and in the popular media (Horstman, 2010, pp. 80–83).

Limitations

Neuromarketers should keep the following limitations in mind:

1. *Brain scans images are not photographs. They are more like complex charts.* The colors on a brain scan image do not arise directly from whatever signal (e.g., radio wave or gamma ray) the scanner is detecting. When neuroscientists analyze brain scan data, they carry out statistical tests to determine which color to paint each part of the image. Therefore, reading a brain scan requires as much care and skepticism as reading a bar graph of a survey result (Klein, 2010).

2. *A brain scan image is, typically, created by comparing the experiment scan against a baseline or control.* The brain is always doing more than one thing. If it weren't, you'd stop breathing every time you got lost in thought. To account for this, techniques like fMRI, typically, require the researcher to subtract a baseline level of activity from the result. For example, a researcher might compare two conditions, one in which the participant looks

at an advertisement and one in which the participant looks at a white screen. If the brain activity in these conditions is different, it does *not* necessarily mean that the advertisement content caused this difference. Perhaps the white screen was boring. Perhaps it hurt the participant's eyes. The choice of a control or baseline condition is important to the meaning of the results.

3. *Parts of the brain do more than one thing.* We have already said that the brain can handle more than one task, and that is true at the local level too. For instance, seeing the Coca-Cola logo before tasting the drink increases activity in the dorsolateral prefrontal cortex (McClure, Li, Tomlin, Cypert, & Montague, 2004), linking the dlPFC to brand information. However, the dlPFC also responds in other contexts, such as word-recognition tasks (Fiebach, Ricker, Friederici, & Jacobs, 2007). So what does it tell us when a company logo makes the dlPFC light up? It is important not to rely solely on labels like "reward center" or "judgment center" and instead to consider the range of possible reasons for a particular brain area's response.

4. *Neuroimaging studies are rarely done in a real-world setting.* It would be fantastic if there were a lightweight, portable fMRI machine. Then we could just strap it to our participants' heads and set them loose in a shopping mall. However, the current reality is that the kinds of techniques that let you pinpoint the location of brain activity (PET, fMRI, and MEG) constrain the participants and, at the very least, provide a tangible reminder that they are in an experiment. At worst, they can deny a random sample when some participants don't feel like sticking their heads in the scanner. That is not to say that experiments aren't valuable, but rather to suggest that experimental findings might be less applicable to situations where the consumer experience and the experimental participant experience are substantially different.

5. *Most neuroimaging studies are conducted among small samples, usually in a single location.* Forget about representative sampling among segments or geography or usage rates; forget about random sampling or statistically reliable sampling (in the traditional sense). Typical studies employ a sample of just 20 respondents, which may be fine for medical research on brain function. It is less clear that these small samples will provide marketers what they seek, and it is quite clear that they require marketers to take a leap of faith that the technology's promise will overcome its current limitations in target audience representativeness.

6. *Neuroimaging studies (so far) are very expensive and beyond the budgets of any but the largest of marketers.*

So where does that leave neuromarketing? To say it succinctly, *caveat emptor*. Businesses aiming to use neuroscience to have an edge over their competition should be informed and discerning and know the right questions to ask when someone pitches them a marketing solution based on their forays into the black box. As Brainard (2008) notes, "There are many responses associated with each area of the brain, however, and as promising as imaging may be, it hasn't come close to directly identifying the exact emotions in play" (para. 5).

In sum, there is the appeal of new technology, tempered by caution. As Northrop (24) so elegantly put it "Men everywhere . . . begin with the aesthetic emotional principle in the nature of things, and come to the rational principle . . . only later, if at all. One feels the beauty of the sunset before one learns of the internal constitution of the stars" (p. 62).

THE FUTURE OF NEUROIMAGING

Neuroimaging and the field of neuromarketing that has emerged from it are both in their infancy, yet already, they appear to be at a crossroads. If neuroimaging is seen as an invasive process that calls to mind a hospital, laboratory, or interrogation room, it is likely to be viewed very warily and very much with a jaundiced eye. However, it has the potential to extend its influence well beyond science and theory and into practical day-to-day marketing.

So in all this hope of finding a Holy Grail into the consumer's mind via neuroimaging, there are objections, limitations, and caveats. Let's recapitulate them.

1. At a very basic level, it can be argued that neuroimaging, such as psychoanalysis, is a medical matter, plain and simple, and results should be used only for medical purposes, and not for selling things.

2. Use of neuroimaging makes some ethically queasy. Although neuroimaging vendors claim to offer special insights into consumer behavior, do we really want to risk exploring the brains of those who are not necessarily that aware among adults—to say nothing of those with fewer defenses, such as children?

3. There are many influencing factors on consumer behavior in general and on responses to research inquiries beyond what we as marketers proffer. These include influences from personality, family, friends, many groups, the culture, noncommercial messages of all sorts, and just plain chance.

4. There is limited validity to date showing that neuroimaging results relate to actual buying behavior in the marketplace. Studies involving wines, coffee, and soft drinks are cited (Harris, 2008), but correlations and effects are limited.

5. There is the potential for massive and dangerous oversimplification. As noted, the tools of neuroimaging are varied, and the brain itself is frighteningly complex. To say it yet again, we are not dealing with bulbs on a Christmas tree that light up (or don't) in any neat, clear, or simple way.

6. Will marketers (and the public) be able to distinguish real scientific breakthroughs from overblown claims? Will consultants employing exotic machines, but very little real scientific knowledge try to entice businesses into spending real money on "junk" science? (After all, if X number of wires gives us useful information, why not 2X or 3X . . . or nX? See Luck, 2005, pp. 122–124 for a technical discussion of using large numbers of electrodes in EEG recording.)

7. Isn't it possible that much of the appeal of neuroimaging as a contemporary hot marketing research tool comes from the fact that it is part of a techno-wave that has engulfed and enchanted a new generation of marketing researchers?

On the other hand, we may find that, over and above everything else, this dramatic new tool can bring forth fruits that may, by themselves, justify our attention to it. Thus, in methodology, "A key advantage of the use of imaging procedures in marketing is primarily the possibility of developing new theories about marketing-related behaviors through the use of the inductive method" (Kenning, Plassmann, & Ahlert, 2007, p.66; translated by the authors with the aid of Google translate). And in the realm of business itself: "[Marketing] researchers have an unparalleled opportunity to adopt cognitive neuroscientific techniques [to] . . . significantly redefine the field and possibly even cause substantial dislocations in business models" (Lee, Senior, Butler, & Fuchs, 2009).

Neuroimaging is part of the broader domain of cognitive neuroscience; it is used as a tool in the business sphere of neuromarketing; and meuromarketing can be thought of as part of the yet broader realm of neuroeconomics.

It is not just an abstract idea. It is a service, *sold* in a variety of forms and for various applications by different research companies. And it exists in the rough-and-tumble world of business, where claims of efficacy naturally are made. Think of the many suppliers of copy testing and of customer satisfaction research and their claims and counterclaims to get a sense of the challenge of evaluating neuromarketing as a whole. There is competition, which sometimes sheds light and which sometimes sheds only heat.

NEUROMARKETING . . . SO FAR

Let's look briefly at neuroimaging in that world of marketing research.

The solidity of the neuroimaging idea is well illustrated by the fact that a patent for a neuroimaging device exists. The inventors Gerald Zaltman and Stephen M. Kosslyn (2000) state,

> Neuroimaging [is] a means of validating whether a stimulus such as [an] advertisement, communication, or product evokes a certain mental response such as emotion, preference, or memory, or to predict the consequences of the stimulus or later behavior such as consumption or purchasing . . . based upon the non-subjective evidence of neuroimaging. . . . [T]he neuroimaging device [to be used] is selected from a group of neuroimaging devices consisting of positive emission tomography, functional magnetic resonance imaging, magnetoencephalography, and single photon emission computer tomography. (p. 1)

The neuroimaging idea can be further explored by looking briefly at just one of the companies, EmSense, whose website (http:// www.emsense.com) is rich with applications that the company makes of the technique.

Its broad view of neuroimaging in marketing research is summed up by their belief that

> Traditional methods suffer from the need to rely upon the consumer's ability—or inability—to accurately explain reactions, feelings, and preferences. EmSense provides marketers with a window into the mind of the consumer with a scientifically validated, quantitatively based means of bio-sensory measurement . . . through the EmSense neuromeasurement devices—[a] scalable non-invasive physiological and brainwave measurement technology. (EmSense, 2010, para. 1)

The various areas in which they execute their work include ad copy testing, in-store research, and package testing. Featured are measures of emotion and cognitive engagement, norms, and quantitative-size samples.

In the real world of marketing, companies are not in the habit of broadcasting what they have learned about customers, nor how they learned it, so the applications literature is actually limited. We can share the following few examples.

In one case (Burkitt, 2009),

> thirty men and women study a sporty silver test model of a 2011 Hyundai. [They] are asked to stare at specific parts of the vehicle, including the bumper, the windshield, and the tires. Electrode-studded caps on their heads capture the electrical activity in their brains as they view the car for an hour. The information is recorded in a hard drive (that) each person wears on a belt. Their brain activity is supposed to show preferences that could lead to purchasing decisions. . . . The carmaker will tweak the exterior (of the car) based on the encephalograph reports, which tracks activity in all parts of the brain. (para. 1)

Other companies cited in the same article (Burkitt, 2009) as neuroimaging users include Google and Disney (who work with NeuroFocus and who was the supplier in the Hyundai example previously), Microsoft (with EmSense), and PepsiCo's Frito-Lay. The latter used neuroimaging to test (interalia) packaging, and found that matte paper bags didn't trigger activity in the anterior cingulate cortex, an area associated with guilt, as much as shiny packaging did.

And in another case (Plambeck, 2010), with NeuroFocus as the supplier,

> *New Scientist* (magazine) . . . (had) men connected to an encephalograph machine, which measures brain waves, and shown three different covers . . . [ratings of the results] were based on factors like memory activation and emotional engagement. . . . The lowest scoring cover, [had] a shattered clock and the New Scientist logo in yellow. . . . The top-scoring cover had the logo in red and a single main image of space. (paras. 1–5)

CONCLUSION

So are neuroimaging and marketing research a hook up, a passing love affair, or a lasting marriage?

We like to quote Dan Ariely, Duke University, and Gregory S. Berns, Emory University:

> It is too early to tell, but, optimists as we are, we think that there is much that neuromarketing can contribute to the interface between people and businesses, and—in doing so—foster a more human-compatible design of the products around us. At the same time, neuromarketing as an enterprise runs the risk of quickly becoming yesterday's fad. . . . If we take neuromarketing as the examination of the neural activities that underlie the daily activities related to people, products, and

marketing, this could become a useful and interesting path for academic research, and, at the same time, provide useful inputs to marketers. (Ariely & Burns, as quoted in Hernandez, 2010, p.8)

Alternatively, in the also developing field of neuroethics, researchers have already raised concerns about the use of neuroimaging technology to exploit vulnerable populations and undermine free will (Farah, 2005).

And tensions have risen between entrepreneurs using neuroscience techniques commercially and researchers who question the foundation of their work. For example, the "Farwell Brain Fingerprinting" technique for applying neuromeasurement to criminal investigation has faced scrutiny (Rosenfeld, 2005), and a neurologist has questioned Dr. Daniel Amen's use of brain scans in the diagnosis of psychological disorders (Burton, 2008).

The perception of neuromarketing as trustworthy and viable rests not on any particular article or controversy or marketing initiative but on how it comes to be viewed by the three spheres: marketing, consumer, and scientific. If scientists reject neuromarketing as pseudoscience; if marketers come to view it as unproven, gimmicky, or too complicated or expensive to be useful; or if the public grows defensive or suspicious of neuromarketing research, it may not take root, irrespective of its scientific merit, its utility for businesses, or its potential to benefit consumers.

It doesn't have to be that way. In fact, it could *add* richness rather and promote ethical choices rather than discourage them. It is possible that neuroimaging (and neuromarketing) could, according to Lee, Broderick, and Chamberlain (2007),

contribute to marketing ethics in many ways . . . (and) research into advertising effectiveness . . . can contribute more than just finding . . . (that) "buy button" in the brain. In fact, exploring exactly what elements of an advertisement are critical to awareness (of), attitudes (towards), and evaluations of products . . . should reduce firms' reliance on the "blunt instruments" of blanket coverage, shock tactics, or sexual imagery. (p. 203)

No doubt the excitement and controversy surrounding neuroimaging and neuromarketing—reading my brain and then leading me into buying temptation—will continue. As Farah (2005) puts it, "The question is, therefore, not whether, but rather when and how, neuroscience with shape our future" (p. 39).

Do we, finally, hear a call for business pragmatism as we look into the matter? Here's one from de Abitua (2009):

While some are attracted to neuromarketing's promise of monitoring the emotional responses of an individual's brain, other experts feel that the answer to emotional engagement lies . . . in the domain of signs and symbols, known as semiotic analysis. Many brand managers will engage a grab bag of these feuding experts and pick and mix from their advice. The various sects and dogmas of Marketing are treated expediently by their clients . . . they just want an approach that works. (para. 3) Or, to paraphrase the Scarecrow in *The Wizard of Oz,* we could really move ahead in our science and in our marketing "If we only had the brain."

Maybe we do.

ACKNOWLEDGMENTS

We would like to thank Eric Halata, Prof. Larry Hawk, and Prof. Scott Wersinger for their invaluable assistance with this manuscript and especially to thank Chief Analytics Officer Elissa Moses for providing us with the opportunity for an interview and for her insights into EmSense, neuromarketing, and biosensory metrics. We would also like to thank the National Institute of Health and the Public Library of Science for making content available for use in this article. Note that use of said content does not imply that the NIH or the PLoS have endorsed this book chapter in any way.

APPENDICES

Appendix 13.1 An Overview of Common Neuroimaging and Related Terms and Techniques

Biosensory metrics: Measurements of the physiological response to sensory stimuli. This includes neuroimaging, EEG, eye-tracking, and other techniques, and can be used to estimate a participant's cognitive and emotional engagement with advertising.

Consumer neuroscience: The scientific study of how the consumer's brain activity relates to consumer behaviors, such as purchasing decisions, brand preferences, and response to advertisement (Hubert & Kenning, 2008).

Electroencephalography (EEG): A technique for measuring electric potentials on the scalp using electrodes. Because EEG is a measurement at the scalp, it does not reveal the precise three-dimensional location of activity within the brain (Luck, 2005).

Functional magnetic resonance imaging (fMRI): A technique for detecting changes in brain activity indirectly by measuring changes in the proportion of oxygenated to deoxygenated hemoglobin in the blood (Senior et al., 2007).

Magnetoencephalography: A technique for recording magnetic field changes at the scalp using sensitive detectors known as superconducting quantum interference devices (SQUIDs) (Ioannides, 2009).

Neural correlate: A pattern of brain activity that accompanies a behavior, experience, or mental process (for example, a preference for one brand over another). Note that brain activity could be correlated with an event without either causing or being caused by that event.

Neural network: A collection of neurons or representations of neurons that can carry out functions like learning and decision making. Typically, this refers to artificial neural networks in which groups of neurons are represented by nodes and synaptic connections are represented by connection weights (Rumelhart & McClelland, 1986).

Neuroeconomics: A parent discipline of consumer neuroscience and neuromarketing; it is the science of the brain's role in economic activity, particularly financial decision making (Clithero, Tankersley, & Huettel 2008).

Neuroimaging: The process of arriving at a picture of the brain and its activity. Typically, this refers to fMRI and PET, but it can also include EEG and MEG (Henson, 2005). Functional neuroimaging techniques provide information about what the brain is doing (e.g., the activity level of a particular brain area), while structural neuroimaging can provide information about the size and shape of brain structures.

Neuromarketing: The application of our knowledge of the consumer's brain to techniques and strategies for selling products (Fugate, 2007).

Neuroscience: The interdisciplinary study of nerve cells (neurons) and the nervous system. Neuroscience draws upon biology, chemistry, physics, psychology, and other fields (Fugate, 2007; Senior et al., 2007).

Positron emission tomography (PET): A neuroimaging technique that measures metabolic activity in the brain by injecting the participant with radioactive material (usually fluorodeoxyglucose) and detecting gamma rays that are released within the head as a result of radioactive decay (Muehllehner & Karp, 2006).

Transcranial magnetic ttimulation (TMS): A technique to stimulate or disrupt neural activity producing pulses of magnetic energy near a part of the head. TMS is often used to create a virtual lesion in the brain to determine which brain areas are important for a particular mental process (Senior et al., 2007).

Appendix 13.2 Brain Areas That Have Been Linked to Consumer Behavior

Brain Region	Location	Marketing-Related Processes That It Is Associated With	Other Associated Processes (Not An Exhaustive List)
Anterior Cingulate Cortex (ACC)	Above and in front of the corpus callosum, between it and the prefrontal cortex	Attractive packaging (Stoll, Baecke, & Kenning, 2008)	Conflict monitoring, response selection (Botvinick, Cohen, & Carter, 2004); Cravings in addiction (Kilts et al., 2001)
Anterior Insula	A fold within cortex, near the junction of the temporal, parietal and frontal lobes	Perceived unfairness (Sanfrey, Rilling, Aronson, Nystrom, & Cohen 2003) Risk-aversion (Kuhnen & Knutson, 2005)	Awareness, orgasm, cravings (Craig, 2009); Taste (Cerf-Ducastel, van de Moortele, MacLeod, Le Bihan, & Faurion, 2001); Language (Augustine, 1996)

Brain Region	Location	Marketing-Related Processes That It Is Associated With	Other Associated Processes (Not An Exhaustive List)
Dorsolateral Prefrontal Cortex (dPFC)	In the upper part of the frontal lobe	Preference for product based on brand logo (McClure et al., 2004)	Distinguishing words from meaningless nonwords (Fiebach et al., 2007); Taste (Kringelbach, de Araujo, & Rolls, 2004)
Ventromedial Prefrontal Cortex (vmPFC)	In the middle of the prefrontal cortex, that is, where the left and right halves of the frontal lobes are close together	Preference for products based on sensory qualities (McClure et al., 2004); Framing Effect (Deppe Schwindt, W, Krämer et al., 2005) First-choice brand effect (Deppe Schwindt, Kugel, Plassmann, & Kenning 2005)	Personal moral judgment (Ciaramelli et al., 2007); Judgment of another person's intent to harm (Young et al., 2010)
Nucleus Accumbens	Part of the striatum (not the cortex) located just behind the OFC	Anticipation of financial gain (Knutson, Adams, Fong, & Hommer, 2001); Product preference (Knutson, Rick, Wimmer,., Prelec, & Loewenstein 2007) Risky financial decisions (Kuhnen & Knutson, 2005)	Goal-directed behavior (Gruber Hussain, & O'Donnell, 2009); Cravings in addiction (Kilts et al., 2001)
Occipital and Parietal Lobes	Lobes of the cortex located at the back and top of the head, behind the frontal lobe	Attractive packaging (Stoll et al., 2008)	A host of visual processes, including the allocation of visual attention
Orbitofrontal Cortex (OFC)	Lower part ("floor") of the prefrontal cortex	Experienced pleasantness (Plassmann, O'Doherty, Shiv, & Rangel, 2008)	Taste, flavor (Rolls, 2004) the reward value of sensory stimuli (Murray O'Doherty, & Schoenbaum, 2007)
Posterior Cingulate Cortex	Behind the anterior cingulate cortex, between the corpus callosum and cortex in the rear of the head (that is, parietal and occipital lobes)	Attractive packaging (Stoll et al., 2008)	Risk (McCoy & Platt, 2005); Anticipatory allocation of spatial attention (Small et al., 2003); Reward outcome of behavior (Hayden, Nair, C., McCoy, & Platt, 2008)

Appendix 13.3

The consumer's impression of the neuroimaging experience is likely to depend at least in part on whether the experience is perceived as alien and restrictive or, alternatively, as reassuring, convenient, and trustworthy. The science fiction depiction of mind-reading equipment in movies such as *Back to the Future* often entails some sort of cap with tubes or wires that somehow draw thoughts out of the head. Many real-world devices conform to this expectation; some EEG devices are, in fact, just that, caps with wires coming out of them. Some newer EEG devices are smaller and more like headbands, allowing their use in familiar surroundings.

In contrast, fMRI and PET scanners are larger machines that require the participant to lie down with his or her head in the scanner, immobilized to prevent motion artifacts. MEG is in between these extremes, allowing the participant to be seated but requiring that the head be immobilized within the detector. It is possible that future devices will enable accurate neuroimaging with high temporal and spatial resolution without encumbering the participant at all, but for now, neuromarketers should keep in mind that the different techniques place different degrees of constraint on the participant and that these constraints certainly limit how closely a neuroimaging study resembles a normal shopping experience.

Participants who have reported their experience with neuroimaging technology have indicated that their sense of being properly informed about the procedure was an important part of their positive views of the technology, while others complained about physical discomfort, particularly in the case of MEG (Senior et al., 2007).

Appendix 13.4 A Special Interview With EmSense Chief Analytics Officer, Elissa Moses

On December 13, 2010, we were pleased to have a special interview with Elissa Moses, Chief Analytics Officer of EmSense Corporation, a leading provider of neurometric research to the market research community. EmSense's EmBand is an EEG device to help track the consumer's brainwaves, and it is totally wireless and gel-free—a modern advancement on the traditional cap that is rooted in medical and academic research to record brainwaves.

Ms. Moses began by noting that the industry is rapidly changing to embrace understanding of neuroscience applications to consumer reactions and preference, particularly EEG measured brainwave patterns for understanding immediate emotional and cognitive response. "Marketers have been trying to measure emotional response and cognitive engagement for decades," said Ms. Moses, "because we know that emotion largely drives purchase decisions and that without some level of true engagement, marketing communications have no shot at making an impact. However, traditional methods have seriously fallen short. Now with breakthroughs in neuroscience and technology, we have a much better understanding of how the brain works and how the precision of biosensory response metrics can exponentially enhance consumer understanding."

As a broad term, she suggests that we might better speak of "*biosensory*" metrics to include eye-tracking and other secondary physiological response patterns, and "*neurometrics*" for that which relates specifically to brain response, such as EEG brainwave patterns. (Note: Biometrics, which is sometimes misused in this regard, is technically a way to identify individuals through fingerprinting, voice recognition, etc.)

The essential output generated by neurometrics is the study of valanced (positive or negative) *emotions*. Also, *cognitive engagement* is determined by analyzing brainwave patterns using proprietary algorithms. Neurometrics are the evolution of the researcher's quest to study implicit responses to marketing stimuli. Over the last two decades, market research has explored biosensory metrics such as eye-tracking, galvanic skin response (GSR) and voice-pitch analysis to understand visceral reactions to marketing stimuli. She argues that with the breakthrough of EEG for indicating positive and negative emotional response and intensity of active mental processing, the market research industry has been able to leap forward in offering more actionable, meaningful insights. Current neurometrics represent a significant advancement in psychomechanical, non-question-asking research.

It should be noted, according to Moses, that biosensory metrics are intended to be used *in addition to* traditional research tools and not necessarily as a replacement. They have been applied in the development and evaluation of advertising communications, web design, packaging, new product concepts, and assessing the shopper experience. The broad spectrum of survey metrics, projective techniques, qualitative interviewing, and ethnographic research can all be employed in various combinations depending on the researcher's objectives to gain complete understanding of consumers' considered and visceral response patterns.

The goal is to add the value of these new biosensory tools to define a true representation of consumer thinking and reactions to offer products and services that address what consumers genuinely want and need.

Another major theme Ms. Moses discussed was the quest for better understanding through neurometric response profiles of what drives consumer decisions and marketplace behavior. A great deal of work is currently being done to correlate pretesting predictions with ultimate in-market results. "To date," she said, "the correlations are positive and the growing body of validation is impressive." Striving for validity is essential in the sense of *relevance* to the issue(s) under investigation, *concurrence* with other measures, and, ultimately, *prediction*: Does what we learn in the laboratory play out in the marketplace?

Finally, Ms. Moses explained that the goal of these new neuroscience applications are to leverage scientific breakthroughs in the understanding of the brain, emotion, cognition, and decision making for understanding consumer response patterns. If neuromarketers are successful, all the advertising, merchandizing, packaging, and innovation investment that marketers waste can be optimized for success with better understanding of that which truly reinforces brands, communicates benefits, elicits positive emotion, and inspires purchase. Given the typical inability of consumers in other forms of research to sort out whether the emotional or the rational predominates at any time, biosensory metrics become highly useful tools. In this way, consumers are helped to shed additional light on the research matter under examination.

In sum, she argues that neuroscience may provide powerful new tools to the market research toolbox, offering precision and insight for understanding the directionality of emotional reactions and levels of engagement. These new tools can work in concert with other research methodologies—qualitative, quantitative, and behavioral—to provide marketers with more richness and precision of consumer understanding.

FURTHER READING

Tarran, B. (2010). Eight firms take part in neuroscience validation study. *Research*. Retrieved from, http://www.research-live.com/news/technology/eight-firms-to-take-part-in-arf-neuroscience-validation-study/4003667.article.

Further Viewing

Neurofocus: http://www.neurofocus.com/video.htm

EmSense: http://www.emsense.com/downloads.php and Chief Analytics Officer, Elissa Moses discusses EmSense: http://scribemedia.blip.tv/rss

Using Empathy and Narrative to Ignite Research

NEIL GAINS

Tapestry Works

THE IMPORTANCE OF EMPATHY AND NARRATIVE

Listening and storytelling have always been critical skills for market researchers. With the increasing democratization of research, easier access to customer and market data, and the need for inspiration as well as information (and quickly, too), these skills have never been in greater demand. Stan Sthanunathan wrote in *Admap* (Sthanunathan, 2010) that, "insight is a passive concept. We (market researchers) must be active participants in providing inspiration. Through inspiration you motivate people to take action and provoke their desire to create something really new and different" (p. 24).

Listening and Market Research

The origins of market research were in listening—specifically in the golden age of radio and the blossoming of the advertising industry. Advertisers needed to understand audiences to sell sponsors. From small beginnings in the 1920s, the industry blossomed in the 1940s with the use of focused groups and theories of human motivation to improve the measurement of audience reactions. In the 1960s, the publication by Carl Rogers (1961) *On Becoming a Person: A Therapist's View of Psychotherapy* had a profound impact on qualitative research practice, placing the research participant (or in Rogers's case the client) at the center of study.

In the middle of the 1960s, George Gallup and others pioneered the use of public opinion polling and the belief that all consumer behavior could be measured through scientific research. These approaches became prevalent in the 1990s, with the globalization of the industry as well as many of the industry's leading companies.

In the 21st century, market research has come full circle, and recent years have seen a return to earlier thinking, with an emphasis on the centrality of the consumer to the insight process and increasing skepticism of more rational and directed approaches to questioning (Graves, 2010). Empathy and narrative are central to the way we *all* communicate, remember, and learn, including clients, market researchers, and customers (Rifkin, 2009).

A New Mindset for Research

Market research has become a big global industry (almost 30 billion U.S. dollars in 2009), with the top five companies accounting for 48 % of turnover (ESOMAR, 2010b). This dominance is built on the process orientation of the large firms, but if market researchers are to inspire clients, we must strive to develop the skills of other creative professionals from advertising, design, journalism, and similar industries, using the whole brain to help us understand consumers' situations and engage with clients.

Daniel Pink (2005) describes these skills well in *A Whole New Mind*, arguing that they are central to future professional success in industries based on information, communication, and creative thinking. He discusses six core skills: (1) design, (2) story, (3) symphony, (4) empathy, (5) play, and (6) meaning.

Design Thinking

Design skills help researchers go beyond the functional and literal meaning of data and use them to create something emotionally engaging (and often beautiful or entertaining too). John Heskett (2002) once said, "Design, stripped to its essence, can be defined as the human nature to shape and make our environment in ways without precedent in nature, to serve our needs and give meaning to our lives" (p. 1).

Design thinking has become a buzz term, and IDEO and other companies are the darlings of innovation (as well as design). In reality, design thinking is based on many of the principles of good research, focusing on understanding problems, observing and talking to consumers, and using feedback to improve designs. Researchers can learn much from the importance placed on empathy with the consumer problem, with storytelling a key component of this (Brown, 2009).

I Wanna Tell You a Story

Stories are easier to remember than facts because stories are *how* we remember facts, not as isolated bites of information, but as sensory impressions connected together by their relationships to one another, their emotional relevance to our lives, and the order in which they occur over time. In essence, stories provide context enriched by emotion.

As Mark Turner (2006) says, "Narrative imagining—story—is the fundamental instrument of thought" (p. 4). Most of our experience, our knowledge and our thinking is organized as stories.

A Symphony of Data

Symphonies emerge from orchestras of musicians, who coordinate their efforts to create something much greater than the sum of their individual parts. Individual data are subject to analysis, but researchers must find the connections between these pieces of information to develop a synthesis. Businesses need to understand broad market trends and patterns of behavior, as well as answer specific questions, and this requires the ability to create symphonies of data.

The brain is designed for pattern recognition, and works in analogies (e.g., metaphors), which help it to take isolated sensory inputs, connect them to previous experience, and then make predictions about future events (Hofstadter, 2007). Comedian, Sid Caesar said, "The guy who invented the wheel was an idiot. The guy who invented the other three, he was a genius" (Caesar quoted in Pink, 2005, p. 142).

Standing in the Customer's Shoes

Empathy is the ability to imagine oneself in someone else's position and to feel what they are feeling. This is not the same as sympathy, but rather to sense what it would be like to be somebody else and experience the world from their perspective (Rifkin, 2009).

That is, empathy is about mimicry, something that is wired into all of us via mirror neurons in the brain, which behave the same whether we feel something ourselves or watch someone else feeling it. Emotions drive the decision making of consumers (Damasio, 2006), and as Daniel Goleman (1995) says, "People's emotions are rarely put into words; far more often they are expressed through other cues. Just as the mode of the rational mind is words, the mode of the emotions is nonverbal" (p. 96–97).

Play for Success

Being playful is one of the keys to triggering your creativity, opening your brain to new possibilities and unlimited connections. Innovation companies focus on play as a key tool of creativity, and that's not just because they are grown kids.

In fact, the open curiosity of our youth is critical to the learning process and to discovering new ideas, and Mihalyi Csikszentmihalyi (1996) sees a high correlation between creative individuals and a playful attitude. Even Albert Einstein acknowledged, "Games are the most elevated form of investigation."

Making Meaning

The motivational engine driving all our lives is the search for meaning (Bruner, 1990), and the purpose of market researchers is to identify the meaning in the data that we collect so we can guide and inspire our clients. Meaning emerges naturally from well-designed research, which playfully engages consumers allowing us to empathize with their individual situations and connect this to our client's business through a clear and simple story.

Researchers start their search for meaning by listening to customers and prospects.

LISTENING TO UNDERSTAND

There Are Many Ways to Listen and Observe

New technologies are increasing the accessibility of consumer voices (through mobile and web-based platforms) and behavioral data (through transactional databases). This technology gives researchers access to online interactions and chatter, social networks, location-based data, picture and video capture of moments in time, purchase and consumption patterns, and much more. Alongside more established tools, the following (nonexhaustive) list provides an introduction to the latest approaches to listening.

Online research is now the largest data-collection methodology at more than 20% of revenues (ESOMAR, 2010b), but it has not fundamentally changed the nature of the problems addressed, the questions asked, or the analyses used for quantitative research. However, increasingly, online research employs panels of prerecruited and profiled participants, ensuring fast and cheap access to target groups and improved ability to collect information longitudinally and cross-sectionally to better integrate behavioral, attitudinal, and demographic information. Such integration and databasing will increase in the future, and it will be especially powerful when used to correlate customer relationship marketing (CRM) data with other customized information.

In the qualitative sphere, the Internet has facilitated online focus groups and longer-term discussions (i.e., over days and weeks), allowing participants to interact with one another when appropriate (e.g., bulletin board discussions). This has further developed into developments such as netnography (ethnography devoted to the study of online cultures and communities; Kozinets, 2009) and the use of mobile devices for data collection.

Online communities have become a growing tool in research, paralleling the growth of social media, reflecting the rise of the use of peer-to-peer platforms online (or moving from a one-to-many to a many-to-many model of research). This includes the collection and interpretation of user-generated media (blogs, photos, videos) and the growth of techniques such as crowd sourcing, enabling participants to take much greater control of the research process.

Interpretation of such content has seen the development of analytic tools including the ability to mine textual information to identify patterns of common response. Buzz mining has developed through both commercial software (often brought in-house by multinational research companies) and free applications, such as those developed by Google and Twitter to track popular online topics.

All of these developments are merging in the rapid growth of online research communities (or MROCs), which are panels of participants recruited specifically to facilitate market research and, usually, devoted to a specific brand, category, or client. Such communities cross the qualitative-quantitative divide with relatively few members who are highly engaged and involved in the activities of the community. They are often set up to provide an ongoing resource for a client, allowing fast and cost-effective feedback on a wide range of business issues.

Poynter (2010) provides an exhaustive description of methods and many case studies, including well-documented examples such as EasyJet's online community and the use of buzz mining by RTL Nederlands to give weekly feedback on the X Factor TV show. Perhaps one of the best-known examples of an online community is Starbucks's use of MyStarbucksIdea (http://mystarbucksidea.force.com/), through which Starbucks have received thousands of ideas for new products, services, and improvements, more than 100 of which have already been successfully introduced.

The Ears Use Many Senses

Thus, market research listens to consumers in many ways, methods falling along a continuum of directed closed questions in surveys through increasingly open questions and dialogue and, finally, to completely undirected observation, content analysis of online interactions and opinions, and statistical analysis of behavioral databases.

Although interrogative styles (e.g., surveys and focus groups) have dominated research in the past, the increasing accessibility of transactional data and online content outlined previously (Poynter, 2010), and increasing skepticism of the value of directed questioning (Graves, 2010), are leading to a shift to less-directed research and greater two-way dialogue. This has many advantages, allowing the more natural expression of consumers' real opinions, beliefs, reactions, and behavior.

However, researchers must always beware that opinions stated online are just as subject to social biases as face-to-face interactions, and often more so. Indeed, behavioral scientists know that very little of human interaction and communication is based on language (the words we use), and studies of public speaking and mass audience communication put the importance of words at about 7% of the overall impact of a presentation. This compares with voice (tone, inflection, pauses, etc.) at 38% and body language at 55% (Mehrabian, 1971). Evolutionary biology and psychology have recently claimed that color vision evolved specifically to help us better understand other humans, by reading the color of their faces (Changizi, 2009)!

Thus, while listening is important for research, this author believes that observation of real behaviors will almost always be the most accurate approach to understand the *why* of consumer behavior, allowing researchers to develop true empathy for the consumer's situation.

Should Researchers Participate?

The directedness or openness of an interaction with a research participant defines one important dimension of an interaction. Another critical dimension is the level of involvement of the researcher, defining the likely influence of a researcher's behavior on the participant, from overt (active) interaction in a face-to-face interview, through less direct interactions on the phone, via e-mail, or in online communities through to covert (passive) observation, web scraping, or database mining.

Covert observation and listening reduce the bias of the researcher's influence on participant, but this is not always a good thing. Graves (2010) argues that covert observation always gives more accurate information, but this is only true if you believe that there is no value in questions or dialogue (as he does).

However, empathy is not passive, and listening should not always be a silent process. Good listeners are dynamically engaged in a conversation, even if they only contribute a small amount to it. Interruptions and questions help us get more out of a conversation, clarifying where unclear, probing for more detail, and also acknowledging and encouraging the participant's contribution to the conversation. Empathy is always *overt*.

Perhaps the best approach is to watch and listen first, studying the consumers' emotions and seek clarification through questioning last.

THE RIGHTS AND WRONGS OF LISTENING

Ethical Issues

The increasing access to data brings new ethical challenges to the research industry, too. Historically, market research has relied on approaches based on trust and transparency, with voluntary informed consent and confidentiality being important keystones of participation. Recent publicity surrounding web scraping has highlighted the difficulties in using web-based data, which can compromise both of these principles. For example, in "Scrapegate," Nielsen BuzzMetrics accessed discussions within a closed (or walled) online community of PatientsLikeMe.com and reported them back in some form to a private client to the consternation of some members of the community (Angwin & Stecklow, 2010).

ESOMAR and other organizations such as the Market Research Society (MRS) in the UK are running hard to keep up with developments in the industry, constantly updating guidelines to reflect new practices, and both published new draft guidelines in 2010 (ESOMAR, 2010a; Market Research Society, 2010). Privacy is challenging in the online environment, with many arguing that there should be an assumption that what is written online is in the public domain.

However, even Facebook has had to back down on completely public access, and current codes of conduct reflect that market research professionals must not abuse the trust of participants or exploit their lack of experience or knowledge. In other words, the onus sits with market research to ensure that participation is voluntary and that participants have no expectation of privacy (in cases where they are not informed of the research).

Similarly, the onus is on market research to maintain confidentiality of respondents. Even when aggregating responses, for small and niche target samples (e.g., business to business [B2B] or employee research), there is clearly a danger that individual participants may be identified unintentionally through personal details or attributable comments and opinions.

As tools and techniques develop, codes of conduct will need to adapt to new realities, but we should never forget that good research needs partnership. Participation rates for traditional research have plummeted, and we must focus relentlessly on improving the experience of research for everyone by adapting approaches to suit the needs of participants. Use of game-based approaches, flexible questioning, and simpler and easier tasks must all be used to create more enjoyable engagements.

Listening Is All About Timing and Context

Our minds work through networks of associations, so the first ideas (setting the frame of reference) at the start of any conversation are very important to framing the rest of a dialogue and the direction it takes. Context has a dramatic effect on our decisions, as can be seen in the experiments of behavioral economists (Ariely, 2008). That's why it is so important to think carefully about how questions are asked and to consider the context in which they are framed.

While vision helps us see what is happening around us (and where), our hearing helps us interpret when things happen, giving us a sense of time and causality. Timing and order are very important when listening to consumers, giving a sense of those things most important to them, the relationships between their ideas, and the certainty of their opinions.

For example, the first responses of a participant reflect those ideas most closely and directly associated with the idea in the question. Later responses may reveal less directly connected thoughts, triggered by their initial responses. In addition, the speed of a response to a question provides a clear indication of spontaneity and, therefore, of the real feelings of the participant. The longer a participant thinks about a question before responding, the more likely it is that their answer reflects consideration of its social acceptance and rationalization of a behavior, of which they may not be fully conscious.

In normal social interactions, words constitute a very small proportion of communication, and, where possible, observation of expressions and body language should be used to provide context to any interpretation of a consumer's responses.

FROM DATA TO STORIES

Making Ideas Stick

In *Made to Stick,* Chip and Dan Heath (2007) discuss the key rules of making ideas sticky, and demonstrate how to successfully communicate information and ideas so they are remembered and acted on by your audience. These are important lessons for preparing and presenting research findings, and empathy and narrative play critical roles in creating memorable meaning!

Their formula (Heath & Heath, 2007) spells SUCCESs: simple, unexpected, concrete, credible, emotional stories, and their book summarizes these rules clearly and engagingly, although the same ideas are central to countless other guides to screenwriting, copywriting, presentation skills, and the use of stories in business.

Acronyms are useful ways to make messages stick, and can be applied to any presentation, by reducing the key messages to a few simple ideas and, ultimately, to one word or phrase. For example, I recently worked on an insight mining exercise to reduce multiple research presentations and reports down to a simple summary. What worked most effectively in summarizing was to provide five key themes: simplify, humanize, attract, persuade, and explain. Having presented the summary to several very different audiences, I am pleased to say that everybody remembers the central message to SHAPE the path to purchase!

Less Is More

Simplicity is critical in an age where clients and researchers are deluged with data. This does not mean dumbing down, but rather keeping a clear and fixed focus on what are the key insights in your data, and what is their meaning for the client.

For researchers, concreteness and credibility should come naturally from the data (provided the research is well designed and executed), but again, focus is important to ensuring that your message is clear. Credibility and concreteness are obscured by too much information, which inevitably sends mixed messages, so focus attention on the most important (and believable) evidence and leave out less important details.

Emotional connection through real consumer stories should be at the heart of all research presentations and reports, but always provide an element of surprise to maintain your audience's interest in the plot. Our brains anticipate events and their sequence, making constant reference to prior and present experience, and, therefore, unexpected elements create much more interest and engagement than long-anticipated ones.

Some of the best lessons in storytelling come from masters of the craft in Hollywood (and Bollywood). I recommend watching at least one good movie every week, and don't be ashamed to steal ideas for your presentations and reports. Dorothy Parker once said that, "the only 'ism' Hollywood understands is plagiarism."

I have used movies and TV shows (as well as mythology) on many occasions to make my material more interesting, including *Star Wars*, *The Godfather* trilogy, and *Toy Story*. One of the most enjoyable presentations I have seen reviewed habit and attitude data under the theme of *Mythbusters*, setting up a series of current myths about the category that were refuted by the evidence from the research.

Equipment for Business

One of the masters of the craft is Robert McKee (1998), who has trained many successful Hollywood scriptwriters. He quotes Kenneth Burke at the beginning of his book *Story: Substance, Structure, Style, and the Principles of Screenwriting*: "Stories are equipment for living" (p. 1), and he goes on to provide a master class in how to create insightful and inspiring narratives.

The importance of stories explains why quantitative researchers often struggle to gain the same acceptance as their qualitative colleagues. Our brains are designed for understanding specific examples (by experience or by watching or listening to others), and not to compile data and evaluate evidence in the same way as the discipline of statistics would.

Our ancestors did not have access to large data sets, but had to rely on real-life examples! All of us tend to generalize from one example to the population (hence, Hume's problem with induction), and our memories for such inferences are inherently sticky. In marketing, word of mouth will always beat the polished ad campaign because evidence is evaluated based on trust in the source.

That's why engaging your audience to empathize with your subject is so important. If we identify with a story, we literally feel it ourselves, imprinting its characteristics on our mind much more powerfully than any array of numbers can do. And this is the basis of successful storytelling.

THE CRAFT OF STORYTELLING

Substance, Structure, and Style

Storytelling in research consists of three main elements. The **substance** of your story will be the individual data and facts that are used within the story to provide the content. The **structure** is the way in which the data are arranged around a series of events within a narrative, highlighting key relationships and important patterns. The **style** is the way you present the narrative and color the events, gradually revealing the development of the ideas toward a strong conclusion.

Thus, narrative and empathy are key components of your story, supporting the substance of your data with an internally consistent structure and a personal style.

The Substance of Your Story

The starting point is your data and all the related information you consider might be relevant for putting together your story. This could include information from other projects conducted for the client, secondary data, your personal experience with the product and category (always try to experience the product or service you research for yourself), the client briefing, and background of the project.

In fact, backstory is a very important concept in plotting narrative and critical to good screenwriting. Good writers know their subjects inside out and outside in, and they use this understanding to drive narrative and create tension. Think of the *Star Wars* films where Luke Skywalker's lineage is only revealed at a crucial moment as he fights Darth Vader, and with the revelation, much of the previous action suddenly makes sense.

Similarly, you know much about your client's business that lies outside the research itself but can inform the way you present information, helping you create tension and drama by revealing key pieces of history as you develop your story. That doesn't mean that you need to document this information in your presentation or report. As with all your data, you should focus only on those elements critical to the flow and substance of the narrative, ensuring it is internally consistent and takes your audience on an inevitable course to a logical conclusion.

The core of your substance should be a protagonist (or protagonists) who is (are) the central character(s) in your narrative—the brand or product or the consumer. Make sure you really know your protagonists, and develop your narrative around them. What are their goals, dreams, and aspirations? What are the barriers that they need to overcome to reach their goals? What is their relationship with other characters in the story, and where are the tensions in their relationships (which will be the most interesting part of the story)?

In a good story, there will always be an inciting incident, an event that is the reason for the story to exist. Try to see this event from the protagonist's perspective, and understand clearly the end goal of the protagonist. This should be a specific business goal. If your protagonist is a brand or product, then business value is created by growing share, increasing penetration (growing the category), increasing price (and profits), or cutting costs (and increasing profits). What is their goal, and what is stopping them achieving the goal? If your protagonist is the consumer, then think about where value is created for them: What is their personal situation, and what are the jobs that they need to get done in their life (which will be where brands come in to the picture)? Above all, what does the protagonist have to lose or gain? If the answer is nothing, then the story will have no interest for your audience.

Plotting the Structure

The first structural decision in a story is to find the controlling idea of the plot. How and why does your protagonist undergo change in the story, moving from one condition to a new (and hopefully better) place? There should always be a cause and a value underlying the controlling idea. Put simply, what is the outcome of the story (what does the client need to do), and why is that the outcome (why do they need to do it)?

Structure will revolve around key events in your story, which will be the key insights from the research. In screenwriting, the law of conflict (or antagonism) is a key principle of plot development: Nothing moves forward without conflict, and progression depends on setting up and resolving tensions between characters in the story. When I used *Star Wars* as the theme of a presentation, guess which character represented the brand and which characters represented the (then fast-growing) competitors?

So you need to decide what are the key events in your story and what information you should include and exclude. The best time to do this is *before* you start writing or opening your presentation software. Put all the relevant information on a table (or sit with the data tables and/or transcripts) and highlight only those data without which you are not able to reach your outcome (the reasons why within the controlling idea). The process should be the same as storyboarding a commercial.

Take these data and draw the relationships between them. Which data support the outcome, and which do not? Which data relate to each of your key insights (insights will always come from connecting different data together rather than from individual data points)?

You should also challenge whether the data are completely consistent. Do they show a clear pattern of events leading to an inevitable outcome? Consider alternative ways to read the data and what impact that might have on the outcome. Is there a different way of reaching your conclusion? Is there any way that the data would support the opposite conclusion? If there is, then step back and reevaluate your original research hypotheses.

Plot is your choice of events and their design in time (McKee, 1998). Or to put it another way, plot is there to navigate your way through a story so when you are confronted with many different alternatives, you inevitably choose the correct path.

In selecting the events that you include in your plot, think of unity and variety. Your plot should be internally consistent and largely inevitable, but including a variety of ideas and different points of view will help keep the story interesting and engaging.

Use an Involving Style

Language is a tool for self-expression and never an end in itself, and the great scriptwriters always add language as the last part of the puzzle. In fact, in some great movies, language features very little—in *2001: A Space Odyssey,* the first words are spoken 20 minutes into the film! So always, develop the plot and events first, adding commentary only at the last moment.

While I don't advocate keeping silent with your client, "show don't tell" is a great principle to follow when communicating results. Invisible expression empowers your audience to work out the answers for themselves and feel greater empathy with your protagonist and the events in your plot, creating a much more powerful engagement with the material. This means that messages are more likely to be remembered and acted on.

To build empathy and interest, always think about your characters and how they would interpret the events in your story. First from the point of view of your protagonist, but also consider other perspectives. How would competitor brands see events? What would the consumer think? All the characters will have expectations and much of the interest in your story will lie in how closely the course of events matches these expectations.

Above all, consider the expectations of your audience. What are they expecting to see, and how can you use their expectations to pique their interest in your narrative? Surprising your audience with unexpected plot twists will ensure they stay interested, but any surprise should be consistent with the plot and previous events (so avoid the *deus ex machina* ending).

Several tricks can be used to build engagement, introduce surprise, and reinforce messages. Metaphors and analogies help your audience create an emotional connection with your material, enabling them to link ideas to previous experience and broader themes and ideas. And always use humor, if and when appropriate, to lighten the tone.

Jokes are based on the element of surprise, delivering a payoff that is not expected from an initial set up. Juxtapositions and combinations of unusual elements can also help introduce unexpected elements, which help lead to new connections and insights, especially when these elements are taken from outside the research itself.

Finally, repetition is an important principle of learning, and do not be afraid to repeat key messages or even key events (perhaps with a shift of emphasis or a new point of view). Also, use emphasis and pauses to help dramatize the story and give focus to the most important messages. Pauses also help your audience absorb material and reflect on important ideas. So silence is a golden opportunity for you to take a breather and let your audience catch up.

Aristotle wrote that the ending of any story should be "inevitable but unexpected" (Aristotle, as quoted in Russell & Winterbottom, 1972, p. 74), or as William Goldman wrote more recently, "Give the audience what it wants, but not the way it expects" (Goldman, as quoted in McKee, 1998). Thus, the payoff at the end of your presentation or report must be consistent with all the events leading up to it, but if it is completely predictable, then it will be uninteresting and unlikely to engage the client.

Above all, the payoff should bring your audience to a different place than where they started. Progression is the key to any great story, providing the audience with the satisfaction that they have been on an enjoyable journey and discovered something new. In particular, always consider whether you can generalize findings, developing universal truths or ideas from the specific results of the research and providing the most satisfying progression of all.

TOP-10 TIPS FOR STORYTELLING

Here are my top-10 tips for storytelling, with examples from one of the best presenters in the world (see *The Presentation Secrets of Steve Jobs* by Carmine Gallo [2009] for more examples).

1. Spend as much time as possible preparing your thoughts and identifying your controlling idea (the inner truth of your narrative). You should be able to write this in a single sentence (no more than 50 words). This will guide you as you develop the material, providing clarity on where the story should end and what events will be included in the journey. Steve Jobs was a master at this, creating short punchy

headlines as focal points for his narratives (for example, "Today Apple reinvents the phone," "The world's thinnest notebook," and "1,000 songs in your pocket"). SHAPE and *Mythbusters* served a similar purpose for me.

2. Be clear on the protagonist of the story (brand, product, consumer). What does the protagonist want? What is their motivation? Who and what is getting in the way of them achieving their ambitions? Steve Jobs was messianic in selling Apple as a hero, frequently pitting his company against an evil protagonist, most notably Big Blue in the famous 1984 Super Bowl commercial and more recently Microsoft.

3. The story should be structured around your key insights, and these events will drive your narrative forward. Make sure you control the flow of information, only revealing what is important to the plot of the story. Steve Jobs always set out a roadmap of his (sometimes quite long) presentations, providing clear markers of what is to come. For more straightforward-results presentations, I often reveal the key messages at the start of the presentation and then provide the supporting evidence around these messages in the main part of the presentation. This "tell them what you're going to say, tell them, and then tell them what you have just said" style of presentation provides very clear structure around key insights and actions, and it helps communicate important messages in a style many consultants and clients prefer.

4. Set up the story clearly at the beginning, using your opening statement to set expectations and provide clear direction. Remember that the enjoyment of the story depends greatly on audience expectations and how they are met, so the opening is critical to managing your audience's reactions throughout. For example, in 2007, Steve Jobs's opening statement on unveiling the iPhone was that he would that day be introducing three revolutionary new products: a widescreen iPod with touch controls, a revolutionary mobile phone, and a breakthrough Internet-communication device, going on to finally explain that all three breakthroughs were in fact one device. Research audiences like to have clear direction (as mentioned in the previous point), which sets expectations and still leaves room to combine key insights into unified recommendations.

5. Decide on your persona (or personas), and narrate your story from one or more perspectives to create empathy and engagement. Focus on your protagonist, but use other points of view to help create interest and tension in the story, making sure that you are authentic and believable in each persona. Steve Jobs is strongly identified with the Apple brand, and presents a consistent, passionate, and engaged persona.

6. Always know where you are headed, and ensure that your audience only knows at the conclusion of the story. Manage events and flow of information to ensure that there is always some element of surprise, even if the conclusion is inevitable. Surprise is key to keeping your audience engaged. In an earlier example, Steve Jobs presented "three" new products, building suspense and tension until he eventually announced, "Today, Apple reinvents the phone."

7. Every story has a beginning, middle, and end, or to put it more formally, a complication and denouement. The middle of the story will be where most interest lies and where tension and conflict should appear. Within these three movements, a story should be unified, with all elements clearly connected. Steve Jobs usually builds a presentation or communication in three parts, provides clear signposts throughout, and always saves the best part until last. John F. Kennedy and Barack Obama have also benefited from the rule of threes (as have I)!

8. Make sure that you periodically pull together the threads of the story, using key events or insights to make clear the connections between characters and any change in their relationships. Steve Jobs provided regular signposts and breaks throughout his presentations. A good rule of thumb is to take a breather every 10 minutes, before your audience's brains overload on information, and this is a good opportunity for a quick rewind and reminder.

9. Focus on the meaning of the story for the audience. Clearly communicate how the protagonist changes during the course of the narrative and what that means for your client. Steve Jobs always focused on the question, "Why should I care?" talking to the benefits for the end consumers rather than the product features (compare and contrast with some of Bill Gates presentations). For instance, he introduced Apple's presentation software, "Using Keynote is like having a professional graphics department to create your slides. This is the application to use when your presentation really counts" (p. 64). I always bring my presentations back to the four sources of client value, which brings the findings to life, making the implications real, tangible, and valuable.

10. Always leave a few loose ends and some unfinished business. By leaving some unanswered questions, you allow your audience flexibility in bringing their interpretation to the story and their ideas within the framework that you have provided. Steve Jobs would often add a "and one more thing" at the end of a presentation, answering at least one of the questions that are still in the audience's minds.

Most marketing research presentations are not global marketing events, but the principles and examples in these 10 tips apply to any presentation where you need to engage and communicate. My experience (from the perspective of presenter and audience) has always been that the best presentations have a clear protagonist, plot, purpose, and payoff. This is easy to develop when you focus on the meaning you want to convey to your audience, summarized best in three questions to ask yourself before every presentation. What would I like my audience to know? What would I like them to feel? And what would I like them to do?

THE PAYOFF

Clients and researchers alike learn most successfully through the mental simulation of events rather than the anticipation of outcomes. In any form of communication or learning, behavioral change comes from the journey itself and not from reaching a particular destination.

Pop psychology tells us all to visualize success, but this is wrong. Success comes from practice, and mental practice is two-thirds as good as real practice (Medina, 2008)!

Mental simulation works because our imagining brain is using the same neural circuits as our doing brain. The brain mirrors activity so the simulation of an event feels the same as the event itself, and mental simulation is strongly tied to our emotions. The most effective stories are simulations triggering the same emotions and mental connections in you or your audience as if you had made the journey yourselves.

Empathy and narrative are powerful because they provide the context and emotions missing from words and numbers on a page. Stories put information and knowledge into a framework, which is more true to life and helps us understand the situation of others, feeling as if we were in their shoes experiencing the same events.

Above all, empathy and narrative automatically bring us into a state of readiness, mentally prepared to internalize and act on the behaviors we have just simulated. If market researchers are to truly drive business change, we must understand consumers' situations and stories, connect them to our lives and the needs of clients, and share their true meaning.

We must ignite our research with empathy and narrative.

FURTHER READING

Armstrong, K. (2005). *A short history of myth*. Edinburgh, UK: Canongate.

Duarte, H. (2010). *Resonate: Present visual stories that transform audiences*. Hoboken, NJ: John Wiley & Sons.

Tierno, M. (2002). *Aristotle's poetics for screenwriters: Storytelling secrets from the greatest mind in western civilization*. New York, NY: Hyperion.

CHAPTER 15

Standing Waves

Stasis, Contagion, and Consumer Trends

J. WALKER SMITH

The Futures Company

Trends research is a funny business. It thrives despite itself, for if accuracy in predicting the future were the metric that mattered, trends research would be done for.

No matter how confidently they carry themselves, experts are on shaky ground when they claim to know the future, something that has been demonstrated repeatedly by research into the ability of experts to make accurate predictions.

In 1964, two researchers at the RAND Corporation studied the ways in which 82 experts went about making long-range predictions in the six areas of scientific breakthroughs, population control, automation, space progress, war prevention, and weapons systems. What they observed were experts sorting through information and options in ways that were vulnerable to many identifiable biases. In other words, the experts they studied were plying the trade of predicting the future in ways sure to make their forecasts unsound and unreliable (Gordon & Helmer, 1964).

This RAND study (Gordon & Helmer, 1964) was one of many precursors of the groundbreaking research done by social psychologists Daniel Kahneman and Amos Tversky from the late 1960s to the mid1990s, a series of studies that gave rise to the field of behavioral economics for which Kahneman received the 2002 Nobel Memorial Prize in Economics. Kahneman and Tversky identified many flawed and recurring cognitive biases in the heuristics that people, experts included, use to make decisions (Kahneman, Slovic, & Tversky, 1982).

Subsequent studies have confirmed, repeatedly, that experts are simply inexpert at predicting the future (Batchelor, 2007; Freedman, 2010). Perhaps the most telling of these studies is the two-decade-long work completed by University of California at Berkeley business professor Philip Tetlock (2005). He cataloged 82,361 political and economic predictions made by 284 experts and then scored their accuracy. Not only were these experts wrong more often than they were right, they were less accurate than chance. Literally, they would have had a better record rolling the dice!

So why worry about studying trends if prediction of the future is little more than a snipe hunt? Because nothing is more important for successful marketing than properly understanding the future. Every aspect of marketing is an exercise in managing the future. First-movers realize an enormous order-of-entry market share advantage that persists over time (Gurumurthy, Robinson, & Urban, 1995). Limited resources require that marketers put scarce time and money behind brands with greater future potential. And brands must evolve continuously to keep up with innovations by competitors and sudden shifts in the marketplace. Even when marketers stand pat, an implicit bet is being made that the future will require nothing different. Every decision made by marketers embodies some expectation about impending events. For marketers, the future is always at hand.

The future is no less important to consumers. The 2010 U.K. MONITOR study of The Futures Company found that the characteristic of "anticipates the future better than its competitors" is the sixth most important attribute that U.K. consumers believe is "characteristic of a leading brand." A vision of the future is also a top-ten characteristic that U.K. consumers expect of a "great business leader" (Smith, 2010).

The quandary facing marketers is that forecasts of the future, while stubbornly wide of the mark, are utterly essential.

METAMORPHOSES

Marketers study trends and futures to steal a march on competitors and pioneer new revenue streams for their businesses. It's all about being the first to capitalize on change. Marketers care about change not trends per se. Marketers don't care about trends for trends sake; they care about trends because they care about change. Their interest in the next big thing focuses marketers on studying change, an orientation, a bias even, which ripples out to marketing research.

When marketing researchers tackle change, they usually conflate two aspects of change that must be understood separately—change as outcome and change as trigger.

All that marketers care about is a change in outcomes. Marketers want to be the first to know which aspects of the marketplace are going to metamorphose. What triggers a new outcome is not always germane to responding to it.

On the other hand, marketing researchers must focus on change both as outcome and as trigger. Marketing researchers focus on change as outcome because that's what their marketing clients want. They focus on change as trigger because they want to understand what's causing new outcomes and even use that knowledge sometimes to make predictions. This is where the bias in orientation kicks in because it leads to an unstated, often unrecognized, presumption that change in one thing is the only trigger that can cause change in something else. It's assumed that only other prior, precipitating changes can trigger changes in outcomes. In fact, more often than is appreciated, changes in outcomes are triggered not by other things changing but by things continuing as before. This is to say that no change at all is the biggest trigger of change.

While speaking in paradoxes underscores the proper way to approach the study and management of change, it is not how marketing researchers or their marketing clients frame what they do. Business-speak is plainspoken, not metaphorical or ironic. Nuances must connect directly to tactics. What needs to be done must be articulated in a straightforward and unambiguous way. Common sense is preferred over complexity.

In business, embellishment and embroidery get in the way because byzantine marketing concepts are difficult if not impossible to put into action. Explaining them is difficult. Defining expectations or setting milestones becomes unworkable. Collaboration is frustrated. The paradoxical pie in the sky winds up on your face.

So it's only natural that marketing researchers take a literal approach to change. Change means change; therefore, the triggers of changes in outcomes must, by definition, be other kinds of changes. The idea that no change could precipitate change seems nonsensical, and, thus, it is typically not considered.

Obviously, this is an exaggerated description of how marketers think, but it is an overstatement to underscore a basic reality about trends research. Certainly, marketing research is not anti-intellectual. Nor are cerebral marketing concepts beyond the ken of marketer researchers. That said, there is a widespread feeling among marketers, and indeed among all business people, that Peter Lynch's oft-quoted investment tip is also the smartest way to do business, to wit, "Go for a business that any idiot can run because sooner or later, any idiot probably is going to run it" (Investopedia.com, Quotes). In short, simplicity is the best guarantee of success. Marketers share a tacit partiality for unadorned, straightforward thinking.

Yet for all the wisdom in this preference for simplicity, sometimes it is not the wisest thing to do, particularly when it comes to trends, futures, and change.

RESEARCHING CHANGE

There are as many approaches to trends research as there are consumer-marketing companies, but amid this diversity, there are similar fundamentals. As typically practiced, the objective of trends research is to identify emerging changes in consumer attitudes. Working from an implicit assumption that attitude change has causal sway, marketing researchers look for the early signs of attitude change in the belief that changes in marketplace behaviors are triggered by changes in attitudes. Finding early evidence of changing attitudes is, thus, a harbinger of changes in behaviors to come.

But marketing researchers want to do more than just track emerging changes in attitudes. They want to anticipate such changes as well. So they also look for changes in the antecedents or roots of attitudes. In their search for these headwaters, marketing researchers range everywhere, studying such factors as other attitudes, the economy, technology, demographics, historical cycles, competitors, the environment, politics, religion and spirituality, societal institutions, social relationships, and more.

Trends researchers try to predict changes in these antecedent factors, but this is impossible to do in a reliable, structured, and replicable way. In particular, trends researchers look for turning points, reversals, synergies and, most elusive of all, black swans. Even in reciting this list of changes, the hopelessness of the task is evident. Certainly, these are uncertainties for which businesses need to be prepared. Many will occur with a measurable statistical likelihood, but none is predictable with any kind of repeatable, pinpoint accuracy.

Turning points, reversals, synergies, and black swans can be hypothesized for contingency planning. Through techniques, such as scenario planning and Delphi methods, future contingencies can be managed, just not predicted. But the management of such contingencies is the day-to-day job of marketing researchers who support line managers running ongoing businesses. It's not what trends research is all about.

Trends researchers believe that deeper, more careful study of antecedent factors will make them more accurate in anticipating changes in triggering events. There are certainly instances in which this has been the case, but these instances are actually the exceptions that prove the rule.

Oxford University economist Jerker Denrell and New York University management professor Christina Fang cataloged the predictions made from July 2002 to July 2005 by the panel of economists surveyed by the *Wall Street Journal* for its twice-yearly Survey of Economic Forecasts (Keohane, 2011). They zeroed in on those economists who had correctly predicted extreme events and found that economists who had missed the so-called "big one," their overall accuracy across all forecasts was much worse than average. As Denrell and Fang summed it up, "The analyst with the largest number as well as the highest proportion of accurate and extreme forecasts had, by far, the worst forecasting record" (p. 9). They likened success in making extreme predictions to the broken clock that is dead-on twice a day but nowhere close at any other time.

Denrell's (Keohane, 2011) prior work on forecasting accuracy reveals an inveterate bias in the ways in which people study success. The emphasis on looking at successes not failures leads to an oversimplified view of what it takes to succeed. In reality, the thin line between success and failure depends on chancy events springing from an enormous complexity of moving parts. What are ignored are the base rates of success and failure, which are far better predictors of what is likely to occur. Base rates, of course, are not things that change; they are, instead, the things that stay the same. What causes a change in outcomes is not a change in triggers. It's the things that don't change. These are the best guides to changes yet to come.

Trends researchers, though, are always looking for the big one. It is an obsessive focus on short-term shocks in the belief that changes in triggers are the only way to understand and anticipate changes in outcomes. But these kinds of contingencies, as important as they are in the successful management of brands, are not the key when it comes to trends. This is one of the lessons of the so-called Great Recession of 2008/2009.

A media consensus emerged during 2009 that the economic downturn of 2008/2009 had ushered in a new normal of frugality that would utterly change the consumer marketplace forever (The Hartman Group, 2011). But no sooner had these pronouncements taken root as Gospel truth than they were proven false. This kind of hyperbolic overreaction to economic downturns is typical. Catherine Rampell (2009), editor of the Economix blog for *The New York Times*, noted in early 2009, that while the phrase "the Great Recession" was acquiring currency as the moniker of choice for the downturn, almost every recession in the U.S. since the end of WW2 had been dubbed by one or more experts and media pundits as the Great Recession. Like Fred Sanford, it seems we're always suffering the big one.

Despite bubbles and busts, the course of the U.S. economy persists in a relatively constant and predictable upward trajectory. In early 2011, Rampell (2011) attended the annual conference of the American Economics Association at which Harvard economist David Laibson presented a paper he coauthored with two of his doctoral students. In it, they noted that the fixation on short-term changes and shocks overlooks the overriding importance of long-term regularities in determining the future. Rampell summed up his thesis in this way,

> Professor Laibson argued that the economy will always revert back to its long-term growth trend, but people still tend to freak out about sudden shocks to the system in the short-term and assume they present a permanent diversion from that long-run trend. . . . This obsession with a "new normal" lends some momentum for the current catastrophe or craze, but nonetheless subsides as things eventually return to their long-run trend (para. 3).

What's important in trends research is not what changes; it's what stays the same.

STANDING WAVES

To say that things stay the same is not to suggest that there is no dynamism to these regularities. Perhaps the best metaphor is one of standing waves, which is a phenomenon of energy waves that remain in a constant position notwithstanding the power propagating them. Standing waves don't change, yet they trigger changes, as any pilot or kayaker who has encountered one can attest. Packed with force, standing waves are able to energize many changes.

Standing waves is a useful metaphor for trends researchers studying the triggers of changes in outcomes. The forces responsible for trends are those that exert a regularity of pressure on the marketplace, not those that burst into view capriciously and unpredictably.

A focus on standing waves means a different approach to trends research. The breathless, faddish search for the next big thing gives way to a more deliberate, more measured tracking of long-term regularities and their consequences. There are five key components of a standing-waves approach to trends research, all of which represent a change in priorities for trends research.

First, the central focus is not on consumers *per se*. It's on the structural dynamics that shape the context within which consumers encounter the marketplace and make choices.

Second, the important elements of change are not attitudes. Indeed, attitudes may not figure into the equation at all. Some structural dynamics (if not all according to attribution theorists and many behavioral economists) will trigger behavioral changes directly, without any shift in intervening attitudes.

Third, the relevant causal linkages from triggers to outcomes are no longer those of attitudes to behaviors. Instead, the causal linkages of greatest relevance are those mapping the ways in which standing waves of regularities energize change.

Fourth, the time horizon of trends research stretches out. Prognostications about the year ahead are explicitly recognized to be issues for researchers supporting ongoing brand management. The immediate term is about the contingencies of the moment, and there should be plans in place to manage near-term issues. But trends research informs the longer term.

Finally, trends research must be focused as much if not more on contagion than on origins. Ultimately, the origins of changes are less relevant than the speed and direction with which changes spread. It is more fruitful for trends researchers to identify where a new development is headed than to anticipate the new development beforehand. For marketers, it is more important to know where change is headed than simply to be made aware that change has occurred.

These five elements of trends research are known, but they do not shape the fundamental structure and focus of trends research today. The current practice of trends research is almost wholly consumer focused, with a microscope on attitudes and a stress on things that are unfolding today. To put itself on solid footing, trends research needs to focus instead on the standing waves that trigger change, of which there are three types of particular interest: fixed, evolving, and discordant.

FIXED STANDING WAVES

Some dynamics are stable and never really change. Certain fixed needs are always present. Yet it is this very stability that sparks changes in the marketplace.

Some of these fixed needs are basics, things that fall at the bottom of Maslow's (1987) hierarchy of needs, such as food, water, sleep, sex, security, employment, health, and so forth. These basic unchanging needs give rise to many changes in the marketplace, as companies compete to better satisfy these needs. This continual interplay of necessities and satisfactions drives an evolution in the marketplace that can be plotted over time. Other structural dynamics are evolving, too, unlocking new possibilities for better satisfying these unchanging needs. The marketplace is shaped by the fixed nature of needs, a constant that is best understood as a form of stasis or a regularity that gives rise to new outcomes.

This sort of constancy is true of many things, some of which, while bound by culture, are enduring for consumers. For example, a fixation on weight loss is widespread in the U.S. marketplace. Over a long time, it is unchanging. Weight-loss fads come and go, but the desire for weight-loss products is always present. There is nothing new to discover here. The underlying desire is fixed. The future will be determined by the ability of new technologies to satisfy this desire, not by an abrupt turning point or reversal that creates a desire for weight-loss products.

Perhaps a political analogy helps bring fixed waves into sharper focus. One fixed, invariant element of American politics is a four-year election cycle for president. This constant, unchanging element leads to significant changes. At least, every eight years and, often, every four, there is a change in the occupant of the presidency. This change occurs not because of some sudden, abrupt shift in political infrastructure. No *coup d'etat* is required. Instead, a constant feature of the political system precipitates change. The very thing that is the most unchanging about politics is what leads to political change.

EVOLVING STANDING WAVES

Not all constancies in the marketplace stay exactly the same over time. Some things that are constant about the marketplace are the direction of change or the rate of change. These elements are unchanging in the ways in which they are evolving. While these elements change shape as they evolve, they continue along on an unchanging arc of evolution that can be traced and anticipated.

The best illustration of this is Moore's (1965) Law, the well-known assertion by Intel cofounder Gordon Moore that the number of transistors put into an integrated circuit would double every two years. Moore's Law was a statement about a constant rate of change in computing power and processing speed. Based on this stable evolutionary dynamic, the future of computing could be anticipated because all aspects of computing are harnessed to power and speed. The future is simply a function of the point at which certain thresholds of power and speed will be crossed.

The marketplace is shaped by many dynamics such as this. In particular, demographics have a trend line driven by a certain momentum that cannot easily or rapidly change. For example, when China introduced its one-child-per-family policy in 1979, demographic changes in China were not immediately affected. Population still grew by virtue of the enormous size of the total population, and young people born in the 1950s and 1960s continued to put pressure on the government and society as they came of age in the 1970s and 1980s. It is only now that the full effects of the one-child-per-family policy are starting to be seen, effects that have a momentum that will play out for decades to come irrespective of whatever else happens.

Another good illustration of how evolving dynamics influence trends appeared in a story in the *Financial Times* about the impact of the Chinese economy on the centuries-old Chinese cultural preference for sons over daughters (Waldmeir, 2010). The rapid rise of the Chinese economy in recent decades has meant greater prosperity for many, as well as a shift from a rural to an urban economy. Both have undermined the need for sons to work the fields and to provide for aging parents. Added to that is a housing boom in China that has driven up prices, making it impossible for many Chinese parents to abide by another tradition of providing a separate home for their son so he is able to marry. In the face of these economic pressures, cultural values have shifted. The demographic gender imbalance of boys over girls peaked in 1995, and has steadily weakened since then. Technology has abetted this trend in the form of Internet chat rooms where women exchange tips on how to conceive girls instead of boys.

The value that Chinese tradition places on boys has been so strong that it is estimated that in recent decades tens of millions of girls have been aborted or killed. A cover story in *The Economist* dubbed it "Gendercide" (*The Economist*, 2010a). This cultural value preference can be traced as far back as the *Book of Songs*, the earliest known collection of Chinese poems and songs that first appeared in 1,000 B.C. (Baculinao, 2004). Yet, with the steady, unchanging evolution of structural changes in 21st century China, a new structure of values and choices is rising.

For students of modernization, it is well known and long documented that economic development has a profound effect on cultural values. Structural changes have an observable impact across generational cohorts. Ronald Inglehart (1997) of the University of Michigan, who oversees the three-decade-old World Values Survey and is best known for his theory of postmaterialism, has shown that the evolution of values associated with economic prosperity tends to be observed on a generational time lag. Other generational researchers, including this author, have also found these patterns of evolutionary changes in values as well (Smith & Clurman, 2007).

The blogosphere has even weighed in on this subject. George Mason economist Tyler Cowen (2010) writes a widely read economics blog, and in one post, he joined in speculation by other bloggers that the evolution of structural dynamics will radically change future ethical values. Cowen wondered, for example, whether the evolution of technology would change the moral status of things such as abortion, euthanasia, preemptive warfare, and changes made to the natural environment. All that's required for these values to change is the steady, unchanging direction of evolution in the dynamics that are currently in place and already at work.

DISCORDANT STANDING WAVES

Sometimes, a standing wave will mask the discordant energies that constitute it. Indeed, the classic form of a standing wave is the combination of two waves of equal amplitude traveling in opposite directions. This coming together of opposing forces is a common sort of marketplace regularity that generates changes in outcomes.

Usually, this sort of discordance is referred to as tension. Many dynamics are present only in concert with a contrary dynamic. For example, the tension between traditional identities and economic modernization is an ever-present dynamic in all emerging economies. Similarly, the tension between limits of time and legions of data is a pervasive dynamic is all developed societies. Indeed, all opposites create ongoing tension: gender, social class, religion, geography, age, and so forth.

Tensions or discordances are always around. Sometimes, one element will have the upper hand; other times, the other element will hold sway. But it is the unceasing tension between dynamics that is the trigger of changes in marketplace outcomes.

One of the biggest tensions marketers face is the conflict between an ever-increasing torrent of advertising and media and upper limits in the cognitive capacities of people to process information. There is much debate about the actual amount of advertising to which people are exposed, but there is no debate that the aggregate amount of advertising, media, and other information confronting people each day has increased substantially over the past three decades (AAAA, 2007; Bohn & Short, 2009; Vedrashko, 2007). Yet people simply do not have the ability to absorb, understand, and act on all of this information. In a comprehensive research review, psychologist George Miller (1956) noted in a famous, often-cited paper that the largest number of things people could hold in working memory at any one time is seven, plus or minus two. In 1992, evolutionary biologist Robin Dunbar presented evidence that approximately 150 people are the upper-size limit for the circle of friends that any one person can maintain.

This tension between available information and cognitive capacity is a permanent dynamic in every economy that has advanced beyond the most primitive level of sophistication. Managing this tension triggers changes that create business opportunities, particularly as technologies evolve and offer new solutions. It's also kinds of content, visual versus textual expressions of data, feelings of pace and pressure, the need for leisure, and the style of work and the approach to work/life balance, just to name a few.

EXCEPT WHEN IT DOES CHANGE

Putting priority on the unchanging regularities of standing waves invites at least one obvious objection. As the renowned futurist Jim Dator (n.d.) put it,

> Trend analysis is very useful. It helps you see what might be the case 'if trends continue' in the future as they did in the past. But trend analysis is seldom an accurate 'prediction' because 'trends seldom continue.' Something always seems to happen to interrupt most trends. (p. 3)

In this context, Dator means trends in the same sense in which standing waves are discussed here. His point is simply that eventually everything changes, even things that seem to be unchanging.

While Dator's (n.d.) observation is true, even Dator doesn't prescribe a trends research agenda focused on predicting turning points, reversals, synergies, and black swans. Instead, what he recommends is a program of "environmental scanning" that surveys the marketplace for "crazy people, marginal people, off-beat publications . . . the recesses of the mind of some scientist or engineer. The concern of some artist or poet, or unpublished novelist" (p. 6). Such inputs would then be subordinated within the study of unchanging regularities for any clues offered about the state of the "the life cycle of everything." The scanning prescribed by Dator is not a substitute for standing waves; he sees it as a better way of understanding standing waves.

Of course, standing waves don't stand forever. These overarching regularities in the marketplace must end sometime, an eventuality for which trends researchers must be prepared. Standing waves collapse when turning points, reversals, synergies, or black swans bring them to an end, but there's no sense in trying to forecast these things because these are exactly the kinds of things that are inherently unpredictable, as the research cited here has shown. Besides, most standing waves rebound once a crisis has passed anyway. Although the contingencies of the moment must be addressed, trends researchers need to remain focused on where the marketplace is headed over the long term, and that involves a deeper study of regularities, not a search of the heavens for the visit from E.T. that will change everything.

CONTAGION

One of the biggest gaps in trends research is the study of how new things are disseminated. Trends researchers are focused, almost exclusively, on what's coming next, not on how it is spread around. But this is a needed shift in focus.

The study of change in the form of predicting turning points, reversals, synergies, and black swans is all about spotting new developments. But something new won't become something big until it becomes something widespread. So it is not enough to identify what's bubbling up. It is also necessary to determine if, and if so, how, it's going to catch on.

In this regard, the science of network analysis is just as essential for trends research as it is for media research. What has become quite clear is how little we knew before about the nature and processes of dissemination and contagion. Now that technology made available the databases it takes to assess and analyze the network connections that tie people together, we see that everything spreads in a network fashion, whether it's happiness, loneliness, anxiety, obesity, smoking, altruism, voting, tutor recommendations, media choices, or product preferences (Christakis & Fowler, 2009).

A growing body of recent research covering a wide variety of domains has found social influences to be far more controlling than previously recognized, not because of anything new in the marketplace, although there are new things going on, but because our understanding of the marketplace has improved. Not only have such studies provided new insights about what influences decision making, they have raised a fundamental challenge to the traditional understanding of what should be researched.

Marketing models from hierarchy of effects to conjoint and discrete choice focus on the individual to the exclusion of social influences. Diffusion, two-step flow, and word-of-mouth models put primary focus on individual agents and little or none on the networks of connections and context that bind people together. Media buying models target individual consumers, oblivious to the context, conversations, and cues that determine how and whether a message gets through, and at what cost. New learning from the growing body of research on connections and context raises deep-seated questions about the models that guide marketing planning.

It is not as if marketers have ignored the context of social influences in the past. What's changed is knowledge of the primary importance of social influences. The structural dynamics captured in the study of standing waves encompass the interconnections of consumers networked together by their social ties. Although trends research looking for new fads has flagged social networking as a change in the marketplace, it is the study of marketplace regularities that point to the ways in which social networks control and accelerate the spread of new outcomes.

MANAGING FORESIGHTS

Megatrends and macroforces, often distilled from newspaper headlines, research abstracts, or bestsellers, are routinely trumpeted as the next big world-changing phenomenon. It's hype.

Trend spotters scour the globe for unusual finds and then spotlight them with catchy names that make them seem earth shattering. It's hit or miss.

Futurologists and lay sociologists look for hidden patterns in the flow of events that can be explained by some obscure cycle woven into the warp and woof of the world. It's conspiratorial.

Marketers need more than an anecdotal portrait of what's to come. Marketers need to take control. Marketers don't want to see the future as much as they want to create it. Marketers don't want to respond to the future; they want to invent it. The purpose of trends research is not to paint a picture of the future. It is to show marketers how they can change the course of the future in their favor.

Trends research to identify opportunities for active intervention is fundamentally different from forecasts about how the future will turn out. In the latter, the unfolding of the future is fixed and will take shape as things play out. In the former, the unfolding of the future is yet to be determined and, thus, open to change, taking shape as those caught in it take charge.

The purpose of trends research is to define alternatives, and that can come only from a study of the standing waves of change. Marketers need to know possible courses of action. The real value of trends research comes not from charting future events but from identifying the challenges likely to be posed by these events.

This understanding of the purpose of trends research puts to bed the most common question asked of trends researchers: "Is this a fad or a trend?" As if the answer to this question should count in what marketers decide to do. The crucial question for marketers is not whether a marketing opportunity is a fad or a trend but whether it offers a profitable avenue for a brand to pursue. If that avenue happens to be a fad, then marketers should go after it, fad or not.

None of this is meant to imply that quantitative surveys are the only valid sources of information about trends and futures. It is only to say that whatever and however data and examples are collected, collated, and synthesized, such input should be not be accumulated and analyzed haphazardly, but in a focus on the broader dynamics and regularities at work in the marketplace.

The Futures Company continues to judge the success of its trends and futures work by the criteria articulated early on for the Yankelovich MONITOR. As noted in the management summary for the second year of MONITOR in 1972, there are five critical things for which marketers rely on trends and futures research (Daniel Yankelovich, Inc., 1972).

1. An early warning system

2. A source of ideas for new products and new initiatives

3. A source of new approaches for existing brands

4. A reference for marketing tactics being considered

5. A "device" for "mind stretching"

These MONITOR (Daniel Yankelovich, Inc., 1972) applications run the gamut and constitute core ways in which trends research provides value irrespective of precise future predictions. Of course, the same thing could be said about any stimulus, however wacky. The unique value of trends research is the ability to use structured techniques and to vet plans and strategies. Unsystematic approaches might get it right, but only by happenstance and without an underlying method or foundation to ensure a thorough definition of alternatives. The odds of success are greater and better managed when an exacting procedure is followed to bring trends, futures, and marketing together in a proper study of the regularities driving change. A focus on standing waves best informs the quest for the next big thing.

FURTHER READING

Armstrong, J. S. (1980, June/July). The seer-sucker theory: The value of experts in forecasting. *Technology Review, 83,* 16–24.

Marketing Research Industry Trends

Mixed Methods in Marketing Research

MELVIN PRINCE

Southern Connecticut State University

MARK A. DAVIES

Heriot-Watt University

CHRIS MANOLIS

Xavier University

SUSAN TRATNER

Empire State College

INTRODUCTION

For most of the past 50 years, marketing researchers relied on quantitative *research* to answer their research questions. Analytical techniques employed included cluster, factor, and discriminant analyses, Chi Square Automatic Interaction Detector, multidimensional scaling, and correspondence analysis. However, before the turn of the century, many marketing researchers turned to an increased use of qualitative research, which included in-depth interviewing, case-based research, focus groups, observation studies, and ethnography.

In recent years, marketing researchers have increasingly cultivated an understanding of and appreciation for both quantitative and qualitative approaches, and they also have begun increasingly combining these two approaches in studies using mixed methods designs. Spurred on by developments in brand and communications research, as well as buzz measurement and network monitoring, mixed methods marketing research has broadened its scope and emerged as an increasingly popular major methodological option. Marketing researchers are starting to view it as a third approach to research, alongside quantitative and qualitative research.

One firm employs a technique that uses quantitative and qualitative online sessions and uses of stimuli for interactive research experiences. Close-ended rating responses are systematically followed by open-ended qualitative explanations. The qualitative data are rich and provide depth of insights into quantitatively measured attitudes (Invoke Solutions, 2008). Mixed methods are eminently suited for projects that rely heavily on emotion. Based on a survey of marketing researchers, mixed methods is considered an invaluable tool for concept tests, message tests, ad tests, naming studies, and packaging tests (iModerate, 2010).

Marketing researchers, in general, need a systematic overview of mixed methods marketing research so that they are familiar with its definition and can judge when it is the appropriate design to choose for a given research problem. They also need practical examples of how marketing researchers are applying this approach in research studies.

In this chapter, we present an introductory overview of mixed methods research. We begin with its definition and discuss reasons that researchers choose this approach and the value that it can bring over other designs. Then we illustrate with unique case illustrations how mixed methods can be applied in practice for a range of research objectives (i.e., survey questionnaire design, explanation of consumer buying styles, and examination of interorganizational cooperation and conflict). These cases represent the different major types of mixed methods designs, discuss the important features that distinguish these designs, and provide concrete applications of mixed methods. Importantly, these same formal mixed methods design and analysis strategies apply to all forms of data, including those obtained observationally via new media, such as consumer brand communities. Finally, we consider the challenges that researchers face when choosing to implement a mixed methods approach and offer our advice for researchers considering mixed methods designs for their studies.

In formulating research designs to respond to marketing problems, a frequent and familiar question arises: Which approach would be best to use for our problem—quantitative or qualitative research? The answer is generally quantitative or qualitative research. The standard rationale supplied for the marketing researcher's answer is conditional: If we are testing hypotheses for decision making, quantitative research is recommended; if we wish to generate rich, in-depth insights and understanding for strategic direction, qualitative research is recommended. This chapter is about a third, and less-familiar option, the recommended use of mixed methods. Mixed methods are research designs that employ both quantitative and qualitative approaches in a research study.

Mixed methods research can result in unanticipated serious political crises between marketing researchers and their clients. Onwuegbuzie and Collins (2007) offer the following insights about this process:

> This crisis refers to the tensions that arise as a result of combining quantitative and qualitative approaches, including any conflicts that arise when different investigators are used for quantitative and qualitative components of a study, the

contradictions and paradoxes that come to the fore when quantitative and qualitative data are compared and contrasted, the difficulty in persuading the consumers of mixed methods research (e.g., stakeholders and policy makers) to value the results stemming from both the quantitative and qualitative components of the study, and the tensions ensuing when ethical standards are not addressed within the research design. (p. 308)

Involvement in mixed methods projects should not be entered into lightly and without careful forethought (Collins & O'Cathain, 2009). For the mixed methods research formulation phase, this calls for fully understanding the mixed methods paradigm; applying mixed model thinking at every phase of the research process; using knowledge of typologies of mixed designs; selecting the reason, rationale, and purpose for mixing; and determining the research question that initiates the mixed methods mode.

For the mixed methods research planning phase, this necessitates selecting a mixed methods research design and determining the overall sampling design. One area of special concern involves sampling issues. Sampling decisions should take into account the type of mixed methods design that is employed, whether methods are concurrent or sequenced by a particular order and whether they are identical or nested (Onwuegbuzie & Collins 2007). Integrated sample selection choices in mixed methods might include respondents for maximizing the range of perspectives, those who are similar or have specific characteristics, deviant or normal cases, and so on. Finally, for the mixed methods implementation phase, this requires collecting mixed types of data, conducting data analysis (including correlation, consolidation, comparison, and integration) and legitimating inferences or formulating generalizations.

Qualitative research connected with quantitative research can assist the researcher in offering new insights for interpreting market facts. Qualitative and quantitative methods have been used in tandem to assure valid classifications of products into high and low involvement groups. Such groups were used to establish treatments in a subsequent quantitative experiment of the effects of such treatments (Rahtz & Moore 1986). Another study employed quantitative techniques followed qualitative analyses to explain themes responsible for attention levels for televised advertisements (Berry et al., 2009). A third study involved the concurrent use of quantitative and qualitative techniques. This research explored the psychological bases of ratings given by constituencies to a school expansion plan (Miller & Gatta, 2006).

Each of these diverse mixed methods designs can also unearth contradictory evidence and false premises for decision making. A mixed methods design can serve as a quality-control check on individual research techniques used. Some basic marketing research designs involving different objectives, sequences of mixed methods, and labels are shown in Figure 16.1.

In this chapter, we will explore these types of mixed methods designs in some depth, illustrate circumstances that favor the use of such designs, and discuss the advantages and limitations of these mixed methods. We will codify the optimal integration of interpretations in mixed methods research, as well as barriers to engaging in such studies (see also Bryman, 2007).

Figure 16.1   Major Mixed Methods Design Types

Design Type	Timing	Notation
Exploratory	Sequential: qualitative followed by quantitative	QUAL $\longrightarrow$ quant
Explanatory	Sequential: quantitative followed by qualitative	QUAN $\longrightarrow$ qual
Triangulation	Concurrent: quantitative and qualitative at same time	QUAN + QUAL

Source: Adapted from Creswell and Plano-Clark (2007).

Now let us turn to several specific case examples of mixed methods applications, illustrative of exploratory, explanatory, and triangulated research designs, respectively. Among the case applications are (a) qualitative research as an exploratory first stage for market segmentation studies; (b) quantitative brand personality research and qualitative research as a second, explanatory stage; and (c) a concurrent quantitative-qualitative triangulation design for a study of interorganizational relations.

In unfamiliar or complex product categories, quantitative segmentation research may be preceded by an earlier qualitative phase. Information from this first phase is used to develop quantitative measures to explore critical topics addressed the survey phase. This case illustrates the mixed methods exploratory-instrument development model—a model that is important when there is no standard preexisting instrumentation and the strategic marketing issue is incompletely understood.

In the brand personality case, previous quantitative research was involved in scale development. Marketing implications of relationships between brand personality and other consumer variables, such as satisfaction and loyalty, may surface only when follow-up qualitative research is conducted. This mixed methods design is classified as exploratory and sequential, with quantitative research followed by qualitative research.

The third case examines the quality of interorganizational relations. In this example, the mixed methods research involving survey projections and ethnographic inquiry evaluates convergent and divergent findings between concurrent quantitative and qualitative research. Technically, this is known as triangulation research, which may be defined as cross-validation that may be based on joining several data sources to study the same subject matter to gain a fuller understanding (Sale, Lohfeld, & Brazil, 2006).

MARKETING RESEARCH CASE APPLICATIONS OF MIXED METHODS

Qualitative Research as a First Stage for Market Segmentation Studies

The use of qualitative research for survey-instrument design quality makes intuitive sense. However, no systematic codification of methodologies has enable researchers to use the approach to full advantage. This section fills the void in the literature. It illustrates how qualitative research informs questionnaire design in key areas, such as the discovery of market segmentation criteria, emotional motives, and consumer vocabularies for product categories. We also discuss how qualitative analysis of nonverbal behavior may be valuable for questionnaire construction and the essential logic of qualitative research for screening questions for meaning in questionnaires.

The use of qualitative research for questionnaire development is well known and widely touted. Most marketing researchers are keenly aware that prior qualitative research may improve the quality of survey instruments. However, few marketing researchers have a full appreciation of *applications* where qualitative research is most fruitful, the *range* of benefits that accrue, and the special qualitative *methodologies* that may be employed to maximize these benefits. Thus, general codification of the methodology of qualitative research for questionnaire design is an urgent need for marketing researchers and their clients. The present section examines how protocols, developed through qualitative research as a first stage, can be used for substantially improving survey questionnaires.

The overall aims of qualitative research in questionnaire design are to improve the quality and validity of information obtained in surveys.

As a means of achieving these aims, qualitative analysis provides insights and understanding of study subject matter, develops hypotheses for the quantitative study, discovers new content areas, refines and classifies survey content, and eliminates meaningless questions from the final questionnaire. It is useful to enumerate the range of benefits of qualitative analysis for questionnaire design. However, it is even more important to develop guidelines to achieve what is desired.

The present section codifies situations and methods to show how qualitative research can be used for questionnaire development. Much is known about basic criteria of suitable questionnaire design. What is generally unknown is how qualitative analysis may be used to determine appropriate question wording, issues to explore, and the structure of scales that are employed. Questions determined from practitioner intuition or casual consumer encounters are extremely risky, as they do not represent actual user feelings, opinions, attitudes, and behavior.

CASE 1: MIXED METHODS RESEARCH FOR AN ORGANIC EGGS MARKET SEGMENTATION STUDY

Note: The authors wish to acknowledge the generosity of the Organic Valley Company in providing these case materials.

A focus group study was conducted to gain a deeper understanding of the organic eggs market. Specifically, the focus groups had the following objective: create a consumer-generated list of attributes and lifestyle elements to quantify in a follow-up study of the organic egg market.

The focus groups were the first phase of a two-phased market research study. Phase 2 of the study is a segmentation study of the organic egg market. Two focus-group discussions, with eight respondents in each group, were conducted among women who, within past three months, had purchased organic eggs. The discussion of primary concern focused on purchase and use of organic eggs.

Results

Phase 1

Consumers have a clear understanding of what constitutes organic eggs (i.e., natural feed, the hen has access to the outdoors, and the absence of antibiotics and hormones). Although many look for "cage-free" or "free-range" eggs, they understand that these claims reference the treatment of the chickens, and might not be enough to make the eggs organic. However, these claims make them feel good enough about buying the eggs, even if the eggs aren't officially organic.

When the price of organic eggs is too expensive, consumers may compromise with the less expensive cage-free or free-range options. Thus, Phil's Eggs, although not organic, offers enough claims to make the purchaser feel better about buying these eggs rather than regular eggs. Amish eggs, which adhere to even lower standards, are also deemed "organic enough" to some, just based on the popularly understood reputation of the Amish community. Most prefer organic eggs for the health benefits of no added chemicals or hormones, as well as the psychological satisfaction of supporting the humane treatment of chickens. While many agree organic eggs are more flavorful than nonorganic eggs, this taste difference is noticeable only when the eggs are consumed as an entrée. Some report a dozen organic eggs can be as much as $1 to $2 more expensive than nonorganic eggs. Because of the additional expense of organic eggs, many use them only when they are the entrée, but will not use the more expensive organic eggs in baking or as a secondary ingredient in other entrees.

> "I buy nonorganic eggs if I have a baking project, especially if it is bulk-baking around the holidays. I buy organic for breakfast or my own foods."

> "I don't cook with organic eggs. It is just too expensive. If we are having eggs for breakfast, though, I'll use organic."

In addition to the USDA certified organic seal, consumers want additional information about the organic eggs listed on the package. Information includes, type of feed; cage-free/free-range; omega-3 enhanced; no hormones, antibiotics, additives, or preservatives; location of farm; expiration date; and an 800 number for questions or inquiries

Knowing the geographical location of the farm ensures product freshness. Many Chicago consumers prefer buying products produced in the Midwest or from local farmers to support their local growers.

Brand preference for organic eggs is often determined by availability and price. Although many have a preferred brand, they are willing to switch to another brand for a lower price, if the price difference is one dollar or more.

> "Sometimes I look at brand, but I usually go with the one I have had experience with."

> "I tend to go with the same brand each time."

> "If I have time, I'll shop around. Otherwise, I grab what I'm familiar with."

Organic Valley eggs, "look healthier with a more yellow yolk," are available at a variety of grocery stores, but they are considered more expensive than other brands of organic eggs.

Eggland's Best is known for the individual "quality" stamp on each egg, omega-3 enhanced, quality taste, and frequent sale pricing.

Egg packaging reflects the company's commitment to organic farming. Consumers agree the packaging must be simple and environmentally friendly (i.e., recyclable or made from recycled materials).

Phase 2

The Organic Eggs Market Segmentation Survey Questionnaire

Next, we'd like to ask you about some egg attributes, including some that you may know and others that you may not know. Thinking about how you typically shop for eggs, please indicate how important each of the following attributes is when you decide which eggs to buy.

Attributes related to ingredients: Rate each attribute on a seven-point scale where seven is the highest level of importance and one is the lowest level of importance. (Rate *each* attribute.)

The eggs are a good source of lutein

No pesticides were used

No artificial flavors were used

No artificial ingredients were used

No artificial preservatives were used

The eggs are a good source of choline

No antibiotics were used

No hormones were used

The eggs are a good source of omega-3s

The eggs are a good source of vitamin D

No artificial colors were used

The eggs are a good source of DHA

The eggs are a good source of vitamin B12

Attributes related to product characteristics: Rate each attribute on a seven-point scale where seven is the highest level of importance and one is the lowest level of importance. (Rate *each* attribute.)

The eggs were produced by family famers

The eggs came from Amish or Mennonite farms

The eggs are certified fair trade

The eggs are natural

The eggs are certified organic by the USDA

The eggs are certified humane

Attributes related to production: Rate each attribute on a seven-point scale where seven is the highest level of importance and one is the lowest level of importance. (Rate *each* attribute.)

The production processes supports the environment

The animals were not caged

The animals had free access to water

The eggs are more nutrient dense

The eggs are produced by a familiar brand

The eggs are not mass-produced

The animals have access to the outdoors

No genetically modified organisms (GMOs) were used in the feed

The eggs are produced locally

The eggs are fresh

Vegetarian feed was used

Integration of the Organic Eggs Mixed Methods Studies

The focus group research identified an extensive list of important attributes of organic eggs for incorporation into the segmentation survey questionnaire. The list can be augmented when related attributes, not salient in the qualitative analysis, are added from the company's research archives of organic eggs consumer research. Note that the qualitative research increases our confidence that the attributes selected for the survey questionnaire will represent the attribute space, or universe of attributes.

By clustering related attributes of organic eggs, it is apparent that these attributes can be grouped into three major concepts or factors. These factors are (1) ingredients of organic eggs, (2) organic eggs product characteristics, and (3) production of organic eggs. In fact, these were used to organize and label sets of attribute items that appear on the questionnaire. Although the items or variables themselves were presented in random order on the questionnaire, the qualitative analysis makes it clear that the three major factors of attributes can be further partitioned—dimensions containing smaller subsets of attributes.

So, for example, the factor *ingredients* can be classified as negative additives (pesticides, antibiotics, etc.) or as nutritional sources (omega 3s, vitamin D, etc.). The *product characteristics* can be classified as certified, labeled organic by USDSA, fair trade, and so on, or from traditional farmers (family farmers, Amish or Mennonite farms, etc.). The *production factor* can be classified as humane animal treatment (not caged, free access to water, etc.) or feed quality (vegetarian feed, feed free, genetically modified organisms, etc.).

Although these classifications do not appear on the questionnaire, they have been identified by the qualitative analyst and will enhance understanding, stimulate analyses, and provide further insights for the interpretation of segmentation survey results. Through mixed methods, the process of interpretation and strategic insights proceeds through the channels of the overall design of the mixed method approach, designs for each separate phase, development of the qualitative interview guide, the qualitative analysis, and the content and language of the survey questionnaire.

Why Qualitative Research Is Useful for Questionnaire Design

Qualitative research is especially useful in questionnaire design for each of the following problems associated with questionnaire design: (a) finding more effective segmentation criteria, (b) eliciting emotional motives, (c) learning consumer language for communications programs, and (d) screening measurement areas. In sections to follow, we discuss each of these problems and provide some illustrations of techniques that may be employed. It should be noted the techniques that are illustrated might be applicable to a variety of questionnaire design problems.

Segmentation Criteria

There is an increasing need to segment more precisely in consumer research since today's consumers exhibit a varied, complex, and sometimes conflicting set of preferences.

Supportive techniques to develop segmentation criteria include using a psychological projection. For example, respondents to a discussion group might be asked to draw a figure of a person who they feel would subscribe to a particular magazine, purchase a candy bar, or join a particular charity. They are later asked to draw a figure of a person who would not use these products.

If the objective is to reposition a brand, debate groups or individuals advocating rival brands may be quite useful. Another outcome of the brand debate approach is that the list of attributes and benefits will be reduced to those most salient to brand acceptance or rejection.

Recruitment and Sampling of Market Segments

In the case of survey sample selection, using scales to qualify respondents, such as loyal brand users, qualitative research can uncover additional qualifying characteristics. Such characteristics can be used to supplement screening scales during any follow-up surveys. The structure of qualifying scales in the number of response options can affect the quality and projectability of the survey sampling process.

Emotional Motives

It is not obvious or easy to penetrate the emotional side of behavior. First, it involves a deeper understanding from merely examining previous purchase behavior. Second, low involvement items (routine, low-ticket items) are unlikely to be subjected to personal scrutiny each time a purchase is made, so the researcher must consider ways to examine purchasing motives from alternative perspectives to direct questioning.

Psychological projective techniques that adopt oblique questioning have been used to uncover emotional motives. Projective techniques have been used to encourage consumer openness about their motives and feelings, beliefs and actions, and they tend to encourage more negative responses. This might follow a strange context for the purchase of a low involvement item, or by asking how other people might use the product of the inquiry.

Qualitative research may be used to identify the hidden drama in products that appear the most mundane on the surface. Reification of a brand can reveal the relative strengths and weaknesses from an emotional perspective. Describing brands as epitaphs, or as houses in which a brand lives, achieves personification, creating the kind of refined imagery necessary.

Consumer Language

Dialogue with or between consumers elicits consumer language that is expressed about marketable objects. The advantage is that nuances of meaning can be identified from slang and from words that share a diffuse imagery (for example, words that share similar meanings that could easily be used out of context). The process enables the analyst to probe beneath the mind's surface for the meanings of words. For example, the word "crunchy" applied to a snack bar might indicate crispness to one group of consumers (suggesting positive associations), whereas to another, it might indicate hard to digest (negative associations).

Consumer language suggests expectations (e.g., this must have a biscuit base or a nutty core) or reveals how the product is accepted by others if consumed in public (e.g., makes a crackly, embarrassing noise when bitten, implying negative associations). The number of identifiable and distinctive positive and negative associations can be useful for designing questions that will elicit product imagery in a survey.

Analyzing Nonverbal Behavior

Analyzing and interpreting data may require moving beyond the spoken word (since people often do things other than what they say).The qualitative analyst, if suitably skilled, can also pick out nonverbal behavior that may be relevant (e.g., gestures) when discussing products, and it can reveal much about acceptability. By using neurolinguistic programming, the analyst can identify patterns in eye movements, hand gestures, and head and body movements that indicate whether respondents are talking truthfully or simply acting on stage.

Screening Measurement Areas

Qualitative analysis can be as important for deciding what to exclude from a questionnaire as to what is included. Qualitative data can act as filtering or screening mechanisms for the narrowing of ideas for hypotheses generation that may be tested in questionnaires. Here, the experience and judgment of the analyst may be critical in determining an inventory of attributes. Attributes selected for a survey should not be entirely dependent on votes or frequency of mention because these have not always been found to be reliable indicators of degree of importance.

An attribute may be particularly important despite seldom occurring in practice, say, in a product. Personal experiences might indicate why or how an attribute is important and offer more information than frequency of mention alone. Indicators of importance also include stress on words, excitement conveyed, interests captured by other members, changes in tone, and body language. Supportive techniques that include Kelly's Repertory Grid techniques (Kelly, 1955) can lead to a qualifying inventory of attributes suitable for a survey instrument.

Constructing questionnaires often involves knowledge of criteria used for market segmentation. Further problems include discerning emotional issues that drive consumer behavior, incorporating the language of consumers into questionnaires, and screening items for inclusion. Using qualitative research can reduce these problems in questionnaire design. In exploratory research, qualitative analysis is particularly productive in establishing a broad range of marketing issues beyond consumer attitudes and usage. Once the broad range of issues has been identified, further discussion can establish the boundaries of these issues. The results are a precise focus on issues that are critical to the inquiry.

Qualitative research is especially useful for establishing quickly (and efficiently) the range of issues for determining attitudes, opinions, and behaviors and for determining the range of attitudes, opinions, and behaviors for each critical issue. Speed (and cost effectiveness) is based on the cross-fertilization of ideas allowed in focus groups. This information enables an optimal battery of attributes and range of response options to be identified. This includes appropriate scale semantics and metrics. Intervention techniques involve projective methods and skilled probing. Qualitative research allows an experienced researcher to check on the general strength of feeling based on intensity of agreement and through signals of nonverbal behavior.

More work needs to be done in future research to determine the kinds of research problems and instruments where qualitative research can be most productive and the specific approaches that work best under these varying conditions. Among the important considerations are the samples used, the character of the interventions, and the methods of analysis that are employed. Sample strategies include the use of homogeneous samples to refine perceptions or, adversary, interactive samples that argue different positions and diverse small groups that are cohesive in problem solving. Suggested projective techniques include personal experience stories, brand personification, role-play, reification, and compare and contrast questioning techniques.

CASE 2: MIXED METHODS AND BRAND PERSONALITY RESEARCH

Quantitative scales for concepts such as brand equity, brand loyalty, brand identity, and brand personality have been widely used in marketing research. This section examines the importance and role of mixed methods in the specific case of brand personality. However, it should serve as a paradigm for use of mixed methods for a variety of marketing concept measures.

Brand personality was defined as "the set of human characteristics associated with a brand" (Aaker, 1997). Brand personality scale development is closely identified with Aaker's landmark work. This brand personality scale was purported to be generalizable (i.e., applicable to all brands, categories and consumer populations). Scale dimensions were adapted from the psychological literature on human personality.

Traits used as potential scale items were culled from three sources: (1) personality scales from psychology, (2) personality scales used by academic and practitioner marketers, and (3) original qualitative research. The qualitative research was based on a sample of $n = 16$ subjects, half of whom were female. Subjects were asked to write the personality traits that first came to mind when thinking about two brands in three types of product categories. Thus, mixed methods were employed in scale development, although the term was never employed.

The research confirmed the existence of the theoretical dimensions of brand personality, based on aggregate results for 40 brands and 114 personality traits. The personality dimensions of this scale are sincerity, excitement, competence, sophistication, and ruggedness.

Practical marketers generally operate at the individual brand level or at the product category level for specific sets of competitive brands. To provide sensitive and reliable information on brand differentiation, scales for brand personality must be customized for specific marketing research assignments.

This conclusion is based on logical, conceptual, and empirical analyses. One strategic finding is that different brands in varied categories prompt consumers to interpret the same traits differently. Using scales based on highly aggregated data invites the problem of cross-loading items and poor fit to confirmatory factor analyses. It follows that scale factor structures are likely to be unique at the brand and product level. Finally, mixed methods assume greater importance for brand personality applied studies. Such studies require revising quantitative scales for relevance and interpreting scale-based analyses.

Qualitative research can assist the researcher in offering guidance for interpreting the underlying pattern of quantitative results. It can also offer salutary effects in revealing contradictory evidence. For example, this might be applied to factor analysis, where variables unexpectedly load on factors contrary to prior qualitative insight. Therefore, a mixed methods design can serve as a quality-control check on multiple research techniques used because the prior qualitative study informs about the later quantitative study. When results are mutually supportive, managers are more likely to use research findings in a constructive manner.

Several published studies illustrate the application of mixed methods to brand personality problems where methodological innovation is necessary.

Example A. Mixed Method Approach to
Understanding Brand Personality (Arora & Stoner, 2009).

This study of brand personality was aimed at providing information for strategies of product design, positioning, and promotion within a specific marketing context. Quantitative scale results, by themselves, may offer little help for advertising programs. Qualitative analysis taps the full range of brand impressions, experiences, and perceptions.

General scales are suspect in their generalizability to specific categories and consumer populations. Scales may be unreliable between custom sponsored studies, hence, not be transferable between applied marketing research assignments. Scaled data may not be sufficiently descriptive and overly complex, requiring qualitative methods for a full understanding. Additionally, qualitative approaches serve to tailor the research to the specific brand and category context.

Concurrent and independent studies (qualitative and quantitative, respectively) were used to measure brand personalities for retail establishments and athletic products. The qualitative leg of the research used no assumptions from the quantitative work and vice versa. There are limitations of using only one type of analysis.

Mixed methods research was found to provide richer perspectives and deeper insights. Qualitative research unearthed brand traits not detected by theory-driven quantitative methods. Furthermore, modifications of brand personality through mixed methods enabled meaningful differentiation between brands. For the qualitative analysis, qualitative data analysis (QDA) software was employed. Two of Aaker's (1997) five brand personality dimensions, sophistication and excitement, were fused in the analysis, resulting in four dimensions. Some of the scale items loaded on different dimensions than Aaker's data showed.

The authors conclude that although mixed methods may be extremely fruitful, caution must be exercised in the selection of qualitative software (for analytical richness) and the specific qualitative methodology (e.g., phenomenology, grounded theory, narrative psychology, and focus groups). One should not expect complete convergence between results of quantitative and qualitative studies. Where there is convergence, reliability is implicit and understanding deepens. Unique information in each data set expands knowledge limits. These mixed methods benefits provide additional opportunities for differentiating brands and improving market positions.

Mixed methods lead to unique and more appropriate measurement of brand personality within a specific category. The result is the achievement of greater insights into brand symbolism. Brand differentiation strategies are more informed.

CASE 3: A MIXED METHODS
DESIGN FOR INTERORGANIZATIONAL RESEARCH

This section illustrates prospects and problems of using mixed methods in a comprehensive study of a specific marketing problem. Two parts of this study involved (1) a cross-sectional survey of relationships between automotive franchisees and a franchisor and (2) an independent ethnographic investigation of the same marketing problem involving a series of depth interviews with an unduplicated small, purposive sample of franchisees from the same franchisee network that was surveyed. The two studies were conducted independently, and were concurrent.

Quantitative Analysis

The research objective for the quantitative analysis was to describe and explain franchisee trust of the franchisor, based on other aspects of the franchise relationship. All respondents were owners of automotive repair franchises. Based on an input from an association of independent dealers (franchisees) affiliated with the auto repair franchise firm, the survey was mailed to a subset of outlets. This dealer association provided 550 names and addresses of independent franchised outlets across the United States. After adjusting for incomplete and/or unusable surveys, we obtained 135 surveys yielding a response rate of approximately 25%. The survey research instrument consisted largely of relevant quantitative scale items culled from research literature and included measures of franchisee trust and satisfaction.

Results

In this quantitative section of the paper, we analyze the relationships between the two components of trust (i.e., technical competence trust and fiduciary responsibility [Integrity] trust) and satisfaction with relationships. We begin by evaluating the relationship between technical competence trust and the construct satisfaction. Next, we consider the relationship between fiduciary responsibility (integrity) trust and the same construct. Finally, we examine the means of the individual variables.

Technical Competence Trust

We find that as levels of technical competence trust increase among franchisees so do levels of satisfaction. In other words, as this component of trust is elevated, the franchisee experiences more satisfaction with the franchisor. The relationship between technical competence trust and satisfaction is also very strong ($p < .01$) and positive. In this case, we find that as levels of technical competence trust increase among franchisees so do levels of satisfaction. In other words, as this component of trust is elevated the franchisee experiences more satisfaction with the franchisor. Here again, we see the importance of the franchisee trusting the technical competence of the franchisor.

Fiduciary Responsibility (Integrity) Trust

Although fiduciary responsibility (integrity) trust and technical competence trust behaved similarly with respect to the pattern of relationships between the satisfaction construct, the relationships themselves were stronger for fiduciary responsibility (integrity) trust. The relationship between fiduciary responsibility (integrity) trust and satisfaction is exceptionally strong and positive, and is stronger than the same relationship involving technical competence trust. The pattern of findings for fiduciary responsibility (integrity) trust and the construct of satisfaction suggest that higher levels of franchisee trust are associated with less conflict and more compliance and satisfaction regarding the franchisor. Clearly, trust in its various manifestations serves as a critical component of effective franchisor-franchisee relations.

Variable Means

The means of the factors provide us with additional insights into how both technical competence and fiduciary responsibility (integrity) trust and the construct of satisfaction operate in a franchised business system. First, we find that the mean for fiduciary responsibility (integrity) trust is lower compared with the mean of technical competence trust. Franchisees investigated in this study trusted the franchisor more from a technical perspective than from an integrity-oriented perspective. The criteria for establishing and maintaining technical-based trust are, for instance, more rigid and less subjective compared to the same criteria for integrity-based trust. Also, there is a clear lack of satisfaction inherent in the current franchisor-franchisee relationships.

Ethnographic Analysis

The research objective for the ethnographic analysis was to generate new insights and understanding about various concepts associated with franchise relationships, the linkages of these concepts, and the explanations for processes inherent in the relationships. The ethnographic work built on previously published material (Prince, Manolis, & Tratner, 2009). All respondents are owners of automotive repair franchises.

The sample was comprised of automotive male franchisee owners who were interviewed in depth for between 45 minutes to an hour and a half. All respondents were contacted through cold calling from franchise listings found on a major automotive company's website, and are located in the greater New York City region. All of the interviews took place via telephone conference call, which were recorded and downloaded for transcription and verbatim quotes. The interviews were unstructured. The advantages of the conference-call interview include, digital recording, the increased ability of the researcher to take notes, and the flexibility to schedule interviews at the respondent's convenience. Further, the interview context is relatively free of distraction because of in-person interaction in an automotive repair location.

The research instrument was created as a qualitative tool to elicit in-depth information from respondents. Specific areas of measurement of that tool include, risk, benefit, competence, integration, confidence, commitment, compliance, and satisfaction. The initial contact and establishment of rapport was implemented via telephone and then the interview itself was scheduled. There were multiple assurances of anonymity, and all respondents understood how the recording of the interview would be used.

Results

Trust

All of the respondents said that they respected the franchisor's expertise, meaning that they thought that the people in the home office knew their business (competence-based trust). Competence trust occurred either because they believed in the product or the individuals who ran the company. The value of understanding the brand image and that the franchisor was competent were essential elements for each franchisee entering into the original contract, and years later, most still felt that the home office was competent.

In contrast with the franchise's strong competence-based trust, there was a perceived lack of franchisor support for their business and the changes that have taken place in the automotive repair industry recently. This highlights problems associated with fiduciary or responsibility based trust (i.e., franchisor integrity). This perceived lack of franchisor integrity impairs the franchisor-franchisee relationship; effective support is a central reason that one enters into a franchise relationship. "That's what I need them for, keeping me up to date" or current in the automotive field. A few respondents indicated that because they did not regard the home office highly in both types of trust, there has been a significant negative effect on their satisfaction as a franchisee.

Frequency of contact with individuals who represent the franchisor is an important dimension affecting trust, and many of the respondents specifically mentioned this as a problem. A few found that the lack of continual contact with the official franchisor representative causes them to have less trust in the franchisor than they might. Most indicate that they did not have a strong relationship with the regional representative from the home office. "He comes in once every few months. He covers, like, ninety shops, so I can't blame him." All of the respondents feel that the representative is in the shop primarily as a spy for the home office rather than their support. These sorts of interactions lead the respondents to feel that the franchisors do not trust the franchisees. The work-around appears to create a close relationship with someone at the home office and to use that person as a jumping-off point for further assistance. In this way, the trust is repaired.

Unfortunately, hardly any of the respondents had created this relationship. Instead, most felt as if they were on their own, and they trusted no one from the home office. Those who had strong personal relationships with individuals either in the home office or with the field representatives appeared to have greater trust in the franchisor (and, therefore, fewer conflicts and greater satisfaction).

Satisfaction

Some of the respondents said that they were fully satisfied with their business relationship with the franchisor. There were two types of dissatisfaction discussed by the respondents. The first was with the franchise system as a whole. These respondents were chafing under the level of control that any franchisor would have over the services offered in an attempt to maintain the consistency of the brand. In this way, the respondents were probably not a good fit to become franchisees, but would have been more satisfied as an independent entrepreneur. The second was with changes within the business itself. The particular automotive repair franchise under review here has altered its service offerings and has grown significantly. These changes were viewed negatively by a few of the respondents, and it impacted their satisfaction with the relationship as a whole.

All of the respondents felt that they would be more satisfied with their relationship with the franchisor if the home office gave more attention to local needs, even though the nationwide policies and practices are the customer advantage of patronizing a franchise.

Most frequently mentioned was couponing and pricing with consideration of the higher rents associated with the Northeast as well as advertising with local flavor.

As has been mentioned before, having the staff (either the franchisee or another employee) creates a greater feeling of both trust and confidence. These, in turn, appear to have an implication for satisfaction. The few respondents who have this connection feel more satisfied with their relationship with the franchisor. Some of this is tied to the relationship decreasing conflict, but it also influences feelings of overall satisfaction. Respondents noted that their personal connection allowed them to feel more connected to the brand. "Yeah, because X worked there, I get the feeling that I have insider knowledge. This allows me to get more done, run my business better, which makes my life easier."

Integration of the Franchise Mixed Methods Studies

Main variables of trust and satisfaction were measured in both the quantitative and qualitative studies. This permitted evaluation of findings for mutual confirmation about the general description of franchise relationships. For example, satisfaction with the franchisor was only modest in both studies, and conflict was common. Additionally, levels of competence trust of the franchisor were consistently high across studies, relative to integrity trust. Interrelationships between variables were also found to be consistent between the mixed methods (e.g., in both cases problems of integrity trust more seriously impact satisfaction with the franchisor than do problems of competence trust).

There are additive findings from the qualitative analysis that enrich the quantitative results and provide greater understanding of the problem. Frequency of contact with the franchisor was an important ingredient in franchisee trust and satisfaction with the relationship.

The analysis of quantitative data may be facilitated by qualitative fieldwork. The additive or joint impact of two forms of trust on satisfaction is discussed in the qualitative section. However, this analysis is not available in the quantitative phase, but may easily be addressed by such methods as multiple regression. Future quantitative studies may investigate a typology of interorganizational conflicts, such as goals, domain, and customer relations-related conflict.

Additional benefits of mixed methods are seen from the use of qualitative analysis to facilitate and refine scale construction for future quantitative work. Qualitative findings suggest that competence trust items should relate to belief in the franchise product and belief in the franchise management. Satisfaction was found to have several components that included satisfaction with the franchise system and its regulations, changes imposed by franchisors, and attention given to local needs of franchisees.

CONCLUSION

We have presented three illustrative cases of different mixed methods designs in marketing research. Many more marketing research applications of these same designs exist in actual practice. Additional examples might include concurrent mixed methods for analysis of consumer experiences in the world of Avatars, health-care practitioner communications patterns, and the effectiveness of social marketing programs (Ivankova & Kawamura, 2010).

The analysis and reporting of the mixed methods research is probably the most problematic aspect of this type of research. Qualitative and quantitative results tend not to be integrated or to be integrated to a limited extent.

Bryman (2007) lists the following barriers to successful integration.

1. The presentation of mixed methods research is skewed since there are different audiences, based on the nature of the topic, and the researcher's impressions of audience predispositions.

2. The researcher has distinct methodological preferences.

3. The way the research project is structured (i.e., the qualitative or quantitative part contains the principal orientation).

4. Timelines of the two methods are at variance because of different needs and rhythms.

5. Researchers often have skill specializations and are predominantly qualitative or quantitative in their training and experience.

6. One set of data may emerge as more interesting or striking than the other set.

7. Philosophical considerations about reality, involving its objective or subjective nature.

8. The lack of examples of successful integration of mixed methods.

The difficulties of merging qualitative and quantitative data to provide an integrating analysis should not be underestimated (Bryman, 2007). Bryman (2007) asserts that the findings from each component should not be compartmentalized or simply parallel accounts. Rather, they should be mutually informative and lead to an analysis of their *joint meaning*. A recommended research strategy is to revisit the initiating rationale for the selection of a mixed methods approach to the specific marketing research problem under investigation.

Additionally, guidelines should be employed for assessing the quality of integration between the mixed methods used for a research investigation. Enrichment of the value delivered by the research should be evident from both the qualitative and quantitative facets of a study. The researcher should evaluate the ways by which decision alternatives, execution options, consumer understanding, and the like become richer because of each method.

In actual practice, the design for mixed methods in marketing research is often unplanned. Designs emerge only after the fact of a management review of a first study. A second phase of mixed methods research may emerge will-nilly, as marketers sense the need for additional information to improve understanding, generate further insights, and fine-tune marketing strategies. It is recommended that after-the-fact research designs be considered during the initial planning phase, as part of the formal research plan.

This approach would promote appropriate introduction of mixed methods and better integration of its results, as well as greater timing and cost efficiencies for such designs.

We now have come full circle. We have demonstrated the use of mixed methods research applications in marketing, under special conditions. However, mixed methods may be impractical for certain kinds of problems in the light of fixed and modest financial budgets. For example, problems that involve products that are easily understood and have a rich history of prior research are less attractive for mixed methods research approaches. On the other hand, when the consequences of marketing strategies are great, data quality from one method alone are dubious, and research findings leave room for considerable risk, it is time to bring the option of mixed methods research to the table.

FURTHER READING

Bergman, M. M. (2008). *Advances in mixed methods research: Theories and applications*. Thousand Oaks, CA: Sage

Biber, S. N. (2010). *Mixed methods research: Merging theory with practice*. New York, NY: Guilford Press.

Greene, J. C. (2007). *Mixed methods in social inquiry*. San Francisco, CA: Jossey-Bass.

Teddie, C., & Tashakkori, A. (2009). *Foundations of mixed methods research: Integrating qualitative and quantitative approaches in the social and behavioral sciences*. Thousand Oaks, CA: Sage.

Improving a Firm's Financial Performance Using Advanced Analytical Insights

MARCO VRIENS

The Modellers LLC

DAVID ROGERS

ConvertClick LLC

INTRODUCTION

Various recent books, such as *Competing on Analytics* (Davenport & Harris, 2007) and *Super Crunchers* (Ayres, 2007) and several papers (e.g., Vriens, 2003; Yunes, Napolitano, Scheller-Wolf, & Tayur, 2007) have illustrated how certain firms have leveraged advanced analytics to improve operational efficiency, grow revenues or market position, or all of the above. Firms often cited as having leveraged advanced analytics in this way include Harrah's entertainment, Netflix, Capital One, Google, Amazon, Dell, Ebay, Intuit, and John Deere. There are many more, some of which will be discussed in this chapter. Yet many large and leading firms, and for that matter smaller not-yet-leading firms, have not been able to do this or do this in a sustained way. There are three reasons for this: (1) Firms may simply not be aware or familiar enough with what can be done with advanced analytics; (2) leveraging advanced analytics to generate winning insights is not easy, and misapplications of advanced analytical techniques resulting in invalid insights and incorrect recommendations; and (3) it is hard to build and sustain an advanced analytical capability that can consistently deliver valid, impactful insights. Firms may simple not have the right tools, processes, and people to build momentum to move the needle from gut-feel decision making to decision making using analytical insights.

In this chapter, we focus primarily on the foundational elements around *tools*, *processes*, and *people* that are needed for successfully scoping out and implementing an advanced analytical function in a firm that has not yet developed such a capability. Specifically, we review (1) what we consider to be advanced analytics and why a firm needs it, (2) the key areas in which advanced analytics have a proven track record, (3) how quality execution can become the norm, and (4) some emerging developments need to be watched. We end our chapter with a few concluding remarks on building an analytics capability and a short section with some further reading recommendations.

WHAT IS ADVANCED ANALYTICS, AND WHY DO WE NEED IT?

Advanced analytics is not a well-defined term, and depending on whom one asks, one may get a different answer. In our experience, any person or group who pursues or practices advanced analytical approaches will recognize the elements listed next. They will do the following:

- *Consider data as a strategic component in the search for actionable insights*. For example, in designing surveys, advanced data-collection approaches are selected that go beyond the standard questioning approach, such as conjoint tasks, best-worst tasks, and laddering tasks, or they may design surveys so they can be connected to or build on to other existing or planned surveys/data sources.

- *Use more advanced statistical or data-mining tools*. To dig deeper into the data and uncover new and better insights, an advanced approach would include a more realistic and vigorous modeling of consumer or market behavior. For example, one looks for interaction effects between attributes in a conjoint study. One looks for interaction effects between marketing mix instruments when determining if online ads may increase the effectiveness of off-line sales efforts. Other examples would be that one would want to capture context effects in choice modeling (extremeness aversion, etc.), or one could capture lagged advertising effects in time series analysis.

- *Execute analysis and modeling in multiple stages*. Analytics is an iterative process and often the initial pass through, or review of, the data does not give the desired results. In our experience, it is common to analyze one specific data set, with one set of variables, in four or five (or more) different ways before we figure out what the best way is to capture the insights.

- *Multiple data sources are being used*. Combining different data sources can often bring unique perspectives and can uncover new insights. For example, we can combine (1) attitudinal, financial, and transactional data or (2) micro- and macrodata (e.g., survey data mixed with population and macroeconomic data). A common scenario is to use internal transaction data and match this with external survey data. In this way, we would pull a sample of customers and their transactions (both internal data sources) and then fuse them with external satisfaction data. Next, driver models could be estimated on the fused dataset.

There are many other examples of the value of merging multiple datasets, some of which will briefly be mentioned in later sections.

There are two key reasons why a firm needs advanced analytics:

1. A first reason is because it enables you to generate more and better insights in a way that a more basic analytical approach would not be able to do. Using more advanced techniques will produce more actionable insights and more strategic insights.
2. A second reason is that an advanced analytics methodology simply performs better than more basic analytics. Advanced analytics allows us to produce more valid insights. This is especially important for prediction and optimization.

Example 1: Latent Class Segmentation Insights

This is an example of how a more advanced approach could generate more insight than what would have been possible with more basic approaches. Greene, Carmone, and Wachspress (1976) used a basic cross-tab analysis technique (using chi-squared test) to assess if there was a relationship between two categorical variables: whether people watched *All in the Family* and *Upstairs/Downstairs*. This analysis showed that if audience members watched one show, then they were very unlikely to watch the other one. The authors then applied latent class analysis and found two segments. In one segment, the relationship was still negative, similar to the aggregate cross-tab analysis, but a second segment emerged that actually showed a segment of the audience that was likely to watch either both shows or neither of the shows. Latent class regression allows one to model situations where there is heterogeneity in the market. In the previous example on TV shows, one would have found that education level would have predicted whether an audience member would be in the first segment or in the second segment.

Example 2: The Benefit of Using Advanced Missing Data Imputation Techniques

This is an example of where advanced methods don't generate more insight but generate better (more valid) insights. In their paper, Ramaswamy, Raghunathan, Cohen, & Ozcan (2001) studied (1) how regression coefficients would be recovered in situations with missing data, and the data were analyzed without any missing data recovery approach; (2) how well the regression coefficients would be recovered when simple methods were applied to recover the missing values; and (3) how well regression coefficients were recovered when advanced statistical approaches (Bayesian Multiple Imputation) were applied. With the exception of the advanced treatment, all analyses resulted in biased estimates. This is a clear example how advanced analytics can lead to more valid insights because all the recommendations that would have been made from the basic analyses would have been incorrect (see Vriens & Sinhara, 2006).

The question often arises, Does a firm really need an advanced approach? The answer is usually a resounding yes. The next section shows the proven record of an advanced analytical insights approach, and it will also show that the benefits of advanced analytics to large firms can equally apply to small firms and that it applies to a wide range of industries from business-to-business (B2B), to consumer focused and from products to services, and so on.

THE SCOPE AND IMPACT OF ADVANCED ANALYTICS

Figure 17.1 illustrates some of the key areas where we have seen advanced analytics make a proven impact. We note that our framework is by no means representative of everything that has been done in the area of advanced analytics in marketing, but based on our combined experience, it does show those areas where we have seen the most tangible and documented impact on successful decision making and firm performance.

Market Dynamics

Market dynamics consists of two key areas. The first area deals with how analytics can be used to define and size markets and to help forecast how these *markets* will grow/shrink as well as what is driving that change. A second area pertains to measuring and understanding (quantitatively) what is driving market *share*.

Market Definition, Sizing, and Forecasting

A very foundational step for organizations embarking on an analytical journey is to start measuring and benchmarking how they are doing. To do this, the company first needs to understand the *size of the markets* they are playing in. This is often not as simple as it seems because such data may not be readily available, or if available, it may need to be adjusted so it accurately reflects the true market size (especially if companies want to track this on a quarterly or biannual pace). For example, one can know the market size that is covered by several major competitors but not know what part of the market is captured by several smaller competitors who may have captured a (sometimes growing) niche. The challenge here is to get data that is credible enough to be accepted by the various stakeholders in the business and that is solid or valid enough that the numbers can be used for further analysis and interpretation leading to a correct set of recommendations and business decisions. This adjustment process is often done analytically.

Second is the area of forecasting. The goal is to ensure that a company is not disadvantaged by unexpected market dynamics. Specifically, forecasting can help the company to understand (1) what the sizes of the various markets are going to be over the next 4 to 12 quarters and (2) what the major contributors driving these forecasts are. This can be a challenging exercise, as forecasting often involves many different internal functions within the firm. The sales department is going to have a point of view (conservative if they want more bonuses, aggressive if they want to add headcount), finance is going to have a point of view (they want to ensure proper allocation of budgetary resources), operations, and many other departments will also have their perspectives. On top of that, it seems all of these departments usually come back with more questions if they see changes in the environment or if they feel the next forecast is off. Do we need to adjust

Figure 17.1   The Scope of Advanced Analytics in Marketing

Market Dynamics		Marketing Dynamics	
Market Sizing and Forecasting Market Growth/Declines	**Predicting Market Share Growth/Declines**	**Campaign Efficiency**	**Customer Efficiency**
• Defining and sizing markets • Identifying early technological threats • Forecasting market sizes • Identification of what drives the forecast	• Identifying the drivers of market share • Understanding acceptance of new products • Feature optimization • Product line optimization • Understand how fast a new product will be adopted (Bass models) • Brand positioning	• Effect of promotions on sales • Testing effects of other campaign components • Short-term and long-term marketing effects on sales, and firm value/marketing ROI • Understanding structural shifts in marketing effectiveness	*Identifying Unmet Needs/ Pain Points* • Quantifying unmet needs • Customer segmentation • Finding actionable insights in structured and unstructured data *Customer Selection and Acquisition* • Sales lead or direct marketing list scoring *Customer Development* • Logical next product • Cross-selling • Customer lifetime value modeling *Customer Retention* • Why/when do customers leave or switch brands (customer churn) • Understanding what drives customer satisfaction/loyalty

our three-year forecast often, and if so, why, and by how much? It is beyond the scope of this chapter to fully cover what forecasting entails.

Rather than using basic exploration or autoregressive integrated moving average (ARIMA) models, an advanced analytics approach would use advanced multivariate time series techniques. This will have the benefit that one not only produces the forecast and can measure its accuracy (and, therefore, can have an insight into likely deviations) but can also have insights as to what economic, demographic, and other variables are driving this forecast. The latter insights are what are needed to adjust the forecasts if conditions are changing. The impact, on a company's performance, when done well, can be tremendous. One company we've worked with in the past, not having yet a solid forecasting function, selling expensive equipment (market annually $200 million) underestimated their demand by 300%, resulting in lost orders and dissatisfied customers. Few companies, we believe, have achieved good, let alone best practice, in this area.

Frito-Lay may be one example of a best practice company. They developed forecasting models and forecasting simulators covering 900 products. Since 2006, forecasting accuracy rate has been on average around 1%, and their forecasting models clearly demonstrated what snack categories would shrink or grow (Girju, Adams, & Ratchford, 2009). Divakar, Ratchford, and Shankar (2005) discuss a sales forecasting model for a soft drinks company that saved the company $11 million on an investment of less than $1 million. Procter and Gamble and Kraft recently upgraded their short-term forecasting accuracy, and were better able to optimize inventory levels. Procter and Gamble expect that this new approach to short-term forecasting will yield them more than $100 million. Olive Garden uses data on store operations to forecast almost every aspect of its restaurant, including demand for staff and individual menu items. By using advanced analytical approaches to forecasting, unplanned staff hours have been reduced by 40% and food waste cut by 10% (Salter, 2009).

Understanding and Predicting Market Share Drivers

Advanced analytics can be used to understand market share dynamics by focusing on understanding what the foundational drivers are in a market that leads customers to prefer or buy one brand or product instead of another. Depending on what data one has available, there are different approaches possible. In one case, one of the authors had access to very reliable quarterly market share data over a significantly lengthy amount of time (approximately eight years) and had access to data over a similar time on how the various brands were rated on a small set of brand attributes. This allowed us to run multivariate time-series regression analyses to assess to what degree any of the brand ratings were predictive of market share. It is beyond the scope of this chapter to describe the details of such an approach, but an example can be found in Vriens, Franses, and Grigsby (2002).

Often, one will not have enough data, or long enough time series, to perform advanced analytical techniques. In such cases, one can take a survey-based approach and apply discrete choice models to gain these types of insights. For example, ABB Electric used this technique to analyze survey data where customers where asked which brand they preferred. Customers also rated the brands on a set of product and brand attributes. A predictive model was built that showed the likelihood of a customer preferring a certain brand based on its attributes ratings. Subsequently, ABB used the analytical insights to improve its performance on the most impactful attributes and managed to grow its market share very significantly. The return of analytics/marketing research investment was estimated to be $50 million (see Gensch Aversa, & Moore, 1990, and Vriens, 2003).

Several approaches can be used to predict how well new or improved products will fare in existing markets. One commonly used technique is concept testing combined with some type of forecasting or prediction component (this can be done *ad hoc* or can be based on data from internal historical databases). Another popular advanced analytics approach is the conjoint choice technique. This research method can estimate the likely market share that a new or improved product will get and what percentage of the target population will buy the product. Though the use and usefulness of conjoint and choice analysis is well known, the impact of the insights derived from this set of tools is less documented possibly because of the proprietary nature of the product and product line insights that come out of this type of advanced analytics. One exception is the study by Wind, Shifflet, and Scarbrough (1990) that documented how Courtyard by Marriot was developed using conjoint insights and how these insights were deemed to have a significant impact on profitability and growth for the hotel chain. The advantage of this advanced approach over more basic approaches was that it generated more valid insights and, hence, led to better decisions. Another real-life example of the impact of conjoint insights is how John Deere reconfigured their product lines. Using a combination of conjoint insights and optimization practices, they were able to simplify their product lines by reducing the number of possible configurations by 20% to 50%, as a result saving production costs and increased profits in the 8% to 18% range (Yunes et al., 2007). They could only do this by combining several advanced analytical approaches, and reducing their product lines without hurting their profits would have been impossible without the advanced analytical insights.

However, to estimate the likely market size when a completely new product is introduced for a new market is harder if one doesn't know the size of the likely consumer base. The first step one needs to take is to identify the likely consumer segments and the size of these segments. In such cases, one often has to develop customized analytical approaches involving multiple data sources.

Marketing Dynamics

We call the first pillar of the marketing dynamics **campaign efficiency**. The core questions that we are trying to answer are, "How effective/efficient are our marketing efforts of the various marketing vehicles: advertising, direct mail, online, and so on, and should we, as a result of these insights, change how much money we allocate to these vehicles," and, "How can we improve the overall impact of our marketing?" The second pillar of marketing dynamics is customer efficiency and includes consumer-level dynamics, such as identifying opportunities and issues and developing the customer relationship, both in an effort to gain insights that lead to more satisfied experiences and for business growth. This is an area where analytics has been shown having tremendous impact and potential.

Campaign Efficiency

The key question answered in this subarea is, How do marketing efforts affect outcome metrics, such as revenues, profits, and shareholder value? It aims to answer specific questions such as, (1) What is the short-term and long-term impact (on sales, awareness, preference) of various types of advertising? (2) Does one marketing channel affect the effectiveness of another marketing channel? (3) Does the impact of certain marketing channels change over time?

One of the most compelling published real-life case studies can be found in Wiesel, Pauwels, and Arts (2010). This work showed how even a small company that sells office furniture (80 employees) can take huge advantage of advanced analytics. During the recent recession, this company saw many competitors pulling back their marketing investments, but Inofec decided they wanted to be smarter about how to best do marketing, so instead of making allocation decisions purely on gut feelings, they wanted these decisions to be informed by validated insights. The challenge was to find out which of a set of marketing activities (e-mail campaigns, faxes, catalog mailings, and Google Adwords) had the most impact on influencing the consumer decision funnel (request for information, requests for quotes, and actual purchases) and profits. Using daily marketing activity (including marketing cost) and customer-response data over a two-year period, they gained several insights as to what marketing activities were most effective in the past. To validate these insights, they also conducted a field experiment in which the current marketing mix was compared with several alternatives that were recommended by the insights. Compared to the previous way of allocating the marketing budget, the insights-driven marketing budget yielded a 14 times higher net profit. We note the authors of the study used four databases (transactions, marketing, off-line, and online), and they actually spend much time preparing the data so it was ready for the right analysis, and applied advanced statistical time series techniques vector autoregression (VAR) models. Again, the type of powerful insights that were generated here would not have been identified without this advanced approach.

Customer Efficiency

The potential of analytics to provide actionable insights in this area has an immediate huge upside because of the vast amounts of data we have available nowadays coming from internal customer databases, consumer surveys, and data pulled from the web, although it is beyond the scope of this chapter to review all these areas. The majority of successful applications of advanced analytics have been done for the areas of (1) customer acquisition and selection, (2) customer development, and (3) customer retention (see Bijmolt et al., 2010, for an excellent review).

Analytics for customer acquisition and selection has mostly focused on generated insights for sales (sales force and territory optimization) and on optimization of direct-mail campaigns (by selecting those people on the list who are most likely to respond, or by improving the mail offer and getting more people interested in responding). For example, Zoltners and Lorimer (2000) showed that 55% of sales territories in a typical company are either too large or too small. Examples of how advanced analytics can be applied to direct mail can be found in Vriens, van der Scheer, Hoekstra, and Bult (1998). In their study, they showed, using a conjoint field experiment by creating an optimal mailing, that the response rate to the mailing increased by almost 10% and that the average amount donated increased by 5%. Given that such mailings may go to tens of thousands of people regularly, these efficiency improvements are by no means trivial.

A good example of using advanced analytics for customer development is the case study done for IBM. They applied a lifetime value (LTV) approach to a set of 35,000 customers and through reallocation of marketing resources (direct mail, telesales, e-mails, catalogs) to their most valuable customers was able to increase revenue by about $20 million (Kumar, Venkatesan, Bohling, & Beckman, 2008).

Customer retention has received much attention, and advanced analytics have shown that leading-edge customer satisfaction (or the opposite as indicated by negative word of mouth) can drive stock price increases (Gruca & Rego, 2005) or decreases (Luo, 2005). Within firms, advanced analytics are often used to gain insight in to when customers are most likely to leave, or defect, and what type of customers are most likely to do so. A good example of how to use advanced analytics for customer retention is presented in Li (1995), who explains how AT&T used survival models to study how to offer a service offering that would retain frequent business travelers when customers are most likely to switch and who these customer are. The service under study was membership based: Customers may either sign up or terminate (and then switch to a competing offering or stop using the service altogether). Three types of insight came from this work:

1. Customers are most likely to switch early on. Within the first six months, relatively more subscribers switched, after which it seemed to stabilize.

2. It identified a number of customer characteristics that were predictive of the likelihood of switching.

3. The top 10% most likely to switch customers were identified who had a 42% probability of switching, which was more than three times higher than the average switching rate in the sample.

These examples illustrate how the use of advanced analytical techniques and methodologies consistently allow for gleaning better insights that drive best decisions within marketing and market dynamics. Without them, one would be handicapped and unable to access insights with the best, proven outcomes.

QUALITY EXECUTION = QUALITY OUTCOMES

In complex data environments, meaning we have complex survey data with many variables or we have many different data sources from which to draw from, many insights are not going to be immediately obvious or are not easily detectable and remain hidden unless analytically extracted. This is an area where many firms consistently underperform for a multitude of reasons, including scarcity of skills at the level of the advanced analytical producers and consumers. Not only does this undermine a firms' insights productivity but it may also affect the perception of low-analytical capability and, as such, undermine the success of getting analytical insights acted on that may affect a firm's performance (Hoekstra & Verhoef, 2010).

We recommend a process that an analytical team or individual can follow to

- help screen out analytical suppliers/consultants that may not have deep enough skills to avoid mistakes,
- help internal analytical teams more consistently,

- help suppliers of research and analytics perform better and more consistently for their clients, and
- help increase the confidence that the supplier has the ability to deliver on its promises.

This process improves the odds that one will find gold nuggets using *a consistent and rigorous* set of questions; a full description can be found in Vriens and Verhulst (2008).

Figure 17.2 shows a simple overview of the basic steps we propose.

The Advanced Analytics Quality Process consists of a number of steps: (1) review data quality, (2) perform univariate and bivariate analyses, (3) perform multivariate analyses, (4) perform more advanced analyses, and (5) integrate analyses done across multiple data sources. In each step, we recommend the analyst ask a standard set of questions. For example, one of the questions in Step 1 would be, Could missing data in our dataset have a negative impact on the validity of the insights extracted? If yes, what is the best way to mitigate this problem (see Vriens & Sinhara, 2006)? Reviewing data quality is typically a step that can easily be overlooked. Ayres (2007) gives an example of how an error in the coding can lead to a policy decision that was quite the opposite of what would have been recommended if the error had been fixed (as Ayres shows after reanalyzing the data and fixing the error). We also know from the literature on missing data that missing data can reduce the ability to find significant relationships in the data.

In the second step of the Advanced Analytics Quality Process, the analyst needs to apply univariate and bivariate analyses to understand initial relationships in the data. Again, to avoid missing insights, it is important to always do this step. The decision to not do this and assume there is nothing in the data of interest runs the risk of missing important insights. The activities in this step, like the others, should be guided by a standard set of questions

Figure 17.2 Five-Step Advanced Analytics Quality Process

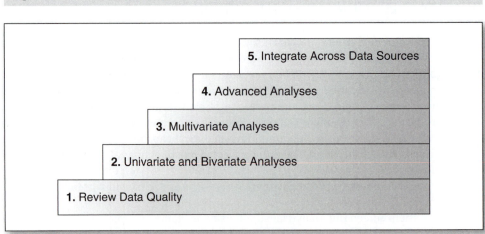

to ensure quality output. For example, what are appropriate statistics and analyses given the measurement levels of the variables?

In the third step, we recommend starting to apply multivariate approaches. Many researchers and analysts already do this, but we have been surprised by the number of times this is not done, and when it is done, it is often not done in the best way. The key is to do it in most if not all cases, and in our experience, following a systematic approach going over a standard set of key questions pays off in the end, with better and more useful insights. For example, what (statistical) models seem most appropriate give the characteristics of the data and variables? The key insight here is that given the characteristics of the data, some techniques or approaches may be more suitable than others and are more likely to uncover the right insights.

Following this process minimizes the risks of missed or suboptimal insights because of (within or across) researcher variability in how to do this step.

In Step 4, the analyst needs to ask if there could be even deeper insights. For example, could there be interaction effects, nonlinear effects? Could we expect heterogeneity across respondents for which we haven't accounted for? We recommend always doing this step, even if the previous step has led to solid insights. This further reduces the chances that insights are left undiscovered. More strategic insights are often the result of doing deeper analyses (e.g., multilayer analyses, digging deeper on certain aspects, and making it more difficult for the competition to replicate what you did).

Dr. Lynne Weber, Managing Director at Duff & Phelps, for example, leveraged the result of a detailed conjoint measurement study to uncover a valuable insight. First, her research quantified the value of 16 attributes, each with multiple levels. The analysis identified a minor feature that was moderately attractive that also lowered the cost of goods sold, making the feature a no-brainer. In fact, the industry was already moving rapidly to incorporate this feature. Dr. Weber didn't stop with the obvious, uninteresting and low-impact result, though. Deeper, advanced analysis illuminated that the feature was disproportionately appealing to an unprofitable market segment. Accordingly, she recommended that the client consider eliminating this feature from a new product launch. The net result of the new product, over the next three years, added an estimated $1 billion to the client's bottom line while the organization's market-leading share grew by five percentage points.

In the final step of the Five Step Advanced Analytics Quality Process, we search for integrated insights by looking and integrating across different waves, different survey studies, internal customer data, and qualitative data. This step has three advantages. First, new insights can be found. Second, such new insights are more hidden and are more strategic because it will be more unlikely that competitors will have the same access to the multiple sources used when doing this integration exercise (e.g., Cooper, 2006). Third, it can make insights more compelling. There are several techniques that can be used to facilitate the process of integration of qualitatively and quantitatively generated insights. For example, the first author created an insights search engine, a dynamic database for insights. This database collects all of the insight garnered from any qualitative and quantitative project so that it can be subjected to rigorous analysis to look for patterns between insights.

RECENT AND FUTURE DEVELOPMENTS

The entire field of analytics is growing rapidly both from a technical-possibilities perspective and an adoption-by-the-businesses perspective. It would be far beyond the scope of this chapter to remotely capture all new and exciting developments from people in academics and from those organizations leading with analytics, but two related areas that we believe deserve some immediate attention and are expected to continue growing rapidly are (1) digital analytics and (2) text analytics.

Digital Analytics

The emergence of online companies and brick-and-mortar companies who added an online channel to their business has given rise to a new field we now refer to as digital analytics. Used interchangeably, digital analytics and web analytics is defined by the Web Analytics Association (n.d.). as, "The measurement, collection, analysis and reporting of Internet data for the purposes of understanding and optimizing Web usage" (para. 1), probably developed a little more than 15 years ago and encompasses a broad human capability and technology solution set focusing on increasing online revenue as well as understanding the consumer.

There is still much debate over what and how to do digital analytics, though, and it seems the field is still mostly in a reporting-only mode. We define digital analytics as all analytical work that is being done on data that is either online specific or used for the purpose to compete work intelligently by using the online channel. This includes consumer data pulled from the Internet directly, as well as integrating that type of data to other data sources for analyses. In this section, we discuss three areas that comprise much of today's practice: (1) data collection, (2) analysis of online data with the primary purpose to improve the performance of the website, (3) analysis of online data with the primary purpose to deepen ones insights into customer-level dynamics.

Data Collection

Behavioral data can be collected at the aggregate level of a website (e.g., number of visitors, average time spent on site, bounce rate, etc.) and at the level of the individual (e.g., which pages a user visited, in what order, as well as whether they successfully completed a goal—such as purchase) through reviewing a website visitor's clickstream activity. A handful of technology vendors exist today to assist with collecting this consumer website data. Website tracking entails the measurement and reporting capability of online behavior only, and it is considered to answer the "what" and sometimes "how many" questions: How many visitors came to your website? What did they do?

While web analytics evolved with log file technology, many could argue that digital analytics grew up with the advent of JavaScript tagging, which was based on an inherent effort to be able to report on individual, business-related behaviors and not just log all technical events. To measure consumer behavior online, all one must do is add some JavaScript code to each page of their site. This code activates a cookie on the users' computer on each visit that allows the web analytics tool the ability to understand this user is the same as a previous visit, allowing immediate analyses and trending over time.

The use of clickstream data is turning quickly into an integral component of consumer learning, and we're now seeing a growing research field on the topic with many disciplines emerging. Bucklin and Sismeiro (2009) review major developments in browsing, site-usage behavior, and online-shopping behavior. Montgomery, Li, Srinivasan, and Liechty (2004) have looked at page sequence to suggest that the path a visitor takes may reflect their goal and could be predictive of future behavior on the site. Moe and Fader (2004) have discovered a model reviewing customer behavior over time at a site finding that those that visit a retail site more frequently are more likely to purchase. In her recent dissertation theses, Lee (2009) linked search behavior to purchase behavior while Mintz, Currim, and Jeliazkov (2010) find propensity to buy is based on type of search pattern. We can now review academic research that predicts off-line orders using clickstream (Huang & Mieghem, 2009), evaluates business-to-business website performance (Wilson, 2010), and a handful of articles try to explain cart abandonment (e.g., Kukar-Kinney & Close, 2009).

Attitudinal and consumer intent data can be collected through online surveys (pop-ups or through less-intrusive survey invitation methods) or/and through scraping stated opinions from social media websites. We explain these techniques in more details in the next subsections.

Improving the Website

Many advanced analytics organizations structure their marketing teams into two distinct functions: those who focus on bringing the most and best qualified traffic to the site and those who optimize the traffic once the visitor has landed on site. We can learn much from visitors based on traffic source and keywords used to find the site, but once there, many new technologies allow for the principle role of improving the website.

Online surveys are often used to answer the "why" question of consumer behavior. For example, web analytics can tell us that a particular visitor spent a considerable amount of time on the site, but without asking the consumer about the experience, we don't know if the consumer had a positive experience (presumably browsing category and other pages and enjoying themselves) or that they were disgruntled (perhaps not being able to complete their task, such as find a product or information they needed to make a purchase decision). Online surveys are a great technology that can help to ascertain that difference—whether a consumer is either highly engaged with the brand. Typically, with this sort of technology, visitors are asked about their immediate experience with the site, such as navigation, search, content, usability, and whether they were able to complete their desired task. Often, the consumer is asked to provide some open-ended feedback about what could be improved. Data are collected at the individual level, and the value of this data should not be overlooked, not only in improving the website, such as adding new functionality or features that would make it easier or more intuitive for the consumer but also by the ability to be able to better the marketing message through content management and e-mail programs in the future.

Another newer capability focuses on replays (often real-time) of the consumer experience. This technology records full sessions of consumer behavior (clicks, navigation, and time on pages and site) that allows the organization to discover online pain points to address. Use cases might incorporate site or checkout abandonment concerns, issues with conversion, or general improvement of site usability. Sometimes called a shared-view, linking website experience to customer support centers is a best practice to define and solve these customer disputes with website issues.

Another more popular technique to optimize online conversion is using A/B or multivariate testing strategies. One of the authors has been doing this for the past decade, achieving significant success. In one particular example, he executed an initial trial case to determine if a testing solution for the online e-commerce firm would be warranted. Eight different changes were made to the product page of this e-commerce site that focused on unique and personalized gifts. The product page is the typical page one views that contains details needed to make a decision whether to add it to the cart, such as images, a description, cost, shipping information, and so on. We ran a multivariate test that produced more than 570 unique combinations of those eight variables shown across randomly selected website visitors. The new and improved page created a 4.4% lift in conversions to adding a product to a shopping cart, generating $5.5M in additional annual revenue. With this sort of success, using testing and other website optimization techniques as a valuable part of the online marketing toolkit cannot be ignored.

Extracting Insights on Customer Dynamics

Gaining consumer insights from understanding online consumers happens in multiple of ways. Similar to collecting data to improve website performance, online surveys are often used with the sole purpose to understand the consumer. What is mildly different with this approach is the type of questions asked and, usually, the length of the survey (such as asking about product and brand awareness, purchase decision attributes, and intention). Extrapolating from these sampled respondents, organizations can use this gathered data to make product and multichannel marketing decisions. ForeSee Results is one such organization that uses online survey technology to glean insights on the consumer. Tied to the American Customer Satisfaction Index (ACSI), their customer satisfaction methodology provides a substantial amount of data to mine and compare to benchmarks of industry for insights. The success of ForeSee Results as a sophisticated consumer-learning tool cannot be argued, with their methodology of using the ACSI, which correlates improved site satisfaction scores to increased stock-market value.

With a vast amount of available online data, defining and using segmentation techniques is quite powerful within digital analytics to find actionable insights. In one case study, one of the authors of this chapter worked closely with the web analytics team that noticed a relatively large amount of traffic hitting an error page. That is, the online visiting consumer would be navigating onsite and would then find a page announcing that there was an error. Although this might not seem like the best consumer experience, some inexperienced web analysts might argue that perhaps it is not the biggest issue to control, that consumers would just hit the back button and continue navigating another way, but in fact, by deploying a segmented view of this clickstream activity, we found the opposite; many times users were frustrated and left the site, resulting in losses predicted in the double-digit millions annually for this firm. Rigorous analyses at the segment-level highlighted where many of the error pages were coming from and solving for these initial issues saved more than half of the estimated loss immediately.

Another advanced analytics approach to deepening consumer insights is combining online data with off-line data. One of the authors worked with a large finance company to measure the effectiveness of website experiences by joining survey and website data sources. The technology of the survey partner, OpinionLab, allows the consumer to choose to participate and give feedback about their experience by clicking on a "feedback" link. This feedback is page-specific, allowing one-to-one matching of consumer's information to a particular page. Those data were collected by the survey partner and passed to the organization where it was matched by page and by a higher category of an experience (i.e., all customer service pages, account review pages, product pages, checkout flow pages, etc.). For each type of experience on the site, the product owner of that experience received a timely report composed of satisfaction ratings for each particular page in their experience (survey data), the number of visits for each of those pages (website visit data), and open-ended text comments (again, survey data). The user of the report could then easily prioritize which pages needed most attention as well as find consumer-generated issues by reading the comments left for those pages that have been determined by consumers to be most unsatisfactory (low-satisfaction ratings) and of high importance (high number of visits). Rolling out this sort of solution not only allowed the organization to quickly understand where consumers where having the most difficulty and then solve the issue, but it also opened the door for a discussion on how each specific team could be evaluated for their quantifiable individual contribution and performance, based on continuous increased levels of satisfaction by addressing consumer needs.

Text Analytics

More and more data and information is becoming available in the form of (semi-) unstructured text data. Some estimates state that more than 80% of all information is stored as text (Anderson Analytics, 2009). Think about how this type of information inside the organization is growing fast (e.g., complaints records, responses to open-ended questions, transcripts of customer support calls, etc.). It is common to see a large company collect thousands, if not tens of thousands, of customer satisfaction surveys each year, each of which contains one or several responses to open-ended questions. Think about how this type of information outside the company is exploding (e.g., web forums, blogs, social media, patent filings, financial reports, etc.). For example, Intuit will scrape comments from Twitter that pertain to them (contain the word Quicken) and analyze this data using text-mining techniques to extract insights that have led to new product (feature) ideas.

Anderson analytics offers interesting examples, as well. One such example is from Unilever. In 2007, Unilever launched Pro-Age, a beauty skin product designed for mature women. The commercial for this product was considered too shocking for public viewing and was not aired. Consumers instead visited the Pro-Age website to watch the original commercial, and it resulted in thousands of comments. Unilever then quickly needed to understand what they could find in the data in case customer issues would require a swift response, and the company also wanted to know how to best find and use those and other insights to their advantage. By scraping the text from the website and subsequently analyzing it, Unilever was quickly able to gain an understanding of what thousands of women were thinking and whether additional marketing effort would be needed.

Another example provided by Tom Anderson (2008) dealt with how Starwood hotels leveraged text analytics to extract actionable insights from the comments and suggestions from about 1,000,000 guest responses. Once the initial text processing had been done, Anderson was able to link the text data to the quantitative survey data, which enabled inclusion of qualitative text elements into a quantitative driver analysis. This yielded very specific actionable insights for Starwood, such as how much more will a customer be likely to return if say the ventilation system and resulting noise was improved.

With limited space, we can only illustrate a handful of concepts and case studies on many emerging themes within advanced analytics, but we urge the reader to review the Further Reading section outlined near the end of the chapter.

CONCLUSION

In this chapter, we have outlined a selection of the vast field of advanced analytics. We have focused on showing how analytical insights can be the engine of marketing impact and firm performance. The breadth and depth of the discipline of advanced analytics has quite dramatically increased over the past 10 years. The impact of analytics goes much beyond marketing and its impact in domains, such as operations, finance, strategy, medicine, warfare, and so on has been extensively documented. However, as we also discussed, despite the many success stories, many executives, decision makers and/or middle managers are still unaware of the true potential advanced analytics could offer. Therefore, we reviewed in this chapter why one needs an advanced analytical approach, and we presented the scope of advanced analytics in marketing illustrated by many real-life case studies.

Further preventing an accelerated pace of adoption is the fact that doing advanced analytics right is far from easy. Hence, we also presented in this chapter a process of how to do advanced analytics that can ensure quality outcomes project after project. We do see an increased number of firms dipping their toes in the analytical pond. Some authors (May, 2009) expect that analytics soon will take off and become a key strategic function in firms, driven by necessities because of economic and business trends and driven by increased possibilities to find gold with analytics. For any student in marketing, marketing research, or business in general, knowing about analytics is going to increasingly be a career requirement.

However, it is impossible to even remotely name, let alone discuss, all developments in the advanced analytics field. The topics in this chapter have been selected based on our joint assessment as what matters most in the practice today. In addition, we want to note that there are still several areas that we believe are very important for anyone entering the field of analytics either as a hands-on implementer or as a manager that we did not address here.

- *Data.* Of course, without data there is no advanced analytics. Data in most organization is messy and, often, far from ready to be analyzed. That said, there is an abundance of data available, and one key issue is that many (from analysts to CEOs) are overloaded, without a firm direction on where to begin or ability to understand what data are crucial to their business.

- *Getting people to act on the insights.* Still, many people in many firms tend to prefer making decisions based on gut feelings instead of allowing insights to influence their decision making. Some papers have addressed this issue (Hoekstra & Verhoef, 2010; Vriens & Grover, 2006; Vriens & Verhulst, 2008). Related to this last issue is the topic of marketing decision-support tools that are often necessary to ensure the right insights can be made available to the right people at the right time (Van Bruggen & Wierenga, 2006).

- *Building the advanced analytical competency.* We have not discussed how to go about if a firm wants to bring in or build an advanced analytical competency. The skill level and general expertise of the consumers of analytical insights (i.e., senior executive decision makers and middle managers who are often commissioning the analytical projects) is quite often lacking or insufficient. Even skills of some consultants or suppliers that are hired to do the actual work can be inadequate, especially if the firm is purchasing advanced analytical services. Inadequate skills will result in several undesired effects for the firm:

- First, advanced analytical projects that could have generated value are not done because the internal project manager did not know enough about the possibilities of analytical tools and techniques.

- Second, advanced analytical projects executed contain errors resulting in incorrect or nonuseful findings and subsequently lead to incorrect recommendations.

- Third, inadequate skills may cause inadequate commercialization of the advanced analytical insights and/or an ability to get the organization to act on such insights. Especially, if the work is solely done by outside consultants who lack the appropriate access within the client organization, the company cannot commercialize the analytical insights. This decreases the appetite of firms to fully embrace this relatively new business tool. Advanced analytics are sometimes seen as hocus-pocus, and consequentially, internal clients are reluctant to adopt the results if these insights can't be communicated clearly and be given sufficient credibility. Taking someone else's advice or insight also means you are exposing yourself to information usage risk (see Grover & Vriens, 2006). Especially when decision-makers don't fully understand the origin of the insight, this becomes a significant hurdle. We refer to Vriens and Grover (2006) for a discussion of how to structure an insights organization for impact.

Though the discipline may be daunting and may seem to offer too many alternatives, which as we know may delay choice or cause one not to act at all, we hope that our chapter has offered a simple framework that can make it easier for firms to choose an initial analytical target area in the firm to start a framework that can be used to start generating analytical insights successfully. As the managers and executives in the firm start knowing more, the firm will win more.

Note: The authors would like to thank Chris Diener for his useful comments and suggestions to this chapter.

APPENDIX

Appendix 17.1   The Analytical Toolbox

Market Dynamics		Marketing Dynamics	
Market Sizing and Forecasting Market Growth/Declines	Predicting Market Share Growth/Declines	Campaign Efficiency	Customer Efficiency
• ARIMA models • Multivariate time series regression (e.g. polynomial distributed lag model)	• Logit choice models • Conjoint (Choice) models • Hierarchical Bayes Choice Models • Source of Volume Source Models • Bass Models • Agent based Models	• Time series models (VAR, VAR-X) • Field Experiments • Eye Tracking Analysis	• RFM • CHAID • Latent Class/Segmentation Models • Regression Analysis • Logit Regression • Survival Models • Data Fusion • Data Squashing • Bagging & Boosting/Random Forests • Text Analytics

FURTHER READING

Armstrong, J. S., Brodie, R. J., & McIntyre, S. H. (1987). Forecasting methods for marketing: *Review of Empirical Research, 3,* 335–376.

Burby, J., & Atchison, S. (2007). *Actionable web analytics: Using data to make smart business decisions.* New York, NY: Wiley.

Davenport, T. H., & Harris, J. G. (2009). The prediction lovers's handbook. *MIT Sloan Management Review, 50*(2), 32–34.

Davenport, T. H., Harris, J. G., & Morison, R. (2010). *Analytics at work.* Cambridge, MA: Harvard Business School.

Diener, C. (2008). *Using choice modeling to supercharge your business.* Ithaca, NY: Paramount Books.

Gupta, S., & Steenburgh, T. J. (2008). Allocating marketing resources. In Kerin, R. A., & O'Regan, R. (Eds.), *Marketing mix decisions: New perspectives and practices* (pp. 3–37). Chicago, IL: American Marketing Association.

Kaushik, A. (2010). *Web analytics 2.0: The art of online accountability and science of customer centricity.* New York, NY: Wiley.

Leeflang, P. S. H., Wittink, D. R., Wedel, M., & Naert, P. H. (2000). *Building models for marketing decisions.* Netherlands: Springer.

Lemmens, A., & Croux, C. (2006). Bagging and boosting classification trees in predictive churn. *Journal of Marketing Research, 43*(2), 276–286.

Sinha, P., & Zoltners, A. (2001). Sales-force decision-models: Insights from 25 years of implementation. *Interfaces,* 31(3), s8–s44.

Sterne, J. (2010). *Social media metrics: How to measure and optimize your marketing investments.* New York, NY: Wiley.

Vriens, M. (1994). Solving marketing problems with conjoint analysis. *Journal of Marketing Management,* 10(1), 37–55.

Vriens, M., & ter Hofstede. (2000, winter). Linking attributes, benefits, and values: A powerful approach to market segmentation, brand positioning, and advertising strategy. *Marketing Research Magazine,* 5–10.

Wedel, M., & Kamakura, W. A. (2000). *Market segmentation: Conceptual and methodological foundations* (2nd ed.). Norwell, MA: Kluwer Academic.

Wilson, R. D. (2010). Using clickstream data to enhance business-to-business web site performance. *Journal of Business & Industrial Marketing, 25*(3), 177–187.

Web Source

OpenID. http://openid.net/add-openidh

Panel Online Survey and Research Quality

RAYMOND C. PETTIT

PRN Corporation

INTRODUCTION

The use of panels to measure people's purchase behavior, media consumption, opinions, habits, and attitudes emerged in the 1940s, primarily through direct application of engineering and economic techniques. Thus, panels were developed because they could be and because of a desire for more science in advertising (Barton, 1949; Webber, 1944). Lester G. Telser, in a 1962 article, reported that panels were well established by the 1960s. He described the Market Research Corporation of America (MRCA) panel as a national consumer panel of 6,000 families, who completed diaries on brands they bought, price and quantities they purchased, types of stores they shopped in, and on what date they purchased.

From this nascent beginning, panels evolved from diary to access panels available for custom and syndicated research via mail and eventually through telephone interviews. When telephone penetration was nearly universal, random digit dialing methods were developed to exploit the complete sampling frame that could be used to obtain probabilistic and representative samples, as well as do surveys more efficiently and effectively (Waksberg, 1978).

With the rise of the Internet in the 1990s, researchers quickly realized another source of surveys and access panels, with essentially the same benefits touted for telephone research decades earlier—faster, better, and cheaper (Pettit & Monster, 2002). Although the Internet never provided a complete sampling frame and, thus, could not provide a truly representative sample of a population, this detail was often overlooked because of the lower cost and quickness of online market research. As technology marched forward, mobile phones, first in Europe and Asia, then in North America, quickly supplanted landlines.

This disrupted the previous gold standard probability sampling method that telephone interviewing enjoyed.

Online research, too, had its share of woes in a noticeable lack of consistency of results reported by major clients of research. This all came to a head in 2006, when several public and private meetings and conferences made it clear that online research *quality* was in question (personal communication, Lederer, 2006).

The response to this dilemma was an interesting mixture of commercial, academic, and practical activities. Associations, in particular ESOMAR, The Advertising Research Foundation (ARF), The American Association of Public Opinion Research (AAPOR), and The Council of American Survey Research Organizations (CASRO), issued white papers and guidelines. In particular, ESOMAR's 26 Questions was meant to be a checklist of questions that each online research vendor should be asked to ensure many quality checkpoints were in place for buyers of research to be confident that a minimum (undefined) level of quality was in place.

AAPOR, a bastion of scientific random sampling principles and, often, critical of online research, sponsored a special task force that concluded that there is no theoretical basis to support population inferences or claims of representativeness when using online survey panels recruited by nonprobability methods. Nonetheless, in an 81-page report issued in March 2010, after nearly 18 months of study, the task force also recognized that samples drawn from nonprobability panels can be valuable for other kinds of research and hypothesis testing, as long as one of the goals is not inference to a larger population.

CASRO in the United States embraced the International Organization for Standards (ISO) Guidelines that had been successfully applied in the area of technology, manufacturing, and production, and were just beginning to be applied to online research outside the United States. Resistance from U.S. online research vendors has served to mitigate the introduction of ISO standards in the United States, based primarily on the cost to complete an audit, as well as the extremely low standards engendered by this system. CASRO, possibly as a result, has supported an enhanced conference and call for papers. For example, in 2011, their comprehensive agenda includes the following:

- *The impact of technology solutions to enhance the quality process*: name and address verification, IP checks, machine IDs, geofencing, speeder and pattern response, and survey engagement.
- *The use of an ever-expanding variety of devices to participate in surveys*. The growth of mobile applications and innovations in location-specific research are opening new avenues of research.
- *Social networking*. Changes in the way people interact have also created opportunities for new research techniques.
- *Online communities for marketing research continue to grow*, possibly at the expense of other research methods. What biases may be present in an online community?
- *The use of routers*. Respondent sources that are blended come through a router while other respondent sources on the same project do not. We need to understand the bias of a respondent source separately from the bias created by a router.
- *Survey design and layout that has a significant impact on the data that is collected*.

The ARF marshaled extraordinary forces to field a large primary research study, titled the Foundations of Quality (FoQ), which sought to get fact-based answers to many issues plaguing online research quality. Much of this chapter will review the comprehensive findings and deliverables of what is, to date, the largest research study ever completed by the ARF for the industry.

Outside of industry organizations, some notable individuals and academics pursued research of their own. Robert Lederer (2008), the respected publisher of a popular research newsletter, exploited the information gathered at a major conference he sponsored in 2007 into a concise guidebook of online research quality. NOPVO (Ossenbruggen, Vonk, & Willems, 2006) was a unique effort to explore the consistency of Dutch online panels. Their nascent work provided valuable insights into the general problem facing online research panels: comparability of results across multiple panels. Jon Krosnick of Stanford University, funded by IBM SPSS, also contributed a timely reanalysis of research he had completed five years earlier to provide further evidence of the inconsistency of online panels and, indirectly, the issue of representativeness (Yeager et al., 2009). Finally, Steve Gittelman (Gittleman & Trimarchi, 2009), founder of MKGTING Inc., has self-funded an extensive research program to assess not just the consistency problem but also to recommend new ways to improve consistency. Note that his work is admirable in that he is attempting to find a solution, not to just identify and confirm a problem.

In fact, Gittleman and Trimarchi (2009) have provided an excellent treatise on the difficulties affecting online panels today. The authors have a commercial business that is actively involved in funded research and development, particularly what they call the Grand Mean Project, producing valuable guidance to users of online research. Their research is focused on blending of online panel sources, achieving panel consistency, and improving reliability of results using optimization and calibration approaches borrowed from the field of ecology.

THE PROBLEM

As a careful reading of the literature suggests, although online panels can provide highly useful information, there are some important challenges they face. Panels require a great deal of effort to recruit and maintain. Bias can be introduced by many factors, such as nonrandom attrition, the mix of tenured and new panelists, and recruiting techniques, which needs to be carefully monitored. Conditioning or the **testing effect** arises from continued participation on any panel. Being a panel member may influence responses as well as actual purchase behavior as the panel member is sensitized over time (Smith & Albaum, 2010).

Panel data may also be systematically biased through **instrument effects**. The majority of online panels use self-administered, structured questionnaires. This means that the quality of respondent behavior in filling out surveys, diaries, and so on is extremely important. Underlying the observed behavior of taking surveys are numerous psychological artifacts mediating response, such as cognitive burden, speed (rapidity) of completion, and the respondent's mental model, that is what is expected of them and how they interpret that (Tourangeau, Rips, & Rasinski, 2000).

Professional respondents: The general concept of a professional respondent is based on three things: (1) They frequently complete surveys; (2) they tend to belong to multiple panels, and (3) they establish longevity; that is, they remain panel members for a long time.

There is evidence that respondents who remain in panels over time actually change during that period. Inexperienced respondents tend to respond more favorably to brand purchase intent questions than experienced respondents (Coen, Lorch, & Piekarski, 2005). The issue in the scant research available is that there is no agreed on quantification of "frequently," "multiple," and "longevity."

Belonging to Multiple Panels

Major attitudinal differences were found in demographically similar respondents who belonged to multiple panels (Casdas, Fine, & Menictas, 2006). Yet, is this a problem? Research presented at the 2007 ESOMAR Congress indicated that those who belonged to multiple panels were better respondents in the following ways: (1) more positive toward the survey-taking process, (2) willing to complete additional surveys, and (3) viewed others in the panel process in a positive light. The most striking finding was that respondents who belonged to multiple panels had slightly superior response quality, and they seemed motivated more by intrinsic motivations such as the need to learn new things and the desire to help others. Interest in financial rewards was much further down the list than expected (De Wulf & Berteloot, 2007).

In reality, online survey research is comprised of a complex mixture of activities and processes that must work together to produce reliable results. A variety of online panel firms have developed techniques, methods, and systems for sourcing, aggregating, managing, rewarding, sampling, and surveying panelists. Since unprecedented levels of marketing and advertising research are completed today using an online panel system—and we can expect the growth of online survey research to continue—it is critical that the results be accurate, precise, and trustworthy because companies use them to make important business decisions, involving billions, if not trillions, of dollars around the globe.

THE FOUNDATIONS OF QUALITY GENERATIVE MODEL

What is quality? Part of the issue and challenge in the industry is that the term "quality" has many potential meanings. Is it a quality online sample one gathered without duplication? Or does it need to also include survey responses that are well considered, thoughtful, and genuine? Does a nonrepresentative sample mean a sample lacks quality?

To achieve a better sense of the phenomenon under study, a basic process model (see Figure 18.1) is presented to frame initial explorations, measurements, and, eventually, guiding metrics.

Briefly, the model consists of four layers.

Panel membership layer: This layer is made up of a pool of panel members, who potentially can overlap (i.e., they can be a member of multiple panels). There are attributes of being a panelist that contribute to the quality of an online survey response; for example, how long

Figure 18.1 Generative Model

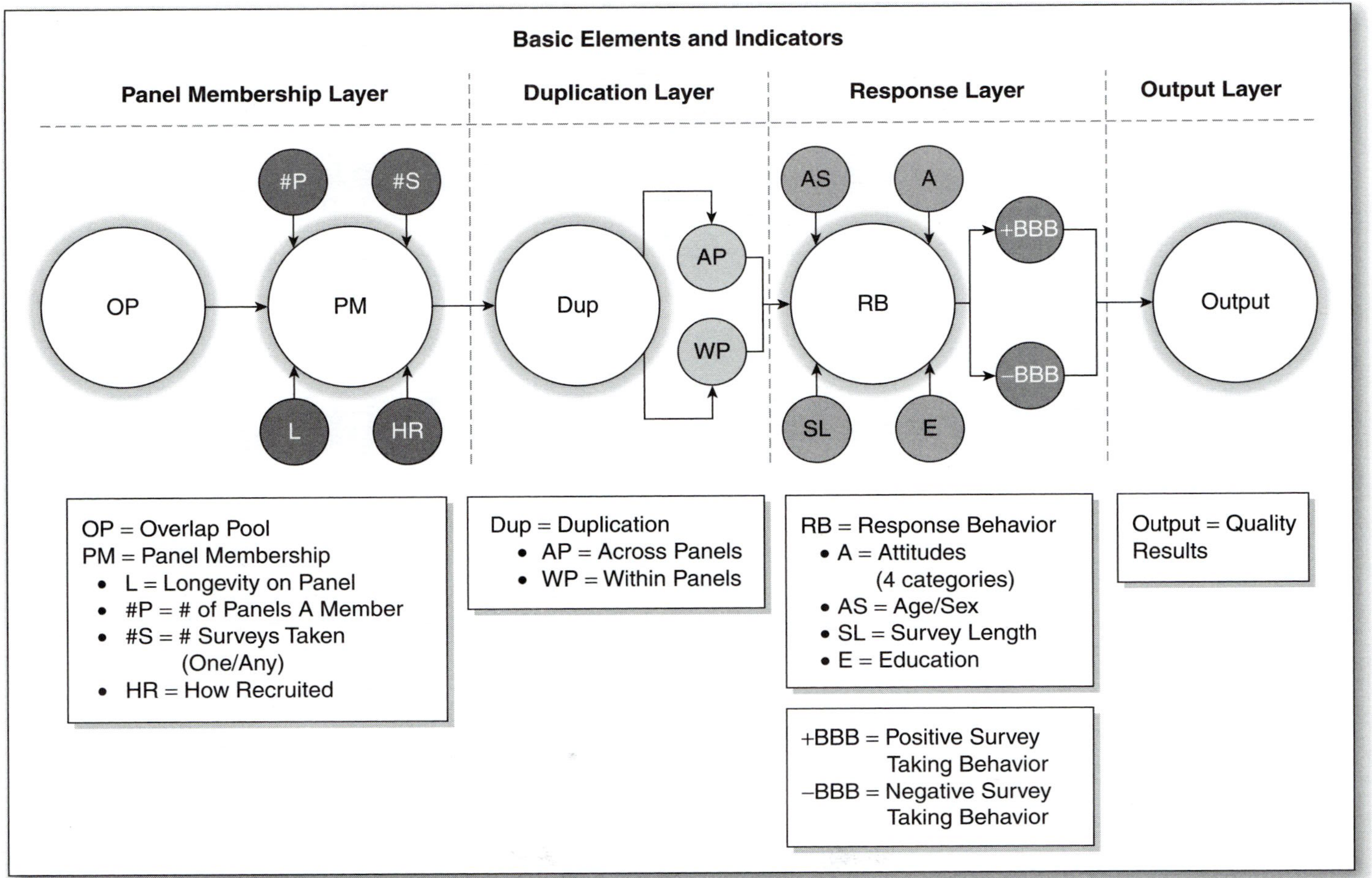
Basic Elements and Indicators
Panel Membership Layer
Duplication Layer
Response Layer
Output Layer
OP
PM
#P
#S
L
HR
Dup
AP
WP
RB
AS
A
SL
E
+BBB
–BBB
Output
OP = Overlap Pool
PM = Panel Membership
• L = Longevity on Panel
• #P = # of Panels A Member
• #S = # Surveys Taken (One/Any)
• HR = How Recruited
Dup = Duplication
• AP = Across Panels
• WP = Within Panels
RB = Response Behavior
• A = Attitudes (4 categories)
• AS = Age/Sex
• SL = Survey Length
• E = Education
+BBB = Positive Survey Taking Behavior
–BBB = Negative Survey Taking Behavior
Output = Quality Results

a person has been a panelist and how many surveys have been taken in a given period. There are also many panel characteristics, such as recruiting method, the form of incentives, the monetary value of incentives, and the like that can subtly influence survey responses at an endogenous level.

Study/duplication layer. Given the fact that people can be members of more than one panel, and that panels are often blended to achieve sampling objectives, the real possibility exists that within a single study, a person can be asked to take the same survey multiple times, either within a panel, across panels, or within a supplier who is working with multiple panels on a given study. In addition, panel members may be contacted to take a related study (by another panel to which they may belong) within a time where they would have been excluded if they were a member of only one panel.

Response layer. This includes attributes such as demographics, survey length, attitudes, and motivations that impact either desirable or undesirable survey taking behaviors.

Output layer. This layer represents the survey responses. Data quality questions center around trustworthiness of the results, interstudy comparability, and whether in aggregate form they are comparable across studies (e.g., reliable results are achieved).

Description of the model: From the pool of online users, people join panels. Panel membership is a construct an individual respondent embodies, with several exogenous characteristics shaping it. These include, number of panels a member is on, number of surveys taken (with one panel or across all panels a member) in a given time, longevity on the panel, and how one was recruited. Attitudes and motivations are endogenous factors that operate throughout the experience of being a panelist and taking surveys (e.g., across all layers).

Since, in reality, there *is* multipanel membership, the opportunity for duplication manifests. The duplication layer is referred to as an operational or infrastructure component. Logically, it should be managed and controlled so that, ideally, duplication is eliminated or significantly reduced.

In the purest state, minus the duplication layer, there is a complicated multivariate covariance between response behavior and panel membership. Attitudes and motivations in both layers interact with each other in influencing survey quality. Consistent with existing research, response behavior is influenced directly by survey length, education, income, attitudes, and age/gender—this was confirmed by regression analysis of the ARF's FoQ data described later in this chapter. But there is also unique evidence that the character of a panel can also subtly influence responses, supporting the notion that online panels, at least today, are not comparable.

The ARF's FoQ analysis found that the majority of respondents exhibited "diligent" (socially responsible) behavior, and a much smaller percentage exhibited "bad" (undesirable) behavior—their responses differ noticeably from each other. To explore this aspect in more detail, a bad behavior score was developed as an indicator to further understand, clarify, and filter out undesirable survey takers; that is, those who may taint the results and create reliability issues.

To complete the model, the output layer represents the results of an individual survey, which can be aggregated with other results to produce findings used by clients to make a variety of business decisions. The goal for the industry is to ensure consistency and reliability of results.

Factors impacting data quality. The FoQ study enabled us to better understand and calibrate the influence of many factors that impact data quality. In the academic literature, the problem we studied empirically is related to the issue of errors in survey results. These errors are traditionally divided into two categories: sampling error and nonsampling error. Sampling error occurs because only part of an entire population is studied. Nonsampling error encompasses all other factors that contribute to the total error of a sample survey estimate. This error source may occur because of nonresponse, errors in the sampling frame, mistakes in recording and coding of data, and other variables, such as the way data is collected and processed or response bias or tendencies. This represents just part of the total error. We note that relative large sampling variance does not automatically disqualify a survey, just as a small sampling variance does not assure good data quality. The important point is distinguishing between accuracy and precision. Accuracy relates to the quality of survey results. A precise survey can exhibit small sampling variation, but the results can be wrong. Accuracy takes into account bias, as well as precision. In the experimental design literature, this distinction is mirrored by the reliability-validity continuum.

Total survey error models were developed in a series of important academic articles in the 1950s and 1960s. The general model assigns the total error into fixed (known) biases and variable errors. To be useful in an actual survey situation, the model must be specified. Today, we are far from realizing an integrated treatment of survey errors within one model and of connecting these errors to cost implications. The work to be done involves a careful balance of results from mathematical statistics and empirical studies involving the primary influences on data quality

THE ARF'S FOUNDATION OF QUALITY RESEARCH PROJECT

While the genesis of the public concern about online research quality is somewhat clouded, Kim Dedeker (formerly of Procter & Gamble) is on record expressing dissatisfaction with the reliability of online (panel-based) survey research at a meeting held at the Advertising Research Foundation (ARF) in New York City in September 2006. Soon thereafter, a chorus of others joined Kim and related their similar experiences that centered on the following problems:

- Replicating results
- Questionable survey taking behavior
- Suspicion that a few heavy respondents were taking most online surveys

The ARF soon assembled researchers, suppliers, and advertisers to discuss the issues in greater detail. From the supplier perspective, there was the sense that advertisers and their

Figure 18.2 Primary Influences on Online Survey Data Quality

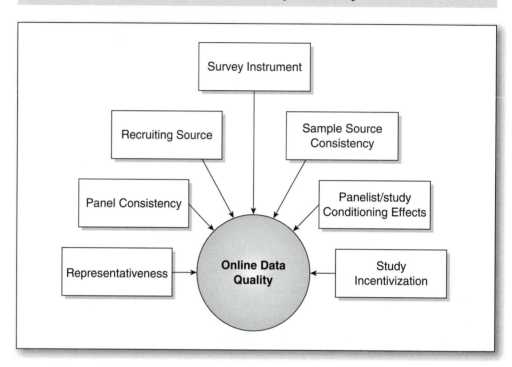

procurement people were stressing "cheap and fast" online research (which was the initial promised benefit of online survey research). In addition, there was a sharp rise of nonresearchers entering the business (because of a low barrier to entry) and offering untested solutions. Finally, it was noted that generally accepted myths, such as heavy responders accounting for a high proportion of surveys, were promulgated with little fact-based research.

This intense scenario set the stage for an industry initiative run jointly by suppliers and advertisers under the auspices of the ARF. The results of the research-on-research activities form the bulk of this chapter.

The Foundations of Quality (FoQ) *Study*: The ARF formed a membership council, called the Online Research Quality Council (ORQC), in August, 2007, with the goal to provide fact-based answers to client questions about the quality of online research. The ORQC leadership originally consisted of a Supplier Steering Committee (SSC) and a Client Advisory Board (CAB).

In conversations with the CAB, as well as with other clients, a diverse range of questions about the quality of online research rose. To assess the dimensions of the problem, and to help in the design of the FoQ study, the ORQC's Define Quality Committee conducted a stakeholder survey and confirmed that data and sample quality issues, including replicability, accuracy, representativeness, survey length, response rates, and undesirable respondent behavior.

Given the diversity of client needs, the ORQC recognized that some issues might have to be addressed in future studies. Thus, the ORQC Steering Committee jointly determined that the initial focus of the FoQ study would be on online consumer samples with expansion into mobile panels/samples or business-to-business samples later.

Because of the limitations of existing knowledge on online research quality, the reasons for the study became clear. It was acknowledged that the industry could benefit from the following:

- A unified, public body of knowledge
- A mechanism to review the data or the details of a survey behind the conclusions reached
- A means to study difficult questions beyond using only a single online sample source
- A way to test conflicting results
- A method to evaluate or validate a plethora of new and evolving technologies and their full impact on quality

Centering on online consumer samples, the ORQC determined that the first areas it would investigate were the following:

- Effects of multipanel membership on survey results
- Effects of respondent motivations and engagement on survey results
- Replication and the reliability/consistency of results across waves
- Connections between proposed or commonly used metrics and data quality

As with any research, it was recognized that one design cannot answer all questions and that the initial study would likely yield further questions for investigation. But the feedback indicated that clients and suppliers were satisfied that the FoQ study would add to an industry knowledge base and serve as a useful starting point.

Scope of the Foundations of Quality (FoQ) study. This landmark study involved the fielding of a survey across 17 online panels and a telephone and mail panel. There were five versions and two waves of the study, and in the end, 100,000 interviews were gathered for analysis. The completed online surveys were further enhanced by appending the historical survey-taking activity of the panelist from the panel's records. Each panel supplier completed a questionnaire about their panel's protocols, maintenance, and characteristics. In addition, a separate analysis looked at 675,000 encrypted e-mail addresses representing the entire online panel universe covered by the 17 panel providers. It was estimated that the book value cost of doing the study exceeded one million dollars.

Study purpose and goals. The purpose of the FoQ study was to create a comprehensive dataset to provide empirical, fact-based results. This information, in addition to being shared in a public report, was used to guide industry solutions and inform the creation of new quality metrics for online panels. The intent was to provide both learning and guidance for the industry so online panel quality and transparency could be improved.

The key objectives of the FoQ study were to complete the following:

- Measure the degree to which duplication occurs when multiple sample sources are used on both a national and local (smaller geographic area) basis
- Measure multipanel membership or multisource participation

- Assess the effects of survey length on survey results and on respondent survey-taking behavior; identify correlations among survey length, multipanel membership, and levels of undesirable responses and investigate the effects on survey results
- Measure respondent motivations, attentiveness, and reporting accuracy
- Assess how respondent segments based on motivation and attention vary in survey-taking behavior
- Compare the wave-over-wave consistency (reliability) of survey results for independent samples from the same provider/mode, compare survey results for consistency across sample providers and across modes, and compare survey results to external benchmarks to assess comparability

Principle areas that were addressed include the following:

- Do frequent survey takers, speeders, or those with multiple panel memberships bias survey results?
- What are the strengths and limitations of different methods for identifying duplicate respondents when multiple sample sources are used?
- What is the impact of undesirable respondent behavior, and what drives it?
- To what degree is inattentiveness, errors, or fraud caused by respondent motivations? Survey length? What is the effect of conditioning bias or panel tenure?

This chapter focuses primarily on the Foundation of Quality research study and concludes with an update on other commercial and industry activities related to the topic.

METHODOLOGY

A specially designed usage and attitude survey was created by a committee of industry research experts (both buyers and sellers) to capture specific and common forms of questions used in online survey research. This included trap and reversed questions, attribute lists, purchase intent, and white-card concept questions. In addition, benchmark questions from CDC, NHIS, and other governmental surveys were integrated verbatim to allow for post hoc comparisons.

The survey was administered online by Decipher, a third-party vendor, to ensure consistency of delivery across all 17 panels. In addition, a mail and phone panel was used to capture responses in those modalities for further comparative analysis.

Specially, the FoQ research consisted of the following:

- Two waves of surveys, 15- and 30-minute versions, were conducted.
- Wave I surveys were conducted October 28 through November 4, 2008, and Wave II surveys were conducted November 11 through November 18, 2008.
- Online 15-minute core surveys were conducted in Wave I, repeated in Wave II (excludes home improvement questions).
- Online-enhanced, 30-minute surveys were in Wave I only, two versions, containing sections on grocery and home improvement shopping behaviors.

- Mail and telephone modalities for the 15-minute version were in Wave I only; best-practice randomized sampling methods (of panels) were used, but no cell-phone-only coverage (for phone interviews) was included because of cost.
- A version of the online survey was also conducted separately at the local market level (Tampa, Florida).
- Historical survey-taking activity data were appended to online data from the individual's panel record.
- A provider/supplier questionnaire, which detailed company/panel characteristics, was provided.
- A hashed (encrypted) e-mail exercise (pooled samples) gathered 675,000 e-mail addresses that represent the total universe of panelist contained in the 17 online panels.
- Three forms of duplicate detection methods were used on the dataset:
  o Two types of digital fingerprinting technology
  o A proprietary telephone, address matching system
  o Browser cookies

Research Design: Key Dimensions

The research as designed allowed collection of multiple types of data to achieve the goals of the project. Key dimensions within the research design included the following:

- Mode of data collection: online, telephone, and mail
- Sample frame: random digit dialers (RDD; for phone), access panel (online or mail), aggregation, or database
- Observed respondent behavior: historical activity (e.g., recency and frequency of taking surveys) and survey-taking tenure
- Survey length: 15 and 30 minutes
- Geographic area: national and market level
- Measures to detect duplicate respondents: technology-based, real-world identifiers
- Waves: two independent national cross sections.

Sample specifications. The sampling unit for this study was the individual, not the household. Each provider (17 in total) was asked to provide samples that met the following specifications for each wave:

- 1,500 national 15-minute interviews among U.S. adults (18+)
- 1,500 national 30-minute interviews among U.S. adults (18+)
- 150 market-level, 15-minute interviews among U.S. adults (18+) in the Tampa, FL and St. Petersburg, FL areas (CBSA #43500)

These national and market-level samples of completed interviews matched the general populations on key demographic variables. Sample providers were asked to draw or recruit these samples following the best practices they use in typical consumer research.

The Tampa-St. Petersburg CBSA was chosen because the demographic composition of this market is similar to the demographic composition of the nation, and it will allow us to compare results across demographically matched populations, one larger and one smaller.

Online sample providers were asked to provide, 250 national 15-minute interviews among U.S. adults, 18 and older, who had joined the panel, database, or list within the three months prior to field start. These over samples of completed interviews matched the U.S. national 18 and older population on key demographics and, minimally, for a 50-50 male-female distribution. To the degree possible, sample providers were asked to draw or recruit these samples following the best practices they use in typical consumer research.

Historical Respondent Activity

In addition, sample providers were asked to provide the following historical respondent-level activity (for the six months prior to field start) or other stored data that was appended to the respondent records for those who respond to the survey:

- Number of survey invitations sent or survey contacts initiated
- Number of survey responses received (includes break-offs, suspends, abandonments, dropouts, closed survey hits, or any activity associated with attempting to enter the survey but does not include nonresponse)
- When relevant, number of times a survey-taker responded but the survey was closed (closed survey hits)
- Number of surveys completed regardless of completion status
  - Number of surveys completed as qualified and quota not filled
  - Number of surveys completed as qualified but quota filled
  - Number of surveys completed as not qualified
- Month and year respondent joined panel or first interaction with respondent for nonpanel sources
- Category/topic for each of the last three qualified completed interviews
- Stored demographics—sex, year of birth, household income, marital status, race, ethnicity, education level, and the like
- Types of recruitment/sample source

The historical data were used as appropriate to conduct analyses, such as the effects of types of recruitment source on survey results, the effects of prior category participation on survey results, correlations between observed and reported number of surveys completed for a single panel, and consistency checks across stored and reported demographics. Reports comparing historical data across sample providers used the phrase, "Sample provider does not store these data" for instances in which historical data is not submitted.

Supplier practices survey. A special survey was administered to each of the 17 panel companies asking them to specify core practices for recruiting, managing, and maintaining their panels.

FOQ RESULTS SET 1: PANEL OVERLAP, DUPLICATION, AND MULTIPANEL MEMBERSHIP

Executive Summary

The objective of this research set was to provide clarity by delineating the concepts of panel overlap and duplication in the act of survey taking and in assessing the impact on data quality. There is much concern in the research arena that "it's all one big panel with heavy responders doing all the surveys"—with few facts to guide judgments or opinions.

In today's world of online survey research, some people belong to more than one panel, known as (panel) overlap. Using an encrypted e-mail matching exercise, the FoQ study found a 43% match at an aggregate level. But to put it in a more realistic light, we looked at the proportion of people/panelists this represents, and the percentage of overlap is, conservatively, around 16%, assuming that each e-mail address is unique. This proportion was not as high as many in the industry had estimated.

Further, just because someone belongs to multiple panels, it does not necessarily mean that degradation in survey response quality will occur: Most online panelists appear diligent and responsible. In fact, whether a respondent belonged to one or to many panels, the FoQ study found virtually no difference in survey results. Statistical modeling confirmed this finding. Multiple panel membership is not a significant driver of survey response quality. But there are other factors in this complex process that are at work, and these are presented in further sections of this chapter.

To put the overlap percentage in perspective, if the proportions are projected to the total population of the 17 panels in the FoQ study, there would be roughly 5,500,000 unique panelists active and available to respond to surveys (the figure would undoubtedly be higher if we consider all U.S. online panels). This is comparable to the numbers reported in past research about research on telephone-survey participation rates (Bickart & Schmittlein, 1999).

Duplication, or evidence of a respondent being asked to take a survey in the same study more than once, also exists. Recent duplication levels reported to the industry have seemed alarmingly high and may be confusing the issue. The reason for this is that the duplication level being reported is across online panels *in their entirety*. But surveys don't work that way: In surveys, a sample is drawn for a particular study and the respondents are placed back in the pool for the next study. So multiple probabilities of being selected and agreeing to participate and actually completing a survey are at the study level.

While duplication *can* occur when people belong to multiple panels, the likelihood of it is *much less* than the percentages reported when looking at the aggregate level. In fact, the numbers being reported to the industry may actually be an indicator of overlap, and, thus, they may be confusing the issue. Regardless, it points out the need to create common and accepted definitions and acceptable standards across the industry.

The FoQ study measured duplication at the study (survey) level, and found that because of the process of first being invited to the survey and then getting past the screening criteria and actually taking the survey, the duplication rate that occurs is a fraction of the total panel duplication percentage.

For example, on a typical per study basis, when another source of sampling is needed (conservatively, 85% to 90% of blending occurs across two panels), the duplicate percentages we found are generally in the low single digits. Because the FoQ study ran across 17 panels, some higher percentages (mostly correlated with high overlap levels of particular panels) were seen.

The FoQ study included a local market sample to assess duplication levels on a restricted sample universe of respondents. In this case, duplication levels did approach unreasonable levels, signaling that great care and effort be exercised when this situation occurs.

It is important to remember that, although the FoQ findings are empirical, the exercise of looking at all combinations of panels to assess duplications levels merely provides a theoretical scaffold. In practice, only certain panels will source or blend with certain others (we don't know which, as the panel suppliers identities are not known to us). We do note, however, that within panel duplication is troubling—seven panels exhibited *internal* duplication levels from 10% to 16% (the remainder averaged 4% to 5%). Why this occurs is unknown for certain, but it does signal a red flag for further investigation.

Further analysis identified a small segment of duplicators (survey takers) who had marked differences in response patterns when compared to nonduplicators. This finding offers some clues for data quality improvement when working with highly specialized or difficult-to-find (low incidence) samples. Even though the *blatant* duplicator segment was quite small, logic dictates that duplication should not be allowed to occur in any form.

Bottom line, the FoQ study reoriented the perspective the industry had started to internalize and even believe—the facts show a manageable problem but that duplication needs further attention—as long as overlap and multipanel sourcing (to meet sample requirements) exists.

What did we learn about overlap?

Across the 17 panel providers, who supplied a representative portion of their panelist's encrypted e-mail addresses for a matching exercise used to assess overlap, the FoQ study identified that 41% of e-mail addresses had two or more matches (this was a weighted average based on the size of the panel). From this, we can ascertain the following:

- Netting up, we estimate there are more than 5,500,000 unique people on the 17 online panels who took part in our study and possibly as many as 7,000,000 across all people taking online surveys.
  - This is comparable with historical levels in mail and phone panels.
- When we look at the respondent (person) level (based on an average of 3.7 matches that we determined empirically across the 17 panels), the percentage of overlap is approximately 16% (unique matches $N = 376,581$; multiple matches unique $N = 69,679$; total $N = 446,260$).
- This overlap varies widely by panel provider because of their methods of recruitment, panel structure, set up, and maintenance.
- In fact, recruitment method is an indicator of overlap:
  - Higher levels of online registration correspond with *lower* overlap levels.
  - Higher levels of referrals correspond with *higher* levels of overlap.

What did we learn about multipanel membership?

Although multipanel membership is a reality, little evidence was found that it impacted data quality to any significant degree. Of respondents in the study, 64% reported they belonged to more than one online panel, and the average number of panels they reported belonging to was four. This percentage and count is higher than the overlap figures calculated from the 17 sample providers in the study. That is because, in the survey, respondents were asked to self-report belonging to any panels and not just limited to the panel suppliers in the study. Based on the survey results, higher multipanel membership occurs with the following forms of recruitment:

- Unsolicited registrations
- Affiliate networks
- E-mail invitations

Little or no impact on survey responses was found, however, because of multipanel membership. This included impacts on purchase intent and product concept uniqueness ratings, poor survey-taking behavior (confirmed by modeling), or speeding and completion time.

Duplication

Duplication is a natural outgrowth of multipanel membership, but it can also occur *within* a panel, if not controlled. Duplication, if it is allowed to manifest, can have a noticeable effect on response patterns, and it is a threat to data quality.

Duplication, for the purposes of the FoQ study, was defined as the proportion of a study sample drawn from the available universe that was *not unique*. This could occur both within and across panels, as panel firms sometimes blend sample from other panels or sources to meet survey requirements, and may duplicate their sample lists.

Using the FoQ online survey data, three methods for gauging duplication levels across all 17 panel suppliers were compared. These included the following:

- Digital fingerprinting technology (two forms)
- Telephone number/physical address matching based on personally identifiable information provided with consent by the respondent
- Browser cookies

All methods were applied to the FoQ survey data only (i.e., there was no cross-referencing of databases as part of the detection exercise). And, it is important to reiterate that the net duplication results were across all 17 panels—this is not the norm in practice, but it represents a worst-case scenario. Typically, one or two additional panels may be used when large samples are needed or when screening is required to fulfill low-incidence sample or lockout quotas.

In the study, it was found that digital fingerprinting methods appear to capture the most duplicates, and they have similar rates to telephone/address matching for studies where personally identifiable information (PII) is available. However, the fact that telephone/address matching *requires* PII is a potential limitation that needs further study.

It was noted that digital fingerprinting methods work at the machine level, and, thus, they would not be able to detect a multiuse machine, unless unique profiles are set. The extent that this occurs in the panel population would affect the possibility of Type 2 errors, incorrectly identifying a duplicate when, in fact, it was not. Browser cookies are an alternative, but because cookies can be deleted, they are not as effective as a duplication detection method. In addition, they also identify machines and not people.

What did we learn about duplication?

- When assessing a realistic scenario of two-panel combinations at the study (survey) level, duplication rates range from 2% to 19%.
  - The majority is in the low single digits, but there are some exceptions.
- Duplication levels for the 17 panels vary, but they correlate with overlap rates.
  - The average *across* panel duplication rate is 8.2%.
  - When we look *within* panels to assess internal duplication, we found rates ranging from 2.5% to 16%.
  - Seven panels exhibited internal duplication levels from 10% to 16% (the remainder averaged 4% to 5%).
- In the FoQ study, the *net* level of duplication, using all four duplication detection methods, was 25% across all 17 panels.
- Duplication rates are excessive (on average, around 40%, when two panels are used) when surveying at the local market (restricted geographic area) level.
  - This confirms the notion that duplication may be more acute at the local market level and will require special attention, rules, or procedures.
- Digital fingerprinting methods, overall, are more likely to capture duplicates, when PII is an issue.
- Telephone and address matching is just as effective as digital fingerprinting, but it requires personal identifying information.

A profile of duplicators was drawn from the survey results, and represents a small segment of older, lower-income, and educated males and a segment of hard-to-capture race/ethnic respondents. For these segments, as duplication rates increase, we observe marked differences in response patterns when compared to nonduplicators. Duplicators are

- more promotionally/incentive-driven;
- engaged (perhaps overly) in the survey-taking process; and
- provide more socially desirable answers, especially pronounced in new product reactions.

Interestingly, the proportion who are nonwhite (either black or Latino) nearly triples among those identified as duplicates five or more times. This is likely a function of hard-to-recruit panelists, among certain providers.

RESULTS SET 2: SURVEY RESPONSE QUALITY

Executive Summary

This section explores and analyzes the significant influences, including the impact of membership in multiple panels, on survey-taking behavior (e.g., are respondents diligent and providing thoughtful answers, or are they potentially gaming the system?).

While multipanel membership is a reality, we found little evidence that it impacted data quality to any degree. Tangentially, "years on the Internet" and "hours per week on the Internet" had *no* significant impact on data quality that we could find.

Survey length and people's attitudes toward surveys (tempered by demographics), however, were more likely to discriminate good or bad survey-taking behavior, whivh *does* impact data quality. Using a metric developed from the design of the survey, called the bad behavior score (BBS), a series of models was developed that clearly captured the influence of survey length, demographics, and attitudes on good or bad survey-taking behavior. This metric (the BBS) was also used to create rules for the optimal number of surveys taken by age/gender.

Recent academic research on speeding (elapsed survey completion time) suggests that total interview time may be a biased indicator of quality because it doesn't take into account endogenous variables such as diligence, accessability of attitudes, and speed of thinking, which may vary by age (Otter, Allenby, & van Zaldt, 2008). Given the difficulty of isolating speeding as a key influencer of data quality, we opted to present some preliminary results in this report, but continue our analysis seperately.

KEY FINDINGS

Many factors are intertwined when we look at response quality in surveys, all working together to shape the eventual outcome (a completed survey). The key elements studied included multipanel membership, speeding, appropriate survey-taking behavior, demographics, attitudes, survey length, and survey frequency.

Multipanel membership is a given: 64% of respondents report they belong to more than one online panel. Higher multipanel membership occurs with the following forms of recruitment:

- Unsolicited registrations
- Affiliate networks
- E-mail invitations

Little or no impact was found on survey responses because of multipanel membership. This included impacts on purchase intent (PI) and uniqueness ratings, bad behavior score (confirmed by modeling), or speeding or completion time.

Attitudes. People participate in surveys because they can be rewarded with incentives and also because they can diligently voice their opinions. The study results showed evidence that most panel members are socially responsible in their survey-taking behavior. This aligns with our modeling results and prior research on the topic. Perhaps not surprisingly, long surveys are the primary reason people do *not* participate in surveys.

A factor analysis of the general attitudinal battery presented in the FoQ survey suggests that a large group of socially responsible panel members exists; only a small group has an affinity with noticeably bad behavior.

Survey-taking behavior. To that end, the FoQ study was designed to capture undesirable survey behaviors, such as straightlining, disinterest (lack of attention), and speeding. The bad behavior score is a measure constructed to reflect good to bad survey-taking behaviors. It consists of counted errors or incidents based on trap questions and observed response behavior (such as straightlining), which we categorized from "good" to "bad" as follows:

- Good: 0 or 1 incident
- Moderately bad: 2 to 5 incidents
- Bad: 6 to 9 incidents
- Very bad: 10 to 17 incidents

For the reasons mentioned previously, we kept the analysis of speeding separate from the bad behavior score metric. To that end, speeders (defined as respondents below the 30th percentile in our study on total interview time) are more likely to exhibit bad behavior (as measured by the bad behvior score). Heavy speeders (defined as respondents below the 10th percentile in our study on total interview time) are more likely to exhibit straightlining behavior.

Speeders are more affected by survey length (which was confirmed by modeling). Younger respondents (18 to 34) with a college degree are more likely to speed relative to the rest of the sample. While this may be an empirical fact, recent research suggests that total interview time may be a biased indicator of data quality (Otter et al., 2008). Specifically, there are endogenous factors, such as diligence, the ability to access attitudes, and the speed of one's thinking, that underly the time it takes to complete a survey. Some people are quick to think; others are quick to judge. Solutions that exclude speeders based on time alone may be, in fact, eliminating respondents who should not be eliminated.

Survey length. Exploratory FoQ analyses and secondary research (la Bruna & Rathod, 2006) suggested that survey length may be a substantive factor impacting data quality.

With that in mind, a cross tabular analysis of survey length (15- and 30-minute survey result comparison) did *not* reveal any real differences on grocery attitudes, soup purchase intent, soup concept uniqueness ratings, or on favorable and unfavorable attitudes, in general, toward survey taking.

The bad behavior score, however, demonstrated considerable differences on all of the variables we looked at in the crosstabular analysis, including on the rating of retail stores, home improvement attitudes, paint concept purchase intent, and uniqueness ratings (30-minute survey only).

Most, but not exclusively, we observed a bimodal difference (lowest and highest ratings are stronger or weaker across the bad behavior score categories), with a step-pattern (increasingly higher or lower) on the middle scale points of the rating scale. So although survey length doesn't *appear to* contribute to data quality and variability in our simple comparisons, it does work *in tandem* with the bad behavior score.

To go further toward capturing the significant impacts on bad behavior, a logistic regression analysis derived the variables with the most influence on bad behavior as defined by the bad behavior score. The logistic regression model clearly identified survey length as the most influential factor. In fact, increasing the length of survey from 15 to 30 minutes resulted in raising the odds of bad behavior (defined as four or more bad behavior occurences [counts]) appearing by nearly six times.

The logistic regression model produced many substantive results:

- Longer survey length increases the likelihood that bad behavior will occur by nearly six times.
- The 18 to 29 age cohort is nearly twice as likely to evidence bad behavior than the 50 to 65+ age-group.
  - But bad behavior is spread throughout all age levels.
- Taking fewer surveys a month increases the odds of exhibiting bad behavior; but taking more actually lowers the odds slightly (see Appendix 18.1 for further analysis).
- The impact of education on bad behavior is more pronounced at the lowest levels of education (some college or less).
- Gender effects are differentiated, but being female raised the odds of bad behavior slightly.
- Race/ethnicity has only a modest effect, and it is limited to Hispanic and black (non-Hispanic) respondents.
- *Increasing* panel membership actually lowers the odds of bad behavior occurring by as much as 32%.

Clearly, survey length is a key determinant of bad behavior. This was not evident in the simple cross tabs analysis. Age/gender and educational level are secondary indicators of this phenomenon, as well. Attitudes also mediate the bad behavior score in dramatic ways, as we will see.

To explore in more detail, a classification and regression tree (CART) and Chi Square Automatic Interaction Detector (CHAID) analysis was completed, which took into account the interaction effects among the primary variables discriminating good and bad behavior. This analysis also showed quite clearly that survey length is a major factor in discriminating good and bad survey-taking behavior.

Given the robustness and clarity of the CART results, CHAID analysis was used to enhance the usefulness of the model by capturing the optimal number of completed surveys (in the last 30 days) by demographic segment before a negative effect is seen on the bad behavior score. Using a technique called Exhaustive CHAID, many cut points of the variable: "number of surveys completed in the last 30 days (overall)" by survey length and by age/gender were identified. This guided the choice of an inflection point for determining when excessive survey taking may degrade survey-taking behavior and, ultimately, data quality.

RESULTS SET 3: PANEL RELIABILITY AND CONSISTENCY

Executive Summary

Benchmarking is the process of comparing the quality of a specific process or method to another that is widely considered an industry standard or best practice. The result is often a strategic, tactical, or metrics solution for making adjustments or changes to make improvements. Benchmarking may be a onetime project, but it is often treated as a process in which organizations continually seek to challenge and improve their practices.

Benchmarking can also be used to test the reliability, or the consistency, of a set of measurements or of a measuring instrument. There are two forms: the measurements of the same instrument over time (test-retest) or, in the case of more subjective situations, such as personality or trait inventories, whether two independent raters give similar scores (interrater reliability). The FoQ study was designed to address the first form of reliability (test-retest).

The focus, then, is on repeatability, which is different from reproducibility. **Repeatability** is achieved when test/survey results across time, within/across different panels, different vendors, or similar (product) categories, agree within certain accepted limits or parameters. For the purposes of the FoQ, these repeatability conditions included the following:

- Comparing the same measurement procedure (online panel surveys)
- Using the same measuring instrument, under the same conditions (survey design was identical across all samples)
- Collecting data from the same sample (all panels used the same sample specifications)
- Collecting data over a specified period of tie (two waves)

A benchmark analysis was a way to study the repeatability conditions within and across online panels, not research vendors. The major findings include the following:

- Although within panel results are consistent, *across* panels, we see a wide variance, particularly on attitudinal and/or opinion questions (purchase intent, concept reaction, and the like).
- Panel best practices reduced variance only slightly.
- Sample balancing (weighting) survey data to known census targets, minimally on age within gender, education, income, and region removed variance, but it did not completely eliminate it.
  - o Likewise, the test of a pseudodemographic weighting variable (panel tenure) did not eliminate variance.
- The data suggest that panel practices work together in subtle ways to build groups of respondents with distinctive attitudinal profiles. Although panel tenure may be one such factor, the way panels recruit, the type and amount of incentives offered, and possibly even the character of an individual research/panel company may encourage distinctive panels to emerge whose members share attitudinal and motivational propensities that drive results that may vary from panel to panel.

The findings suggest strongly that panels are not interchangeable. Guidelines and transparency about sourcing is needed, when blending or multiple panels are used to fulfill sample requirements. In addition, buyers of research should be aware of the attitudinal tendencies provoked by panel practices and seek ways to assure that suppliers carefully blend and balance samples to achieve a harmonious result.

Results

The FoQ study included questions designed to permit comparison to known benchmarks. One of these is the National Health Interview Survey (NHIS), the principal source of information on the health of the U.S. civilian population. (The National Health Interview Survey [NHIS] is the principal source of information on the health of the civilian noninstitutionalized population of the United States and is one of the major data collection programs of the National Center for Health Statistics [NCHS], which is part of the Centers for Disease Control and Prevention [CDC]). For example, the FoQ results on smoking behavior have been compared to NHIS.

It should be noted that NHIS data are collected via computer-assisted personal interviews, and their standard of accuracy is very high.

The FoQ survey included questions worded specifically to permit comparison to known benchmarks for interpreting survey data. That is, we used exact forms of the questions asked in the benchmark about smoking and cell phone ownership. Results were also compared from 15-minute Waves I and II of the FoQ study. As well, preliminary information on a soup concept was tested for further evidence on variation.

There was moderate variability across providers in the percentage who have *ever smoked,* yet there is a high degree of consistency between mail, phone, and NHIS/CDC benchmark data. Weighting and cleaning adjustments have a minimal impact on these percentages.

Moderate variability across providers is seen in the percentage who *currently smoke*, with consistency between mail, phone, and NHIS/CDC benchmark data. Across waves (i.e., over time), data for *ever smoked* shows consistency within provider. We hypothesize that more clear-cut (e.g., behavioral) measures *may* show less variability over time.

Slight variability across providers is seen in the percentage who *owns a cell phone*. Also, online respondents may be legitimately higher in actual cell phone use (e.g., more technology savvy or dependent). Across waves, cell phone use is relatively consistent *within* the provider. Slight variability across providers is seen in the percentage of calls received on a cell phone (percentage of "all" or "almost all" calls received on a cell phone).

For a hypothetical soup concept, significant variability was observed *across* providers with general wave-to-wave consistency *within* provider on both purchase intent and uniqueness (top two box basis).

It is likely that more variability may naturally exist in sample-based attitudinal results. Whereas, self-reporting behaviors (like cigarette smoking) are relatively accessible via cognition; self-reported attitudes are more complex and a function of numerous dimensions: experience expressing the attitude, opportunities for review or rehearsal of the beliefs and behaviors associated with the attitude, direct experience with the attitude question, and anticipation of future instances of the attitude question.

Seminal research from Ron Gailey (Gailey, Teal, & Haechrel, 2008), formerly of Washington Mutual, showed that like anything based on associative learning, attitude strength varies. The stronger the attitude, the more accessible it is. Correlations between attitudes and behavior are much higher among people with highly accessible attitudes. Highly accessible attitudes are linked to selective processing of information and even selective attention. This protects a person against counterattitudinal information and potentially inconsistent attitude/behavior responses.

Revisiting Sample Balancing

Demographic and behavioral differences (e.g., smoking) were seen among duplicates and those belonging to multiple panels. What happens if we eliminate these from our data? What happens if we also combine a uniform sample balancing approach across all 17 providers?

Sample balancing, plus filtering out the most egregious duplicates, dampens variance further, though not entirely: Other sources still exist.

Sample balancing (weighting) survey data to known census targets, minimally on age within gender, education, income, and region, does appear to control variance for straightforward questions, such as smoking or cell phone use.

But, a more typical example, a white-card concept description, shows more variability across panels for both mock concepts.

Figure 18.3 Controlling Variance Using Sample Balancing

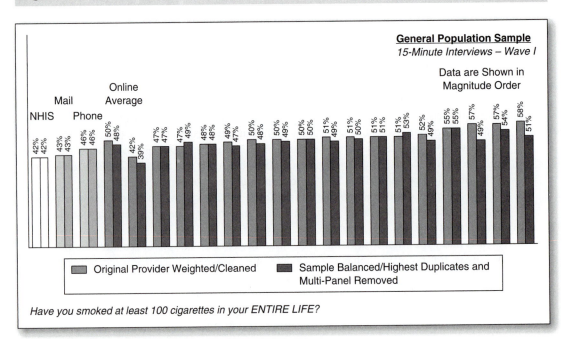

The Effect of Panel Characteristics

The FoQ study contained a wealth of information about panel practices. Standard weighting methods were not able to achieve comparability across panels, thus, panel characteristics and their potential influence on survey response was explored. The first, and some would say most obvious, choice would be panel tenure, including the mix of how long people are on panels—does it matter?

In the FoQ results, newer panelists scored higher on concept reaction questions from the FoQ survey. Self-reported panel tenure exhibits the same trend. When looking across panels, we see a mix of distinctive combinations of tenure, both from company records and self-reported membership information.

Given this seemingly powerful indicator, results were balanced using a psuedodemographic (panel tenure). Panel tenure impact on product demand was found to be a significant factor by Gailey et al. (2008), who also suggested it may be useful as a weight. However, as we can see in Figure 18.4, when applying the psuedodemographic to a purchase intent question, the variability in response across panels still exists.

Clearly, other factors are at work and are most likely working interactively to influence survey results. To explore this, the relationships between panel tenure (longevity), frequency of survey taking, and the bad behavior score were studied.

Figure 18.4 Sample Balanced With Tenure Adjustment

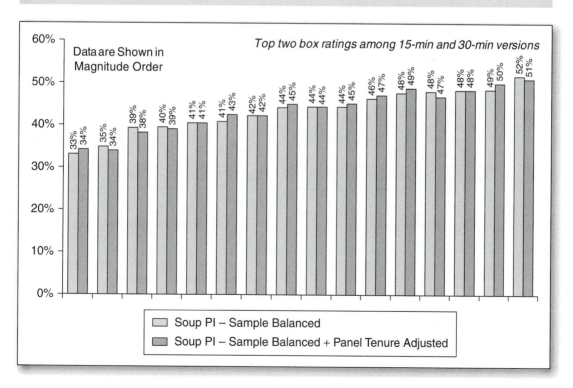

Panelists with tenure of three years or more tend to take more surveys, while less-experienced panelists take fewer surveys, in general. Note this relationship mirrors the logistic regression result presented previously: Those who take more surveys tend to exhibit less bad behavior. Panelists with tenure of three years or more tend to take more surveys—panelists taking fewer surveys show appreciably less tenure. Note this relationship also mirrors the logistic regression result: Those who take more surveys tend to exhibit less bad behavior. Finally, this relationship also mirrors the logistic regression result: Panel tenure is not a significant driver on the bad behavior score. The levels of tenure vary 5% or less across the bad behavior score categories.

Further exploration into panel practices. In a comparison of high and low responses across the 17 panels on the purchase intent and concept questions, panels that were associated with the low and the high scores (top two box in Figure 18.5) by their reported panel practices were identified and compared

Figure 18.5 Panel Practices Comparison

Panel Practice	Lower Responses (top two box)	High Responses (top two box)
How often do you update panels?	Annual	Annual
Do you offer respondent rewards?	Yes	Yes
Do you offer monetary incentives?	No	No
Do you use a point system?	Yes	Yes
Do you use a lottery system?	No	No
Do you use a sweepstakes?	Yes	Yes
What is the cumulative monetary value of rewards (one-year average)	$15	$25
Do you prescreen on an individual basis?	No	Yes
Do you have any exclusion rules?	Yes	Yes
Do you have any contact/invite rules?	Three to nine times a month	Three to nine times a month
What type of research company are you?	Research Company with own panel	Panel management only
What is the percentage of surveys completed last year with different panel sources?	16%	14%
Definition of active panelist	1 survey in last year	Taken a survey in last six months

Many practices differ, specifically, monetary incentives, cumulative dollar value of rewards, and percentage of surveys completed with a different panel source. A comparative analysis of the panels showed that higher scores on the purchase intent questions were related to panels that offered monetary incentives. To test whether there may be an attitudinal relationship, answers were compared on questions related to incentives in the survey. Panels that offered a monetary incentive produced a higher (top two boxes) rating on these two key attitudinal questions.

To further delve into the effect of panel practices, the recruitment method used, and its impact on purchase intent, concept questions, smoking, and cell phone usage were examined, using a high/low break based on whether the panel was above or below the online panel average on purchase intent and response to the unique proposition for the soup and paint concepts.

Consistently, a lower score was found (below the average) for eight panels that averaged six recruitment sources. The sources most used by these panels include the following:

- Referrals/affiliate networks
- E-mail invites, partner, ISP, client website, or purchased lists
- Off-line recruitment—all types
- Online registration at own website—unsolicited respondent

For the higher score, seven panels were identified that averaged only four recruitment sources. The sources most used by these panels were (1) online registration at partner, ISP, or client website, (2) online recruitment—all other types, and (3) e-mail invite, partner, ISP, client website, or purchased lists.

What about monetary incentives? The data revealed that the cumulative (average yearly) dollar value for the 17 panels ranged from $0 to $42, regardless of the reward or incentive system. For the purposes of analayis, a three-category cumulative yearly dollar variable was created. The correlation with the bad behavior scorewas statistically significant but low ($r = 016$). The correlation with the third factor (so called "bad attitude" group from the factor analysis of attitudes) was also statistically significant ($r = 116$). However, when the difference in response across these three categories on purchase intent, concept, smoking, or cell ownership was studied, there was none.

Could attitudes be a mitigating factor? Indeed, the study found that more dollars equals stronger agreement (top box of Figure 18.5 "completely" agree) on two attitudinal questions.

The third leg of this exploration looked at the percentage of total completed surveys conducted with external sample sources and the possible influence on variability in responses. The percentage this occurred was from 0% to 86% across the 17 panels. Even with this wide variation, there was little difference in bad behavior scores across panels, and the correlation with panel tenure was negligble. Note also that the number of self-reported surveys did not increase substantially as the percentages moved from 0% to 86%.

However, when household and grocery product concept and purchase intent were examined, the higher the percentage of surveys completed from external sources, the higher the top box score. For attitudes, an interesting trend emerged: Top box scores increase; but on the bottom, we notice they decreased or stayed level.

Clearly, attitudes vary based on the presence of a monetary incentive and on having a higher/lower average cumulative yearly dollar value and on the percentage of surveys completed from sources external to the primary panel. And this affects response and bad behavior score directly and indirectly (as identified in the CART analysis).

It is conceivable that panels may build, recruit, and maintain demographically equivalent panels, but because of particular panel practices and protocols, they may encourage or create a panel with underlying latent (lurking) variables related to attitude (engagement, diligence, etc.) that affect response. This could explain the discrepancies across panels, based on hidden aspects of the panel (e.g., panelists degree of diligence, their feelings of social responsibility, or their affinity regarding incentives). A complex swirl of variables that are interacting with one another to produce noticeable differences in response.

Thus, panel practices, particularly around tenure and incentives, may produce a variation in panels that is latent—an overall attitudinal effect somewhat hidden from sight but causing real variability in responses across panels.

We know that attitudes are closely aligned with motivation—people who are diligent respondents (socially responsible) and engaged with surveys for the right reasons (the majority) also value the incentives and monetary awards. But when compared to a group that is not rewarded because of panel practices/protocols (or just in it for the money, a small minority) they may answer differently because of the subtle influence of an underlying attitudinal factor.

MANAGERIAL IMPLICATIONS

Managerial Implications Study 1

Overlap. Overlap exists. In the FoQ study framework, there appeared to be a significant proportion of people on multiple panels. These guidelines emerged for managers:

- Overlap varies widely by panel provider.
- There appears to be a recency effect: More overlap is seen in the most recent month of panel activity (October 2008, in the FoQ study).
- Recruitment method is an indicator of overlap.
- Higher levels of online registration correspond with *lower* overlap levels.
- Higher levels of referrals correspond with *higher* levels of overlap.
- Education and income are also indicators of overlap.
- Less than a high school education corresponds with higher levels of overlap.
- Lower-income levels (less than $50,000) correspond with higher levels of overlap.
- Age, panel tenure, average monetary incentive, and gender did not appear as indicators of overlap.

As we saw in the FoQ analyses, multiple panel membership does not necessarily lead to degradation in survey quality. Other factors in this complex process are at work.

Duplication. Duplication is a natural outgrowth of multipanel membership, but it can also occur within a panel. Duplication is not a direct contributor to data quality, but if it is allowed to manifest, it can have a noticeable effect on response patterns.

Digital fingerprinting methods appear to capture the most duplicates and have similar rates to name/address matching for studies where PII is captured, if 100% of the sample's PII can be provided. However, the fact that name/address matching *requires* PII is a potential limitation that needs further study. We note that digital fingerprinting methods work at the machine level, and, thus, would not be able to detect a multiuse machine. The extent this occurs in the panel population would determine the possibility for Type 2 error, incorrectly identifying a duplicate when, in fact, it was not. Browser cookies are an alternative, but because cookies can be deleted, they are not as effective as a method to identify duplication.

- Digital fingerprinting methods, overall, are more likely to capture duplicates when PII is an issue.
- Telephone and address matching is just as effective, but requires PII.
- In the FoQ study, a realistic portrayal of duplication across panels (two panel combinations) uncovered an average 8% duplication level, with a range from 2% to 19%.
  - Within-panel duplication was on average 8.8%, with a range from 3% to 16%
  - The net level of duplication was 25% across 17 panels.
- Duplication rates vary widely by provider (and are related to the percentage of overlap).
- Duplication rates are nearly double when surveying at the local market level (across all 17 panel providers).
  - This suggests that a limited sampling frame needs to be carefully managed for duplicate identification.

Cross-panel duplication is an operational or infrastructure problem that needs addressed by an industry-wide solution. Buyers should look for a profiling overlap statistic that falls within an acceptable range. In addition, panel management procedures should be in place to prevent the possibility of duplication, defined as taking the same survey twice (or more) by the same person. Within-panel duplication should be strictly controlled, with the most up-to-date systems and procedures in place to avoid this.

Of greatest concern, however, is the duplication finding in the local-market scenario. This finding suggests that special attention, rules, and procedures need to be in place whenever a sample restriction is in force, whether it is geographical, segment-imposed, or category limiting.

Managerial Implications Study 2

Response quality. Survey length must be controlled. Buyers and research firms can work together to create surveys that foster good survey-taking behavior. The bad behavior score can function as an indicator to assess response quality. More analysis needs done to infuse the effect of interview time (speeding) into the equation.

Attitudes are a clear indicator of response quality. Firms can build off favorable attitudes to generate more engaged and diligent respondents: assess and adjust practices via regular panel satisfaction and attitudinal studies. Vendors can also consider using an attitudinal battery at recruitment time to classify panelists and flag ones who may potentially be poor.

The FoQ study ascertained an optimal range of survey taking frequency *overall* that was between 3 to 10 (each month), with some variation depending on the age/gender segment; thus, survey invites as often as every other day may be acceptable. However, a primary consideration is that if a person belongs to multiple panels, stricter rules must be in place so the overall optimal point is not crossed. Protocols for assessing multipanel membership are a requirement to keep survey taking frequency at an optimal point.

Managerial Implications Study 3

Consistency. Based on the FoQ data analysis, the following areas can be addressed in sample management and study execution:

- Sample balancing (weighting) survey data to known census targets, minimally on age within gender, education, income, and region will reduce variance, but not completely eliminate it.
- Attempts at balancing based on panel tenure represent a promising avenue, but it does not completely eliminate variance.
- The data suggest that panel practices interact to build groups of respondents with distinctive attitudinal profiles. Although panel tenure may be one such factor, the way panels recruit, the type and amount of incentives offered, and the percentage of surveys completed from external panel sources may encourage distinctive panels to emerge that share attitudinal and motivational propensities that drive results that may vary from panel to panel.

The findings suggest strongly that panels are not interchangeable. Guidelines and transparency about sourcing are needed. But, in addition, buyers of research should be aware of the attitudinal tendencies provoked by panel practices and look for attempts to carefully blend and balance samples to achieve a harmonious result.

CONCLUSION

Since the completion of the ARF's FoQ study in 2009, many developments have occurred. Although much industry-wide works begs to be completed, the ARF did use the FoQ results to create a Quality Enhancement Process (QeP; Pettit, 2010) to help buyers and sellers of online research create more transparency while attending to the improvement of consistency in results in a collaborative manner. The ARF has created workshops to train the industry in QeP principles and practices that have been successfully delivered in public forums, as well as private, custom work with some Fortune 100 firms (see www.thearf.org).

CASRO has continued to foster yearly conferences on the technical aspects of online data quality and its improvement. Some industry vendors, in particular Markettools; Marketing, Inc.; and a consortium titled Prometheus (global research vendors Kantar and GfK), have formed independent efforts to address singular aspects of quality. It appears that the industry has taken the quality challenge seriously, and these efforts are all admirable. As the use of technology grows beyond the online panel world, it will be interesting to see how these new sources will be adapted to enrich and extend the ability of marketers and advertisers to further touch the consumers to see, hear, and learn what they are thinking and feeling.

CHAPTER 19

RFID in Research

19 Things You Can Do With RFID That You Couldn't Do Before

MICKEY BRAZEAL

Roosevelt University

A SEARCH ENGINE FOR THINGS

Radio frequency identification (RFID) is an old technology for automatically identifying things in the physical world—but with many new uses and recent improvements. It was borne out of the need to distinguish enemy fighters from friendly fighters over London in the Battle of Britain. It became immensely more useful when the same functionality could be shrunk into individual computer chips and manufactured for pennies per unit. Today, RFID systems are used for keycard entry and subway tickets and shoplifting defense and tracking cows, and, perhaps most important, *for inventory control*. In the supply chains of U.S. manufacturers and retailers, there is perhaps $45 billion worth of stuff that is not accounted for (BEA Systems, 2006). It's out there somewhere, probably. Where it needs to be is on the shelf. Items that are out of stock on the retail shelf cause lost sales each year of perhaps $50 billion (BEA Systems). RFID is beginning to shrink that, and its widespread deployment for inventory control has made the technology more robust and less expensive than ever before.

Think of RFID technology as a *search engine for things* in the physical world. Our lives have been transformed by search engines that can locate nothing but digits in servers somewhere. Now there's a way to know where a particular *thing* is and what condition it's in, pretty much anywhere. Not just a category of things, but a particular thing. This individual pork chop. This particular pill bottle, puppy, or polar bear.

In research, RFID is a way to see things you couldn't see before. Find patterns you couldn't find before. Collect data that you could not possibly collect before. Respond to consumer behavior in ways and at a speed that you couldn't hope for before. It is a way to integrate research with action in real-time. It is in many situations, it is a cheaper, less obtrusive, and more objective means of data collection than has ever been available. It is a source of measurements and insights and even operational improvements in marketing.

And it is transformative. RFID permits changes in the capabilities and economics of research that almost change what the word "research" means.

Sometimes, for example, we think of research as a *batch* of measurements on a *sample* of a population of interest. Is it still research when it becomes affordable and practical to collect the same data on that total population, for as long as we are interested?

Sometimes, we think of research as an activity separate from operations, an activity that ends when insights and measurements are delivered to managers. Is it still research if *sense-and-respond* processes create an automated real-time follow-up to the research result, instead of a delayed response?

It will still take the researcher's imagination to figure out what and where and when to measure, who should respond, and how. But the report-writing part sort of goes away.

Our new powers make it necessary to *reimagine* what kinds of things the marketer and the manager would like to know and how they would use research results in an ideal world. In this chapter, I will assume that any systematic collection of data that serves to improve management's strategy or operational efficiency is research.

Figure 19.1 TAGSYS Chip

A small and inexpensive chip designed for individual-item-level tagging. Price depends on quantity, but it is not high enough to be a significant part of most research budgets.

Source: TAGSYS.

HOW RFID WORKS

Think of it as a four-part system.

First is a tag, a very small radio transceiver. It is attached to the steak or socks or snow tire that you wish to follow. It can be thinner than a thumbnail, about the diameter of a nail head, or maybe, with its antenna laid out around it, as big as a postage stamp. (See Figures 19.1 and 19.2)

There are specialized tags the size of glitter, but the ones that go for less than a nickel apiece are stamp-size. The tag is perpetually broadcasting, "Here I am, and who I am." There are active tags, with batteries, and passive tags that get their energy from radio waves sent by the reader.

Second is a reader or interrogator. This, too, can be chip-size. The reader is in a known place, so whenever a tagged item gets close to the reader, and talks to it, you know where that item is. You can put readers in a doorway, on a shelf, in a cell phone, wherever.

Third, we need software to make sense of all the millions of readings, to throw out most of them and direct our attention to the moment when a reader first detects a tag and the moment when it moves away.

Finally, there are sensors. Tiny microelectromagnetic (MEMS) sensors can reside on the tag. They can sense, record, and report on some aspect of the condition of the tagged item. There are sensors for temperature, vibration, shock (did the item get dropped?), light, radiation, chemicals, bacteria, certain sounds (was a shot fired?), acceleration, humidity, and so forth. With sensors, you can know the condition of the item right now, how it has changed over time, or whether it reached some designated level at some point in the past.

Sensors can be strewn across an area in a network of nodes. Each acts as a router and a repeater for the other nodes in the network, sending out a message of condition and location to a reader at the edge of the network. Like the Internet, it's reliable because of all its alternative, redundant pathways.

RFID is more powerful than barcodes because it identifies an individual item

Figure 19.2 Example of an RFID Tag Used on a Book

A typical chip design from a book-locating application

Source: TAGSYS.

rather than a category, because it doesn't depend on line of sight, and because it doesn't have to be oriented by somebody such as checkout clerk picking it up and wiggling it back and forth. Unlike barcodes, RFID works in the dark, inside a box, under a layer of mud, or whatever. The tagged item could be facing the wrong way, or in the middle of the stack, and still be readable. Barcodes are easy to forge. RFID tags are not.

Now, look at some applications. Following are some basic ways in which RFID transforms research. In some cases, I have used applications from pure research in the sciences because they are the best early examples. But *every one* of these methods is directly applicable to the needs of the manager and the marketer.

By the time you finish this chapter, you will have invented several more.

19 THINGS YOU CAN DO WITH RFID-BASED RESEARCH THAT YOU COULDN'T DO BEFORE

1. You can collect, unobtrusively, information on consumer behavior in a bricks-and-mortar retail store.

Herb Sorensen (2009), the shopper-marketing guru, did a famous study of where the shopping carts go in a supermarket and where they don't go. He put tags on the carts and readers along the aisles—simple and inexpensive and extremely important. He found that the particular items in an aisle are not nearly as important in generating traffic as how wide the aisle is. Many shoppers will simply never enter a narrow aisle unless they need one of a few can't-do-without items in that aisle. The other items in that aisle won't see much traffic. Yet many supermarkets still have a broad racetrack around the outside, and many narrow aisles in the middle. That single insight will have a powerful impact on supermarket design. And measuring retail traffic by aisle becomes a new operational tool.

As products are commoditized and price competition gets ever tighter, marketers focus more and more on the quality of the customer experience. As a driver of loyalty, customer experience may be more important than either price or perceived product quality. One study puts *quality of customer experience* higher in importance than either price or product quality in air travel, banking, hotels, and landline phone service and within a few percentage points of product quality in auto purchase, department stores, fast-food restaurants, full-service restaurants, supermarkets, and cell phones (Thompson, 2008).

Yet the customer experience is a very hard thing to measure. RFID gives you some important new opportunities.

Museums sometimes offer a handheld audio device with a headset that provides background information on the exhibit you are closest to. RFID tags on the exhibit tell the device which exhibit you're close to and, thus, which story to tell. But in addition, the device can track exhibits attended, time spent on each, and go-backs, so the museum knows what you are interested in and what you skip. It would be easy to do that with a shopping cart or basket, or with a mobile shopping app.

A cosmetics marketer has experimented with a smart shelf, with a built-in reader. Individual nail polish bottles have tags. So the marketer can know not only the product purchased but also which alternatives were considered and then put back (Heinrich, 2005; Hughes, 2006). A similar model is already in use in jewelry stores. At retail, jewelry is often removed from a glass case and displayed to the customer on a velvet countertop tray. One version of that tray contains a built-in reader. The jewelry's price tag has an RFID tag. So managers can see which pieces were viewed but not purchased (O'Connor, 2007a). Both brand managers and retailers see "putbacks" as valuable information.

Clothing at retail is a particularly difficult business. Size and color variations make it necessary to carry large inventories. The short lifespan of style variations creates a brief window in which you can move them at full price. Yet, with all that investment, the majority of trips to a woman's clothing retailer do not produce a sale. The customer "couldn't find anything" (Wasserman, 2007). One small piece of remediation requires tags on garments and readers in the fitting room. Women take several items to the fitting room and leave some or all of them behind. Until they are back on the rack, they become an out-of-stock item. You cannot sell that color in that size. But now the reader tells the sales associate what needs to be carried back to the rack as soon as the fitting room door is opened and closed. And again, you get a record of things considered but not purchased.

2. You can deliver data in real-time—fast enough that it can be responded to while the customer is still in the store.

Knowledge at the Point of Action (RightNow Technologies, 2006) has long been seen as the key to the customer experience. With RFID applications, it can sometimes be collected and delivered in time to influence a customer experience in progress.

The leading example is Harrah's, which has used loyalty cards to transform the customer experience in casinos. Harrah's has a real-time view of the casino floor including game preference, age, amount spent, drink preference, and so on. This enables, for example, individualized promotions using a patron's favorite drink. RFID cards make this more granular and less expensive than cards inserted in a machine. And again, the application can provide behavior data without being obtrusive (Schloter & Hamid, n.d.).

Another early application of this idea puts tags on the name badges worn by the people who attend a trade show. When you visit a vendor's booth, the tag can be read and your contact information collected for follow-up, if the people operating the booth think you are a good prospect (Ferguson, 2006).

3. You can create sense-and-respond applications, where research data are delivered to customer-facing applications and generate a predetermined instant response.

Sense-and-respond is the future for retail and other service businesses. Right now, there's much information processing at retail stores, but most of it is in the backroom or at checkout. The next step is its distribution across the area where we can study consumer behaviors and address them automatically. This will create a much more personal and predictable customer experience (RightNow Technologies, 2006).

A key part of the customer experience in air travel is reliable baggage tracking. Before RFID, lost bags were at 4 million per year, worldwide. RFID is expected to eliminate 98% to 99% of this (McCartny, 2007). But the sense-and-respond part that could affect the customer experience is this: You could now get an automatically generated text message, before takeoff, reassuring you that your bag made it onto the plane (*Science Spectra,* 2000). Passengers say they'd like that.

4. You can create sense-and-respond applications, where data collected on the spot is combined with data from an individual customer's previous behavior to create a response tailored to that individual.

Have you heard about Media Cart? It's a computerized shopping assistant that rides on a shopping cart through the supermarket. It can locate items, keep lists, remind a customer of things on their list that they've walked past, and run a total cost.

Figure 19.3 Media Cart

Media Cart can make real-time, individualized promotional offers in-store, right at the moment of truth, and test how well they work.

Source: TAGSYS.

Imagine you're shopping. You start by feeding the cart your RFID loyalty card. Now the cart has a database. Not your name or your address or anything about you, except a history of what you buy at that supermarket. A smart-shelf reader sees you coming, recognizes you as a buyer of premium cat food, and a flat-screen on the cart makes an individualized offer on a new cat food brand. (Why put the same things on sale for everybody? Everybody doesn't want the same things.) Not everybody buys fresh seafood, for example. But you do, so for you, salmon is on sale. Once you've bought in a category, you stop getting offers about it.

Right now, it's expensive to put a computer on every shopping cart. But it's happening. And when this application makes it to the cell phone, we'll have mass-market, real-time individualized relationship retailing.

A similar application involves coupon distribution. Right now, there are systems that give consumers coupons based on purchase data or loyalty card data as they check out of the supermarket. That's lame. They're *leaving*; the coupons got there too late. Surely, it's smarter to let a customer show a card to a kiosk on the way into the store and obtain behavior-based coupons then. A particularly interesting tactic in this space would be to respond to a brand-defector with a win-back, super coupon.

In places where product cost is high enough for individual product tagging, a shopper could use a cell phone to find out, without human intervention, whether a particular product is in stock before entering the store. That's research carried out by the customers on their behalf, and it might create an advantage in categories such as hardware, where stores with more limited inventory must compete with big boxes.

5. You can create multistage sense-and-respond interactions, like artillery, so successive responses change as previous responses are measured.

This model got its start in biomedical applications. There's a chip for diabetics with a blood glucose sensor. In response to sensor messages, it releases insulin from a pocket-borne intravenous system. Then, it measures the result and decides whether to release a little more (personal communication Steve Sabicher, 2008; Bacheldor, 2006; Brazeal, 2009). That's a lot better than the sticks-and-shots model currently used. There's also a heart monitor that reads an RFID sensor *over the phone* and adjusts the electrostimulation from an implanted pacemaker, *without a trip to the doctor's office* (Gregory, 2006). But multistage sense-and-respond doesn't have to be life-and-death.

Think about packaged goods promotions at retail. Marketers get measurably better responses if special promotional packages and displays are on the selling floor when the advertising breaks. But a supermarket, for example, has lots of promotions and may not get yours set up on schedule. Checkers can be sent around, but they are expensive. And they can't be in all the stores on Day 1, and they have many promotions to check for, and maybe, sometimes, they fib a little bit.

Now there's a better way. Put a tag on the display being shipped to the store. Add a reader on the store's backdoor and another on the door from the backroom onto the selling floor. Day 1, you call the supermarket manager and observe that your promotional display isn't up yet. He says they didn't get it yet. You say it went through his back door. He says we already put it up. You say it didn't go through the door to the selling floor yet.

If it goes back and forth through the selling floor door, it means they are using your display pack to replenish out-of-stocks. If it gets to the reader at the box crusher, then they threw your display away. Sometimes, there's an agreement that links your promotional price to putting up the display. Now, for the first time, there's some chance of getting what's been paid for (Swedberg, 2007c). What's more, the marketer can tell, also for the first time, whether the response rate was because of the promotional idea or to the retailer's execution (Collins, 2006).

Mass transit businesses find it tough to maximize revenues. Now that they have mostly switched to RFID-based ticketing, they can do promotions based on segments of their audience—on students or seniors or occasional users or nonweekend users—see in real-time what is working and what is not. Promotional e-mails can spread the word to the targeted segment that a promotion has been extended while it's working or offer a last chance when it's time to stop.

6. You can detect events of interest in the most problematic locations, quickly and reliably.

Kodak has patented an application to measure pill-taking compliance. It's an RFID microtag attached to each pill, which digests in the stomach at the same speed as the pill does. It reports from inside the patient on the moment at which the medication has actually entered the bloodstream (RFIDupdate.com, 2007). There is no better way to measure. Rule of thumb, prescription compliance in the United States is about two-thirds. Now you know how to change that.

A biologist has tagged European eels and tracked their seasonal migration from the coast of Ireland to the Sargasso Sea, in the middle of the North Atlantic, and back, through the ocean and along the ocean floor. Nobody knew they did that till now (Swedberg, 2009). These were not five-cent tags, and the reader was in a satellite, but absent RFID, it is hard to see how these events could have been detected. Scientists track the population and range of peccaries (wild pigs) across Mexico and Central America primarily by RFID tags (Rajewski, 2007) because if you get too close you risk being eaten by your respondents.

7. You can provide objective, unassailable data about highly emotional or disputed behaviors.

There's a problem with the detection of *preventable medical errors* in hospitals. A study by the U.S. Institutes of Medicine, reported in the *New York Times*, documented almost exactly a million deaths per year from such mistakes, plus another 770,000 nonfatal "adverse events" (Bacheldor, 2007c; Harris, 2006). Self-reports of errors are not widespread in this highly judgmental environment. Hospitals do share-of-error studies to try to detect recurring patterns and problem caregivers.

One category is drug errors. Nurses learn the five rights: (1) the right medication in the (2) right form and the (3) right dosage at the (4) right time to the (5) right patient. But some nurses come on shift at night and have to work quickly, and patients look alike and are asleep, and doctors write badly, and things happen. Think, one error, per patient, per day, which is the actual finding (Associated Press, 2006). (Does that make you need to take a pill?)

Here, RFID-driven research has been both the pattern identifier and the first line of defense. Put a tag on the patient, a tag on the medication, and a tag on the nurse's name badge, and show them all to the reader when it's time to medicate. If they don't all match, the bottle doesn't open (Wessel, 2007). A dangerous event has been identified, and its consequences prevented, simultaneously.

For a more marketing-oriented information need, consider the vexing problem of manufacturer/wholesaler/retailer relationships. Imagine that a small manufacturer (names withheld by request) ships to a large retailer. The retailer notifies the manufacturer that nothing arrived. The poor manufacturer, who only knows what happens at the other end from the people at the other end, has no choice but to ship again. It's much worse when there's a wholesaler and a distribution center, or two in-betweens, and there is no good way to figure out where the problem is. But put RFID tags, perhaps only at the pallet level, which can make the specific problem disappear, and identify the underlying cause.

8. You can economically measure entire populations over very long time spans.

Many businesses want to keep an eye on their employees, for one reason or another. Here is one application that serves two very different populations.

Casinos want to watch dealers, who disperse large sums of money at a high rate of speed. The casino wants to know that the dealer is not taking advantage of an individual customer and not colluding with a customer to take advantage of the casino. But no one can afford to watch them all, all the time. The convenience store operator wants to know that its solitary and isolated employees are not endangered by a customer who wants to rob the store.

There's an RFID innovation that appears to meet both needs. It's a biosensor on a wristband. Measuring pulse rates, it notices when an employee's heart starts racing. In the casino, it can be set to turn a camera toward the dealer and alert the surveillance staff. For the convenience store employee, it can be set to call 911 and ask for help (Swedberg, 2007a).

9. You can measure unobtrusively, without changing behaviors.

There is an RFID application that tracks page turning in a magazine (Britt, 2005). It permits the researcher to measure time spent overall and time-of-exposure for a specific ad or article, as accurately as TV watching has traditionally been measured. It's inexpensive, self-tabulating, and data are available right now. Presumably, it would be used with a longitudinal panel, such as the Nielsen data. You would have to get the respondent's permission, but it is completely in the background and does little to create a consciousness of assessment.

Shiseido is a major Japanese cosmetics marketer. Mitsukoshi is a high-end department store in Tokyo's Ginza, among other places. Together, they launched a smart shelf and smart mirror application in the cosmetics section (Swedberg, 2007b). A smart shelf combines a shelf-fixed reader with tagged individual items in a store. A smart mirror lets the customer hold tagged products up to the mirror to get information about them.

In this application, an "electronic concierge" sees the cosmetic product that is held up to the mirror. It provides product features and instructions, and it shows, on the reflection in the mirror, what that particular shade would look like *on the customer's face*. It is real-time virtual sampling. It's designed as a sales tool, but it also tracks which products are picked up, which ones are sampled, and which of the sampling behaviors results in a sale. So the marketer can know, not just what gets considered, but what, to the customer, looks best on her face. You couldn't know that till now.

10. With sensors, you can measure the current state of an item, a change over time, or the moment at which a particular condition reached a predetermined level.

There's a sensor that can "smell" a bad apple in a produce display before it has a chance to spoil the barrel (Machrone, 2003).

There are five bacteria that appear when milk goes sour. A sensor-cluster that can detect all five could be installed as a single tiny tag in the mouth of a milk jug, so no one would ever buy a sour one (Wan, et al., 2007). This is still being commercialized, and it might happen first in bigger volume applications, like food service. But there will be a lot of spinoffs from this one. It's not going to cost much. And there are a many places where a researcher, who can lie in wait for a bacterium and sound the alarm when it shows up, will add enormous value.

You can know the life history of a high-priced bottle of wine when you buy it, secure in the knowledge that it has never been exposed to extremes of heat or cold that would have damaged its flavor and bouquet (Peeters, 2005).

A retailer can sell fresh fish knowing *for sure* that it has never been frozen and sell frozen fish knowing *for sure* that it thawed in the truck on the way to the store and, thus, made likely to rot before it is sold (Ferguson, 2002; Meyer, 2003). Both of these were merely convenient fictions before RFID.

Chile ships avocados (paltas) by sea to the United States. It's not easy to measure temperature in a big area like a ship: There are many interior microclimates. But the Paltag Program, a network with tags as individual nodes, can detect a temperature issue, locate it, and provide both an alarm and location directions (Swedberg, 2007d).

11. Monitoring a condition and a location simultaneously, you can describe, dynamically and in real-time, the boundaries of a phenomenon.

Where in a huge and valuable vineyard will there be trouble with fungus on the growing grapes? Could only the vines that are going to have the problem be treated and the rest be left alone? An algorithm using air temperature, soil temperature, hours of sunshine exposure, and humidity can identify the problem vines in time to prevent fungal damage. Battery-powered sensor pods, combined with tags and readers to identify vineyard rows and individual plants, can send a vine-specific fungus alert. So the vintner only sprays where it's needed. The system can also predict the perfect pruning moment (Culler, 2004).

12. You can collect customer information with precise and reliable privacy controls, tailored to the situation and to respondent preferences.

Privacy is complicated. It's hard to know what people want. We combine extreme statements about absolute concealment of all personal data with widespread use of Facebook and other social sites essentially dedicated to strewing personal information to the winds. We pay extra for OnStar and smart phones and EZPass tollgate tags so that unknown numbers of people, we've never met, can know exactly where we are and have been.

As a practical matter, it may be easier to get respondent cooperation if you can give some assurances about data security and personal control of personal data. It is not widely understood that privacy protection is an advantage, rather than a disadvantage of RFID systems. That story is greater than the scope of this article. But note a few data protection advantages. Tags can be designed to be "killed" at the checkout counter. They can have short read ranges. (Someone else's tag won't be read if it has a quarter-inch read range.) Data on tags can be encrypted. Tag data can be just a serial number, identifying one cell in a database, and the database can be physically protected (Brazeal, 2009).

13. You can instantly and accurately measure complex interactions in the behavior of groups of people and things.

Rugby (seen by a nonplayer) is a bunch of thick-necked thugs in a scrum, pushing one another backward and forward and trying to get loose to run away with the ball. Be the coach for a moment. How can you possibly tell which thick-necked thug is adding the most value and should be retained at all costs despite his occasional lapses in hygiene and decorum?

Guinness, which owns a rugby team, and Gilbert, the premier manufacturer of rugby balls, have developed a very sophisticated RFID app that does precisely that (Guinness, 2009). There's a tag inside the ball, tags on the ankles of players, and 12 long-range readers around the stadium. The moment-by-moment contributions to success of each individual player can be measured and compared. A player's progress through the season can be tracked. Specific mistakes and specific winning strategies can be identified. This will be hard to beat. Managers of teams in free-flowing systems, from construction to baggage handling to the NFL, take note.

14. As more and more marketers sell *the way an item was produced*, (organic, free-range, halaal, wild-caught, etc.), it becomes more important to perform process authentication.

Process authentication is the child of greenwashing. Today, some markets are segmented by production process. Some people would rather buy the best-looking apples or the cheapest apples. Others want organic apples. Some buy chicken by price or by brand. Others want free-range chicken or fair-traded coffee. How do consumers know their getting what they paid for?

One way is because an independent authenticator gave that product a seal of approval. And how does the independent authenticator know? One way is to track that product from the tree or the chicken farm or wherever to the retailer, using RFID tags. It takes classic qualitative interviewing to know what's being authenticated, but it takes RFID to confirm that verdict at the point of sale.

15. You can measure service behaviors, even complex ones, to identify patterns that maximize customer satisfaction or efficiency.

Service businesses create business rules for how to get things done, but it can be hard to measure compliance with business rules. And if compliance isn't tracked, well, there can be departures. RFID-based research designs are particularly effective at addressing this. Tags give identities to individual assets. Thus, where they are, when they are there, and for how long can be known. Previously, uncovered and invisible violations, mistakes, and inefficiencies can lead to opportunities for process improvement.

One Greek municipality got improvements just by keeping track of time elapsed for each task. It's a garbage collection service. Each bin has a tag, and each truck has a reader, and each time a bin is emptied into the truck, the time is automatically recorded. If there are long pauses between nearby bins, that's noted, too. Tag and timing data are uploaded by phone to the municipal government (Ferguson, 2002; O'Connor, 2007b). This is not to disparage Greeks or garbage collectors. It is to point out a method for tracking the performance of services. (If only they had it in Chicago, where I live.)

Healthcare workers use much mobile equipment: respiratory therapy machines, IV stands, wheelchairs, and so on. Hospitals found that highly paid workers, tracked by badge-tags, were spending large amounts of time looking for the equipment necessary for their work. There were multiple instances of hiding shared equipment (over the ceiling tiles will work) to ensure its availability. In this case, the solution was putting tags on the equipment and readers in the halls, so their location could be seen on a computer screen at the nurses' station. That's happening all over the country now. Hospitals that had a shortage of expensive equipment suddenly have a surplus (Bacheldor, 2007b; McCoy, 2006).

16. You can identify high-quality respondents for intercept research.

Not everybody wants to carry around an RFID loyalty card that would identify them as a top quintile customer as they walk through the door. There are many privacy issues in our society, and they are getting more complicated rather than less. But there are interesting—and huge—exceptions.

High rollers in the casino environment prize their loyalty card status and won't be caught without the badge of it. And that's who you'd want to talk to if you did an intercept study there.

People in collectivist cultures, such as Japan, China, India and Mexico, do not have anything like the same privacy issues that Americans have. RFID applications where customers carry a card that can be read on entering a bank or a retailer have been in place in Japan, for example, for a long time. They empower customized service and are seen by the customer as a way to improve the shopping experience. But, as a side benefit, if a retailer wanted to talk to a store's most valuable customers in-store, they could quickly be identified (Banham, 2003).

As the loyalty card and the payments card migrate inside the cell phone, there will be more and more situations where an RFID loyalty identifier could be used to know whom to intercept in store.

17. You can associate individual items or products with the production line/ shift that created them or the corner of the field in which they were grown to manage recalls and eliminate repeated problems.

The rise of relationship marketing has changed the priorities of marketers. Today, we spend much time on the experience after the sale and how to improve that experience to create loyalty. In the extreme case, when a product doesn't work right, or some part of a food shipment turns out to be unhealthy, we need to engineer a quick recall and a quick solution to the problem that made a recall necessary.

Food recalls are all about lot size. If you have a small lot size and you get some bad hamburger, maybe you throw away 500 pounds. If you don't track by lot size, maybe you throw away 60,000 pounds (Gregory, 2006; Rasco, & Bledsoe, 2005). Tags on each separated lot can associate it with a date, a shift, and a production location or one little corner of a grower's field. If you know where, you can use conventional research techniques to figure out why.

Manufactured goods recalls are either about purchased components or production-line errors. Again, with a tag you can associate a tire or strut or carburetor with both a supplier and a moment in time on a particular production line. And again, if you know where and when, you can figure out why.

18. You can embed behavior-data collection in products.

Coke machines could indicate what they're running out of before the resupplier arrives at their location, and air conditioners could tell the repairman when they are about to need repair (Heinrich, 2005). Hospital medicine cabinets can warn when they're running low on a critical medication (Bacheldor, 2007a). Cars could be made to deliver much more specific information than "check engine soon," if that were demanded of their makers.

19. In complex, large-scale research, such as the clinical trials of drugs, you can eliminate most of the sources of experiment failure and redos.

This is a much more mechanical use of RFID, but one of the most mature because of the importance of the problem and the urgent need for improved performance.

Pharmaceutical companies spend an average of $802 million to develop a single new drug. A very large share of that is spent on clinical trials. Trials for a single drug may take 12 years. It's a big business. The Clinical Research Organizations (CRO) outsourcers of clinical trials did $14.4 billion in 2007. A key problem they face is tracking both drug samples and biological specimens (Rangarajan & Vijaykumar, 2005).

Medicine samples get lost, misrouted, misplaced onsite among many scattered research locations. Often, they must be held at a particular temperature or efficacy is degraded. In typical research designs, there is no good way to be sure they were always in the proper environment, and many good reasons to suspect they were not.

Biological specimens in test tubes are not usually tracked at all. Test tubes sent to the investigator's site go missing and are not returned. Wrong tubes are returned. The result may simply be a reduction in sample size, or it may be that critical data does not get collected and tests are canceled entirely. The time and money wasted are significant.

The RFID applications are not less urgent for being obvious. Test tubes can be tagged and tracked. Temperatures can be tracked. RFID wristbands can match patients with specimens during the collection process. In an EPC global study, errors were reduced, patient dropouts were reduced, and management interventions were reduced. Immediate response to sensor alerts essentially eliminated temperature degradation issues. Chain-of-custody problems were eliminated, and time goals were actually exceeded (Rangarajan & Vijaykumar, 2005).

WHAT HAPPENS NEXT?

Foiled pundits abound, and it is not practical to pick which applications will come first, or how quickly they will come, or which will be most successful. Nevertheless, here are some predictions:

- Tags will get cheaper, though it took longer to get from a dime to a nickel than it did to get from a dollar to a dime.
- Tags will get more specialized, wherever big volume markets exist.
- Tags are already in touch-less credit cards. These are migrating into cell phones, and that probably means many mobile applications. Research initiated and conducted by the customer, via readers in smart phones, will make big changes at retail.
- RFID projects are now easier to start than they used to be, more like plumbing and less like art. This trend will continue.
- Business analytics applied to Internet and mobile-device behaviors have created a process model that will be applied to customer behaviors in retail and service environments.
- Marketing researchers are notoriously timid about new technologies, perennial late-adopters (Fisher, 2007). If the adoption of RFID identification tools should happen to emulate the adoption of bar-code identification tools, then a few pioneers will build large, lucrative, syndicated products. But there are so many diverse applications of RFID that it might lend itself to a small-business consultant model as well.

New Applications Are Added Every Month

If you have a goal that involves the location or condition of objects in the world, the intersection of objects with people, with their co-operation, or the presence and behavior of people in the world, consider the possibility that RFID might provide a solution. It is a search engine for things.

HOW TO GET STARTED

Companies that start new RFID applications mostly do not have anyone on staff who knows about tag frequencies and reader ranges and RFID middleware. Giant companies go right to the giant manufacturers of RFID equipment—Motorola and Alien Technologies and many others. But imagine a small manufacturer who just wants to track ingredients coming in and finished packages going out. That company will go to a small, local, and inexpensive RFID project firm that can design a system, cost it out, and pick the right tags and readers. Researchers can use that same supplier. Just do a web search for RFID and add a city name (e.g., RFID Chicago). If you don't see one nearby, the big tag suppliers can direct you. (They showed me local resources.)

The critical thing to understand is that *the whole ecosystem is already in place*, with carefully developed and exhaustively tested standards for tags and readers and middleware and measurements. All the pieces are designed to fit together. It might be a mistake to try to go it alone at first (though some academic researchers appear to have done so). But if you develop a niche in a particular kind of study, you may soon develop the ability to figure out each new project yourself. How about becoming one of the first to combine the behavioral understanding derived from RFID with qualitative and/or quantitative research on what was being thought about during a specific action or the reasons that action was engaged in? Call me; we'll talk.

FURTHER READING

Brazeal, M. (2008). Green revolution: RFID and the rise of convenient environmentalism. Proceedings: *RFID World*.

Brazeal, M. (2009). *Varieties of efficiency: How RFID asset tracking changes the way businesses work in the culture of efficiency*. New York, NY: Peter Lang.

Finkenzeller, K. (2003). *RFID handbook: Fundamentals and applications on contactless smart cards and identification*. Chichester: John Wiley & Sons.

Glover, B., & Himanshu B (2006). *RFID essentials*. Sebastopol, CA: O'Reilly Media.

Peppers, D., & Rogers, M. (2004). *Managing customer relationships: A strategic framework*. Hoboken, NJ: John Wiley and Sons.

Want, R. (2006). *RFID explained: A primer on radio frequency identification technologies*. San Francisco, CA: Morgan & Claypool.

Is the Future in Their Hands?

Mobile-Based Research Options and Best Practices

DARREN MARK NOYCE

SKOPOS Market Insight

INTRODUCTION

The mobile-platform device is becoming the most powerful, flexible, and essential tool consumers own—effectively a handheld minicomputer. As such, it will ultimately revolutionize the way marketing researchers interact with the platform and, by extension, respondents.

This chapter provides a snapshot of mobile/cell phone research in early 2011, outlining justifications for its trial and adoption, current options for use, choices, and applications (along with the associated advantages and limitations of the platform), plus it examines mobile's strong future potential.

The catalysts driving this quiet revolution, and their interlinkage with mobile research, will be explored, such as hard and soft technological advances like smartphones (e.g., iPhone and Android) as well as increased consumer interaction with social media networks, blogs, and news websites, which influence consumer behavior in accessing the mobile Internet.

The chapter also describes 21 real-life mobile research applications that exemplify the wide array of research possibilities including several that could *not* be accomplished prior to mobile technology.

THE CURRENT STATUS OF MOBILE-BASED MARKETING RESEARCH

In March 2010, *AdWeek* magazine in the United States reported the findings of a GfK/Advertising Research Foundation (ARF) study (among 250 ARF members) regarding the future of market research. "Atop the ranking of what issues will be 'cutting edge' in the current decade, mobile marketing was named first" (Dolliver, 2010).

So a robust future for mobile research is envisioned, but the current reality is very different. For example, in Europe (United Kingdom, France, Germany, Spain, and Italy), the share of the iPhone, now in its fourth generation, as a harbinger of smart phone, usage is just at 4%. What's interesting though is the potential, for already those 4% represent 12% of all mobile phone *media* users and exhibit a "voracious consumption of mobile media: 94% use mobile media, 87% use applications and 85% browse the mobile Internet" (McCarthy, 2010, para. 3).

And as of the year 2010, I have been personally exploring mobile as a channel and method for research for *more than a decade*. One of my first true studies on the mobile was for U.K. mobile network, One2One, back in 2000. We tested SMS (short messaging service) versus WAP (communications protocol) versus online surveys as alternative data-gathering methods for a general satisfaction survey. Of course, SMS was fast, but it lacked the depth and richness of online (and even WAP, although the proportion of WAP respondents was *very* low back then). Then, we presented a paper to ESOMAR in 2003, regarding a test of SMS versus online versus computer-assisted telephone interviewing (CATI) among online panelists (Hofmann, Menti, & Noyce, 2003). Again, we showed similar findings, with online winning the test, based on a balance of speed, data depth, and detail. Our findings concluded with three text messages sent to the audience:

- SMS samples have a natural bias and skew younger.
- Method and sample, therefore, have to be controlled, and clear instructions for completion must be given.
- SMS does have some role for *instant* data collection with dedicated panels, especially for those on the move, but it is *not* better than online surveying and CATI to mobile phones for online panels.

Limitations including the lack of data depth and detail (for quantitative mobile studies) have certainly been key inhibitors to date (more detail on challenges and inhibitors later) and possibly help explain evidence that even after 10 to 20 years of existence just 1% of research volume is conducted via mobile devices (Macer, 2009).

Does mobile research matter if so little is being done just yet?

As Figure 20.1 suggests, mobile matters because it offers researchers speed, unequaled respondent access, efficiencies, and enriched insights, and respondents benefit from a truly convenient response channel that they are *engaged,* the latter being something that increasingly is lacking in virtually every other data-collection method.

What's more, although everyone agrees that mobile is ideal for gathering data from respondents on the move—away from their home or office—it turns out it also is very

Figure 20.1   Yes, It Matters!

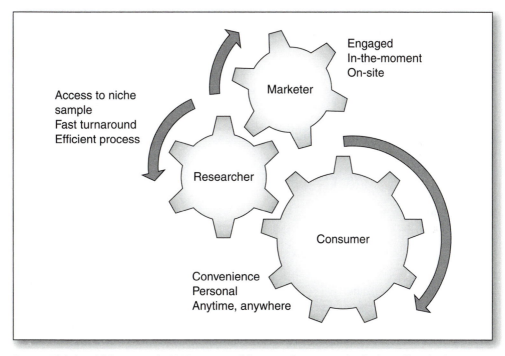

Source: Global Park/Fly Research (2009, June). *Mobile research: Best practice for immediate, in-the-moment feedback*. [Webinar]. Retrieved from, http://www.slideshare.net/FlyResearch/mobile-research-webinarwith flyf9june1020.

adequate for respondents when they are not traveling. *The clear fact of the matter is that when we contact someone on their mobile, they will usually be at home or at work.*

What is mobile research? Is it the fifth methodology?

Traditionally, research involving interviews has mainly been conducted via face-to-face, written (including mail and some shopper intercept studies), telephone (including interactive voice response [IVR]), and online methodologies. I would like to suggest that mobile (or cell phone, from here on, interchangeable terms in this chapter) is the fifth methodology, adding a new dimension to modern marketing research.

Here's an exact definition of mobile-based research: the *self-administered participation* in surveys and research panels using mobile devices. It also refers to *active and prompted questioning* rather than just passive measurement or voice calls made to mobile handsets. Methods and channels include mobile web, WAP, SMS, and MMS (more on these later.) This chapter is *not* about CATI calls to mobiles, CAPI or mobile assisted personal interviewing (MAPI), nor about software that collates mobile-user behavior (although this latter item is described toward the end).

Table 20.1 More than 80% at Home/Work When on Mobile

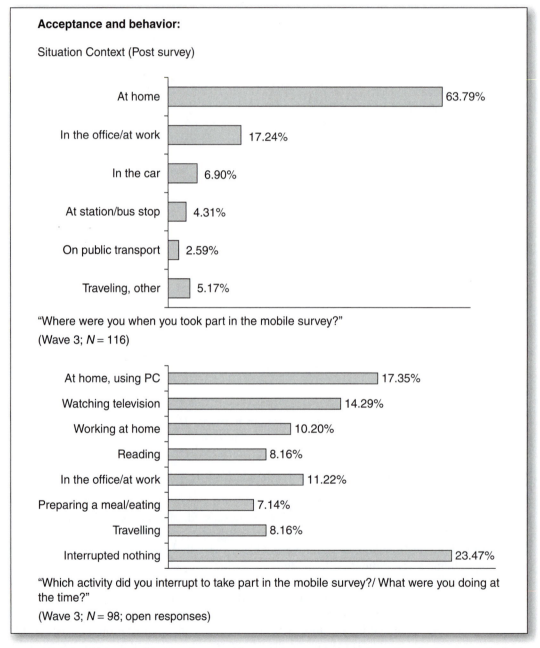

Acceptance and behavior:

Situation Context (Post survey)

At home	63.79%
In the office/at work	17.24%
In the car	6.90%
At station/bus stop	4.31%
On public transport	2.59%
Traveling, other	5.17%

"Where were you when you took part in the mobile survey?"
(Wave 3; N = 116)

At home, using PC	17.35%
Watching television	14.29%
Working at home	10.20%
Reading	8.16%
In the office/at work	11.22%
Preparing a meal/eating	7.14%
Travelling	8.16%
Interrupted nothing	23.47%

"Which activity did you interrupt to take part in the mobile survey?/ What were you doing at the time?"
(Wave 3; N = 98; open responses)

Source: Global Park/Fly Research (2009, June). *Mobile research: Best practice for immediate, in-the-moment feedback.* [Webinar]. Retrieved from, http://www.slideshare.net/FlyResearch/mobile-research-webinarwithflyf9june1020.

THE OPPORTUNITIES AND RATIONALE

Is mobile the next big thing in research?

The following 12 reasons lend heavy weight to the positive assertion that mobile *is* the next best thing:

1. Mobile is hot and now.
2. Enhanced adoption is partially driven by the media.
3. People are attached to their mobile phones.
4. Accessing the Internet via mobile is taking off.
5. The depth and length of mobile web usage are increasing.
6. Mobile is maturing.
7. M-commerce will be important.
8. Young people have embraced social media.
9. Mobile-only households are more prevalent.
10. Users are deeply engaged with their cell phones.
11. Data quality *can* be good.
12. There are a multitude of options and possibilities.

Let's look at each of these now, in turn.

Mobile Is Hot and Now

The global reach for mobile phones is around 50%, and far outweighs that of PCs. Mobile Internet access is increasing fast (Cisco, 2011); and it is also evermore a successful channel for marketing (an indirect measure of the potential for research, if there ever was one).

Research by the Internet Advertising Bureau (IAB) has shown that in the United Kingdom, mobile marketing spend increased year on year by 100% (IAB/ PwC, 2009). It also found that 11 million users access the Internet via mobiles each month. Usage of mobiles and marketing via mobiles is now extensive and still increasing. Surely, research should follow.

Enhanced Uptake Is Partly Driven by the Media

Indeed, media owners the world over are embracing mobile as a channel and justifying this with their research (sometimes using mobile). In doing this, they are helping to push the channel for marketing and research while elucidating the matter with their findings. Research by Yahoo! Europe (Yahoo, 2010) for instance, has indicated an increase in consumer uptake of mobile media by 4.5 million from 2008 to 2010, a figure forecasted to repeat for the following period.

People Are Attached to Their Mobile Phones

Research by Global Park/Fly Research (2009), shown in Table 20.2, clearly indicates that among 13 different sources of wellbeing—including parents and siblings—the absence of a mobile handset would be missed the most if it were unavailable for a day. This modern-day mobile addiction (and the ubiquity of the devices/channel) has emotional strength behind it.

Accessing the Internet Via Mobile Is Taking Off

Figure 20.2 from Morgan Stanley indicates that the number of new subscribers to Internet services among mobile phone owners far surpasses those from desktop users. Further, the speed of adoption via mobile has also been dramatically quicker than desk-based access.

Table 20.2 Mobile Phone Missed Most If Not Available

Which of these things would you miss most if you had to spend a day without them?		
Sources of Wellbeing	**Ranking**	**Percentage**
Mobile phone	1st	63
Friends	2nd	60
Internet	3rd	50
Parents	4th	39
Brothers/sisters	5th	29
iPod/MP3 players	6th	28
TV programs	7th	19
Computer games	8th	14
Magazines & newspapers	9th	11
Books	10th	10
Radio	11th	7
Teachers	12th	1
Advertising	13th	0

Source: Global Park/Fly Research (2009, June). *Mobile research: Best practice for immediate, in-the-moment feedback.* [Webinar]. Retrieved from, http://www.slideshare.net/FlyResearch/mobile-research-webinarwithflyf9june1020.

Figure 20.2 Mobile Internet Outpaces Desktop Internet Adoption

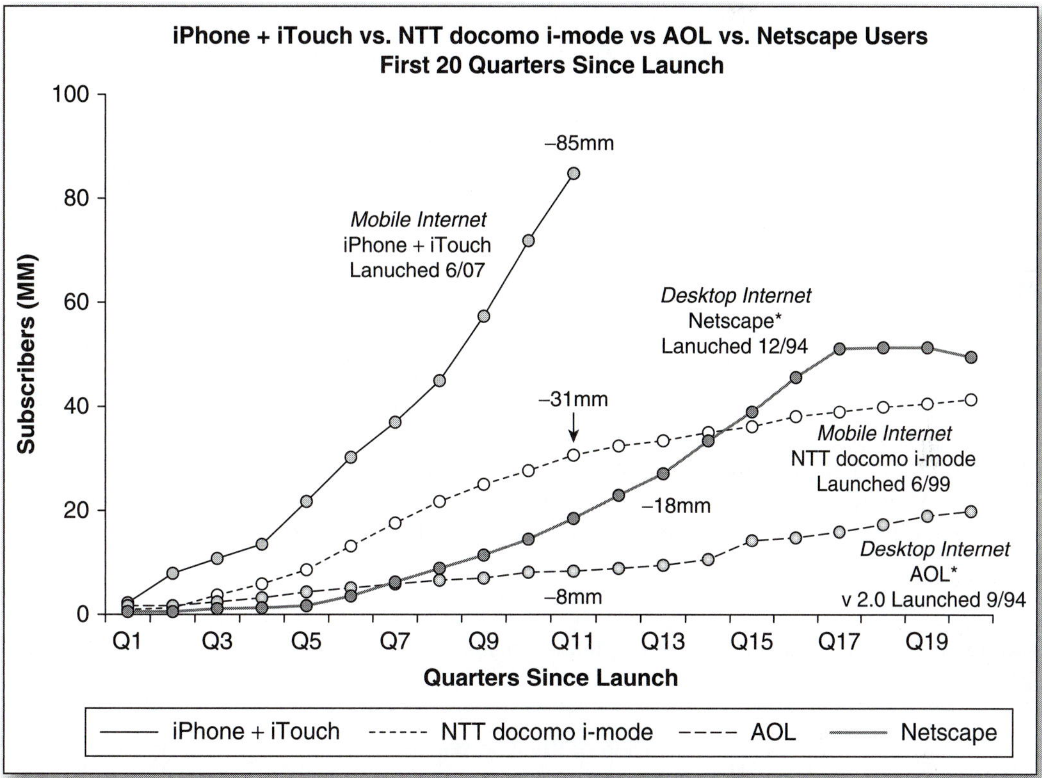
iPhone + iTouch vs. NTT docomo i-mode vs AOL vs. Netscape Users
First 20 Quarters Since Launch
Subscribers (MM)
100
80
60
40
20
0
~85mm
Mobile Internet
iPhone + iTouch
Lanuched 6/07
Desktop Internet
Netscape*
Lanuched 12/94
~31mm
Mobile Internet
NTT docomo i-mode
Launched 6/99
~18mm
Desktop Internet
AOL*
v 2.0 Launched 9/94
~8mm
Q1
Q3
Q5
Q7
Q9
Q11
Q13
Q15
Q17
Q19
Quarters Since Launch
iPhone + iTouch
NTT docomo i-mode
AOL
Netscape

Source: Morgan Stanley, Internet Trends, April 2010.

Depth and Length of Mobile Web Usage Increasing

Research by Yahoo! (2010) has also found that the length of mobile Internet sessions is lengthening, with 77% of their respondents spending more than five minutes per average mobile Internet session. As they say, "Less snacking, more real web" (on the mobile) (slide 6). Consumers are clearly shifting their Internet usage to the mobile, and again, researchers should look to follow.

Mobile Is Maturing

To momentarily sum things up, we could simply say mobile is maturing for the following reasons:

- Consumers' emotional needs are being met, as we have shown.
- 4.2 million in the United Kingdom are three-screeners (TV-PC-mobile, Yahoo, 2010).

- Literally, hundreds of thousands of apps (for the iPhone, Android, and Blackberry systems) deepen and richen the experience and most aren't available *except* on the mobile platform. And these apps include practical (and whimsical) lifestyle aids, business tools, and entertainment.
- M-commerce will be the next growing development as we will outline below.

In a recent study by Yahoo! (2010), the large majority of respondents declared they used/viewed more than one of TV/PC/laptop/mobile at the same time; some 22% claimed to use three devices/screens simultaneously. Anyone with teenage children may have seen this in action!

M-Commerce Will Be Important

And the moment is now for M-commerce as well (buying and ordering things via the mobile). Existing e-tailers and retailers are leading the way here, including eBay, Amazon, and so on. This excellent verbatim from Yahoo! (2010) points to the potential: "It's like with the Internet in its early days—everyone was reluctant to buy things online a few years ago. Now we all do it. It'll be the same with mobile" (slide 11).

Moreover, newer forms of purchasing abound as well—especially as retailers install radio frequency identification (RFID) readers, handset manufacturers add RFID chips, and

Table 20.3   Rise of Multiscreening (TV, laptop, mobile)

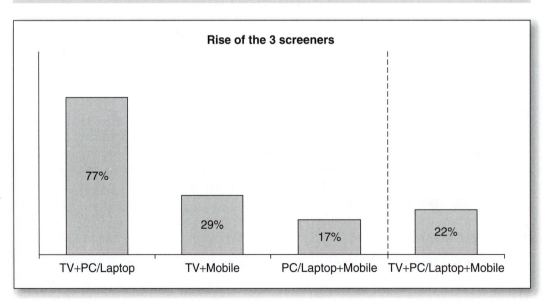

Source: Yahoo! (2010).

retailers develop proprietary apps employing the camera-reading capability of most smart phones. For example, Starbucks announced that its 6,800 U.S. stores plus 1,000 of its outlets in Target stores will allow payment via mobile apps available to owners of Blackberries, iPhones, or iPod Touches (Miller, 2011).

Young People Have Embraced Social Media

Further rationale for the present and future importance of the mobile channel is evidenced by the movement of social network usage from desktops to mobiles among the younger population. This is driven by better devices, contents, data plans, familiarity, and the social media themselves. As Nielsen put it, "Brands targeting youth must consider the mobile as a channel" (Weber, 2010, slide 16). This applies to both marketers and researchers.

Mobile-Only Households Are More Prevalent

Few argue that the ways people are spending time with media has profoundly shifted. Yes, a landline phone and a mobile phone are both media. Medium was defined most trenchantly by Marshall McLuhan (1964) as "any extension of ourselves." Among the more notable changes has been the rise in mobile-only (cell-only) households.

Increasingly, this is an issue for traditional fieldwork models as access to respondents can be inhibited in a number of ways, including absence from sample frames and simple lack of relevant channel/technology (home/fixed line phone). And random digit dialers (RDD) typically exclude cellular customers because inbound calls are often paid for by the handset owner.

Not surprisingly, the Council of American Survey Research Organizations (CASRO) has suggested that the industry needs to make cell-phone research "viable, productive and acceptable" (Bowers quoted in Bain, 2008, para. 5), as 2008 figures show 29% of U.S. households now rarely or never use a landline.

Consumers Are Deeply Engaged With Their Cell Phones

Data from Nielsen (Weber, 2010) as shown in Table 20.4 indicate that subscriptions on smartphones are significantly higher compared to those on traditional feature phones. In mobile media consumption and mobile engagement, clearly the rise of smartphones has had a huge impact, and this will continue and continue (especially as the Apple versus Android versus Blackberry battle intensifies). Smartphones are already helping researchers via mobile Internet surveys, apps, and even full Internet survey taking.

Data Quality *Can* Be Good

Thinking from a researcher's perspective, quality of data has been one of the biggest criticisms of the cell phone as a research platform. A recent interesting evaluation by Ipsos, however, brings this assumption into question. Using a quality index based on

Table 20.4 Consumers Are Deeply Engaged With Their Cell Phones

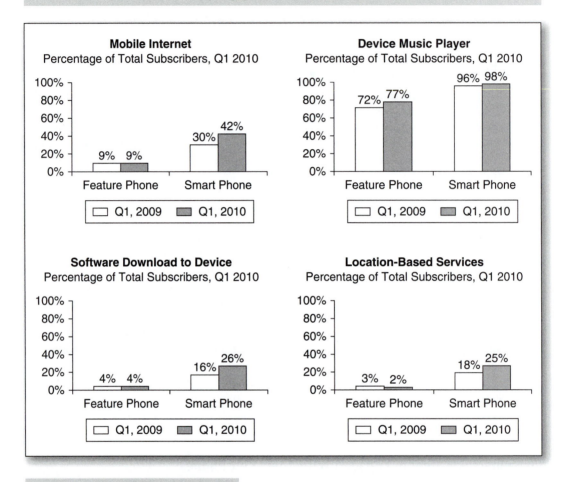

Table 20.5 Wide Range of Research Options Are Practicable

Quantitative	Qualitative
Short surveys	Verbatims/opens
Quick polls	Txt-depths
Ad hoc	Vox-mobs
Tracking	Life diaries
Verbatims/opens	
Access panels	
Bespoke panels	
Omnibuses	

response and contribution rates to an ad recall study, they have shown that scores are significantly higher (for quality) from mobile responders versus online responders (IPSOS, 2010). Researchers should be very careful when assuming online is always better than mobile.

There Are a Multitude of Options and Possibilities

Table 20.5 quickly indicates that a wide range of research paradigms are possible employing the mobile platform.

Unique to mobile is that it is a multichannel channel, a mixed-mode method in itself. It can be used for many types of quantitative surveys and for highly innovative qualitative research—as will be seen in coming sections.

THE FIVE *Rs* THAT WILL DRIVE MOBILE ADOPTION AND SUCCESS

Mobile-based research of today and tomorrow will be successful because of a number of key factors. They can be summarized as the 'Five *Rs*', and they are depicted in Figure 20.3.

Relevance and Fit

The greatest success is likely when the needs of the audience, the marketer, and the research topic are well matched. So far, in my experience, greatest use and demand for mobile-based methods has been from mobile networks, mobile media, and mobile advertisers. This is clearly driven by the combined and cumulative relevance to the audience (respondents), the topic, and the marketer (Noyce, 2011).

The opportunity for the researcher is to have mobile as part of the toolkit for these companies, as well as to increase the relevance beyond these in the future.

Figure 20.3   The Five *Rs* that Drive Mobile

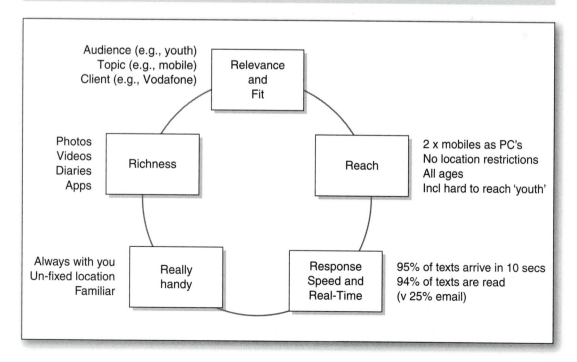

Reach

Mobiles are nearly ubiquitous and usable in most locations and for *most* audiences unlike other data-gathering tools. Mobile has been the most rapidly adopted (new) technology in history. Estimates of global penetration vary from 50% to 60%, clearly exceeding access/penetration rates for TVs, the Internet, PCs, and so on.

Mobile is not just a viable method for developed countries, but also increasingly a primary method for the weaker economies that often have by-passed fixed-line telecommunications infrastructure (and can have wide geographic population dispersal). This penetration provides unique access to both broad and niche groups in many countries around the world today.

Response Speed and Real-Time

Experience and evidence show that mobile, especially SMS/text, has a relatively instant (real-time) data-capture dimension; *this has never been available before among survey-size audiences.*

Research by my company SKOPOS (presented at ESOMAR in 2003), and by others, indicates that those who respond to mobile surveys (most data/testing for SMS/text) do so almost instantly. Lightspeed Research (Coates & Corcoran, 2010), for instance, has found that 60% of completed surveys were returned within 15 minutes of distribution and 90% within an hour. This implies near real-time impact for mobile research.

Think of it this way: Mobile surveys get most response within a few hours, online within a few days, CATI/paper within a few weeks, and so on. Speed is a key strength of mobile, even compared to online.

Table 20.6   Massive Global Reach Achieved in Record Time

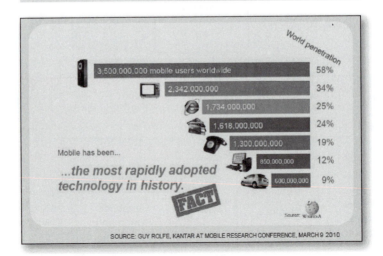

Case Study 1: Speed and Real-Time Research, U.K. General Election 2010 (Source: SKOPOS)

During the U.K. general election in 2010, for the first time, there was a series of leader debates. The news media were keen for the instant evaluation of performance for each participant, and they commissioned a variety of polls. Some used traditional CATI (telephone) methods while others used SMS/text to poll the home viewing, general public (in-studio polls used press-button technology). Results were often available and reported at the end or straight after the broadcast of the TV show. Real-time research seemingly produced instant insight in action.

Case Study 2: *In-Situ* and In-The-Moment Retail and Restaurants (Dodgson, 2010).

The ease and convenience of mobile can also capture *in-situ* and in-the-moment evaluations of experiences, including retail and restaurants. As results are returned in real-time, it is a very powerful tool for consumers to report their satisfaction at the point of consumption while still in consumer/shopper mode. (Later, we show a similar example for hospitals.)

Figure 20.4   Mobile Being Used to Evaluate Results of a Political Debate

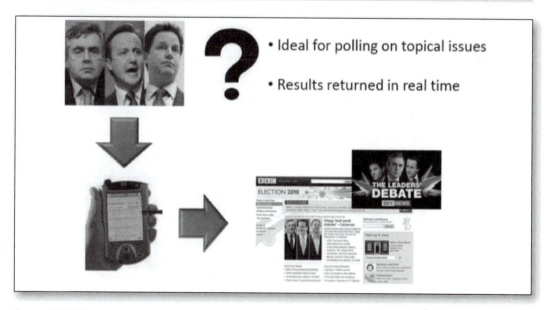

Source: SKOPOS.

Really Handy

As shown earlier, respondents tend to always have their mobile with them. Consumers miss it when it's not there. Also, most get to know how their phone works and, hence, find using it very handy.

In fact, some spend a remarkable amount of time on their phones. Consider these quotes: "A new generation of 'multi-media' children are spending an average of 7 hours a day glued to smartphones, iPods and video games" (Hastings & Warren, 2010). And "I'm on my Blackberry all day—I'm never not on it. Most of my friends have one. I message people on the way to school, and listen to my iPod on the bus, and soon as I get home from school, I turn on my laptop to do my homework and go on Facebook. I'm friends with literally everyone I've ever met" (Katie, 17-year-old student, as quoted by Rolfe, 2009).

Consider the mobile for a moment; it is (always) with you, it is yours (alone), it is portable, and your engagement and use (and relationship) with this device/channel is continuously increasing. You can use it virtually anywhere. It is personal, private, and portable. What an opportunity for researchers!

Richness

This is the most recent dimension to evolve for mobile, and it covers the ever-improving ability of handsets (and users) to take photos and video, as well as the emergence of apps. Again, this is a *unique attribute of the mobile platform*.

Figure 20.5 Mobile Offers Enriched Insights

Source: Global Park/Fly Research (2009, June). *Mobile research: Best practice for immediate, in-the-moment feedback.* [Webinar]. Retrieved from, http://www.slideshare.net/FlyResearch/mobile-research-webinarwith flyf9june1020.

The newer tools and applications available on modern handsets are already being used by innovative research suppliers, clearly adding richness (and value, and insights) to these projects. Examples include photo-ethnography, VoxMobs (mobile voxpops), diary applications, geotracking/location, and so on. Portable multimedia and visualization are key attributes of the modern mobile research proposition.

OBSTACLES, KEY CHALLENGES, AND LIMITATIONS

As with any data-gathering method, there are weaknesses and barriers to full adoption. They can be summarized as the following:

- Irrelevance and bad fit
- Technicalities and technology
- Psychological barriers
- Long/complex surveys are difficult
- International variance (differences by country)

Irrelevance and Bad Fit

Let's ask ourselves a question: Will a survey regarding health provision among respondents over age 60, including a conjoint exercise, work over the mobile? As with any research method, relevance is always a matter for consideration. The researcher must consider the fit between the method, the audience (sample), the topic, the coverage/questionnaire, and the marketer. If mobile data collection can deliver against a majority of these considerations (versus other methods), then it is certainly worth consideration.

In answer to the previous question, mobile would, at least for now, be unsuitable for research on older or less tech-savvy respondents. Further, research will compete with other activities carried out on mobile phones, and it would be naïve to believe that research can capture the attention of a respondent for long periods.

Technical Matters

There are numerous networks, handsets, operating systems, screens, subchannels, and so on. All have to be considered and planned for when designing mobile research. SMS/text is the most universal and, perhaps, easiest to employ, but equally, it is usually the least rich method.

Here are a few of the technical considerations:

1. What handsets do potential respondents have?
2. Will they use touch screens or keyboards to respond?
3. What mobile browser do they use (old school WML, modern HTML or X-HTML)?
4. Might they respond via an iPad?

Making the right choices and working with knowledgeable staff/partners are paramount for success.

Psychological Barriers

As it is still a relatively new method, uncertainty and reluctance are often encountered from all parties—companies, research agencies, and respondents. Simply, clear reassurance, instructions, and incentives can make all the difference here for everyone (as well as experience, of course).

Respondent uncertainty and reluctance mainly include the following:

- Cost of messages/data ("What is this going to cost me?" This is the key barrier so far among respondents, but its importance seems to be diminishing.)
- Technical (e.g., how to use mobile Internet? "What do I do?")
- Privacy ("Is this private?")
- Intrusion ("How did they get my phone number?")
- Plus usual research resistance

Figure 20.6 Why Have You Not Taken a Mobile Survey Answers *Before* Taking A Survey?

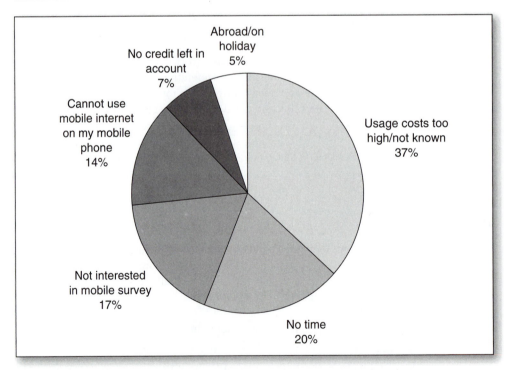

Source: Global Park/Fly Research (2009, June). *Mobile research: Best practice for immediate, in-the-moment feedback.* [Webinar]. Retrieved from, http://www.slideshare.net/FlyResearch/mobile-research-webinarwith flyf9june1020.

The adjacent table illustrates respondent concerns about a mobile diary with geotracking research that they had just taken. Clearly, again, cost of data is a concern, but so are concerns about privacy and tracking.

However, most people enjoy mobile surveys when taken, as can be seen in Table 20.8.

Research agencies also have reservations, and these can include design matters, technicalities (e.g., with data collection and fusion with and transition from other methods), and cost. Of course, knowing who to work/partner with is another challenge (and a key solution).

Currently, mobile is not a *successor* to online or traditional survey methods. It should be seen as a complimentary technique rather than a substitute.

Companies have reservations as well, such as this 2009 quote from Paul Hardcastle, head of consumer research and insights, Yahoo! Europe: "I have reservations over privacy, and, moreover, robustness and reliability—but I can see potential—indeed my concerns may be overcome once I have more experience of this as a method for delivering true insight (rather than just data)" (Noyce & Dodgson, 2010, slide 54).

Table 20.7   Respondent Concerns: Percentage of Top-Two-Box ("Strongly Agree," "Tend to Agree")

Concerned about cost of data use	32%
Concerned about having location tracked	23%
Diary too intrusive into my private life	3%
Receiving text/SMS reminders are intrusive	6%

Source: IPSOS, 2010.

Table 20.8   Respondent Feelings *After* Taking a Mobile Survey

Complete a mobile diary again?	100%
Enjoyed?	97%
Interesting?	97%
Innovative?	90%
Recommend a mobile diary to others?	77%

Source: IPSOS, 2010.

Interestingly, clients are also gradually opening up to the idea of mobile-based research, as seen in Paul Hardcastle's later note from 2011,

"I have seen this method of research collection being applied in a variety of studies across the industry and therefore have a lot more exposure to this method now but I still think this collection method is still in its infancy compared to online for data capture. Regarding the robustness/reliability of respondents' answers via mobile, I still have some reservations but I do see mobile's advantages now and the method will mature over time and it is something we are starting to consider using here at Yahoo". (personal communication)

The most obvious concern many have with mobile is undertaking a longer/more complex survey this way. The challenges are certainly there, including the small screens, short

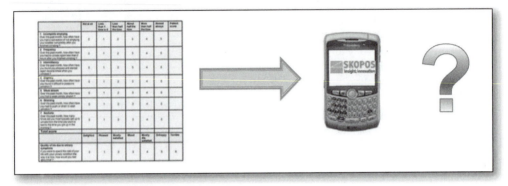

Figure 20.7 Long/Complex Surveys Are Currently Infeasible Via Mobile

Source: SKOPOS.

respondent attention spans, and simple lack of familiarity (and guidance, as it is self-completed). As a rule of thumb, six questions are just about the limit in an SMS interview.

International Differences

Companies such as OnePoint are conducting mobile studies around the globe. Each country has its own considerations such as the following:

1. The economy
2. Geography
3. Telecoms regulation
4. Money/finance regulations (incentives)
5. Network operators
6. Handsets/devices

A word to the wise, be sure you understand these, or work with a supplier who does, when researching across international boundaries (via mobile).

Table 20.9 Examples of Country Differences in Cell-Phone Regulations

Country	Market Regulation
Malaysia	RM 0.00, shared short codes, keywords in answers
France	Masking of phone numbers with 16 digit ids, red flag list
China	2 short codes—1 for each operator
Australia	Government tax $10k p.a. (6 digits)
India	Do-not-contact database

Source: Snaith, 2010.

THE OPTIONS

One of the clear strengths of this data-gathering tool is its array of applications, both quantitative and qualitative. In the following section, there is more detail and elaboration on both practices.

Mobile Quantitative Research: The Options, Platforms, and Technical Choices

Under the heading of mobile quantitative research, there are two key dimensions for choice, subchannel (e.g., SMS) and technical.

The choices for subchannel chiefly include the following:

- Messaging via SMS (text) and MMS (multimedia)
- WAP (mobile Internet)
- JavaScript/apps (embedded/downloaded/activated)
- Apps (embedded/downloaded/activated)
- Full Internet (emerging and definitely part of the future)

The more technical among us might also ask if the display format is HTML, X-HTML, WML, or other. **Rendering** is a key principle for the display of surveys, and this is chiefly a function of device/manufacturer, operating system, and subchannel. The easiest example to give is that even text messages look very different on the iPhone compared to other (more traditional) handsets (see the hospital case study (3) that follows for iPhone text screen shots).

A range of question formats is possible when executing mobile quantitative research as can be seen in Figure 20.8.

As shown in the shots here, increasingly modern devices are capable of rendering most types of quantitative question types, from dichotomous to semantic differential.

SMS/Text

SMS surveys are simple, short text questions and answers. They are best for short polls or surveys, and can include coded and open data collection. Opt-in mobile numbers are required, and the invite message is broadcast to this group. Responses are returned and received via text message too, according to predesignated parameters (open versus closed, scale versus dichotomous choice, etc.). Costs of messages can be covered by the researcher if they work with appropriate partners and use short-code text numbers for example.

Case Study 3: U.K. Health Self-Completion Via SMS/Text (Source: Princess Alexandra Hospital, Harlow UK)

The three images in Figure 20.8 illustrate how hospitals in the United Kingdom are obtaining live, in-the-moment feedback from patients and visitors, via an advertised text survey/number. Quick and easy to complete, with six key questions, perhaps the only criticisms might be the absence of an incentive, an assumption that the acronym PAH meant something to respondents, and perhaps an assumption that "free" was understood and positive in this context. Overall, it is an excellent example of good practice for self-completion SMS surveys.

Case Study 4: Ferry Company Customer Satisfaction Survey Via SMS/Text

In this particular case study, a ferry company shifted their customer satisfaction measurement from face-to-face to SMS having observed many passengers playing with their phones while in transit. This, of course, saved them money.

Figure 20.8 Hospital Satisfaction SMS Survey

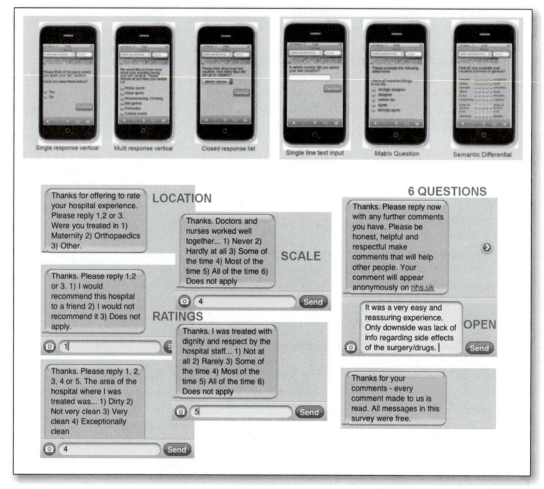

Source: From author's SHUTTERSTOCK account.

This example clearly illustrates the power and potential of mobile delivering for all research triumvirates (respondents, marketer, and research firm). The client ultimately saved money and improved research engagement and response, with a relevant, convenient, mobile method.

Case Study 5: Texts and TV Viewing Diary Via SMS/Text (Source: Sparkler/Channel4) (Hodge & Cox, 2010)

Later, more examples of multimode research employing mobile technology will be offered, but this is an excellent example of how SMS text prompts/surveys can be used in a multimode research project and enable the simple capture of longitudinal observation and behavioral data.

Figure 20.9   Using SMS Texts in a Multimode TV Viewing Study

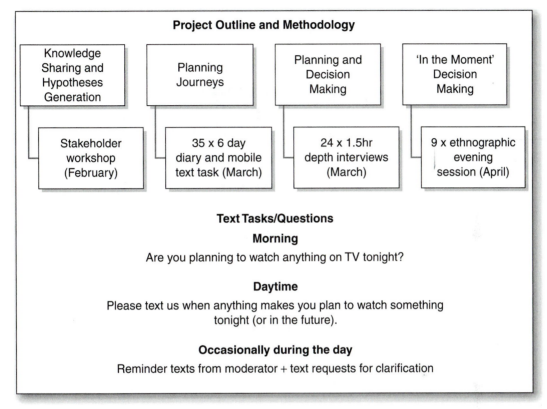

Source: Sparkler/Channel14.

Case Study 6: T-Mobile M-Customer Satisfaction Research SMS/Text (Source: T-Mobile; Sugden, 2010)

Most mobile networks conduct one form of their user satisfaction research via mobile/text. T-Mobile has implemented an enhanced form of this with a simple text survey as the front-end, but powerful back-end tools including the automated coding of open-ended responses and instant flow of data to relevant departments within the business. The former functions shape many detailed answers into something traceable over time while the latter allows for direct action by the responsible department (with permission).

A simple relevant method can still deliver powerful research.

Case Study 7: Orange B2B SMS Panel SMS/Text (IPSOS, 2010)

This study was titled The Orange Business Jury. In 2008, Orange, a European mobile network, established an SMS panel of business people for the express purpose of gaining

Figure 20.10 T-Mobile Customer Satisfaction Auto-Coding

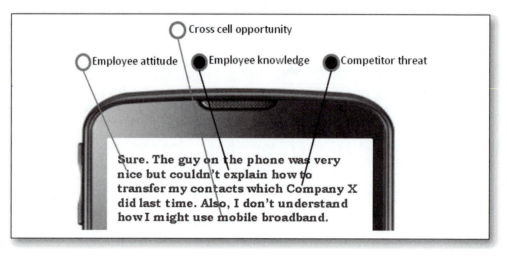

Source: T-Mobile.

instant insight on relevant and topics of breaking news, for same-day reporting (often back to the media).

The timeliness of the insight was certainly a key factor in any subsequent media reporting.

Figure 20.11 Orange B2B SMS Panel

- A three-year project using mobile technology, conducted on behalf of Orange.
- The panel was recruited from IIS Panel consisting of 1,000 small-business owners, managers, and decision makers.
- Surveys were used to gain instant insight into breaking-news stories and events from the business community's point of view, when they happen. The flexibility and speed of the research enabled instant results.
- Example: Bank of England increased U.K. interest rates from 5.5% to 5.75% in July 2007. The SMS surveys were released on the same day as the announcement and results were available at 4:00 PM with a high-response rate (more than 62%) for the questions asked.
- Other surveys asked of the business panel received a 70% response from the jury in less than 10 minutes.

Source: IPSOS, 2010.

Case Study 8: Q1000 Panel/Omnibus SMS/Text Global Park/Fly Research (2009)

Research panels have been key to the broader implementation of mobile research and often fundamental, unless the client can supply opt-in mobile numbers. This example shows how research company, Fly, operates a targeted instant omnibus via mobile.

Figure 20.12   Q1000 Panel/Omnibus

Every week Fly Research conducts an omnibus to its rapidly responding teen panel and young professional panel of 11- to 25-year-olds, with 1,000 balanced responses guaranteed!

Notify Fly by Monday evening to include your questions.

Surveys are answered on Wednesday/Thursday with results delivered on Friday!

No other omnibus responds so well and so rapidly, but then no other omnibus has the dual benefit of youth and mobile phone technology creating a more representative sample than can be achieved with online research and an even more rapid response.

Source: Fly Research.

Mobile Quantitative Surveys Using WAP/Mobile Web

For all intents and purposes, WAP and the mobile web are the same thing; cut-down versions of the full Internet for mobile devices. As such, this method offers a richer survey experience and capability, including visuals, mobile-ad testing, and more dynamic/interactive questioning than SMS/text.

Usually, respondents are invited to take part via a text message (with a link), or they will click on an ad on a mobile website. Unlike with apps, no downloads are required. However, data charges may be incurred by respondents (and may need to be paid for/covered via incentives).

WAP/mobile web surveys are considered by some to be best for inviting or intercepting users of mobile web/WAP sites, but they can also be used with opt-in panels.

Case Study 9: Government Mobile Web Usability Via Intercept and WAP (Source: IPSOS, 2006)

This WAP example from IPSOS used an advertised link (intercept) to the mobile survey while stating a charity incentive at the same time. Its purpose was to evaluate users' opinions of the U.K. government website Directgov *in situ* and onsite.

Figure 20.13   Directgov Mobile Web Usability

- Targeting site visitors to understand the reasons participants access the site, its usability, and perceived quality of information.
- Users click on one of the "Do Our Survey—Help Sport Relief" links, which were located throughout Directgov mobile.
- The first wave collected 340 complete interviews over 12 weeks.

Source: IPSOS, 2006.

Case Study 10: Live Soccer Study via Panel and WAP

The alternative study shown here is an example of the SMS-invited WAP method. Lightspeed Research contacted a panel of 7,000 during halftime of the 2007 European Champions League Final soccer match. Results showed that the event itself was an ideal time to conduct the survey, as 63% of surveys were completed during the halftime break. It was also found that younger respondents were more likely to undertake the mobile survey, and 21% were "out of home."

Through this medium, Lightspeed Research was able to find out if respondents were currently watching the game, where they were watching it, if they were drinking beer, as well as the beer brands they were consuming.

Figure 20.14   Lightspeed Research Champions League Survey

- 1,484 completed surveys
- Younger respondents were slightly more likely to undertake the mobile survey, with 26% respondents age 18 to 24 versus 19% age 34 to 44
- 63% completed it during the halftime break
- 51% were watching the game, of which 41% were watching it "out of home" (21% of the full sample)

- 36% of people who watched the game at home drank beer
- 64% of people who watched the game in a bar drank beer
- Most popular beer brand in homes was Stella while in bars it was Carling

Source: Lightspeed Champions League Mobile Study, half-time on July 2007.

Mobile Quantitative Research Using Mobile Apps

Apps or applications are pieces of mobile software that require embedding/downloading and deploying/activating on mobile devices. Some come preloaded on the phone (embedded); others require downloading. Employed in research, they are survey engines delivering richer, more relevant, and easier to read survey experiences. Surveys appear more visual or animated, and they can be used for event-driven (activated) or in-the-moment polls and customer-satisfaction surveys.

These apps can be written in various programming languages, which should be appropriate to the handset and/or operating system. Common examples are Java Applets (scripts) and iPhone apps. Two non-Apple iPhone examples are shown in this section—Broca (now 2 Ergo) and MoSurvey. Key is that both offer *services* that any organization can employ to create and field mobile surveys.

Case Study 11: MoSurvey Mobile App (Source: SKOPOS)

MoSurvey is a proprietary Java application, which consists of a Java MIDlet for respondents (containing the survey engine) and a website for businesses (to create their surveys, deploy them, view live results, and also analyze the data). It can be deployed over the air (GPRS, WAP, or SMS) or via infrared.

According to their literature, MoSurvey has been developed to (1) solve some of the challenges in customer surveys, (2) offer businesses an alternative solution, (3) provide businesses with better quality data through uniformity, and, at the same time, (4) offer customers a more convenient, user-friendly experience.

The major benefit to businesses is the ability to create surveys and deploy them within minutes. This is because (1) new surveys can be sent to respondents, who already have MoSurvey, at any time; (2) a respondent's mobile phone is always at hand, so the survey is always at hand; (3) it is less expensive than telephone and face-to-face surveys; and (4) a high response rate is achieved because of end-user friendliness and simplicity. Plus, the service offers (5) real-time reporting, (6) the ability to export data, and (7) a consistent data quality.

Figure 20.15   Mobile Apps, Broca, and SAMS Customer Experience Examples

Source: Broca PLC (now 2Ergo).

Case Study 12: Network and Handset Maker Repair Satisfaction Mobile App (Source: SKOPOS)

SKOPOS undertook this study as a response to a two-fold need: to experiment with mobile apps research and to measure customer satisfaction after a handset repair. With the respondent's permission, the Java app was embedded on the handset during repair, and it would self-activate a survey once the phone was being used again. Using a short survey and derived importance statistics, we were able to prioritize actions for T-Mobile and Sony Ericsson, such as recommending better loan phones.

Figure 20.16   SKOPOS Case Study: Network and Handset-Maker (Noyce & Dodgson, 2010)

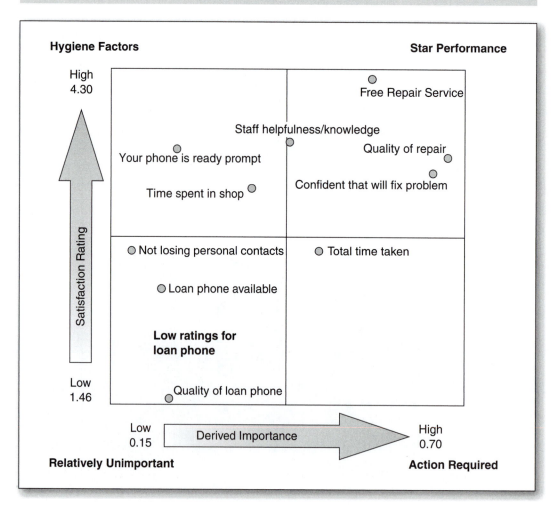

Case Study 13: iPhone Apps (Mobile Apps) (Source: SKOPOS)

The iPhone App store has no doubt been a huge success, and this is exemplified by the number of survey apps that can be found there, including Surveyor and Have a Sec—and those recently launched by OnePoll, Revelation, and Thumbspeak. Naturally, the key limitation here is that only iPhone users can take the surveys. Of course, that weakness is also a strength if iPhone users are your target audience; and research firms such as Thumbspeak have embraced this concept with dedicated iPhone communities.

Mobile Qualitative Research

There is again a range of alternative qualitative methods possible via the mobile. These include the following:

- Text depths
- VoxMobs
- Diaries (life diaries)
- Ethnography/observation (employing pictures or video)

Text Depths

Text depths are two-way, iterative, open-ended conversations between interviewer and respondent. As both parties carry their mobile with them, these exchanges can theoretically be at any time, in any place (for both parties). Naturally, all exchanges are automatically captured as text, and increasingly, visuals can be exchanged either as stimuli or as data from respondents.

VoxMobs (Source: HHBD)

Nowadays, most mobile handsets have video-capture capabilities, some with two-way video calling. If you have the latter. and a 3G (or better) network provider, instant mobile vox-pops (Vox Mobs) can be captured if you have an opt-in recruited panel.

Case Study 14: Skype VoxMobs (Source: SKOPOS)

SKOPOS has undertaken such VoxMobs, and one example is the fast-turnaround work for Skype. Undertaken

Figure 20.17   Mobile Qualitative Research: VoxMobs

over a weekend and analyzed/edited on the Monday, results of a five-minute VoxMob regarding attitudes toward Internet telephony were presented as PowerPoint and video on Wednesday (Attitudes to Internet Telephony).

Diaries

Research diaries are also an emerging success for the mobile channel, and the three case studies that follow exemplify this. To summarize the learning from these, we will borrow from Fly/Mintel: "Keep it short and simple," and "Keep them engaged, interested, and 'sweet'" (Corcoran, 2010, slide 8). The IPSOS case study also shows how capturing behavior, moods, and movements enables rich research stories to be told.

Case Study 15: Drinking and the Young Diary (Corcoran, 2010)

In 2009, Mintel/Fly Research launched a research project to discover the dynamics of young people's drinking behavior. They sought to understand where, when, who with whom, what, how much, how drinking behaviors changed, and respondents' attitudes toward getting drunk. Mobile research enabled accurate information by allowing *in situ* interviewing, whereby respondents reported on *current* behavior. Real-time feedback ensured that their responses were unclouded by morning-after recollections. The mobile medium enabled the researchers to garner a high response rate and fast turn-around time.

Young adults age 18 to 24 have historically been a difficult audience to reach and motivate; hence, it is important to keep them engaged. The few simple steps that were taken to ensure this were to make it easy for them, to send reminders to nonresponders *every day*, to simplify the questions, and to use incentives for completing the *full* set of surveys.

Case Study 16: Day-In-A-Life Diary

In this particular case study, again from Fly Research (Global Park/Fly Research, 2009), a small panel of young people were required to record daily events in their lives via their mobile phones. An example of the rich gleanings included the following (from Wakefield, age 15, social class AB, ethnicity white, British:) "If there was one thing I would miss most it would be my mobile phone, as it has everything from talking to my friends, to going on MSN for free to surfing the Internet and most important making free calls via Skype; and I would not be able to cope without having my daily dose of texting after school."

Case Study 17: Moods and Moments Diary (Source: Johnson & Contry, 2010)

A panel of respondents were asked to record their moods and activities during the day. An example for a tech-savvy grandma follows:

Table 20.10   Case Study: Moods and Movements

Time	Activity	Mood	Summary
2:32 PM	Half working at my daughter's house, half playing with my 18m old granddaughter	Happy	On Friday evening, Grandma managed to half work at her daughter's house and half play with Scarlett, her 18-month-old granddaughter. After a busy day, she relaxed while checking out Facebook. Woke up late the next morning, and she was in a relaxed mood. Later that afternoon, she was excited getting her paintings ready for art exhibition next week. Watched TV before going to bed. Next day, she went to her interesting Pastel workshop.
7:49 PM	Settled on sofa with laptop to check out Facebook	Relaxed	
11:56 AM	Still in bed—what a lazy day	Relaxed	
1:49 PM	Getting my paintings ready for the art exhibition next week	Excited	
11:53 PM	Watching TV	Relaxed	
10:32 AM	On a Pastel workshop	Other	

Source: IPSOS and Techneos.

Ethnography/Pictography

And finally, under the mobile qualitative heading, let's take a look at photo/picture and video capture. Sufficiently motivated respondents can really enrich the research process by capturing relevant images as they go about their day (or task). These pictures (or video) can both augment diaries and simply enable ethnographic analysis.

Case Study 18: Global Picture Diary/Ethnography (Source: Snaith, 2010)

A global brand owner embarked on a research project with the aim to understand sweet cravings among U.S. females. It studied 150 panelists across three time zones in the United States over seven days. As a result, 508 lunch diaries were sent in with 70 photographs. Findings were that sweet cravings occur:

- At home (51%)
- At work (31%)
- Peak between 11a.m. to 2 p.m. (25%)
- Alone (25%)
- With family (15%)
- Want something sweet (29%)
- As part of general hunger (27%)
- And type of craving varied by day part: baked goods (a.m.), chocolate (afternoon), ice cream (p.m.)

Here mobile research enabled picture capture of the moment whenever and wherever.

THE OUTLOOK AND FUTURE OPPORTUNITIES

Having looked at what's happening with mobile research, let us turn to what is next or might be. The following are emerging and evolving now and will hugely influence (and even drive) mobile-based research in the coming years:

1. Better devices and screens
2. Location-based technologies
3. Full Internet on the mobile
4. Mobile programming and Internet standards
5. New mobile technologies and applications
6. Multimode/fusion/hybrid

Smart Phones and Touch Screens

Undoubtedly, new devices, evermore capable and exciting, will offer research more and more opportunities. The evidence is that Smartphone users want to do research this way too, as when given the choice, iPhone users would rather complete a survey on their handset, than switch to online. The reverse is true of older and more traditional handset users.

Figure 20.18   Smart Phone Users Prefer to Do Research Via Mobile "Do you want to continue answering the survey mobile or online (in this case you will get a link via e-mail)?" (N = -40)

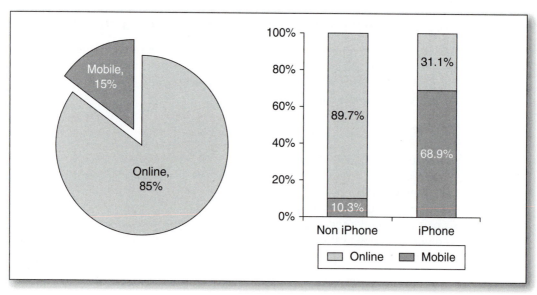

Source: GlobalPark.

Location-Based Research (LBR)

Increasingly, GPS location technology is being embedded in devices, enabling the locating and tracking of respondents. The IPSOS case study here (Johnson & Conry, 2010) hints at the possibilities, where they geotracked various "tribes/segments" over the course of a day (or two), via their mobile device.

A quick word of caution though. As always, a transparent, informed, opting-in is crucial to avoid privacy issues (i.e., identifying a respondent's location without permission). For some business-to-business (B2B) samples, employment contracts may imply opt-in. For consumers, however, the formal opt-in is crucial.

Case Study 19: Day in the Life Via Geotracking (Source: IPSOS)

This IPSOS study fused GPS coordinates and corresponding descriptions provided by respondents to facilitate a detailed understanding of their habits and behavior. This enabled IPSOS to not only observe respondents' movements across the city during a bank holiday weekend but also be privy to participants' activities and feelings at the reported venues. Such data provided an invaluable insight to the behavioral patterns of demographic segments within the population.

Full Web and Convergence

Anyone with a smartphone and a good data plan/tariff may already have taken an online survey over their mobile. Full mobile web (think 3G, iPhone, and WIFI) is developing fast and is the future of mobile research for many because it offers the richest, most engaging

Figure 20.19 An Application of Geotracking

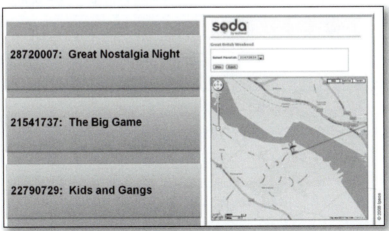

Source: IPSOS and Techneos.

(longer) experience and, hence, a better dataset. WAP and cut-down Internet surveys are currently prominent, but they are expected to yield to full web options.

Standards are already being developed for the mobile web/Internet convergence.

Advanced Technologies

All channels and technologies evolve or they die. The same is true for mobile, and advances that may play a part in the future for mobile include augmented reality, the implementation of game mechanics, employment of quick response (QR) codes, and passive measuring software. In this regard, there have already been some advances.

Quick Response Codes/Tags

As an example of the existing technology, although still in the early adoption phase, QR codes/tags are increasingly being printed on goods, packaging, in media, and on advertising. These are activated by taking a photo of the code on your mobile, and they could be used to trigger mobile surveys.

Figure 20.20 How Quick Response (QR) Codes Work

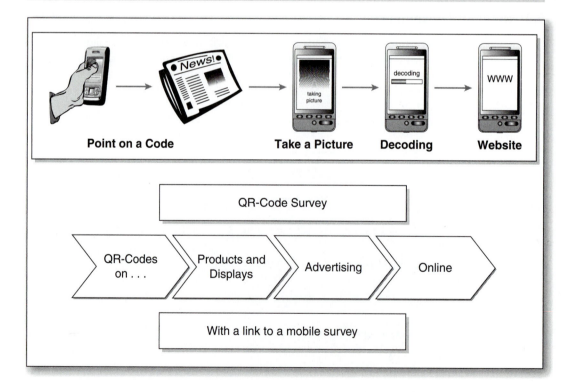

Passive Measuring

Of course, this chapter has chosen to focus on traditional and less-traditional qualitative and survey research methods. It wouldn't be accurate though to completely omit passive measuring software and the ability to automatically capture a *remarkable array* of data including behavior via a mobile device, including calls, texts, Internet, apps, and so on.

Passive measuring software enables the automatic capture of data on the mobile device, functioning similarly to Internet cookies. This is certainly an area of opportunity and involves the download of a small application to the handset. Once loaded, this software automatically captures and sends data to the research office.

Fusion and Linkage

The evolution of mobile research has been arguably slow, from texts, to WAP, to visuals, and to apps. However, this evolution points to a dazzling future of linked, multichannel, multimethod research. Whether it's texts to trigger diary responses, online/mobile survey options, image capture, or video interviews, fusion with more traditional methods can make very good sense.

Figure 20.21   How Passive Data Collection Might Work on a Mobile Device

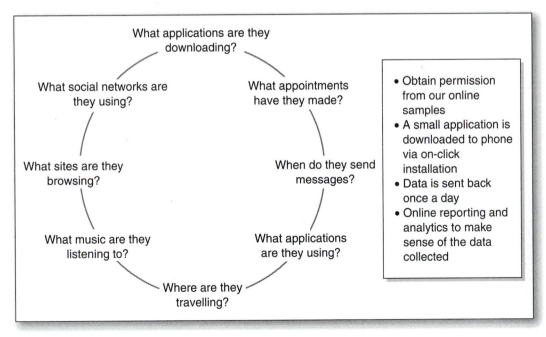

Source: IPSOS, 2010.

Figure 20.22   Example of Photo Capture and Commentary During a Day in the Life

Item	Note
	3.00PM - Mall – Striking Saw this in the shopping mall and found it striking. Reminded me I needed to buy some washing powder.
	4.25PM – Metro – Strong This was at the Metro station. I thought the message was strong and I also like the design

Source: SKOPOS.

For example, participants could take notes, photos, and videos of relevant items during their day, which then are automatically uploaded to an online diary. (See Figure 20.22.)

Capturing images and videos can help to provide a greater richness of response, as well as being far more engaging for participants. The final two case studies embody this fusion and linkage principle.

Case Study 20: Video Portraits (Source: SKOPOS)

The case study from SKOPOS shows how even traditional projects (here, focus groups with customer segments for a global bank) can benefit from the infusion of some mobile magic. In this example, during recruitment for the groups, all respondents were tasked and incentivized to also complete a one-week online diary, and provide a self-shot mobile video portrait of themselves; each adding real, individual-level insight to their personalities and lives prior to the focus groups.

SKOPOS conducted a multi-phased research for a global bank. The qualitative stage involved focus groups combined with Online Diary and Mobile Pen Portraits. Each respondent provided a 5 min 'meet me' video profile to complement the other findings.

CONCLUSION

So that is an overview of mobile-based research: a look at the opportunities, the obstacles, the options, and the outlook. Although there has been a slow take up of this method to date, no doubt because of some real and some perceived challenges and limitations, there is strong evidence and a powerful argument that the time is now for the mobile channel for research.

Marketing and media practitioners have embraced the mobile channel, and so should research. Indeed, mobile data collection allows for opportunities that could never have been realized any other way. If there is such a thing as a leading edge, 21st century research tool, the mobile handset with supporting technical infrastructure is it.

If you have not tried mobile research already, you *must* give it a go.

Figure 20.23

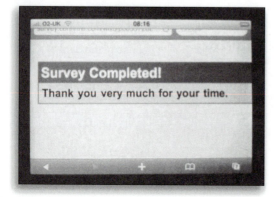

CONTRIBUTOR CREDITS: A THANK YOU FROM THE AUTHOR

The following companies and events helped in the preparation of this chapter:

HHB Dialogue	www.hhbdialogue.com
Fly Research	http://flyresearch.com/
Broca Mobile	www.brocaplc.com
Dialogue Mobile Marketing	www.dialogue.net
OnePoint Surveys	www.onepointsurveys.com
Globalpark	www.globalpark.org.uk
IPSOS	http://www.ipsos.com/
Lightspeed Research	http://www.lightspeedresearch.com/
Meaning	www.meaning.uk.com
Kantar Media	www.kantarmedia.com
Mobile Research Conference 2009/2010	www.mobileresearch09.com
MRS Conferences	http://www.mrs.org.uk/conference/index.htm

FURTHER READING

Maxl, E., Döring, N., & Wallisch, A. (2009). *Mobile market research*. Köln: Herbert Von Halem Verlag.

Michael, A., & Salter, B. (2006). *Mobile marketing: Achieving competitive advantage through wireless technology*. Oxford, UK: Butterworth-Heinemann.

Krum, C. (2010). *Mobile marketing: Finding your customers no matter where they are*. Upper Saddle River, NJ: Pearson Education.

Whitlock, W., & Micek, D. (2008). *Twitter revolution: How social media and mobile marketing is changing the way we do business & market online*. Las Vegas, NV: Xeno Press.

Websites

Globalpark: http://www.mobileresearchconference.com/

ESOMAR: http://www.esomar.org/index.php/professional-standards-codes-and-guidelines-guideline-on-research-via-mobile-research.html

Videos

Merlien: http://vimeo.com/merlien/skopos

The Futures of Marketing Research

ROBERT MORAN

StrategyOne, US

INTRODUCTION

Facing rapid social, technological, and economic change, the traditional marketing research industry will either adopt new tools and talent, repositioning itself in a more strategic, consultative space, or it will fall into decline.

The rate of change in marketing research will accelerate as new entrants from the wider emerging marketing research insights industry (management consulting, customer relationship management [CRM], customer experience management [CEM], data mining, DIY desktop tools, predictive analytics, neuromarketing, social media analytics, prediction markets, and cocreative digital consultants) converge with and redefine the traditional marketing research space.

With all this change, it is not surprising that some have even predicted that "the consumer-research industry as we know it today will be on life support by 2012" (Neff, 2008, para. 2).

The situation may not be this dire, but the industry's transformation over the next decade is likely to be significant. Certainly, marketing research firms will still exist, but whether they exist under the name "marketing research firms" is an open question. More likely, the marketing research industry will transition from long-standing references to a more forward-thinking term such as, "consumer insights," "business insights," or "business intelligence industry."

Instead, the industry is likely to reposition, rebrand, and rename itself. It will shift focus from asking to observing, questioning to discussing, collection to analysis, insight to foresight, rational to emotional, large surveys to data streams, quarterly trackers to 24/7 insights communities, geographically fixed to mobile, siloed to converged, cognitive self-reporting to precognitive neurosensing, and project-based work to engagement-based consulting. It will find ways to integrate itself across the strategic decision-making process, will help its clients pull insights from disparate data streams, will aggressively leverage foresight tools, will be nimble, and will make speed a core competence by fully leveraging the 24-hour global clock.

This chapter explores four questions about the plausible, plural futures of marketing research:

1. What forces are shaping the futures of marketing research?
2. What might these industry futures look like?
3. How might those in the field adapt to compete in these futures?
4. How might those in the field (or currently outside it) create preferred futures?

To explore these questions, we will use futuring tools from the field of strategic foresight (Hines & Bishop, 2006) to analyze the social, technological, economic, and political forces driving probable marketing research futures. We will review a baseline forecast for the industry's evolution, explore 22 plausible developmental futures, and close with some general strategic observations about how actors at the corporate and individual level might compete for the future (Hamel & Prahalad, 1994).

FORCES SHAPING THE FUTURE OF MARKETING RESEARCH

There was a time when the marketing research industry was fairly predictable and orderly. There were clearly defined roles, spaces, and processes with professionals either working in the insights function of a corporation or working for a supplier. One typically became a researcher by completing a social science education followed by what amounted to a series of white-collar apprenticeships. There were a standard set of tools. These tools were built on an interrogatory model. And the heart of this asking-based system was the survey instrument, the industry's premier data-collection vehicle and central paradigm.

There was quite a bit of stability and predictability in this system. But nothing lasts forever. Although not entirely gone, this era of classical marketing research is clearly passing. Consider the future of the two primary workhorses of traditional research, the standard 15- to 20-minute survey and the two-hour focus group.

The traditional survey is a beleaguered tool, struggling with low participation rates, respondents speeding through surveys, data quality issues, and projectability concerns. As Donna Goldfarb, vice president of consumer market insights for Unilever Americas, has noted, "I don't know if we are going to have a choice but to move away from survey research" (Goldfarb, as quoted in Neff, 2008, para. 3). Surveys are almost certainly going to become much shorter, more interest based, and triggered by a respondent's physical location.

Now, consider the focus group. Focus groups, with their relatively short time spans and high travel costs are likely to be squeezed by insights communities (also known as marketing research online communities or MROCs), which act like a large, free-ranging, 24/7 focus group discussion. Although far from doomed, traditional surveys and focus groups are likely to play a diminished role relative to next-generation tools.

The Industry of the Future

The marketing research toolbox is clearly in transition. A recent Advertising Research Foundation (ARF) member survey segmented research tools into four categories: (1) passing, (2) timeless, (3) transitional (so named because some see them as fads while others see them as the future), and (4) emerging (Wittenbraker, 2010).

Table E.1   Research Tool Segmentation

Passing Tools	Timeless Tools	Transitional Tools	Emerging Technologies
Telephone surveys	Marketing mix modeling	Social media	Mobile research
	Online surveys	Insight communities	Passive data (GPS, RFID)
	Focus groups	Text analytics	Web-use tracking
	Ethnography	Virtual reality	
	Econometric modeling	Neurobiometrics	

One look at the transitional tools and emerging technologies featured in the previous research toolbox chart highlights the significant amount of change on the horizon and the emergence of more passive, observational tools. Practitioners clearly believe mobile research, passive data collection via GPS and radio frequency identification (RFID) and web-use tracking will define the futures. And many in the industry see social media analytics, insights communities, virtual reality environments, and neurobiometrics as either trendy or cutting edge.

Moving beyond research tools, two statistics hint at the significant change about to overtake the traditional marketing research industry. First, 80% of global research spending is currently dedicated to quantitative, survey-based, research (ESOMAR, 2010b). As spending shifts toward observational, cocreative, and anticipatory tools, we can expect significant reallocation of spending within the industry. Second, two-thirds of all traditional marketing research is conducted in the five aging industrial democracies of the United States (30%), the United Kingdom (11%), Germany (9%), France (9%), and Japan (6%) (ESOMAR, 2010b). Eventually, there will be a strong influx of research spending into emerging economies. When combined, the implications of these two data points are staggering. The growth of noninterrogatory tools and emerging markets will reshape the industry.

TRADITIONAL MARKETING RESEARCH VERSUS EMERGING MARKETING RESEARCH

In thinking about the futures of marketing research, it is critical to distinguish between the traditional marketing research industry and the wider emerging marketing research industry.

The traditional $28.9 billion global marketing research industry (ESOMAR, 2010b) is defined by the corporate insights function; their large suppliers; the core research tools, such as the survey and the focus group; and a skill set focused on project management, questioning, and statistical analysis. Created in the 20th century industrial age, the traditional marketing research industry often displays what Mike Cooke of Gfk has called an "over reliance on an industrialized view of research" (ESOMAR, 2009, p. 51). It is defined by the first evolutionary stage in marketing researching, the asking epoch.

In the beginning of the asking epoch, data were expensive. Large suppliers built the equivalent of a vertically integrated, industrial corporation to collect, process, structure, analyze, report, and consult on data. Many still struggle with this organizational legacy long after the closing of the industrial era.

The organizing framework in this epoch was the survey, especially the quarterly tracking survey, a product on which many of the larger firms still depend. The traditional marketing research industry has many positive qualities, but it and the asking epoch, in which it flourished, have several significant weaknesses. These include a dependence on self-reported behavior; a focus on the present and past; limited ability to engage subjects in a protracted, cocreative dialogue; and a reliance on periodic, as opposed to continuous, reporting. These weaknesses have left the traditional marketing research industry open to significant competition from the wider insights industry.

In contrast, the emerging marketing research industry includes new entrants from management consulting, social media, software, and business intelligence that are increasingly providing insight-driven consulting in competition with traditional marketing research. The wider insights industry was created in the information age. It surrounds traditional marketing research with next-generation technologies and firms defined by observation and listening. Examples of these wider insights industry tools are illustrated in Table E.2 and include social media analysis, neuromarketing research, insights communities (MROCs), predictive markets, and mass simulation gaming.

Can traditional marketing research firms adapt to this new reality by adding next-generation tools and practices from the observational epoch? Maybe. Many traditional research companies are buying neuromarketing firms, experimenting with eye-tracking technology, learning how to build and maintain insight communities, and exploring social media listening platforms. For example, the marketing research giant Kantar owns traditional and social media analytics firm Cymfony, and research agency Maritz recently acquired social media analytics firm evolve24. But, if history is any guide, many of today's marketing research suppliers, including some of the larger players, will struggle through the transition.

Table E.2 Traditional Versus Emerging Marketing Research Industry

	Traditional Marketing Research	Wider Insights Industry
Firm Types	Full-service custom suppliers Syndicated research suppliers Niche Sector expertise firms	Management consulting Social media Software CRM Business intelligence Data mining
Founding Time Period	Industrial age	Information age
Example Firms	Ipsos Gfk Synovate Harris Interactive ORC	McKinsey BCG SPSS IBM Communispace Clarabridge Nunwood Comscore HYVE Conversition Autonomy
Methodological Focus	Asking (survey data collection)	Observing
Signature Tools	Custom survey research Tracking surveys Live focus groups	Data mining Text analytics Insight communities Model building
Customer Engagement	Project work Tracking studies	Retainer-based consulting Software as a service
Buyer	CMO Insights Function	C-suite CMO Insights Function

THE FIVE GREAT CHALLENGES
FOR THE FUTURE OF MARKETING RESEARCH

Marketing researchers have identified detailed lists of challenges to the industry. In fact, ESOMAR's Global Marketing Research 2010 report specifically identifies DIY research, commoditization, alternative data sources, new entrants, overreliance on technology, and respondent fatigue as the top threats in its strengths, weaknesses, opportunities, and threats (SWOT) analysis (ESOMAR, 2010b).

But at a macrolevel, the industry faces five primary challenges that will shape its future:

1. Data abundance

2. Asking-observing shift

3. Convergence

4. Democratization

5. The strategic imperative

Data Abundance

As noted earlier, marketing research was born in the industrial age when data and information were still scarce and expensive. Increasing geometrically, data has gone from scarce to abundant within a generation. As far back as 1998, a marketing research textbook was pronouncing that "at least in developed economies, data has moved from being a scarce commodity to a burdensome surplus" (Lehmann, Gupta, & Steckel, 1998, p. 15). We are drowning in a torrential stream of data.

The central challenge now is the creative intelligence needed to synthesize these vast data flows into information, knowledge, insight, foresight, and strategy. Our technical ability to gather data outstrips our creative ability to synthesize it. T. S. Eliot (1934) captured this problem best in his 1934 work "The Rock":

Where is the wisdom we have lost in knowledge?

Where is the knowledge we have lost in the information?

Unfortunately, like many institutions born in one era and competing in another, marketing research is struggling to keep up. The marketing research industry created data collection and information processing factories when data were scarce commodities. But the problem with basing a business on information collection and control is that, to quote Stewart Brand at the first Hacker's Conference, "Information wants to be free."

The industry now must adapt to a world of abundant data in which insight-driven strategy, as opposed to simply the reporting of data, is scarce. If the industry cannot make the transition from industrial collector of data to strategic sifter of data flows, it will be caught in a commodity trap.

Moreover, the marketing research industry, broadly, and the corporate insights department, in particular, are no longer central information choke points in a world of scarce data. Consumer information can be accessed and analyzed without the help of the insights function via DIY tools such as, Google Analytics, SurveyMonkey, and a host of free or inexpensive syndicated products. Employees across the corporate structure can access this information without going through the corporate insights department. The corporate insights function is no longer the only gateway to critical business data.

Consider the experience of the travel agent, real-estate agent, and stockbroker. All three operated as the informational conduit to their buyers. The travel agent and the real-estate agent operated in a system in which data about vacation options and houses was scarce. Consumers didn't have the time, skill, or wherewithal to search through myriad travel options or access the multiple listing service. But now, consumers plan much of their vacations using online databases and marketplaces, such as Orbitz and Priceline. And the real-estate agent's stranglehold on data is now gone, as consumers shop for their next home with powerful online search tools.

The case of the stockbroker may be the most relevant to marketing research. Discount brokerages and superabundant investing information have forced the profession to move toward financial planning. Executing trades became a commoditized service, so the industry migrated up the value chain to advisory services. We can anticipate marketing researchers and the industry attempting a similar strategy.

For us to better explore the industry's migratory repositioning, we need a model for thinking about the underpinnings of insight-driven strategy. One useful model to draw on is the knowledge hierarchy explored by T. S. Elliot, Russell Ackoff, Milan Zeleny, Chaim Zins, and others (Ackoff, 1989). Ackoff's foundational knowledge hierarchy moves from data to information to knowledge to understanding to wisdom. Customizing this model for marketing research creates what I call the "insight-driven strategy superstructure." Without this supporting superstructure, insight driven strategy is impossible.

The superstructure begins with data, progresses to information, and is converted by analysts into basic knowledge. These are based on the past and present. The flow then switches to a future orientation at the insight stage.

Based on this model, traditional marketing research should ask itself these three difficult questions.

1. Which one of these six stages best describes marketing research's product today?
2. Which one of these six stages best describes the corporate customer's expectation of marketing research?
3. Which one of these six stages should best describe marketing research in five years?

Asking-Observing Shift

Flowing directly from the challenge of abundant data is the epochal shift in marketing research from asking to observing/listening. The shift from collecting scarce data via questioning to sifting abundant data via listening and observing is tectonic, and it will radically change how marketing research harvests insights. This does not mean that the survey will

Table E.3   Insight-Driven Strategy Superstructure

	Data	Information	Knowledge	Insight	Foresight	Strategy
Defining Traits	Recorded observations	Dataset Datafile Topline Data cross tabulations	Descriptive facts	Narrative Understanding of relation and causation	Understanding projected into the future	Planned activity to achieve a goal within a competitive framework
Generative Activity	Collecting	Processing Structuring	Analyzing	Synthesizing Probing Causation	Anticipating	Planning
Temporal Focus	Past Present	Past	Past	Present / Future	Future	Future
Deliverable	Raw data	Datafile Topline data Cross tabulations	Useful facts "know how"	Actionable knowledge Implications	Probable and preferred futures	Sequenced actions Resource allocation

cease to exist or that the industry will stop asking questions. But it does mean that the age of the survey as dominant tool is fading.

Convergence

The next great challenge for the industry is domain, tool, and data convergence. New entrants from management consulting, social media, software, strategic foresight, and predictive markets are on the brink of redefining the traditional marketing research industry. New tools, such as, social media listening platforms, insights communities, advanced data mining, predictive markets, DIY desktop survey applications, eye tracking, and neurological monitoring, are poised to merge with, and in some cases replace, the traditional marketing research workhorses. Finally, the abundance of data from many sources will spawn firms and professionals that can sift through, connect, and pull insights from multiple data streams.

In fact, the traditional marketing research industry is likely to experience many new entrants. As ESOMAR's Global Marketing research 2009 pointed out,

Advisory and consulting skills are growing in importance as researchers are increasingly called upon to draw conclusions and provide advice based on their findings. While trying to reposition themselves higher up the value chain, research agencies come across other organizations that, perhaps, beforehand, were not considered to be competitors (such as management consultancies). (ESOMAR, 2009, p. 36)

Although prescient, this likely *understates* the issue. It is not just that some traditional marketing research firms are migrating up the value chain and discovering new competitors there but that these competitors are migrating into the traditional marketing research space as well.

For example, with their move into data-based consulting and their purchase of SPSS for $1.2 billion, IBM is clearly moving into the insights space. Another example of this phenomenon is the formation of NM Incite, a joint venture between Nielsen and McKinsey that combines Nielsen's social media measurement prowess (BuzzMetrics) with McKinsey's powerful business consulting brand. Management consulting is clearly moving into the insights ecosystem to strengthen its core business.

Besides several industries converging to redefine the marketing research space, we are also likely to see the convergence of research tools and data streams. Ultimately, these multiple data streams will be incorporated into a robust and customized customer voice portal with streaming social media analytics, CRM/CEM data, complaint data, project-based insights, and proprietary online community (MROC) data all occupying digital real estate on the same platform and knitted together with a knowledge-management system. This portal will act as a desktop insight hub, and the marketing research industry should strive to own this portal outright, as opposed to fighting over real estate within it. In this endeavor, IT firms, such as, Clarabridge and Nunwood Knowledge Management, seem to have made the most progress.

Democratization

One of the tenets of traditional marketing research has been the concept of the controlled experiment with research participants, a stimulus and a measured response. Transitioning away from the controlled experiment and toward more open, cocreative systems will be a challenge for traditional marketing research. The possibilities for insight democratization are endless.

Consider soft drink brand Mountain Dew and its "DEWmocracy 2010" campaign in which Mountain Dew fans whittled the initial field from seven new products to three and, finally, chose White Out. DEWmocracy had consumers openly picking flavors, names, packaging, and advertising.

There is no reason why this approach couldn't be replicated across any number of product categories using open- or closed-insights communities with predictive markets, similar to those employed by organizations such as Betfair, Intrade, TradeSports, Inkling, and the Iowa Electronic Markets. Companies such as Brainjuicer are already using predictive markets to replace traditional concept testing via monadic cells. In the end, more open, cocreative, and peer-to-peer methodologies will evolve.

The Strategic Imperative

The only legitimate use for data-driven insights is informing business strategy and, ultimately, increasing competitive advantage, which, in turn, produces company growth. With data now abundant and the traditional marketing research industry faced with the threat of commoditization, traditional marketing research suppliers have one of only two options. They can accept commoditization and focus exclusively on efficiency and accuracy of data collection, or they can migrate to insight-driven strategy. Neither will be easy, but the latter appears to be more preferable.

One of the challenges to this migration up the value chain is the image many insights functions have within their organization.

The Boston Consulting Group's 2009 report on this topic (Egan, Manfred, Bascle, Huet, Marcil, 2009) found that (1) most of the work being done was tactical as opposed to strategic (p. 5), (2) only 40% of line managers felt that the insights teams was viewed as "thought leaders within the organization" (p. 15), (3) only 35% of executives describe their insights function as best in class (p. 4), (4) only 34% of line managers agreed that the insights team "consistently answer the question 'so what'" (p. 4), and (5) only 32% of line managers could agree that the insights function translates "research findings into clear business recommendations for senior executives" (p. 15).

Alex Batchelor, chairman of the Marketing Society and CMO of TomTom, summarizes the problem best when he writes,

> In a 20 year career in which I have worked for Unilever, Orange, Royal Mail and TomTom, as well as in advertising and brand consultancy—it is disappointing to report that I have met only one CEO, who spontaneously asked me about marketing research, and none who came from a marketing research background. (Batchelor, 2010, p.17)

Both sides are clearly to blame for this, as management engagement is often weak, leading to fuzzy research objectives and poor project scoping (Rathjen, 2008). But this only makes the strategic migration more difficult.

How does the traditional marketing research industry ascend the strategy ladder?

The BCG model (Egan et al., 2009) for this ascension places insights functions into four stages of development leading from today's traditional function to a strategic foresight organization.

1. The traditional marketing research function
2. The business contribution team
3. The strategic insight organization
4. The strategic foresight organization

As has been pointed out, the first stage is the traditional marketing research function. In this phase, the focus is knowledge creation, and the methods are surveys, focus groups, and other qualitative approaches. The work is generally tactical and project driven, and the professionals are masters of the classic, technical skills.

The next stage is the business contribution team. In this phase, the focus is insight discovery, and the methods are a mix of traditional and innovative (ethnography and social media). The work is a mix of strategic and tactical, and projects build on one another.

The third phase is the strategic insight organization. Functions that have achieved this development phase are focused on insights that drive business results. They expand "beyond the consumer to economic data and trend work" (Egan, Manfred, Bascle, Huet, & Marcil, 2009, p. 28). The work is largely strategic and a "knowledge capture system spans past research studies" (p. 28). The professionals have shifted from a focus purely on methodology to a focus on "integrated thinking, pattern recognition, and communication" (p. 28). At this stage, professionals have a more eclectic background and not purely in marketing research.

The fourth and final stage of evolution is a strategic foresight organization. At this level, the work is focused on driving competitive advantage. It is predictive and future driven. Methods include the traditional and innovative but have expanded "beyond the consumer to economic data and trend work" (Egan et al., 2009, p. 28).

Where would you place the industry today?

Where would you place your organization?

If you could not place your organization in the third or fourth evolutionary phase, then what is your strategy to get there?

HOW TO COMPETE IN THE FUTURE

Given the five great challenges to the industry today, what industry futures exist?

Which futures are most advantageous to you, your function, or your firm?

What futures could you create that would advantage you, your function, or your firm?

A traditional approach in the field of strategic foresight is to review what Smith and Raspin (2008) call "remote environment factors" and analyze trends within the so-called STEEP framework (Hines & Bishop, 2006). The STEEP framework is composed of *s*ocietal, *t*echnological, *e*conomic, *e*cological, and *p*olitical forces that we can identify in the present and believe will have a significant impact on the future. In this instance, we will modify the STEEP framework and quickly look at the social, technological, economic, and political (STEP) forces likely to shape the future of marketing research and the wider insights industry.

Social Drivers

There are three societal game changers likely to impact marketing research in a significant way. They are (1) fragmentation, (2) the rise of social networks, and (3) privacy consideration.

The first driver is fragmentation of values, lifestyles, audiences, communication channels, and consumption habits. Here we need to think about what society looks like when we apply the so-called "long tail" of online retailing to everything. Extreme, individualized choice may be a challenge to societies, especially traditional ones, but it could be a boon to marketers and marketing researchers focused on selling to niches and nanoniches.

The second, and related, societal trend is the rise of digital social networks, user-generated content (UGC) and peer-generated tribes. These networks are channels and authorities unto themselves, and are replacing an era of vertical, top-down communication, with horizontal, peer-to-peer communication. Marketers won't be able to control these communications channels. They may influence them with authentic dialogue, but as the mass market, mass-advertising age grows smaller in the rearview mirror, new marketing models will emerge. Here, we can expect a shift from creating advertising and messaging that moves a mass audience in a top-down manner to crafting ideas that replicate horizontally across social networks like viruses.

In this case, fields such as epidemiology and memetics, the study of self-replicating ideas first proposed by Richard Dawkins (1976) in the *Selfish Gene*, may have a significant role to play in the future of marketing research. We already see the power of viral campaigns and the viral spread of videos on YouTube. As social media replaces broadcasting, viral campaigns will become *big buzzness.*

The third and final societal driver is how consumers react to the explosion in personal, consumer data. Some consumers will recoil in shock and fear at the data being amassed on them. Some of these consumers may even become the new "off-griders," citizens valuing their privacy more than the convenience that data sharing can give them.

The other extreme of this privacy continuum could be the world's youth. With more *laissez faire* attitudes about personal privacy, the young may view highly customized offers and highly detailed purchase recommendations as a modern convenience and not an incursion.

How individuals react to privacy issues will dramatically impact research cooperation levels.

How societies and their governments react will impact marketing research in the political sphere.

Technological Drivers

Although we are living in a time of rapid technological change, four general technological changes will have a significant impact on marketing research. These are (1) technology-created time compression, (2) the data explosion, (3) new observational tools at the macro- and microlevel, and (4) mobile telephony and geolocation.

The first is simply the increasing velocity of life. Time compression and velocity seem to be constants among the consumers we study and the business environment in which we operate. For the foreseeable future, this makes speed of data collection, analysis, and reporting a competitive advantage. The implications of this are explored in the Need for Speed scenario later. Like it or not, we are all competing against time (Stalk & Hout, 1990).

The data explosion is the second great technological driver of change for the industry. Whether in the form of transactional data, customer feedback, syndicated research, proprietary research, or observational data in the social media space, it is plentiful and ubiquitous. And yet many organizational structures have not kept pace. In fact, many research suppliers still labor under organizational structures built around data scarcity, designed as vertically integrated data collection factories vacuuming data.

If the image for marketing research in the past was the vacuum cleaner sucking in hard-to-collect data, then the new image is the filter separating the key insights from the mass of abundant data. This has profound implications for the futures of marketing research.

Supplier business models based on the industrial model are likely to struggle. Relative to analysis and synthesis, staff mastery of the data-collection process will be less valuable. Data mining and analysis across multiple data sets will grow in value.

Other technological drivers are observational tools at both the macrosocial (social media, data mining, geolocation data) and microindividual (eye tracking, fMRI, neuromarketing) level. These observational tools are likely to create a paradigm shift in marketing research as the industry is pushed from an era of asking via surveys and focus groups to an era of observing and listening. Tobii eye-tracking equipment and Clarabridge's social media analytics are just two excellent examples of this trend toward observation and listening. These new observational tools will not fully replace the traditional survey. But coupled with declining survey respondent cooperation rates, it is conceivable that these tools will significantly displace survey work.

Mobile telephony would be a technology-based change agent by itself, but coupled with GPS dependent geolocation, it is a very strong futures driver. The initial rise of mobile telephony challenged the traditional landline-based telephone survey, transitioning a significant amount of survey work online. But the rise of smart phones with the ability to prompt consumer feedback based on their location could be a quantum leap forward. Location-dependent social media services, such as Foursquare, Facebook Places, or Gowalla, are already surging among the young. It is not hard to imagine researchers conducting very short and extremely targeted surveys to coffee drinkers when they enter a Starbucks, frequent fliers when they enter a major airport, and shoppers when they enter a mall. Nor is it difficult to imagine even more finely tuned geobased research conducted, for example, among affluent shoppers across national markets, as they enter the frozen-food section of a supermarket.

What will consumers think of this? Will they find it too intrusive?

Certainly, location-dependent research (LDR) could ignite the kind of privacy concerns we reviewed earlier as a social driver. Ultimately, some LDR tools will be useful to researchers and acceptable to research subjects, but at this early date, it is difficult to gauge what LDR tools will be considered in and out of bounds.

Finally, we need to conclude our thinking about technological drivers with a note of caution. Andrew Odlyzko (2010), a mathematics professor at the University of Minnesota and a 26-year veteran of research and research management at AT&T reminds us, "While the general impression that technology forecasts are far too optimistic is true, it is not universally true" (p. 7). As he points out, "We don't live in underwater cities, nor do we commute in helicopters" (p. 7). But "There are many technologies that have surprised not only the general public, but sometimes even their inventors and promoters with their success" (p. 7).

The primary difficulty in technology forecasting is the human factor (Odlyzko, 2010). How will research subjects react to these technologies? How will suppliers and insights functions choose to use these tools?

Most of us fall into the trap of assuming that one technology, after sufficient introduction, replaces another. But as Odlyzko (2010) points out, this is not always the case. In fact, far from outright replacement, some new technologies "serve to strengthen their predecessors" (p. 7).

Odlyzko cites the railroad as a new technology that actually increased the use of a previous technology for a time. The rail was expected to kill the horse, but the number of horses in Great Britain did not peak until 1905. Why? Because, by expanding the volume of goods that could be transported and sold, the railroad increased the need for horses to haul goods to and from railroad depots. The classic "first mile, last mile" challenge unique to transportation hubs required more horses to transport products shorter distances.

Today, many of us in emerging marketing research believe that social media listening posts will replace some traditional survey work. Although it seems unlikely, could social media listening prompt so many additional lines of inquiry that large amounts of short, focused surveys are needed to explore these questions?

Economic Drivers

The economic drivers likely to impact the industry can be divided into four general segments. Moving from the general to the specific, these are (1) globalization, (2) consumers in the emerging economies, (3) client demands, and (4) nontraditional substitutes.

Globalization will require insights functions and research suppliers to broaden and deepen their cross-national research capacities. Assuming that they deepen their expertise across the globe, this may be one of the few trends that help the larger, transnational research suppliers. Globalization will also unlock marketing research talent pools worldwide and make globally dispersed, but integrated, analytical teams the norm. These globally positioned teams will work the 24-hour clock and quicken the pace of organizational learning.

Tied to this will be the growth in research conducted within emerging economies. Billions of consumers with improving standards of living in emerging markets will shift the focus of research from North America and Western Europe to the Pacific Rim, Brazil, and the Middle East. Paradoxically, this could push marketing research in two very different directions. First, the heavy mobile phone usage in emerging economies should create a surge in mobile survey research. But because many emerging economies also have cultures where face-to-face research is preferred, we may see an increase in this methodology globally.

Client demands for faster, better, and cheaper are likely to continue, with an emphasis on strategic insights (not a data dump), speed, a better understanding of emotional triggers and neurological function, stronger models for understanding communication and influence within social networks, and insight management.

Finally, we are already witnessing and can anticipate the rise of additional, nontraditional substitutes, both of DIY desktop tools and search and social media corporations. It is not difficult to imagine Google, Facebook, Foursquare, and, its Chinese equivalent, Jiepang, providing increasingly sophisticated interrogatory, observational, and cocreative tools.

Political Drivers

Finally, we come to the *P* in STEEP, the political drivers. In this case, there is only one driver, and this is how the political system grapples with privacy issues related to observational research and data mining. Unless citizens old and young adjust to the digital version of Jeremy Bentham's panopticon, a cylindrical prison design in which every prisoner can be watched at all times by guards in a central tower, it seems likely that civil rights advocates and predigital notions of privacy will produce at least some new regulation outlined in the do-not-disturb future.

Privacy regulation would strengthen opt-in insight communities, old-fashioned panels, and focus groups. If the reaction is muted, then marketing research will have truly entered a brave new world described in the What Was Privacy? (McCreary, 2008) scenario.

BASELINE FORECAST FOR MARKETING RESEARCHER'S EVOLUTION

After reviewing likely futures drivers across the societal, technological, economic and political categories (STEP), a baseline forecast for the industry begins to emerge. But, as Herman Kahn is famous for saying, "The surprise-free future isn't." (Hines & Bishop, 2006)

The futures are filled with constants, trends, cycles, and novelties. The novelties, often low-probability, high-impact, wild-card events, can wreak havoc on even our best estimates. This is why this baseline forecast is followed by numerous future scenarios.

The foundational model for this baseline forecast is a schema dividing marketing research's development into eras and epochs past, present, and future. This model tracks marketing research's development across the asking, observational, cocreative, and anticipatory epochs. Each epoch has one or more eras nested within it. Like all other historical shifts, bright dividing lines between epochs are difficult to draw, and there is some overlap between the end of one epoch and the beginning of another. Slide rules and computers coexisted for a time, just as petroleum-fueled mobility coexists with battery-powered mobility today.

As Table E.4 details, each epoch has unique challenges, favored methodologies, prized skill sets, and temporal focus.

Table E.4   The Epochs of Marketing Research

Epoch	Era	Challenges	Favored Methods	Prized Skill Sets	Temporal Focus
Asking	Face-to-face	Data scarcity Efficiency	Survey	Project management Questioning	Past Present
Asking	Telephone	Participation	Survey	Project management Questioning Analytics	Past Present
Asking	Online	Participation Projectability	Survey	Project management Questioning Analytics	Past Present

Epoch	Era	Challenges	Favored Methods	Prized Skill Sets	Temporal Focus
Asking	Geo-Mobile	Privacy Participation Projectability	Survey	Project management Questioning Analytics	Present
Observational	Listening	Privacy Data volume Projectability	Listening Posts MROCs Text analytics	Analytics Data set synthesis Cultural context	Present
Observational	Neurological	Interpretation Philosophical	fMRI, Eye tracking	Neuroscience Psychological training	Present Future behavior
Observational	Behavioral	Privacy Data volume Philosophical	CRM software Sales data Experimental marketing Geotracking Clickstreams Ethnography	Analytics Data mining Knowledge management Interpersonal skills	Present Future behavior
Cocreative	UGC	Purpose Ownership Expectations	MROC Design communities	Interpersonal skills Creativity	Preferred future
Anticipatory	Simulation	Interface Models	Online games Agent-based computational modeling Predictive markets Foresight tools	Game development, Systems thinking Creativity	Plausible future Preferred future

As pointed out previously, the asking epoch came first and is at the crux of the marketing research industry as it exists today. This epoch is dominated by the fading problem of data and computational scarcity. The challenge has been largely data collection, and this challenge has been met successively with face-to-face research, telephone research (defined by nearly ubiquitous landline phone penetration and random digit dialers [RDD]), and now online research. Face-to-face, telephone, online, and geomobile survey research are each distinct eras within the asking epoch.

Marketing research is currently in the last stages of the asking epoch, beginning its transition into the geomobile and listening eras. As Survey Sampling International's Kees de Jong writes, "We're now on the edge of a completely new era, where everything will be much different. I think we're in for more change in the next five years than we've had in the last 15" (ESOMAR, 2010b, p. 30).

At the doorstep of the observational epoch, marketing research is entering a developmental stage that relies on passive surveillance of behavior, expression, and neurobiological response. This represents a shift from an authoritarian and interrogatory question-and-answer system to a passive, observational, and listening-based system, from stimulus-response to serendipity, from projects and periodic tracking to real-time monitoring and a tighter feedback loop, from statistical probability based on random samples to directional data based on multiple sets of streaming observations, and from vertically integrated data collection factories to analytic consultancies.

This epochal shift is what most marketing researchers today are focusing on and concerned with. They should be. The transition is likely to be difficult for organizations built in and professionals trained during the asking epoch. Years of project managing and training in survey construction may not easily convert to the skills needed in the observational epoch.

But within the observational epoch, the listening era faces two existential threats. These threats are the two *P*s of (1) projectability and (2) privacy. The projectability-representativeness challenge directly threatens the ability of social media listening tools to expand beyond the realm of qualitative, directional feedback. And certainly, the privacy threat to observational research is also significant.

At what point do consumers begin to view social media monitoring as surveillance? Already, we can find weak signals of this issue as web scrapers begin to challenge societal privacy norms. *Wall Street Journal* coverage of NM Incite's recent scraping of posts from the semiprivate community PatientsLikeMe is just one example (Angwin & Stecklow, 2010). If a significant number of consumers choose to shield their conversations, projectability-representativeness suffers. In this way, privacy and projectability could create a mutually reinforcing restraint on the observational epoch.

Although they are likely to overlap significantly, the observational epoch will be followed by the cocreative epoch. The fundamental transition here will be the shift from observing via listening to social media, recording behavior, or tracking neurological response to engaging in a massive, running dialogue with consumers in real-time. This is the world of UGC, but on a scale and at a speed that is likely to make YouTube look very 20th century.

In this epoch, insights communities or MROCs will dominate. The creation of massive design communities will flourish. Some of these communities will be open invitation, but many will be proprietary to protect intellectual property and support competitive advantage. Design or innovation community participants may be screened for right-brain strength. Researchers and corporations will struggle with heightened consumer expectations, not only among their core buyers but among their prospects.

After all, once consumers have been brought into the process, expectations can only be escalated. These design communities may, in time, challenge the foundational ideas we have about how a company identifies a need, develops a product, prices it, and brings it to market. If all these functions are conducted by a company's customers via innovation communities, we will have arrived at a very new model for a corporation.

Finally, this will transform many marketing researchers from project directors to community managers, shifting skill emphasis from project management to interpersonal relationship with the many market segments the company seeks to serve.

The last marketing research epoch on the edge of the horizon is the anticipatory epoch. Here digital gaming, agent-based computational modeling, predictive markets, and foresight tools will simulate and explore future consumption patterns, interests, and desires. Unlike previous epochs, the anticipatory epoch will focus exclusively on the futures. Game development, creativity, and systems thinking will be prized skills. The challenge will be building entertaining and usable interfaces for participants. If the project director was the center of the marketing research world in the asking epoch, the game designer and analyzer will become the core here. Game design will replace survey design as a core competence.

In reviewing this baseline forecast for the development of the insights industry, several implications emerge.

Listening and Observing

The industry is at the edge of an evolutionary jump from asking to listening and from focusing on what people say within the construct of a survey to what people do and discuss with their networks. This is a very big change. Surveys won't disappear, but they will become shorter and less central to marketing research. We will always need to ask questions, but we'll do so after listening much more.

Transition

The volume and rapidity of change about to hit the industry will challenge client side insights functions, suppliers, and professionals. Some will be unable to make this transition.

Privacy

The privacy concerns of citizen-consumers and their governments may threaten, limit, or cripple the observational epoch. This may force the industry more quickly into the cocreative and anticipatory epochs.

Geographic Shift

Although 66% of the world's marketing research is concentrated in five aging economies today, it is likely to shift heavily to the emerging economies in Asia, South America, and the Middle East.

Temporal Shift

The insights industry will shift its focus over time from past, reported behavior to present data streams to anticipated future desires and behavior. Currently, marketing research is like a man driving a car by looking in the rearview mirror and out his side window. He takes what he sees and projects it onto the road ahead. But marketing research is likely to develop a much greater future focus, especially with cocreation, gaming, agent-based modeling, prediction markets, and foresight tools.

Iterative Insight Streaming (IIS)

The baseline forecast strongly suggests the move from a periodic questioning format (quarterly tracking and the occasional exploratory focus groups) to iterative insight streaming (IIS), where multiple data sources are harnessed and the insights are recorded within a knowledge-management system that assists strategists in continual learning. In this new paradigm, strategists are accessing and knowledge banking insights from survey data, CRM, social media listening posts, insights communities, and predictive markets. These insights will be hubbed on a portal and continually build on one another.

CREATING THE RIGHT DEVELOPMENT PATH FOR YOUR FUTURE

Presently, many plausible futures exist. Instead of thinking about one future, we should think about plural futures. Imagine a cone with today's reality the beginning point and the number of possible futures expanding rapidly out in time from that point. This is the concept those in the field of strategic foresight refer to as the futures cone or the cone of plausibility. It will serve as a useful model as we explore the futures of marketing research.

Based on the STEP drivers, 22 plausible futures have been created. These futures are arranged into socially, technologically, and economically driven clusters. Many of these futures are the result of combinations of numerous drivers, but they are sorted by their dominant driver for ease of reading. They are not mutually exclusive.

Readers will have to judge for themselves how their organizations and their individual careers are impacted by each scenario. Ideally, readers will begin to develop strategies that help them achieve a preferred future, help them avoid unfavorable futures, and help them develop mitigation strategies for undesirable futures. This is a more flexible and deeper approach I call "scenario dependent strategy."

And now, a general warning is in order.

Some of these scenarios will seem likely. Readers will have considered the contours and implications of these before. An example of this might be the incredible-shrinking-survey scenario.

Other scenarios may seem absurd or at least far-fetched. I expect many readers will place E-Agency, Let's Play a Game, and Back to the Future in this category.

At this point, consider the words of noted futurist Jim Dator (1995), "Any useful statement about the futures should appear to be ridiculous."

Readers should create an attractiveness-likelihood matrix and place each scenario within this matrix. Which scenarios do you identify as highly attractive and highly likely? Which scenarios do you identify as unattractive, but highly likely?

Build on these scenarios. Create scenario mash-ups, and begin formulating a strategy.

Socially Driven Futures Scenarios

There are eight socially driven futures scenarios. The first four are concerned with changes in data collection rising from social change. The next four emerge from shifts in values, expectations, engagement, and communication.

The Incredible, Shrinking Survey

In a classic example of a "tragedy of the commons," the insights industry loaded too many surveys onto too few people and effectively overfished the ocean of participants. In the ever-busier 21st century, consumers simply don't take surveys longer than a few minutes.

Concerned with poor data quality driven by low completion rates, the industry moves en masse to much shorter surveys. The rise of mobile research makes these surveys even shorter. As social media listening increases, traditional survey research continues its decline. Although the need to ask consumers questions will remain, the questioning will become more conditional, shorter, and iterative. The survey persists, but in a smaller form.

Do Not Disturb

A privacy movement incorporating changing values, behaviors, and increased legislation dramatically reduces respondent cooperation rates, increases research costs, and reduces statistical projectability. Opt-in panels become incredibly valuable, turning the panel companies into powerhouses. In some cases, research in the developed world reverts to face-to-face interviewing. Blog monitoring and analysis flourishes, but the privacy movement destroys social media listening as a methodology and a business.

Back to the Future

Lack of projectability becomes the top concern among clients, as online convenience samples and social media listening posts are criticized for their lack of projectability. The industry moves to mixed mode research that includes a reversion back to door-to-door data collection. Mass, in-home, ethnography built on a short survey model becomes the new normal, and marketing research strangely returns to its door-to-door interviewing roots.

What Was Privacy?

Younger generations using social media drop any remaining privacy concerns and allow research firms to purchase their social media and behavioral *lifestreams*. Seizing a business opportunity, Google, Facebook, Foursquare, and numerous other search and social media platforms become mass panel providers and then research firms, in their own right, with subscription-based, desktop research tools. Clients begin mass use of DIY, desktop research tools, eliminating most internal insights functions. Insights communities (MROCs) become a tool within the Google Insights platform, but clients stay with bespoke communities because of the unique rapport that must develop for these communities to be successful.

Power to the People

A cocreative approach to marketing research establishes primacy and destroys the traditional product development paradigm, blurring the historically bright lines between innovator, producer, and consumer. Traditional marketing research is turned on its head and goes from a screening mechanism that kills bad product ideas to a creative engine that develops good ones. Corporations begin asking how they control "their" product innovation.

In this future, consumer-populated online design communities (a variant on today's MROCs) are the core tool. Munich-based HYVE's Innovation Communities are an example of what this future might look like. These design communities are merged with prediction markets, providing real-time, forward-looking feedback. Research project directors become community facilitators. Some corporations make democratic cocreative engagement a core, differentiating value.

From Value to Values

To catch up with emerging world mores, corporations move dramatically to competition on values and purpose. In fact, values and purpose become the key competitive differentiator, transcending brand, and focus on things like justice, shared aesthetic sense, ecological preservation, and community aspirations. This trend migrates from premium brands downward into almost every sector and even into business-to-business (B2B). Values research becomes a very hot commodity. Branding becomes seen as a narcissistic relic of the 20th century. Functional product attributes comes to mean the product's value to society. In this future, formal philosophy training is a prized credential for marketing research staff.

Tribal Rituals

As competition increases and consumption becomes more about experience and purpose, marketers turn increasingly to the creation of community and ritual, with the product embedded within the ritual. Marketing researchers look to NFL tailgating, Coca Cola's "pause that refreshes," scrapbooking parties, motorcycle weekends, and teatime for inspiration. This approach works because of three intersecting trends: (1) the rapid pace of social change creates a need for stabilizing ritual, (2) 21st century society places a higher value on meaning and purpose, and (3) location-based social media makes planned and impromptu tribal gatherings much easier. A signal of this future is Starbucks' new marketing slogan "take comfort in rituals."

Epidemiology

The peer-to-peer world directly challenges the mass market, mass advertising, stimulus-response pattern of traditional marketing research. **Memetics**, the study of self-replicating ideas first proposed by Richard Dawkins (1976) in his book *The Selfish Gene*, replaces advertising research. In this future, pioneering thinkers like Susan Blackmore (The Meme Machine) and Robert Aunger (The Electric Meme) provide the foundation for a very different kind of marketing research. Epidemiologists turned memetic engineers become the hottest talent as clients seek to create self-replicating, exclusive, and sticky ideas in a marketing world obsessed with the Darwinian struggle for mind share. They design idea viruses that promote their product or service as they spread from one brain to the next.

Technology-Driven Futures

These seven technology driven futures represent the logical extrapolations of advances in location-based social media, IT, data mining, simulation, and biometrics.

Geotimed Feedback

The combination of mobile phones, social media, and geotracking creates a suite of products that allow researchers "just in time—just in place" feedback. In this future, prerecruited and incentivized participants respond to simple survey questions at a certain time of day or location, delivering much deeper insights. Location-based social media also revolutionizes qualitative research, creating "just in time qual," where consumers are invited in real-time, based on their location to product parties, brief focus groups, and fun cocreation events.

Rapid In-Market Experimentation (RIME)

Standard concept and product-testing research is replaced by rapid, in-market experimentation (RIME) with prototype products rapidly introduced into physical and virtual test markets to better gauge consumer interest. Marketers frequently eschew exploratory research altogether. Instead, they follow the lead of their online design communities, take the highest valued products on their prediction market, and begin RIMEing.

Iterative Insight Streaming (IIS)

The industry moves away from periodic, interrogatory research (e.g., four focus groups and then a survey) to a flexible, iterative, and evolutionary research design that includes social media monitoring, CRM/CEM data, insights communities (MROCs), prediction markets, and traditional research tools. IIS becomes the new research paradigm, replacing research projects with exploratory engagements and moving marketing research from a pricing model based on data collection to one based on consulting.

Portal Power

Insights portals integrate sales data, CRM/CEM data, social media monitoring, insights communities (MROCs), proprietary predictive markets, quarterly brand tracking, and all past reports into one online interface. The insights portal becomes analogous to enterprise software for marketing researchers. Technology companies such as Clarabridge, already specialists in analyzing unstructured text, are already far down this path. The awareness and knowledge gaps between CRM/CEM data, sales data, social media, and primary research begin to close. Software companies developing these portals are quickly acquired by the large suppliers. Corporate insights departments become the guardians of this portal.

Let's Play a Game

Survey research begins a rapid decline as the pool of respondents dwindles and exhaustion with even short surveys appears. Social media fails to deliver future leaning insights. Corporations cast about for new methods to generate hard, anticipatory data. Online shopping simulation games surge. Participants actually enjoy the experience, as gaming activates the human need to play. Game design and analysis replaces survey design and analysis. While participant-based online gaming becomes the norm, agent-based computational modeling is employed, especially for pricing strategy.

Limbic

The dominant marketing research model of man, as a rational animal, collapses as behavioral economics and brain-scanning reveal the true power of instinct and emotion. Neuromarketing explodes. Deep qualitative, ethnographics, mass collage work, fMRI brain scans, and eye tracking begin to replace traditional survey research. Social media monitoring becomes heavily focused on emotion-laden phrases, as every company, brand, and product is given a social media "emotional quotient" score. Neuroscientists take command of many insights functions. Cries of manipulation erupt within society as the insights industry explores the concept of free will.

Nanotargeting (or Farewell Pareto Principle)

Marketing research begins to approach the N of 1, making MicroTrends look like MegaTrends. Microargeting is replaced by nanotargeting, as Chris Anderson's "long tail" of widening product diversity becomes 8 billion customized consumer tails. Research teams are redesigned to include ethnographers, data miners, and RIMEers. All billboards become interactive marketing platforms pitching products based on a passing consumer's digital profile, time of day, estimated gender and age, and facial expression. Civil libertarians label this brave new world "nanny-targeting" and protest by digital off-gridding, paying with cash, and deliberately randomizing their purchase behaviors (McCreary, 2008).

Economically Driven Futures

These seven economically driven futures focus on either the configuration of the insights industry or commercially driven changes in the way it functions.

Dispersive Convergence

Marketing research ceases to exist as a term or identifiable industry. Paradoxically, the industry convergence outlined in this chapter disperses the corporate insights function and splinters marketing research into dozens of tools and competencies purchased across many siloed marketing and consulting disciplines. Google, Facebook, and Foursquare offer robust sampling, surveying, and analytics tools, making DIY research only a few keystrokes away. Marketing researchers lose any remaining group or professional identity, but their analytical skills provide them solid career paths. In this future, "marketing research department" sounds as odd as "typing pool" does today.

Lilliput

The traditional, large, multinational research suppliers struggle. No longer able to buy their future by acquiring smaller, more innovative companies, they compete harder and harder over shrinking, procurement-guarded, marketing research budgets. Smaller, new entrants from the wider insights industry block the large suppliers' evolutionary path, and the giants are overwhelmed by the next-generation Lilliputians.

E-Agency

The traditional model of a marketing research firm is atomized and replaced by individual e-lancers, each specializing in a niche. In a future that looks like a cross between Amazon's "Mechanical Turk" and eBay, online talent markets allow insights functions to hire research professionals from around the world based on their ratings across many metrics.

Taking a page from Cory Doctorow's (2003) science fiction novel *Down and Out in the Magic Kingdom*, marketing research professionals are hired based on their "whuffie" score or overall reputation. Uncover crucial strategic insights for a company and your whuffie soars. Overbill for a poorly designed study yielding zero actionable insights and your whuffie plummets. Does this sound far-fetched? It isn't. The nonprofit Whuffie Bank, an experiment in reputational currency, launched in 2009. Workable social currency systems are possible today. Will they develop faster in Western, celebrity-crazed societies or duty-driven, traditional or Confucian societies?

Global Depth

In a future that is comforting for large research suppliers, globalization requires corporations to have deep insights in nearly every market simultaneously. Smaller suppliers with only a national footprint cannot compete in this future, and the large suppliers win comfortably based on their global reach and local depth. Although it could be possible for client side insights functions to piece together many local suppliers, it is simply too time consuming. Large, global suppliers win because they can execute face-to-face interviews in Bahrain and Sao Paulo simultaneously with elite indigenous staff.

Need for Speed

The speed of decision making shortens to such an extent that real-time data are dramatically more valued than periodic tracking data. Real-time products like insight communities (MROCs) and other passive listening posts eliminate the traditional quarterly tracker and destroy most traditional industry incumbents in the process. Rapid, survey-based research is measured in hours and not days, as the survey-research process transitions from one long survey to an iterative stream of very short surveys. Research and analytical teams are distributed across the globe to work the 24-hour clock.

Space Invaders

As companies continue to search for competitive advantage, they begin mapping mental market space and competing outside traditional sectors, within consumer conceptual space. In this future, the focus is less on product category and more on the consumer's conceptual space.

This means that Volvo, an automotive brand that has a strong presence within the safety marketspace, begins competing in injury-reducing clothing, protective sporting gear, and baby strollers. Nike, with its strength in the fitness market space, begins competing in sporting and wellness vacations, supplements, and exercise equipment. In this future, mapping these mental market spaces and building strategies to reinforce mindshare within them is critical. Syndicated market space tracking becomes highly valuable.

Anticipation

Anticipatory customer strategies (ACS) replaces marketing research and insights as the temporal focus of the industry shifts heavily into the future. Insights functions achieve BCG's fourth stage of development, the strategic foresight organization (Egan et al., 2009). Strategic foresight tools are used in conjunction with trend watchers, social media listening posts, real-time Delphi panels, and insights communities with prediction markets. Scenario dependent strategy (SDS) is the new deliverable, and each area of exploration is mapped in three dimensions (scenario likelihood, scenario attractiveness, and ease of execution). Design and marketing strategies are built on preferred futures identified in the research. "Insight" has been replaced by "foresight."

CONCLUSION

Based on this analysis, I see three potential outcomes for the traditional marketing research industry. These are transcendence, convergence, or stagnation.

The first outcome, transcendence, is that traditional marketing research renames, rebrands, and repositions itself at the center of the wider insights industry. In this scenario, traditional marketing research absorbs and integrates tools and knowledge from the wider insights industry, placing itself at the top of the strategic insights value chain.

This outcome is best described by Reineke Reitsma of Forrester,

> There are new playing fields, new players and new rules. Marketing researchers are not playing the whole field anymore. They need to get much closer to all this kind of information, and make sure that they become the conscience and voice of reason, handling this large stream of information. In time, they should work towards taking on a new role that combines all the customer insights from social media, email, a variety of website statistics and primary research data. (ESOMAR, 2010b, p. 27)

Convergence, the second outcome, is produced by a crowded collision of marketing research, management consulting, social media analytics, data mining, and software producing a synthesis of tools and a blurring of roles. Unlike the transcendence scenario, convergence is forced on traditional marketing research and the adjustment is difficult.

In the outcome, stagnation, traditional marketing research refuses to evolve, preferring to stay with questioning rather than observing tools. It continues to execute tactical research projects while the wider insights industry passes it by.

Finally, based on what's been discussed in this chapter, there are (1) general implications for the industry, (2) implications for corporate insights functions, and (3) implications for marketing research suppliers.

General Implications

The marketing research industry must rename, rebrand, and reposition itself as the central, strategy-building hub of a wider insights industry. It must aggressively move beyond the asking epoch in which it was created and embrace observational, cocreative, and anticipatory methods. It must excel at harvesting insights across multiple data streams. It must shift its temporal focus from the present into the future, possibly renaming itself "anticipatory customer strategies."

Finally, it must focus on the three enduring constants of curiosity, creativity, and communication. Marketing researchers are curious by nature, and they need to feed this strength. But the industry will need to become more right-brained, as the need for left-brained project managers is eclipsed by the need for creative listeners. And it will need to keep honing its communications skills. Finding actionable insights is one thing, but communicating them with impact across an enterprise is quite another.

Implications for Insights Functions

Insights functions must have greater C-suite access. If the insights function is expected to be a center of corporate learning, the insights head must hold an executive level position. The function must move beyond periodic, tactical, asking-based research to the role of strategic counselor based on IIS. The insights function must become the strategic custodians of digital portals that harness multiple data streams and methodologies. They cannot fight for real estate on these portals. They must run the portal.

To adjust to the evolution of marketing research, insights functions will need to diversify their talent sets through the addition of staff conversant in data mining, social media monitoring, insights communities, neuromarketing, prediction marketing, and foresight.

Implications for Suppliers

What got you here, won't get you there. Prepare to make the leap from the asking epoch to the observing epoch. Diversify talent away from a focus on the survey and toward data mining, knowledge management, social media, insights communities, and prediction markets. Develop solutions that merge all of these into iterative insights streams. Move beyond the role of data provider and add value at the strategy level or risk becoming commoditized. *Innovate.*

FURTHER READING

Chadwick, S., Lewis, J., & Dedeker, K. (2009, April). Engaging people in their backyards. *Research World, 8,* 35–37.

The Listening Posts. (2009, May). *ResearchTalk*. Retrieved from, http://www.researchtalk.co.uk/rt/2009/05/27/the-meme-hunters/.

References

AAAA. (2007). *How many advertisements is a person exposed to in a day.* Retrieved from, http://ams.aaaa.org/eweb/upload/faqs/adexposures.pdf

Aaker, J. L. (1997, August). Dimensions of brand personality. *Journal of Marketing Research, XXXIV,* 347–356.

Ackoff, R. L. (1989). From data to wisdom. *Journal of Applied Systems Analysis, 16,* 3–9.

Agrawal, A. (2011). Nudging to save lives! [weblog]. Retrieved from http://mostlyeconomics.wordpress.com/2011/05/09/nudging-to-save-lives/

Allen, R.C. (1983). Collective invention. *Journal of Economic Behavior and Organization, 4*(1), 1–24.

Amerine, M. A., Pangborn, R. M., & Roessler, E. (1965). *Principles of sensory evaluation of food.* New York, NY: Academic Press.

Anderson Analytics. (2009). *Data mining & text analysis.* Retrieved from, http://www.andersonanalytics.com/index.php?page=data-mining

Anderson, T. (2008). *Text analytics in market research: Gaining an innovative advantage.* Amsterdam, Netherlands: ESOMAR.

Angwin, J., & Valention-Devries, J. (2010, December 2). FTC backs do-not-track System for web. *Wall Street Journal.* Retrieved from, http://online.wsj.com/article/SB10001424052748704594804575648670826747094.html

Angwin, J., & Stecklow, S. (2010, October). "Scrapers" dig deep for data on the Web. *Wall Street Journal.* Retrieved from, http://online.wsj.com/article/SB10001424052748703358504575544381288117888.html

Ariely, D. (2009). *Predictably irrational: The hidden forces that shape our decisions.* New York, NY: Harper Collins.

Arora, R., & Stoner, C. (2009). A mixed methods approach to understanding brand personality. *Journal of Product and Brand Management, 18*(4), 272–283.

Associated Press. (2006). Drug errors injure more than 1.5 million a year. *MSNBC.com* Retrieved from, http://www.msnbc.msn.com/id/13954142/

Ataman, M., van Heerde, H., & Mela, C. (2009). The long-term effect of marketing strategy on brand sales. *Journal of Marketing Research, 47,* 866–882.

Audit Bureau of Circulation. (2010). Virtual press room. Retrieved from, http://www.accessabc.com/press/industryscoop.htm#august

August, S. (2010). *Why mobile will be huge. And why it won't.* Retrieved from http://www.revelationglobal.com/news/thinking/why-mobile-will-be-huge-and-why-it-wont

Augustine, J. R. (1996). Circuitry and functional aspects of the insular lobe in primates including humans. *Brain Research Reviews, 22,* 229–244.

Avruch, M. (2010). Shift in world economic power means a decade of seismic change. *PricewaterhouseCoopers.* Retrieved from, http://www.pwc.com/pt_BR/br/sala-de-imprensa/assets/release-pib-2030-uk.pdf

Ayres, I. (2007). *Super crunchers: Why thinking-by-numbers is the new way to be smart.* New York, NY: Bantam.

Bacheldor, B. (2006, October 31). Digital angel developing an implantable glucose-sensing RFID tag. *RFID Journal.* Retrieved from, http://www.rfidjournal.com/article/view/2783

Bacheldor, B. (2007a, September 24). ASD healthcare deploys RFID refrigerated drug cabinets. *RFID Journal.* Retrieved from, http://www.rfidjournal.com/article/view/3632

Bacheldor, B. (2007b, April 3). At Wayne Memorial, RFID pays for itself. *RFID Journal.* Retrieved from, http://www.rfidjournal.com/article/view/3199

Bacheldor, B. (2007c, July 10). RFID-enabled handheld helps nurses verify meds. *RFID Journal.* Retrieved from, http://www.rfidjournal.com/article/view/3470

Baculinao, E. (2004). China grapples with legacy of its "missing girls." *NBC World News.* Retrieved from, http://www.msnbc.msn.com/id/5953508/ns/world_news/

Bain, R. (2008). *Industry must make cellphone research more acceptable*. Retrieved from, http://www.research-live.com/news/industry-must-make-cellphone-research-'more-acceptable/3004651.article

Bain, R. (2010a). Brain sells: Cutting through the neuromarketing hype. *Research*. Retrieved from, http://www.research-live.com/comment/brain-sells-cutting-through-the-neuromarketing-hype/4003572.article

Bain, R. (2010b). Thoughts into action. *Research*. Retrieved from, http://www.research-live.com/magazine/thoughts-into-action/4002149.article

Baldwin, C., & Clark, K. (2006). The architecture of participation: Does code architecture mitigate free riding in the open source development model? *Management Science, 52*(7), 1116–1127.

Balik, B. S. (2010, July 26). Behavioral economics is helping marketers better understand consumers. *Advertising Age*, p. 24.

Banham, R. (2003). CRM, as you like it. *CFO.com*. Retrieved from http://www.cfo.com/article.cfm/3009214?f

Banks M. (2001). *Visual methods in social research*. Thousand Oaks, CA: Sage.

Barton, S. G. (1949, March 15). *What you can and can't do with a consumer panel*. Presentation at the meeting of the American Marketing Association, March, Boston MA.

Batchelor, R. (2010, February). Getting research noticed. *Research World*. Retrieved from, http://www.esomar.org/uploads/rw/2010.02/Research-World-February-2010-Getting-research-noticed.pdf.

Batchelor, R. (2007). Bias in macroeconomic rorecasts. *International Journal of Forecasting, 23*(2), 189–203.

BEA Systems. (2006). *Retail operations and asset management: Enhancing retail operations and supply-chain management with RFID*. [white paper]. Retrieved from, http://wp.bitpipe.com/resource/org_928437302_173/BEA_RFID_9941_edp.pdf?site_cd=ssn

Belenzon, S., & Schankerman, M. (2008). *Motivation and sorting in open source software innovation*. (CEPR discussion paper number DP7012). Centre for Economic Policy Research, London. Retrieved from, http://papers.ssrn.com

Benkler, Y., & Nissenbaum, H. (2006). Commons-based peer production and virtue. *Journal of Political Philosophy, 14*(4), 394–419.

Bernard, H.R. (2000). *Social research methods: Qualitative and quantitative approaches*. Thousand Oaks, CA: Sage.

Berry, T. R., Spence, J. C., Plotnikoff, R. C., Bauman, A., McCargar, L., Witcher, C., Clark, M., et al. (2009, May). A mixed methods evaluation of televised health promotion advertisements targeted at older adults. *Evaluation and Program Planning, 32,* May, 278–288.

Bickart, B., & Schmittlein, D. (1999). The distribution of survey contact and participation in the United States. *Journal of Marketing Research, 36,* 286–294.

Bijmolt, T. A., Leeflang, P. S. H., Block, F., Eisenbeiss, M., Hardie, B. G. S., Lemmens, A., & Saffert, P. (2010). Analytics for customer engagement. *Journal of Service Research, 13,* 341–356.

Bohn, R., & Short, J. (2009). *How much information? 2009 report on American consumers*. Retrieved from, http://hmi.ucsd.edu/pdf/HMI_2009_ConsumerReport_Dec9_2009.pdf

Bosman, J. (2006, April 4). Chevy tries a write-your-own-ad approach, and the potshots fly. *New York Times*. Retrieved from, http://www.nytimes.com/2006/04/04/business/media/04adco.html?pagewanted=print

Boston Consulting Group (2009). "The Consumer's Voice: Can Your Company Hear It?" Retrieved September 10, 2010, from, http://www.bcg.com/documents/file35167.pdf

Botvinick, M. M., Cohen, J. D., & Carter, C. S. (2004). Conflict monitoring and anterior cingulate cortex: an update. *Trends in Cognitive Sciences, 8,* 539–546.

Boudreau, K., Lacetera, N., & Lakhani, K. (2008). *Parallel search, incentives and problem type: Revisiting the competition and innovation link*. (Research paper 1264038). Harvard Business School Technology & Operations Management Unit, Boston, Massachusetts. Retrieved from, http://papers.ssrn.com

Boudreau, K., & Lakhani, K. (2009). How to manage outside innovation. *Sloan Management Review, 50*(4), 69–76.

Box, G. E. P., Hunter, J.. & Hunter, S. (1978). *Statistics for experimenters*. New York, NY: John Wiley and Sons.

Brabham, D. (2008). Crowdsourcing as a model for problem Solving: An introduction and cases. *Convergence: the International Journal of Research into New Media Technologies, 14*(1), 75–90.

Brainard, C. (2008). Beware of "neuropunditry." *Columbia Journalism Review*. Retrieved from, http://www.cjr.org/campaign_desk/beware_of_neuropunditry.php

Brand Finance.(n.d.). Branding: The invisible business. Retrieved from http://brandfinance.dda.co.uk/docs/invisible_business.asp

Braselton, J. & Blair, B. (2007). Cementing relationships: A short menu of high value offerings builds profits. *Marketing Management, 16*(3),14–17.

Brazeal, M. (2009). *RFID: Improving the customer experience*. Ithaca, New York. Paramount Market.

Brennan, M., Benson, S. & Kearns, Z. (2005). The effect of introductions on telephone survey participation rates. *International Journal of Market Research, 47*(1), 65–74.

Britt, P. J. (2005, July/August). RFID positioned to aid measurement of traditional print. *eContent 28*(7/8). Retrieved from http://www.econtentmag.com/Articles/News/News-Feature/RFID-Positioned-to-Aid-Measurement-of-Traditional-Print-Pilots-Offer-New-Possibilities-8262.htm

Brown, T. (2009). *Change by design: How design thinking transforms organizations and inspires innovation.* New York, NY: HarperBusiness.

Bruner, J. (1990). *Acts of meaning.* Cambridge, MA: Harvard University Press.

Bryman, A. (2007). Barriers to integrating quantitative and qualitative research. *Journal of Mixed Methods Research, 1*(1), 8–22.

Bucklin, R., & Sismeiro, C. (2009). Click here for internet insight: Advances in clickstream data analysis in marketing. *Journal of Interactive Marketing, 23*(1), 35–48.

Buckner, R. L. (1998). Event related fMRI and the hemodynamic response. *Human Brain Mapping, 6,* 373–377.

Burkitt, L. (2009, November 16). Neuromarketing: Companies use neuroscience for consumer insights. *Forbes.* Retieved from http://www.forbes.com/forbes/2009/1116/marketing-hyundai-neurofocus-brain-waves-battle-for-the-brain.html

Burton, R. (2008). Brain scam. *Salon.* Retrieved from, http://www.salon.com/life/mind_reader/2008/05/12/daniel_amen/

Carr, A. (2010). *The most important leadership quality for CEOs? Creativity.* Retrieved from, http://www.fastcompany.com/1648943/creativity-the-most-important-leadership-quality-for-ceos-study

Casdas, D., Fine, B., & Menictas, C. (2006). Attitudinal differences: Comparing people who belong to multiple versus single panels. Panel Research: 2006 ESOMAR World Research Conference.

Caul, J. F. (1957). The profile method of flavor analysis. *Advances in Food Research, 7,* 1–40.

Cefkin, M. (2010). Business, anthropology, and the growth of corporate ethnography. In M. Cefkin (Ed.), *Ethnography and the corporate encounter* (pp. 1–37). New York, NY: Berghan Books.

Cerf-Ducastel, B., van de Moortele, P. F., MacLeod, P., Le Bihan, D., & Faurion, A. (2001). Interaction of gustatory and lingual somatosensory perceptions at the cortical level in the human: a functional magnetic resonance imaging study. *Chemical Senses, 26,* 371–383.

Changizi, M. (2009). *The vision revolution: How the latest research overturns everything we thought we knew about human vision.* Dallas, TX: BenBella Books.

Christakis, N., & Fowler, J. (2009). *Connected: The surprising power of social networks and how they shape our lives.* New York, NY: Little, Brown and Company.

Christensen, C., Cook, S., & Hall, T. (2006, January 16). What customers want from your products. *Harvard Business School Working Knowledge: Research Ideas.* Retrieved from http://hbswk.hbs.edu/item/5170.html

Christensen, G. L., & Olson, J. C. (2002, June). Mapping consumers' mental models with ZMET. *Psychology & Marketing, 19,* 477–502.

Churchill, G. Jr. (1995). *Marketing research: Methodological foundations* (6th ed.). Hillsdale, IL: Dryden Press.

Ciaramelli, E., Muccioli, M., Làdavas,, E., & di Pellegrino, G. (2007). Selective deficit in personal moral judgment following damage to vetromedial prefrontal cortex. *Social Cognitive and Affective Neuroscience, 2,* 84–92.

Cisco. (2011, February 1). *Cisco visual networking index: Global mobile data traffic forecast* (Update, 2010–2015). [White paper]. Retrieved from, http://www.cisco.com/en/US/solutions/collateral/ns341/ns525/ns537/ns705/ns827/white_paper_c11-520862.html

Clancy, K., & Krieg, P. (2000). *Counterintuitive marketing.* New York, NY: John Wiley & Sons.

Clancy, K., Krieg, P., & Gamse, H. (2006). An end to door stops: Segmentation studies should do more than sit on your floor. *Marketing Research,* 16–24.

Clark, A. (1997). *Being there: Putting brain, body and world together again.* Cambridge MA: The MIT Press.

Clithero, J. A., Tankersley, D., & Huettel, S. A. (2008). Foundations of neuroeconomics: from philosophy to practice. *PLoS Biology, 6,* 2348–2353.

Coan, J. A., & Allen, J. J. B. (2004). Frontal EEG asymmetry as a moderator and mediator of emotion. *Biological Psychology, 67,* 7–49.

Coates, D., & Corcoran, L. (2010, June). Mobile research: Best practices for immediate, in-the-moment feedback. [Webinar]. Retrieved from, http://www.slideshare.net/FlyResearch/mobile-research-webinarwithflyf9june1020

Coen, T., Lorch, J., & Piekarski, L. (2005, April). The effects of survey frequency on panelists' responses. Presented at ESOMAR World Research Conference, *Developments and Progress,* Budapest, 409–424.

Cohen, D. (2007). Methods in cultural psychology. In S. Kitayama & D. Cohen (Eds.), *Handbook of cultural psychology* (pp. 197–236). New York, NY: Guilford Press.

Collins, J. (2006). P&G finds RFID "sweet spot." *RFID Journal*. Retrieved from, www.rfidjournal.com/article/view/2312.

Collins, K. M. T., & O'Cathain, A. O. (2009). Ten points about mixed methods research to be considered by the novice researcher. *International Journal of Multiple Research Approaches, 3*(1), 2–7.

Connell, J., & Voola, R. (2007). Strategic alliances and knowledge sharing: Synergies silos? *Journal of Knowledge Management, 11*(3), 52–66.

Cook, W.A., & Plummer, J. (2007). *Idea engagement: Feeling stirred, not shaken.* New York, NY: White Paper, Advertising Research Foundation.

Cooper, T. (2006). Enhancing insights discovery by balancing the focus of analytics between strategic and tactical levels. *Database Management and Customer Strategy Management, 13*(4), 261–270.

Corcoran, L. (2010, June). *Mobile research: Young adults drinking behavioural study.* Paper presented at MRS Mobile Conference 2010, London. Retrieved from, http://www.slideshare.net/FlyResearch/mrs-mobile-conference

Cornell, J. A. (1973). Experiments with mixtures: A review. *Technometrics, 15,* 437–455.

Cornish, E. (1981, June). *Telecommunications: What's coming.* Paper delivered at the America Marketing Association 1981 Annual Conference, San Francisco, California.

Council for Marketing and Opinion Research (CMOR). (2003). *Respondent Cooperation and Industry Image Survey.* Port Jefferson, NY: Author.

Council of American Survey Research Organizations (CARSO). (2011). *CARSO code of standards and ethics for survey research.* Retrieved from http://www.casro.org/codeofstandards.cfm

Cowen, T. (2010, September 29). On which issues will we become less moral? *Marginal Revolution Blog* Retrieved from, http://www.marginalrevolution.com/marginalrevolution/2010/09/which-current-practices-will-be-con demned-by-the-future.html

Craig, A. D. (2009). How do you feel—now? The anterior insula and human awareness. *Nature Reviews Neuroscience, 10,* 59–70.

Creswell, J. W., & Plano-Clark, V. L. (2007). *Designing and conducting mixed methods research.* Thousand Oaks, CA: Sage

Csikszentmihalyi, M. (1996). *Creativity: Flow and the psychology of discovery and invention.* New York, NY: HarperCollins.

Culler, D. E. (2004, June). Smart sensors to network the world. *Scientific American.* Retrieved from, www.intel.com/research/exploratory/smartnetworks.htm

Damasio, A. (2000). *Descartes' error: Emotion, reason, and the human brain.* New York, NY: HarperCollins.

Daniel Yankelovich, Inc. (1972, July). *The Yankelovich MONITOR, 2*(3), [Unpublished].

Das, T., & Teng, B. (2000). 'A resource-based theory of strategy alliances. *Journal of Management, 26*(1), 31–61.

Dator, J. (1995). Newt's sweet dreams. *Hawaii Research Center for Futures Studies.* Retrieved from, http://www.futures.hawaii.edu/dator/governance/Newt.pdf

Dator, J. (n.d.). *Trends analysis compared with emerging issues analysis.* [Unpublished manuscript.].

Davenport, T. H., & Harris, J. G. (2007). *Competing on analytics.* Cambridge, MA: Harvard Business School.

Dawkins, R. (1976). *The selfish gene.* New York, NY: Oxford University Press.

de Abitua, M. (2009). The neuroadvertising paradox. *Bad Idea.* Retrieved from, http://www.badidea.co.uk/2009/12/the-neuroadvertising-paradox/

Deci, E., Koestner, R., & Ryan, R. (1999). A meta-analytic review of experiments examining the effects of extrinsic rewards on intrinsic motivation. *Psychological Bulletin, 125*(6), 627–668.

Denny, R. (2002). Communicating with clients. In S. Squires & B. Byrne (Eds.), *Creating breakthrough ideas* (pp. 147–159). Westport, CN: Bergin & Garvey.

Deppe, M., Schwindt, W., Krämer, J., Kugel, H., Plassmann, H., Kenning, P., & Ringelstein, E. B. (2005a). Evidence for a neural correlate of a framing effect: Bias-specific activity in the ventromedial prefrontal cortex during credibility judgments. *Brain Research Bulletin, 67,* 413-421.

Deppe, M., Schwindt, W., Kugel, H., Plassmann, H., & Kenning, P. (2005b). Nonlinear responses within the medial prefrontal cortex reveal when specific implicit information influences economic decision making. *Journal of Neuroimaging, 15,* 171-182.

De Wulf, K., & Berteloot, S. (2007, October). Duplication and multi-source online panel recruitment: Real quality differences or idle rumors? *Good Quality, Good Business.* ESOMAR World Research Conference, Panel Research 2007, Orlando, FL.

Diakopoulos, N. (2009, July 28). Mechanical turk lets you make a few bucks online. *Sacramento Bee.* Retrieved from http://www.ics.uci.edu/community/news/articles/view_article?id=142

Divakar, S., Ratchford, B. T., & Shankar, V. (2005). CHAN4CAST: A multi-channel, multi-region sales forecasting model and decision support system for consumer packaged goods. *Marketing Science, 24*(3), 334–350.

Doctorow, C. (2003). *Down and out in the magic kingdom* (Rev. ed.). New York, NY: Macmillan.

Dodgson, S. (2010, April). *The future's in their hands: Exploring the application of digital research technology across the mobile platform.* Presented at the Association for Survey Computing (ASC), ASC Conference. London, United Kingdom.

Dolliver, M. (2010, March 29). Researchers look into a mobile future. GfK survey also foresees more attention to social media as phone surveys fade. *AdWeek.* Retrieved from, http://www.vnuemedia.com/aw/content_display/our products/in-print/news/e3ie9fc421daf51cf821a5f781292347273

Donal, R. J. (2002). Emotion, cognition, and behavior. *Science, 298,* 1191.

Drolet, A., Luce, M. F., & Simonson, I. (2009, June). When does choice reveal preference? Moderators of heuristic vs. goal based choice. *Journal of Consumer Research, 36*(1), 137–147.

Dunbar, R. (1992). Neocortex size as a constraint on group size in primates. *Journal of Human Evolution, 22*(6). Retrieved from, http://bit.ly/95HaA7

Economist Magazine. (2010, November 30). Don Tapscott on mass collaboration. [Video file]. Retrieved from http://www.youtube.com/watch?v=WbeST8H05dI

Egan, M., Manfred, K., Bascle, I., Huet, E., & Marcil, S. (2009, November). *The consumer's voice—Can your company hear it?* Boston Consulting Group. Retrieved from, http://www.bcg.com/documents/file35167.pdf

Ekman, P. (2004). *Emotions revealed: Understanding faces and feelings.* New Haven, CT: Phoenix Press.

Ekman, G., & Akesson, C. A. (1964). Saltiness, sweetness and preference: A study of quantitative relations in individual subjects. *Psychological Laboratories, University Of Stockholm, Report 177.*

Eliot, T. S. (1934). *The rock.* London: Faber & Faber.

Emsense. (2010). *A window into the mind of the consumer.* Retrieved from, http://www.emsense.com/

Engel, R. (1928), Experimentelle Untersuchungen Uber die Abhangigkeit der Lust und Unlust Von der Reizstarke beim Geschmacksinn. *Pfluegers Archiv fur die Gesamte Physiologie, 64,* 1–36.

ESOMAR. (2009). *Global market research 2009: ESOMAR industry report.* Amsterdam, Netherlands: ESOMAR.

ESOMAR. (2010a). *ESOMAR world research codes & guidelines: Passive data collection, observation and recording.* Amsterdam, Netherlands: ESOMAR.

ESOMAR. (2010b). *Global market research 2010: ESOMAR industry report.* Amsterdam, Netherlands: ESOMAR.

Farah, M. J. (2005). Neuroethics: The practical and the philosophical. *Trends in Cognitive Sciences, 9,* 34–40.

Ferguson, G. T. (2002). Have your objects call my objects. *Harvard Business Review, 80*(6), 138–144.

Ferguson, R. (2006, February 27). RFID: Still searching for payoff? *eWEEK.com.* Retrieved from http://www.eweek.com/c/a/IT-Management/RFID-Still-Searching-for-Payoff/

Festinger, L. (1957). *A theory of cognitive dissonance.* Stanford, CA: Stanford University Press.

Fiebach, C. J., Ricker, B., Friederici, A. D., & Jacobs, A. M. (2007). Inhibition and facilitation in visual word recognition: Prefrontal contribution to the orthographic neighborhood size effect. *NeuroImage, 36,* 901–911.

Fisher, L. E. (2007, March). Fifty years and counting in marketing research. *Alert,* pp. 18–22.

Fishkin, J. S. (2009). *When people speak: deliberative democracy & public consultation.* Oxford UK: Oxford University Press.

Fiske, S. T., & Taylor, S. E. (2008). Social cognition: From brains to culture. New York, NY: McGraw-Hill

Fitch, D., & Herr, P (2002, October). *Yes Virginia, there is a media multiplier.* Proceedings from ARF Workshops, New York, NY.

Fransella, F., Bell, R., & Bannister, D. (2004). *A manual for repertory grid technique* (2nd ed.). West Sussex, England: Wiley

Freedman, D. H. (2010). *Wrong: Why experts keep failing us—And how to know when not to trust them.* New York, NY: Little, Brown and Company.

Friedman, T. (2006). *The world is flat.* New York, NY Penguin.

Fugate, D. L. (2007). Neuromarketing: A layman's look at neuroscience and its potential application to marketing practice. *Journal of Consumer Marketing, 24,* 385–394.

Fuller, J. (2009). *Heads, you die: Bad decisions, choice architecture, and how to mitigate predictable irrationality.* Retrieved from, http://www.percapita.org.au/_dbase_upl/Heads,%20You%20Die_full%20report%20final_colour_reduced%20file%20size.pdf

Gailey, R., Teal, D., & Haechrel, E. (2008, June). *Sample factors that influence data quality.* Presented at ARF Online Research Quality Council meeting, New York, NY.

Gladwell, M. (2004, February). *Spaghetti sauce*. Presented at TedTalk. (Technology, Entertainment, Design) Conference, Long Beach, CA.

Gallo, C. (2009). *The presentation secrets of Steve Jobs*. New York, NY: McGraw-Hill

Gaudoin, T. (2010). Mickey Drexler retail therapist. *Wall Street Journal Magazine*, Retrieved from http://magazine.wsj.com/features/the-big-interview/retail-therapist/

Gensch, H. D., Aversa, N., & Moore, S. P. (1990). A choice-modeling market information system that enabled ABB Electric to expand its market. *Interfaces, 20*(1), 6–25.

Gibbs, R. (1992). Categorization and metaphor understanding. *Psychological Review 99*(3), 572–577.

Gilovich, T., & Griffin, D. (2002). Heuristics and biases: Then and now. In T. Gilovich, D. Griffin, & D. Kahneman (Eds.), *Heuristics and biases: The psychology of intuitive judgment* (pp. 1–18). Cambridge: Cambridge University Press.

Girju, M., Adams, M., & Ratchford, B. T. (2009). *Demoimpact: Modeling, forecasting, and managing the impact of major U.S. sociodemographic trends on multi-category snack consumption*. (Working Paper). University of Texas, Dallas.

Gittelman, S., & Trimarchi, E. (2009). *On the road to clarity: Differences between sample sources*. East Islip, NY: Mktging Inc.

Gladwell, M. (2006). *Blink: The power of thinking without thinking*. New York, NY Penguin.

Global Park/Fly Research (2009, June). *Mobile research: Best practice for immediate, in-the-moment feedback*. [Webinar]. Retrieved from, http://www.slideshare.net/FlyResearch/mobile-research-webinarwithflyf9june1020

Goldcorp Challenge Winners! (2001, March). *The Goldcorp challenge*. Retrieved from, http://www.goldcorpchallenge.com/challenge1/winnerslist/chaleng2.pdf

Goldstein, N., Martin, S. J., & Cialdini, R. B. (2007). *Yes! 50 secrets from the science of persuasion*. London: Profile Books.

Goleman, D. (1995). *Emotional intelligence: Why it can matter more than IQ*. New York, NY: Bantam.

Gordon, J. (1965). Evaluation of sugar-acid-sweetness relationships in orange juice by a response surface approach. *Journal of Food Science, 39*, 903–907.

Gordon, T. J., & Helmer, O. (1964). *Report on a long-range forecasting study: P-2982*. The RAND Corporation. Retrieved from http://www.rand.org/pubs/papers/2005/P2982.pdf

Gordon, W. (2010, June). What's the buzz about behavioral economics? *Admap, 45*(6), 38–39.

Graves, P. (2010). *Consumerology: The myth of market research, the truth about consumer behavior and the psychology of shopping*. London, UK: Nicholas Brealey.

Green, P. E., Carmone, F. J., & Wachspress, D. P. (1976). Customer segmentation via latent class analysis. *Journal of Marketing Research, 3*, 170–174.

Greenwald, A. G., Carnot, C. G., Beach, R., & Young, B. (1987). Increasing voting behavior by asking people if they expect to vote. *Journal of Applied Psychology*, (72), 315–318.

Greenwald, A. G., McGhee, D. E., & Schwartz, J. L. K. (1998). Measuring individual differences in implicit cognition: The implicit association test. *Journal of Personality and Social Psychology, 74*(6), 1464–1480.

Greenwald, A. G., Poehlman, T. A., Uhlmann, E. L., & Banaji, M. R. (2009). Understanding and using the implicit association test: III. Meta-analysis of predictive validity. *Journal of Personality and Social Psychology, 97*(1), 17–41.

Gregory, J. (2006). RFID and SAP: A strategic vision. *Computer Sciences Corporation*. Retrieved from, www.csc.com/aboutus/leadingedgeformum/knowledgelibrary/uploads/1128_1.pdf

Grover, R., & Vriens, M. (Eds.). (2006). *Handbook of marketing research*. Thousand Oaks, CA: Sage.

Gruber, A. J., Hussain, R. J., & O'Donnell, P. (2009). The nucleus accumbens: A switchboard for goal-directed behaviors. *PLoS, 4*, 1–10.

Gruca, T. S., & Rego, L. L. (2005). Customer satisfaction, cash flow and shareholder value. *Journal of Marketing, 69*, 115–130.

Grunwald, M., (2009, April). How Obama is using the science of change. *Time*. Retrieved from, http://www.time.com/time/magazine/article/0,9171,1889153,00.html

Guinness. (2009). It's alive inside. [Video file]. Retrieved from http://www.youtube.com/watch?v=9NNL0aHF-Y8

Gurumurthy, K., Robinson, W. T., & Urban, G. L. (1995). Order of market entry: Established empirical generalizations, emerging empirical generalizations, and future research. *Marketing Science, 14*(3), G212–G221.

Gutman, J. (1982, spring). A means-end chain model based on consumer categorization processes. *Journal of Marketing 46*, 60–72.

Hagins, B. (2010). The ROI on calculating research's ROI. *Quirk's Marketing Research Review*, 52–57.

Hale, T. (2010, May 3). Store brands flex muscle in weak economy. *Nielsen Wire*. Retrieve from, http://blog.nielsen.com/nielsenwire/consumer/store-brands-flex-muscle-in-weak-economy

Hamel, G., & Prahalad, C. K. (1994). *Competing for the future.* Boston, MA: Harvard Business Review Press.

Hansen, F. (1981). Hemispheral lateralization: implications for understanding consumer behavior. *Journal of Consumer Research, 8,* 23–36.

Harris, G. (2006, July 21). Report finds a heavy toll from medication errors. *New York Times.* Retrieved from, http://www.nytimes.com/2006/07/21/health/21drugerrors.html

Harris, P. (2008). Neuromarketing: Marketing insights from neuroimaging research; Insights. University of Melbourne. Retrieved from, http://insights.unimelb.edu.au/vol4/15_Harris.html

Hastings, C., & Warren, G. (2010). Children spend 7 hours a day in "electronic life." *The Sunday Times* [Online]. Retrieved from, http://www.timesonline.co.uk/tol/life_and_style/health/child_health/article7009738.ece

Hauser, J., & Griffin, A. (1993). *The voice of the customer.* (Working Paper 92-106). Marketing Science Institute, Cambridge, MA

Hayden, B. Y., Nair, A. C., McCoy, A. N., & Platt, M. L. (2008). Posterior cingulated cortex mediates outcome-contingent allocation of behavior. *Neuron, 60,* 19–25.

Heath, C., & Heath, D. (2007). *Made to stick: Why some ideas take hold and others become unstuck.* London, UK: Random House.

Heinrich, C. (2005). *RFID and beyond.* Indianapolis, IN: Wiley.

Henson, R. (2005). What can functional neuroimaging tell the experimental psychologist? *Quarterly Journal of Experimental Psychology, 58A,* 193–233.

Hernandez, C. (2010). Neuroimaging: The future of marketing. *Smart Planet.* Retrieved from, http://www.smartplanet.com/blog/pure-genius/neuroimaging-the-future-of-marketing/2634

Heskett, J. (2002). *Toothpicks and logos: Design in everyday life.* Oxford, UK: Oxford University Press.

Hines, A., & Bishop, P. (2006). *Thinking About the future: Guidelines for strategic foresight.* (p. 85, 87). Washington, DC: Social Technologies,

Hobday, M., Davies, A., & Prencipe, A. (2005). Systems integration: A core capability of the modern corporation. *Industrial and Corporate Change, 14*(6), 1109–1143.

Hodge, L., & Cox, A. (2010, June). *Channel 4 case study: Using text-based research to uncover key drivers for watching TV programmes.* Paper presented at MRS Mobile Insights Conference 2010, London. Retrieved from, http://www.research-live.com/Journals/1/Files/2010/7/1/Leonie%20Hodge%20and%20Anthony%20Cox.pdf

Hodgson, G. M. (2003). The hidden persuaders: Institutions and individuals in economic theory. *Cambridge Journal of Economics, 27,* 159–175.

Hoekstra, J. C., & Verhoef, P. (2010). *The customer intelligence—Marketing interface: Its effect on firm performance.* [Working paper] University of Groningen, The Netherlands.

Hofmann, O., Menti, M., & Noyce, D. (2003, January). *Txt message surveys: Return to sender?* Paper presented at ESOMAR Technovate 2003, Cannes.

Hofstadter, D. (2007). *I am a strange loop.* New York, NY: Basic Books.

Horstman, J. (2010). *The Scientific American brave new brain.* San Francisco, CA: Jossey-Bass.

Howe, J. (2006a, June 2). Crowdsourcing: A definition. *Crowdsourcing: Tracking the Rise of the Amateur* (weblog). Retrieved from, http://crowdsourcing.typepad.com/cs/2006/06/crowdsourcing_a.html

Howe, J. (2006b, June 15). Pure, unadulterated (and scalable) crowdsourcing. *Crowdsourcing: Tracking the Rise of the Amateur* (weblog). Retrieved from, http://crowdsourcing.typepad.com/cs/2006/06/pure_unadultera.html

Howe, J. (2006c, June 14). The rise of crowdsourcing. *Wired.* Retrieved from http://www.wired.com/wired/archive/14.06/crowds.html

Huang, T., & Mieghem, V. (2009, January). *Are web visitors really saying something? An empirical study of predicting offline orders and lead times using online click data.* Working paper, Kellogg School of Management, Northwestern University.

Hubert, M., & Kenning, P. (2008). A current overview of consumer neuroscience. *Journal of Consumer Behaviour, 7,* 272–292.

Hughes, S. (2006). P&G: RFID and privacy in the supply chain. In Simpson, G., & Rosenberg, B. (Eds.), *RFID: Application, security, and privacy* (pp. 404–405). New York, NY: Addison-Wesley.

Huston, L., & Sakkab, N. (2006, March 1). Connect and develop: Inside Proctor and Gamble's new model for innovation. Harvard Business Review, 58–66.

Hutton, W. (2010). *Them and us: Changing Britain—Why we need a fair society.* London: Little Brown.

iModerate Research Technologies. (2010). *Demystifying hybrid research.* Retrieved from, http://www.imoderate.com

Inglehart, R. (1997). *Modernization and postmodernization.* Princeton, NJ: Princeton University Press.

International Organization for Standardization. (2009). *Access panels in market, opinion and social research—Vocabulary and service requirements.* ISO 26362: 2009.

Internet Advertising Bureau (IAB)/PricewaterhouseCoopers (PwC). (2009). *Mobile Adspend 2008.* Retrieved from, http://www.iabuk.net/en/1/mobileresearch.html

Investopedia.com. (2011). The greatest investors: Peter Lynch, http://www.investopedia.com/university/greatest/peterlynch.asp

Invoke Solutions. (2008, September 23). Using qual/quant research for faster, more fluid decisions. Esomar Congress Presentation, Montreal, Canada.

Ioannides, A. A. (2006). Magnetoencephalography as a research tool in neuroscience: State of the art. *Neuroscientist, 12*, 524–544.

Ioannides, A. A. (2009). Magnetoencephalograpy (MEG). In Hyder, F. (Ed.), *Dynamic brain imaging: Multi-modal methods and in vivo applications* (Vol. 489, pp. 167–188). Clifton, NJ: Humana Press.

IPSOS. (2010, June). *Time for new thinking: Using mobile to gain greater consumer insights.* Presented at MRS, Mobile Research Conference. London, U.K.

Ivankova, I., & Kawamura, Y. (2010). Emerging trends in the utilization of integrated designs in the social, behavioral and health sciences. In A. Tashakkori & C. Teddie (Eds.), *The Sage handbook of mixed methods in social and behavioral research.* Thousand Oaks, CA: Sage

James, J. M., & Bolstein, R. (1992). Large monetary incentives and their effect on mail survey response rates. *Public Opinion Quarterly, 56*, 442–453.

Jenkins, H. (2006). *Convergence Culture: Where Old and New Media Collide.* New York: New York University Press.

Johnson, A. J., & Conry, S. (2010, June). *Mobile research: New platform, new thinking.* Paper presented at CASRO Technology Conference 2010. Retrieved from, http://www.ipsos.fr/sites/default/files/attachments/survey_apps.pdf

Johnson, E. J., & Goldstein, D. (2003, November 21). Do defaults save lives? *Science, 302*(5649), 1338-1339. DOI: 10.1126/science.1091721. Retrieved from, http://www.sciencemag.org/content/302/5649/1338.short

Johnston, G. (2009). *Ethnography: Your guide to doing it right.* Retrieved, from http://www.aipmm.com/html/newsletter/archives/000362.php

Kaden, R., & Linda G. (2009). *MORE Guerrilla Marketing Research: Asking the right people, the right questions, the right way, and effectively using the answers to make more money.* London: Kogan Page.

Kahneman, D., Slovic, P., & Tversky, A. (1982). *Judgment under uncertainty: Heuristics and biases.* New York, NY: Cambridge University Press.

Kaplan, R. S., & Norton, D. P. (1996). *The balanced scorecard: Translating strategy into action.* Cambridge, MA: Harvard Business Press.

Kaplan, R., & Norton, D. (2000). The strategy focused organization. *Harvard Business Review*, Retrieved from http://hbswk.hbs.edu/item/1746.html

Kahneman, D., Knetsch, J. L., & Thaler, R. H. (2001, winter). Anomalies: The endowment effect, loss aversion, and status quo bias. *The Journal of Economic Perspectives, 5*(1), 193–206.

Kahneman, D., & Tversky, A. (1979). Prospect theory: An analysis of decision under risk. *Econometrica, 47*(2), 263–292.

Katz, A. (2010). *Building your own brand foundation to drive your business and your brand.* Retrieved from, http://www.continuinged.ku.edu/programs/brand_foundation/webinar.php

Kearon, J., & Earls, M. (2009). *Me-to-we research.* ESOMAR Congress. Retrieved from http://herd.typepad.com/files/brainjuicer-paper---me-to-we-research-2.pdf

Kelly, G. A. (1955). *The psychology of personal constructs.* New York, NY: Norton

Kenneth, J. H. (1927). An experimental study of affects and associations due to certain odors. *Psychological Monographs 37*, 1–64.

Kenning, P., Plassmann, H., & Ahlert, D. (2007). Consumer neuroscience: Implikationen neurowissenschaftlicher Forschung für das Marketing. *Marketing: ZFP, 29*, 57-68.

Keohane, J. (2011, January 9). The guy who called the big one? Don't listen to him: Inside the paradox of forecasting. *The Boston Globe*, p. 9.

Kidney, R. (Producer), & Luketic, R. (Director). (2001). *Legally blonde* [Motion picture]. USA: MGM.

Kilts, C. J., Schweitzer, J. B., Quinn, C. K., Gross, R. E., Faber, T. L., Muhammad, F., Ely, T. D., et al., (2001). Neural activity related to drug craving in cocaine addiction. *Archives of General Psychiatry, 58,* 334–341.

Kjeldgaard, D., & Askegaard, D. (2004). Consuming modernities: The global youth segment as a site of consumption. *Advances in Consumer Research 31,* 104–105.

Klein, C. (2010). Images are not the evidence in neuroimaging. *British Journal for the Philosophy of Science, 61,* 265–278.

Klimesch, W. (1999). EEG alpha and theta oscillations reflect cognitive and memory performance: a review and analysis. *Brain Research Reviews, 29,* 169–195.

Korzybski, A. (1948). Science and sanity: An introduction to non-Aristotlean systems and general semantics (5th ed.). Englewood, NJ: Institute of General Semantics.

Kotler, P. (2004). *Ten deadly marketing sins: Signs and solutions.* New York, NY: John Wiley & Sons.

Kotler, P., & Keller, K. (2006). *Marketing management* (12th ed.). Upper Saddle River, New Jersey: Pearson.

Kövecses, Z. (2006). *Metaphor in culture: Universality and variation.* Cambridge, MA: Cambridge University Press.

Kozinets, R. (2009). *Netnography: Doing ethnographic research online.* Thousand Oaks, CA: Sage.

Knutson, B., Adams, C. M., Fong, G. W., & Hommer, D. (2001). Anticipation of increasing monetary reward selectively recruits nucleus accumbens. *Journal of Neuroscience, 21, RC159,* 1–5.

Knutson, B., Rick, S., Wimmer, G. E., Prelec, D., & Loewenstein, G. (2007). Neural Predictors of Purchases. *Neuron, 53,* 147–156.

Kringelbach, M. L., de Araujo, I. E. T., & Rolls, E. T. (2004). Taste-related activity in the human dorsolateral prefrontal cortex. *NeuroImage, 21,* 781–788.

Krugman, H. E. (1971). Brain wave measures of media involvement. *Journal of Advertising Research, 11,* 3–9

Kuhnen C. M., & Knutson, B. (2005). The neural basis of financial risk taking. *Neuron, 47,* 763–770.

Kumar, V., Venkatesan, R., Bohling, T., & Beckmann, D. (2008). The power of CLV: Managing customer lifetime value at IBM. *Marketing Science, 27*(4), 585–599.

Kukar-Kinney, & Close, A. (2009). The determinants of consumers' online shopping cart abandonment. *Journal of the Academy of Marketing Science,* 38(2), 240–250.

la Bruna, A., & Rathod, S. (2006). *Questionnaire length and fatigue effects.* SSI White Paper #5. Survey Sampling International.

Lakhani, K., & E. von Hippel, E. (2003). How open source software works: "Free" user-to-user assistance. *Research Policy, 32*(6), 923–943.

Lakoff, G., & Johnson, M. (1980). *Metaphors we live by.* Chicago, IL: University of Chicago Press.

Lassiter, L. (2005). *The Chicago guide to collaborative ethnography.* Chicago, IL: The University of Chicago Press.

Lawless, H. T., & Heymam, H. (1998). *Sensory evaluation of food: Principles and practices.* New York, NY: Chapman & Hall.

Lederer, R. (2008). *Quality progress: The client's guide to rapid improvement of online research.* Chicago, IL: RFL Communications.

LeDoux, J. (1998). *The emotional brain: The mysterious underpinnings of emotional life.* New York NY: Simon & Schuster.

Lee, N., Broderick, A. J., & Chamberlain, L. (2007). What is neuromarketing?: A discussion and agenda for future research. *International Journal of Psychophysiology, 63,* 199–204.

Lee, M. (2009). *Airline passenger online search and purchasing behavior.* Georgia Institute of Technology. Retrieved from ProQuest dissertations and theses.

Lee, N., Senior, C., Butler, M., & Fuchs, R. (2009). The feasibility of neuroimaging methods in marketing research. *Nature Precedings.* Retrieved from, http://hdl.handle.net/10101/npre.2009.2836.1

Leefling, P., & Hunneman, A. (2010). Modeling market response: Trends and developments. *Marketing, Journal of Resource and Management, 6,* 71–80.

Leeflang, P., Bijmolt, T., van Doorn, J., Hanssens, D., van Heerde, H., Verhoef, P., & Wieringa, J. (2008). Creating lift versus building the base: Current trends in marketing dynamics. *Marketing Science Institute.* Retrieved from, http://www.anderson.ucla.edu/faculty/dominique.hanssens/Website/content/Lift_Base_IJRM_2009.pdf

Lehmann, D., Gupta, S., & Steckel, J. (1998). *Marketing research.* New York, NY: Addison-Wesley.

Lehrer, J. (2008, September). Metaphors of the mind: Why loneliness feels cold and sin feels dirty. *Scientific American Mind.* Retrieved from, http://www.scientificamerican.com/article.cfm?id=metaphors-of-the-mind

Lenskold, J. (2003). *Marketing ROI: The path to campaign customer and corporate profitability.* New York, NY: McGraw-Hill.

Levi Strauss & Co. (2010). *Levi Strauss & Co. Launches dENiZEN™; A New Jeanswear Brand in Asia.* Retrieved http://www.denizen.com/news/press-releases/levi-strauss-co-launches-denizen-a-new-jeanswear-brand-in-asia

Lévy, P. (1997). *Collective intelligence: Mankind's emerging world in cyberspace.* New York, NY: Plenum.

Lewin, K. (1947). Force field analysis and frontiers in group dynamics. *Human Relations, 1*(1), 5–41.

Lextant. (2008). *Case study: Samsung.* Retrieved from, http://www.lextant.com/clients/casestudies/samsung/

Li, S. (2005). Survival analysis. *Marketing Research, 7*(4), 17–23.

Lindstrom, M. (2008). *Buyology: Truth and lies about why we buy.* New York, NY: Doubleday.

Luck, S. J. (2005). *An introduction to the event-related potential technique.* Cambridge, MA: The MIT Press.

Lukavitz, K. (2009). *BCG: Blue chips drop market research ball.* Retrieved from, http://www.mediapost.com/publications/?fa=Articles.showArticle&art_aid=117788&passFuseAction=PublicationsSearch.showSearchReslts&art_searched=bcg&page_number=0

Luo, X. (2005). Quantifying the long-term impact of negative word-of-mouth on cash flows and stock price. *Marketing Science, 28*(1), 148–165.

Ma, Q., Wang, X., Shu, L., & Dai, S. (2008). P300 and categorization in brand extension. *Neuroscience Letters, 431,* 57–61.

Macer, T. (2009, February). *Snapshot of mobile interviewing.* Presented at GlobalPark, Mobile Research 2009 Conference, London, United Kingdom.

Machrone, B. (2003, November). RFID: Promise & peril. *PC Magazine.* Retrieved from, http://www.pcmag.com/article2/0,2817,1369158,00.asp.

Mahajan, V., & Wind, J. (1992). New product models: Practice, shortcomings and desired improvements. *Journal of Product Innovation Management, 9,* 128–139

Marcus, G. E. (1995). Ethnography in/of the world system: The emergence of multi-sited ethnography. *Annual Review of Anthropology, 24,* 95–117.

Marcus, G. E. (2002). Beyond Malinowski and after writing culture: On the future of cultural anthropology and the predicament of ethnography. *The Australian Journal of Anthropology, 13*(2), 191–199.

Marcus, G. E. (2007). How short can fieldwork be? *Social Anthropology, 15*(3), 353–357.

Market Research Society. (2010). *Guidelines for online research: August 2010 Draft.* London, UK: Market Research Society.

Martin-Loeches, M., Sel, A., Jiménez, L., & Castellanos, L. (2009), Encouraging expressions affect the brain and alter visual attention. *PLoS ONE, 4,* e5920.

Maslow, A. (1987). *Motivation and personality.* New York, NY: HarperCollins.

Matthews, R., & Wacker, W. (2008). *What's your story?* Upper Saddle River, NJ: Pearson Education.

May, T. (2009). *The new know: Innovation powered by analytics.* New York, NY: John Wiley & Sons.

McCarthy, C. (2010, June 23). The iPhone reality in Europe: Low overall penetration, enormous impact. *Comscore.* Retrieved from, http://www.comscore.com/ger/Press_Events/Press_Releases/2010/6/The_iPhone_Reality_in_Europe_Low_Overall_Penetration_Enormous_Impact

McCartny, S. (2007). A new way to prevent lost luggage. *Wall Street Journal Online.* Retrieved from, www.volweb.cz/horvitz/os-info/news-feb07-028.html

McClure, S. M., Li, J., Tomlin, D., Cypert, K. S., Montague, L. M., & Montague, P. R. (2004). Neural correlates of behavioral preference for culturally familiar drinks. *Neuron, 44,* 379–387.

McCoy, A. N., & Platt, M. L. (2005). Risk-sensitive neurons in macaque posterior cingulate cortex. *Nature Neuroscience, 8,* 1220–1227.

McCoy, J. (2006). Spot by InnerWireless: A rational solution for healthcare asset tracking. *InnerWireless.* Retrieved from, www.antennason-lin.com/images/whitepapers/innerwireless.pdf

McCracken, G. (2010). How Ford got social marketing right. *Bloomberg BusinessWeek,* Retrieved from http://www.businessweek.com/managing/content/jan2010/ca2010018_445530.htm

McCreary, L. (2008, October). What was privacy? *Harvard Business Review.* Retrieved from, http://www.ncbi.nlm.nih.gov/pubmed/18822675

McGraw, T. (2007). *Prophet of innovation: Joseph Schumpeter and creative destruction.* Cambridge, MA: Harvard University Press.

McKee, R. (1998). *Story: Substance, structure, style, and the principles of screenwriting.* London, UK: Methuen.

McLuhan, M. (1964). *Understanding media: The extensions of man.* New York, NY: McGraw Hill.

McNichol, T. (2007). The wales rules for Web 2.0. *Business 2.0.* Retrieved from, http://money.cnn.com/galleries/2007/biz2/0702/gallery.wikia_rules.biz2/index.html

Medina, J. (2008). *Brain rules.* Seattle, WA: Pear Press.

Mehrabian, A. (1971). *Silent messages.* Belmont, CA: Wadsworth.

Menin, A., & Wilcox, J. B. (1994). USER: A scale to measure use of market research. *Marketing Science Institute Technical Working Paper,* 94–108.

Meilgaard, M, Civille, G. V., & Carr, B. T. (1999). *Sensory evaluation techniques.* Boca Raton, FL: CRC Press.

Meiselman, H. L., & Schutz, H. G. (2003). History of food acceptance research in the U.S. Army. Lincoln, NE: University of Nebraska-Lincoln.

Milgram, S. (1974). *Obedience to authority: An experimental view.* New York, NY: Harper & Row.

Miller, C. (2011, January 24). Now at Starbucks: Buy a latte by waving your phone. *The New York Times,* p. B5.

Miller, George. (1956). The magical number is seven, plus or minus two. *Psychological Review, 63*(2). Retrieved from, http://psychclassics.yorku.ca/Miller/

Miller, Greg. (2008). Growing pains for fMRI. *Science, 320,* 1412–1414.

Miller, S. I., & Gatta, J. L. (2006). The use of mixed methods models and designs in the human sciences: Problems and prospects. *Quality and Quantity, 40,* 595–610.

Mintz, O., Currim, I., & Jeliazkov, I. (2010). *Consumer search and propensity to buy.* Retrieved from, http://www.economics.uci.edu/~ivan/MCJ2010.pdf

Moe, W., & Fader, P. (2004). Capturing evolving visit behavior in clickstream data. *Journal of Interactive Marketing, 18*(1), 5–19.

Montgomery, A., Li, S., Srinivasan, K., & Liechty, J. (2004). Modeling online browsing and path analysis using clickstream data. *Marketing Science, 23*(4), 579–595.

Moore, G. (1965). Cramming more components onto integrated circuits. *Electronics Magazine, 38*(8). Retrieved from, ftp://download.intel.com/museum/Moores_Law/Articles-press_Releases/Gordon_Moore_1965_Article.pdf

Moore, K. (2005). Maybe it is like brain surgery. *Marketing Magazine, 110*(5), 12.

Moskowitz, H. R. (1985). *New directions in product testing and sensory evaluation of food.* Westport, CT: Food and Nutrition Press.

Moskowitz, H. R. (2000). Sensory driven product development: Optimization approaches and analyses. *Australasian Journal of Market Research, 8,* 31–52.

Moskowitz, H. R. (2004). Just about right (JAR) directionality and the wandering sensory unit. In data analysis workshop: Getting most out of just-about-right data. *Food Quality and Preference, 15,* 891–899.

Moskowitz, H., & Gofman, A. (2007). *Selling blue elephants: How to make great products that people want before they even know they want them.* Upper Saddle River, NJ: Wharton School Publishing.

Moskowitz, H. R., Wolfe, K., & Beck, C. (1978). Sweetness and acceptance optimization in cola-flavored beverages using combinations of artificial sweetener. *Journal of Food Quality, 2,* 17–26.

Muehllehner, G., & Karp, J. S. (2006). Positron emission tomography. *Physics in Medicine and Biology, 51,* R117–R137.

Murray, E. A., O'Doherty, J. P., & Schoenbaum, G. (2007). What we know and do not know about the functions of the orbitofrontal cortex after 20 years of cross-species studies. *Journal of Neuroscience, 27,* 8166–8169.

Myers, T. (2003). RFID shelf-life monitoring helps resolve disputes. *RFID Journal.* Retrieved from, http://www.rfidjournal.com/article/articleview/3357/1/128/

Neale, M. (2008). *Habit: The 95% of behavior marketers ignore.* Upper Saddle River, New Jersey: Pearson Education.

Neff, J. (2008, September). The end of consumer surveys? *Advertising Age.* Retrieved from, http://adage.com/article?article_id=130964

NeuroFocus. (2011). *Advertising.* Retrieved from http://www.neurofocus.com/Advertise.htm

Nolan, J. M., Schultz, W., Cialdini, R., Goldstein, N., & Griskevicius, V. (2008, July). Normative social influence is underdetected. *Personality and Social Psychology, 34*(7), 913–923.

Norretranders, T. (1999). *The user illusion: Cutting consciousness down to size.* New York, NY: Penguin Books.

Northrop, F. S. C. (1960). *The meeting of east and west.* New York, NY: Macmillan.

Nosek, B. A. (2005). Moderators of the relationship between implicit and explicit evaluation. *Journal of Experimental Psychology, 134*(4), 565–584.

Nosek, B. A., Smyth, F. L., Hansen, J. J., Devos, T., Lindner, N. M., Ranganath, K. A., et al. (2007). Pervasiveness and correlates of implicit attitudes and stereotypes. *European Review of Social Psychology, 18,* 36–88.

Novak, T. P., & MacEvoy, B. (1990). On comparing alternative segmentation schemes: The list of values (LOV) and values and life styles (VALS). *The Journal of Consumer Research, 17,* 105–109.

Noyce, D., & Dodgson, S. (2010, September). Mobile-based research: Options and best practices. [Webinar]. Retrieved from, http://www.skopos-mr.co.uk/articles-papers.php

Noyce, D. (2011, July). Relevance, relevance, relevance! A call to arms (hands, fingers & thumbs) for mobile research. [Video]. Retrieved from, http://vimeo.com/27792101

O'Connor, M. C. (2007a, March 27). Display-maker integrates RFID for security, inventory apps. *RFID Journal.* Retrieved from, http://www.rfidjournal.com/article/view/3173

O'Connor, M. C. (2007b, January 15). Greek RFID pilot collects garbage. *RFID Journal.* Retrieved from, http://www.rfidjournal.com/article/view/2973

Odlyzko, A. (2010, fall). The manifold problems of technology forecasting. *Phi Beta Kappa Key Reporter,* p. 7. Retrieved from http://www.dtc.umn.edu/~odlyzko/doc/pbk2010.txt

Office of Management and Budget. (2009). *A new era of responsibility, Proposed budget.* Retrieved from, www.budget.gov.

O'Mahony, M. (1995). Who told you the triangle test was simple? *Food Quality and Preference, 6*(4), 227–238.

O'Mahony, S., & Ferraro, F. (2007). The emergence of governance in an open source community. *Academy of Management Journal, 50*(5), 1079–1106.

Onwuegbuzie, A. J., & Collins, K. M. T. (2007). A typology of mixed methods sampling designs in social science research. *Qualitative Report, 12*(2), 281–315.

Ostrow, A. (2009, Ferary, 19). *82 million user generated content creators and counting.* Retrieved from, http://mashable.com/2009/02/19/user-generated-content-growth

Otter, T., Allenby, G. M, & van Zaldt, T. (2008). An integrated model of discrete choice and response time. *Journal of Marketing, 19*(3/4), 593–607).

Packard, V. (1957). *Hidden persuaders.* New York, NY: David Mackay.

Paddison, G. (2010). *Movie goers 2010.* Stradella Road Consultants. Retrieved from, http://www.stradellaroad.com/what-we-do/

Park, R. (2008). Unlocking the power of enterprise segmentation. [Webinar]. *Merkle Insight Inc.* Retrieved from, http://www.merkleinc.com/wmspage.cfm?parm1=687

Patnaiak, D., & Mortensen, P. (2009). *Wired to care.* Upper Saddle River, New Jersey: FT Press.

Peeters, J. P. (2005, April). Ask the experts: John Peeters, pres & founder, Gen Tag. *Contactless News.* Retrieved from, http://www.rfidnews.org/2005/04/03/ask-the-experts-john-peeters-president-and-founder-gentag/

Penn, D. (2008, April). *Metaphors matter.* Paper presented at the ARF Conference, New York, NY.

Petabyte. (n.d.).*Wikipedia.* Retrieved from, http://en.wikipedia.org/wiki/Petabyte#cite_note-6

Pettit, R. (2010). *The ARF's quality enhancement process.* New York, NY: The Advertising Research Foundation.

Pettit, R. C., & Monster, R. W. (2002). *Market research in the internet age: Leveraging the internet for marketing measurement and consumer insight.* Singapore, Asia: John Wiley & Sons.

Pine, B. J., II. (1999). *The experience economy: Work is theatre & every business a stage.* Boston, MA: Harvard Business School Press.

Pink, D. H. (2005). *A whole new mind: Why right brainers will rule the future.* London, UK: Riverhead.

Pink, S. (2004). *Home truths: Gender, domestic objects and everyday life.* Oxford, NY: Berg.

Pink, S. (2005). *Doing visual ethnography.* Thousand Oaks, CA: Sage.

Pink, S. (2009). *Doing sensory ethnography.* Thousand Oaks, CA: Sage.

Pinker, S., (2007). *The stuff of thought: Language as a window into human nature* (pp 332–333). United Kingdom: Allen Lane.

Pisano G., & Verganti, R. (2008). Which kind of collaboration is right for you? *Harvard Business Review, 86*(12), 78-86.

Plambeck, J. (2010, August 8). A magazine tests neuromarketing. *The New York Times.* Retrieved from, http://www.nytimes.com/2010/08/09/business/media/09neuro.html

Plassmann, H., O'Doherty, J., Shiv, B., & Rangel, A. (2008). Marketing actions can modulate neural representations of experienced pleasantness. *PNAS, 105,* 1050–1054.

Poldrack, R. A. (2006). Can cognitive processes be inferred from neuroimaging data? *Trends in Cognitive Sciences, 10,* 59–63.

Poynter, R. (2010). *The handbook of online and social media research: Tools and techniques for market researchers.* Chichester, UK: John Wiley & Sons.

Prince, M., Manolis, C., & Tratner, S. (2009). Qualitative analysis and the construction of causal models. *Qualitative Market Research, 12*(2), 130–152.

Rahtz, D. R., & Moore, D. L. (1986). Q-Tips: Using qualitative and quantitative techniques in tandem to assure valid manipulations. *Advances in Consumer Research, 13,* 291–296.

Rajewski, G. (2007, June). Not just for retailers, RFID helps track rainforest wildlife. *WIRED.* Retrieved from, www .wired.com/gadgets/miscellaneous/news/2007/06/rfid_pigs

Ramachaandran, A. (2010). *Crowdsourcing.* Retrieved from http://crowdsourcingexamples.pbworks.com

Ramaswamy, V., Raghunathan, T. E., Cohen, S. H., & Ozcan, K. (1999). A multiple imputation approach for the analysis of missing data in marketing research. Working paper, University of Michigan.

Rampell, C. (2009, March 11). Great recession: A brief etymology. *Economix Blog,* Retrieved from, http://economix .blogs.nytimes.com/2009/03/11/great-recession-a-brief-etymology/

Rampell, C. (2011, January 11). The "new normal" is actually pretty old. *Economix Blog.* Retrieved from http://economix .blogs.nytimes.com/tag/american-economic-association/.

Rangarajan, T. S., & Vijaykumar, A. (2005). *RFID in clinical trials.* Retrieved from, www.tcs.com/SiteCollectionDocuments/ White%20Papers/RFID%20in%20Clinical%20Trials.pdf.

Rasco, B. A., & Bledsoe, G. E. (2005). *Bioterrorism and food safety.* New York, NY: CRC Press.

Rathjen, G. (2008, December). No more begging for a seat at the table. *Quirk's Marketing Research Review, XXII*(12), 68.

Reynolds, T. J., & Craddock, A. B. (1988). The application of the MECCAS model to the development and assessment of advertising strategy: A case study. In T. J. Reynolds & J. C. Olson (Eds.), *Understanding consumer decision making: The means-end approach to marketing and advertising strategy* (pp. 163–184). Hillsdale, NJ: Erlbaum Associates.

Reynolds, T. J., & Gutman, J. (1988). Laddering theory, method, analysis, and interpretation. *Journal of Advertising Research, 28,* 11–31.

RFIDupdate.com. (2007, May). *RFID invention to detect esophageal reflux.* Retrieved from, www.rfidupdate.com/articles/ index.php?id+1371

Rolfe, G. (2009, March). *The future for mobile research: What will the landscape look like in two years time?* Kantar at Mobile Research Conference, London, UK.

Rifkin, J. (2009). *The empathic civilization: The race to global consciousness in a world of crisis.* London, UK: Penguin Books.

RightNow Technologies. (2006). *Knowledge at the point of action.* Retrieved from, http://www.rightnow.com/files/ whitepapers/Knowledge_at_the_Point_of_Action.pdf

Rogers, C. (1961). *On becoming a person: A therapist's view of psychotherapy.* London, UK: Constable & Robinson.

Rolls, E. T. (2004). The functions of the orbitofrontal cortex. *Brain and Cognition, 55,* 11–29.

Rosenfeld, J. P. (2005). Brain fingerprinting: A critical analysis. *The Scientific Review of Mental Health Practice, 4,* 20–37.

Rothschild, M. L,. & Hyun, Y. J. (1990). Predicting memory for components of TV commercials from EEG. *Journal of Consumer Research, 16,* 472–478.

Rothschild, M. L., Hyun, Y. J., Reeves, B., Thorson, E., & Goldstein, R. (1988). Hemispherically lateralized EEG as a response to television commercials. *Journal of Consumer Research, 15,* 185–198.

Rubin, H., & Rubin, I. (1995). *Qualitative interviewing: The art of hearing data.* Thousand Oaks, CA: Sage.

Rubinson, J. (2009). *Transforming consumer research.* Retrieved from, http://www.slideshare.net/joelrubinson/trans forming-consumer-research-warc-conference-rubinson-vf

Rubinson, J. (2010, October 15). *The future of consumer insights.* Retrieved from, http://www.slideshare.net/joelrubinson/ the-future-of-consumer-insights

Rumelhart, D. E., & McClelland, J. L. (1986). On learning the past tenses of English verbs. In J. L. McClelland, D. E. Rumelhart, and the PDP Research Group (Eds.), *Parallel distributed processing: Psychological and biological models* (Vol. 2). Cambridge, MA: MIT Press

Russell, D. A., & Winterbottom, M. (1972). *Classical literary criticism.* Oxford, UK: Oxford University Press.

Rust, R. T., Zeithaml, V. A., & Lemon, K. N. (2000). *Driving customer equity.* New York, NY: The Free Press.

Salari, S. (2008). *Ethnographic panels.* Retrieved September 12, 2010, from, http://www.youtube.com/watch?v=bPP4 lqxB7e8&feature=related

Salari, S. (2009). *iPhone app for ethnographic research.* Retrieved September 12, 2010, from, http://www.insights qualitativos.com/2009/12/iphone-app-for-ethnographic-research.html

Salari, S. (2010). *Using mobiles to uncover new ethnographic insights into consumer behavior.* Retrieved September 12, 2010, from, http://www.research-live.com/Journals/1/Files/2010/7/1/Sieamack%20Salari.pdf

Salter, C. (2009, July/August). Why America is addicted to Olive Garden. *Fast Company. 137,* 102–121.

Sanfrey, A. G., Rilling, J. K., Aronson, J. A., Nystrom, L. E., & Cohen, J. D. (2003). The neural basis of economic decision-making in the ultimatum game, *Science, 300,* 1755–1758.

Schoenberg, S. O., Reiser, M. F., Meindl, T. M., & Poeppel, E. (2006). MRI shows brains respond better to name brands. *RSNA.* Retrieved from http://www.rsna.org/rsna/media/pr2006-2/name_brands-2.cfm

Schkade, D. A., & Kahneman, D. (1998). Does living in California make people happy? *Psychological Science,* 9, 340–346.

Schloter, P., & Hamid A. (n.d.).*Wireless RFID networks for real-time customer relationship management.* Paper Presented at the First International Workshop on RFID and Ubiquitous Sensor Networks. Retrieved from, http://dl.ifip.org/index.php/lncs/article/view/25456

Schraidt, M. (2009). Penalty analysis or mean drop analysis. *American Society for Testing and Materials, Digital Library/Manuals and Monographs/MNL63-EB/MNL11493M.*

Science Spectra. (2000). The case for smart luggage. *21,* 12–14.

Selden, L., & Colvin, G. (2003). M & A needn't be a losers game. *Harvard Business Review, 81*(6), 71–79. Retrieved from, http://www.ncbi.nlm.nih.gov/pubmed/12800718

Senior, C., Smyth, H., Cooke, R., Shaw, R. L., & Peel, E. (2007). Mapping the mind for the modern market researcher. *Qualitative Market Research, 10,* 153–167.

Shefrin, H. (2002). *Beyond greed and fear: Understanding behavioral finance and the psychology of investing.* Boston, MA: Harvard Business School Press.

Shepard, B. (2006). The growing market for marketing researchers. *Wisconsin Business Alumni Update.* Retrieved from, http://www.bus.wisc.edu/update/winter06/marketing_research.asp

Shore, B. (1996). *Culture in mind: Cognition, culture, and the problem of meaning.* New York, NY: Oxford University Press.

Shweder, R. A. (1997). The surprise of ethnography. *Ethos, 25*(2), 152–63.

Slutsky, I. (2010). Chief listeners use technology to track, sort company mentions. *Ad Age Digital.* Retrieved from, http://adage.com/article/digital/marketing-chief-listeners-track-brand-mentions/145618/

Small, D. M., Gitelman, D. R., Gregory, M. D., Nobre, A. C., Parrish T. B., & Mesulam, M. M. (2003). The posterior cingulate and medial prefrontal cortex mediate the anticipatory allocation of spatial attention. *NeuroImage, 18,* 633–641.

Smith, D. V. L. (2010, May 19). *Continuing the market research success story. A report on an ESOMAR debate held in London.* Retrieved from, http://www.brainjuicer.com/xtra/ESOMAR_Debate.pdf

Smith, J. W. (2010). *Leading by looking ahead.* Keynote speech at Marketing Society Annual Conference, London, England, United Kingdom. Retrieved from, http://blog.marketing-soc.org.uk/2010/11/judie-lannon-annual-conference-report-j-walker-smith/

Smith, J. W., & Clurman, A. (2007). *Generation ageless: How baby boomers are changing the way we live . . . and they're just getting started.* New York, NY: Collins.

Smith, S. M., & Albaum, G. S. (2010). *An introduction to marketing research.* Retrieved from, http://www.qualtrics.com/university/wp-content/uploads/2010/05/Chapter%2000%20Title%20Page-TOC-Preface.pdf

Smith, B., & Raspin, P. (2008). *Creating market insight* (pp. 15–20). West Sussex, England: John Wiley & Sons.

Snaith, T. (2010, June). *Securing foundations, defining the future.* Paper presented at MRS Mobile Insights Conference 2010, London. Available at http://www.research-live.com/Journals/1/Files/2010/7/1/Tim%20Snaith.pdf

Sorensen, H. (2009). *Inside the mind of the shopper.* Upper Saddle River, NJ. Wharton School Publishing.

South Lanarkshire Council. (2007). *Speed signs reduce you to a smile.* Scotland, UK.

Spanos, Y. E., Zaralis, G., & Lioukas, S. (2003). Strategy and industry effects on profitability: Evidence from Greece. *Strategic Management Journal, 25*(2), 139–165.

Spence, M. T., & Brucks, M. (1997, May). The moderating effects of problem characteristics on experts and novices' judgments. *Journal of Marketing Research, 34*(2), 233–247.

Srinivasan, S., VanHuele, M., & Pauwels, K. (2010). Mind-set metrics in market response models: An integrative approach. *Journal of Marketing Research, 47,* 672–684.

Stevens, S. S. (1975). *Psychophysics: An introduction to its perceptual, neural and Social prospects.* New York, NY: John Wiley and Sons.

Stalk, G., & Hout, T. M. (1990). *Competing against time: How time-based competition is reshaping global markets.* New York, NY: The Free Press.

Sthanunathan, S. (2010, July/August). Don't explain the past, predict the future, in *Admap*.

Stoll, M., Baecke, S., & Kenning, P. (2008). What they see is what they get? An fMRI-study on neural correlates of attractive packaging. *Journal of Consumer Behaviour, 7*, 342–359.

Strohmetz, D. B., Rind, B., Fisher, R., & Lynn, M. (2002, February). Sweetening the till: The use of candy to increase restaurant tipping. *Journal of Applied Social Psychology, 32*(2), 300–309.

Sugden, G. (2010, June). *Measuring customer satisfaction using an SMS feedback tool to optimise future customer experiences*. MRS Mobile Insights Conference 2010, London. Retrieved from, http://www.research-live.com/Journals/1/Files/2010/7/1/Gavin%20Sugden.pdf

Surowiecki, J. (2004). *The wisdom of crowds: Why the many are smarter than the few and how collective wisdom shapes business, economies, societies, and nations*. New York, NY: Doubleday.

Sutherland, R. (2010, October). *Why advertising should care about behavioral economics—Red hot or red herring*. Geneva, Switzerland: IPA.

Sunderland, P. L., & Denny, R. M. (2007). *Doing anthropology in consumer research*. Walnut Creek, CA: Left Coast Press.

Swedberg, C. (2007a, March). New RFID system takes security to heart. *RFID Journal*. Retrieved from, http://www.rfidjournal.com/article/view/3170

Swedberg, C. (2007b, January). Mitsukoshi and Shiseido test tagged cosmetics. *RFID Journal*. Retrieved from, http://www.rfidjournal.com/article/view/3011

Swedberg, C. (2007c, March). OATSystems launches solutions for tracking in-store product promotions. *RFID Journal*. Retrieved from, http://www.rfidjournal.com/article/view/3164

Swedberg, C. (2007d, April). RFID helps keep avocados fresh. *RFID Journal*. Retrieved from, http://www.rfidjournal.com/article/view/3188

Swedberg, C. (2009, November). Eeliad project tracks eels odyssey. *RFID Journal*. Retrieved from, http://www.rfidjournal.com/article/view/537

SYSTAT (2008). *SYSTAT 12 User Manual*. Richmond,CA: SYSTAT Software, Inc., a subsidiary of Cranes Software International Ltd.

Tapscott, D., & Williams, A. D. (2006). *Wikinomics: How mass collaboration changes everything*. New York, NY: Portfolio Books.

Tapscott, D., & Williams, A. D. (2010). *Macrowikinomics: Rebooting business and the world*. New York, NY Penguin.

Tarran, B. (2009). New P&G chief talks up value of research in innovation. Retrieved from, http://www.research-live.com/news/financial/new-pg-chief-talks-up-value-of-research-in-innovation/4000617.article

Terranova, T. (2004). *Network culture: politics for the information age*. London, England: Pluto Press.

Telser, L. G. (1962). The demand for branded goods as estimated from consumer panel data. *The Review of Economics and Statistics, 44*(3), 300–324.

Tetlock, P. (2005). *Expert political judgment: How good is it? How can we know?* Princeton, NJ: Princeton University Press.

Thaler, R. H., & Sunstein, C. R. (2008). *Nudge*. New Haven, CT: Yale University Press.

The Economist. (2010a, March 4). Gendercide: The worldwide war on baby girls. Retrieved from, http://www.economist.com/node/15636231

The Economist. (2010b, September 4). Untangling the social web (p. 13).

The Hartman Group. (2011, January). *A Hartman Group white paper: The new frugality? The sky that never fell*. Retrieved from, http://www.hartman-group.com/hartbeat/the-new-frugality-the-sky-that-never-fell

The London Collaborative. (2009, August). *The capital ambition guide to behavior change*. Retrieved from,

The London Collaborative. (2009, August). *The capital ambition guide to behavior change*.

Thompson, B. (2008). *Customer experience management: The value of "moments of truth."* Retrieved from, http://retaintogain.com/pdf/customer_exp1.pdf

Toffler, A. (1970). *Future shock*. New York, NY: Random House.

Totman, P. (2010, March). *The Rashomon effect: An exploration of the meaning of qualitative analysis*. Paper presented at the MRS Conference Research 2010: The Annual Conference/festival of ideas, innovation and inspiration, Park Plaza Riverbank, London.

Tourangeau, R, Rips, L. J., & Rasinski, K. (2000). *The psychology of survey response*. Cambridge, MA: Cambridge University Press

Turner, M. (1996). *The literary mind: The origins of thought and language*. Oxford, UK: Oxford University Press.

U.S. Census Bureau. (2008). An older and more diverse population by midcentury. Retrieved from, http://www.census.gov/newsroom/releases/archives/population/cb08-123.html

U.S. Census Bureau. (2011). *Geographic areas reference manual* (GARM). Retrieved from http://www.census.gov/geo/www/GARM/Ch11GARM.pdf

USA Today. (2007). *How the internet took over.* Retrieve from, USAToday, http://www.usatoday.com/tech/top25-internet.htm

Van Bruggen, G., & Wierenga, B. (2006). Marketing management support systems and their implications for marketing research. In R. Grover & M. Vriens (Eds.), *Handbook of marketing research* (pp. 646–667). Thousand Oaks, CA: Sage.

van Ossenbruggen, R., Vonk, T., & Willems, P. (2006). *Results Dutch online panel comparison study* (NOVPO). Retrieved from, www.nopvo.nl

Vedrashko, I. (2007, November 14). The elusive advertising clutter. *Hill Holliday Blog.* Retrieved from, http://www.hhcc.com/blog/2007/11/the-elusive-advertising-clutter/

Vigna, S. D., & Malmendier, U. (2006). Paying not to go to the gym. *The American Economic Review, 96*(3), 694–719.

Vriens, M. (2003, winter). Strategic research design. *Marketing Research*, 21–25.

Vriens, M., Franses, P. H., & Grigsby, M. (2002). Time series models for advertising tracking data. *Canadian Journal of Marketing Research, 20*(2), 62–71.

Vriens, M., & R. Grover, R. (2006). Structuring market research departments and process for optimal impact. In R. Grover & M. Vriens (Eds.), *Handbook of marketing research* (pp. 18–31). Thousand Oaks, CA: Sage.

Vriens, M., & Sinharay, S. (2006). Dealing with missing data in surveys and databases. In R. Grover & M. Vriens (Eds.), *Handbook of marketing research* (pp. 178–191). Thousand Oaks, CA: Sage.

Vriens, M., van der Scheer, H., Hoekstra, J. C., & Bult, J. R. (1998). Conjoint experiments for direct mail optimization. *European Journal of Marketing, 32*(¾), 323–339.

Vriens, M., & Verhulst, R. (2008, winter). Unleashing hidden insights. *Marketing Research*, 13–17.

Waaser, E., Dahneke, M., Pekkarinen, M., & Weissel, M. (2004). How you slice it: Smarter segmentation for your salesforce. *Harvard Business Review.* Retrieved from, http://hbr.org/product/how-you-slice-it-smarter-segmentation-for-your-sal/an/R0403H-PDF-ENG

Waksberg, J. (1978). Sampling methods for random digit dialing. *Journal of the American Statistical Society, 73*(361), 40–46.

Waldmeir, P. (2010). China bubble erodes preference for sons. *Financial Times.* Retrieved from, http://www.ft.com/cms/s/0/d7749a7a-e5eb-11df-af15-00144feabdc0.html#axzz16tuIT7IQ

Walker, B. A., & Olson, J. C. (1991). Means-end chains: Connecting products with self. *Journal of Business Research, 22*, 111–118.

Wan, J., Shu, H., Huang, S., Fiebor, B., Chen, I. H., Petrenko, V. A., & Chin, B. A. (2007). *Bacterial sensors for food.* Retrieved from, http://www.reeis.usda.gov/web/crisprojectpages/206993.html

Wasserman, E. (2007, February 19). RFID is in fashion. *RFID Journal.* Retrieved from, http://www.rfidjournal.com/article/purchase/2408

Web Analytics Association. (n.d.). About us. Retrieved from http://www.webanalyticsassociation.org/?page=aboutus.

Weber, T. (2010). *Mobile Innovation, Usage and Trends.* Presented at the Market Research Society (MRS), Mobile Research Conference, The Nielsen Company 2010, London, United Kingdom

Webber, H. H. (1944). The consumer panel: A method of media evaluation. *The Journal of Marketing, 9*(2), 137–140.

Wedel, M., & Kamakura,W. A. (2000). *Market segmentation: Conceptual and methodological foundations.* Dordrecht, Netherlands: Kluwer Academic.

Wells, W. D. (1975). Psychographics: A critical review. *Journal of Marketing Research, 12*, 196–213.

Wernerfelt, B. (1984). A resource based view of the firm. *Strategic Management Journal, 5*, 171–180.

Wernerfelt, B. (1989). From critical resources to corporate strategy. *Journal of General Management, 14*, 4–12.

Wessel, R. (2007, June 1). Jena University Hospital prescribes RFID to reduce medication errors. *RFID Journal.* Retrieved from, http://www.rfidjournal.com/article/view/3360

WhatIf. (2002). *Sticky wisdom.* West Sussix: Capstone.

Wiesel, T., Pauwels, K., & Arts, J. (2010). *Marketing's profit impact: Quantifying online and offline funnel progression.* [Working Paper]. University of Groningen, The Netherlands.

Williams, A. (2010). Macrowinkinomics. [Weblog]. Retrieved from http://anthonydwilliams.com/books/

Williamson, O. E. (1979). Transaction-cost economics: The governance of contractual relations. *Journal of Law and Economics, 22*(2), 233–261.

Wilson, A., & Calder, R. (2006, February). *Powerful brands: Learning from the Greeks.* Paper presented at ESOMAR *Brand Matters* conference, New York, New York.

Wilson, A., Johns, R., Miller, K., & Pentecost R. (2010). *Marketing research: An integrated approach.* Frenchs Forest, NSW, Australia: Pearson.

Wind, J., Green, P. E., Shifflet, D., & Scarbrough, M. (1989). Courtyard by Marriott: Designing a hotel facility with consumer-based marketing. *Interfaces, 19*(1), 25–46.

Wittenbraker, J. (2010, August). Now and for the future. *Quirk's Marketing Research Review*, pp. 52–57. Retrieved from, http://www.quirks.com/pdf/201008_quirks.pdf

Womelsdorf, T., & Fries, P. (2007). The role of neuronal synchronization in selective attention. *Current Opinion in Neurobiology, 17,* 154–160.

Wood, F., Parry, B., Breeze, J., & Wormald, T. (2009, September). *Building citizen dialogue: New approaches for involving the citizen in policy making.* Paper presented at ESOMAR CONGRESS, Montreux, Switzerland.

Wood, O. (2010). Using an emotional model to measure ad effectiveness. *Admap, 45*(1), 40–41.

Yahoo. (2010, March). *Appetite: The hunger for mobile media.* Retrieved from, http://pdfcast.org/download/yahoo-research-rsquo-appetite-rsquo-the-hunger-for-mobile-media.pdf

Yankelovich, D. (1964). New criteria for market segmentation. *Harvard Business Review, 42,* 1.

Yankelovich, D., & Meer, D. (2006). Rediscovering market segmentation. *Harvard Business Review, 84*(2), 122–131.

Yeager, D. S., Krosnick, J. A., Chang, L. C., Javitz, H. S, Levindusky, M. S., Simpser, A., & Wang, R. (2009). *Comparing the accuracy of RDD telephone surveys and internet surveys conducted with probability and non-probability samples.* Palo Alto, CA: Stanford University.

Yoon C., Gonzalez, R., & Bettman, J. R. (2009). Using fMRI to inform marketing research: Challenges and opportunities. *Marketing Research, 46*(1), 17–19.

Young, L., Bechara, A., Tranel, D., Damasio, H., Hauser, M., & Damasio, A. (2010). Damage to ventromedial prefrontal cortex impairs judgment of harmful intent. *Neuron, 65*(6), 845–851. doi:10.1016/j.neuron.2010.03.003.

Yunes, T.H., Napolitano, D. Scheller-Wolf, A., & Tayur, S. (2007). Building efficient product portfolios at John Deere and Company. *Operations Research, 55*(4), 615–629.

Zaltman, G. (1997, November). Rethinking market research: Putting people back in. *Journal of Marketing Research, 34,* 424–437.

Zaltman, G. (2003). *How customers think.* Boston, MA: Harvard Business School Press.

Zaltman, G., & Coulter, R.H . (1995, July/August). Seeing the voice of the customer: Metaphor-based advertising research. *Journal of Advertising Research, 35,* 35–51.

Zaltman, G., & Kosslyn, S. M. (2000). *Neuroimaging as a marketing tool.* Retrieved from, http://www.freepatentsonline.com/6099319.html

Zaltman, G., & Zaltman, L. (2008). *Marketing metaphoria.* Boston, MA: Harvard Business School Press.

Zoltners, A., & Lorimer, S. (2000). Sales territory alignment: An overlooked productivity tool. *Journal of Personal Selling & Sales Management. 20*(3), 139–150.

Zuckerberg, M. (2010). 500 million stories. The Facebook Blog. Retrieved from, http://www.facebook.com/blog.php?post=409753352130

Index

About the Editors

Bob Kaden is the author of *Guerrilla Marketing Research*, coauthor of *MORE Guerrilla Marketing Research*, and President of The Kaden Company, a marketing research company. He has been in marketing research his entire career, spending many years in the research departments at various Chicago advertising agencies and, in the early 1970s, becoming President of Goldring & Company. Goldring became one of Chicago's premier research suppliers, employing a staff of more than 40 marketing research professionals. He and his partners sold Goldring to MAI, plc, a U.K. financial and market research conglomerate, in 1989. In 1992, he started The Kaden Company and continues to serve his marketing research clients.

Bob has worked extensively in the retail, banking, credit card, food, consumer package goods, health care, educational, toy, technology, and direct marketing industries. He has been involved in more than 3,500 focus group and survey studies, and has pioneered many unique quantitative and qualitative market research approaches.

Over the years, he has written numerous articles on marketing research and new product development approaches for a variety of business websites and professional journals. He speaks frequently to business and university audiences on a wide range of research topics, with particular attention to the "Guerrilla" approach to marketing research. He has lectured widely and conducted numerous virtual seminars. His speaking engagements have taken him to many U.S. cities, as well as London, Paris, and Moscow, where he addressed audiences on the use of attitude research in the direct marketing industry as well as on the application of creative problem-solving principles to marketing research problems. Additionally, he has lectured as adjunct professor in the Medill Graduate Program at Northwestern University.

Gerald Linda, the coauthor of *MORE Guerrilla Marketing Research*, reestablished the marketing consulting firm, Gerald Linda & Associates, in 1994. The firm provides marketing strategy, planning, and research services to a mix of large, sophisticated marketers, as well as smaller, entrepreneurial companies. A second service is aiding advertising and public relations agencies with their new business and account planning efforts. And a third service area is assuming senior marketing leadership/executional roles on an interim basis.

Mr. Linda received a BS in business administration and a MBA at Northeastern University, Boston. He received the Candidate in Philosophy degree from the University of Michigan for completing his doctoral course work. He is a frequent writer, whose thinking has appeared dozens of times in refereed (*Journal of Marketing Research, Journal of Advertising Research, Views,* and the *Journal of the Qualitative Research Consultants Association*), trade, and professional publications. And he has made more than 100 presentations and speeches at professional and trade association meetings and conferences. He is on the marketing faculty of the American Management Association, and has served on the faculty of the American Marketing Association's School for

Marketing Research. He also serves on the editorial review board for the *Journal of Current Issues in Research and Advertising*.

Melvin Prince holds a PhD from Columbia University. He is a professor of marketing at Southern Connecticut State University. He teaches graduate courses in marketing research, consumer behavior, and advertising. Past academic appointments include teaching and research positions at Brandeis University, Fordham University, Pace, Iona College and Quinnipiac University.

Dr. Prince is also President of Prince Associates, and provides analytic counsel to research companies and their clients. He spearheaded the research and development of the instant coupon machine, a breakthrough in-store promotional device. His previous industry experience includes marketing research directorships at advertising agencies, manufacturing companies, and the media. He worked in this capacity for BBDO and Marsteller agencies, National Brand Scanning, J. B. Williams, M & M's Candies, and Scholastic magazines. He is a member of the American Marketing Association, American Statistical Association, Association for Consumer Research, and the Society for Consumer Psychology, a division of the American Psychological Association.

He has delivered addresses before the Advertising Research Foundation, the Association of National Advertisers, and the Market Research Council. He has written three books, including *Consumer Research for Management Decisions*. His articles have previously appeared in such journals as *Journal of Business Venturing, Journal of Economic Psychology, Business Horizons, Business Strategy Review, Journal of Advertising, and Journal of Advertising Research*. A major theme of his articles include cutting-edge issues in research methodology, such as the reliability of positioning studies, innovative approaches to focus groups, and potentials of mixed methods studies. He is a member of the editorial board of the Journal of Business Research.

About the Contributors

Ami Bowen is the Vice President and Director of Corporate Communications at Copernicus Marketing Consulting and Research. Prior, she supervised the McDonald's public relations account at Arnold Worldwide. She holds an MBA from Boston University and a BA in Political Science and American Studies from Princeton University.

Mickey Brazeal is an Associate Professor of Marketing Communication at Roosevelt University. He spent 28 years as an advertising agency creative, most of them as Executive Creative Director at Lois (formerly Grey-Chicago). He is the author of *RFID: Improving the Customer Relationship,* and he is a frequent speaker on issues involving green marketing and marketing technologies.

Katja Bressette is a Director at Olson Zaltman Associates, responsible for global initiatives and projects, and cofounder and coeditor of *Deep Dives,* a global newsletter about the mind and marketing. She regularly speaks at business schools, and has presented at ESOMAR Qualitative. Katja studied in Aix-en-Provence, France, Oxford, U.K., and Regensburg, Germany, and holds an MBA with focus on international marketing. She began her career at Audi before moving to the United States to work for OZA.

Simon Chadwick is the Managing Partner of management consulting firm, Cambiar LLC. He has held a number of leadership positions in market research firms and the industry globally. He is a Fellow of the Market Research Society and holds an MA from Oxford University in Philosophy, Politics, and Economics.

Kevin J. Clancy (PhD, New York University) is the Chairman of Copernicus, a research-driven marketing consulting firm. A member of the Market Research Hall of Fame, Kevin began his career at BBDO Advertising and moved into academia as an Assistant Professor of Marketing at the Wharton School. He later became the chairman of Yankelovich Clancy Shulman.

Mark A. P. Davies (PhD, University of Leeds) is a Senior Lecturer in Marketing at Heriot-Watt University, Scotland. Mark has extensive teaching experience in cognate areas of marketing, and has published in a variety of European and North American journals.

Sharon Dimoldenberg, Divisional Director GfK Business & Technology, London, is a qualitative research specialist with over 20 years agency experience. She conducts workshops on qualitative research trends for ESOMAR and is a Visiting Lecturer at Said Business School, Oxford University. She holds an MA in Information Studies and BSocSc. Jt Hons, Political Science/Economic History.

Dorothy Fitch is a Global Analyst at Millward Brown. She edits the Millward Brown *Point of View* series and worked closely with Nigel Hollis, chief global analyst at Millward Brown, on his 2008 book, *The Global Brand.* Her *Point of View* article, "Whose Brand is it Anyway?" was highly commended in the 2009 WPP Atticus awards.

James Forr is a Director at Olson Zaltman Associates. During his tenure, four ARF David Ogilvy Research Award winners have featured OZA as a research partner. James holds a master's degree in Business Administration from the Smeal College of Business at the Pennsylvania State University.

Neil Gains is the owner of Tapestry Works and focuses on weaving richer connections from research through insight mining, insight activation, and coaching. Neil has more than 20 years of research experience on both the client and agency side, and has a doctorate in consumer psychology and sensory science.

Alastair Gordon is a Managing Partner of Gordon & McCallum, a consultancy providing support to the market research industry. Alastair has held senior management and product leadership roles with the Nielsen Company and Survey Research Groups. A well-known speaker and trainer, Alastair's key research interests are in the areas of emotion research, shopper insights, and consumer-decision processes.

Jamie Gordon is Vice President of Consumer Anthropology at Northstar Research Partners. She specializes in bringing a sociocultural perspective to brand, marketing and new product development strategy solution development. Since receiving her BA in Anthropology and MA in Applied Sociology from The University of Central Florida, Jamie has spent more than a decade delivering solutions for her global roster of clients and evolving human and cultural insight approaches and methodologies.

Sean Green (PhD, Cognitive Psychology, University at Buffalo, The State University of New York, SUNY) is currently teaching psychology in Singapore with the University at Buffalo program at the Singapore Institute of Management. He has a Bachelor of Science in Biology and Asian Studies (University of North Carolina at Chapel Hill) and an MA in Psychology (University at Buffalo, The State University of New York, SUNY). Sean has carried out research on topics including visual perception and auditory learning. Current research interests include metacognition and visual search.

Paul M. Gurwitz is Managing Director of Renaissance Research & Consulting, Inc., a firm specializing in applying statistical models to data to obtain actionable solutions to marketing problems. He holds a PhD from the University of California, Berkeley. Dr. Gurwitz's special area of expertise is multivariate statistical analysis of social and market research data, including optimization, decision, and segmentation analysis.

Philip Herr (BA Hons) is a Senior Vice President at Millward Brown, responsible for corporate intelligence. He consults across the organization on issues of analytics and marketing. Educated in South Africa, his career spans advertising agencies, research companies, and Coca-Cola. In addition, he is an Adjunct Professor in Marketing at Fairfield University in Connecticut.

Neil Holbert (PhD NYU) has worked in marketing research since the 1950s, with Metropolitan Life, Forbes Research, Chesebrough-Pond's (Unilever), Grey Advertising, and Philip Morris (Altria). He has taught in 10 countries on four continents, currently in the SUNY-Buffalo program in Singapore, and has written on many subjects including segmentation, strategy, branding, and global matters. He has studied at Columbia (AB, MBA) and NYU (PhD), and, latterly, is a determined autodidact.

Crawford Hollingworth is an applied social psychologist and founder of The Behavioral Architects, a new global consultancy, which leverages frameworks and understanding derived from behavioral sciences to deliver insights into consumer behavior and behavioral change. He was Global Executive Chairman of The Futures Company from January 2008 until June 2010. Earlier, he developed HeadlightVision, a global futures company that provided strategic intelligence and research to many of the biggest companies in the world; it was acquired by the WPP Group in 2003.

Larry Irons (PhD, Washington University in St. Louis) is a Principal at Customer Clues, LLC. His research focuses on the effect of sociocultural practices on innovation and collaboration in human relationships, including relationships between brands and consumers. Larry leads strategy, ideation, design, and development projects for major brands.

Bert Krieger (MBA University of Connecticut) is the Executive Vice President and Chief Research Officer at Moskowitz Jacobs, Inc. His principal responsibilities have been in client service, project consultation, and study design. Highly experienced in concept, package, and product optimization, he brings a broad range of experience to his position based on his past employment at leading package goods manufacturers and research suppliers.

Judy Langer, president of Langer Qualitative, is a qualitative research specialist. Author of *The Mirrored Window: Focus Groups from a Moderator's Point of View,* she leads workshops on qualitative research trends for ESOMAR and other organizations. She conducts a wide range of consumer and business-to-business research, using a variety of qualitative methodologies. She was a founder and first president of the Qualitative Research Consultants Association. Her BA from Smith College and MA from Columbia University are in political science.

Ian Lewis is the Director of Research Impact Consulting for Cambiar LLC. He previously led market research functions for Time Inc., Sterling Winthrop, Pfizer, and Unilever. He has published articles about research transformation in *Research World* and *Quirk's,* and coauthored the March, 2011, *JAR* article, "The Shape of Marketing Research in 2021."

Linda Ettinger Lieberman is the Editorial Coordinator at Moskowitz Jacobs Inc., editing, researching, writing, and coordinating publications. She holds a BA Cum Laude from the University of Bridgeport and MEd., Summa Cum Laude, from the University of Virginia. Her career has spanned the corporate, government, nonprofit, and private business sectors.

A. Dawn Lesh is the President of A. Dawn Lesh International, a marketing consulting practice that focuses on planning, research, and implementation to achieve business goals. She is also the Executive Director, Center for Measurable Marketing at the Stern School of Business at New York University and is an Associate Adjunct Professor at Stern and Columbia.

Chris Manolis, (PhD, University of Kentucky) is a professor of Marketing at Xavier University. His research has appeared in a number of journals and conference proceedings, including, but not limited to, the *Journal of the Academy of Marketing Science, Journal of Consumer Psychology, Journal of Business Venturing, Journal of Business Research, Journal of Personal Selling and Sales Management,* and the proceedings of the *Association for Consumer Research.*

Robert Moran is the President of the U.S. Region at StrategyOne, a global insights-driven consulting firm. His writing on the futures of marketing research has been featured in the *Journal of Advertising Research, Quirk's Marketing Research Review,* and his blog, the *Future of Insight.* He is also a frequent contributor to Pollster.com.

Howard R. Moskowitz, (PhD) is the president of Moskowitz Jacobs, Inc., a strategic marketing research company in White Plains, NY. The winner of Sigma Xi-The Research Society's 2010 Walston Chubb Innovation Award, he has authored 20 books, including *Selling Blue Elephants: How to Make Great Products That People Want Even Before They Know They Want Them* (Wharton School Publishing) and several hundred refereed papers. Dr. Moskowitz frequently contributes to business and scientific journals on messaging, product optimization, and the emerging area of psychophysics and the law.

Darren Mark Noyce (MMRS, MCIMA, marketing graduate). Darren cofounded and comanages SKOPOS Europe. He has spent the last two decades understanding customer needs through research and refining and optimizing clients' products, processes, and communications. Gadgets, technology, media, and digital are his passions, and these have fused into his pioneering spirit for insight and research.

Robin Pentecost (PhD Bond University, Australia) is a lecturer at Griffith University in Australia. His research interests are in events marketing and social marketing. Along with coauthoring a marketing research textbook, he has authored articles in a number of journals including *Psychology and Marketing*.

Raymond C. Pettit (EdD, University of Illinois) is the Vice President, Market Research for PRN Corporation. He has worked as a marketing science consultant for numerous corporations during his career, in addition to adjunct teaching at Baruch College's Zicklin School of Business. Pettit is the author of two books on marketing and advertising research, and most recently was SVP, Research and Standards at the Advertising Research Foundation.

William Pink, (PhD, politics, NYU) is a Partner, Client Solutions, at Millward Brown. Bill is a thought leader in the field of marketing accountability. He leads Millward Brown's marketing science, cross media, and ROI teams in North America. Bill is an elected member of the Market Research Council.

Joe Plummer (PhD, Ohio State University) is an adjunct Professor in the Columbia Business School and Senior Adviser at Olson Zaltman Associates. He is former EVP at McCann Worldgroup and at Young & Rubicam. Joe also is the past editor of the *Journal of Advertising Research* and the author of more than 25 journal articles.

David J. Rogers is the principal of ConvertClick, LLC, a digital analytics agency focusing on developing successful online marketing strategies, identifying consumer behavior insights, and employing best-in-class optimization and testing approaches that drive opportunities to increase customer satisfaction, thus business growth.

Diane Schmalensee is the President of Schmalensee Partners in Boston. She researches, writes, and consults on the keys to success for market researchers. Her work also focuses on B2B and B2C customer experience management, combining her research and quality management disciplines. She serves on many boards of directors.

J. Walker Smith (PhD, University of North Carolina at Chapel Hill) is the Global Executive Chairman of The Futures Company, a foresight and futures consultancy. He was the President of Yankelovich and Research Director at DowBrands. He is coauthor of four books and an authority on generations, consumer trends, and marketing strategy.

Mark Spence received his PhD in Marketing from the University of Arizona where he specialized in consumer behavior. He has published in top journals, including the *Journal of Marketing Research,* the *Journal of Consumer Research, Psychology & Marketing,* and the *European Journal of Marketing.*

Susan W. Tratner is an Associate Professor at SUNY Empire State College. Her market research interest is in qualitative interviewing and analysis, and she has experience in the food and beverage, automotive, and pharmaceutical industry. She has done anthropological research in the United States, Mexico, the Dominican Republic, and Costa Rica.

Marco Vriens is the Senior Vice President at the Modellers LLC., and he has led analytics, research, and insights teams at Microsoft, GE Healthcare, and marketing research firms. He is the coeditor of the *Handbook of Marketing Research* (published with Sage, 2006). His new book, *The Insights Advantage,* will appear in 2011.

SAGE Research Methods Online

The essential tool for researchers

**Sign up now at
www.sagepub.com/srmo
for more information.**

An expert research tool

- An **expertly designed taxonomy** with more than 1,400 unique terms for social and behavioral science research methods

- **Visual and hierarchical search tools** to help you discover material and link to related methods

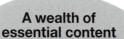

- Easy-to-use navigation tools
- Content organized by complexity
- Tools for citing, printing, and downloading content with ease
- Regularly updated content and features

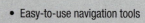

A wealth of essential content

- The most comprehensive picture of quantitative, qualitative, and mixed methods available today

- More than **100,000 pages of SAGE book and reference material** on research methods as well as editorially selected material from SAGE journals

- More than **600 books** available in their entirety online

Launching 2011!

$SAGE research methods online